CONTEMPORARY ISSUES IN **HUMAN RESOURCE**

3rd edition **MANAGEMENT** gaining a competitive advantage

We live in a time of chaos, marked by
breathtaking technological advances, tectonic
cultural and political shifts, and vigorous international
competition. Our workforce grows more diverse
every day, while our attitudes about work are
constantly changing. At the same time customers are
demanding intensive service in near-perfect quality.
Everything has to be better, cheaper, faster.

Robert H. Rosen with Paul B. Brown, 1996.
*Leading people: transforming business from the
inside out.*
New York, Viking Penguin, p. 10.

CONTEMPORARY ISSUES IN
HUMAN RESOURCE
MANAGEMENT

3rd EDITION

gaining a competitive advantage

C Brewster
L Carey
P Grobler
P Holland
S Wärnich

OXFORD
UNIVERSITY PRESS
Southern Africa

OXFORD
UNIVERSITY PRESS

Southern Africa

Oxford University Press Southern Africa (Pty) Ltd

Vasco Boulevard, Goodwood, Cape Town, Republic of South Africa
P O Box 12119, N1 City, 7463, Cape Town, Republic of South Africa

Oxford University Press Southern Africa (Pty) Ltd is a wholly-owned subsidiary of
Oxford University Press, Great Clarendon Street, Oxford OX2 6DP.

The Press, a department of the University of Oxford, furthers the University's objective of
excellence in research, scholarship, and education by publishing worldwide in

Oxford New York

Auckland Dar es Salaam Hong Kong Karachi
Kuala Lumpur Madrid Melbourne Mexico City Nairobi
New Delhi Shanghai Taipei Toronto

With offices in

Argentina Austria Brazil Chile Czech Republic France Greece
Guatemala Hungary Italy Japan Poland Portugal Singapore South Korea
Switzerland Turkey Ukraine Vietnam

Oxford is a registered trade mark of Oxford University Press
in the UK and in certain other countries

Published in South Africa
by Oxford University Press Southern Africa (Pty) Ltd, Cape Town

Contemporary Issues in Human Resource Management: gaining a competitive advantage 3e
ISBN 978 0 19 576804 6

© Oxford University Press Southern Africa (Pty) Ltd 2008

The moral rights of the author have been asserted
Database right Oxford University Press Southern Africa (Pty) Ltd (maker)

First published 2000
Third edition published 2008
Second impression 2009

Publishing director: Marian Griffin
Publisher: Mthunzi Nxawe
Project manager: Nicola van Rhyn
Editor: Patricia Myers Smith
Designer: Oswald Kurten
Cover designer: Oswald Kurten

Set in Minion Pro 10 pt on 12 pt by Orchard Publising
Printed and bound by ABC Press, Cape Town
110778

Contents in brief

Table of contents

8 Ethical issues and challenges in human resource management 167

Acknowledgements

Many people deserve thanks for the successful completion of this project, and we would particularly like to thank Mthunzi Nxawe from Oxford University Press (Southern Africa), the Publisher for the project, for his guidance and Cecilia du Plessis from the University of South Africa library, for her assistance with searching for articles and books. Babs Marais's assistance with the typing of the manuscript is much appreciated!

The authors

About the authors

CHRIS BREWSTER is Professor of International Human Resource Management and Director of Henley's HR Centre of Excellence. Prior to joining Henley Management College, he was Professor of International HRM at the South Bank Business School, South Bank University, UK, and before this, Professor of European Human Resource Management at the Cranfield School of Management, UK. He has substantial experience in trade unions, government, specialist journals, personnel management in the construction and air transport sector and consultancy. In addition to his teaching role, Professor Brewster has acted as a consultant to British and international organisations mainly in the areas of personnel policies (the subject of his PhD thesis) and management training. He is a frequent conference speaker around the world, presenting papers at the Association of International Business, the Academy of Management, and the European Association of Personnel Management, amongst others. He is author and co-author of some twenty books and over a hundred articles. In 2002 he received the Georges Petitpas Memorial Award from the World Federation of Personnel Management Associations (WFPMA) for advancing knowledge and practice in the international management of people at work.

LORRAINE CAREY (TPTC, *Vic College*; BA, *Monash*; MDiv, *Harvard*; MBA, *Monash*: PhD, Canberra) is Senior Lecturer and MBA Programme Director at the University of Canberra, where she lectures in business ethics and organisational behaviour. She recently completed her PhD at the University of Canberra in the operationalisation of corporate ethics. Dr Carey previously held appointments in the USA as director of campus ministry at Trinity College in Washington, DC, and as a medical administrator in Boston, and in Australia as a consultant and an educator in a range of settings, including women's prisons and detention centres.

PIETER GROBLER (BCom, BCom (Hons), MCom, DCom, MHRP, MIAC) is Professor of Human Resource Management in the Department of Human Resource Management at the University of South Africa (UNISA).

He received his DCom in strategic human resource management from UNISA in 1991. He joined the teaching profession in 1986 following a career in human resource management in the government.

He has authored numerous articles for local as well as international journals, including the *Bond management review* in Australia, the *SAM advanced management journal* as well as the *Journal of transnational management development* in the USA and the Danish management journal *LEDELSE I DAG*. In South Africa his articles have appeared in *Management dynamics*, *Human resource management* (now *Management today*) and the *South African journal of business management*. He has addressed numerous international and local conferences on strategic human resource management, organisational competitiveness, and leadership.

Internationally, he serves as a Director on the International Board of the Society for Advancement of Management in the USA. The Society was established in 1912 by the father of Scientific Management, Frederick Taylor. He is also a member of the international network of researchers at the Centre for European Human Resource Management at the School of Management at Cranfield University, UK. Additionally he serves on the Editorial Boards of the *SAM advanced management journal*, published by the Society for Advancement of Management and distributed to more than sixty countries, the *Journal of international business and technology*, the *Journal of teaching in international business* and the *Journal of transnational management development*, all published in the USA. Locally he serves on the Editorial Board of the *South African journal of labour relations*. Professor Grobler is registered as a Master HR Practitioner in the Generalist category with the South African Board for Personnel Practice. He is also a member of the Institute of Administration and Commerce of Southern Africa, the Institute of People Management, the Southern Africa Institute for Management Scientists, and the Southern Africa Institute of Management Services.

He is a contributor to the very popular publication *Global impact: Award winning performance programs from around the world*, published by Irwin Professional Publishing, USA, *Introduction to business management* and *Managing tourism in South Africa* by OUP (Southern Africa); and *Successful labour relations: Guidelines for practice*, published by JL van Schaik (South Africa). He is co-author of the books *Human resource management in South Africa*, published by Pearson Publishing (South Africa), and *Human resource management in South Africa*, second and third editions, published by Thomson Learning, London, UK. He has also been a contributor to the handbook *Management concepts/Managementkonzepte*, published by the DaimlerChrysler AG Headquarters in Stuttgart, Germany, and has undertaken work for the General Motors Corporation in the USA as well as the International Labour Organisation (ILO), in Geneva, Switzerland.

PETER HOLLAND (MA, *Kent at Canterbury*; PhD, *Tasmania*) is Senior Lecturer in Human Resource Management at Monash University, Melbourne, Australia, and has practised human resource management in the Australian finance industry. His areas of research include new patterns of work, reward management, and employee relations. He has also held visiting appointments at the University of Auckland, New Zealand; Kings College, University of London, and the University of Kent at Canterbury. He is author and co-author of some six books and numerous articles in the fields of human resource management and development, as well as employee relations. He is a member of the Australian Human Resources Institute and Australian Industrial Relations Society.

SURETTE WÄRNICH (BCom, BCom (Hons), MCom) is Senior Lecturer in Human Resource Management at the Department of Human Resource Management at UNISA. During 1999 she completed her Industrial Psychology internship at a leading banking group in South Africa and is a registered psychometrist with the Health Professions Council of South Africa. She is also a member of the Southern Africa Institute for Management Scientists. She has been involved with the Standards Generating Body (SGB) for HRM since 1999 in the capacity of writing unit standards for the National Qualifications Framework in South Africa. She is a co-author of the very popular book *Human resource management in South Africa*, published by Pearson Publishing (South Africa) and the second and third editions, published by Thomson Learning, London, UK. Internationally she has also published in the *Journal of transnational management development* in the USA and locally in *Management today*.

Preface

This book is intended to give all managers within an organisation (human resource managers included) insight into the changing role of the human resource management (HRM) function and to indicate how it can contribute towards enhancing the competitiveness of a company. Although there are numerous titles giving a solid account of the various functional areas in which HRM operates – such as recruitment, placement, performance appraisal, compensation, and training and development – it is essential for the HR manager to find the optimum framework in which each of these functional areas can contribute towards the competitiveness of the organisation.

The changing role of HR has led to a shift in activities and objectives, which has been the result of a number of new challenges:
- Globalisation – the restructuring of world markets
- Technology and structure – work roles and skill requirements, work teams, the role of managers, company structures, information
- Social – the changing composition of the labour market, employee values, legislation, skills deficits
- Quality – meeting customers' needs, service needs and product needs.

These are crucial influences on the world of business and the world of HRM, and they will be addressed in the chapters that follow.

Key changes

For this third edition of *Contemporary issues in human resource management*, new material has been added on talent management, measuring HRM within organisations, corporate citizenship and governance, change management and the learning organisation. Case studies, as well as interesting Web sites and additional reading sources, have also been added at the end of each chapter. Besides these new additions, each chapter also contains a chapter purpose, a chapter outcome, a chapter overview, review questions and activities, and a list of key concepts.

Instructor's ancillary material

Oxford University Press will provide supplementary packages to adopters who qualify under our adoption policy. Please contact Oxford University Press at www.oxford.co.za to learn how you may qualify.

Test bank

A comprehensive test bank to assist lecturers is also available. Included per chapter are:
- 25 multiple choice questions
- 25 true/false questions
- 25 complete-the-statement questions and comprehensive answers for the review and case study questions
- A number of experiential exercises.

PowerPoint slides

A set of PowerPoint slides is also available for instructors. These slides include graphics of the illustrations within each chapter.

1

Human resource management's role in the evolving paradigm

Learning outcomes

After reading this chapter you should be able to:

▶ Identify the origins of human resource management
▶ Describe the new role of human resource management within organisations
▶ Explain the new employee–employer relationship
▶ List and discuss new innovative approaches to human resource management

Purpose

The purpose of this chapter is to introduce you to the changing world of human resource management.

Chapter overview

This chapter focuses on the evolving role of human resource management. It begins with a discussion of the origins of human resource management. It considers the new role of human resource management within the changing organisational environment. Thereafter it describes the new employee–employer relationship within this environment. The chapter also contains a discussion of new innovative approaches to human resource management. The concluding case study illustrates how to apply this chapter's theory to a practical situation.

Introduction

The role human resource management (HRM) plays within organisations has changed dramatically. Having excluded HRM from participating actively in business decisions for most of its existence, organisations now require HRM to play an active role in the fight to be successful and remain competitive.[1-2] They ask the HR function to respond by cutting costs and finding creative ways to add value to the business. Doing so, however, appears to require a repositioning of the HR department, which will involve not only new roles but also new competencies, new relationships, and new ways of operating[3] (see Chapters 2 to 13). To understand the role of HRM, one must understand, firstly, its historical evolution, and, secondly, the challenges facing HR today.

In this chapter we shall discuss the origins and new role of HRM, the new employee–employer relationship, and innovative approaches to HRM.

1.1 The origins of HRM

Although some HR activities had been taking place in the early 1800s in areas such as agriculture and small family businesses, more formal HR practices evolved only at the beginning of the Industrial Revolution, when factories required large numbers of employees with specific skills to operate their machines.[4] To recruit and train these workers, companies started employing persons who would be responsible for these activities. Since then, rapid changes, which have had a profound impact on the role played by the HRM professional, have taken place within organisations.[5-6]

The researcher McKee[7] has successfully described these paradigm shifts in business life and has also identified the evolving role of the HRM function during these periods. Before we take a closer look at McKee's work, it may be appropriate to define briefly what is meant by 'a paradigm'. According to Barker (1989), a futurist, as quoted by Belohlav[8], the term 'paradigm' can be described as a set of rules and regulations that define boundaries and tell us

what to do to be successful within those boundaries. Thus, the term 'paradigm' refers to a particular way of thinking about, seeing, and doing things within one's environment.

The categories of change which McKee has identified within businesses can be grouped into four distinct periods:

- *The mechanistic period.* This period can be associated with the 1940s and 1950s, when manufacturing was the driving force in industry. This period saw the birth of the personnel/industrial relations profession. The main focus of the HR function was of an administrative nature, e.g. interpreting union contracts, keeping manual records, and hiring and paying people. This period also saw the emergence of benefit programmes as an area of interest.[9]
- *The legalistic period.* The 1960s and 1970s saw an unprecedented amount of legislation in the social and employment areas. This legislation had a major impact on the workplace and the roles and responsibilities assumed by the personnel officer. The legislation began a trend towards the regulation of the workforce beyond the union contract and company rules. Training and development began to emerge as a separate and specialised area of HRM and continues to play an important and vital role. Also in the early 1970s, the first HR information systems application (the computerisation of the salary database) was started.[10]
- *The organistic period.* Tremendous organisational change started to take place in the 1980s. Here we think of globalisation, mergers, acquisitions, re-engineering, and downsizing. These activities brought about radical changes in the workplace and created an environment in which the HRM function faced numerous challenges (e.g. an increasingly diverse workforce and an increase of awareness of work and family issues). During this period the movement towards cost and profit centres became an important issue for HRM, as did the implementation of more command-and-control policies and procedures to save the

organisation from failing to deal with the turbulent environment. This period can also be seen as the height of HRM specialisation.[11]

- *The strategic period.* The period of the 1990s has become known as the strategic period. During this time strategic thinking and planning emerged as the most prominent activity to deal with the continual change faced by corporate organisations. In this period organisations were in flux, with structures ranging from webs to networks and matrices. Owing to the fierce competition, organisations turned to the HRM function to assist them in their struggle to remain successful and competitive. The HRM function now became a true strategic partner, reporting to the CEO and interacting with the Board of Directors. HR professionals also played an active role in determining the future direction of organisations.[12]

Beyond 2000, McKee projected the trends described above and called this period the catalytic period. In this period, she argued, the following issues would play major roles[13]:

- An increase in cross-border employment
- A workforce that will be comfortable in, and with, other cultures
- Fewer organisations as a result of continued mergers and acquisitions
- The use of just-in-time professional workers
- An increase in outsourcing of administrative functions
- More innovative compensation practices
- A more selective approach by employees regarding their careers
- Telecommuting and other forms of flexible work being widely introduced
- Teams playing a major role.

Thus, to summarise, the good old days of HRM are over, and in the future HRM will emerge as an even more critical factor in developing and maintaining a company's competitive edge. However, if HRM is to play this significant part successfully, it is important to take a look at how the function is adapting to its new role in order to meet the needs of the future.

1.2 The new role of HRM

As indicated in the previous section, rapid changes have taken place within the organisation as well as in the role HR professionals play. Thus, few successful businesses can continue to rely on past policies and practices, while their HR professionals can ill afford to continue to be functional experts.[14-16] Management and HR professionals must become partners in decision-making and share accountability for organising the work to be performed – including where it is to be performed. To be successful, the HR professional will have to[17]:

- Become involved with line managers in strategy formulation and implementation, resulting in the design of HR strategies that will support the overall company strategy
- Become an expert in the way work is organised and executed
- Become involved in reducing costs through administrative efficiency, while at the same time maintaining high quality; this can be achieved by delivering state-of-the-art, innovative HR practices
- Become a reliable representative for employees when putting their concerns to management
- Become involved in efforts to increase the employees' contribution to the organisation
- Become an agent for continuous transformation, shaping processes and culture to help organisations improve their capacity for change.

If all these tasks are done well, the HR professional will receive the recognition he or she deserves within the organisation.

The strategic alliance between management and HR has received substantial attention in both popular and academic literature. However, a study of these articles reveals a focus on the strategic partnership role (e.g. getting to know the needs of the business and where it is going), while no mention is made of HR's past operational role.

Figure 1.1 HRM's roles in building a competitive organisation

	Future/strategic focus (short–long term)		
Processes	**Cell 1** Management of strategic human resources **Deliverable/outcome** Executing strategy **Activity** Aligning HR and business strategy: 'Organisational diagnoses' **Role** Strategic partner	**Cell 3** Management of transformation and change **Deliverable/outcome** Creating a renewed organisation **Activity** Managing transformation and change: 'Ensuring capacity for change' **Role** Change agent	**People**
	Cell 2 Management of firm infrastructure **Deliverable/outcome** Building an efficient infrastructure **Activity** Reengineering organisation processes: 'Shared services' **Role** Administrative expert	**Cell 4** Management of employee contribution **Deliverable/outcome** Increasing employee commitment and capability **Activity** Listening and responding to employees: 'Providing resources to employees' **Role** Employee champion	
	Day-to-day/operational focus		

SOURCE: Adapted and reprinted by permission of Harvard Business School Press. From ULRICH, D. 1997. *Human resource champions: The next agenda for adding value and delivering results*. Boston, M.A.: Harvard Business School Press. This figure is a combination of Figure 2.1 on page 24 and Table 2.1 on page 25 of the text. Copyright © 1999 by the President and Fellows of Harvard College, all rights reserved.

In his popular book *Human resource champions*, Ulrich[18-19] warns about this one-sided view and proposes a multiple role model for HRM, which addresses these as well as other issues. Ulrich is of the opinion that for HR professionals to be successful, they will have to play at least four different roles, namely strategic partner, administrative expert, employee champion and change agent.[20] He also proposes that HR professionals should focus on what they can deliver before they look at the activities or work of HR. As his model has been successfully implemented by major corporations around the world (e.g. Hewlett-Packard, General Electric, and Sears), it would be wise to take a closer look at the model.

The axes of Ulrich's model (see Figure 1.1)

represent two aspects, namely focus (i.e. short term and long term) and activities (managing processes, HR tools and systems, and managing people). The HRM roles mentioned earlier are depicted in the four quadrants of the model. To clarify these roles, each quadrant also contains the outcome of each role as well as the activities the HR professional is to perform. For example:

- *Top left quadrant (Cell 1)*. In this cell (management of strategic human resources) the HR manager works to be a strategic partner by focusing on the alignment of HR strategies and practices with the overall business strategy (see Chapter 4 for more detail). By fulfilling this role, HR professionals increase the capacity of the business to execute its strategies.[21]

- *Bottom left quadrant (Cell 2).* This role (management of firm infrastructure) requires HR professionals to design and deliver efficient HR processes, e.g. staffing, training, appraisal, rewarding, and promotion. HR professionals must ensure that these organisational processes are designed and delivered efficiently. This process is ongoing.[22]
- *Top right quadrant (Cell 3).* The third key role to be played by the HR professional is management of transformation and change. This entails making fundamental cultural changes within the organisation.[23]
- *Bottom right quadrant (Cell 4).* The employee-contribution role of HR professionals encompasses their involvement in the day-to-day problems, concerns, and needs of employees. Where, for example, intellectual capital becomes a critical source of a company's value, HR professionals should be active and aggressive in developing this capital.[24]

Thus, by turning the four HRM roles into specific types of behaviour and actions, a world-class HR organisation can be created, as seen in companies such as Hewlett-Packard and some others already mentioned. According to Ulrich, the business partner concept has changed to become a more dynamic, all-encompassing equation, thus replacing the simple concept of business partner (i.e. only working with general managers to implement strategy), with:

> Business partner = strategic partner + administrative expert + employee champion + change agent.[25]

In conclusion, being an effective HR professional does not mean simply moving from operational to strategic work as the new challenges demand; it means learning to master both operational and strategic processes and people. For today's HR professionals to deliver value to a company, they must fulfil multiple roles.

1.3 The new employee–employer relationship

From the discussion thus far it has become clear that successful and competitive organisations are able to turn their strategies into action quickly, manage their processes efficiently, and maximise their employees' contributions and commitment. For this to be possible, organisations must abolish the old way of doing things and implement new practices. This can take place through re-engineering, restructuring, downsizing, and other activities.

These changes will inevitably result in employees being dismissed, not only those working in factories, but also those who, traditionally, were offered long-term careers within the organisation. Thus, the psychological contract – what employees and employers want and expect from each other[26-27] – will change dramatically in the new work environment. The question now is: what will this new contract look like?

The psychological contract that is dynamic, voluntary, subjective, and informal accomplishes two tasks: firstly, it defines the employment relationship, and, secondly, it manages mutual expectations.[28-29]

Perhaps the most significant change in the new work environment is the lack of job security offered to employees. In the old paradigm, an employee's current and future position were very clear and predictable, which resulted in employee loyalty being fostered. For this loyalty, employers would provide good pay, regular promotion, and benefits, and would also invest in the training and development of their staff. The relationship between the employer and the employee was a good one. However, this happy marriage has become strained in the new work environment, in which cutting costs and improving productivity are management goals. The flexible, de-layered, slimmer organisation is constantly changing to suit volatile and shifting markets, and can logically no longer sustain secure career progression.[30]

What is interesting is that, while these changes are occurring from the employer's side, new values, trends, and workplace demographics have resulted in revised expectations from employees themselves. For example, there seems to be a significant shift in employees' attitudes and values as regards career management, leadership style, motivation, and working conditions. This highly educated new generation of workers wants more opportunities for development, autonomy, flexibility, and meaningful experiences. These workers also value independence, imagination, tolerance, and responsibility.[31]

Thus, with changes taking place on the employer's as well as the employee's side, a new type of psychological contract is emerging – one that is more situational and short term and assumes that each party is much less dependent on the other for survival and growth.

According to Hiltrop, this new contract can be defined as follows[32–33]:

There is no job security, the employee will be employed as long as he or she adds value to the organisation, and is personally responsible for finding new ways to add value. In return the employee has the right to demand interesting and important work, has the freedom and resources to perform it well, receives pay that reflects his or her contribution and gets the experience and training needed to be employable here or elsewhere.

SOURCE: HILTROP, J-M. 1995. The changing psychological contract: the human resource challenge of the 1990s. *European management journal*, 13(3):287, September.

As the old employment contract, which is based on security and predictability, is withdrawn, it will be replaced with one of faint promises. Thus employees will give their time but not much more.

According to Grant (1997), as quoted by Niehoff and Paul[34], Kodak has one of the most innovative applications of paying attention to psychological contracts. Kodak has, for example, formalised the development of a 'social contract' with each employee, whereby the employee pledges to understand the business and the customers and also give 100 per cent of his or her effort on the job. The company, from its side, pledges to provide extensive training, career-development opportunities, and appraisal of managerial performance. The main purpose of Kodak's actions, according to the authors, has been to take the 'psychological' out of the contract by putting both parties' obligations in writing. Besides this formal approach from the employer's side, employees can also play an active role in minimising any problems with the psychological contract. This can take place by engaging organisational agents (e.g. HR managers and supervisors) in explicit discussions of obligations to ensure that both their perceptions of the terms of the employment relationship are shared and that those terms are as clear as possible.[35] These types of discussion are especially important when there are cultural differences between the employee and the organisational agents responsible for executing the terms of the psychological contract and when the employee lacks knowledge regarding the norms of the organisation.

Consequently, when psychological contracts go unfulfilled or are perceived to have been violated, employees may experience reduced organisational commitment, stronger intentions to quit, and other disaffections, such as the likelihood for sabotage, theft, and other aggressive types of behaviour which can impact negatively on the organisation and its efforts to gain and sustain a competitive advantage[36] (see Figure 1.2).

Two types of violation of the psychological contract can occur, namely reneging and incongruence.[37] Reneging occurs when either party to a psychological contract knowingly breaks a promise to the other. Reneging may also occur because one party is unable to fulfil its promise or because one party does not want to fulfil the terms of the agreement. In contrast, incongruence occurs when the parties have different understandings of their obligations in terms of the contract. Those different understandings occur because the terms and conditions of psychological contracts are often perceptual. On the opposite end of the continuum, employers who understand and

Figure 1.2 A process model of the links between contract violation, trust, cynicism, and organisational change

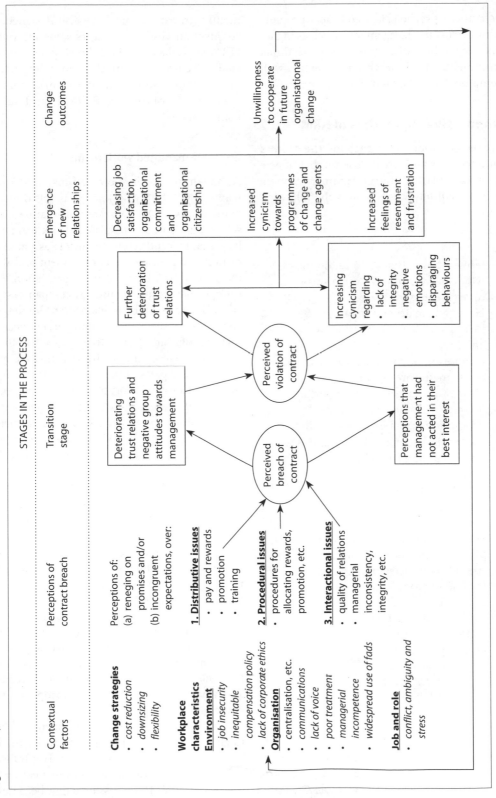

SOURCE: Adapted from PATE, J., MARTIN, G. & STAINES, H. 2000. Exploring the relationship between psychological contracts and organisational change: a process model and case study evidence. *Strategic change*, 9:482. 2000© John Wiley & Sons Limited. Reproduced with permission.

uphold these psychological contracts promote employee trust in management as well as higher levels of job satisfaction, organisational commitment, and the intention to remain with the employer – the desired state.[38]

1.4 Innovative approaches to HRM

There is no doubt that each of the factors mentioned thus far is creating a number of new challenges for HRM. Hiltrop summarises these challenges skilfully when he asks the following questions[39]:

> - How can we attract and retain people who can live with and often thrive upon uncertainty?
> - How can we get and maintain the loyalty and commitment of our employees when job security, promotion opportunities and career entitlements are declining?
> - How can we meet career expectations of employees who expect rapid promotions in an organisation that is becoming flatter and leaner and is not expanding enough?
> - How can we encourage (older) employees to take more responsibility for their own personal and professional development?
> - How can we develop procedures and processes that help managers and specialists understand and commit themselves to working together?
> - How can we build an organisation culture and structure in which employees feel satisfied, challenged and empowered?

SOURCE: HILTROP, J-M. 1995. The changing psychological contract: the human resource challenge of the 1990s. *European management journal*, 13(3):288, September.

To manage this complex and challenging environment, HR professionals have not only adopted new roles within the workplace, as was mentioned earlier, but have also designed, in conjunction with line managers, some innovative HR approaches. In the following section we shall discuss some of the more important approaches: self-managed work teams, alternative workplaces, E-HRM, and talent management.

1.4.1 Self-managed work teams

Although not totally new, self-managed work teams (SMWT) – also known as self-directed work teams (SDWT) or as self-maintaining, self-leading and self-regulating work teams[40] – have again recently come to the fore as a method of improving employee commitment and thus the general well-being of the organisation.[41] In Europe, these teams are used by companies such as Volvo, Saab, and (in Spain) the Mondragon cooperative movement, resulting in significantly higher profits and productivity gains than those of the average operator. These teams are also used in other parts of the world.[42] For example, in a recent survey of Fortune 1 000 companies in the USA, the results indicated that 79 per cent of the companies and 81 per cent of manufacturing organisations used SMWTs or so-called 'high-performance' teams.[43] Some reported successes of SMWTs appear in Table 1.1.

As the term 'self-managed' implies, these teams within the work environment are responsible for determining what they want to do, how they want to do it, and when they want to do it. The teams are thus empowered to use their initiative in solving problems and managing themselves.[44] The advantage of these teams is that they can respond quickly to the needs of a particular situation, which is of great importance for companies finding themselves in a turbulent environment. Team members participate in decisions regarding, for example, who to hire for their teams, what equipment to purchase, and what training is necessary to operate the equipment.

The most profound implication for establishing these teams appears to be in the overall role of HRM.[45] Moving from a centralised functional staff position, as indicated earlier in the chapter, the HR professional now becomes a

Table 1.1 Reported successes of self-managed teams

Characteristics	Reported benefits
Monsanto	Quality and productivity improved by 47 per cent in 4 years
Harley-Davidson	Returned to profitability in 6 years
Johns Hopkins Hospital	Patient volume increased by 21 per cent Turnover was reduced Absenteeism was cut
Logan Aluminum	Turnover reduced by 20 per cent Absenteeism reduced to 1,2 per cent in 2 years
Hallmark	200 per cent reduction in design time Introducing 23 000 new card lines each year
Liberty Mutual	50 per cent reduction in contract process time Savings of more than $50 million per year
Saab and Volvo	40 per cent reduction in time spent on each car 4 per cent increase in production output Inventory turnover increased from 9 to 21 times a year

SOURCE: Reprinted with permission from the Institute of Industrial Engineers, 3577 Parkway Lane, Suite 200, Norcross, 6A 30092, 770-449-0461. ©1995 from ATTARAN, M. & NGUYEN, T. T. 1999. Succeeding with self-managed work teams. *Industrial management*, July/August:26.

coach or counsellor or advisor to the team. For example, when hiring or selecting people for the company, the team members play an important role in deciding whether the applicants will be good team members or not. Also, in the job-analysis process, the team plays an important role.[46] Not only are certain kinds of behaviour necessary to perform a specific job, but the team members also have to learn new sets of behaviour to be able to work together successfully. These sets of behaviour have to be identified during the job-analysis stage. In training, the SMWT assesses its own training needs and, with the input and advice from the HR professional, participates in the design, delivery, and evaluation of the training programmes. Besides its own job-training requirements, the team also needs training in communication, listening and supervisory skills, conflict resolution, decision making, running meetings, and time management. For overall business responsibility, the team needs to learn customer relations and how to deal with suppliers and unions.[47]

Owing to the teams' unique situation, changes will also have to be made to the compensation system within the company. In the past, individuals were paid according to the job category in which they were classified. Now, however, with teams, the most prevalent pay system used is pay for knowledge. Thus, team members are paid according to how many team tasks they can perform. Other innovations in the compensation system for teams include gainsharing or suggestion-system payments in order to encourage team initiative.[48]

New procedures to determine the critical factors of performance for teams must also be implemented. Team members must become involved in both the design and the appraisal itself. The team will also be responsible for its own work schedule and vacation policy. It is clear that the development of team-based work systems has the potential to create a more productive, creative, and individual-fulfilling working environment and thus plays a critical role in the new challenges facing HRM.

However, despite these successes, there are a number of 'no-gos' which can doom SMWTs to near-certain failure and thus need to be noted. These include the following[49]:

• The company is not willing to commit the time and resources (including problem-solving resources) necessary for the teams to succeed

- The work does not allow employees time to think, meet, and discuss ideas
- Employees work independently much more than interdependently
- Employees do not have highly developed technical competencies
- The organisational leader or champion of the team concept cannot guarantee a personal commitment for at least two years, perhaps due to retirement or a pending transfer.

With the greater availability of technology within companies, the SMWTs have now also evolved into virtual teams.[50] According to Townsend, De Marie, and Hendrickson, these teams can be defined as follows[51]:

> Virtual teams are groups of geographically and/or organisationally dispersed co-workers that are assembled using a combination of telecommunications and information technologies to accomplish an organisational task. They rarely meet face to face, they may be set up as temporary structures existing only to accomplish a specific task or may be more permanent structures to address ongoing issues.
>
> SOURCE: TOWNSEND, A. M., DE MARIE, S. M. & HENDRICKSON, A. R. 1998. Virtual teams: technology and the workplace of the future. *Academy of management executive*, 12(3):17–29.

Virtual teams have become important for a number of reasons, including[52]:
- The change in organisation structures to flat or horizontal formats
- The emergence of environments that require interorganisational cooperation as well as competition
- Changes in workers' expectations regarding their involvement in organisations
- The globalisation of trade and organisation activity.

Virtual-team formation can expand telecommuting potential by allowing employees involved in highly collaborative teamwork to participate from remote locations. However, these teams will be successful only if all the members became proficient in a wide variety of computer-based technologies and learn new ways to express themselves and understand others in an environment with a diminished sense of presence. Also, in many organisations, virtual-team membership crosses national boundaries, involving a variety of cultural backgrounds, which will require additional team development in areas such as cultural diversity.[53] Table 1.2 shows some critical success factors for global virtual teams.

A further new development in this area has been the establishment of the interorganisational virtual organisation. This new term is defined by Fuehrer and Ashkanasy[54] as

> ... a temporary network organisation, consisting of independent enterprises (organisations, companies, institutions or specialised individuals) that come together swiftly to exploit an apparent market opportunity. The enterprises utilise their core competencies in an attempt to create a best-of-everything organisation in a value-adding partnership (VAP), facilitated by information and communication technology (ICT). As such these virtual organisations act in all appearances as a single organisational unit.
>
> SOURCE: FUEHRER, E. C. & ASHKANASY, N. M. 1998. *The virtual organisation: defining a Webrian ideal type from the interorganisational perspective*. Annual meeting of the Academy of Management. San Diego: C.A.:19. [Paper.]

From this definition it is clear that three important characteristics of these organisations can be identified, namely[55]:
1. The central role to be played by ICT
2. The cooperative character of these organisations
3. Their temporary nature.

Table 1.2 Critical success factors for global virtual teams

Virtual team challenge	Critical success factors for effective global virtual teams
Communication	Emphasise continuous communication
	Set meeting schedules and rules of engagement
	Conduct periodic face-to-face meetings
	Engage in team-building activities at onset of virtual team creation
Culture	Instill a sense of cultural awareness
	Create teams from complementary cultures
Technology	Utilise multiple computer mediated communications systems (CMCS)
	Train team members in the use of various CMCS
	Ensure infrastructure compatibility among geographic locations
	Assess political and economic barriers to international telecommunications
Project management (leadership)	Set clear team goals and provide continuous performance feedback
	Build team cohesiveness
	Express flexibility and empathy towards virtual team members
	Exhibit cultural awareness

SOURCE: Reprinted from KAYWORTHY, T. & LEIDNER, D. The global virtual manager: a prescription for success, *European management journal*, 18(2):190, April. © with 2000 with permission from Elsevier Science.

Although not much research is at present available on these types of organisation, they undoubtedly have HRM implications such as, for example, building trust, which is essential for the functioning and success of these organisations.

1.4.2 Alternative workplace

Besides the SMWTs and virtual teams, other approaches have been developed to increase employee commitment and productivity. The alternative workplace is such an effort by HR management to transform the workplace by moving the work to the worker instead of the worker to the work.[56] The alternative-workplace approach is a combination of non-traditional work practices, settings and locations that is beginning to supplement traditional offices. It can also give companies an edge in vying for talent as well as in keeping it. Today, AT&T in the USA is just one among many organisations pioneering the alternative workplace. By recent estimates, nearly 18 million US workers currently spend at least a portion of their workweek in virtual mode and that number has increased by almost 100 per cent since 1997.[57] Virtual work is important because of its increasing prevalence and also because virtual organisations and virtual workers may be the key factors in the 'new economy'.[58]

Other reasons of importance include the following[59]:

• The ability of a field sales or service organisation to function effectively as a team without having to come to the office to collect messages, attend meetings, and interact with co-workers
• The desire to eliminate wastage of time in commuting, thus giving workers more free time for personal or business needs
• The interest in spending more time at home with family members by virtue of conducting business from a home office
• The significant cost savings for companies over time, as fewer employees require expensive office space and other support services
• The perceived increase in productivity when employees have more time to spend on their jobs without having to commute to the workplace.

Although different companies use different variations on the alternative-workplace theme to tailor work arrangements to their own needs, Apgar IV has identified a number of options available, namely[60]:

- *Placing workers on different shifts or travel schedules.* This enables them to share the same desk and office space.
- *Replacing traditional offices with open-plan space.*
- *Implementing the concept of 'hotelling'.* As in other shared office options, 'hotel' work spaces are furnished, equipped, and supported with typical office services. These spaces can then be reserved by the hour, day or week instead of being permanently assigned. In addition, 'hotels' may appoint a concierge to provide employees with travel and logistical support.
- *Creating satellite offices.* Such offices are the result of breaking up large, centralised facilities into a network of smaller workplaces that can be located close to customers or to employees' homes.
- *Introducing telecommuting or virtual offices.* This is one of the most commonly recognised forms of alternative workplace and has been used for some time. Telecommuting – performing work electronically wherever the worker chooses, e.g. from home – generally supplements the traditional workplace rather than replacing it.

Some interesting information pertaining to these different options appears in Appendices 1.1 and 1.2 to this chapter.

Although these different forms of alternative workplace have been identified separately, they are sometimes also found in combination within organisations (e.g. shared offices and telecommuting); see the article in Box 1 on the next page, entitled 'One company, two telecommuting arrangements'. It is also interesting to note that a dynamic, non-hierarchical, technologically advanced organisation is more likely to use these practices than a highly structured, command-driven company is to do so.

One of the most critical HR issues in setting up these alternative workplace practices is that of measuring the employees' performance. It is very clear that the traditional approaches will not work and new methods have to be devised. This also applies to the manner in which

employees receive rewards. As a result of the different locations at which the employees will be working, a culture change within the company will be necessary as employees learn new ways of connecting with one another.[61] It is also important to note that some personalities suit working alone for extended periods from a remote location better than other personalities do. When choosing telecommuters for example, one should look for:

- Self-motivation
- High level of job knowledge and skills
- Flexibility
- Strong organisational skills
- Strong communication skills
- Low need for social interaction
- Team-player mentality
- Enjoyment of responsibility
- Trustworthiness and reliability.[62]

The decision to implement alternative workplace practices is normally based on a number of assumptions, for example that certain jobs either do not depend on specific locations and types of facilities or depend only partly on them. For the successful implementation of the different workplace practices, Apgar IV suggests asking the following questions[63]:

- What function does the job serve?
- Is the work performed over the phone?
- How much time does the employee have to spend in direct contact with other employees/customers and business contacts?
- Is the location of the office critical to performance?
- Is it important for others to be able to reach the employee immediately?

SOURCE: APGAR IV, M. 1998. The alternative workplace: changing where and how people work. *Harvard business review*, May/June:121–136.

Having answered these questions satisfactorily, the company will also have to look at a number of other issues before proceeding with the

BOX 1: One company, two telecommuting arrangements

Lucent Technologies, a high-tech firm that split off from AT&T in 1996, continues to promote telecommuting for several reasons, according to company spokesman William T. Price: 'First, it offers a recruiting advantage because flexible work arrangements weigh heavily with today's employees. Second, and very important for a company like Lucent, telecommuting uses the technology we provide to the world. We can promote our own products; we can use our own workforce as pioneers in telecommunications; we gain marketing knowledge and product knowledge.'

Unlike AT&T, which places the decision to allow telecommuting squarely in the laps of its department heads, Lucent has people who go from unit to unit and division to division, prescreening individual employees to determine whether they're suitable candidates. According to Price, they ask questions like: 'Do you have a need for a lot of personal contact? Are you comfortable enough with technology to download files, do routine maintenance and so on? Are you a self-starter? A self-motivator? On the other hand, will you not be able to stop working?' They also interview supervisors, asking questions like: 'Are you comfortable supervising a person you don't see every day? How will you measure the employee's performance?'

'Rarely does an employee have to be brought back to the office, once given a work-at-home arrangement,' Price claims, 'because with this prescreening system, we ensure that each telecommuter can work well from home.'

Lucent uses two telecommuting arrangements – 'formal' and 'casual'. In a 'formal' arrangement, employees have no office space in the Lucent building. Instead, they're provided with the necessary equipment, telephone connections and coaching. They're rarely seen on the company premises.

Employees with 'casual' work-at-home arrangements work at home only occasionally, for instance if there's bad weather or a family illness. Price estimates that 20 per cent of Lucent's 150 000 employees worldwide have some sort of telecommuting arrangement. Of that 20 per cent (most are based in the US), more than half use the formal system.

Price asserts that monitoring the performance of telecommuters is not a problem. Lucent has an extensive performance management plan, by which key objectives are set every year, and supervisors give out semi-annual assessments.

Lucent's telecommuting policies would work in many other industries, he believes. 'In general, the line between people's personal and professional lives has become blurred, and having the flexibility to work at home, whether you're in your own business or working for a paper company, makes you a more productive worker and family person.'

SOURCE: SANDLER, S. (Ed). 1999. *HR focus*, December:12, 212/2440360. http://www.ioma.com. Reprinted by permission © HR focus.

---

implementation of alternative-workplace programmes. One such aspect that needs attention is the attitude of middle management. These employees normally see their roles being diminished when their subordinates work at home. Informing them of the positive contribution these programmes can make to the company – as well as their crucial role therein – is vital. Undertaking programmes with only partial support from the staff results only in confusion and frustration for the employees at home, with a consequent drop in productivity.[64]

The company will also have to look at the cost aspects of implementing the programmes. These programmes need hardware, software, and other support, which can involve large sums of money. The company also needs to budget for ongoing costs such as allowances, phone charges, and technical support, as well as the time necessary to reorientate and train the employees involved.[65]

Besides these problems, certain external barriers may exist. For example, in Japan people's homes are so small that they cannot contain a home office. Also, in many other countries around the world, some citizens' homes either do not have electricity or are structures not conducive to housing highly sophisticated technical equipment. Thus, when an employee at home cannot communicate with other employees or clients, gain access to the right information or easily reach a help desk to solve a technology problem, the initiative is destined to fail.[66]

Thus, to improve the chances of an alternative-workplace programme, those involved must have a full set of tools, relevant training, and appropriate and flexible administrative support.

If all these problems are solved satisfactorily, the company is then in a position to implement such a programme. It is advisable to start with simple activities, for example functions such as telemarketing and personal sales, before moving to more complex ones.

It is also important to inform the employees involved of how their performance will be monitored. Setting clear goals from the outset and agreeing on what to monitor is critical. The success of a programme will also depend on how successfully the individuals can distribute their time between their work and family at home.[67]

A major US company, Merrill Lynch, has reduced its people risk by setting up tele-commuting laboratories at a number of its offices. After extensive pre-screening, employees spend about two weeks at work in a simulated home office. Here, the prospective tele-commuters communicate with their managers, customers, and colleagues by phone, email or fax. If they do not like this way of working, they can drop out.

This approach has proved very valuable to Merrill Lynch in that it has enabled the company to minimise the risk of placing people in jobs they do not like. Interestingly, approximately 17 per cent of IBM's total worldwide workforce is sufficiently equipped and trained to work in alternative-workplace programmes.[68]

1.4.3 E-HRM

One of the more innovative methods of managing employees efficiently is using the World Wide Web for HR applications.[69] Although this development is still limited in its application, HR departments worldwide are showing a keen interest in it. E-HRM includes a wide range of functions, ranging from something as simple as making a company's HR policies and procedures available through its intranet to managing the development and deployment of the company's most strategic skills.

In this section we shall focus on the work reported by Letart, an employee at the TALX Corporation. This company is responsible for the design and implementation of interactive Web and interactive voice response (IVR) solutions for HR. It is based in St Louis, USA.[70]

According to Letart, there are five stages of Web deployment within organisations. These stages can be used to determine where an organisation stands. Let us take a brief look at each of these stages.

- *Stage I – information publishing.* Many companies find themselves at this stage of development. Here the HR policies and procedures of the company are published for general scrutiny. Other information also available includes the company history, a directory of services, and information on the management team. This is a very cost-effective way of making up-to-date company information available to employees.[71]
- *Stage II – database inquiry.* Like the previous level, this level provides one-way communication to employees. However, increased security requirements now exist, as the user is given the opportunity to gain some personal information from the system. Examples include current benefit coverage, personal demographic data, and work schedules. The advantage of this stage of development is that it reduces phone calls and emails to the HR department; this reduction can, ultimately, have a major

impact on staffing needs. This level begins to change the way companies do business.[72]

- *Stage III – simple HR transactions*. At this stage, paperwork is replaced with transactions using electronic input. Here the employee updates personal information, such as bank particulars for salary deposits, on the HR database available in the company. This is the first step in HR transaction processing and represents a much bigger change in the way HR departments work.[73]

- *Stage IV – complex HR transactions*. Stage IV applications differ from those of the previous stage in the complexity of the interaction between the user and the HR transactions being processed. In addition to updates, calculations or other internal processing of data take place – for example, an employee may access the employee benefits database and make a selection of items which will be calculated by the system, approved within the budget limits allowed, and confirmed by email to the employee.[74]

- *Stage V – HR workflow over the Web*. This is the ultimate stage of development. Here HR executives give employees and managers a way to administer their own HR data and processes without paperwork or administrative support. The users are walked through all the steps necessary to complete whole processes rather than just discrete transactions. For example, an employee who gets divorced may need to change her or his address, contacts, income-tax particulars, benefits profile, and pension contributions.[75]

It is clear that the Web application for HR departments is enormous. It can lead not only to improved services, better communication, and cost reduction, but also to the ultimate goal of making the organisation more successful and more competitive, especially when deployed globally, increasing the capability to manage a global workforce. See Chapter 10 for further aspects of conducting HRM entirely online.

1.4.4 Talent man...

A concept only emer... closely related to th... approaches already discusse... talent management.[76] In the kno... of the twenty-first century, talent... the scarcest of scarce resources – ... companies compete for, depend on, and s... with in today's highly competitive busi... environment.

Insofar as talent is the greatest competitive instrument, skills, competencies, and aspirations are its building blocks.[77] If competencies are to talent as investments are to wealth, why then can most investors list their holdings in detail, while HR departments usually do not even have a basic concept of the competencies at their organisations' disposal? Analysts attribute this to numerous reasons, but the fact is that excellence in the management of talent is complex, the data collection and management elements are enormous, and the proper analysis of the data is even more challenging.[78] However, as the literature indicates, to be successful, companies have no choice but to acquire and use modern types of HR technology, as mentioned in the previous section, to manage their talent pools effectively.[79]

But what then does talent management entail and what role does the HRM department and HR professional play in this process?

According to Schweyer[80] talent management can be defined as follows:

> ... the sourcing (finding talent); screening (sorting of qualified and unqualified applicants); selection (assessment/testing, interviewing, reference/background checking etc. of applicants); on-boarding (offer generation/acceptance, badging/security, payroll, facilities etc.); retention (measures to keep the talent that contributes to the success of the organisation); development (training, growth, assignments, etc.); deployment (optimal

From Figure 1.3 it is clear that proper planning is essential to ensure the availability of the right talent for the job at the right time.

According to a recent benchmarking study on talent management, conducted by the American Productivity and Quality Centre and the Centre for Creative Leadership, as reported by McCauley and Wakefield[83], organisations that excel in talent management follow eight best practices, namely:

- Define talent management broadly
- Integrate the various elements of talent management into a comprehensive system
- Focus talent management on the most highly valued talent
- Get CEOs and senior executives committed to talent-management work
- Build competency models to create a shared understanding of the skills and types of behaviour the organisation needs and values in employees
- Monitor talent needs within the organisation to identify potential gaps
- Excel at recruiting, identifying, and developing talent, as well as at performance management and retention

and in the future. It is important to note that the concept not only enhances the value of outsiders, but also looks at the talent an organisation already possesses.[81] Although the HRM activities to manage talent within organisations are not new, the approach used – bundling together the activities to produce a more coherent whole that can be a vehicle for obtaining, developing, and retaining talent the organisation needs – is new.[82] In Figure 1.3 the elements of talent management and their interrelationships are shown.

Figure 1.3 The elements of talent management

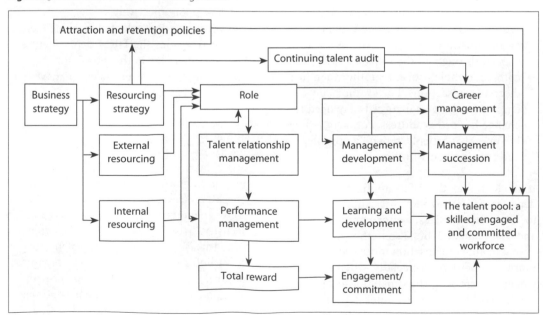

SOURCE: ARMSTRONG, M. 2006. *A handbook of human resource management practices* 10th ed. London: Kogan Page:391. Used with permission.

- Regularly evaluate the results of the talent-management system.

Thus, for talent management initiatives to be effective, organisations need formal processes (see Figure 1.3) with many people involved and with strong links between leadership and talent to translate into specific organisational value-based behaviour.[84] To tie all these activities together successfully, the leaders in HRM (normally the person known as the chief learning officer (CLO) within the HRM department) should actively pursue a number of activities.[85] These activities can include informing management and employees about why talent management is important, how it works, and what the benefits to the organisation are. Therefore regular and effective communication is essential. Besides this, the HRM department also needs to manage a number of risks to the business. These risks include[86]:

- *A vacancy risk.* To safeguard key business capabilities, focus on scarce skills, and fit to position.
- *A readiness risk.* To accelerate leadership development, provide full business exposure to rising stars.
- *A transaction risk.* To avoid loss of key talent, select successors with leadership ability, and hire for organisation capability.
- *A portfolio risk.* To maximise strategic talent leverage, focus on senior management's commitment to development and performance standards.

Consequently, effective talent-management policies and practices that demonstrate commitment to human resources will ultimately lead to more engaged employees and lower turnover of staff. See Chapter 6 for more details regarding the management of talent within organisations.

SUMMARY

This chapter describes an evolution within both the management of organisations and the role played by HR professionals. The old way of doing business has gone forever, and a new flexible, fluid, and ever-changing environment is a reality. Changes are taking place not only within organisations but also in the people working in them. Gone are the days of job security and numerous fringe benefits. Companies are prepared to employ only individuals who can add value, and individuals are interested only in selling their labour to the highest bidder. Thus the challenges facing HRM are multiple. HR professionals have responded with innovative ideas to address challenges such as self-managed work teams, creating virtual teams with available technology, implementing alternative-workplace programmes, and talent management, all of which offer profound opportunities to benefit both the individual and the company. HRM has also moved into the area of the World Wide Web to deliver its own services.

KEY CONCEPTS

- Alternative workplace
- Global virtual teams
- High-performance teams
- HR technologies
- Incongruence
- Information and communication technology (ICT)
- Interorganisational virtual organisation
- Intranet
- Knowledge economy
- Legalistic
- Mechanistic
- Multiple role model for HRM
- New economy
- Organistic
- Paradigm
- Portfolio risk
- Psychological contract
- Readiness risk
- Reneging
- Self-directed work teams (SDWT)
- Self-leading work teams
- Self-maintaining work teams
- Self-managed work teams (SMWT)
- Self-regulating work teams
- Strategic
- Talent management
- Transaction risk
- Vacancy risk
- Value-adding partnership (VAP)
- Virtual HRM
- Virtual offices
- Virtual teams

CASE STUDY

Objective: To understand the role of HRM in a changing environment

Just putting you on hold ... Protea Bank

Protea Bank was founded in Cape Town during the late nineteenth century and by 2005 had become a traditional bank with branches in most South African towns and cities. Its main business is in personal banking and financial services for individual customers and small businesses. It has subsidiary business units which handle personal insurance, mortgages and share-dealing, but these are managed separately from the banking concern.

The development of Procall

By mid 2005 all traditional banks were feeling the pressure of fierce competition in financial services, intensified by the arrival of new entrants such as supermarkets and other well-known brands. With an eye to the growing commercial success of direct-line banking organisations, Protea Bank decided to enter the telephone-banking sector, and was recently able to improve shareholder value by switching a significant proportion of its general account management and enquiry activity to a dedicated call centre named Procall. This resulted in the closure of many smaller, unprofitable branches and a consequent need for redundancies. Protea Bank attempted to redeploy existing employees where possible, but also needed to recruit new staff to work in the national call centre. True to its origins, and mindful of the relatively high unemployment rates in Cape Town, Protea Bank decided to locate Procall just outside Cape Town. However, none of this was achieved easily, since the press and public expressed concern and dismay at the closure of so many small local branches, and there was strong trade-union resistance to the job losses. Thus, it is true to say that, currently, staff morale is low, there is considerable anxiety and discontent with the new arrangements, and the staff at Procall itself are beginning to feel somewhat exposed as the debate about branch closures rages in the media.

The work at Procall

At present, Procall employs 150 staff and operates 24 hours a day, 7 days a week on a 4-shift system. The majority of staff work on the daytime shifts. Staff work at sets of four desks, wear headsets with microphones to take the calls and operate terminals with access to all the required account and product information. Supervisors are responsible for each shift and there are two call-centre managers and a deputy manager, one of whom is always either available at the centre or can be contacted by telephone. Pay scales are standardised; there is a starting rate of R40 000 per year, which applies to newly recruited staff during their six-month probationary period, after which they are placed at the bottom of a four-point scale that rises by increments to R50 000. Employees proceed up the scale by annual increments until they reach the top point, after which further increases are dependent on promotion to supervisory or managerial work. Supervisory grades start at R60 000 and rise similarly to R70 000. There is no performance-management system in place, and as yet the idea of an appraisal system has not been developed. Procall is located in pleasant, airy open-plan offices, which are nicely decorated and have good basic facilities, including a snack and sandwich service, a rest room, a separate smoking room, and a kitchenette for the preparation of hot drinks and snacks; thus the 'hygiene' factors are fairly good.

Problems with Procall

The history of Procall has been mixed. After a patchy first six months, it seems to be picking up business very rapidly as customers begin to see the advantages of this service. While this is encouraging, it has led to a new range of problems. The existing number of Procall staff is now clearly inadequate for the growing demands for the telephone-banking service. Recruitment is under way, but this is likely to place existing induction programmes and initial training programmes under strain. Complaints are beginning to be heard from customers who are being 'put on hold' for anything from 30 seconds to 5 minutes during busy periods (especially early in the evenings and at weekends).

There are also problems associated with the use of the computer system itself; these centre on the apparent inability of some staff to extract accurate information about relatively simple enquiries, or on the length of time that such interrogations take. Monitoring systems, which measure the number and duration of different types of call, add weight to these complaints, with enquiries relating to standing orders and direct-debit arrangements appearing to take up to 50 per cent longer than they should, according to the authors of the software. There have been customer complaints about rudeness, staff's apparent inflexibility when dealing with complex account problems, and the fact that different operators seem to give different answers to the same questions. There are additional knock-on effects for customers who prefer to visit their local branch. Here the problem seems to be that branch staff themselves have to telephone the call centre in order to deal with certain very simple transactions such as opening new accounts, and that they too are often kept 'on hold', to the annoyance of clients and their own considerable frustration.

The call-centre staff are also beginning to complain about aspects of the work. Protea Bank carried out a staff survey six months after the start of the operation and again after a further three months. The findings of the second survey reflect the increased pressures by revealing a higher degree of discontent than was noted in the first survey. Workers say that they often feel very isolated from their colleagues, which leads to a certain unhealthy rivalry both within and between shifts. Many feel that they are 'like battery hens', working in an intensive manner, with little control over the number and type of calls they receive and with limited opportunity to recover from one call before receiving the next. They are also under constant surveillance, with calls being monitored both to determine the productivity of the operators and

to check the accuracy of the information given and general quality of their work. This causes some resentment, and it appears that the operators often find informal ways to control the number of calls they receive and the time between calls. Some groups have worked out a method by which calls can be redirected to one of their numbers, thus allowing them all to appear busy while only one is actively taking calls. This way they take it in turns to give themselves an informal break from calls while still giving the appearance of working. On occasion this technique has been used to 'soak' new or unpopular members of staff, who find themselves the victims of such redirection, not realising that they are the only person on their team who is actually busy and appears to have a backlog. Supervisors are aware that this is happening, but they find it very difficult to detect.

Some of the redeployed staff remain unhappy with the type of service they are being asked to give and find it too impersonal. Some of the new recruits, especially in the younger age groups, believe that they work better and more effectively than other staff, and are beginning to feel that the standardised pay structure does not recognise or reward their individual skills and efficiency. Some are concerned about their employability and want formal recognition for their skills, which would be transferable to other similar employers, of which there is an increasing number in the region. Indeed, Procall has already lost a number of its staff to other local call centres which have a more varied clientele and better career prospects.

Procall and Proline, the future strategy

Protea Bank remains aware of the way in which the banking and personal-finance sector is likely to develop and management recently decided to expand the service at Procall to include the provision of mortgages and insurance, thus providing more of an integrated 'one-stop shop' service. Furthermore, work has already started on the development of an online banking system, Proline, in parallel with the telephone service. Protea Bank has been somewhat late in appreciating the importance of online banking, and thus finds itself at something of a disadvantage here. The new operation, Proline, is located in the same set of buildings as Procall, and urgently needs both programming staff and others, with knowledge of banking and financial services, who can help to both develop and run the initial trials of Proline. It is also clear that if the local labour market is unable to supply this type of expertise at a competitive rate, then Protea Bank will have to consider alternative approaches.

Questions and activities

1. Identify the key HRM issues at Procall.
2. Recommend and justify HRM interventions which will improve business performance.

(Contributed by Fill Christy, University of Portsmouth)

SOURCE: Adapted from: Call centres in the financial services sector – just putting you on hold .... (*In* PILBEAM, S. & CORBRIDGE, M. 2006. *People resourcing: Contemporary HRM in practice* 3rd ed. Harlow: Pearson Education:23–26.) Used with permission.

REVIEW QUESTIONS AND ACTIVITIES

1. Describe the issues that will play a major role in the future in McKee's catalytic period.
2. Describe the present ways in which HR professionals can be successful.
3. Give a definition of the new psychological contract.
4. Give four reasons why virtual teams have become important.
5. Give some examples of the training needs of self-managed work teams.
6. Give a brief explanation of the evolving role of HRM during the four periods of organisational change as described by McKee.
7. Explain Ulrich's multiple role model for HRM.
8. Discuss the employee–employer relationship in the new work environment.
9. According to Mahlon Apgar IV, a number of options are available for the alternative workplace in order to tailor work arrangements to one's own needs. Discuss these options.
10. Briefly describe what you understand by talent management.

FURTHER READING

REDDINGTON, M., WILLIAMSON, M. & WITHERS, M. 2005. *Transforming HR: Creating value through people.* Oxford: Elsevier Butterworth-Heinemann.

BURKE, R. J. & COOPER, C. L. (Eds.) 2005. *Reinventing HRM: Challenges and new directions.* Oxon: Routledge.

DYCHTWALD, K., ERICKSON, T. J. & MORISON, R. 2006. *Workforce crisis: How to beat the coming shortage of skills and talent.* Boston, Massachusetts: Harvard Business School Press.

WARNER, M. & WITZEL, M. 2004. *Managing in virtual organisations.* London: Thomson Learning.

WEB SITES

www.shrm.org – Society for Human Resource Management
www.humancapitalinstitute.org – Human Capital Institute
www.ilo.org – International Labour Organisation
www.cornell.edu/iws – Institute for Workplace Studies
www.conference-board.org – The Conference Board

ENDNOTES

1. ULRICH, D., BROCKBANK, W., YEUNG, A. K. & LAKE, D. G. 1995. Human resource competencies: an empirical assessment. *Human resource management*, 34(4):473–495, Winter. See also WRIGHT, P. M., MCMAHAN, G. C., SNELL, S. A. & GERHART, B. 2001. Comparing line and HR executives' perceptions of HR effectiveness: services, roles and contributions. *Human resource management*, 40(2):111–123; GALFORD, R. 1998. Why doesn't this HR department get any respect? *Harvard business review*, March/April:24–26; BECKER, B. E., HUSELID, M. A. & ULRICH, D. 2001. *The HR scorecard: Linking people, strategy and performance.* Boston, Massachusetts: Harvard Business School Press.

2. PFEFFER, J. 1995. Producing sustainable competitive advantage through the effective management of people. *Academy of management executive*, 9(1):55–68. See also RUSSEL, S. & DEUTSCH, H.

1999. People performance: the ultimate competitive advantage. *Journal of compensation and benefits*, 14(6):21–25; HUNTER, R. H. 1999. The new HR and the new HR consultant: developing human resource consultants at Andersen Consulting. *Human resource management*, 38(2):147–155; ARMSTRONG, G. 2005. Differentiation through people: how can HR move beyond business partner? *Human resource management*, 44(2):195–199.

3. SCHULER, R. S. 1990. Repositioning the human resource function: transformation or demise? *Academy of management executive*, 4(3):49–59. See also SPELL, C. S. 2001. Organizational technologies and human resource management. *Human relations*, 54(2):193–213; FERRIS, G. R., HOCHWATER, W. A., BUCKLEY, M. R., HARRELL–COOK, G. & FRINK, D. D. 1999. Human resources management: some new directions. *Journal of management*, 25(3):385–415;

MCLAGAN, P. A. 1999. As the HRD world churns. *Training and development*, 53(12):20–30; CHIAVENATO, I. 2001. Advances and challenges in human resource management in the new millennium. *Public personnel management*, 30(1):17–26; LIPIEC, J. 2001. Human resources management perspective at the turn of the century. *Public personnel management*, 30(2):137–146. ALTMAN, Y. 2000. Work and careers in the new millennium: a landscape. *Strategic change*, 9:67–74; BURTON, T. & WALSH, D. 1998. The role of personnel in change processes: introducing the charabanc of change typology. *Strategic change*, 7:407–420. ARMSTRONG, G. 2005. Differentiation through people: how can HR move beyond business partner? *Human resource management*, 44(2):195–199.

4. SIMS, R. R. & SIMS, S. J. 1994. *Changes and challenges for the human resource professional*. Westport, Connecticut: Quorum Books:2; SWART, J., MANN, C., BROWN, S. & PRICE, A. 2005. *Human resource development: Strategy and tactics*. Oxford: Elsevier Butterworth–Heinemann.

5. ULRICH, D. 1998. A new mandate for human resources. *Harvard business review*, January/February:124–134; BURUD, S. & TUMOLO, M. 2004. *Leveraging the new human capital: Adaptive strategies, results achieved and stories of transformation*, Palo Alto: Davies–Black Publishing.

6. CAPELLI, P., BASSI, L., KATZ, H., KNOKE, D., OSTERMAN, P. & USEEM, M. 1997. *Change at work*. New York: Oxford University Press. See also KAUFMAN, B. E. 1999. Evolution and current status of University HR programs. *Human resource management*, 38(2):103–110.

7. MCKEE, K. D. 1997. The human resource profession: Insurrection or resurrection? (*In* Ulrich, D., Losey, M. R. & Lake, G., *Tomorrow's HR Management*. New York: John Wiley & Sons:182–189.)

8. BELOHLAV, J. A. 1996. The evolving competitive paradigm. *Business horizons*, 39(2):11–19, March/April.

9. MCKEE, K. D. 1997. The human resource profession: Insurrection or resurrection? (*In* Ulrich, D., Losey, M. R. & Lake, G., *Tomorrow's HR Management*. New York: John Wiley & Sons:185.)

10. Ibid.:185–186.
11. Ibid.:186.
12. Ibid.:187–188.
13. Ibid.:188–189.

14. MORTON, M. S. 1995. Emerging organisational forms: work and organisation in the 21st century. *European management journal*, 13(4):339–345, December.

15. LAABS, J. J. 1996. Eyeing future HR concerns. *Personnel journal*, 75(1):28–37, January; BURKE, R. J. & COOPER, C. L. 2005. The human resources revolution: why putting people first matters. (*In* Burke, R. J. and Cooper, C. L. (eds.) *Reinventing HRM: Challenges and new directions*. Oxon: Routledge, an imprint of the Taylor & Francis Group:3–13.)

16. JACKSON, S. E. & SCHULER, R. S. 1995. Understanding human resource management in the context of organisations and their environments. *Annual review of psychology*:237–264.

17. ULRICH, D. 1998. A new mandate for human resources. *Harvard business review*, January/February:124–134. See also SVOBODA, M. & SCHRÖDER, S. 2001. Transforming human resources in the new economy: developing the next generation of global HR managers at Deutsche Bank AG. *Human resource management*, 40(3):261–273.

18. ULRICH, D. 1997. *Human resource champions. The next agenda for adding value and delivering results*. Boston, Massachusetts: Harvard Business School Press.

19. DAWSON, P. 1995. Redefining human resource management. *International journal of manpower*, 16(5/6):47–55.

20. ULRICH, D. 1997. *Human resource champions: The next agenda for adding value and delivering results*. Boston, Massachusetts: Harvard Business School Press:24–25; HUNTER, I., SAUDERS, J., BOROUGHS, A. & CONSTANCE, S. 2006. *HR business partners*. Hants: Gower Publishing.

21. ULRICH, D. 1997. *Human resource champions: The next agenda for adding value and delivering results*. Boston, Massachusetts: Harvard Business School Press:25–27.

22. Ibid.:27–28.
23. Ibid.:30–31.
24. Ibid.:29–30.
25. Ibid.:37.

26. HILTROP, J-M. 1995. The changing psychological contract: the human resource challenge of the 1990s. *European management journal*, 13(3):286–294, September. See also SINGH, R. 1998. Redefining psychological contracts with the US workforce: a critical task for strategic human resource management planners in the 1990s. *Human resource management*, 37(1):61–69; PALMER, B. & ZIEMIANSKI, M. 2000. Tapping into people. *Quality progress*, April:74–83; TSUI, A. S. & WU, J. B. 2005. The new employment relationship versus the mutual investment approach: implications for human resource management. *Human resource management*, 44(2):115–121.

27. HILTROP, J-M. 1996. The impact of human resource management on organisational performance: theory and research. *European management journal*, 14(6):628–637, December. See also TURNLEY, W. H. & FELDMAN, D. C. 1998. Psychological contract violations during corporate restructuring. *Human resource management*, 37(1):71–83, Spring.

28. HILTROP, J-M. 1995. The changing psychological contract: the human resource challenge of the 1990s. *European management journal*, 13(3):287, September;

CONWAY, N. & BRINER, R. B. 2005. *Understanding psychological contracts at work: a critical evaluation of theory and research*. Oxford: Oxford University Press:32; BOSSIDY, L. 2007. What your leader expects of you and what you should expect in return. *Harvard business review*, 85(4):58–65, April.

29. OVERMAN, S. 1994. Re-engineering HR. *HR magazine*, June:50–53. CULLINANE, N. & DUNDON, T. 2006. The psychological contract: a critical review. *International journal of management reviews*, 8(2):113–129.

30. HILTROP, J-M. 1995. The changing psychological contract: the human resource challenge of the 1990s. *European management journal*, 13(3):287, September.

31. Ibid.

32. Ibid.:289.

33. CAPPELLI, P., BASSI, L., KATZ, H., KNOKE, D., OSTERMAN, P. & USEEM, M. 1997. *Change at work*. New York: Oxford University Press:203–204.

34. NIEHOFF, B. P. & PAUL, R. J. 2001. The just workplace: developing and maintaining effective psychological contracts. *Review of business*, 22(1):5–8.

35. MORRISON, E. W. & ROBINSON, S.L. 1997. When employees feel betrayed: a model of how psychological contract violation develops. *Academy of management review*, 22(1):226–256.

36. NIEHOFF, B. P. & PAUL, R. J. 2001. The just workplace: developing and maintaining effective psychological contracts. *Review of business*, 22(1):5; MORRISON, E. W. & ROBINSON, S. L. 1997. When employees feel betrayed: a model of how psychological contract violation develops. *Academy of management review*, 22(1):226; PAUL, R. J., NIEHOFF, B. P. & TURNLEY, W. H. 2000. Empowerment, expectations and the psychological contract – managing the dilemmas and gaining the advantages. *Journal of socio-economics*, 29:471–485.

37. NIEHOFF, B. P. & PAUL, R. J. 2001. The just workplace: developing and maintaining effective psychological contracts. *Review of business*, 22(1):6.

38. ROBINSON, S., KRAATZ, M. & ROUSSEAU, D. 1994. Changing obligations and the psychological contract: a longitudinal study. *Academy of management journal*, 37:137–152. See also ROBINSON, S. & MORRISON, E. 1995. Organizational citizenship behaviour: a psychological contract perspective. *Journal of organizational behaviour*, 16:289–298; Robinson, S. L. 1996. Trust and breach of the psychological contract. *Administrative science quarterly*, 41:574–599, December.

39. HILTROP, J-M. 1995. The changing psychological contract: the human resource challenge of the 1990s. *European management journal*, 13(3):288, September. See also PFEFFER, J. 1998. Seven practices of successful organizations. *California management review*, 40(2):96–124; LOSEY, M., MEISINGER, S. R. & ULRICH, D. 2005. Conclusion: reality, impact and professionalism. *Human resource management*, 44(2):201–206.

40. CLIFFORD, G. P. & SOHAL, A. S. 1998. Developing self-directed work teams. *Management decision*, 36(2):77–84. See also ATTARAN, M. & NGUYEN, T. T. 1999. Succeeding with self-managed work teams. *Industrial management*, July/August:24–28; DENTON, D. K. 1999. How a team can grow: goal is to become self-directed. *Quality progress*, June:53–57.

41. BANNER, D. K., KULISCH, W. A. & PEERY, N. S. 1992. Self-managing work teams (SMWT) and the human resource function. *Management decision*, 30(3):40–45. See also RATLIFF, R. L., BECKSTEAD, S. M. & HANKS, S. H. 1999. The use and management of teams: a how-to guide. *Quality progress*, June: 31–38; HICKMAN, G. R. & CREIGHTON-ZOLLAR, A. 1998. Diverse self-directed work teams: developing strategic initiatives for 21st century organisations. *Public personnel management*, 27(2):187–200.

42. BANNER, D. K., KULISCH, W. A. & PEERY, N. S. 1992. Self-managing work teams (SMWT) and the human resource function. *Management decision*, 30(3):40. See also CHASTON, I. 1998. Self-managed teams: assessing the benefits for small service-sector firms. *British journal of management*, 9:1–12.

43. DUMAINE, B. 1994. The trouble with teams. *Fortune*, 130(5):86–87. DRUSKAT, V. U. & WHEELER, J. V. 2004. How to lead a self-managing team. *MIT Sloan management review*, 45(4):65–71; KATZENBACH, J. R. & SMITH, D. K. 2005. *Harvard business review*, 83(7), July–August:162–171; FISCHER, B. & BOYNTON, A. 2005. *Harvard business review*, 83(7), July/August:117–123.

44. KIRKMAN, B. L. & ROSEN, B. 2000. Powering up teams. *Organizational dynamics*, Winter:48–66.

45. Ibid.: 41. See also ADAMS, S. & KYDONIEFS, L. 2000. Making teams work. *Quality progress*, January:43–48; MUELLER, F., PROCTER, S. & BUCHANAN, D. 2000. Teamworking in its context(s): antecedents, nature and dimensions. *Human relations*, 53(11):1387–1424; BACON, N. & BLYTON, P. 2000. High road and low road teamworking: perceptions of management rationales and organizational and human resource outcomes. *Human relations*, 53(11):1425–1458. LONGENECKER, C. O. & NEUBERT, M. 2000. Barriers and gateways to management cooperation and teamwork. *Business horizons*, 43(5): no page numbers; WEST, M. 2001. How to promote creativity in a team. *People management*, 8 March: no page numbers.

46. BANNER, D. K., KULISCH, W. A. & PEERY, N. S. 1992. Self-managing work teams (SMWT) and the human resource function. *Management decision*, 30(3):40–45. See also FINDLAY, P., MCKINLAY, A., MARKS, A. & THOMPSON, P. 2000. In search of perfect people: teamwork and team players in

the Scottish spirits industry. *Human relations,* 53(12):1549–1574; SALAS, E., KOSARZYCKI, M. P., TANNENBAUM, S. I. & CARNEGIE, D. 2005. Aligning work teams and HR practices. (*In* Burke, R. J. and Cooper, C. L. (eds.) *Reinventing HRM: Challenges and new directions.* Oxon: Routledge, an imprint of the Taylor & Francis Group, p. 133–147.)

47. BANNER, D. K., KULISCH, W. A. & PEERY, N. S. 1992. Self-managing work teams (SMWT) and the human resource function. *Management decision,* 30(3):40–45.

48. Ibid.

49. YANDRICH, R. M. 2001. A team effort. *HR magazine,* 46(6):136–146. HARVEY, T. R. & DROLET, B. 2004. *Building teams, building people* 2nd ed. Maryland, USA: Scarecrow Education, an imprint of The Rowman & Littlefield Publishing Group.

50. TOWNSEND, A. M., DE MARIE, S. M. & HENDRICKSON, A. R. 1998. Virtual teams: technology and the workplace of the future. *Academy of management executive,* 12(3):17–29. See also HUGHES, J. A., O BRIEN, J., RANDALL, D., ROUNCEFIELD, M. & TOLMIE, P. 2001. Some 'real' problems of the 'virtual' organisation. *New technology, work and employment,* 16(1):49–64; MALHOTRA, A., MAJCHRZAK, A. & ROSEN, B. 2007. Leading virtual teams. *Academy of management perspectives,* 21(1):60–70, February; COMBS, W. & PEACOCKE, S. 2007. Leading virtual teams. *Training & development,* 61(2):27–28, February; ROSEN, B., FURST, S. & BLACKBURN, R. S. 2006. Training for virtual teams: an investigation of current practices and future needs. *Human resource management,* 45(2):229–247, Summer: KIRKMAN, B. L. & MATHIEU, J. E. 2005. *Journal of management,* 31(5):700–718, October.

51. TOWNSEND, A. M., DE MARIE, S. M. & HENDRICKSON, A. R. 1998. Virtual teams: technology and the workplace of the future. *Academy of management executive,* 12(3):18.

52. Ibid.

53. Ibid.:19–29. See also KIRKMAN, B. L., GIBSON, C. B. & SHAPIRO, D. L. 2001. Exporting teams: enhancing the implementation and effectiveness of work teams in global affiliates. *Organizational dynamics,* 30(1):12–29; GOVINDARAJAN, V. & GUPTA, A. K. 2001. Building an effective global business team. *MIT Sloan management review,* 42(4):63–71; LAROCHE, L. 2001. Teaming up. *CMA management:*22–25, April; MCDERMOTT, L., WAITE, B. & BRAWLEY, N. 1999. Putting together a world-class team. *Training and development,* 53(1):47–51.

54. FUEHRER, E. C. & ASHKANASY, N. M. 1998. *The virtual organisation: defining a Webrian ideal type from the interorganisational perspective.* Annual meeting of the Academy of Management. San Diego: C.A.:19. [Paper.]

55. FUEHRER, E. C. & ASHKANASY, N. M. 2001. Communicating trustworthiness and building trust in interorganizational virtual organizations. *Journal of management,* 27(3):236.

56. APGAR IV, M. 1998. The alternative workplace: changing where and how people work. *Harvard business review,* May/June:121–136.

57. WIESENFELD, B. M., RAGHURAM, S. & GARUD, R. 2001. Organizational identification among virtual workers: the role of need for affiliation and perceived work-based social support. *Journal of management,* 27(3):213. See also WELLS, S. J. 2001. Making telecommuting work. *HR magazine,* 46(10):34–44.

58. CARR, N. G. 1999. Being virtual: character and the new economy. *Harvard business review,* May/June:181–186. See also TAPSCOTT, D. 1997. Strategy in the new economy. *Strategy & leadership,* 25(6):8–14, November/December.

59. GREENBAUM, T. L. 1998. Avoiding a 'virtual' disaster. *HR focus,* February:1.

60. APGAR IV, M. 1998. The alternative workplace: changing where and how people work. *Harvard business review,* May/June:122–124.

61. Ibid.:125. See also RAGHURAM, S., GARUD, R., WIESENFELD, B. & GUPTA, V. 2001. Factors contributing to virtual work adjustment. *Journal of management,* 27(3):383–405; BROADFOOT, K. J. 2001. When the cat's away, do the mice play? *Management communication quarterly,* 15(1):110–114; KERRIN, M. & HANE, K. 2001. Job seekers' perceptions of teleworking: a cognitive mapping approach. *New technology, work and employment,* 16(2):130–143.

62. SCHILLING, S. L. 1999. The basics of a successful telework network, *HR focus,* June:10.

63. APGAR IV, M. 1998. The alternative workplace: changing where and how people work. *Harvard business review,* May/June:121–136.

64. Ibid.:126.

65. Ibid.:127–130. See also DEEPROSE, D. 1999. When implementing telecommuting leave nothing to chance. *HR focus,* October:13–15. PEARLSON, K. E. & SAUNDERS, C. S. 2001. There's no place like home: Managing telecommuting paradoxes. *Academy of management executive,* 15(2):117–128.

66. APGAR IV, M. 1998. The alternative workplace: changing where and how people work. *Harvard business review,* May/June:121–136. See also ALLERT, J. L. 2001. You're hired, now go home. *Training and development,* 55(3):55–58, March; ALFORD, R. J. 2001. Going virtual, getting real. *Training and development,* 53(1):35–44; HARTMAN, J. L. J., OGDEN, B. K. & GEROY, G. D. 2000. Electronic communication training: reconciling gaps created by the virtual office. *Performance improvement quarterly,* 14(1):11–25.

67. APGAR IV, M. 1998. The alternative workplace: changing where and how people work. *Harvard business review,* May/June:121–136. See also ENDESHAW, A. & TUNG, L. L. 2000. Emerging

patterns of teleworking in Singapore. *Human systems management*:161–167.

68. APGAR IV, M. 1998. The alternative workplace: changing where and how people work. *Harvard business review*, May/June:121–136. See also MARKUS, M. L., MANVILLE, B. & AGRES, C. E. 2000. What makes a virtual organisation work? *Sloan management review*, 42(1): no page numbers, Fall.

69. Baker, S. 2000. From your intranet and extranet strategies. *Journal of business strategy*, July/August:41–43. See also GALE, S. F. 2001. The HRMS tune-up: keep your system running smoothly. *Workforce*, 80(7):34; PILBEAM, S. & CORBRIDGE, M. 2006. *People resourcing: Contemporary HRM in practice* 3rd ed. Harlow: Pearson Education Ltd.

70. LETART, J. F. 1998. A look at virtual HR: how far behind am I? *HR magazine*, June:33–42.

71. Ibid.:36.

72. Ibid.

73. Ibid.:36–37.

74. Ibid.: p. 38.

75. Ibid.:36–39.

76. ARMSTRONG, M. 2006. *A handbook of human resource management practices* 10th ed. London: Kogan Page:289; REINDL, R. 2007. Growing talent at Edwards Lifesciences. *Training & development*, 61(2):38–41, February; OAKES, K. 2006. The emergence of talent management. *Training & development*, 60(4):21–24, April; SILVERMAN, L. L. 2006. How do you keep the right people on the bus? Try stories. *The journal for quality and participation*, 29(4):11–15, Winter; BECKER, F. 2007. Organizational ecology and knowledge networks. *California management review*, 49(2):42–61, Winter; MEISINGER, S. 2006. Talent management in a knowledge-based economy. *HR magazine*, 51(5):10, May; CORSELLO, J. 2006. The future is now for talent management. *Workforce management*, 85(12); INGHAM, J. 2006. Closing the talent management gap? *Strategic HR review*, 5(3):20–23; GOFFEE, R. & JONES, G. 2007. Leading clever people. *Harvard business review*, 85(3):72–79; LANDES, L. 2006.

Getting the best out of people in the workplace. *The journal for quality and participation*, 29(4):27–29, Winter; JOERRES, J. & TURCQ, D. 2007. Talent value management. *Industrial management*, March/April:8–13.

77. SCHWEYER, A. 2004. *Talent management systems*. Canada: John Wiley & Sons Ltd:22; GRIGORYEV. P. 2006. Hiring by competency models. *The journal for quality & participation*, 29(4):16–18.

78. SCHWEYER, A. 2004. *Talent management systems*. Canada: John Wiley & Sons Ltd:22.

79. Ibid.:35.

80. Ibid.:38–39.

81. ARMSTRONG, M. 2006. *A handbook of human resource management practices* 10th ed. London: Kogan Page:289.

82. Ibid.:290.

83. MCCAULEY, C. & WAKEFIELD, M. 2006. Talent management in the 21st Century: help your company find, develop and keep its strongest workers. *The journal for quality & participation*, 29(4):4–7, Winter.

84. Lockwood, N. R. 2006. Talent management: driver for organisational success. *HR magazine*, 51(6):2–10.

85. ELKELES, T. & PHILLIPS, J. 2007. *The chief learning officer: Driving value within a changing organisation through learning and development*. Oxford: Butterworth-Heinemann, an imprint of Elsevier; DYCHTWALD, K., ERICKSON, T. J. & MORISON, R. 2006. *Workforce crisis: How to beat the coming shortage of skills and talent*. Boston, Massachusetts: Harvard Business School Press.

86. LOCKWOOD, N. R. 2006. Talent management: driver for organisational success. *HR magazine*, 51(6):5; BERGER, L. A. & BERGER, D. R. 2004. *The talent management handbook*. New York: McGraw-Hill; BOUDREAU, J. W. & RAMSTAD, P. M. 2005. Talentship, talent segmentation and sustainability: a new HR decision science paradigm for a new strategy definition, *Human resource management*, 44(2):129–136; GROSSMAN, R. J. 2006. Developing talent. *HR magazine*, 51(1):40–46, January.

Appendix 1.1

Teleworking – organisational, societal, and individual advantages and challenges

Table A1 Organisational advantages and challenges of teleworking

	Advantages	**Challenges**	
Home-based telecommuting	Greater productivity Lower absenteeism Better morale Greater openness Fewer interruptions at office Reduced overhead Wider pool of talent Lower turnover Regulation compliance	Performance monitoring Performance measurement Managerial control Mentoring Jealous colleagues Synergy Informal interaction Organisational culture Virtual culture	Organisation loyalty Interpersonal skills Availability Schedule maintenance Work coordination Internal customers Communication Guidelines (e.g. expenses) Technology
Satellite office	Greater productivity Better morale Wider pool of talent Lower turnover Customer proximity Regulation compliance Corporate culture intact	Performance monitoring Performance measurement Managerial control	Jealous colleagues Virtual culture Internal customers
Neighbourhood work centre	Greater productivity Better morale Wider pool of talent Lower turnover Customer proximity Regulation compliance	Performance monitoring Performance measurement Managerial control Mentoring Jealous colleagues Synergy	Informal interaction Organisation culture Virtual culture Organisational loyalty Schedule maintenance Work coordination Internal customers
Mobile work	Greater productivity Lower absenteeism Customer proximity	Performance monitoring Performance measurement Managerial control Synergy Informal interaction Organisational culture Virtual culture	Organisational loyalty Availability Schedule maintenance Work coordination Communication Guidelines (e.g. expenses) Technology

Table A2 Individual advantages and challenges of teleworking

	Advantages	Challenges	
Home-based telecommuting	Less time commuting Cost savings Less stress No need for relocation More autonomy Schedule flexibility Comfortable work environment Fewer distractions Absence of office politics Work/family balance Workplace fairness More job satisfaction	Social isolation Professional isolation Organisation culture Reduced office influence Work/family balance Informal interaction	Conducive home environment Focusing on work Longer hours Access to resources Technical savvy
Satellite office	Less time commuting Cost savings Less stress No need for relocation Work/family balance More job satisfaction	Professional isolation Reduced office influence	Access to resources
Neighbourhood work centre	Less time commuting Cost savings Less stress No need for relocation More autonomy Absence of office politics Work/family balance More job satisfaction	Social isolation Professional isolation Organisation culture	Reduced office influence Access to resources
Mobile work	More autonomy Schedule flexibility Absence of office politics	Social isolation Professional isolation Organisation culture Reduced office influence	Longer hours Access to resources Technical savvy

Table A3 Societal advantages and challenges of teleworking

	Advantages	**Challenges**	
Home-based telecommuting	Less traffic congestion Less pollution Less neighbourhood crime Greater community involvement	Telework culture	Loss of ability to interact with others
Satellite office	Less traffic congestion Less pollution Greater community Involvement		
Neighbourhood work centre	Less traffic congestion Less pollution Greater community involvement		
Mobile work		Telework culture	

SOURCE: KURLAND, N. B. & BAILEY, D. E. 1999. Telework: the advantages and challenges of working here, there, anywhere, and anytime. *Organizational dynamics* 28, (2):56–58. Copyright Elsevier, used with permission.

Appendix 1.2

Addressing the risks of working at home

Cigna Corp has strict guidelines for its employees regarding the work-at-home environment. The firm's Risk Management group publishes information on the company's intranet about the workspace, productivity, health, personal safety, and information security. Table A4 gives the highlights.

Table A4 Guidelines for the workspace, productivity, health, personal safety, and information security

The workspace	• Create a space where there is minimal traffic and distraction. • Make it comfortable, with adequate room for computer, printer, fax machine, and storage. • Keep it off-limits to family and friends (for security reasons). • Use the proper furniture and equipment, some of which may be supplied by the company. • Be sure to have proper lighting and telephone service.
Health	• Be sure the workspace is ergonomically sound, if possible. • Try to avoid eyestrain by having enough light and having the computer at a comfortable level. • Use a headset or speakerphone with the telephone instead of propping it between your head and shoulder. • Keep space well ventilated. In particular, place printers, fax machines, and copiers away from walls, because this type of equipment produces ozone.
Information security	• Remember that the home office is an extension of the company office. • Be vigilant about avoiding computer viruses and protecting information. • Be sure to back up and store data and other information in a safe place, and also provide a copy to the office in case the home set is damaged.
Personal safety	• Be cautious; 100 000 people are injured in their homes every year. • Be careful of visitors. Don't hold meetings in your home. • Have working smoke detectors and an adequate number of fire extinguishers. • Know first aid. • Use a post office box rather than giving out your home address.

SOURCE: Adapted from material by CIGNA Corp., based in Philadelphia, as it appeared in SOLOMON, C. M. 2000. Don't forget your telecommuters. *Workforce*, 79(5):58. Used with permission. www.workforce.com.

2

Human resources and the competitive advantage

Learning outcomes

After reading this chapter you should be able to:

▶ Explain what a competitive advantage is
▶ Distinguish between the different sources of competitive advantage
▶ Discuss the role of human resources within the competitive-advantage paradigm
▶ Discuss the different paradigms regarding the contribution of human resources to company performance

Purpose

The purpose of this chapter is to introduce you to the role of human resources in gaining a competitive advantage for a company.

Chapter overview

This chapter focuses on the competitive advantage of companies. It begins with a discussion on what the concept of competitive advantage entails. It then considers the different sources of competitive advantage and goes on to discuss the role of human resources in this regard. The chapter also contains a discussion of the various paradigms regarding the contribution of human resources to company performance. The concluding case study illustrates how the theory in this chapter can be applied practically to companies.

Introduction

It is an accepted fact that governments do not make profits, but do create the environment in which organisations and employees can interact to the advantage and benefit of all concerned. Thus, the well-being of the citizens of any country is inextricably linked to the effectiveness of their organisations. However, for organisations to achieve their goals, they must constantly look for better ways to organise and manage their work.[1] Although this is not an easy task, a substantial body of evidence indicates that many organisations can obtain a competitive advantage by adopting a management style that involves employees in the business of their organisation.[2] Employee involvement and most of the management practices that are part of it have been shown to have significant positive effects on organisational effectiveness.[3] There is thus a growing recognition that a primary source of competitive advantage derives from a company's human resources; also that this source of advantage may be more inimitable and enduring than a particular product is.

This was not always the case, as human resources – both as labour and as a business function – have traditionally been seen as a cost to be minimised. However, the new interest in HR as a strategic lever that can have economically significant effects on a company's bottom line appears to be shifting the focus more towards value creation.

In this chapter, we shall see what a competitive advantage is, what its sources are, and what HRM's role is in gaining a competitive advantage.

2.1 **What is a 'competitive advantage'?**

As observed in the literature, understanding the phrase 'competitive advantage' is an ongoing challenge for many decision makers.[4] Historically, competitive advantage was thought of as a matter of position; companies occupied a competitive space and built and defended their market share.[5] With this strategy, the competitive advantage depended on the area in which the business was located and where it chose to provide its goods and services. This was known as the strategic model.

This strategy seemed to work well in a stable environment, especially for large and dominant organisations.[6] However, with rapid competition appearing, it outlived its popularity and a new meaning of the phrase 'competitive advantage' emerged.

One of the earlier researchers in this area was Barney, who, besides defining the concept, provided some interesting insight into the total area of competitive advantage.[7-8] Barney defined the term as follows[9]:

> A firm is said to have a sustained competitive advantage when it is implementing a value creating strategy not simultaneously being implemented by any current or potential competitors and when these other firms are unable to duplicate the benefits of this strategy.
>
> SOURCE: BARNEY, J. 1991. Firm resources and sustained competitive advantage. *Journal of management,* (17)1:101.

From the above description, it appears that company resources have a major role to play in obtaining a competitive advantage. Companies cannot create strategies if they do not utilise their resources in the process. This approach is known as the resource-based view (RBV), and is based on two assumptions[10]: first, that companies within an industry or group may be heterogeneous with respect to the strategic resources they control; and second, that these resources may not be perfectly mobile across the industry or group. If this is not the case, companies will be able to retain a competitive advantage only for a very short period; they will also have to be the first to utilise their resources in the marketplace to make this possible.

2.2 **Sources of competitive advantage**

As indicated in the previous section, the RBV plays a key role in achieving a competitive advantage. This view describes a company as a

Figure 2.1 An example of a strategic specialised bundle*

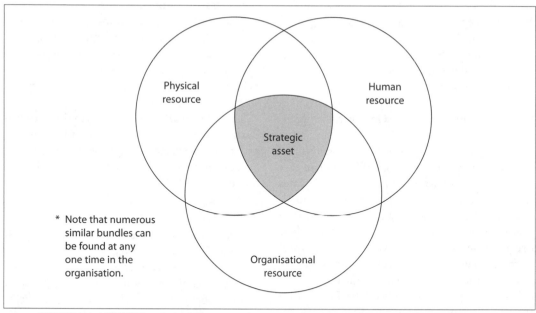

SOURCE: WINFREY, F. L., MICHALISIN, M. D. & ACAR, W. 1996. The paradox of competitive advantage. *Strategic change*, 5:206. Copyright John Wiley & Sons Ltd, used with permission.

bundle of resources (see Figure 2.1) that enables it to conceive and implement strategies that will lead to above-average industry returns.[11-12]

Thus the differences in company resources across an industry will be reflected in the variability in profits generated by them. No two companies are alike, because no two companies have had the same set of experiences, acquired the same assets and skills or built the same organisational culture. Each company, therefore, is unique.[13]

It is also important to note that the RBV of competitive advantage differs from the traditional strategy paradigm mentioned earlier, in that the RBV is company focused, whereas the traditional strategic analysis has an industry-environment focus.[14] The traditional strategy model also sees company resources as homogeneous and mobile across companies in an industry, i.e. companies can purchase or create resources held by a competing company, which is not the case with the RBV.[15]

Barney indicates that a company's resources can be classified into four groups, namely[16]:

- *Financial capital resources.* These include debt and equity-retained earnings.
- *Physical capital resources.* These include physical technology, machines, manufacturing facilities, and buildings.
- *Human capital resources.* These include knowledge, experience, insight, and wisdom of employees associated with a company.
- *Organisational capital resources.* These are the history, relationships, trust, and organisational culture that are attributes of groups of individuals associated with the company, as well as a company's formal reporting structure, explicit management-control systems, and compensation policies.

However, not all these resources can be classified as strategic resources (assets). For example, some might even prevent the company from implementing valuable strategies. To determine a resource's value, managers must address four questions[17] concerning value, rarity, imitability, and organisation. We shall briefly discuss these.[18]

- *The question of value.* The first question to ask is: do a company's resources add value by enabling it to exploit the opportunities and/or neutralise the threats in the company's environment? By answering this question, managers link the analysis of internal resources with the analysis of environmental opportunities and threats. This is important as the resources of a company cannot be valuable in a vacuum; the company must be able to exploit opportunities and/or neutralise threats.[19]

- *The question of rarity.* The second question to ask is: how many other companies already possess the valuable resources? The valuable resources must be rare among the competing companies in order to be a source of competitive advantage. However, this does not mean that a common but valuable resource is not important; it might be essential for a company's survival.[20]

- *The question of imitability.* The third question to ask is: do companies without a resource face a prohibitive cost disadvantage in obtaining the resources other companies already possess? Having a valuable and rare resource can at least provide a company with a temporary competitive advantage. However, if a competing company does not find it too expensive to imitate this resource, the competitive edge will soon disappear. If imitation is too expensive, the first company will retain its competitive advantage. According to Barney, imitation can occur in at least two ways: by duplication or by substitution. Duplication occurs when an imitating company builds the same kind of resources it knows the competitor possesses; with substitution a imitating company may find a similar resource that provides the same result. It is important to note that some competing companies might find the imitation of a company's resources difficult as a result of historical reasons. For example, many resources are built up over years through

trial and error within companies, making them unique reflections of personalities, experiences, and relationships that can exist only in one company. Another obstacle might be the social integration of resources through trust, friendship, teamwork, and culture, which will make them virtually impossible to imitate.[21]

- *The question of organisation.* The fourth question that can be asked is: is a company organised to exploit the full competitive potential of its resources? As indicated thus far in this chapter, a company's competitive-advantage potential depends on the value, rarity, and imitability of its resources. However, to fully realise what it has, a company needs a proper organisational structure. Issues that are important in this regard are a formal reporting structure, explicit management-control systems, and compensation policies. These components are also referred to in the literature as complementary resources, as they have – in isolation – only a limited ability to generate a competitive advantage. In combination with other resources, however, they are capable of releasing a company's full competitive advantage.[22]

Before we conclude this section of the chapter, it is important to look at the aspect of flexibility, which has not been mentioned. By aligning its strategy and its resources with the environment, a company can achieve superior performance. In the literature this alignment is termed 'strategic fit'.[23-27] However, with rapid external and internal changes taking place, this strategic fit becomes more challenging (see Chapter 4). The ability of a company to adjust to these changes is referred to as 'strategic flexibility'.[28-34]

Winfrey, Michalisin, and Acar[35] make a number of suggestions that will help a company sustain strategic fit while simultaneously enjoying flexibility in a hypercompetitive environment. One of their proposals is to give a system flexibility within the company, which will allow it to create batches of unique products quickly, at a relatively low cost, as and when required. Galbraith[36], as quoted by Winfrey et al., notes that a flexible system's transferability makes it a valuable resource. To enhance this system, companies must also strive to acquire flexible (knowledge) workers and organic structures which in a hypercompetitive environment will play a crucial role. The basis for this flexibility can be made possible by installing a company culture based on creativity and quick response.

2.3 HR's role in gaining a competitive advantage

The role that HR can play in gaining a competitive advantage for an organisation is empirically well documented.[37-45] A number of paradigms in the literature describe the contribution of HR to company performance:

- The first paradigm assigns value to a company's stock of human intellectual capital as a way of measuring the contribution of HR to the company's performance (see Chapter 7).[46] The researchers into human intellectual capital attempt to formalise, capture, and leverage this asset (intellectual capital) to produce higher-value products. This approach can be captured in the RBV.
- The second paradigm attempts to identify HR's best practices. Researchers in this movement specify and measure the bundles of typologies of HR practices associated with the high performance of labour.[47-48]
- The third paradigm is a new perspective, designed by Raphael Amit and Monica Belcourt[49], which is anchored in both the RBV and the best-practices theory, and is known as the 'process' approach. This perspective integrates economic considerations with social-legitimacy aspects.

Before we look at these different perspectives on the role of HR in a competitive-advantage paradigm, it might be useful to evaluate the HR component against the measures of sources of competitive advantage. For this discussion we shall look at the important work done by Wright and McMahan and published in their article 'Theoretical perspectives for strategic human resource management'.[50]

- *The value of HR.* For human resources to exist as a sustained competitive advantage they must provide value to the company. A heterogeneous demand for labour (i.e. companies have jobs that require different types of skills) and a heterogeneous supply of labour (i.e. individuals differ in their skills and level of skills) are assumed. Under these circumstances, human resources can add value to the company.[51]
- *The rarity of HR.* If it is to be a source of sustained competitive advantage, a resource must be rare. Wright and McMahan note that, due to the normal distribution of ability, human resources with high levels of ability are, by definition, rare. For example, the basic premise of a selection process is to select only the individuals who possess the highest ability.[52]
- *The inimitability of HR.* Human resources must be inimitable to be considered a source of sustained competitive advantage. Wright and McMahan use the concepts of unique historical conditions, causal ambiguity, and social complexity to demonstrate the inimitability of human resources:
  - ➤ Unique historical conditions are the historical events that shape the development of a company's practices, policies, and culture.
  - ➤ Causal ambiguity describes a situation where the causal source of the competitive advantage is not easily identified.
  - ➤ Social complexity recognises that in many situations (e.g. team projects) competitive advantage has its origins in unique social relationships that cannot be duplicated.

Thus, Wright and McMahan argue that, due to the fact that many competitive advantages that might be based on a company's human resources are characterised by unique historical conditions, causal ambiguity, and social complexity, it is highly unlikely that well-developed human resources could easily be imitated.[53]

- *The substitutability of HR.* For a resource to be considered a source of sustained competitive advantage it must not have substitutes. For example, if a company has the highest-ability individuals, who constitute a source of competitive advantage, and a competitor develops new technology that provides vast increases in productivity – greater than the productivity differences in the company's ability – it will be only a matter of time before the company obtains the same technology, and then its human resources will again exist as a source of competitive advantage.[54]

From the foregoing discussion it is clear that human resources can serve as a source of competitive advantage for a company. As mentioned earlier in this section, a number of paradigms exist in the literature regarding the contribution of HR to company performance. We shall now discuss each of these paradigms in more detail.

2.3.1 The resource-based paradigm

This approach suggests that HR systems can contribute to a sustained competitive advantage by facilitating the development of competencies that are company specific.[55] However, one of the biggest problems facing the resource-based approach, especially its human resources, is the possibility of employee turnover.[56–58] Building competencies that do not stay long can have a negative effect on the competitive advantage enjoyed by the company. To limit the damage that can occur as a result of losses, companies can design and implement turnover-management strategies. Other approaches that can be implemented include the allocation of a bigger portion of the profits to employees by means of gainsharing or share options. To

further enhance this process, a culture of belonging can also be created within the company.[59]

Performance implications from a HR perspective thus go much further than the knowledge/competencies the HR have; motivation also plays a part. Accordingly, an integral part of all the processes mentioned above is the motivation of employees within a company. In the resource-based literature this is called the 'level of interest alignment', i.e. the degree of alignment of individual interest with organisational goals.[60] Gottschalg and Zollo[61] describe this as 'the improvement in organisational performance due to changes in employee behaviour obtained through increased interest alignment that accrues to the organisation'. Two aspects are important here, namely:

- The degree to which the behaviour helps individuals to meet their goals
- The relevance of each organisational goal to the individual (individual motivational preferences) – individual goals are not always in line with organisational goals.[62]

It is thus helpful, especially in the RBVs of competitive advantage, to use the concept of interest alignment as a measure of the correspondence between individual and organisational goals. Gottschalg and Zollo[63] define organisational interest alignment, in contrast, as 'the degree to which the members of the organisation are motivated to behave in line with organisational goals'. According to Linderberg[64], as quoted in Gottschalg and Zollo[65], a high level of interest alignment can be realised at three levels of motivation by three interest-alignment levers (see Figure 2.2 on the next page).

The three motivation levels in Figure 2.2 are as follows:

1. *The extrinsic motivation level.* This is most directly influenced by the reward system that specifies rewards for a given behaviour. It also includes issues such as power and recognition.
2. *The hedonic intrinsic motivation level.* This is the enjoyment individuals experience in

Figure 2.2 Antecedents of organisational interest alignment

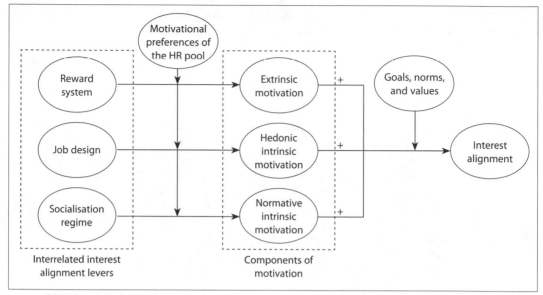

SOURCE: GOTTSCHALG, O. & ZOLLO, M. 2007. Interest alignment and competitive advantage. *Academy of management review,* 32(2):423. Used with permission.

completing the task in the work environment. It can be influenced by changes in the design of individual tasks and the task context.

3. *The normative intrinsic motivation level.* This is driven by the goal of engaging in behaviour that is compliant with the norms and values of the organisation.[66] This can be influenced by the socialisation processes within the organisation.

Thus, organisations can influence interest alignment positively through adjustments of the three interest-alignment levers, namely: the reward system, the socialisation regime, and changes to job design.[67]

Besides the motivational aspects discussed above, it is also important to note that scholars of the RBV have in the past envisioned companies only as independent entitities.[68] This approach yielded only a partial account of company performance. The reason for this is that companies do not exist in isolation; they form alliances with other companies. According to recent empirical work undertaken by Das and Teng (2000), Afuah (2000), Stuart (2000), Lee, Lee and Pennings (2001), and Rothaermel (2001)[69] alliance partners can play a significant

role in shaping the resource-based competitive advantage of the company through network resources. Lavie defines network resources as 'external resources embedded in the company's alliance network – that provide strategic opportunities and affect company behaviour and value'. Thus, the fundamental assumption of the RBV that companies must own, or at least fully control, the resources that confer competitive advantage is incorrect. Ownership or control of resources is not a necessary condition for competitive advantage.[70] It is the services that resources provide, not the resources themselves, that generate value for the company, according to Lavie. The proprietary assumption of the RBV prevents an accurate evaluation of a company's competitive advantage. Thus, when an alliance is formed, each participating company endows a subset of its resources to the alliance with the expectation of generating common benefits from shared resources of both companies. Therefore, each company possesses a subset of shared resources and a subset of non-shared resources that together form its complete set of resources.[71] In view of this new development, it is clear that to gain and sustain the competitive advantage will depend less on conditions of the traditional RBV and more on the relational capability, i.e. a company's capacity to form and maintain valuable interactive relationships with alliance partners.[72] Alliances can take different forms, including joint ventures, franchising, long-term marketing and licensing contracts, reciprocal trade agreements, research-and-development (R&D) partnerships, and affiliation in research consortia. In its broadest sense, it can also include outsourcing partners.

2.3.2 The best-practices paradigm

This approach implies that there is a direct relationship between particular HR approaches and company performance.[73] The literature shows a fair amount of evidence that certain HR practices – such as compensation, selection, and training activities – can be related to company performance.[74] More recently, however, researchers have found that bundles or systems of HR practices have more influence on company performance than individual practices working in isolation.[75] Although support for a best-practices approach to HR exists, there are notable differences across studies as to what constitutes bundles of 'HR best practices'. Most studies focus on enhancing the skill base of employees through HR activities – selective staffing, comprehensive training, and broad developmental efforts like job rotation and cross-utilisation.[76] Other issues include the promotion of empowerment, participative problem-solving, and teamwork.[77] An aspect closely linked to the use of best practices is that of creating role behaviours. Company strategies dictate certain unique attitude and role behaviours from employees, and HR practices are the primary means to make this happen. However, because role behaviours of employees are observable and also transferable from one organisational setting to another, they may be easily duplicated and may not be a source of an enduring competitive advantage.

Going beyond these direct HR-performance relationships however, other evidence suggests that the impact of HR practices on company performance may be further enhanced when practices are matched with the competitive requirements inherent in a company's strategic posture.[78] This new trend came about with the introduction of the strategic HR approach (see Chapter 4).

From the research undertaken in this area three primary perspectives emerged, namely a universal approach, a contingency approach, and a configurational approach.

Huselid's[79] work reflects what has become known as the universalistic approach to strategic HRM. According to the author, this perspective assumes that there are certain best HRM practices that will contribute to, for example, increasing the financial performance of a company, regardless of the strategic goals of the company. Unfortunately, as indicated earlier with the traditional HRM approach, relatively little work has been done to provide a definitive prescription as to which HRM practices should be included in a best-practices system. The work undertaken has either focused on single organisations like banks or on single jobs within organisations, without really considering some other internal or external influences.[80]

In recent work, Delery and Doty[81] identified seven practices consistently considered to be strategic in nature. The practices are internal career opportunities, formal training systems, appraisal measures, profit sharing, employment security, voice mechanisms, and job definition. It is interesting to note that these practices were utilised in several analyses to test the soundness of the three dominant theoretical perspectives mentioned earlier, namely the universal, contingency, and configurational perspectives. The results of the analyses provided some support for each of the three perspectives.

A number of theoreticians and researchers have argued, however, that a contingency perspective is more appropriate to strategic HRM.[82] The contingency approach differs from the universal approach in that research undertaken here attempts to link HRM systems and practices to specific organisational strategies.[83] A closely related body of research calls for a configurational approach to strategic HRM and argues that it is the pattern of HRM practices and systems that contributes to the attainment of organisational goals.[84] Similarly to the contingency approach, the configurational approach argues that the fit of HRM practices and systems with the company strategy is a vital factor; however, it goes on to argue that there are specific 'ideal types' of HRM systems and practices that provide both horizontal and vertical fit of HRM systems and practices to the organisational structure and strategic goals.

The configuration of practices and systems that provides the tightest horizontal and vertical fit with any given strategy is the ideal type for an organisation pursuing that particular strategy. (Horizontal fit refers to the internal consistency of the organisation's HR policies or practices. Vertical fit refers to the congruence of the HR system with other organisational characteristics, such as the company strategy.)

2.3.3 The process paradigm

This approach, as mentioned earlier, is anchored in both the RBV and the best-practices theory.[85] The creators of this approach, Amit and Belcourt, refer to HRM processes as the deeply embedded company-specific dynamic routines by which a company attracts, socialises, trains and motivates, evaluates, and compensates its HR.[86]

Company-specific HRM processes are established by developing and exchanging information throughout the entire organisation. This process, sometimes called organisation learning, creates transfers and institutionalises knowledge throughout the organisation, which increases its adaptability.[87] From the foregoing it can be deduced that HRM processes within a company are evolutionary. In other words, they are continuously evolving and adapting by drawing on past experiences to refine the effectiveness of processes and to meet the changing needs of the organisation. Indeed, the HRM processes can become one of the company's strategic assets if they are able to help it realise superior profitability.[88]

Thus, to summarise, it is clear that the HRM process is an engine of renewal that can be used continually to adjust the way in which a company selects, trains, socialises, and evaluates its human capital, and that enables a company to execute its strategy effectively. The universal adoption of best practices leads to company homogeneity, as people come and go, but processes remain and improve the company. Thus, HRM processes are about how things are done, not what is produced.

SUMMARY

In this chapter, we discussed the growing importance of HRM as a source of competitive advantage. We defined the phrase 'competitive advantage' and identified sources of competitive advantage. We also discussed measures used to identify sources of competitive advantage.

Finally, we considered the various paradigms – i.e. the RBV, the best-practices approach, and the process approach – in the literature regarding the contribution of HRM to company performance.

KEY CONCEPTS

• Alliances	• Normative intrinsic motivation
• Competitive advantage	• Organisational capital resources
• Configurational approach	• Physical capital resources
• Contingency approach	• Rareness
• Extrinsic motivation	• Strategic fit
• Financial capital resources	• Strategic flexibility
• Hedonic intrinsic motivation	• Strategic specialised bundle
• Human capital resources	• Substitutability
• Imitability	• Universal approach
• Interest alignment	• Value creation
• Network resources	

CASE STUDY

Objective: To understand the competitive advantage of interconnected companies from a human resources perspective.

Outsourcing: Can it work?

The people chase

So how are outsourcers equipped to compete in this planetary war for talent? Well, it turns out these organisations are generally far better able to attract, develop, and retain talent in their area of specialization than their customers. 'In fact', says Joe Marciano, president and CEO of Océ Business Services, the New York-based document process management specialist, 'clients today are rethinking outsourcing as a means to accelerate transformation and gain competitive advantage, and that means using outsourcing to gain access to the best people to provide non-core competencies such as document services'.

In Océ Business Services' case, that means having its specialists work with public and private organisations of all sizes to help them effectively manage their business processes through enhanced document management. The life cycle of a document begins with its creation, then evolves through distribution, printing, access, and archiving, and ends with its disposal. It's about technology – but even more importantly, it's about people who can find innovative ways of using it. To make sure its staff is the best at what they do, Océ has a consistent commitment to ongoing employee training and education at all levels of the organisation. Classroom instruction, on-the-job training, and more than 1,500 online courses are woven together into a comprehensive staff education program – ranging from specialized print technologies to how to apply quality improvement methodologies like Six Sigma.

PNC Financial Services Group can attest to the efficiency of Océ's approach. The nation's twelfth-largest bank has been an Océ Business Services client for nine years, relying on its print and mail expertise to help it handle 65 million pieces of customer correspondence per year. According to Dough Lippert, vice president for operations, PNC's relationship with Océ has directly translated into millions of dollars of savings for the bank in reduced production, distribution, and postage costs. 'Océ is not simply an outsourcing vendor, they're another arm of the bank – constantly using its talented people and process knowledge to find ways to improve our operations.'

'Most importantly', notes Marcianio, 'our focus on document process management enables us to attract the best people, because we can offer them a career path not available in most corporations.' In fact, most site managers – 67%, to be exact – placed at client locations have been promoted from within. 'This investment in our people, combined with operational excellence, providing innovative customer support tools, and constantly expanding our services to meet customer needs, is core to how we create value,' says Marciano.

British Airways' relationship with EMCOR – which has managed everything from the airline's energy systems, to security, to its industrial buildings, corporate offices, call centers, and hangars for 14 years – is another example of companies using outsourcing to gain access to the right talent and know-how. Overall, there has been a significant annual saving. But saving is actually the last thing BA considers when contemplating outsourcing. 'We consider EMCOR our strategic partner,' says Bryan Mitchell, manager of BA's global facilities operations at its Heathrow Airport headquarters. That is why in March it extended its contract for three years to include over 8,6 million square feet of facilities at the airport (including the new Terminal 5), and at its headquarters in London. As he explains, 'We describe ourselves as an intelligent client. Managing the contract and EMCOR adds real value. EMCOR is with us for the long haul.'

Leveraging the workforce

As the outsourcing industry matures, companies are realizing that service providers are strategic partners that aim not to replace an organisation's in-house staff, but augment it. This allows corporations to focus their attention on the most valuable activities and not burden Grade-A players with back-office tasks. Gary Rappeport, CEO of Northbrook, Ill.-based Donlen Corp., clearly sees this trend in his industry, vehicle fleet management. There was a time when customers only saw companies like his as providers of leasing or financing for the cars, trucks, and other vehicles used in their operations. 'Today companies use us for all aspects of fleet administration – everything from acquiring and maintaining their vehicles to being the first point of contact for their drivers,' he says. This frees their internal fleet departments to become business managers, linking their fleet operations to company strategy and goals.

In addition, outsourcing partners can provide access to proprietary know-how. Donlen, for example, offers clients access to its unique online fleet management software, FleetWeb. The business intelligence application lets users stay in control of their fleet's operations and analyze cost-effectiveness by monitoring many industry variables including fuel and maintenance costs. According to Rappeport, the technology has helped many customers make more-informed decisions about their fleets and reduce costs. Often they are surprised to learn that replacing a fleet of vehicles makes sense earlier in the vehicles' life than expected.

Champions of innovation

Sometimes outsourcing partners can help speed up innovation. Their expertise can help corporate clients redesign business functions so they become more efficient and leapfrog competitors. That was the experience of a major automobile manufacturer who began outsourcing about two years ago with Pitney Bowes Management Services (PBMS), a wholly-owned subsidiary of Pitney Bowes Inc., that designs and manages customized print, mail, and document management solutions. Within the first few weeks, PBMS helped streamline the automaker's entire process for producing marketing packages distributed directly to consumers. Where once it was a matter of pulling together and mailing a folder of preprinted brochures stored in a warehouse, prospects now receive totally personalized packages – right down to the model and colour of the automobile they expressed interest in – printed in real time using the latest digital variable print technology. The result: More prospects are becoming customers.

According to Vincent De Palma, executive vice president and president, PBMS, 'It really takes a combination of new technologies, new management techniques, and talented people to produce results like this.' Pitney Bowes, the mail and document management-industry giant based in Stamford, Conn., is probably less well-known for its ability to manage a client's entire 'mailstream'. This includes all aspects of inbound and outbound document design, production, processing, and distribution. 'There's actually been a dramatic shift over the past decade in the very nature of corporate mail,' points out De Palma. The focus has gone from correspondence mail to inbound transactional and direct mail, including items such as claim forms, mortgage applications, bills, and statements, that are tied right to a company's bottom line.

At the same time, the convergence of technology and globalization is leading companies like PBMS to search the world for solutions and talent to meet changing customer needs. Even with 'physical' mail, much of the work is now done using digital technology, Six Sigma processes, and an on-site/off-site management strategy. A case in point: Through its global partner network, PBMS now handles imaging and records-management operations for many of its clients at locations all around the world, offering them lower costs and 24-hour-a-day processing capabilities.

'The real payoff for companies', says Joe Hogan, vice president of Global Outsourcing solutions for Unisys based in Blue Bell, Pa., 'is when great technology, talent, and know-how come together to create tremendous expertise in an industry segment.' As an example, he cites the vertical process knowledge that Unisys has gained by processing, on behalf of its customers, more than $10 billion of residential mortgage loans in Australia and 70% of the paper checks in Britain. 'It gives our people a level of understanding – not only about the process itself, but about the tools and technologies needed to make it work – that few others possess.'

For Unisys, all of these forces converged when it launched its 3D Visible enterprise in 2003, a proprietary approach to align IT to business goals with a comprehensive set of modelling tools and methods. The resulting 'blueprints' can be used to identify business process and IT infrastructure that can be effectively outsourced. Hogan says clients are amazed at what they uncover, and the model helps them work with Unisys to tailor an outsourcing program.

So how will the outsourcing industry shake out in the months and years ahead? It will likely continue to morph into a transnational business spread across continents, transcending cultural and political barriers. For companies, the challenge will be managing their extended far-flung operations and workforce. Hogan sums it up best: 'In this environment only the best-of-breed will flourish.' Brain power will be the great equalizer.

Questions and activities

1. Based on the descriptions of the experiences of the various companies mentioned in the case study, what is the unifying theme of the role played by HRM from a competitive-advantage perspective?
2. What were the environmental influences stimulating the actions described for each of the companies?
3. What managerial trends are indicated in the experiences of these companies?

SOURCE: CORBETT, M. F. 2007. Winning the global talent war. *Fortune* (European edition), 155(7):S4–S8, April. Used with permission.

REVIEW QUESTIONS AND ACTIVITIES

1. Write a short paragraph on the rareness of HR.
2. According to Barney, imitation can occur in at least two ways. Explain briefly.
3. Explain the RBV paradigm and its application in interconnected firms (also refer to the motivation component of the HR assets as it relates to this paradigm).
4. Explain the best-practices paradigm.
5. Explain the process paradigm.
6. Give a brief explanation of the term 'competitive advantage'.
7. According to Barney, an organisation's resources can be classified into four groups. Name them.
8. Briefly discuss the four questions which determine a resource's value.
9. Write a short paragraph on the universal, contingency, and configurational approaches.
10. Write a brief essay on HRM's role in gaining a competitive advantage.

FURTHER READING

LEI, D. & SLOCUM, J. W. 2005. Strategic and organisational requirements for competitive advantage. *Academy of management executive*, (19)1:31–45.

FELIN, T. & HESTERLY, W. W. 2007. The knowledge-based view, nested heterogeneity, and new value creation: philosophical considerations on the locus of knowledge. *Academy of management review*, (32)1:195–218.

PRIEM, R. L. & BUTLER, J. E. 2001. Is the resource-based 'view' a useful perspective for strategic management research? *Academy of management review*, 26:22–40.

SIRMON, D. G., HITT, M. A. & IRELAND, R. D. 2007. Managing firm resources in dynamic environments to create value: looking inside the black box. *Academy of management review*, (32)1:273–292.

BOWMAN, C. & COLLIER, N. 2006. A contingency approach to creation processes. *International journal of management reviews*, (8)4:191–211.

WEB SITES

www.shrm.org/research – Society for Human Resource Management Research Division

www.imd.ch/research – IMD World competitiveness report (The Institute for Management Development – IMD)

ENDNOTES

1. LAWLER, E. E. III. 1992. *The ultimate advantage: Creating the high involvement organisation.* San Francisco, Jossey-Bass Publishers:xi; LEI, D. & SLOCUM, J. W. 2005. Strategic and organisational requirements for competitive advantage. *Academy of management executive,* 19(1):31–45.

2. LAWLER, E. E. III. 1992. *The ultimate advantage: Creating the high involvement organisation.* San Francisco, Jossey-Bass Publishers:xi. See also MONGALISO, M. P. 2001. Building competitive advantage from ubuntu: management lessons from South Africa. *Academy of management executive,* 15(3):23–33; DUNCAN, W. J., GINTER, P. M. & SWAYNE, L. E. 1998. Competitive advantage and internal organisational assessment. *Academy of management executive,* 12(3):6–16; PFEFFER, J. & ULRICH, D. 2001. Competitive advantage through human resource management): best practices or core competencies? Human relations, 54(3):361–372.

3. LAWLER, E. E. III. 1992. *The ultimate advantage: Creating the high involvement organisation.* San Francisco, Jossey-Bass Publishers:xi; CARMELI, A. & FISHLER, A. 2004. Resources, capabilities and the performance of industrial firms: a multivariate analysis. *Managerial and decision Economics,* 25(6/7):229–315, September–October.

4. DUNCAN, W. J., GINTER, P.M. & SWAYNE, L. E. 1998. Competitive advantage and internal organisational assessment. *Academy of management executive,* 12(3):7. See also Christensen, C. M. 2001. The past and future of competitive advantage. *MIT Sloan management review:* no page numbers, Winter.

5. Ibid.

6. Ibid.

7. BARNEY, J. 1991. Firm resources and sustained competitive advantage. *Journal of management,* 17(1):99–120; ACEDO, F. J., BARROSO, C. & GALAN, J. L. 2006. The resource-based theory: dissemination and main trends. *Strategic management journal,* 27(7):621–636, July.

8. BARNEY, J. 1995. Looking inside for competitive advantage. *Academy of management executive,* 9(4):49–61.

9. BARNEY, J. 1991. Firm resources and sustained competitive advantage. *Journal of management,* 17(1):101.

10. Ibid.:100; LADO, A. A., BOYD, N. G., WRIGHT, P. & KROLL, M. 2006. Paradox and theorizing with the resource-based view. *Academy of management review,* 31(1):115–131.

11. COLLIS, D. J. & MONTGOMERY, C. A. 1995. Competing on resource strategy in the 1990s. *Harvard business review,* July/August:118–125.

12. COFF, R. W. 1997. Human assets and management dilemmas: coping with hazards on the road to resource-based theory. *Academy of management review,* 22(2):374–402.

13. COLLIS, D. J. & MONTGOMERY, C. A. 1995. Competing on resource strategy in the 1990s. *Harvard business review.* July/August:119; MILLER, D. 2005. Advantage by design: competing with opportunity-based organisations. *Business horizons,* 48:393–407.

14. WRIGHT, P. M. & MCMAHAN, G. C. 1992. Theoretical perspectives for strategic human resource management. *Journal of management,* 18(2):295–320.

15. Ibid.:301.

16. BARNEY, J. 1991. Firm resources and sustained competitive advantage. *Journal of management,* 17(1):101; LEASK, G. & PARNELL, J. A. 2005. Integrating strategic groups and the resource-based perspective: understanding the competitive process. *European management journal,* 23(4): 458–470, August.

17. BARNEY, J. 1991. Firm resources and sustained competitive advantage. *Journal of management,* 17(1):105–106.

18. BARNEY, J. 1995. Looking inside for competitive advantage. *Academy of management executive,* 9(4):50–61.

19. Ibid.:50–51.

20. Ibid.:52.

21. Ibid.:53–55.

22. Ibid.:56–57.

23. VENKATRAMAN, N. & CAMILLUS, J. C. 1984. Exploring the concept of 'fit' in strategic management. *Academy of management review,* 9(3):513–525.

24. DRAZIN, R. & VAN DE VEN, A. H. 1985. Alternative forms of fit in contingency theory. *Administrative science quarterly,* 30:514–539.

25. VENKATRAMAN, N. 1990. Environment–strategy coalignment: an empirical test of its performance implications. *Strategic management journal,* (11):1–23.

26. CHORN, N. H. 1991. The 'alignment' theory: creating strategic fit. *Management decision,* 29(1):20–24.

27. NATH, D. & SUHARSHAN, D. 1994. Measuring strategy coherence through patterns of strategic choices. *Strategic management journal,* 15:43–61.

28. HARRINGAN, K. R. 1985. *Strategic flexibility: A management guide for changing times.* Lexington: Lexington Books; SCHULER, R. S. & JACKSON, S. E. 2007. *Strategic human resource management* 2nd ed. Oxford: Blackwell Publishing.

29. NOORI, H. 1990. Economies of integration: a new manufacturing focus. *International journal of technology management,* 5(5):557–587.

30. HARRIGAN, K. R. & DALMIA, G. 1991. Knowledge workers: the last bastion of competitive advantage. *Planning review,* November/December:4–9, 48.

31. GOLDHAR, J. D., JELINEK, M. & SCHIE, T. W. 1990. Flexibility and competitive advantage – manufacturing becomes a service industry. *International journal of technology management,* Special Issue on Manufacturing Strategy, 6(3/4):243–259.

32. SARGE, A. 1991. Strategic fit and societal effect: Interpreting cross-national comparisons of technology organisation and human resources. *Organization studies*, 12(2):161–190.

33. PARTHASARTHY, R. & SETHI, S. P. 1992. The impact of flexible automation on business strategy and organization structure. *Academy of management review*, 17(1):86–111.

34. D'AVENI, R. A. 1994. *Hypercompetition: Managing the dynamics of strategic maneuvering.* New York: The Free Press.

35. WINFREY, F. L., MICHALISIN, M. D. & ACAR, W. 1996. The paradox of competitive advantage. *Strategic change*, 5:206.

36. GALBRAITH, C. S. 1990. Transferring core manufacturing technologies in high-technology firms. *California management review*, Summer:56–70.

37. BECKER, B. & GERHART, B. 1996. The impact of human resource management on organisational performance: progress and prospects. *Academy of management journal*, 39(4):779–801; BURKE, R. J. 2005. Human resources as a competitive advantage. (*In* Burke, R. J. and Cooper, C. L. (Eds.). *Reinventing HRM: Challenges and new directions.* Oxon: Routledge:17–33.)

38. DELERY, J. E. & DOTY, D. H. 1996. Modes of theorizing in strategic human resource management: tests of universalistic, contingency and configurational performance predictions. *Academy of management journal*, 39(4):802–835.

39. YOUNDT, M. A., SNELL, S. A., DEAN, J. W. & LEPAK, D. P. 1996. Human resource management, manufacturing strategy and firm performance. *Academy of management journal*, 39(4):836–866.

40. ARTHUR, J. B. 1994. Effects of human resource systems on manufacturing performance and turnover. *Academy of management journal*, 37:670–687.

41. CUTCHER-GERSHENFELD, J. C. 1991. The impact on economic performance of a transformation in workplace relations. *Industrial and labour relations review*, 44:241–260.

42. HUSELID, M. A. 1995. The impact of human resource management practices on turnover, productivity and corporate financial performance. *Academy of management journal*, 38:635–672; BURUD, S. & TUMOLO, M. 2004. *Leveraging the new human capital: Adaptive strategies, results achieved and stories of transformation.* Palo Alto, CA: Davies-Black Publishing.

43. GERHART, B. & MILKOVICH, G. T. 1990. Organizational differences in managerial compensation and firm performance. *Academy of management journal*, 33:663–691.

44. MACDUFFIE, J. P. 1995. Human resource bundles and manufacturing performance: organizational logic and flexible production systems in the world auto industry. *Industrial and labor relations review*, 48:197–221.

45. AMIT, R. & SHOEMAKER, J. H. 1993. Strategic assets and organisational rents. *Strategic management journal*, 14:33–46.

46. STEWART, T. A. *Intellectual capital.* New York: Doubleday/Currency.

47. BECKER, B. & GERHART, B. 1996. The impact of human resources management on organizational performance: progress and prospects. *Academy of management journal*, 39:779–801; DYCHTWALD, K., ERICKSON, T. J. & MORISON, R. 2006. *Workforce crisis: How to beat the coming shortage of skills and talent.* Boston, Massachusetts: Harvard Business School Press.

48. KOCH, R. & GUNTER-MCGRATH, R. 1996. Improving labour productivity: HR policies do matter. *Strategic management journal*, 17:335–354; REDDINGTON, M., WILLIAMSON, M. & WITHERS, M. 2005. *Transforming HR: Creating value through people.* Oxford: Elsevier Butterworth-Heinemann.

49. AMIT, R. & BELCOURT, M. 1999. Human resources management processes: a value-creating source of competitive advantage. *European management journal*, 17(2):174–181; PILBEAM, S. & CORBRIDGE, M. 2006. *People resourcing: Contemporary HRM in practice* 3rd ed. Harlow: Pearson Education Ltd.

50. WRIGHT, P. M. & MCMAHON, G. C. 1992. Theoretical perspectives for strategic human resource management. *Journal of management*, 18(2):295–320.

51. Ibid.:301.

52. Ibid.:302.

53. Ibid.

54. Ibid.:303.

55. LADO, A. A. & WILSON, M. C. 1994. Human resource systems and sustained competitive advantage: A competency-based perspective. *Academy of management review*, 19(4):700; DOMSCH, M. E. & HRISTOZOVA, E. 2006. *Human resource management in consulting firms.* Heidelberg: Springer Berlin.

56. CASIO, W. F. 1991. *Costing human resources: The financial impact of behaviour in organisations.* Boston: PWS Kent.

57. CHIANG, S. H. & CHIANG, S. C. 1990. General human capital as a shared investment under asymmetric information. *Canadian journal of economics*, 23:175–188.

58. STEFFY, B. D. & MAURER, S. D. 1988. Conceptualizing the economic effectiveness of human resource activities. *Academy of management review*, (13):271–286.

59. COFF, R. W. 1997. Human assets and management dilemmas: coping with hazards on the road to resource-based theory. *Academy of management review*, 22(2):380–382. See also PRIEM, R. L. & BUTLER, J. E. 2001. Is the resource-based view a useful perspective for strategic management research? *Academy of management review*, 26(1):22–40; PRIEM, R. L. & BUTLER, J. E. 2001. Tautology in the

resource-based view and the implications of externally determined resource value: further comments. *Academy of management review*, 26(1):57–66; HAANES, K. & FJELDSTAD, O. 2000. Linking intangible resources and competition. *European management journal*, 18(1):35–36.

60. GOTTSCHALG, O. & ZOLLO, M. 2007. Interest alignment and competitive advantage. *Academy of management review*, 32(2):418–437.

61. Ibid.:419.

62. Ibid.:420.

63. Ibid.:420.

64. LINDENBERG, S. 2001. Intrinsic motivation in a new light. *Kyklos*, 54:317–342.

65. GOTTSCHALG, O. & ZOLLO, M. 2007. Interest alignment and competitive advantage. *Academy of management review*, 32(2):421.

66. Ibid.:420.

67. Ibid.:423.

68. LAVIE, D. 2006. The competitive advantage of interconnected firms: an extension of the resource-based view. *Academy of management review*, 31(3):638.

69. DAS, S. & TENG, B-S. 2000. A resource-based theory of strategic alliances. *Journal of management*, 26:31–61; AFUAH, A. 2000. How much your co-competitors' capabilities matter in the face of technological change. *Strategic management journal*, 21(Special issue):387–404; STUART, T. E. 2000. Inter-organisational alliances and the performance of firms: a study of growth and innovation rates in a high-technology industry. *Strategic management journal*, 21:719–811; LEE, C., LEE, K. & PENNINGS, J. M. 2001. Internal capabilities, external networks, and performance: a study on technology-based ventures. *Strategic management journal*, 22:615–640; ROTHAERMEL, F. T. 2001. Incumbent's advantage through exploiting complementary assets via interfirm cooperation. *Strategic management journal*, 22:687–699.

70. LAVIE, D. 2006. The competitive advantage of interconnected firms: an extension of the resource-based view. *Academy of management review*, 31(3):638.

71. Ibid.:643.

72. Ibid.:449.

73. BECKER, B. & GERHART, B. 1996. The impact of human resources management on organizational performance: progress and prospects. *Academy of management journal*, 39:779–801.

74. YOUNDT, M. A., SNELL, S. A., DEAN, J. W. & LEPAK, D. P. 1996. Human resource management, manufacturing strategy and firm performance. *Academy of management journal*, 39(4):837–838.

75. Ibid. See also ARTHUR, J. B. 1994. Effects of human resource systems on manufacturing performance and turnover. *Academy of management journal*, 37:670–687; HUSELID, M. 1995. The impact of human resource management practices on turnover, productivity and corporate financial performance. *Academy of management journal*, 38(3):635–672; KLEINER, M. M., BLOCK, R. W., ROOMKIN, M. & SALSBURG, S. W. 1987. *Human resources and the performance of the firm*. Madison, W.I.: University of Wisconsin.; KOCHAN, T. A. & OSTERMAN, P. 1994. *The mutual gains enterprise*. Boston: Harvard Business School Press; MACDUFFIE, J. P. 1995. Human resource bundles and manufacturing performance: organizational logic and flexible production systems in the world auto industry. *Industrial and labor relations review*, 48:197–221; OSTERMAN, P. 1994. How common is workplace transformation and who adopts it? *Industrial and labour relations review*, 47:173–188; PFEFFER, J. 1994. *Competitive advantage through people*. Boston: Harvard Business School Press; RUSSEL, J. S., TERBORG, J. R. & POWERS, M. L. 1985. Organisational productivity and organisational level training and support. *Personnel psychology*, 38:849–863.

76. YOUNDT, M. A., SNELL, S. A., DEAN, J. W. & LEPAK, D. P. 1996. Human resource management, manufacturing strategy and firm performance. *Academy of management journal*, 39(4):839.

77. Ibid.:836–866; COLBERT, B. A. 2004. The complex resource-based view: implications for theory and practice in strategic human resource management. *Academy of management review*, 29(3):341–358.

78. CAPPELLI, P., BASSI, L., KATZ, H., KNOKE, D., OSTERMAN, P. & USEEM, M. 1997. *Change at work*. New York: Oxford University Press. See also JACKSON, S. E., SCHULER, R. S. & RIVERO, J. C. 1989. Organizational characteristics as predictors of personnel practices. *Personnel psychology*, 42:727–786; MILES, R. & SNOW, C. C. 1984. Designing strategic human resource systems. *Organizational dynamics*, 13(1):36–52; WRIGHT, P. M., SMART, D. & MCMAHAN, G. C. 1995. Matches between human resources and strategy among NCAA basketball teams. *Academy of management journal*, 38:1052–1074.

79. HUSELID, M. 1995. The impact of human resource management practices on turnover, productivity and corporate financial performance. *Academy of management journal*, 38(3):635–672.

80. GERHART, B., TREVOR, C. & GRAHAM, M. 1996. New directions in employee compensation research. (*In* Ferris, G. R. (Ed.). *Research in personnel and human resources management*: Greenwich: CI JAI Press: 143–203); DYER, L. & REEVES, T. 1995. HR strategies and firm performance: what do we know and where do we need to go? *International journal of human resource management*, 6:656–670; MILGRAM, P. & ROBERTS, J. 1995. Complementarities and fit: strategy, structure and organizational change in manufacturing. *Journal of accounting and economics*, 19(2):179–208.

81. DELERY, J. E. & DOTY, D. H. 1996. Modes of theorizing in strategic human resource management:

tests of universalistic, contingency and configurational performance prediction. *Academy of management journal*, 39(4):802–835.

82. BUTLER, J. E., FERRIS, G. R. & NAPIER, N. K. 1991. *Strategy and human resources management.* Cincinnati: South Western. See also DYER, L. & HOLDER, G. 1988. A strategic perspective of human resource management. (*In* Dyer, L. (Ed.). *Human resource management: Evolving roles and responsibilities.* Washington, D.C., Bureau of National Affairs:1–46); LENGNICK-HALL, C. A. & LENGNICK-HALL, M. L. 1988. Strategic human resource management: a review of the literature and a proposed typology. *Academy of management review*, 13:454–470.

83. FOMBRUN, C. J., TICHY, N. M. & DEVANNA, M. A. 1984. *Strategic human resource management.* New York, Wiley; GOLDEN, K. & RAMANUJAN, V. 1985. Between a dream and a nightmare: on the integration of the human resource management and strategic business planning process. *Human resource management*, 24:429–452; GOMEZ-MEJIA, L. R. & BALKIN, D. B. 1992. *Compensation, organizational strategy and firm performance.* Cincinnati: South Western.

84. DOTY, D. H., GLICK, W. H. & HUBER, G. P. 1993. Fit, equifinality and organizational effectiveness: a test of two configurational theories. *Academy of management journal*, 36:1196–1250. See also DOTY, D. H. & GLICK, W. H. 1994. Typologies as a unique form of theory building: toward improved understanding and modelling. *Academy of management review*, 19:230–251; MEYER, A. D., TSUI, A. S. & HININGS, C. R. 1993. Guest editors' introduction: configurational approaches to organizational analysis. *Academy of management journal*, 36:1175–1195; VENKATRAMAN, N. & PRESCOTT, J. E. 1990. Environment–strategy coalignment: an empirical test of its performance implications. *Strategic management journal*, 11:1–23.

85. AMIT, R. & BELCOURT, M. 1999. Human resources management processes: a value-creating source of competitive advantage. *European management journal*, 17(2):174.

86. Ibid.:175.

87. Ibid.:176.

88. Ibid.:177–179.

3

Human resources and leadership

Learning outcomes

After reading this chapter you should be able to:

▶ Define the concept of leadership
▶ Discuss the ten leadership management roles
▶ Explain the difference between successful leadership and unsuccessful leadership
▶ Identify several individual models of leadership
▶ Identify several group models of leadership
▶ Identify several organisational models of leadership
▶ List the various leadership training and development techniques
▶ Describe the leadership role of human resources

Purpose

The purpose of this chapter is to introduce you to several leadership theories as well as to the leadership role of human resources.

Chapter overview

This chapter focuses on the importance of leadership within organisations. It begins by discussing the definition of the concept of leadership. It then examines what leaders actually do in organisations. Thereafter it describes the three levels of leadership – namely individual, group, and organisational – and highlights the differences between successful leadership and unsuccessful leadership. The chapter concludes with a discussion of leadership training and development techniques and the leadership role of human resources. The concluding case study illustrates how the theory contained in this chapter can be applied in practice.

Introduction

Thus far we have examined the new role that HRM has to play to enable the company to gain and sustain its competitive advantage. Being a good manager in today's flexible, innovative, and dynamic environment is not enough; all managers (HR included) also need to play a leadership role.[1]

In this chapter, we shall begin by defining the concept of leadership. We shall continue by discussing individual, group, and organisational models of leadership, leadership managerial roles, the difference between successful leadership and unsuccessful leadership, leadership training and development techniques, and the leadership role of HRM.

3.1 What is leadership?

The literature contains many definitions of leadership.[2] Bennis, for example, an authority on leadership, claims to have collected more than 300[3] definitions. Nevertheless, they all say essentially the same thing – namely that leadership is:

- The activity of influencing people to strive willingly for group objectives[4]
- The process of influencing the activities of an individual or a group in efforts towards goal achievement in a given situation[5]
- The process of giving purpose (meaningful direction) to collective effort, and causing willing effort to be expended to achieve such a purpose[6]
- The activity of getting people to move in directions, make decisions, and support paths they would typically not have selected[7]
- The process of making sense of what people are doing together, so they will understand and be committed[8]
- The process of articulating visions, embodying values, and creating the environment within which things can be accomplished.[9]

These definitions highlight a number of important issues. The following is clear:

- Leadership is a process and not a position
- It involves a relationship between a leader and followers in a given situation
- It involves influencing people
- Leaders gain the commitment and enthusiasm of followers who are willing to be influenced
- Leadership influences followers to think not only of their own interest but the interest of their organisation
- It involves influencing followers to bring about change towards a desired future for their organisation.[10]

Thus, leadership can be seen as a complex phenomenon involving the leader, the followers, and the situation.

Considering these definitions, what is the difference between leadership and management? According to Hinterhuber and Krauthammer[11], the sources of leadership are alertness to opportunity and the imagination and vision to exploit or capitalise on it, thereby creating value for all the stakeholders – people, society, customers, and shareholders. They see management, in contrast, as creative problem-solving that works within the system and that is easier to learn than leadership. They also believe that, in a time of uncertainty, leadership is more important than management. Figure 3.1 illustrates their views on the complementarity of leadership and management.

This view is echoed by Hughes, Ginnett, and Curphy, who indicate that the term 'management' suggests words like 'procedures', 'control' and 'regulations', while the term 'leadership' is more associated with words like 'risk-taking', 'creativity', 'change' and 'vision'.[12] Hughes et al. come to the conclusion that leadership and management are closely related but distinguishable activities; these authors do not view leaders and managers as different types of people. Thus, the same individual can fulfil both roles.[13]

Bennis[14] also draws a distinction between the two concepts by stating, 'Managers administer and leaders innovate, managers control and leaders inspire, and managers accept the status quo, while leaders change it.'

Figure 3.1 The complementarity of management and leadership

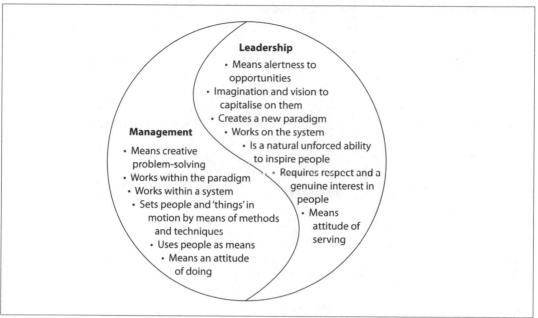

SOURCE: HINTERHUBER, H. H. & KRAUTHAMMER, E. 1998. The leadership wheel: the tasks entrepreneurs and senior executives cannot delegate. *Strategic change*, 7(7):150. Copyright John Wiley & sons. Reproduced with permission.

Howard, as quoted by Leonard[15], expands on the concept of leadership when he remarks that:

- Leaders do not just develop visions of what an organisation is; they develop visions of what an organisation can be
- Leaders do not just inform people about new visions; they energise people to accept and work towards making those visions come true
- Leaders do not just formulate new programmes and policies; they initiate improvements that last by changing organisational culture
- Leaders do not just manage organisations; they seek ways to transform them.

SOURCE: LEONARD, B. 1999. From management to leadership. *HR magazine*, 44(1):34

It is clear from the discussion thus far that leadership and management complement each other and that both are vital to organisational success. This view is shared by Kotler, as quoted by Nur[16], when he states:

A manager who does not have what it takes to be a leader would be bogged down with day-to-day managerial matters, and the leadership needs of the organisation would be neglected – to the eventual detriment of the organisation. Likewise, a manager with leadership qualities but no managerial skills will have an empty vision. Without the requisite power, vision cannot be turned into reality.

SOURCE: NUR, Y. A. 1998. Charisma and managerial leadership: the gift that never was. *Business horizons*, 41(4):20, July/August.

However, to be an effective leader, some critical competencies are required. Today there is a growing agreement on some of these competencies, which include, according to Ketterer and Chayes[17], vision, managing complexity, industry and business insight, a

Table 3.1 The four fundamental capabilities and competencies of emotional intelligence

Self-awareness	Self-management
• *Emotional self-awareness*: the ability to read and understand your emotions as well as recognise their impact on work performance, relationships, and the like. • *Accurate self-assessment*: a realistic evaluation of your strengths and limitations. • *Self-confidence*: a strong and positive sense of self-worth.	• *Self-control*: the ability to keep disruptive emotions and impulses under control. • *Trustworthiness*: a consistent display of honesty and integrity. • *Conscientiousness*: the ability to manage yourself and your responsibilities. • *Adaptability*: skill at adjusting to changing situations and overcoming obstacles. • *Achievement orientation*: the drive to meet an internal standard of excellence. • *Initiative*: a readiness to seize opportunities.
Social awareness	**Social skill**
• *Empathy*: skill at sensing other people's emotions, understanding their perspective, and taking an active interest in their concerns. • *Organisational awareness*: the ability to read the currents of organisational life, build decision networks, and navigate politics. • *Service orientation*: the ability to recognise and meet customers' needs.	• *Visionary leadership*: the ability to take charge and inspire with a compelling vision. • *Influence*: the ability to wield a range of persuasive tactics. • *Developing others*: the propensity to bolster the abilities of others through feedback and guidance. • *Communication*: skill at listening and at sending clear, convincing, and well-tuned messages. • *Change catalyst*: proficiency in initiating new ideas and leading people in a new direction. • *Conflict management*: the ability to de-escalate disagreements and orchestrate resolutions. • *Building bonds*: proficiency at cultivating and maintaining a web of relationships. • *Teamwork and collaboration*: competence at promoting cooperation and building teams.

SOURCE: Reprinted by *Harvard business review*, March/April, from GOLEMAN, D. 2000. *Leadership that gets results*. Harvard Business School Publishing Corporation:80. © 2000 by the Harvard Business School Publishing Corporation; all rights reserved.

general management perspective, drive for success, personal integrity, flexibility, active learning, influencing without authority, extreme humility, developing talent, and teamwork. More recently, authors have seen the role of emotional intelligence also as important. They propose that emotional intelligence – the ability to understand and manage moods and emotions in the self and others – contributes to effective leadership in organisations.[18] Emotional intelligence consists of four fundamental capabilities: self-awareness, self-management, social awareness, and social skills. Each capability is composed of a specific set of competencies (see Table 3.1).

Besides the competencies, practices, and commitment, a further ingredient is necessary for successful leadership – namely effective communication.[19] Knowing what to do, but not being able to communicate this to others, can be a major drawback for effective leadership. According to Platts and Southall[20], organisations need complete, coherent, and efficient communication systems which channel essential information upwards, downwards, and sideways between employees. Sonnenschein[21] defines communication as 'understanding each other as individuals and as members of larger groups'.

It is important that organisations should take note of a number of barriers to good communication. These barriers include poor communication skills, distortion or omission of information flowing through the various levels within the organisation, people hearing only what they expect to hear, and lack of trust between the sender and the recipient.[22] In contrast, the literature identifies a number of common characteristics in organisations that do communicate well. The following keywords describe these characteristics[23]:

- Top management commitment
- Open and honest
- Planned and deliberate
- Upwards, downwards, sideways
- Supported by training
- Agreed objectives
- Interesting, significant content
- Systematic
- Two-way
- Relevant
- Sufficient time and money
- Reliable
- Regular and well timed
- Right amount
- Support in preparation
- Flexible
- Think message then medium
- Supportive attitudes

- Within recipients' horizon
- Constantly reinforced.

3.2 What leaders do on the job

It is important to also establish what leaders actually do on the job – the so-called leadership managerial roles. Mintzberg, as quoted in Lussier and Achua[24], identified 10 managerial roles that leaders perform to accomplish organisational objectives. He grouped these roles into three categories (See Table 3.2), namely:

- Interpersonal roles
- Informational roles
- Decision roles.

These roles have been widely supported by numerous research studies in the literature. As Table 3.2 is self-explanatory, we shall not discuss these roles further.

Table 3.2 Mintzberg's 10 managerial roles of leaders

Interpersonal roles	
Figurehead role	Leaders perform the figurehead role when they represent the organisation or department in legal, social, ceremonial, and symbolic activities
Leader role	The leader role is that of performing the management functions to operate the managers' organisation unit effectively
Liason role	Leaders perform the liason role when they interact with people outside their organisational unit, e.g. networking
Informational roles	
Monitor role	Leaders perform the monitor role when they gather information
Disseminator role	Leaders perform the disseminator role when they send information to others in the organisational unit
Spokesperson role	Leaders perform the spokesperson role when they provide information to people outside the organisational unit
Decision roles	
Entrepreneur role	Leaders perform the entrepreneur role when they innovate and initiate improvements
Disturbance-handler role	Leaders perform the disturbance-handler role when they take corrective action during a crisis or conflict situation
Resource-allocator role	Leaders perform the resource-allocator role when they schedule, request authorisation, and perform budgeting activities
Negotiator role	Leaders perform the negotiator role when they represent their organisational unit during routine and non-routine transactions that do not include set boundaries such as the pay of an employee

SOURCE: Adapted from LUSSIER, R. N. & ACHUA, C. F. 2004. *Leadership: Theory, application, skill development.* Minnesota: South Western/Thomson Corporation: 9–12. Used with permission.

3.3 Successful and unsuccessful leadership[25]

A great deal of knowledge has been generated about what contributes to successful and unsuccessful leadership. Due to the variety of approaches taken to better understand this phenomenon, it is difficult to integrate findings across the many streams of research. However, several approaches in the literature do stand out as having been particularly fruitful. Each of these approaches reflects a unique combination of definition of success, type of predictors of success, and setting for studying leadership. These issues are further illustrated in Table 3.3.

Table 3.3 Examples of successful and unsuccessful leadership as found in different research studies

Successful leadership	Unsuccessful leadership
Theme: Balance concern for task efficiency, human relations, and adaptive change	
• When making decisions, takes into account the needs of the organisation and needs of employees • Gets things done without creating adversarial relationships • Coaches employees in how to meet expectations	• Hires people with good technical skills but poor ability to work with others • In implementing a change, does not take the time to explain the rationale or listen to concerns • Is unable to deal firmly with loyal but incompetent employees
Theme: Develop intrapersonal and interpersonal competence	
• When working with another group, gets things done by finding common ground • Does an honest self-assessment • Quickly gains trust and respect from customers	• Is not adaptable to many different types of people • Is emotionally volatile and unpredictable • Overestimates own abilities
Theme: Engage in transformational and charismatic behaviours	
• Is a visionary able to excite other people to work hard • Rewards hard work and dedication to excellence • Gains commitment of others before implementing changes	• Does not help individuals understand how their work fits into the goals of the organisation • Orders people around rather then working to get them on board • Fails to encourage and involve team members
Theme: Think and act in more complex ways	
• Once the more glaring problems in an assignment are solved, can see the underlying problems and patterns that were obscured before • Understands higher management values and how they see things • Recognizes that every decision has conflicting interests and constituencies	• Is overwhelmed by complex tasks • Cannot make the transition from technical manager to general manager • Prefers to work on day-to-day problems rather than long-range strategies
Theme: Overcome deficiencies that limit success	
• Does not become hostile when things are not going his or her way • Does not blame others or situations for own mistakes • Does not become paralyzed or overwhelmed when facing action	• Does not use feedback to make necessary changes in behaviour • Selects people for a team who do not work well together • Is self-promoting without the results to support it
Theme: Seek a wide variety of leadership experiences	
• Is prepared to seize opportunities when they arise • Is willing to make a lateral move to gain valuable experience • Accepts change as positive	• Resists learning from bad decisions or mistakes • Chooses an overly narrow career path • Feels uncomfortable in situations that call for untested skills

SOURCE: ANTONAKIS, J., CIANCIOLO, A. T. & STERNBERG, R. J. 2004. *The nature of leadership*. Thousand Oaks, CA: Sage Publications:209. Used with permission.

3.4 **Individual models of leadership**

It is amazing that during the twentieth century more than 8 000 studies on leadership emerged.[26-28] However, when one takes a closer look at all the published work, three main streams of research emerge: one looks at individual models of leadership, one at group models of leadership, and the third at organisational models of leadership. We shall now briefly discuss a number of the individual models. In section 3.5 we shall discuss a number of models found in the 'group' category, and in section 3.6 we shall look at organisational models of leadership.

3.4.1 **Traits-based approach**

The early studies on leadership (during the 1930s and 1940s) looked at the various issues concerning the individual leader in the workplace.[29] These studies began with a focus on traits or characteristics (physical or mental), followed by a focus on skills (ability to carry out tasks), and then moved on to behaviours (performing in specific ways).[30] A very extensive

literature on leadership traits (so-called traits-based leadership) exists.[31] Figure 3.2 summarises the traits into four categories, namely physical, social, personality, and intellectual. However, the trait theory was not very successful, as it was found that no particular set of personality characteristics had recurred in leaders.[32] As Hunt correctly states, 'The reverse is more likely to be true – leaders are noted for being different from each other in personality traits.'[33]

3.4.2 **Behavioural-based approach**

The second major development was the behavioural approach popular in the 1950s. Here researchers tried to discover leadership styles that would be effective across all situations.[34] Most studies undertaken in this area used questionnaires measuring task-orientated and relations-orientated behaviour. Researchers conducted these studies to see how these behaviours correlated with criteria of leadership effectiveness, such as subordinate satisfaction and performance. Unfortunately the results from the massive research efforts were mostly contradictory and inconclusive.[35]

Figure 3.2 Leadership traits

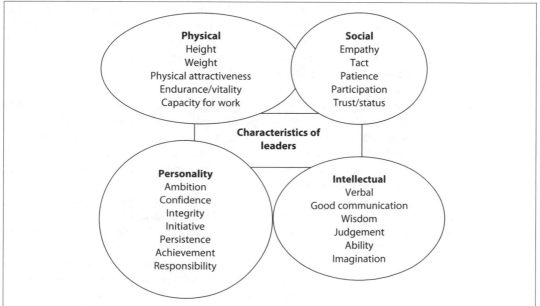

SOURCE: SWIERCZEK, F. W. 1991. Leadership and culture: comparing Asian managers. *Leadership & organisation development journal*, 12(7):7. Reproduced with permission.

The two leading research projects associated with this theory are the Ohio State project and the University of Michigan research.[36]

3.4.3 Situational-based approach

The third approach, developed during the 1960s and 1970s, expanded on trait theory to include tasks to be completed, the factors affecting the situation both leader and followers are in, and the personality traits of the followers.[37] This theory became known as the situational theory, but is also referred to in the literature as the contingency theory. Although it had some shortcomings, the situational theory was a useful way to get leaders to think about how leadership effectiveness may depend somewhat on being flexible with different subordinates, i.e. not acting the same way towards them all.[38] This approach was popularised by Hersey and Blanchard and to a lesser extent by Fiedler, Vroom, and Yetton.

3.5 Group models of leadership

The leadership models discussed thus far in this chapter worked reasonably well within a fairly stable internal environment. However, as Chapters 1 and 2 indicated, this environment has undergone radical changes during the last few years. Issues that have had a major impact on a company's internal environment include downsizing, rightsizing, restructuring (implementing matrix structures and flatter organisations), the introduction of teams, and the empowerment of employees. The acceptance of the resource-based approach as a method to improve the organisation's competitive advantage has also refocused leadership researchers to look at new approaches in the field.[39]

An important movement in this regard has been the implementation of group-leadership approaches and the movement away from the old power-control paradigm (using coercive, expert, referent, legitimate power) to the empowering of others.[40] This new leadership style will require the transformation of the role of managers at all levels within the company,

with more time being spent on initiating problem solving among team members and absorbing internal and external information to ensure the best possible decision-making.[41]

Thus formal authority, as the cornerstone of leadership, is nearly obsolete. Leadership should no longer be restricted to one individual who happens to be entrenched in a formal hierarchical position, but must be dispersed across a wide range of diverse individuals, some of whom will not even be within the organisation. This view is shared by McCrimmon in a thought-provoking article 'Bottom-up leadership'.[42] According to McCrimmon, such dispersed leadership should not only be spread across more individuals, but should also be broken down into components that allow everyone to show some aspect of leadership, however small.[43] He thus suggests that one should stop characterising leadership solely in terms of personality or behavioural attributes and start thinking about leadership acts. McCrimmon defines such an act as 'any initiative which influences how an organisation does business'.[44] Thus, an individual may not be classified as a leader according to the old leadership paradigm, but his or her initiatives that lead to an improvement in the functioning of the organisation are definitely leadership acts. McCrimmon remarks as follows in this regard: 'In any given team, each member might exhibit technical leadership acts on different projects. If each team member has reasonably effective interpersonal skills he or she may also display people leadership acts from time to time'.[45]

Besides considering the leadership acts to be performed by numerous individuals, McCrimmon argues that is also useful to think of leadership functions. Most leadership acts will fall into one or more leadership categories, such as developing new products, enhancing quality, and convincing people to contribute to a new plan. According to McCrimmon, some of these categories should be formalised as leadership functions which would be seen as essential for competitive success. These functions could be fulfilled by a variety of senior executives who can exhibit leadership by ensuring that all critical leadership functions are fulfilled by as many people as possible.[46]

As Chapter 1 indicated, a growing trend in organisations nowadays is to give more responsibility to teams rather than to individuals.[47] These teams have considerable discretion as to how to execute their duties and have a common purpose, interdependent roles, and complementary skills. Although various types of teams can be found, we shall concentrate on three of the more popular types: cross-functional, self-managed, and executive teams.

3.5.1 Cross-functional teams

Organisations are increasingly using cross-functional teams with a view to improving coordination of independent activities among specialised sub-units.[48] This type of team usually includes employees from each of the functional sub-units. These teams allow flexible, efficient deployment of personnel and resources to solve problems as these occur. As a result of the different backgrounds of the team members, cross-functional teams are normally creative in generating various ideas and also in providing interesting solutions to problems.[49] Although cross-functional teams are beneficial to organisations, they do have a number of negative aspects. For example, it is not always possible to get the members to participate sufficiently, and time-consuming meetings may result. A further problem is the possibility of role conflicts as a result of the competing demands of team members.[50]

Barry[51], as quoted by Yukl[52], identifies four leadership functions that appear to be essential for cross-functional teams that solve problems, manage projects or develop policy. These are:

- Envisioning – articulating strategic objectives or a vision and encouraging the team to consider innovative performance strategies
- Organising – planning and scheduling team activities
- Social integration – encouraging mutual trust and open communication among team members
- External spanning – monitoring the external environment to identify client needs and emerging problems, and

promoting a favourable image of the team to outsiders.

3.5.2 Self-managed teams

As Chapter 1 indicated, much of the responsibility and authority for making important management decisions is turned over to self-managed teams (SMTs).[53] These teams are normally responsible for producing a distinct product or service. While the parent organisation usually determines the mission, scope of operations, and budget, SMTs are responsible for setting their own performance goals and quality standards.[54] The internal leadership role of these teams involves management responsibilities assigned to the team and shared by the group members. It is typical for SMTs to have an internal team leader who is responsible for coordinating the team activities. However, it is not unknown for self-managed teams to rotate this position among several team members.[55] According to Yukl, shared leadership in SMTs can take many different forms besides the rotation of the team-leader position. For example, group decisions about important issues can be made at any time, and members may also assume responsibility for providing coordination and direction for specific activities of the team. Members may also collectively perform some supervisory functions and teams may distribute some administrative responsibilities to individual members.[56]

3.5.3 Executive teams

The third group model we shall discuss is executive team leadership. Much early literature on leadership was mainly concerned with supervisors and middle managers in organisations. However, with the rapid changes taking place within organisations, and the intensifying competition between companies, attention has shifted towards the CEO and the top-management executive team.[57]

Although the traditional top-management structure is still popular, there is a new approach in which the CEO shares power with the top-management team. The advantage of this approach is that team members can compensate for weaknesses in the skills of the CEO.[58] Thus, leadership is becoming a team sport. A set of executives now takes on the responsibility for providing leadership to the whole organisation.[59]

The development of executive leadership teams has a number of advantages which include, according to Nadler and Spencer, the generation of more ideas, increased ownership of products, increased commitment and motivation, a wide range of views and perspectives, the sharing of risks, the transfer of expertise, and social support.[60]

The quality of team performance at the executive level is critical, not just because of the obvious impact of the team's decisions on organisational performance, but also because of the team's leadership role as a model of appropriate behaviour.[61]

A model designed by Rivero, containing elements of executive-team effectiveness, appears in Table 3.4.

This model can be used to diagnose threats to the team's effectiveness, and also indicates the team's opportunities. It is important to note that the different elements of the model are linked with one another. For example, the skills and experience of the team have a great impact on core processes such as how to share information and how to make decisions.[62] Another link is that between core processes and performance. The team's performance is directly influenced by, for example, the quality, effectiveness, and appropriate management of the team's work, relationship, and external boundaries.[63]

For the executive team to lead the organisation successfully, it must, according to Nadler and Spencer, perform at least four leadership activities successfully. These activities are[64]:

- *Governance.* This involves a number of activities such as determining and monitoring the company identity and mission; developing internal policies, processes, and rules; managing external and internal relationships; and ensuring future executive capability.
- *Developing strategy.* Developing strategies and choosing the best one are vital for the retention of the company's sustained competitive advantage.
- *Leading strategic-change teams (SCTs).* These teams, which are appointed by the executive team, are responsible for driving

Table 3.4 Elements of executive team effectiveness

Element	Description
Team design	
Composition	Mix of skills and experiences, values, perspectives, and other characteristics
Structure	Includes the size of the team, the boundaries (who's in and out, the specific formal roles, the nature of team and individual roles)
Succession	Team members' perceptions and expectations of how their performance and behaviour affect their succession prospects
Core processes	
Work management	How the team organises and manages itself to perform work
Relationship management	How the team manages the nature and quality of relationships among its members
External boundary management	How the team deals with elements outside the team and beyond the organisation
Team performance	
Production of results	The team's ability to consistently meet the performance demands on it
Maintenance of effectiveness	The team's ability to meet members' needs and for members to work together over time

SOURCE: RIVERO, J. C. 1998. The role of feedback in executive team effectiveness. (*In* Nadler, D. A. & Spencer, J. L. (Eds). *Executive teams.* San Francisco: Jossey Bass:182.) Used with permission.

critical business priorities and initiatives by means of generating innovative solutions for tough issues that strongly affect the organisation's future capabilities, performance, and competitive position in the marketplace. Designing effective SCTs involves the following four important steps (Figure 3.3 gives more detail regarding these issues, which we shall not discuss further):

➤ Firstly, establishing the team charter
➤ Secondly, electing team members
➤ Thirdly, agreeing on key work processes
➤ Fourthly, embedding a quality-assurance process into the work of the team.

• *Creating a high-performance operating environment.* To be successful, the executive team must also create a new operating environment that will support

Figure 3.3 Building framework for SCTs

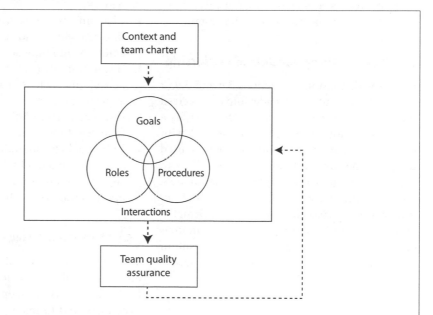

1 Context and team charter
  • What is the role of this team in the larger system?
  • What are the team's performance requirements?
  • What are key relationships with other teams?
  • What are the team's rewards and consequences?

2 Goals
  • What is the value-added work of the team?
  • What is the core content of the team's agenda?
  • What are the measures of team success?

3 Roles
  • What is expected or required of team members?
  • What are the special roles (e.g. leadership)?
  • What do subgroups require of each other?

4 Procedures
  • How are meetings structured?
  • How is the team's agenda created and managed?
  • How are decisions made?
  • How is team output managed?

5 Interactions
  • What behaviour is expected or required of members?
  • Which operating principles will govern behaviour?

6 Team quality assurance
  • How will the team be initiated or launched?
  • How are work sessions started?
  • How are work sessions process reviews conducted?
  • How are periodic process reviews conducted?

SOURCE: Delta Consulting Group, 1991 as it appeared in KETTERER, R. F. & SPENCER, J. L. 1998. Leading strategic change teams. (*In* Nadler, D. A. & Spencer, J. L. (Eds.). *Executive teams.* San Francisco: Jossey Bass:254.) Used with permission.

the successful implementation of the business strategy. Thus, just as organisations need operating plans to implement strategies, they also require appropriate operating environments to execute these plans. According to Thies and Wagner[65], this process will involve changing how decisions are made; how people deal with each other; patterns of leadership behaviour; how people operate individually and collectively; how people think about customers, competitors, and employees; and how the organisation is perceived by the external environment.

3.6 Organisational models of leadership

From the discussions in sections 3.4 and 3.5, it is clear that the subject of leadership has received much attention over the years. However, as a result of various problems experienced with many of these approaches, newer models started to appear during the 1980s and 1990s. We can classify these models as organisational models. Some of the most popular were models of transactional, transformational, charismatic, and strategic leadership. As these models brought a newer perspective on the issue of leadership, a brief discussion of each model follows.

3.6.1 Transactional-based approach

In the transactional leadership approach, leaders are characterised by contingent-reward and management-by-exception styles of leadership.[66] Leaders develop exchanges or agreements with followers. These exchanges or agreements point out what the followers will receive if they do something right (or wrong). The transactional leadership approach thus lasts only as long as the needs of both leader and follower are satisfied by the continuing exchange process. There is consequently not a relationship that binds the leader and follower together in a mutual and continuing pursuit of higher purpose. Thus, one could say that a purely transactional style of leadership may be counter-productive, in a sense.[67]

3.6.2 Transformational-based approach

In direct contrast to the transactional approach, in which the status quo within the organisation is maintained, the transformational-based approach raises both leaders and followers to higher levels of motivation and morality, with a view to changing the present situation by focusing primarily on the external environment.[68] According to Bass, as quoted by Steers, Porter, and Bigley[69], transformational leadership consists of four behavioural components, namely:

- Charisma, which is viewed as the process through which leaders arouse strong emotions in followers
- Inspiration, which refers to leader behaviours such as articulating an appealing vision
- Intellectual stimulation, which encourages followers to be creative in solving problems
- Individual consideration, which includes leader behaviours that provide special support to followers, such as expressing appreciation for a job well done.

3.6.3 Charismatic-based approach

Where transformational leadership seeks to empower and elevate followers, charismatic leadership seeks to keep followers weak and dependent and to instil personal loyalty rather than commitment to ideals. This is especially true in non-business organisations such as religious or political movements. The existence of charismatic leadership within a business organisation is rare, as it occurs only when there is a collapse of formal authority to deal with a severe crisis.[70]

3.6.4 Managerial-based approach

Another leadership model – a combination of both transactional and transformational leadership – which appeared in the literature also deserves some attention. This model is known as managerial leadership.[71] Flanagan and Thompson, who designed this model, found in their extensive research that the pendulum was clearly swinging back from the emphasis on transformational leadership.[72] According to them, this swing could be the result of the exclusive emphasis on the creative component in the transformational leadership approach. It would appear that a combination of both these leadership styles (i.e. transactional and transformational) might be the answer. Empirical research has indicated that the same leader can display both transactional and transformational types of leadership behaviour in varying degrees and intensities, and also in a complementary way.[73–78]

Besides encompassing transactional and transformational leadership components, the proposed model also includes a third major component, situational sensitivity. The managerial leadership model enables management to diagnose the organisational situation and deploy the appropriate leadership response – i.e. the right combination of transformational and transactional leadership. It is important to note that the precise mix will vary from one organisation to the next and also from one time to another. Working from the basic factors of transformation, transaction, and the situation, Flanagan and Thompson found it possible to derive a range of components from these factors. The following are examples[79]:

- Transformational leadership skills
  - › Create a vision
  - › Communicate meaning
  - › Inspire
  - › Empower
  - › Stir
  - › Take risks
- Transactional management skills
  - › Agree on objectives
  - › Communicate information
  - › Motivate
  - › Bargain
  - › Promote security
  - › Stabilise
- Situational sensitivity
  - › Scans organisation
  - › Reads jobs
  - › Understands self.

To be successful, managers need to have the three macro components listed above, by acquiring their underlying capabilities. Once managers have these skills, they need to exercise them holistically; and if their actions and behaviour are in harmony with the demands and expectations of the situation, they will be successful.[80]

It is important to note that each of the components in the model builds progressively on the others. For example, once a vision has been created, it is important to agree on specific objectives that will build that vision. A further critical aspect is that, after this process has been completed, the vision and objectives must also be communicated to the employees. This will give meaning to their work.[81] However, hard facts and information will also be required to set further individual objectives against which to measure performance. Also, if employees see meaning in what they do, this can inspire them to greater efforts. The empowerment of employees should accompany this process. Devolution of authority will enable employees to stir things up and be innovative, thereby resulting in employees taking risks in exploring new ways of managing new situations that will provide opportunities to adapt to change. If the activities mentioned are not in tune or harmony with the company's environment, they will not be successful.[82]

3.6.5 **Strategic-based approach**

According to Ireland and Hitt[83], strategic leadership can be defined as 'a person's ability to anticipate, envision, maintain flexibility, think strategically, and work with others to initiate changes that will create a viable future for the organisation'. From this definition it is clear that this approach will enable an organisation to achieve superior performance when competing in turbulent and unpredictable environments. CEOs who apply practices associated with strategic leadership of the twenty first-century can create sources of competitive advantage for their organisations (see Table 3.5).[84] However, the CEOs will have to cease viewing their

Table 3.5 Strategic leadership practices for the twenty-first century

20th-century practices (past)	21st-century practices (future)
Outcomes focused	Outcome and process focused
Stoic and confident	Confident, but without hubris
Sought to acquire knowledge	Seeks to acquire and leverage knowledge
Guided people's creativity	Seeks to release and nurture people's creativity
Work flows determined by hierarchy	Work flows influenced by relationships
Articulated the importance of integrity	Demonstrates the importance of integrity by actions
Demanded respect	Willing to earn respect
Tolerated diversity	Seeks diversity
Reacted to environmental change	Acts to anticipate environmental change
Served as the great leader	Serves as the leader and as a great group member
Views employees as a resource	Views organisational citizens as a critical resource
Operated primarily through a domestic mindset	Operates primarily through a global mindset
Invested in employees' development	Invests significantly in citizens' continuous development

SOURCE: Republished with permission of *Academy of management executive*, from IRELAND, R. D. & HITT, M.A., 1999. Achieving and maintaining strategic competitiveness in the 21st century: the role of strategic leadership. *Academy of management executive*, 13(1):54. Permission conveyed through Copyright Clearance Center, Inc.

leadership position as one with rank and title, but rather as a position of significant responsibility to a range of stakeholders.[85]

In this process, the CEOs will also have to satisfy the requirements associated with six key leadership practices, namely:

- Determining the company's purpose or vision
- Exploiting and maintaining core competencies
- Developing human intellectual capital
- Sustaining an effective organisational culture
- Emphasising ethical practices
- Establishing balanced organisational controls.[86]

3.6.6 Institutional leadership

A model closely related to the strategic-based model is that of institutional leadership.

What has emerged is the application of a special kind of leadership that appears to be critical during periods of discontinuous organisational change. As a result of this new development, we find it appropriate to discuss this issue briefly. The focus for this discussion will be the work done by Nadler, Shaw, and Walton, and published in the book *Discontinuous change: Leading organisational transformation*.[87]

Nadler et al. identify four different types of change that can occur within the organisation. These are[88]:

- *Tuning*. Here organisations initiate incremental change in anticipation of environmental events. There is thus no immediate need for change. According to Nadler et al., this type of change maintains or enhances the fit between strategy and organisation.
- *Adaptation*. While tuning is initiated internally and is proactive in nature, adaptation takes place as a result of external conditions and is reactive in nature.
- *Reorientation*. Here the company initiates change as a result of an emerging environmental shift that is perceived. This will involve redefining the company's identity, vision, and mission.
- *Recreation*. As companies do not always have visionary leaders, they are sometimes caught unawares regarding certain changes that are taking place. In this situation they must move quickly and change all the basic elements of the organisational system if they want to survive.

Figure 3.4 Institutionalised leadership

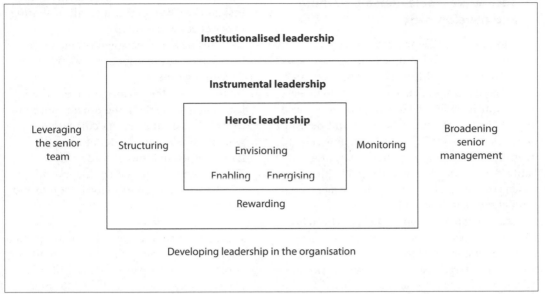

SOURCE: NADLER, D. A., SHAW, R. B. & WALTON, A. S. 1995. *Discontinuous change: Leading organizational transformation.* San Francisco, Jossey Bass:225. Used with permission.

Focusing on the reorientation type of organisation change, Nadler et al. suggest that for success under these circumstances, two types of leadership are required, one 'heroic' and the other 'instrumental'.[89] A heroic leader will excite the employees, shape their aspirations, and direct their energy, while an instrumental leader will make sure that the individuals throughout the organisation do indeed behave in ways needed for the change to occur.[90] It thus appears that effective organisational change (reorientation change) requires both heroic and instrumental leadership.

Although there may be individuals who can fulfil both roles, organisations may be wise to involve other employees as well in the leadership roles. According to Nadler et al.[91], the best option is to extend the leadership role beyond the individual leader and create institutionalised leadership. They consequently suggest extending the leadership to at least three groups – namely the senior team, the broader senior-management group, and the entire organisation[92] (see Figure 3.4.) This makes even more exciting the challenge of leadership in an organisation.

3.6.7 E-leadership approach

The most recent, and what many consider the least traditional, form of leadership is e-leadership.[93] According to Hunt, as quoted in Antonakis, Cianciola, and Sternberg[94], e-leadership can be defined as 'a social influence process mediated by advanced information systems to produce a change in attitudes, feelings, thinking, behaviour, and/or performance with individuals, groups and/or organisations'. According to the author, it can occur at any hierarchical level and can involve both one-to-one and one-to-many interactions within and across large units and organisations. This leadership approach operates within the context of advanced information technology (AIT).[95]

Systems which can be used for this purpose include email systems, message boards, groupware, group-support systems, knowledge-management systems, and executive-information systems.[96] These technologies can help leaders scan, plan, decide, disseminate, and control information within the organisation.

3.7 Techniques for leadership training and development

Creating an effective process for selection is a prerequisite to developing enduring capability for leadership within the organisation.[97] However, it is not sufficient to identify managers with requisite skills; the organisation needs also to give them a chance to broaden and develop their skills through systematic job-related training and developmental experiences.[98] Table 3.6 contains a typical set of questions which you can use to evaluate your own personal competencies in leadership.

According to Cacioppe[99], there has been little research on establishing how much learning from leadership-development programmes has been transferred back into the workplace. Authors such as Cohen and Tichy[100] also question the value of many existing programmes when they remark: 'Most of what has been done in leadership development falls drastically short. It has been too rote, too backward looking and too theoretical. It has rarely been tied to a business's immediate needs, nor has it prepared leaders for the challenges of the future.'

The question thus is: what should companies do in this regard? Numerous studies quoted in the literature[101-104] place the involvement and commitment of the CEO and senior executives of the company as the first priority in the successful design and execution of a leadership-development programme. This involvement can be by means of participating in the design of the programme, giving keynote talks, and serving on discussion panels. For example, the former CEO of General Electric, Jack Welch, participated in the General Electric Senior Leadership Programme for two weeks of every year of his term of office.[105] The CEOs of other successful companies, such as Intel, Hewlett-Packard, Shell. and PepsiCo, have done similarly.[106] Mumford[107], one of the leading authorities on leadership development, as quoted by Cacioppe, indicates that there are many reasons why leaders (CEOs and other senior executives) should develop other leaders. The following are some examples:

- It brings personal satisfaction by helping others grow

- The leaders' own skills, knowledge, and insight are developed as a result of sharing experiences with others
- Real business and personal problems can be resolved as the leaders are working on developing others
- By improving the performance of others, leaders are enhancing the others' ability to deal with tasks the leaders currently do, which can allow the leaders to pursue larger responsibilities of leadership
- The involvement of senior leaders with middle-level managers helps integrate and link together the two groups.

It is also important that the group participating in such a programme should be small, for example around 10 people. This will allow a great deal of interaction with the CEO and other senior executives, which is important.

Besides senior-executive involvement, leadership development should also address issues such as the following[108-120]:

- It should be closely aligned with and used to support the corporate strategy; thus it should be future orientated
- Leadership competencies needed for a particular organisation should be clearly defined and kept up to date through internal and external research – there must be an awareness of changes taking place
- Real-time business issues should form the basis of the programme – it must be action orientated
- It must be linked to an organisation's succession planning
- It should also be linked to all HR systems (e.g. performance management, compensation, selection, etc.)
- The impact of the leadership-development programme should be assessed on a regular basis (e.g. by conducting follow-up research to determine whether staff could see a significant improvement in key performance areas after attending one of the programmes)
- It should be tied to specific development needs, otherwise it will not be effective
- Multiple approaches should be used as everyone does not learn in the same way.

Table 3.6 How good a leader are you?

This quiz is based on the leadership studies of AchieveGlobal. The statements are grouped according to the five leadership strategies of the CLIMB™ leadership model.

To test yourself on these leadership skills, circle the number that best represents the extent to which you agree or disagree with each statement.   Strongly disagree = 1   Somewhat agree = 3   Strongly agree = 5

Strategy 1 Create a compelling future	Agreement
1. I link my work efforts to the organisation's objectives	1 2 3 4 5
2. I use the organisation's core values to guide my decisions and actions	1 2 3 4 5
3. I help others understand their roles in the changing organisation	1 2 3 4 5
4. I help others develop positive approaches to emerging needs in the organisation	1 2 3 4 5
5. I help ensure that my work group or team undertakes appropriate planning activities	1 2 3 4 5
6. I challenge assumptions that may keep the organisation from moving forward	1 2 3 4 5
Your score	

Strategy 2 Let the customer drive the organisation	
7. I meet with customers or review customer feedback regularly	1 2 3 4 5
8. I help ensure that timely, accurate customer data are gathered and distributed	1 2 3 4 5
9. I make sure that people know how their work affects the customer	1 2 3 4 5
10. I am always watching for ways to make it easier for customers to deal with my company	1 2 3 4 5
11. I hold my work group or team accountable for considering the customer in decision-making	1 2 3 4 5
12. I keep informed about what the competition is doing to win customers	1 2 3 4 5
Your score	

Strategy 3 Involve every mind	
13. I seek ideas and opinions from individuals throughout the organisation	1 2 3 4 5
14. I help ensure that people are involved in decisions that affect their work	1 2 3 4 5
15. I encourage people to speak up when they disagree	1 2 3 4 5
16. I involve all relevant stakeholders when engaging in problem solving	1 2 3 4 5
17. I help others learn and grow by providing feedback, coaching and/or training	1 2 3 4 5
18. I seek opportunities to recognise others' contribution	1 2 3 4 5
Your score	

Strategy 4 Manage work horizontally	
19. I look for ways to build teamwork within and across work groups	1 2 3 4 5
20. I challenge unnecessary barriers (policies, procedures, etc.) to working across functions	1 2 3 4 5
21. I apply my technical expertise to help solve problems related to cross-functional work	1 2 3 4 5
22. I help track progress toward improvement of cross-functional work processes	1 2 3 4 5
23. I help plan and implement cross-functional projects	1 2 3 4 5
24. I help ensure that my work group or team meets deadlines that affect the work of other functions	1 2 3 4 5
Your score	

Strategy 5 Build personal credibility	
25. I consistently treat others with honesty and respect	1 2 3 4 5
26. I admit when I've made a mistake	1 2 3 4 5
27. I confront issues with others directly rather than avoid problems or go around them	1 2 3 4 5
28. I actively seek feedback regarding my strengths and weaknesses	1 2 3 4 5
29. I model the behaviours that I expect others to practice	1 2 3 4 5
30. I seize opportunities for personal growth and learning	1 2 3 4 5
Your score	

Although your scores represent your evaluation of your own leadership, they are based on the criteria that others use to judge you. A low score on an item indicates that some additional effort needs to be made in that particular skill; a low score for a strategy suggests a larger area that needs work.

SOURCE: BERGMANN, H., HURSON, K., RUSS-EFT, D. 1999. *Everyone a Leader: A grass-roots model for a new workplace.* New York: Wiley, as it appeared in Bergmann, H., Hurson, K. & Russ-Eft, D. 1999. Introducing a grass-roots model for leadership. *Strategy & leadership*, 27(6):15–20. Used with permission.

Special Report

Developing Leaders for the 21st Century

Providing or creating a vision is the key difference between managing and leading. Managers administer policies, set practices, maintain systems and direct activities. Leaders inspire and acquire followers with a vision.

This type of behaviour or leadership style has not always been the norm. For many leaders in profit-oriented organisations, the modus operandi was simply to increase revenue, decrease expenses and raise the profit margin. Redirecting the organisation and its operating philosophy to a more balanced, humanistic and financial vision and style is a recent occurrence.

Saratoga Institute surveyed Fortune 1 000 companies to obtain a view of the changes both in style and development of today's leaders. Following is a sampling of those findings, and what high-performance companies are doing to enable their leaders to develop the requisite skills necessary for the 21st century.

1 Changing the role of the Leader. Outside forces are now major drivers for the new leadership. Eighty-eight percent of the participants indicated that both the nature of leadership and the method for developing leaders had changed. Successful leaders are embracing a 'people first – activities second' style. They are putting trust in the human asset to develop and achieve, as opposed to controlling the workforce.

2 CEO & Corporate Culture. Over half of all participating companies feel that the CEO is the driving force for determining or changing the culture of the organisation. The CEO's behaviour is emulated by the rest of the organisation's leaders – the more visible the CEO, the greater the impact.

3 Performance Factors. Those who lead successful companies take a cohesive, holistic approach to organisational management. The three most important words were 'values, inspiration and beliefs'. More organisations are focusing on communicating and teaching company core values and beliefs, and value systems are being re-established.

4 A Guide for Effective Leaders. Participating organisations chose six leadership skills or traits that identify a great leader. They are: vision; values and beliefs; teamwork and collaboration; business and technical knowledge; communication; and personal attributes.

5 Focusing on the Next Generation. Identifying the next generation of leaders requires foresight. Potential leaders exist throughout the organisation, yet the process of identification and development is often inadequate. Considering technology, customers, competition and employees is a prime asset. Beyond that, flexibility, openness and communication skills are important.

6 Approaches to Leadership Development. Leadership training is now a corporate priority. Over 70 percent of participants indicate that their organisation has a formal leadership development program. New approaches and topics are indicated by many participating organisations, and case studies outline how several organisations are using these new training approaches.

7 Evaluating Leadership Effectiveness. How will you know that your company's leadership style is effective? Data provides a picture of how organisations can and will measure leaders. The five highest-ranked factors were: profitability; customer satisfaction; employee attitudes/satisfaction; sales revenue increases; and company reputation.

8 The Future Direction of Leaders. What will the 21st century bring in leadership development training? It requires the complete development of a broad array of leadership abilities. Sixty-two percent of companies report future changes to the leadership development process, and indicate how in the report.

This article is based on Saratoga Institute's special report ,'Leadership Development', published by AMACOM. Saratoga Institute, Santa Clara, California, is known for its pioneering research and reports on performance measurement and improvement. Copyright © Saratoga Institute 1997. To order the full report, call 800-262-9699 or e-mail your order to cust_serv@amanet. org.ARTICLE#8951.

A large variety of methods – including lectures, demonstrations, procedural manuals, audio-visual material, and equipment simulations – has been used for leadership training.[121–124] Interactive computer tutorials are used to learn technical skills, while cases, exercises, business games, simulations, and audio-visual material are used to learn conceptual and administrative skills. Lectures, case discussions, role play, and group exercises are normally used to learn interpersonal skills. The literature also identifies techniques for leadership development. These techniques include special assignments, job rotation, action learning, mentoring, multi-source feedback workshops, the consortium approach, developmental assessment centres, outdoor challenges, and personal-growth programmes.[125]

An issue also becoming important in the leadership-development area is that of ethics. The ethics of leadership and leaders' degree of moral development are increasingly becoming essential elements of leadership research. We hope more attention will be paid to this aspect in the future.

Further interesting information pertaining to the development of leaders appeared in the 'Special Report' on the previous page, in a summary of a survey of Fortune 1000 companies by the Saratoga Institute in Santa Clara, California.

3.8 The leadership role of HRM

Being a business partner, the HR professional plays a crucial role in unlocking the organisation's people potential to help it achieve world-class status.[126] However, this will not be possible if it does not shed its control and bureaucratic role and act like a true leader. Thus, instead of orientating employees to their current roles, HR leaders must disorientate them so that they can take on new roles, new relationships, new values, new types of behaviour, and new approaches to

Figure 3.5 Reorientating HRM for its leadership role

work.[127] To be successful in this regard, activities such as creating an HR vision, developing an overall corporate HR strategy, and instilling new values in employees are essential.[128]

Within the work context, developing and maintaining the technology infrastructure to support the organisation's HR programmes and establishing and managing proper communications to and from managers and employees, to name but a few activities, are essential. These activities can all be seen as leadership activities. Thus, according to Alvares[129], HR officers who play a leadership role are held accountable for the bottom line and are less control orientated.

Using a model designed by Rosen and Brown[130] (see Figure 3.5 on the previous page), we suggest that HR leaders should start their own leadership orientation with some basic assumptions about human nature and organisational life. These assumptions will influence their values and beliefs about people and organisations. They should then continue to develop an operating style and build relationships that reflect these basic beliefs. From there, HR leaders should create a work environment of strategies, systems, and practices that grow naturally out of these philosophies. When this is done, all the stakeholders – whether employees, customers, shareholders, or society – will benefit.[131]

SUMMARY

This chapter makes it clear that business as usual will not generate a competitive edge, but that something significantly different – namely effective leadership – is needed. Leaders inspire the creation of a shared and compelling vision, and once they establish this, they articulate it, keep it current, and enrol others in its vigorous support. Various approaches to leadership are available to achieve this goal. In this chapter we looked at individual models of leadership as well as group models, and their contribution to company performance. We discussed training and development methods to enhance an organisation's leadership capability. We also addressed the leadership role of HRM and how to improve it.

KEY CONCEPTS

- Adaptation
- Advanced Information Technology (AIT)
- Attribution approach
- Behavioural-based approach
- Charisma-based approach
- Communication
- Competencies
- Consortium approach
- Cross-functional teams
- Decision roles
- E-leadership
- Emotional intelligence
- Empower
- Executive teams
- Follower
- Group models
- Heroic leadership
- Individual models
- Informational roles
- Institutionalised leadership
- Instrumental leadership
- Interpersonal roles
- Leadership
- Leadership managerial roles
- Leadership training techniques
- Management
- Managerial-based approach
- Organisational models
- Recreation
- Reorientation
- Risk-taking
- Self-managed teams
- Situation
- Situational-based approach
- Strategic leadership practices
- Strategic-based approach
- Traits-based approach
- Transactional-based approach
- Transformational-based approach
- Tuning
- Vision

CASE STUDY

Objective: To understand the role of leadership within organisations

Sam Magubane – Sun Sporting Goods

The Sun Sporting Goods facility in Midrand, Gauteng, was considered one of the least-efficient plants in the corporation. The facility producing golf balls consistently lost money. Midrand's lack of profitability was caused by major problems in the following areas: productivity, quality, cost, safety, morale, and housekeeping. The management and employees displayed an 'us against them' mentality.

Sam Magubane, the plant manager, wanted to change the situation by solving these problems. He wanted Sun to make the best golf balls and have the most efficient production facilities in the world. To achieve that mission, Sam developed five guiding philosophies, or what he wanted to become shared values:

- Employee involvement
- Total-quality management
- Continuous improvement
- Lowest-total-cost manufacturing
- Just-in-time manufacturing.

Sam held meetings with groups of employees to tell them about the vision, mission, and values he wanted them to share. He asked everyone to change radically the facility's way of doing business. He stressed the need to change from the old dictatorial management style to the new employee-involvement style. As a result of those meetings, employees were called associates and empowered to find new solutions to old problems. Managers were trained in employee-involvement management, and through training they developed skills to include employees in decision making, to develop teams, to develop better human relations, to coach employees, to manage time better, and to manage total quality. The old attitude of 'we cannot do it, or we cannot afford to do it' was changed to 'we can do it, and we cannot afford not to do it'.

To solve Sun's problems, Sam instituted a voluntary employee-participation program called Team Sun. Teams of associates were developed to participate in problem solving in the areas of productivity, quality, cost, safety, morale, and housekeeping. Teams focused on reducing operating expenses, increasing cash flow, reducing inventory, and improving safety and housekeeping. To ensure team success, at the beginning of the change in process, all associates on teams were given training similar to that given to managers.

Within a few years, 66 per cent of employees had formed voluntary teams. Each team represents a specific area of the plant. Each team has created its own unique logo, T-shirt, and posters, which are displayed in the plant. Sun holds several picnics and parties each year to show its appreciation to all associates. To recognise team accomplishments, three Team Sun teams are chosen each quarter for awards that Sam presents at a meeting of the entire plant.

Its new vision, mission, and management style dramatically changed the Midrand facility. Sun at Midrand was named one of the 'Best Plants in South Africa' by a leading financial magazine. The following are some team accomplishments:

- Market share increased from 2 per cent to 17 per cent
- Inventory turns per year increased from 6,5 to 8,5
- Inventory was reduced by two-thirds
- Manufacturing losses caused by scrap and rework were reduced by 67 per cent
- Productivity increased by 121 per cent.

Questions and activities

1. Explain how each of the five elements of our definition of leadership applies to this case.
2. Identify leadership roles illustrated in this case. Which role was the most important?
3. Describe how each level of analysis of leadership theory is illustrated in this case. Which level is the primary focus?
4. Explain how each of the leadership-theory classifications applies to this case.
5. Describe how this case illustrates the management-to-leadership paradigm.

SOURCE: Adapted from Case: A Scott Wilson Sporting Goods. (*In* LUSSIER, R. N. & ACHUA, C. F. 2004. *Leadership: Theory, application, skill development* 2nd ed. Minnesota: South Western, part of Thomson Corporation:22.) Used with permission.

REVIEW QUESTIONS AND ACTIVITIES

1. Define the concept of leadership.
2. Explain the difference between leadership and management.
3. Provide five examples of successful leadership and five examples of unsuccessful leadership.
4. Name some of the characteristics of organisations that communicate well.
5. Write a short paragraph on leadership traits.
6. List 10 leadership managerial roles.
7. Briefly discuss the advantages and disadvantages of cross-functional teams.

8. Critically discuss the following individual models of leadership: transactional leadership and transformational leadership.
9. Discuss strategic leadership practices of the past and of the future, according to Ireland and Hitt.
10. Nadler identifies four different types of change that can occur within organisations: tuning, adaptation, reorientation, and recreation. Discuss these changes briefly.

FURTHER READING

BLASS, F. R. & FERRIS, G. R. 2007. Leader reputation: the role of mentoring, political skill, contextual learning and adaptations. *Human resource management*, 46(1):5–19.

FELFE, J. & PETERSEN, L. E. 2007. Romance of leadership and management decision making. *European journal of work and organisational psychology*, 16(1):1–24.

BALLINGER, G. A. & SCHOORMAN, F. D. 2007. Individual reactions to leadership succession in workgroups. *Academy of management review*, 32(1):118–136.

QUINN, R. E. 2005. Moments of greatness: entering the fundamental state of leadership. *Harvard business review*, 83(7):75–83.

AVOLIO, B. J. & GARDNER, W. L. 2005. Authentic leadership development: getting to the root of positive forms of leadership. *The leadership quarterly*, 16(3):315–338. GARDNER, W. L., AVOLIO, B. J., LUTHANS, F., MAY, D. R. & WALUMBWA, F. 2005. 'Can you see the real me?' A self-based model of authentic leader and follower development. *The leadership quarterly*, 16(3):343–372.

WEB SITES

www.ccl.org – Centre for creative leadership.
www.academyleadership.com – Academy Leadership – leadership training.

ENDNOTES

1. NATHANSON, C. 1993. Three ways to prove HR's value. *Personnel journal*, 72(1):19, January.

2. SCHRIESHEIM, C. A. & NEIDER, L. L. 1989. Leadership theory and development: the coming 'New Phase'. *Leadership & organisation development journal*, 10(6):17–26. See also BARKER, R. A. 2001. The nature of leadership. *Human relations*, 54(4):3; LUSSIER, R. N. & ACHUA, C. F. 2004. *Leadership: Theory, application and skill development* 2nd ed. Minnesota: South-Western, part of the Thomson Corporation; MANNING, G. & CURTIS, K. 2007. *The art of leadership* 2nd ed. New York: McGraw-Hill.

3. BENNIS, W. G. 1989. *On becoming a leader*. Reading, M.A.: Addison-Wesley:2.

4. ULRICH, D. & Lake, D. 1990. *Organizational capability: Competing from the inside out*. New York: John Wiley & Sons:259.

5. Ibid.:259.

6. JACOBS, T. O. & JAQUES, E. 1990. Military executive leadership. (*In* Clark, K. E. & Clark, M. B. (eds.). *Measures of leadership*. West Orange, N.J.: Leadership Library of America:281.)

7. LIPPITT, M. 1999. How to influence leaders. *Training and development*, (53)3:18.

8. DRATH, W. H. & PAULUS, C. J. 1994. *Making common sense – leadership as meaning-making in a community of practice*. Greensboro, N.C.: Center for Creative Leadership.

9. RICHARDS, D. & ENGLE, S. 1986. After the vision: suggestions to corporate visionaries and vision champions. (*In* Adams, J. D. (ed.). *Transforming leadership*. Alexandria, V.A.: Miles River Press:206.)

10. HUGHES, R. L., GINNETT, R. C. & CURPHY, G. J. 2002. *Leadership: Enhancing the lessons of experience* 4th ed. New York: McGraw-Hill, Irwin:1; LUSSIER, R. N. & ACHUA, C. F. 2004. *Leadership: Theory, application and skill development* 2nd ed. Minnesota: South-Western, part of the Thomson Corporation:5–8; WOOD, M., 2005. The fallacy of misplaced leadership. *Journal of management studies*, 42(6):1101–1121.

11. HINTERHUBER, H. H. & KRAUTHAMMER, E. 1998. The leadership wheel: the tasks entrepreneurs and senior executives cannot delegate. *Strategic change*, 7:149; ANTONAKIS, J., CIANCIOLO, A. T. & STERNBERG, R. J. 2004. *The nature of leadership*. Thousand Oaks, C.A.: Sage Publications.

12. HUGHES, R. L., GINNETT, R. C. & CURPHY, G. J. 2002. *Leadership: Enhancing the lessons of experience* 4th ed. New York, McGraw-Hill, Irwin:10; KUMLE, J. & KELLY, N. J. 2006. Leadership vs Management. *Supervision*, 67(8):11–13.

13. Ibid.

14. Bennis, W. G. 1989. *On becoming a leader*. Reading, M.A.: Addison-Wesley:18. See also Bennis, W. G. 2000. The end of leadership: exemplary leadership is impossible without full inclusion, initiatives and cooperation of followers. *Organizational dynamics*, 28(4):71–80.

15. LEONARD, B. 1999. From management to leadership. *HR magazine*, 44(1):34; TSUI, A. S., ZHANG, Z-X., WANG, H., XIN, K. R. & WU, J. B. 2006. Unpacking the relationship between CEO leadership behaviour and organisational culture. *The leadership quarterly*, 17(2):113–137.

16. NUR, Y. A. 1998. Charisma and managerial leadership: the gift that never was. *Business horizons*, 41(4):20, July/August.

17. KETTERER, R. & CHAYES, M. 1995. Executive development: finding and growing champions of change. (*In* Nadler, D., Shaw, R., Walton, A. E. & Associates (eds). *Discontinuous change*. San Francisco, Jossey Bass:190–216.) See also KANTER, R. M. 2000. Leaders with passion, conviction and confidence can use several techniques to take charge of change rather than react to it. *Ivey business journal*, May/June:32–36; COLLINS, J. 2001. Level 5 leadership: the triumph of humility and fierce resolve. *Harvard business review*, January:67–76.

18. GEORGE, J. M. 2000. Emotions and leadership: the role of emotional intelligence. *Human relations*, 53(8):1027–1055, August. See also Lewis, K. M. 2000. When leaders display emotion: how followers respond to negative emotional expression of male and female leaders. *Journal of organizational behaviour*, 21:211–234; RICKARDS, T. & CLARK, M. 2005. *Dilemmas of leadership*. London: Routledge, Taylor & Francis Group; ALAN, I. & HIGGINS, J. M. 2005. Global leadership success through emotional and cultural intelligences. *Business horizons*, 48:501–512.

19. YUKL, G. 1998. *Leadership in organizations* 4th ed. New Jersey, Upper Saddle River: Prentice Hall:19.

20. PLATTS, M. & SOUTHALL, A-M. 1994. Employee communications and effective involvement. (*In* Armstrong, M. (Ed.). *Strategies for human resource management*. London, Kogan Page:150–164.)

21. SONNENSCHEIN, W. 1997. *Workforce diversity*. Lincolnwood, Illinois: NTC Business Books.

22. PLATTS, M. & SOUTHALL, A-M. 1994. Employee communications and effective involvement. (*In* Armstrong, M. (Ed.). *Strategies for human resource management*. London, Kogan Page:153.)

23. Ibid.:154.

24. LUSSIER, R. N. & ACHUA, C. F. 2004. *Leadership: Theory, application and skill development* 2nd ed. Minnesota: South-Western, part of the Thomson Corporation:5–8

25. This section is based on work done by Antonakis, Cianciolo, and Sternberg. See ANTONAKIS, J., CIANCIOLO, A. T. & STERNBERG, R. J. 2004. *The nature of leadership*. Thousand Oaks, C.A.: Sage Publications:209.

26. STEERS, R. M., PORTER, L. W. & BIGLEY, G. A. 1996. *Motivation and leadership at work* 6th ed. New York: McGraw-Hill.

27. HUGHES, R. L., GINNETT, R. C. & CURPHY, G. J. 2002. *Leadership: Enhancing the lessons of experience* 4th ed. New York, McGraw-Hill, Irwin:236;

YAMMARINO, F. J., DIONNE, S. D., CHUN, J. U. & DANSEREAU, F. 2005. Leadership and levels of analysis: a state-of-the-science review. *The leadership quarterly,* 15(6):879–919.

28. YUKL, G. 1998. *Leadership in organizations* 4th ed. New Jersey, Upper Saddle River: Prentice Hall:82.

29. STEERS, R. M., PORTER, L. W. & BIGLEY, G. A. 1996. *Motivation and leadership at work* 6th ed. New York: McGraw-Hill:167.

30. HUNT, J. W. 1992. *Managing people at work* 3rd ed. Berkshire, McGraw-Hill:241–242.

31. STEERS, R. M., PORTER, L. W. & BIGLEY, G. A. 1996. *Motivation and leadership at work* 6th ed. New York: McGraw-Hill:167. See also ROMM, C. & PLISKEN, N. 1999. The role of charismatic leadership in diffusion and implementation of e-mail. *The journal of management development,* 18(3):273–290.

32. KIRKPATRICK, S. A. & LOCKE, E. A. 1991. Leadership: do traits matter? *Academy of management executive,* 5(2):48–60.

33. HUNT, J. W. 1992. *Managing people at work* 3rd ed. Berkshire, McGraw-Hill:241.

34. STEERS, R. M., PORTER, L. W. & BIGLEY, G. A. 1996. *Motivation and leadership at work* 6th ed. New York: McGraw-Hill:167.

35. YUKL, G. 1998. *Leadership in organizations* 4th ed. New Jersey, Upper Saddle River: Prentice Hall:64.

36. ROMM, C. & PLISKEN, N. 1999. The role of charismatic leadership in diffusion and implementation of e-mail. *The journal of management development,* 18(3):278.

37. Ibid.

38. HUGHES, R. L., GINNETT, R. C. & CURPHY, G. J. 2002. *Leadership: Enhancing the lessons of experience* 4th ed. New York, McGraw-Hill, Irwin:62.

39. Ibid.:47.

40. ULRICH, D. & Lake, D. 1990. *Organizational capability: Competing from the inside out.* New York: John Wiley & Sons:260.

41. Ibid.

42. MCCRIMMON, M. 1995. Bottom-up leadership. *Executive development,* 8(5):6–12.

43. Ibid.:10.

44. Ibid.

45. Ibid.:11.

46. Ibid.

47. YUKL, G. 1998. *Leadership in organizations* 4th ed. New Jersey, Upper Saddle River: Prentice Hall:351.

48. Ibid.:356; MEHRA, A., SMITH, B. R., DIXON, A. L. & ROBERTSON, B. 2006. Distributed leadership in teams: the network of leadership perceptions and team performance. *The leadership quarterly,* 17(2):232–245; BURKE, C. S., STAGE, K. C., KLEIN, C., GOODWIN, G. F., SALAS, S. & HALPIN, S. M. 2006. What type of leadership behaviours are functional in teams? A meta analysis. *The leadership quarterly,* 17(2):288–307.

49. Ibid.:356–357.

50. Ibid.:357.

51. BARRY, D. 1991. Managing the bossless team: lessons in distributed leadership. *Organisational dynamics,* Summer:31–47.

52. YUKL, G. 1998. *Leadership in organizations* 4th ed. New Jersey, Upper Saddle River: Prentice Hall:358.

53. Ibid.:359.

54. Ibid.

55. Ibid.:360; KETS DE VRIES, M. F. R. 2005. Leadership group coaching in action: The Zen of creating high performance teams. *Academy of management executive,* 19(1):61–76.

56. Ibid.

57. NADLER, D. A. & SPENCER, J. L. (eds). 1998. *Executive teams.* San Francisco: Jossey Bass:3; SRIVASTAVA, A., BARTOL, K. M. & LOCKE, E. A. 2006. Empowering leadership in management teams: effects on knowledge sharing, efficacy and performance. *Academy of management journal,* 49(6):1239–1251.

58. YUKL, G. 1998. *Leadership in organizations* 4th ed. New Jersey, Upper Saddle River: Prentice Hall:409.

59. NADLER, D. A. & SPENCER, J. L. (eds). 1998. *Executive teams.* San Francisco: Jossey Bass :1.

60. Ibid.:5.

61. RIVERO, J. C. 1998. The role of feedback in executive team effectiveness. (*In* Nadler, D. A. & Spencer, J. L. (Eds). 1998. *Executive teams.* San Francisco: Jossey Bass:181.)

62. Ibid.

63. Ibid.

64. NADLER, D. A. & SPENCER, J. L. (eds). 1998. *Executive teams.* San Francisco: Jossey Bass:193–234.

65. THIES, P. K. & WAGNER, D. B. 1998. (*In* Nadler, D. A. & Spencer, J. L. (Eds). 1998. *Executive teams.* San Francisco: Jossey Bass:258.)

66. BASS, B. M. & AVOLIO, B. J. 1994. Transformational leadership and organisational culture. *International journal of public administration,* 17(3&4):541–554.

67. GROBLER, P. A., WÄRNICH, S., CARRELL, M. R., ELBERT, N. F. & HATFIELD, R. D. 2002. *Human resource management in South Africa,* 2nd ed. London: Thomson Learning:641.

68. HUNT, J. W. 1992. *Managing people at work* 3rd ed. Berkshire, McGraw-Hill:255; VINGER, G. & CILLIERS, F. 2006. Effective transformational leadership behaviours for managing change. *SA journal of human resource management,* 4(2):1–9.

69. PICCOLO, R. F. & COLQUITT, J. A. 2006. Transformational leadership and job behaviours: the mediating role of core job characteristics. *Academy of management journal,* 49(2):327–340; BROWN, D. J. & KEEPING, L. M. 2005. Elaborating the construct of transformational leadership: the role of affect. *The leadership quarterly,* 16(3):245–272; STEERS, R. M., PORTER, L. W. & BIGLEY, G. A. 1996. *Motivation and leadership at work* 6th ed. New York: McGraw-Hill:181; SCHRIESHEIM, C. A., CASTRO, S. L., ZHOU, X. & DE CHURCH, L. A. 2006. An investigation of path–goal and transformational leadership theory predictions at the individual level of

analysis. *The leadership quarterly,* 17(1):21–38; CHA, S. E. & EDMONDSON, A. C. 2006. When values backfire: leadership, attribution and disenchantment in a values-driven organisation. *The leadership quarterly,* 17(1):57–78.

70. YUKL, G. 1998. *Leadership in organizations* 4th ed. New Jersey, Upper Saddle River: Prentice Hall:326–327; VAN DE VLIERT, E. 2006. Climatic ecology of charismatic leadership ideals. *European journal of work and organisational psychology,* 15(4):385–403.

71. This section of the chapter is based on the work done by one of the authors (Prof. P.A. Grobler) and published in GROBLER, P. A., WÄRNICH, S., CARRELL, M. R., ELBERT, N. F. & HATFIELD, R. D. 2002. *Human resource management in South Africa,* 2nd ed. London: Thomson Learning:641.

72. FLANAGAN, H. D. & THOMPSON, D. J. C. 1993. Leadership: the swing of the pendulum. *The leadership & organizational development journal,* 14(1):9–15.

73. BASS, B. M. 1985. *Leadership and performance beyond expectation.* New York: Free Press.

74. AVOLIO, B. J. & BASS, B. M. 1988. Charisma and beyond. (*In* Hunt, J. G., Baliga, B. R., Dachler, H. P. & Schriesheim, C. A. (Eds) *Emerging leadership vistas.* Lexington, M.A.: Heath.)

75. BASS, B. M. & AVOLIO, B. J. 1990. *Manual for the multifactor leadership questionnaire.* Palo Alto, CA: Consulting Psychologists Press.

76. BASS, B. M. & AVOLIO, B. J. 1994. Transformational leadership and organisational culture. *International journal of public administration,* 17(3&4):541–554.

77. KOH, W. L., TERBORG, J. R. & STEERS, R. M. 1991. *The impact of transformational leadership on organizational commitment, organizational citizenship behaviour, teacher satisfaction and student performance in Singapore.* Annual Academy of Management Meeting. Miami, Florida. [Paper.]

78. HOWELL, J. M. & AVOLIO, B. J. 1993. Transformational leadership, transactional leadership, locus of control and support for innovation: key predictors of consolidated business unit performance. *Journal of applied psychology,* 78(6):891–902.

79. FLANAGAN, H. D. & THOMPSON, D. J. C. 1993. Leadership: the swing of the pendulum. *The leadership & organizational development journal,* 14(1):10; EPITROPAKI, O. & MARTIN, R. 2005. The moderating role of individual differences in the relation between transformational/transactional leadership perceptions and organisational identification. *The leadership quarterly,* 16(6):569–589.

80. FLANAGAN, H. D. & THOMPSON, D. J. C. 1993. Leadership: the swing of the pendulum. *The leadership & organizational development journal,* 14(1):10–11.

81. Ibid.:12–13.

82. Ibid.:14–15.

83. IRELAND, R. D. & HITT, M. A. 1999. Achieving and maintaining strategic competitiveness in the 21st century: the role of strategic leadership. *Academy of management executive,* 3(1):43; COLVILLE, I. D. &

MURPHY, A. J. 2006. Leadership as the enabler of strategizing and organising. *Long range planning,* 39(6):663–677.

84. IRELAND, R. D. & HITT, M. A. 1999. Achieving and maintaining strategic competitiveness in the 21st century: the role of strategic leadership. *Academy of management executive,* 3(1):54; KAPLAN, B. & KAISER, R. 2006. *The versatile leader: Make the most of your strengths without overdoing it.* San Francisco, C.A.: Pfeiffer, an imprint of John Wiley; HUGHES, R. & BEATTY, K. 2005. Five steps to leading strategically. *Training & development,* 59(December):45–47; VERA, D. & CROSSMAN, M. 2004. Strategic leadership and organisational learning. *Academy of management review,* 29(2):222–240.

85. IRELAND, R. D. & HITT, M. A. 1999. Achieving and maintaining strategic competitiveness in the 21st century: the role of strategic leadership. *Academy of management executive,* 3(1):47.

86. Ibid.:49–52.

87. NADLER, D. A., SHAW, R. B. & WALTON, A. S. 1995. *Discontinuous change: Leading organizational transformation.* San Francisco, Jossey Bass:217–231.

88. Ibid.:25–29; KAVANAGH, M. H. & ASHKANASY, N. B. 2006. The impact of leadership and change management strategy on organisational culture and individual acceptance of change during a merger. *British journal of management,* 17:S81–S103.

89. NADLER, D. A., SHAW, R. B. & WALTON, A. S. 1995. *Discontinuous change: Leading organizational transformation.* San Francisco, Jossey Bass:218–224.

90. Ibid.:222.

91. Ibid.:224.

92. Ibid.:225.

93. ANTONAKIS, J., CIANCIOLO, A. T. & STERNBERG, R. J. 2004. *The nature of leadership.* Thousand Oaks, C.A.: Sage Publications:43.

94. Ibid.:43.

95. Ibid.:43.

96. Ibid.:43.

97. ZEMKE, R. & ZEMKE, S. 2001. Where do leaders come from? *Training,* August:44–48.

98. Ibid.:206. See also WILLIAMS, R. L. & COTHREL, J. P. 1997. Building tomorrow's leaders today. *Strategy & leadership,* 25(5):17–22, September/October; EDGEMAN, R. L., DAHLGAARD, S. M. P., DAHLGAARD, J. J. & SCHERER, F. 1999. On leaders and leadership. *Quality progress,* October:49–54; DELAHOUSSAYE, M. 2001. Leadership in the 21st century. *Training,* August:50–59; GEORGE, B., SIMS, P., MCLEAN, A. N. & MAYER, D. 2007. Discovering your authentic leadership. *Harvard business review,* 85(2):129–138; ANCONA, D., MALONE, T. W., ORLIKOWSKI, W. J. & SENGE, P. M. 2007. In praise of the incomplete leader. *Harvard business review,* 85(2):92–100.

99. CACIOPPE, R. 1998. Leaders developing leaders: an effective way to enhance leadership development programs. *Leadership & organizational development*

journal, 19(4):194–198. See also CACIOPPE, R. 1998. An integrated model and approach for the design of effective leadership development programs. *Leadership & organizational development journal,* 19(1):44–53.

100. COHEN, E. & TICHY, N. 1997. How leaders develop leaders. *Training & development,* 51(5):58–73, May.

101. FULMER, R. M. & WAGNER, S. 1999. Leadership: lessons from the best. *Training & development,* 53(3):29–32.

102. WELLINS, R. & BYHAM, W. C. 2001. The leadership gap. *Training,* March:98–106. See also MERYER, T. W. 2001. Ten tips for leadership trainers. *Training & development,* 55(3):16–18.

103. NICHOLLS, J. 1999. Value-centred leadership – applying transforming leadership to produce strategic behaviour in depth (part 1). *Strategic change,* 8(September/October):311–324.

104. TICHY, N. 1997. The leadership engine: how winning companies create leaders at all levels. *Proceedings of the 2nd Annual Leadership Development Conference:* Linkage Inc.: 57–81.

105. WELCH, J. & BYRNE, J. A. 2001. *Jack: What I've learned leading a great company and great people.* London: Headline Book Publishing.

106. RUSSEL, P. 1997. The PepsiCo leadership center: How PepsiCo's leaders develop leaders. *Proceedings of the 2nd Annual Leadership Development Conference.* Linkage Inc.: 97–138.

107. MUMFORD, A. 1993. *How managers can develop managers.* Gower: Aldershot; MENDENHALL, M. E. 2006. The elusive yet critical challenge of developing global leaders. *European management journal,* 24(6):422–429.

108. BYHAM, W. C. 1999. Grooming next-millennium leaders. *HR magazine,* 44(2):46–50, February.

109. BARNER, R. 2000. Five steps to leadership competencies. *Training & development,* March:47–51.

110. YEAROUT, S., MILES, G. & KOONCE, R. 2000. Wanted: leadership builders. *Training & development,* 54(3):34–42.

111. BYHAM, W. C. 2000. How to create a reservoir of ready-made leaders. *Training & development,* 54(3):29–32.

112. ZENGER, J., ULRICH, D. & SMALLWOOD, N. 2000. The new leadership development. *Training & development,* 54(3):22–27; COHN, J. M., KHURANA, R. & REEVES, L. 2005. Growing talent as if your business depended on it. *Harvard business review,* 83(10):63–70; BURGOYNE, J. & JAMES, K. T. 2006. Towards best or better practice in corporate leadership development: operational issues in mode 2 and design science research. *British journal of management,* 17(4):303–316; ANTONAKIS, J., CIANCIOLO, A. T. & STERNBERG, R. J. 2004. *The nature of leadership.* Thousand Oaks, C.A.: Sage Publications:10.

113. SOMERSET, F. 2001. The softer side of leadership. *CMA management,* October:12–13.

114. FRIEDMAN, S. D. 2001. Leadership DNA: The Ford Motor story. *Training & development,* 55(3):23–29.

115. FULMER, R. M. 2001. Frameworks for leadership. *Organizational dynamics,* 29(3):211–220.

116. SCHULTZ, L. E. 2000. Qualities of an exceptional leader. *Human systems management,* 19:93–103.

117. BENSON-ARMER, R. & STICKEL, D. 2000. Successful team leadership. *Ivey business journal,* May/June:520–533.

118. DROTTER, S. J. & CHARAN, R. 2001. Building leaders at every level. *Ivey business journal,* May/June:21–27.

119. FULMER, R. M., GIBBS, P. A. & GOLDSMITH, M. 2000. Developing leaders: how winning companies keep on winning. *Sloan management review,* 42(1): no page numbers, fall.

120. SMITH, L. & SANDSTROM, J. 1999. Executive leader coaching as a strategic activity. *Strategy & leadership,* 27(6):33–36.

121. BASS, B. M. 1990. *Handbook of leadership: A survey of theory and research.* New York: Free Press.

122. BURKE, M. J. & DAY, R. R. 1986. A cumulative study of the effectiveness of managerial training. *Journal of applied psychology,* 71:232–246; WHITE, D. 2006. *Coaching leaders: guiding people who guide others.* San Francisco: Josey Bass.

123. LATHAM, G. P. 1988. Human resource training and development. *Annual review of psychology,* 39:545–582; LORD, R. G. & HALL, R. J. 2005. Identity, deep structure and the development of leadership skill. *The leadership quarterly,* 16(6):591–615.

124. TETRAULT, L. A., SCHRIESHEIM, C. A. & NEIDER, L. L. 1988. Leadership training interventions: a review. *Organizational development journal,* 6(3):77–83.

125. YUKL, G. 1998. *Leadership in organizations* 4th ed. New Jersey, Upper Saddle River: Prentice Hall:477. See also LAWLER, W. 2000. The consortium approach to grooming future leaders. *Training & development,* 54(3):53–77; SMITH, R. & BLEDSOE, B. 2006. Grooming leaders for growth. *Training & development,* 60(8):47–50.

126. MARKOWICH, M. M., 1995. HR's leadership role in the third wave era. *HR magazine,* September:93.

127. YEUNG, A. K. & READY, D. A. 1995. Developing leadership capabilities of global corporations: a comparative study of eight nations. *Human resource management,* 34(4):529–547, winter.

128. HEIFETZ, R. A. & LAURIE, D. L. 1997. The work of leadership. (*In* Kerr, S. *Ultimate rewards: What really motivates people to achieve.* Boston: Harvard Business Review Book:113–132.)

129. ALVARES, K. M. 1997. The business of human resources. *Human resource management,* 36(1):9–15, spring.

130. ROSEN, R. H. & BROWN, P. B. 1996. *Leading people: Transforming business from the inside out.* New York: Penguin Books:365–376.

131. Ibid.:367.

4

The strategic role of human resource management

Learning outcomes

After reading this chapter you should be able to:

▶ Explain the basic principles of strategic HRM
▶ Discuss critically the relationship between strategic management and strategic HRM
▶ Describe the design of an HR strategy
▶ Describe the various models of strategic HRM

Purpose

The purpose of this chapter is to introduce you to the strategic role of human resource management within an organisation.

Chapter overview

This chapter sets out to explain the major approaches and theories related to the study of strategic HRM (SHRM). It also seeks to explain the broad concepts underlying the theories and throws light on the issues that have led to the emergence of strategic HRM to its current status. The chapter also contains a discussion on the relationship between strategic management and SHRM and focuses on the different SHRM models developed over the years. The concluding case study illustrates how the theory contained in this chapter can be applied to a practical situation.

Introduction

There is no doubt that dramatic changes in both internal and external environments of companies during the past few decades have presented HR professionals with new and important challenges. To address these challenges, the HR function has evolved from playing a limited administrative role to entering into a business partnership with line managers.[1]

As Chapter 1 indicated, HR professionals – in their capacity as business partners – must play a number of new roles to be successful, one being the strategic-partner role, which involves linking the HRM practices, systems, and policies with the strategic initiatives of the company[2] (see Figure 4.1). In the literature, this process is known as strategic human resource management (SHRM).[3-4]

A number of benefits can be derived from this process, including[5-6]:

- Contributing to the goal accomplishment and survival of the company
- Supporting and successfully implementing given corporate and business strategies of the company
- Creating and maintaining a competitive advantage for the company
- Improving the responsiveness and innovation potential of the company
- Increasing the number of feasible strategic options available to the company
- Participating in strategic planning and influencing the strategic direction of the company as an equally entitled member of top management
- Improving cooperation between the HRM department and line managers.

However, despite these benefits, the strategic use of human resources within companies frequently remains an afterthought.[7]

In this chapter, we shall discuss a number of issues relating to how the HRM function can be linked to the company strategy to gain the desired competitive advantage. More specifically, we shall discuss the basic principles of SHRM, the relationship between strategic management and SHRM, the development of an HRM strategy, and the various models of SHRM.

4.1 The basic principles of SHRM

Before we look at some of the basic principles of SHRM, it is necessary to provide a few brief definitions of the concept. Tsui, in one of the early definitions, describes the concept as follows[8-9]:

Figure 4.1 Linking HR practices with the strategic initiatives of the company

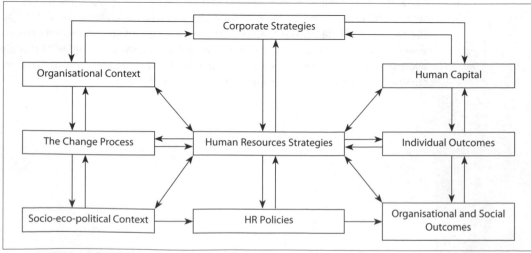

SOURCE: SHARMA, A. & KHANDEKAR, A. 2006. *Strategic human resource management: An Indian perspective.* New Delhi: Response Books, a division of Sage Publications:42. Used with permission.

The concept of strategic human resource management tends to focus on organisation-wide human resource concerns and addresses issues that are related to the firm's business, both short-term and long-term. It is particularly useful for designing specific human resource programmes, policies, systems or management practices at the organisational or business level. It also suggests that the line executive is the most important constituent for the human resource function.

SOURCE: TSUI, A. S. 1987. Defining the activities and effectiveness of the human resource department: a multiple constituency approach. *Human resource management*, 26(1):36

What is interesting about this definition is that it supports the 'proactive' approach to be found within the literature. With this approach, HR professionals participate in the strategic-planning process and can, as a result of limitations in the company's HR situation, potentially influence the formulation of the company strategy. In another definition, Dyer and Holder provide more substance to the concept when they remark[10]:

Strategic human resource management consists of three major tasks. The first task, which arises during the formulation of business strategies, is to assure that the HR issues and implications of various alternatives or proposals are fully considered (their desirability and feasibility). The next task involves establishing HR goals and action plans – that is HR strategies (at all levels) – to support the business strategies. And the final task requires working with line managers as principal clients to ensure that established action plans are indeed implemented.

SOURCE: DYER, L. & HOLDER, G. W. 1988. A strategic perspective of human resource management. (*In* Dyer, L. (Ed.). *Human resource management: Evolving roles and responsibilities*. Washington: The Bureau of National Affairs.)

From the above definitions it is clear that two major issues or aspects need to be in place within the organisation before the SHRM process can function successfully. The first is the presence of a strategic management process; the second is the restructuring of the HRM function itself.[11–15]

Thus, it is clear that if the organisation has no process by which to engage in strategic management at the corporate and business level, it will not be possible for the HR function to develop a strategic thrust, since the HR strategy flows from the corporate or business strategy. Also, as the HR function will be evolving from a reactive administrative focus, it will have to be reorganised to address its strategic responsibilities. Thus the HR system must have its operational house in order before it can afford the luxury of concentrating on the formulation and implementation of an HR strategy.[16–17]

There are numerous descriptions of the concept of strategic management. Briefly, however, it involves a process that deals with organisational renewal and growth, with the development of strategies, structures, and systems necessary to achieve renewal and growth, and with the organisational systems needed to manage effectively the strategy formulation and implementation processes.[18]

For the HR function to operate at the strategic level, it needs to reorganise the existing HR administrative function into three distinct levels, namely strategic, operational, and functional.[19–20] At the strategic level, HR professionals fulfil their role as strategic partners and are involved in corporate and HR planning. Casio identifies the following four features of this role[21]:

- Senior HR professionals meet regularly with their counterparts in line management to formulate and to review broad HR strategies (those designed to promote innovation, quality enhancement, or cost control)
- Senior HR professionals participate fully in all top-level sessions on business strategy; this permits early evaluation of proposals in terms of their feasibility and desirability

from a HR perspective, as well as an early warning of upcoming HRM issues

- HR professionals at all levels work closely with line managers on an ongoing basis to assure that all components of the business strategy are implemented adequately
- The HRM function itself is managed strategically: it has its own departmental strategy that identifies priorities, directs the allocation of resources, and guides the work of various specialists (e.g. compensation, labour relations).

At the operational level, the HR team develops action plans to meet present labour needs, and at the functional level it carries out the many activities which ensure that employees are in the right place at the right time and cost. Consider, for example, the performance appraisal function. At the strategic level a decision will be made regarding what to value in the long term. At the operational level, appraisal systems that relate current conditions and future potential will be set up. At the functional level, the actual appraisal system will be implemented annually and day-to-day control systems will be put in place.

Once the new HR structure has been finalised, it is important that it establishes proper communication links with line management. This relationship can be enhanced by having regular meetings with line managers, circulating relevant HR reports to them, and establishing a computerised HR system that allows access by all stakeholders.[22]

4.2 The relationship between strategic management and SHRM

The discussion makes it clear that if an organisation is to function successfully, managers cannot ignore the relationship between strategic management and SHRM. However, in many cases, this relationship between the two processes within a company is non-existent for a number of reasons. Rothwell and Kazanas have named several[23]:

- Top managers do not perceive a need for a relationship

- HR practitioners are perceived as 'personnel experts' not 'experts in business'
- HR information is sometimes incompatible with other information used in strategy formulation
- Conflicts may exist between short-term and long-term HR needs.

We shall now briefly discuss a model, designed by Tichy, that indicates the important relationship between strategic management and SHRM (see Figure 4.2).[24-25] Although it was developed during the 1980s, we have selected this model, known as the 'human resource management cube', because it has several advantages:

- It has been shown to be a relatively powerful model of organisational effectiveness
- It has important implications for the strategic management of the HR function
- It has been commonly used in the SHRM literature.

According to Tichy, companies are continually confronted by three basic problems that must be managed: a technical problem, a political problem, and a cultural problem (see Figure 4.2).[26]

As far as the technical problem is concerned, Tichy argues that, as a result of the external threats and opportunities and the internal strengths and weaknesses of companies, all companies continually face a production problem. In other words, companies must manage technical resources in such a way that they continuously deliver the required output. To solve problems in this area, management is regularly involved in strategy and goal formulation and the design of organisational and management systems.[27]

As far as the political problem is concerned, companies continually have problems with the allocation of power and resources within the organisational structure. Aspects that are important here are the direction in which power and resources are moving, and who will share in the benefits. The following will reflect decisions in this regard: the compensation the organisation

Figure 4.2 The HRM cube

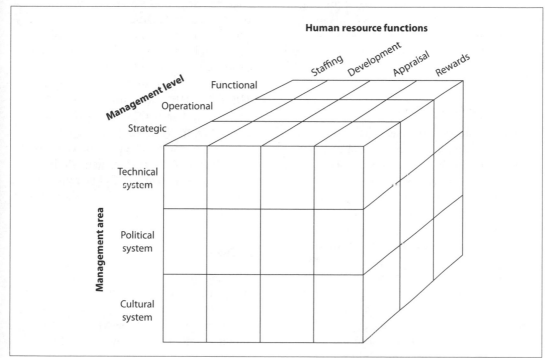

pays, the budget allocations it makes, and the allocation of decision-making power to the different levels within the organisational structure.[28]

Regarding the cultural problem, it is important to remember that a company's 'culture' holds it together. Culture consists of values, beliefs, and views shared by the employees within the company. The organisation must thus continually decide which values, views, and beliefs its employees need to possess and also which sections within the company need to possess which values.[29]

To solve these problems, Tichy suggests that companies design three systems, namely:
• *The technical system.* This will include all those aspects that are required to solve the production problem.
• *The political system.* This will contain all the practices, activities, and elements involved in the allocation problem.
• *The cultural system.* This will contain all the symbols, values, and elements

necessary to address the ideology problem within the organisation.[30]

Tichy suggests that organisations require certain aids for these systems to be managed properly. He identifies the following three as necessary[31]:
• *The mission and strategy of the organisation.* 'Mission and strategy' refer to the setting of goals and the development of a strategy.
• *The structure of the organisation.* The structure will include the tasks, the manner in which workers are grouped and coordinated to perform the tasks, and the management processes of control and information to enable the organisation to function properly.
• *The HRM system of the organisation.* The HRM system will include all the activities such as recruitment, selection, performance appraisal, training and development, and compensation.

Thus, for the organisation to be managed efficiently and effectively, organisations need to manage these issues as an integrated whole (see Figure 4.2). We shall discuss this process briefly.[32]

4.2.1 The technical system

- *Mission and strategy.* Here the traditional tasks of designing a mission and strategy must take place. Through this process the organisation identifies the types of products to manufacture or services to provide and allocates resources to make this possible.
- *Organisational structure.* The organisation designs its structure in such a way as to make the organisation function properly.
- *HRM.* This entails placing individuals properly in posts, determining performance levels and outputs, and developing career and development processes and criteria for filling present and future posts in the company.[33]

4.2.2 The political system

- *Mission and strategy.* It is important to determine who will be responsible for the mission and strategy or who will play the most important role in influencing it, e.g. all the heads of departments, or only the vice-presidents of the company. After the mission and strategy have been accepted, the next step is their physical execution. The strategy might involve establishing new businesses, selling-off present ones or amalgamating two businesses. All these decisions can influence – either negatively or positively – the employees and their jobs. These decisions entail the allocation of resources and budgets and can even have an effect on the quality of relationships between employees.
- *Organisational structure.* The second issue in the management of the political system is the organisational structure. At the technical level, we looked at how the organisation will be structured; here we

shall consider how power will be distributed throughout this structure. In other words, we shall discuss how much power individual division or departmental heads will receive with regard to control over their budgets and their employees.
- *HRM.* The HR system must fit in with the political system within the organisation. Issues like the following will have to be addressed: who will be promoted or not, how the compensation system will be designed, what benefits will be available, and who will be evaluated, by whom and on what grounds.[34]

4.2.3 The cultural system

- *Mission and strategy.* The organisation must address two issues here: the impact of the mission and strategy on the culture of the organisation and the type of culture management desires. This is vital for success.
- *Organisational structure.* The organisation structure must address a number of elements in the cultural system. The first is the development of a management style to fit the technical and political structure developed within the organisation. For example, a company moving from a functional structure to a matrix structure needs an open management style instead of a closed one. The second is the development of different subcultures within the organisation – for example the production division needs a cost-effective culture, while the research-and-development division needs an innovative and creative one. The important issue here is the management of the different cultures within the structure.
- *HRM.* The HRM system provides the final aid in the management of the cultural system, and must be used to develop work-orientated cultures within the organisation. For example, the company's training and development processes can enhance these cultures, and compensation can nurture and develop them (for example by

promoting those whose culture supports the goals of the organisation).[35]

To summarise, the task of strategic management within an organisation involves more than the mere choice of a portfolio of businesses and the design of strategies; it entails the management of all the issues discussed above. To do this successfully, it must include the SHRM approach as well. Thus, without the effective and efficient management of the HRM system, strategic management will not be successful. The HRM practices, systems, and policies must be in line with the strategic initiatives of the company. For example, each of the HRM activities (recruitment, training, compensation, performance appraisal, etc.) must be viewed from a technical, political, and cultural perspective, on a strategic, operational, and functional level.

We have indicated the important and vital role to be played by the HRM function within the organisation. The next question to ask is: how can we design the individual HRM strategies to make this success possible?

4.3 **The design of an HR strategy**

To implement the SHRM process, an organisation needs HR strategies, about which Dyer and Holder make the following remarks:[36-37]

> While a wide variety of issues are addressed in such strategies, at a minimum they include four components:
> - Mission statement or a set of prioritised goals for the function and the major subfunctions (e.g. training, compensation)
> - A proposed organisation structure
> - A programme portfolio to outline priorities and policies
> - A budget to address the issue of resource allocation.
>
> SOURCE: DYER, L. & HOLDER, G. W. 1988. A strategic perspective of human resource management. *In* Dyer, L. (Ed.). *Human resource management: Evolving roles and responsibilities.* Washington: The Bureau of National Affairs:32.

An HR strategy is described by Labelle as 'a set of important decisions an organisation makes about the management of human resources that define an adaptation to both internal and external environments in the pursuit of its objectives'.[38] Hax expands on this with the remark that 'a human resource strategy is a critical component of the firm's corporate and business strategies comprising a set of well coordinated objectives and action programmes aimed at securing a long-term sustainable competitive advantage over the firm's competitors'.[39]

In other words, in view of the above, we can see a strategy as a plan of action which includes both means and ends. HR goals can include, for example, quality of performance (productivity goals), quantity of employees (HR quantity goals), and costs goals.[40] The means, in contrast, can include, for example, HR practices and HR policies. As far as the use of HR practices is concerned, Schuler has provided a practice menu from which a company can make a selection to support a particular strategy (see Table 4.1 on page 81).[41] However, the use of these HR practices can be successful only if the management, in its mission statement, makes a commitment to its employees. According to Nininger, this component could be compiled as follows[42]:

> The people in the organisation will be managed in such a manner as to generate a climate of opportunity and challenge for each employee within which the individual can most effectively contribute to the fulfilment of his or her goals and those of the organisation. This will be accomplished by:
> - Having a clear understanding of all the qualities of each employee, such as skills, knowledge, potential, aspirations and limitations
> - Setting standards of performance that challenge each employee and by ensuring that this performance is attained

- Rewarding excellent employee performance in both material and non-material terms
- Planning properly for human resource needs
- Providing employees throughout the organisation with opportunities for promotion and for developing their job knowledge, skills and satisfaction
- Practising a form of management that allows decision-making authority to be as decentralised as is practical
- Being alert and receptive to new and productive developments in the field of human resources management.

SOURCE: NININGER, J. R., 1982. *Managing human resources: A strategic perspective.* The Conference Board of Canada, Study 71:113.

Thus, an HR strategy will express the intentions of an organisation about how it should manage its human resources. These intentions provide the basis for plans, developments, and programmes for managing change. Typical questions the HR professional would ask when participating in the strategy process would be:

- What sort of people do we need in the business to achieve our mission?
- How can the required changes to our culture and value system be achieved?
- What are the implications of those plans for the future structure, HR systems, and resource requirements?

It is important to note that a number of issues besides the company strategy can influence the formulation of an HR strategy. As we indicated earlier in the chapter, an HR strategy does not take place in isolation but is influenced by both external and internal issues. Externally we think of issues in the economic, technological, social, political, legal, geographic, cultural, and labour-market environments. Internally, issues such as employee demographics, employee skills, productivity, organisational structure, potential of employees, organisational culture, and turnover can all play important roles.

From the above it is clear that many issues need to be considered in the design of a HR strategy. A key aspect in this regard is to understand the strategic imperatives behind important decisions taken either within the HR department or the company.[43] According to Swamy[44], strategic imperatives are 'priority issues that must be addressed to meet long-term objectives'. These imperatives, when properly understood, are used to guide the behaviour of, for example, the HR department or company. Thus, major undertakings within the company or HR department demand a properly evaluated strategic imperative. In other words, when an HR department or company starts a new initiative or addresses a critical or urgent concern that will affect its long-term future, it is very important that management understands the rationale, sets goals, tests the goals with independent and objective reliable tools or systems, considers alternative options, and plans a roadmap for execution.[45] Swamy[46] indicates that organisations can categorise strategic imperatives into two broad categories:

- *An aspiration-driven imperative.* This consists of two components, namely a growth imperative (e.g. a merger or acquisition) and an efficiency-imperative (e.g. informal restructuring). The aspiration imperative comes thus from within.
- *A situation-driven imperative.* This comes from external forces, e.g. a government-facilitated imperative (e.g. regulatory change) or a market-led imperative (e.g. cost cutting to remain competitive).[47]

The question thus is: how can an HR department or company better understand its strategic imperatives? It is clear that the HR department or company needs to identify a priority to address and understand why this is a priority. Depending on whether it is aspiration driven or situation driven, there are different considerations to take into account (see Figure 4.3 on page 82).

We shall briefly describe the steps this figure contains. (Please note that the discussion in this part of the chapter is based on the work done by Swamy and published in his article 'Strategic Imperatives'.[48])

Table 4.1 HRM practice menu

Planning choices

Informal	....	Formal
Short term	....	Long term
Explicit job analysis	....	Implicit job analysis
Job simplification	....	Job enrichment
Low employee involvement	....	High employee involvement

Staffing choices

Internal sources	....	External sources
Narrow paths	....	Broad paths
Single ladder	....	Multiple ladders
Explicit criteria	....	Implicit criteria
Limited socialisation	....	Extensive socialisation
Closed procedures	....	Open procedures

Appraising choices

Behavioural criteria		Results criteria
Purposes: development, remedial, maintenance		
Low employee participation	....	High employee participation
Short-term criteria	....	Long-term criteria
Individual criteria	....	Group criteria

Compensating choices

Low base salaries	....	High base salaries
Internal equity	....	External equity
Few perks	....	Many perks
Standard, fixed package	....	Flexible package
Low participation	....	High participation
No incentives	....	Many incentives
Short-term incentives	....	Long-term incentives
No employment security	....	High employment security
Hierarchical	....	High participation

Training and development choices

Short term	....	Long term
Narrow application	....	Broad application
Productivity emphasis	....	Quality of work life emphasis
Spontaneous, unplanned	....	Planned, systematic
Individual orientation	....	Group orientation
Low participation	....	High participation

SOURCE: From JACKSON, S. E. AND SCHULER, R. S. 2000. *Managing human resources* 7th ed. 128. Copyright © 2000. Reprinted with permission of South-Western College publishing, a Division of Thomson Learning.

- *Step 1.* This step examines the goals management is formulating for a particular setting. In the case of an aspiration-driven imperative it may be necessary to interview key stakeholders to determine their aspirations, institutional biases, and operational preferences. In the case of a situation-driven imperative, adequate documentation needs to be analysed.
- *Step 2.* For aspiration-driven imperatives, testing management's assumptions using objective, fact-based analysis is important. In the case of a situation-driven imperative, management must develop an

Figure 4.3 High-level framework for understanding strategic imperatives

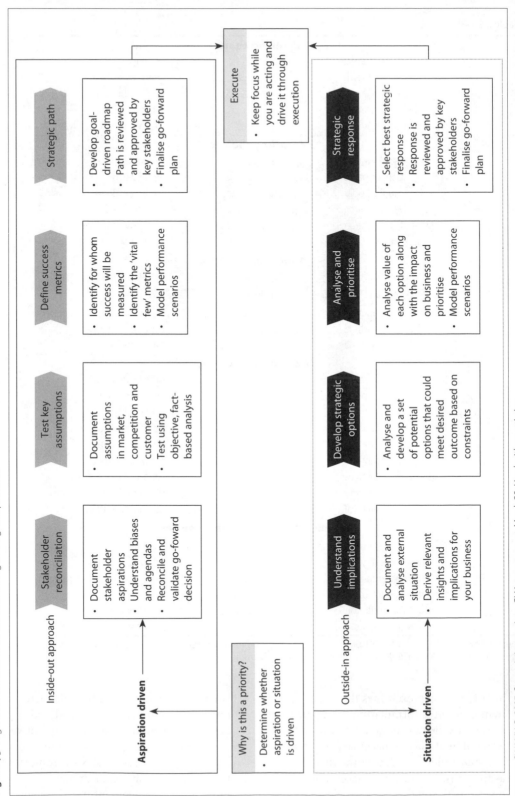

SOURCE: SWAMY, R. 2007. Strategic imperatives. *CMA management*, March:20. Used with permission.

exhaustive set of potential strategic options that could meet the same desired outcome.

- *Step 3.* For a strategic path to be successful on the aspiration-driven side, it is necessary to identify for whom and by whom to measure success. The company should identify a few measurements that will satisfy its stakeholders and should model a number of performance scenarios against these measurements. On the situation-driven side, the company should identify performance scenarios, as they will allow the company to analyse the value of each option it identified in step 2. From this exercise it can then prioritise correctly.
- *Step 4.* This step represents the 'strategy' component of strategic imperatives. In the case of the aspiration-driven imperatives, management needs to develop a goal-driven roadmap – an executable strategy for the imperative – and ensure key stakeholders review and approve the path. In the case of a situation-driven impera-tive, management needs to decide on the best strategic response and finalise a plan for moving forward. Appendix 4.1 at the end of this chapter indicates an example of how this process can actually take place in practice.

In conclusion, note that we can distinguish two types of HR strategy, namely:

- *Organisational strategies.* We can see these as part of the organisational or company strategy. They have a major impact throughout the organisation.
- *Functional strategies.* We can see these as more narrowly focused and involved only with the strategic management of HR divisions or departments.[49]

It is inevitable that with the emergence of SHRM as a field of study and practice, 'how to' models have also emerged. In the next section we shall give a brief overview of the major types of model developed over a period of two decades.

4.4 Models of SHRM

Several SHRM models, which describe how to link the company strategy and HRM, have been developed over the years.[50-58] However, there are two dominant approaches to integration:

- A reactive role of HRM, in which strategy dictates HR policies
- A proactive role, in which the strategy-formulation process itself involves HRM.

In order to understand the SHRM models found in the literature, we shall apply a classification method designed by Dyer. Dyer suggests, in his four-quadrant model, that two dichotomies are important to consider:

- Separating the organisational-level HR concerns from the functional-level HR concerns
- Differentiating between content and process elements.[59]

According to Lengnick-Hall and Lengnick-Hall, content concerns specific choices such as policies and practices in SHRM, whereas process focuses on the means by which to derive and implement these policies and practices.[60] In the literature, it is clear that content versus process distinctions have prevailed throughout. Consequently, we shall discuss the various models according to their specific classification.

4.4.1 Organisational SHRM content models

There are two important models – namely those of Labelle and Wils. In his investigation, Labelle[61] found that company strategy was the determin-ing factor for the content of the organisational HR strategy. He also found that both the content of the organisational HR strategy and the company strategy were influenced by internal and external environmental factors. Labelle identified various types of HRM practices and goals to fit company strategies. Unfortunately, however, the investigation was limited to only 11 companies from diverse sectors.

A similar investigation was carried out by Wils[62] in the USA. He identified a strong correlation between the content of the company strategy and the content of the organisational HR strategy. However, his investigation was limited to only one company consisting of 22 business units.

Although both studies made an important contribution to the content theory of organisational HR strategy, they did not explore the relationship between companies with stable strategies and those with unstable strategies, to determine whether company strategy is a stronger contributing factor in the content of organisational HR strategy in turbulent times or normal times. There is also a need to investigate companies with the same company strategy but different organisational HR strategies.

4.4.2 Functional SHRM content models

A number of diverse models are found in this group. As the purpose of this chapter is not to discuss each model in detail, we shall evaluate only a representative number.

In their model, Baird and Meshoulam[63] argue that two strategic fits must be managed:

- An external fit, whereby HRM practices fit the development stage of the organisation
- An internal fit, whereby the components of HRM complement and support each other.

The content of the HRM practices is thus determined by the developmental stage of the organisation. Two shortcomings of Baird and Meshoulam's approach are that they see the

Table 4.2 The composition of three functional HR strategies

HRM system	Type A (Defender)	Type B (Prospector)	Type AB (Analyser)
Basic strategy	Building human resources	Acquiring human resources	Allocating human resources
Recruitment, selection and placement	Emphasis: 'make' Little recruiting above entry level Selection based on weeding out undesirable employees	Emphasis: 'buy' Sophisticated recruiting at all levels Selection may involve pre-employment psychological testing	Emphasis: 'make' and 'buy' Mixed recruiting and selection approaches
Staff planning Training and development	Formal, extensive Skill-building Extensive training programmes	Informal, limited Skill identification and acquisition Limited training programmes	Formal, extensive Skill-building and acquisition Extensive training programmes Limited outside recruitment
Performance appraisal	Process-orientated procedure (e.g. based on critical incidents or production targets) Identification of training needs Individual/group performance evaluations Time-series comparisons (e.g. previous years' performance)	Result-orientated procedure (e.g. management by objectives or profit targets) Identification of staffing needs Division/corporate performance evaluations Cross-sectional comparisons (e.g. other companies during same period)	Mostly process-oriented procedure Identification of training and staffing needs Individual/group/division performance evaluations Mostly time-series, some cross-sectional comparisons
Compensation	Oriented towards position in organisation hierarchy Internal consistency Total compensation heavily orientated towards cash and driven by superior/subordinate differentials	Orientated towards performance External competitiveness Total compensation heavily orientated towards incentives and driven by recruitment needs	Mostly orientated towards hierarchy, some performance considerations Internal consistency and external competitiveness Cash and incentive compensation

SOURCE: MILES, R. E. & SNOW, C. C. 1984. Designing strategic human resources systems. *Organizational dynamics*, 13(1):49, Summer. (Originally adapted from Canadian Pacific Ltd.) Copyright Elsevier, used with permission.

classification of an organisation into a specific phase as too simplistic, and the fact that the determination of a specific phase is also largely based on subjectivity.

Miles and Snow[64], in their model, identify three company strategies which, in their view, can be found in every company – namely defender, prospector, and analyser. By using these strategies, Miles and Snow identify various types of HRM practices that could support them (see Table 4.2). These practices were based on information gathered throughout various types of companies in Canada. One of the biggest drawbacks of this approach is the idea that strategies are rigid and that the only flexible aspect is human resources.

The last group of models found in this category contains those based on the life-cycle concept. Here development occurs in relatively predictable discrete building blocks of birth, maturity, decline, and death. Authors like Smith[65] and Stybel[66] have used these building blocks to identify the content of various HRM practices (see Table 4.3).

Table 4.3 Characteristics of HR programmes by maturity stages

HR programmes		Development stages			
		Embryonic	**High growth**	**Mature**	**Ageing**
Compen-sation	Fixed vs. variable	High variable; low fixed; non-predictable	High variable; low fixed; big carrot	Less variable relative to fixed; predictable	High fixed; lower variable; security
	Central vs. local control of compensation	Local control; immediate response	Policy centralised; administration local	Policy centralised; consistent administration	All control centralised
	Policy line vs. market	High pay for high risk	High pay for excellence	Median pay; high security	Higher pay; higher risk
	Basis of variable compensation	Sales growth; risk; innovation; survival	Growth of sales and profits; new products; share	Control systems; consistency; cost reduction; hold share	Cash generation; cost control; consistency
	Time focus	Short-term rapidly changing goals	Short term for operations; longer for strategy	Stronger focus on long-term optimisation	Short term
Manpower planning	Forecasting of organisational needs	Not used; future totally unpredictable	Forecasting critical to adequate staffing	Forecasting limited to retirements; major reorganisation	Forecasts only to identify excess
	Individual career planning	Not used	Directional use only; opportunities outnumber qualified people	Need employee retention; optimisation of human resources	Needed; optimise fewer opportunities
Manage-ment style (selection)	Entrepreneurial vs. bureaucratic	Entrepreneurial rapid response; directive	Entrepreneurial for growth, but building systems to preserve gains	Bureaucratic; economy of scale; repetitious quality	Entrepreneurial directive; cuts, reorganises; survives
Employee develop-ment	Hiring vs. training	All skills hired; no training	Much hiring needed but training becomes important	Emphasis on internal development and promotion; little hiring	No hiring, no training
Benefits	Profit-sharing pension	Profit-sharing or nothing; cash or deferred cash	Profit-sharing; some guaranteed benefit like savings	Defined benefit pension; also savings	Pension; security

SOURCE: SMITH, E. C. 1982. Strategic business planning and human resources (part I). *Personnel journal*, 61(8):606–610. Copyright © August 1982. Used with permission of ACC Communications/*Personnel Journal* (now known as *Workforce*), Costa Mesa, C.A. All rights reserved.

One of the drawbacks of these models is the fact that organisations do not follow a cycle which includes death, but constantly reform and renew themselves to fit the environment.

4.4.3 Organisational SHRM process models

There are a very large number of models in this category.[67–77] However, a noticeable limitation of work in this area has been the failure to take a more comprehensive view, matching the HRM function to strategic or organisational conditions.

Nininger's[78] model, for example, provided a framework to enhance organisational effectiveness by integrating the strategic planning and management function with human resources. Golden and Ramanuyum[79] adopted a similar view. Apart from these and a few other studies (an example of Nkomo's[80] model appears in Figure 4.4), little work has been done that takes a comprehensive view of the HRM function at the strategic level. Although these authors provide steps for the integration and implementation of HRM in an organisation, one of the major drawbacks of these models is that they do little to overcome the problems of identifying and analysing the appropriate information, either to characterise the strategic situation or to clarify the HR manager's role under a specific set of conditions. Nor do they consider the inevitable need for change as new products and technologies enter the marketplace.

4.4.4 Functional SHRM process models

While the research regarding the organisational SHRM process models concentrated on the wider organisation, the emphasis in this category is narrowed down specifically to the HR function. Odiorne's[81] model is the only one in this category. It seems that no large-scale systematic attempts have thus far been made to study ways in which HR functions determine their strategies, the factors to which they respond during this process or the quality of results obtained. In his model, Odiorne recommends a process which can evaluate the company's

human resources and classify them into four different groups: 'stars', 'problem children', 'cash cows', and 'dogs'. To classify the workforce, Odiorne uses a matrix whose vertical axis indicates performance and horizontal axis indicates potential.

A management-by-objectives (MBO) approach determines the performance capability of an individual, and assessment centres determine the potential.[82] The matrix is then used as a basis for developing various HRM practices. One of the drawbacks of this approach is that it is not easy to classify an average individual into one of the categories. Subjectivity also plays an important role in the process, and the impression is created that it is a very static and rigid short-term model, one that is not very future orientated.[83]

An examination of the various groups of models, as classified according to Dyer's framework, appears to show that not much attention is given to content models. In contrast, process models – especially the organisational SHRM models – have reached a more advanced stage of development. This is a logical development, as the process of any system must first be implemented before the content can be identified.

4.4.5 General SHRM models

Besides the different types of models already discussed, the literature contains a number of general models which contain elements of the four different categories of models. The models of authors such as Dyer and Holder[84], Rothwell and Kazanas[85], and Lengnick-Hall and Lengnick-Hall[86], as well as Schuler's 5 P model[87], are of importance here. An example of the model of Rothwell and Kazanas – one of the most comprehensive in the field of SHRM – appears in Figure 4.5.

4.4.6 Models of 'fit' versus 'flexibility'

The traditional SHRM models that we have discussed thus far in this chapter have focused on two types of congruence or fit, namely a vertical fit and a horizontal fit[88–89]:

Figure 4.4 A conceptual model of strategic HR planning

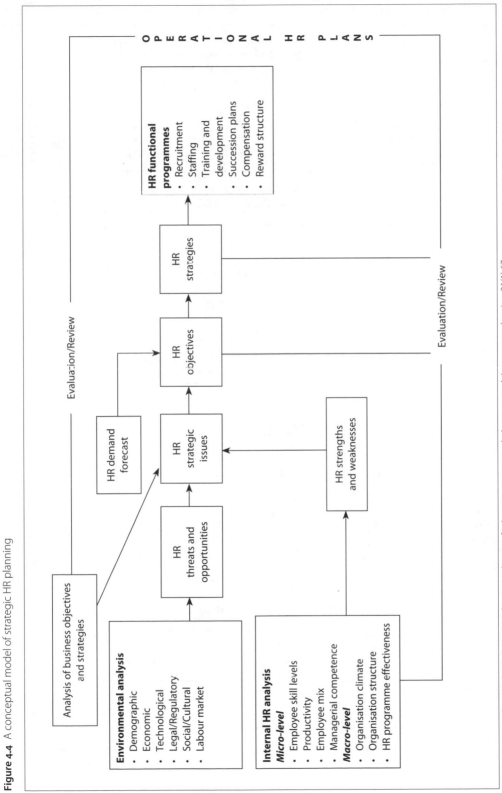

SOURCE: Reprinted from NKOMO, S. M. 1988. Strategic planning for human resources – let's get started. *Long range planning*, 21(1):67. Copyright © 1988, with permission from Elsevier Science.

Figure 4.5 The SHRM model of Rothwell and Kazanas

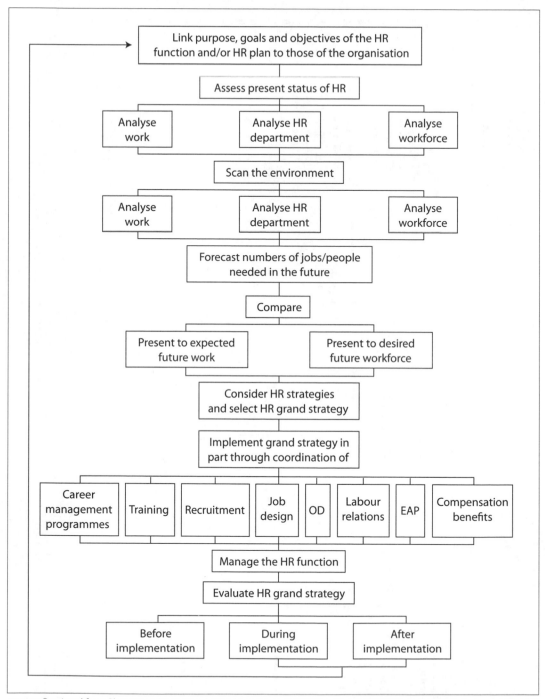

SOURCE: Reprinted from *Planning and managing human resources* by ROTHWELL, W. J. & KAZANAS, H. C. © 1994. Amherst, M.A.: HRD Press. Reprinted by permission of the publisher, HRD Press, Amherst, MA, (800) 822–2801, www.hrdpress.com.

- *A vertical fit*. This involves the alignment of HRM practices and the strategic management process. It involves directing human resources towards the main initiatives of the organisation.
- *A horizontal fit*. This implies a congruence or fit among the various HRM practices. The horizontal fit is viewed as being instrumental in efficiently allocating the resources needed by the horizontal fit.

In addition to the so-called 'fit' approach, a number of articles in the literature emphasise the so-called 'flexibility' in SHRM.[90-91] The authors in this area argue that organisations face a complex and dynamic environment which requires them to be sufficiently flexible to adapt to changing requirements. Thus these authors see 'fit' as a snapshot of a particular short period of time.

The question that arises is: can the two types of models co-exist, or are they in conflict with one another? Nadler and Tushman[92], as quoted by Wright and Snell, define congruence or fit as 'the degree to which the needs, demands, goals, objectives and/or structure of one component are consistent with the needs, demands, goals, objectives and/or structure of another component'. Thus, we can deduce that organisations should be more effective when they achieve fit than when they do not.

In contrast to this, Sanchez[93], as quoted by Wright and Snell, defines flexibility as 'a firm's abilities to respond to various demands from dynamic competitive environments'. Thus flexibility provides an organisation with the ability to modify current practices in response to changes in the environment. By consistently scanning the environment and detecting changes, organisations will have to have a pool of alternatives available to accommodate these changes.

Wright and Snell[94] indicate that, as a result of the existence of 'fit versus flexibility', there are two opposing groups of researchers, namely:

- *The so-called 'orthogonal' group*. This group sees the two alternatives as opposites.
- *The so-called 'complementary' group*. This group argues that the two approaches are

independent of one another. The complementary group views both concepts as essential for organisational effectiveness, since the challenge of strategic management is to cope with change (requiring flexibility) by continually adapting to achieve fit between the firm and its external environment.

We find that the orthogonal group is thus concerned with companies at only one point in time, while the complementary group sees 'fit' over a longer time frame, while exploring adaptation processes. The orthogonal group sees what firms actually do, while the complementary group sees what firms ought to do.[95]

Wright and Snell designed a SHRM model in which they included both views (see Figure 4.6).[96] These authors see 'fit' as an interface between an external and an internal variable, while 'flexibility' is seen as only focusing internally. According to Wright, a company is required increasingly to promote organisational flexibility, in order to achieve a dynamic fit.

A brief discussion of the HR model as it appears in Figure 4.6 follows. In the model, the top half depicts the 'fit' component and the lower half the 'flexibility' part.

Like other SHRM models, this model starts with the mission and goals of the organisation, followed by an examination of internal resources (strengths and weaknesses) and external developments (opportunities and threats). These make up the basic components of the model that lead to the choice of a given strategy. At the same time, the HRM function also gives input regarding the strengths and weaknesses, and opportunities and threats, as seen from the point of view of the company's human resources.[97] As in previous models, this model also uses the company's strategy to dictate the skills and types of behaviour required from employees to implement the strategy successfully. This subsequently drives the HRM practices. These desired HRM practices are then operationalised into actual HRM practices which influence the actual skills and types of behaviour of human resources impacting on the

Figure 4.6   A fit/flexibility model of SHRM

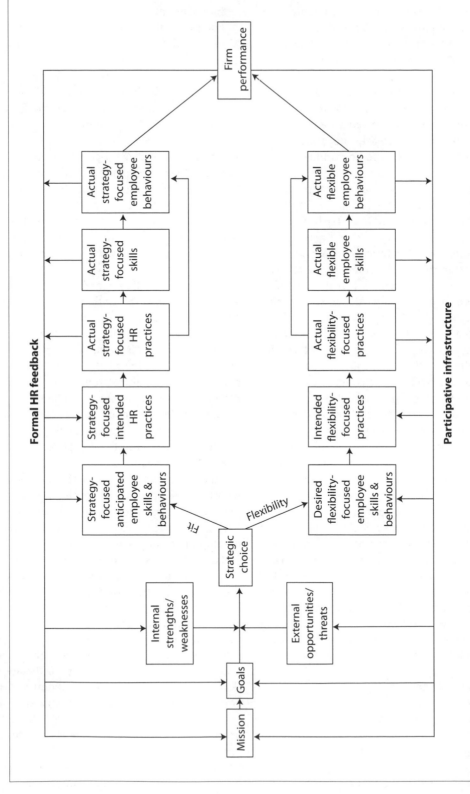

source: Republished with permission of *Academy of management review*, from WRIGHT, P.M. & SNELL, S.A. 1998. Toward a unifying framework for exploring fit and flexibility in strategic human resource management. *Academy of management review*, 23(4):760. Permission conveyed through Copyright Clearance Center Inc.

company's performance. Finally, the company's performance is fed back into the process of strategy formulation that will affect future strategies. This concludes the 'fit' process of the model. It is interesting to note that the model makes a number of assumptions, namely that decision makers are able to identify all the skills and types of behaviour a specific strategy requires, that decision-makers can specify and control all HRM practices, and that the environment stays stable enough to achieve fit.[98]

However, these assumptions cannot always be accepted in an ever-changing environment. Hence the lower part of the model, where flexibility plays an important role. The authors view this part as important in that achieving fit over time may depend upon the extent to which

flexibility exists in the system. The flexibility component expands upon the fit component in a number of ways: that it accepts that HR practices can focus on more than just fit; that there is a broader range of skills than those needed to implement the current strategy; and that the employees possess a broader repertoire of behaviour than simply those relevant to the strategy.[99] These various skills and types of behaviour make it possible to implement various strategies that can respond to a variety of different competitive demands. Finally, the model also highlights the role of the participative infrastructure in developing, identifying, and exploiting emergent strategies.[100] This model is an interesting development within SHRM theory and reflects the future trend in the flexible firm.

SUMMARY

From the discussion it is clear that SHRM plays a critical role in the superior achievement of the company's strategic goals. This, however, is only possible with the availability of a strategic-management process and the restructuring of the traditional HRM function into strategic, operational, and functional levels. There is a strong relationship between strategic management and SHRM, and there is also an important link between HR professionals and line management.

To operationalise the process, HR strategies need to be designed to support company strategies. These consist of means (e.g. HR practices and policies) and ends (e.g. productivity goals). Many models help with the implementation process, but only a few present a total integrated process. The existence of firm flexibility has supplemented the rigid, tight-fit approach with a flexible arrangement which generates numerous alternatives to address the challenges from an ever-changing environment.

KEY CONCEPTS

• Aspiration-driven imperative	• Mission statement
• Cultural system	• Organisational strategies
• Efficiency imperative	• Political system
• Ends	• Proactive approach
• Fit	• Reactive approach
• Flexibility	• Situation imperative
• Functional strategies	• Strategic HR planning
• Growth imperative	• Strategic human resource management (SHRM)
• HR strategy	• Strategic imperatives
• HRM cube	• Technical system

CASE STUDY

Objective: To understand the importance of aligning the HR activities with the corporate strategy of the company

Happy Sky Company: Aligning human resource functions with strategic objectives

John Flack founded Happy Sky and has managed the company's operations from its inception. Happy Sky designs and produces communications software that is sold to customers, ranging from the computer industry to independent businesses. Although Happy Sky has been profitable over the decade of its existence, its productivity has recently declined. Specifically, in the past several years, the workers have displayed diminished innovation, higher turnover and absenteeism, and overall sluggish performance.

Based on these trends, John called a meeting of all the managers to discuss potential courses of action to correct the problems. After a series of discussions, John and the other managers agreed that they needed to hire a full-time manager to assume sole responsibility for human resource management. In the past, the department managers had assumed basic responsibilities for managing their employees. However, the growth of the company – there are now over 300 employees – coupled with recent increases in absenteeism and turnover, suggest that the human resource responsibilities are substantial enough to warrant hiring a full-time manager.

After careful consideration John decided to hire Judith Thompson, in line with the company's new employment equity policy, to assume the primary responsibilities of developing a systematic HRM function for Happy Sky. When Thompson arrived at Happy Sky, she and John met to discuss the strategic objectives of the company. John stated that Happy Sky must achieve two primary objectives to be successful in the future. First, the company must continue its growth strategy to respond to the expanding demands for its services. Second, it must enhance the innovative nature of its workforce to ensure that it remains up to date with competitors and market changes. At the end of their meeting, John gave Thompson the task of developing an HRM function that could tackle the absenteeism and turnover problems while helping Happy Sky attain the two goals he had outlined.

As a first step to achieve this, Thompson began to review the human resource practices used at Happy Sky. It became clear that the company relies primarily upon two practices to meet employment needs. First, it recruits at the local university located just 10 kilometres away. If graduating students are uninterested or unsuitable candidates for a certain job, Happy Sky places advertisements in regional newspapers to seek job candidates with the relevant skills who are willing to relocate. Although this hiring process is not comprehensive, Happy Sky, because of its potential growth opportunities, has not typically experienced much difficulty in recruiting employees.

Second, Happy Sky has relied upon an established compensation system that applies to all employees throughout the company. Workers are paid on a salaried basis, with their compensation levels based on the going rate in the market for similar positions. By linking employee compensation to the market average, Happy Sky has been able to ensure that there is a reasonably high degree of equity between the company's pay levels and the pay levels at other firms. Annual salary increases are calculated by considering inflation and each employee's performance. The average salary increase is between 3 and 7 per cent of employees' base salary.

Thompson realises that besides these recruitment and compensation practices, there is really no consistent use of other human resource practices at Happy Sky. Instead, managers use different methods of managing the workers in their respective units. For example, there are no consistent performance appraisal standards used throughout the organisation. The criteria used to evaluate employees range from counting days absent to measuring innovation and creativity. Similarly, each manager uses somewhat different tactics for training employees. Some units assign new employees to shadow more experienced employees, who serve as the new employees' mentors. Other managers do not offer any training and assume that the employees come to the job with all the knowledge they need to succeed.

In light of the organisation's goals of growth and innovation, Thompson has become quite certain that significant changes need to be made at Happy Sky. The productivity of employees and the success of the company depend on effectively realigning the HR function.

Questions and activities

1. Identify the causes that led to high absenteeism and turnover at Happy Sky.
2. Suggest specific HRM practices that could facilitate the company's strategic objectives of growth and innovation.
3. Happy Sky employs 10 sales associates to sell its software products. List and describe various criteria which can be used to evaluate the performance of sales associates.

SOURCE: Adapted from SHERMAN, A., BOHLANDER, G. & SNELL, S. 1998. Case 5: ConnetPlus: Aligning human resources function with strategic objectives. *Managing human resources* 11th ed. Cincinnati, Ohio: South-Western College Publishing, an ITP company:703–705. Used with permission.

REVIEW QUESTIONS AND ACTIVITIES

1. Write a short paragraph on the benefits organisations can derive from the SHRM process.
2. One of the early definitions in the SHRM literature is Tsui's. Discuss briefly.
3. At a strategic level, HR professionals fulfil their strategic-partner role and are involved in corporate and HR planning. Identify the four features of this role, according to Casio.
4. Give four reasons (according to Rothwell and Kazanas) why there is no relationship between strategic management and SHRM.
5. What are the four essential components of HR strategies, according to Dyer and Holder?
6. Explain Tichy's HRM-cube model, which indicates the important relationship between strategic management and SHRM. In your discussion focus on:

(a) The basic problems that confront organisations
(b) The design of three systems to solve these problems
(c) Aids required to manage these systems
(d) The process of integration of all the issues.

7. Discuss the design of an HR strategy by referring to the issue of strategic imperatives.
8. Explain the two dominant approaches of two models of SHRM and describe Dyer's classification method of these models.
9. Briefly explain Rothwell and Kazanas's model of SHRM.
10. Explain the fit/flexibility model of Wright and Snell.

FURTHER READING

HAMMER, M. 2007. The process audit. *Harvard business review*, 85(4):111–123.
BASSI, L. & MCMURRER, D. 2007. Maximising your return on people. *Harvard business review*, 85(3):115–123.
ZOOK, C. 2007. Finding your next core business. *Harvard business review*, 85(4):66–75.

WEB SITES

www.gao.gov – General Accountability Office (USA) – review reports on human capital
www.fhcs.opm.gov – Office of Personnel Management (USA) – review reports on human capital

ENDNOTES

1. LUNDY, O. & COWLING A. 1996. *Strategic human resource management*. London: International Thomson Business Press:1–6; ROBINSON, D. G. & ROBINSON, J. C. 2004. *Strategic business partner: Aligning people strategies with business goals*. San Francisco: Berrett-Koehler Publishers; LOSEY, M., MEISINGER, S. R. & ULRICH, D. 2005. Conclusion: reality, impact and professionalism. *Human resource management*, 44(2):201–206; ROEHLING, M. V., BOSWELL, W. R., CALIGUIRI, P., FELDMAN, D., GRAHAM, M. E., GUTHRIE, J. P., MORISHIMA, M. & TANSKY, J. W. 2005. The future of HR management: research needs and directions. *Human resource management*, 44(2):207–216.
2. MARTELL, K. & CARROLL, S. J. 1995. How strategic is HRM? *Human resource management*, 34(2):253,

Summer. See also GRUNDY, I. 1997. Human resource management – a strategic approach. *Long range planning*, 30(4):507–517.
3. GRUNDY, I. 1997. Human resource management – a strategic approach. *Long range planning*, 30(4):507–517. See also GRATTON, L., HAILEY, V. H., STILES, P & TRUSS, C. 1999. *Strategic human resource management*. Oxford: Oxford University Press; MABEY, C., SALAMAN, G. & STOREY, J. (Eds). 1998. *Strategic human resource management: A reader*. London: Sage Publications.
4. BOXALL, P. F. 1992. Strategic human resource management: beginnings of a new theoretical sophistication? *Human resource management journal*, 2(3):60–79. See also SCHULER, R. S. & JACKSON, S. E. (Eds). 2000. *Strategic human resource management*.

Oxford: Blackwell Publishers; SHEPPECK, M. A. & MILITELLO, J. 2000. Strategic HR configurations and organisational performance. *Human resource management,* 39(1):5–16, Spring; RICHARD, O. C. & JOHNSON, N. B. 2001. Strategic human resource management effectiveness and firm performance. *International journal of Human resource management,* 12(2):299–310, March; BAKER, D. 1999. Strategic human resource management: performance, alignment, management. *Library career development,* 7(5):51–63; HUANG, T. C. 2001. The effects of linkage between business and human resource management strategies. *Personnel review,* 30(2):132–151.

5. ACKERMANN, K. F. 1989. *Strategic human resource management: concepts and applications for managing people at work in turbulent times.* University of South Africa, Pretoria, July. [Lecture.]

6. ACKERMANN, K. F. 1986. A contingency model of HRM strategy. *Management forum,* 6:65–83; LAWLER, E. E. 2005. From human resource management to organisational effectiveness. *Human resource management,* 44(2):165–169.

7. HUSELID, M. A., JACKSON, S. E. & SCHULER, R. S. 1997. Technical and strategic human resource management effectiveness as determinants of firm performance. *Academy of management journal,* 40(1):171–188. See also BASU, D. R. & MIROSHNIK, V. 1999. Strategic human resource management of Japanese multinationals. *The journal of management development,* 18(9):714–732.

8. TSUI, A. S. 1987. Defining the activities and effectiveness of the human resource department: a multiple constituency approach. *Human resource management,* 26(1):36; TANSKY, J. W. & HENEMAN, R. L. (Eds). 2006. *Human resource strategies for the high growth entrepreneurial firm.* Greenwich, Connecticut: Information Age Publishing (IAP).

9. MCKINLAY, A. & STARKEY, K. 1992. Strategy and human resource management. *The international journal of human resource management,* 3(3):435–449.

10. DYER, L. & HOLDER, G. W. 1988. A strategic perspective of human resource management. *In* Dyer, L. (Ed.). *Human resource management: Evolving roles and responsibilities.* Washington: The Bureau of National Affairs; STAVROU, E. T. & BREWSTER, C. 2005. The configurational approach to linking strategic human resource management bundles with business performance: myth or reality? *Management review,* 16(2):186–201.

11. ANTHONY, W. P., PERREWÉ, P. L. & KACMAR, K. M. 1996. *Strategic human resource management* 2nd ed. Fort Worth: The Dryden Press, Harcourt Brace College Publishers:3–30.

12. WALKER, J. W. 1992. *Human resource strategy.* Singapore: McGraw-Hill.

13. GREER, C. R. 2001. *Strategic human resource management – a general managerial approach* 2nd ed. Upper Saddle river, N.J.: Prentice Hall.

14. TYSON, S. 1995. *Human resource strategy: Towards a general theory of human resource management.* London: Pitman Publishing.

15. BUTLER, J. E., FERRIS, G. R. & NAPIER, N. K. 1991. *Strategy and human resources management.* Cincinnati, O.H.: South Western Publishing.

16. ANTHONY, W. P., PERREWÉ, P. L. & KACMAR, K. M. 1996. *Strategic human resource management* 2nd ed. Fort Worth: The Dryden Press, Harcourt Brace College Publishers:3–30; CHRISTENSEN, R. 2006. *Roadmap to strategic HR: Turning a great idea into a business reality.* New York: Amacom.

17. HUSELID, M. A., JACKSON, S. E. & SCHULER, R. S. 1997. Technical and strategic human resource management effectiveness as determinants of firm performance. *Academy of management journal,* 40(1):171–188.

18. PEARCE II, J. A. & ROBINSON JR, R. B. 1991. *Strategic management: Formulation, implementation and control* 4th ed. Homewood, Il.: Irwin:2–19; BOWER, J. L. & GILBERT, C. G. 2007. How managers' everyday decisions create or destroy your company's strategy. *Harvard business review,* 85(2):72–79.

19. ANTHONY, W. P., PERREWÉ, P. L. & KACMAR, K. M. 1996. *Strategic human resource management* 2nd ed. Fort Worth: The Dryden Press, Harcourt Brace College Publishers:3–30.

20. FOMBRUN, C. J., TICHY, N. M. & DEVANNA, M. A. 1984. *Strategic human resource management.* New York: Wiley:43.

21. CASIO, W. F. 1989. Gaining and sustaining a competitive advantage: challenges for human resource management. *In* Nedd, A., Ferris, G. R. & Rowland, K. R. (Eds). *Research in personnel and human resource management, supplement I.* Connecticut: JAI Press.

22. KAVANAGH, M. J., GUEUTAL, H. G. & TANNENBAUM, S. I. 1990. *Human resource information systems: Development and application.* Boston: PWS-Kent:2; KEARNS, P. 2003. *HR strategy, business focused individually centred.* Oxford: Butterworth Heinemann.

23. ROTHWELL, W. J. & KAZANAS, H. C. 1988. *Strategic human resources planning and management.* Englewood Cliffs, N.J.: Prentice Hall:15–17; SCHULER, R. S. & JACKSON, S. E,. 2007. *Strategic human resource management* 2nd ed. Malden: Blackwell Publishing.

24. TICHY, N. M. 1983. Managing organizational transformations. *Human resource management,* 22(1):45–60. See also VALLE, R., MARTIN, F., RONERO, P. M. & DOLAN, S. L. 2000. Business strategy, work processes and human resource training: are they congruent? *Journal of organizational behavior,* 21(3):283–297; Hiltrop,

J-M. 2006. A diagnostic framework for building HR capability in organisations. *Strategic change,* 15(7/8):341–351.

25. TICHY, N. M. 1983. The essentials of strategic change management. *Journal of business strategy,* 3(4):55–67.

26. TICHY, N. M. 1983. Managing organizational transformations. *Human resource management,* 22(1):48; DERY, K. & WAILES, N. 2005. Necessary but not sufficient: ERP'S and strategic HRM. *Strategic change,* 14:265–272.

27. TICHY, N. M. 1983. Managing organizational transformations. *Human resource management,* 22(1):48–49.

28. Ibid.:49.

29. Ibid.:50.

30. TICHY, N. M. 1983. The essentials of strategic change management. *Journal of business strategy,* 3(4):60.

31. TICHY, N. M. 1982. Managing change strategically: The technical, political and cultural keys. *Organisational dynamics,* 10(2):59–80.

32. Ibid.:68.

33. Ibid.:67–69.

34. Ibid.:70.

35. Ibid.:72.

36. DYER, L. & HOLDER, G. W. 1988. A strategic perspective of human resource management. *In* Dyer, L. (Ed.). *Human resource management: Evolving roles and responsibilities.* Washington: The Bureau of National Affairs:32. DAVID, F. R. & DAVID, F. R. 2003. It's time to redraft your mission statement. *Journal of business strategy,* 24(1):11–14.

37. COOKE, R. 1992. Human resources strategies for business success. *In* Armstrong, M. (Ed)., 1992. *Strategies for human resource management: A total business approach.* London: Kogan Page:25–44. See also MUMFORD, A. 2000. A learning approach to strategy. *Journal of workplace learning: employee counselling today,* 12(7):265–271; POMEROY, A. 2006. HR is mission critical at the FBI. *HR magazine,* 51(6):66–70; TRÉRY, F. 2006. The fundamental dimensions of strategy. *MIT Sloan management review,* 48(1):71–75.

38. LABELLE, C. M. 1984. *Human resource strategic decisions as responses to environmental challenges.* New York. Cornell University, Ithaca. (Master's thesis.)

39. HAX, A. C. 1985. A new competitive weapon: the human resource strategy. *Training and development journal,* 39(5):76. See also BALDACCHINO, G. 2001. Human resource management strategies for small territories: an alternative proposition. *International journal of educational development,* 21:205–215.

40. LABELLE, C. M. 1984. *Human resource strategic decisions as responses to environmental challenges.* New York. Cornell University, Ithaca. (Master's thesis.):141. See also TYLER, K. 2001. Strategizing for HR. *HR magazine,* February:93–98.

41. SCHULER, R. S. 1988. Human resource management practice choices. (*In* Schuler, R. S., Youngblood, S. A. & Huber, V. L. (Eds). *Readings in personnel and human resource management* 3rd ed. St Paul, M.N.: West Publishing.) See also BENNETT, N., KETCHEN, D. J. & SCHULTZ, E. B. 1998. An examination of factors associated with the integration of human resource management and strategic decision-making. *Human resource management,* 37(1):3–16.

42. NININGER, J. R., 1982. *Managing human resources: A strategic perspective.* The Conference Board of Canada, Study 71:113. See also KENG-HOWE CHEW, I. & CHONG, P. 1999. Effects of strategic human resource management on strategic vision. *International journal of human resource management,* 10(6):1031–1045; ULRICH, D. & BROCKBANK, W. 2005. *The HR value proposition.* Boston, Massachusetts: Harvard Business School Press: SUBRAMONY, M. 2006. Why organisations adopt some human resource management practices and reject others: an exploration of rationales. *Human resource management,* 45(2):195–210; SOCIETY FOR HUMAN RESOURCE MANAGEMENT. 2006. *The essentials of strategy.* Boston, Massachusetts: Harvard Business School Press.

43. SWAMY, R. 2007. Strategic imperatives. *CMA management,* March:18.

44. Ibid.

45. Ibid.

46. SWAMY, R. 2007. Strategic imperatives. *CMA management,* March:19.

47. Ibid.

48. SWAMY, R. 2007. Strategic imperatives. *CMA management,* March:19–21.

49. DYER, L. 1985. Strategic human resource management and planning. (*In* ROWLAND, K. M. & FERRIS, G. R. (Eds). *Research in personnel and human resources management,* 3. Connecticut: JAI Press.) See also SHAFER, R. A., DYER, L., KILTY, J., AMOS, J. & ERICKSEN, J. 2001. *Human resource management,* 40(3):197–211; STOREY, J. 1998. Strategic non-HRM – a viable alternative? *Strategic change,* 7:379–406; GRUNDY, T. C. & BROWN, L. 2003. *Value-based human resource strategy: Developing your consultancy role.* Oxford: Elsevier/Butterworth-Heinemann; LAWLER, E. E., BOUDREAU, J. W. & MOHRMAN, S. A. 2006. *Achieving strategic excellence: An assessment of human resource organisations.* Stanford, CA: Stanford University Press.

50. BAIRD, L., MESHOULAM, I. & DE GIVE, D. 1983. Meshing human resources planning with strategic business planning: a model approach. *Personnel,* 60:14–25.

51. DYER, L. 1983. Bringing human resources into the strategy formulation process. *Human resource management,* 22(3):257–271.

52. DYER, L. & HOLDER, G. W. 1988. A strategic perspective of human resource management. (*In* Dyer, L. (Ed.). *Human resource management: Evolving roles and responsibilities.* Washington: The Bureau of National Affairs.)

53. KELLEHER, E. J. & COTTER, K. L. 1982. An integrative model for human resource planning and strategic planning. *Human resource planning,* 5:15–27.

54. NKOMO, S. M. 1988. Strategic planning for human resources – let's get started. *Long range planning,* 21(1):66–72.

55. ROTHWELL, W. J. & KAZANAS, H. C. 1988. *Strategic human resources planning and management.* Englewood Cliffs, N.J.: Prentice Hall.15–17.

56. SCHULER, R. S. 1992. Strategic human resource management: linking the people with the strategic needs of the business. *Organizational dynamics,* Summer:18–32.

57. Grobler, P. A. 1993. Strategic human resource management models: a review and a proposal for South African companies. *Management dynamics: contemporary research,* 2(3):1–21, Winter.

58. KANE, B. & PALMER, I. 1995. Strategic HRM or managing the employment relationship? *International journal of manpower,* 16(5/6):6–21.

59. DYER, L. 1985. Strategic human resource management and planning. (*In* ROWLAND, K. M. & FERRIS, G. R. (Eds). *Research in personnel and human resources management,* 3. Connecticut: JAI Press:3–4.)

60. LENGNICK-HALL, C. A. & LENGNICK-HALL, M. L. 1988. Strategic human resources management: a review of the literature and a proposed typology. *Academy of management review,* 13(3):456.

61. LABELLE, C. M. 1984. *Human resource strategic decisions as responses to environmental challenges.* Ithaca, New York. Cornell University. (Master's thesis.)

62. WILS, T. 1984. *Business strategy and human resource strategy.* Ithaca, New York. Cornell University. (Doctoral dissertation.)

63. BAIRD, L. & MESHOULAM, I. 1988. Managing two fits of strategic human resource management. *Academy of management review,* 13(1):116–128.

64. MILES, R. E. & SNOW, C. C. 1984. Designing strategic human resources systems. *Organizational dynamics,* 13(1):36–52.

65. SMITH, E. C. 1982. Strategic business planning and human resources (part I). *Personnel journal,* 61(8):606–610.

66. STYBEL, L. J. 1982. Linking strategic planning and manpower planning. *California management review,* 25(1):48–56.

67. BAIRD, L., MESHOULAM, I. & DE GIVE, D. 1983. Meshing human resources planning with strategic business planning: a model approach. *Personnel,* 60:14–25.

68. CASSELL, F. H., HARVEY, A. & ROOMKIN, J. 1985. Strategic human resources planning: an orientation to the bottom line. *Management decision,* 23(3):16–28.

69. DYER, L. 1983. Bringing human resources into the strategy formulation process. *Human resource management,* 22(3):257–271.

70. GALOSY, J. R. 1983. Meshing human resources planning with strategic business planning – one company's experience. *Personnel,* 60:26–35.

71. GOULD, R. 1984. Gaining a competitive edge through human resource strategies. *Human resource planning,* 7(1):31–38.

72. KELLEHER, E. J. & COTTER, K. L. 1982. An integrative model for human resource planning and strategic planning. *Human resource planning,* 5:15–27.

73. MANZINI, A. O. & GRINDLEY, J. D. 1986. *Integrating human resources and strategic business planning.* New York: American Management Association.

74. NKOMO, S. M. 1988. Strategic planning for human resources – let's get started. *Long range planning,* 21(1):66–72.

75. ROTHWELL, W. J. & KAZANAS, H. C. 1988. *Strategic human resources planning and management.* Englewood Cliffs, N.J.: Prentice Hall:15–17.

76. SCHULER, R. S. 1992. Strategic human resource management: linking the people with the strategic needs of the business. *Organizational dynamics,* Summer:18–32.

77. DELENY, J. E. & DOTY, D. H. 1996. Modes of theorizing in strategic human resource management: tests of universalistic, contingency, and configurational performance predictions. *Academy of management journal,* 39(4):802–835.

78. NININGER, J. R. 1982. *Managing human resources: a strategic perspective,* 71. Canada: The Conference Board of Canada.

79. GOLDEN, K. A. & RAMANUYAM, V. 1984. Between a dream and a nightmare: On the integration of the human resource management and strategic business planning process. *Human resource management,* 24:429–452.

80. NKOMO, S. M. 1988. Strategic planning for human resources – let's get started. *Long range planning,* 21(1):66–72.

81. ODIORNE, G. S. 1984. *Strategic management of human resources: A portfolio approach.* San Francisco: Jossey-Bass.

82. Ibid.:66.

83. Ibid.:66–67.

84. DYER, L. & HOLDER, G. W. 1988. A strategic perspective of human resource management. (*In* Dyer, L. (Ed.). *Human resource management: Evolving roles and responsibilities.* Washington: The Bureau of National Affairs:1–31.)

85. ROTHWELL, W. J. & KAZANAS, H. C. 1988. *Strategic human resources planning and management.* Englewood Cliffs, N.J.: Prentice Hall:15–17.

86. LENGNICK-HALL, C. A. & LENGNICK-HALL, M. L. 1988. Strategic human resources management: a review of the literature and a proposed typology. *Academy of management review*, 13(3):454–470.

87. SCHULER, R. S. 1992. Strategic human resource management: linking the people with the strategic needs of the business. *Organizational dynamics*, Summer:18–32; MELLO. J. A. 2006. *Strategic human resource management* 2nd edition. Mason, Ohio: South Western, part of the Thomson Corporation.

88. WRIGHT, P. M. & SNELL, S. A. 1998. Toward a unifying framework for exploring fit and flexibility in strategic human resource management. *Academy of management review*, 23(4):756. See also POWELL, G. N. 1998. Reinforcing and extending today's organisations: the simultaneous pursuit of person-organization fit and diversity. *Organizational dynamics*, Winter:50 61.

89. MYNE, L., TREGASKIS, O. & BREWSTER, C, 1996. A comparative analysis of the link between flexibility and HRM strategy. *Employee relations*, 18(3):5–24.

90. KERR, J. L. & JACKOFSKY, E. F. 1989. Aligning managers with strategies: management development versus selection. *Strategic management journal*, 10:157–170.

91. MILLIMAN, J., VON GLINOW, M. A. & NATHAN, M., 1991. Organisational life cycles and strategic international human resource management in multinational companies: implications for congruence theory. *Academy of management review*, 16:318–339.

92. NADLER, D. & TUSHMAN, M. 1980. A diagnostic model for organisational behaviour. (*In* Hackman, J. R., Lawler, E. E. & Porter, L. W. (Eds). *Perspectives on behaviour in organisations*. New York: McGrawHill:83–100.)

93. SANCHEZ, R., 1995. Strategic flexibility in product competition. *Strategic management journal*, 16:135–159.

94. WRIGHT, P. M. & SNELL, S. A. 1998. Toward a unifying framework for exploring fit and flexibility in strategic human resource management. *Academy of management review*, 23(4):757. See also WERBEL, J. D. & JOHNSON, D. J. 2001. The use of person–group fit for employee selection: a missing link in person–environment fit. *Human resource management*, 40(3):227–240.

95. WRIGHT, P. M. & SNELL, S. A. 1998. Toward a unifying framework for exploring fit and flexibility in strategic human resource management. *Academy of management review*, 23(4):757.

96. Ibid.:759–761.

97. Ibid:759.

98. Ibid.

99. Ibid.:757–761.

100. Ibid.:761.

Appendix 4.1

SHRM in the city of Clearwater, Florida (USA)

The city of Clearwater is located on the west coast of Florida, USA. Its population has remained relatively constant between 101,000 and 108,000 residents for the past ten years. Clearwater's market consists of a large tourism-based economy, but it has been able to attract some high-technology companies. The city has no open land, so its strategy has been to improve its infrastructure and aesthetics and try to attract companies to redevelop existing properties.

Clearwater provides a full range of municipal services: police and fire protection; city-operated marina; a business airpark; convention centre and exhibition hall; planning, zoning, subdivision and building code regulation and enforcement; park and recreation programmes; a public library system with four branch locations; solid waste collection and recycling; water supply and distribution, wastewater treatment and disposal, and reclaimed water treatment and distribution; and a citywide parking system.

The members of the city commission decided that a formal strategic vision would articulate their motivating beliefs and intent for the city, serving as a framework for the city's future and for the everyday operations of city government. With the help of the city manager, and after a series of consensus-building steps, new mission and vision statements were drafted. These are geared toward helping achieve a high quality of life today and in the next twenty years. The ultimate goal is to shape a liveable city that eliminates barriers and provides opportunities for all citizens to succeed. Though Clearwater will change over the years, the vision must stay the same to ensure that policy decisions of future commissions, and the resulting progress the city makes, remain consistent and beneficial to all.

Eleven goals were identified in **five priority** areas. The goals were as follows:

- A safe, clean, green environment
- Diverse, high-paying jobs
- High-quality education
- A variety of cultural and recreational offerings
- Efficient, responsive city services
- Safe, comfortable, walkable neighbourhoods
- Well-maintained housing stock in all markets
- A vibrant downtown that is mindful of its heritage
- Well-maintained infrastructure
- Efficient transportation systems
- A quality beach environment

The city integrated these goals into **five strategic priorities**:

Public Safety. All public safety services must concentrate on continual personnel training to be prepared for any emergency on a moment's notice, including large-scale calamities such as terrorist threats or natural disasters.

Economic Development. Strategic public investment in the downtown area and partnerships with private investors and nonprofit entities will spur redevelopment. Preservation of local history and character will be mirrored in all new projects. With public support of local businesses, property values will increase and aesthetics will improve. Clearwater's beaches will continue to remain open to the public. They will be redeveloped through city and county incentives that will address residential, commercial, and transportation issues.

Infrastructure Maintenance. Assessment of the current infrastructure will determine needs for the future. Existing infrastructure assets will be maintained through the repair and replacement of worn parts, and future projects will implement new technologies that improve function and durability and reduce operating costs.

Quality of Life. The high quality of life we enjoy here is why we live, learn, work, and play in Clearwater. It can be reinforced by encouraging diversity in cultural and recreational programs and by supporting neighbourhoods. Beautification programmes and expansion of our nationally known brownfield programme will promote a safe, clean, green environment. We must also continue to provide and improve on the excellent customer service our residents and visitors have come to expect.

Human Resources Issues. None of the vision can become reality without the people to achieve it. Therefore, the city must provide and support a healthy working environment and a competent workforce and must plan for future employment trends.

Human Resources Strategic Plan

As one of the five defined priority levels, the city's Human Resources Management Department developed its own strategic business plan consistent with the city's strategic plan.

The mission of the HRM Department is as follows:

> To help the city of Clearwater provide premier service to our customers by recruiting, selecting, training, developing, and retaining a diverse, highly qualified, satisfied, motivated, and productive workforce.

Its core HR values are to be strategic, responsive, professional, flexible, and caring, and its HR vision is to deliver results that add value and help our customers achieve their goals.

Included in the strategic business plan are five specific goals that are linked with the city's mission statement, key intended outcomes, and measurable objectives, as follows:

Goal 1

Create a high-performance organisational climate that encourages superior customer service and continuous quality improvement through effective recruitment, selection, and retention programmes, development and training initiatives and reward and recognition programmes.

Key Intended Outcomes

- Improve customer satisfaction
- Increase customer trust and confidence in government
- Develop employees who have the skill and commitment to deliver quality service

HR Initiatives for 2003–2004

- Strategic Planning and Management System
- Performance Management System
- HRIS Strategic Implementation System
- New Employee Mentoring Programme
- Employee and Team Reward and Recognition Programme
- Long-Range Training Assessment Plan
- SAMP[a] Incentive Pay system
- SAMP Paid time-Off System
- Labour-Management Partnerships
- Leadership Development and succession Planning Programme

Measurable Objectives

- Increase the percentage of employees who agree with the statement 'HR staff help recruit and retain high-quality employees.'
- Increase the percentage of employees who agree with the statement 'HR staff provide quality and timely service.'
- Increase the percentage of employees who agree with the statement 'I am able to apply the skills and knowledge learned through city-sponsored educational, training, and development programmes to improve my personal and organisational effectiveness.'
- Increase the percentage of employees who agree with the statement 'I am motivated by the city's reward and recognition programmes.'

Goal 2

Improve communication, interaction, and cooperation between HR and its customers.

Key Intended Outcomes

- Improve customer satisfaction
- Increase customer trust and confidence in government
- Strive for overall effective communication
- Initiate capital projects needed to improve the levels of service

HR Initiatives for 2003–2004

- HR Liaison Programme
- Supervisory Leadership Certification Programme
- HR Customer Communication Plan (Newsletter, Internet, intranet)
- Revised SAMP Manuals
- HR Policy Handbook

Measurable Objectives

- Increase the percentage of employees who agree with the statement 'HR seeks and listens to employee input on issues and policies affecting employees.'
- Increase the percentage of employees who agree with the statement 'I am satisfied with HR communication and liaison services.'

Goal 3

Help foster an organisational climate that makes the city of Clearwater a 'premier place to work.'

Key Intended Outcome

- Recognition of Clearwater as a preferred place to live, work, and play.

HR Initiatives for 2003–2004

- Employee Salary and Benefits Survey
- Revised and Modified Light-Duty Programme
- Employee Benefit Analysis

---

[a] SAMP refers to supervisory, administrative, managerial and professional employees who are exempt from belonging to a union under Florida law or are in middle or upper management positions.

- Employee Wellness Programme
- Job Evaluation System

Measurable Objectives

- Increase the percentage of employees who agree with the statement 'I enjoy working for the city of Clearwater.'
- Increase the percentage of employees who agree with the statement 'I am proud to be a city employee and would recommend city employment to a friend.'
- Increase the percentage of employees who agree with the statement 'The city cares about my well-being.'
- Increase the percentage of employees who agree with the statement 'I am satisfied with my salary or wage range.'
- Increase the percentage of employees who agree with the statement 'I am satisfied with my benefits package.'

Goal 4

Promote programmes and activities that expose the city's workforce to community organisations.

Key intended Outcome

Proactive promotion of community well-being.

HR Initiatives for 2003–2004

City-Community Education, Training, and Development Partnership Programmes
City Student Internship Programme

Measurable Objectives

- Increase the percentage of employees who participate in city-sponsored community programmes and activities.
- Increase the percentage of employees who agree with the statement 'The city and community benefit from employees who participate in city-sponsored community programmes and activities.'

Goal 5

Promote an organisational workforce that reflects the city's demographics.

Key Intended Outcome

A city that values diversity

HR Initiatives for 2003–2004

- Support city Diversity Plan
- ESL and Bilingual Language Training Programmes
- Business Case for diversity

Measurable Objectives

- Increase the percentage of minorities and protected-class members in the workforce to more closely reflect city demographics.
- Increase the percentage of bilingual employees.
- Increase the percentage of employees who agree with the statement 'The city promotes a work environment in which diversity is valued.'

SOURCE: PYNES, J. E. 2004. *Human resources management for public and nonprofit organisations* 2nd ed. San Francisco: Jossey Bass, a John Wiley Imprint:36–41. Used with permission.

5

Managing flexible patterns of work for competitive advantage

Learning outcomes

After reading this chapter you should be able to:

▶ Define the concept of flexibility
▶ Distinguish between the different types of flexibility
▶ List 10 organisational/management practices organisations can use to determine whether they are ready for flex work
▶ Discuss the flexible-firm model
▶ Discuss the changing dynamics of the workplace and their impact on new forms of flexibility

Purpose

The purpose of this chapter is to introduce you to the concept of flexibility within the work environment.

Chapter overview

This chapter focuses on the issue of flexible patterns of work. It begins with a discussion of what flexibility is. It considers different types of flexible patterns of work and also lists their advantages and disadvantages. It further describes how organisations can determine whether they are ready to introduce such practices. The chapter also contains a discussion of a flexible-firm model and looks at the changing dynamics of the workplace and their impact of new forms of flexibility. The concluding case study illustrates how the theory contained in this chapter can be applied to a practical situation.

Introduction

In recent years a variety of factors – such as increasing economic volatility, competitiveness, new technology, and, more recently, intensifying shortages of skills – have led many organisations actively to seek more efficient and effective ways of utilising their resources.[1-3] A key aspect in the development of competitive advantage through human resources is management's ability to manipulate flexibly the available internal and external labour-market resources in line with the supply and demand of the market, with minimal disruption to the production process.[4-12]

As Ursell[13] notes:

> A major goal implicit in the idea of flexible labour is to render HRM as a strategic, rather than merely a tactical, activity. ... By this is meant a multifold process involving one or many of the following: (i) for any individual worker, a wider range of tasks and abilities and a willingness to employ them on behalf of the organisation which purchases them; (ii) a greater variety in the time periods of employment; (iii) a greater ability by the employer to dispense with certain workers when not strictly essential to the production process (an ability which may be grounded in the replacement of traditional contracts of employment by franchise and subcontractor relations, and/or the greater use of part-time and temporary employees); and (iv) a greater capacity among workers (in both internal and external labour markets) to be so deployed, necessitating changed attitudes for all, and skill and time-management change for some.

SOURCE: URSELL, G. D. 1991. Human resource management and labour flexibility: some reflections based on cross–national and sectoral studies in Canada and the UK. (*In* Blyton, P. & Morris, J. 1991. *A flexible future? Prospects for employment and organization.* Berlin: De Gruyter:311–327:312.)

The inference from the development of these work patterns and practices is a new-found strategic focus by management, integrating both the 'hard' (or quantitative) approach to human resources, which emphasises the link to organisational strategy, and the 'soft' (or qualitative) approach, which focuses on the developmental aspects of managing human resources.[14-15] In this chapter we shall find out what exactly the term 'flexibility' means. Then we shall consider flexibility and organisational design, look at the advantages and disadvantages of flexible patterns of work, and, lastly, discuss the changing dynamics of the workplace and their impact on new forms of flexibility.

5.1 What is flexibility?

The term 'flexibility' is difficult to define as it has been applied to a wide range of issues and levels of analysis.[16-17] At a national level the debate focuses on rigidities in the regulation of the labour markets.[18] At an organisational level flexibility is concerned with the integrative use of employment practices and organisational structures to create a capacity to adapt and manage innovation.[19-22] However, one such definition in the literature, which describes the term broadly, is that of Pilbeam and Corbridge: 'The ability of the organisation to adapt the size, composition, responsiveness and cost of the people inputs required to achieve organisational objectives'.[23] In the context of these dimensions a number of forms of flexibility have been identified. We shall discuss these next. The categorisation should not suggest that the forms of flexibility are mutually exclusive. Many forms of overlapping flexibility exist, and managers need to distinguish between these forms of flexibility in order to be able to seize opportunities for increasing organisational flexibility. However, managers should also be aware of the problems.

5.1.1 Functional flexibility

Functional flexibility refers to management's ability to deploy and redeploy particular sections of the workforce on a wide range of tasks, in response to market demand, as and when required. To ensure that managers achieve this efficiently, the organisation trains employees in a wide range of skills. As Atkinson notes[24]:

This might mean the deployment of multi-skilled craftsmen from mechanical, electrical and pneumatic jobs; it might mean moving workers between indirect and direct production jobs or it might mean a complete change of career. ... As products and production methods change, functional flexibility implies that the same labour force changes with them, in both short and medium term.

SOURCE: ATKINSON, J. 1984. Manpower strategies for flexible organisations. *Personnel management,* 28–31(August)·28.

The volatility of product markets and the blurring of skill boundaries through technological change provide the environment for the development of this form of flexibility. Central to the development of functional flexibility is the reversal of the Taylorist (or scientific management) practices of fragmentation and de-skilling.[25] Working practices which incorporate elements of functional flexibility include team working, empowerment, muli-skilling, re-skilling, and projectworking.

5.1.2 **Numerical flexibility**

Numerical flexibility is a quantitative approach to the utilisation of the workforce. It is based on the principle of relating the size of the workforce to the levels of economic activity easily and at short notice.[26] As the workload fluctuates, management has the option to adjust or redeploy its human resources accordingly.[27–28] The use of seasonal, casual, part-time, and subcontracted workers typically provides this form of flexibility. The pressures of unpredictable short-term fluctuations in demand, combined with increased competitiveness, make these work patterns efficient and effective to sustain, as

organisations are relieved of the cost of a fixed labour force.[29] While these patterns of work organisation have been traditional aspects of some segments of the labour market (e.g. the service and retail sectors), the use of these work practices to externalise traditional core organisational activities is the major factor in increasing enterprise efficiency through numerical flexibility.[30–31]

5.1.3 **Work-time flexibility**

Work-time flexibility (or internal numerical flexibility) is a further process of adjusting the 'quantity and timing of labour input without modifying the number of employees'.[32] This has been part of the traditional patterns of work organisation (e.g. overtime, shift working, and, now, also flexi-time arrangements), although it has traditionally incurred financial penalties. The incorporation of these patterns of work into contract hours per week, month or year[33] provides the organisation with the flexibility to arrange and adjust work patterns, and leads to a closer correlation between labour utilisation and production demands, without financial penalty or the additional costs of hiring labour.[34]

Job sharing refers to a situation where one job (often full-time) is split between two (or more) employees. The employees may work a variety of combinations, including split day or split week or alternating weeks. These work patterns can provide both functional and numerical flexibility.

Distancing relates to the outsourcing of activities that may include core and non-core activities. The outsourcing of non-core activities (e.g. cleaning, catering, and security) and the increased outsourcing of traditional core activities, particularly in the human resources area (for example call-centre, customer-service work)[35], facilitates the reduction of the core or permanent workforce.

5.1.4 **Financial flexibility**

Financial flexibility is a compensation system designed to facilitate the development of flexible patterns of work, in particular numerical and functional flexibility. As Atkinson outlines[36]:

> Financial flexibility is sought for two reasons; first, so that pay and other employment costs reflect the state of supply and demand in the external labour market. ... Secondly, and probably of greater importance in the long term, pay flexibility means a shift to new pay and remuneration systems that facilitate numerical or functional flexibility, such as assessment-based pay systems in place of rate-for-the-job systems.
>
> SOURCE: ATKINSON, J. 1984. Manpower strategies for flexible organisations. *Personnel management*, 28–31(August):29.

Financial flexibility therefore provides the duality of:
- Allowing market forces to dictate relative wage rates, providing cost-efficient numerical flexibility to the organisation
- Providing the incentive for the core workforce to increase its skill base by relating pay to skill levels.

Other examples of functional flexibility include:
- Gainsharing
- Profit sharing
- Variable executive-pay schemes.

5.1.5 Procedural flexibility

Procedural flexibility is the central tenet in the development of flexible patterns of work. This is particularly the case in the highly regulated labour markets.

Procedural flexibility is concerned with the establishment of consultative mechanisms for introducing changes or negotiating variations in work practices, primarily through changes in both legal and traditional practices covering employment.[37] As Woods notes[38]:

> In most industrialised countries the 'flexibility debate', concerned with changing rigidities in labour and employment patterns, has been an important element in industrial policy making and industrial relations ...
>
> SOURCE: WOODS, S. 1989. *The transformation of work: Skill, flexibility and the labour process.* London: Unwin-Hyman:1.

At the level of the organisation, the process can range from directive through to a participative framework of negotiation. The substantive aspects of the traditional 'Taylorist' relationship between employer and employee and the employee's representative (trade unions) are fundamentally recast for flexible patterns of work to be fully utilised.[39-40] Central to procedural flexibility is the acceptance of, and a role in managing, the new relationship for the employees and their representatives.[41] Such procedures are indicative of commitment to joint administration of labour flexibility within the workplace.[42] Procedural flexibility facilitates the combination of work patterns and practices that increase the utilisation of the enterprise's human resources.[43-46]

5.1.6 Regulatory flexibility

Regulatory flexibility is a process to encourage and facilitate the establishment, development or relocation of enterprises through the relaxation, amendment or exemption of public policy. This may include changes in labour law restrictions or issues of occupational health and safety.[47]

5.1.7 Mobility flexibility

Mobility (or location) flexibility involves a change in the nature of work, or a career change with the same employer.[48] It may also mean a relocation of the work location through telecommuting and virtual teams (see Chapter 1), where the location is incidental to the work.

5.1.8 **Cognitive flexibility**

Cognitive flexibility is the mental frame of reference required to perform effectively in the job and the level of cognitive skill required.[49] The development of new forms of flexibility has significantly changed the psychological contract between the employer and the employee, as we indicated earlier in the book. From the development of less secure forms of employment – even to the extent of zero-based contracts where no hours are actually guaranteed – through to the implementation of multi-skilling requiring the development of new skills, knowledge, and competencies, employees have had to accept and adjust to the differing demands and expectations organisations have placed on them.[50–52]

5.1.9 **Organisational flexibility**

Organisational flexibility is a structural response to the development of the flexible patterns of work described above. Despite increased interest in the development of flexible work practices, little is actually new in any of these patterns of work. What is new, however, is management's explicit desire to seek to develop integrative or multiple forms of flexibility.[53] In this context, the pursuit of multiple forms of flexibility requires a parallel development in organisational forms to accommodate these changes.[54] The contention is that the traditional hierarchical or bureaucratic organisation cannot adequately handle these changes in work patterns, and that organisational structures with the capacity to adapt and manage change and innovation must therefore replace it.[55–56]

5.2 **Organisation readiness for flex work**[57]

The use of flexible work arrangements as discussed above can entail many levels of change, e.g. operational, managerial, organisational, and, even, cultural. The big question is: is the organisation ready to implement any of these techniques? Dychtwald, Erickson and Morison identified 10 organisational and management practices which can assist organisations, to determine organisations' readiness to establish or expand their flexible work arrangements. We shall briefly look at these:

- *Policy.* Are there specific policy and strategy statements approved and communicated by top management that endorse flex work as a component of the employment relationship?
- *Employee commitment.* How deeply are employees committed to the success of the organisation's mission and to high achievement in their own jobs?
- *Management commitment.* Do the actions of management as well as its communications to employees reinforce management's support for flex work?
- *Workforce planning.* How good is the organisation at forecasting projects, deadlines, production quotas, and workloads? How good is it at scheduling workforce needs; and at allocating resources?
- *Technology.* Are information-technology and communication systems in place to support flex work in smooth, efficient, consistent ways?
- *Training and orientation.* How effective are training content and delivery mechanisms for meeting the ongoing needs of flex workers?
- *Teamwork.* To what extent is work done in teams, and is there sufficient coordination to ensure coverage and to compensate for having team members on different schedules?
- *Performance management.* Are there methods for performance measurement, employee appraisal, and staff development that are equivalent, if not identical, for flex workers and others?
- *Decision making.* Who holds decision rights and makes key decisions in the course of everyday work?
- *Communication and information dissemination.* How effective are the means, media, and frequency of communication of everyday business

information and are those processes robust enough to keep flex workers in the loop?

5.3 Flexibility and organisational design

What has emerged from the extensive debate on flexibility is the increasing use of multiple forms of flexible patterns of work, to facilitate more timely responses to the competitive forces of the market.[58-60] This has required the parallel development of organisational structures to facilitate these changes.[61-62] Organisational flexibility therefore provides management with the template to adjust and utilise the available human resources in a flexible manner in response to changing demands.[63-64] The model which has attracted particular attention is the flexible-firm model or core–periphery model.

5.3.1 The flexible-firm model or core–periphery model

Research by the Institute for Employment Studies (IES), formerly the Institute of Manpower Studies (IMS), in the UK identified the development of a distinct organisational structure – the flexible-firm model – to accommodate the development of multiple forms of flexibility, in particular functional, numerical, and financial flexibility.[65-67] Thompson and McHugh note that the flexible-firm mode or core-periphery model provides competitive advantage through the restructuring of the employment relationship[68]: '[The flexible firm model] is based on a break with unitary and hierarchical labour markets and organisation of internal means of allocating labour, in order to create a core workforce and a cluster of peripheral employment relations.'

In place of the traditional hierarchical structures, the flexible-firm model redefines the organisation into two broad segments – the core and the periphery. The make-up of the two segments reflects the different types of flexibility the organisation requires. The core is made up of a permanent, highly-skilled group of employees with internal career paths.[69-71] As a result, 'core' employees experience a high degree of job security, with resources provided for training in firm-specific skills not readily bought in. This segment of the organisation is characterised by functional forms of flexibility.[72-74] In contrast, the peripheral workforce is associated with the organisation's development of qualitative or numerical flexibility. The key function of this sector for the organisation is the undertaking of day-to-day activities that are important but not vital to the organisation.

As Atkinson points out[75]:

> In effect they are offered a job not a career. For example, they might be clerical, supervisory, component assembly and testing occupations. The key point is that their jobs are 'plug-in' ones, not firm-specific. As a result the firm looks to the external market to fill these jobs, and seeks to achieve numerical flexibility and financial flexibility through more direct and immediate links to the external labour market than is sought for the core group.
>
> SOURCE: ATKINSON, J. 1984. Manpower strategies for flexible organisations. *Personnel management*, 28–31(August):20.

Where either the core or peripheral workforce needs supplementing, the secondary peripheral workforce accommodates this through part-time temporary or subcontracting work.[76] This provides increased numerical and functional flexibility with minimal organisational commitment or disruption.

The new organisation therefore takes the form of a core with a variety of peripheral activities to serve its changing requirements, as Figure 5.1 illustrates. The focus of the flexible-firm model is closely to match organisational (labour) resources with work demand, increasing the efficiency of human resource utilisation while dampening the effects of market volatility and uncertainty, thereby increasing organisational effectiveness.[77-79]

Figure 5.1 The flexible-firm model

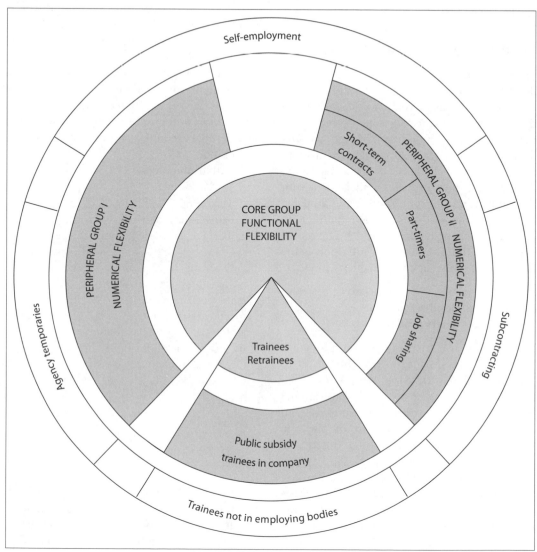

SOURCE: ATKINSON, J. 1985. *Flexibility, uncertainty and manpower management*. Brighton, England: Institute for Employment Studies (formerly the Institute of Manpower Strategies). Used with permission.

Research on the development of the flexible-firm model is less well developed. In the UK, results of the implementation of these strategies remain mixed. In Australia, Burgess found a growth in non-standard employment, including part-time and casual work, although these changes tended to be ad hoc and reactive. Research has generally found the development of the flexible-firm model to be reactive to the demands of the market, rather than a new-found strategic view of management towards the organisation of its human resources.[80]

Despite the mixed evidence relating to the development of the flexible firm, the model has generated significant debate.[81-90] What is distinctive about the flexible-firm model and its approach to the organisation and management of human resources is the extent to which it implies a distinctive strategy on the part of management in developing more efficient and effective utilisation of labour.[91-93] Critics of the flexible-firm model contend that this is simplistic and argue that change is far more uneven and complex: they contend that the model is too abstract to represent reality.[94-99]

The flexible-firm model is also criticised for its promotion of variation in terms and conditions of employment within organisations[100-101]. The outcome of this variation is the creation of a (skill) polarised workforce with an elite core workforce and a disenfranchised low-skilled, low-wage peripheral workforce.[102-104] From a management perspective, it can be argued that the flexible-firm model incorrectly assumes that organisations have uniformly moved from ad hoc to explicit labour strategies in both the short and the long terms.[105-109] In addition, many researchers note the lack of empirical evidence to support the uniform development of the flexible firm.[110-116]

Despite these criticisms, the flexible-firm model does provide a framework for analysis, insight, and explanation with respect to the development of new patterns of work.[117-122]

5.4 The changing dynamics of flexibility

5.4.1 New workers – the changing dynamics of the flexible core worker

At be beginning of the twenty-first century there is a renewed recognition of the key role of flexible work patterns in generating sustainable competitive advantage. At the centre of this is the need to attract, retain, and develop key employees for the core activities and develop a stable supply of workers for the periphery. Consequently, flexibility has become a key platform of the new organisational environment. What is significant about the new core workers in the emerging knowledge economy is that they increasingly own the means of production – knowledge – which attract large rewards. Research by the Australian Centre for Industrial Research and Training (ACIRRT)[123] notes that the changing labour market has also changed the nature of the psychological contract which has significantly transformed the employer–employee relationship.[124] As the ACIRRT research report states:

Sometimes known as 'gold-collar workers' this latter group of workers has benefited considerably from technological change and economic deregulation. Often found in the cutting edge of computer technology in banking or in publishing, 'gold-collar workers' have found high paying jobs which stimulate and challenge them. They often spend extremely long hours at their job, they are young, ambitious and very well paid. Their loyalty, however, is owed less to their employer than it is to their career. As a result, they are highly mobile, lured by new jobs, which offer technical challenges or opportunities for self-development.

SOURCE: ACIRRT. 1999. *Australia at work: Just managing.* Sydney: Prentice Hall.

The management of these strategic resources therefore assumes greater significance. As Newell, Robertson, Scarbrough, and Swan[125] note, the term 'gold-collar worker' implies that organisations need to manage these carefully and provide them with excellent working conditions. It is this group that is at the core of a firm's unique strategic advantage. It is not possible to develop a competitive advantage without the consideration of the people that form the core of a firm's knowledge base. Therefore, the management of these human resources throws out particular challenges to organisations that base their advantage on these 'free thinking' workers and 'managed' resources. Organisations need to focus their employment systems, practices, and organisational structure to ensure they capture this unique resource.[126-127]

The key to developing strategies that attract, develop, and retain these employees is to understand what motivates them. As Barnes[128] points out, these workers think differently and behave differently to the traditional employee and have different needs. Typically, these workers are self-focused and less interested in the traditional benefits of employment such as job security and working conditions. This view is supported by Storey and Quintas[129], who argue that the fundamental issue for organisations to identify is 'employability'. There is an expectation therefore that an organisation will play a part in not only securing employment, but in upgrading employees' knowledge, skills, and abilities, so that they remain in demand in the wider market for employment. Whilst the concept of job-hopping may become the norm, this approach or characteristic of employment paradoxically may be a factor in, at least, reducing turnover. It can even make the organisation an 'employer of choice' to which these increasingly discerning workers will return.[130]

These fundamental changes to the nature of the employment relationship will further accelerate the move away from the traditional employment relationship (see Box 1) as exemplified in the traditional psychological contract based on loyalty and stability of employment. The onus, for gold-collar workers, will be to manage their own careers, which will mean constantly upgrading skills and employment. This will require them to direct their own training and development for a broader range of skills, and accept greater role ambiguity and responsibility.[131] Organisations will have to adapt to this new paradigm in a variety of ways. In particular, terms and conditions of employment and the way work is organised will need to be conducive to these workers (see Box 2). Management must therefore pay careful attention to both structural and cultural conditions within the firm. In other words, organisations will need to organise

---

BOX 1: Work in progress – flexible people planning

'If you build the job around the way people want to work to live their lives, you are more likely to win the services of the best and brightest,' says cultural commentator Bernard Salt, summing up what is likely to be the competitive-edge corporate response to the major long-term changes in the workforce.

The workforce is ageing, and the younger talent has already shown that it has different priorities and motivations to preceding generations. Planners will have to think outside the square and adopt more creative and more *flexible options* [emphasis added] in work practices if they are to ensure their organisations have the skills and experience to face the future.

The concept of drawing on rigid professional competency groups is looking decidedly dated. Organisations need to find new ways to increase the rate of participation in the workforce and maximise talent. The most forward-thinking ones are already taking greater account of the attitudes and needs of different generations at various stages in their life, as well as individual personalities and their motivators.

'For 40 or 50 years', says Salt, a partner at KPMG and author of the 2001 best seller *The Big Shift*, 'companies recruiting people have been quite prescriptive about what they wanted: here is the height of the bar and you must jump it to get into the firm. Now the boot is on the other foot.'

The uncertainty of rapid change in business and society is greatly complicating strategic planning. An employer starts by ascertaining the type of workers they will need to match their vision, but then comes the tricky part – attracting and retaining this talent whilst maintaining a workforce plan flexible enough to meet unforeseen challenges.

While there has been much emphasis on ways to retain the skills of older employees, Salt suggests that employers can't afford to ignore the different attitudes and needs of Generation Y (born between 1978 and 1991), the children of the baby boomers, who will account for 10 per cent more of the population than Gen-X by 2021. He says these younger employees are more experiential than their parents and therefore more inclined to travel and swap jobs and relationships, and less concerned with financial stability.

SOURCE: Adapted from KEEN, S. 2005. Interview with Bernard Salt – cultural commentator. *HR monthly*, February:18. Used with permission.

BOX 2: **Work in progress – flexible people planning**

'Organisations need to look at both skills and personal characteristics including behaviour, personality style, thinking style, general disposition and motivators,' says Matthew Dale. These should be used to develop a capability framework that is applied in recruitment, professional development, performance management and succession planning.

'Organisations are already putting more work into gazing into the crystal ball and deciding what sort of skill sets they need,' says Dale. 'On a deeper level, the smart organisations are defining what type of person will fit with the organisation's culture. A lot of that is value-driven – not just what they are capable of doing, but what satisfies them. If someone is unmotivated, their skill set will walk out the door,' says Dale.

Employers also need to recognise that the top talent is not responding to autocratic management styles. 'Smart organisations are looking to drive a culture of coaching in senior management. They need to engage the individual.'

One workforce planning strategy he suggests is to allow recent university graduates to take time out from their employment to travel and gain overseas experience with no loss of salary. Dale adds that some New Zealand employers are already doing this at a time of serious skill shortages.

SOURCE: Adapted from KEEN, S. 2005. Interview with Matthew Dale – Hudson Consulting – National Practice Manager for Talent Management – Australia. *HR monthly*, February:18. Used with permission.

---

along very different lines compared to more traditional aspects of the employment relationship, which, typically, did not consider workers as the key productive force of the organisation and, in relative terms, found them easy to replace.[132]

5.4.2 New Organisations – the changing dynamics of the flexible organisation

In dealing with these issues of a labour force that is increasingly dynamic, new ways of organising work to access knowledge across traditional boundaries is vital. This brings organisational design into the frame. Because of the lack of loyalty to the organisation relative to their profession and career, the new generation of workers needs an organisational structure to reflect this. Metaphorically, we need to view organisations more as porous systems which do not aim to own the human capital but to manage it. This means accepting and accommodating the movement of human resources into and out of the firm, often via capricious mechanisms such as informal networks, which are largely beyond the firm's control.[133] The trade-off for the loss of employees is the gain through knowledge flow that results from exchanges

through opportunities to create new networks beyond the firm. Also there is evidence to suggest that people who are only weakly associated with the organisation can be the providers of new information.[134] Such weak associations could include peripheral organisational structures. These may range from sub-contracts or fixed-term appointments for specific projects, to encouraging 'core' staff actually to leave to develop themselves and allow new talent into the core organisation, thus developing a hybrid of the core–periphery model.

Increasingly the key issue for organisations is the management of these flexible 'distributed knowledge systems' or networks.[135] The ability to manage distributed systems of knowledge has become a major factor of production as well as a source of competitive advantage for firms in advanced economies (see Box 3). What differentiates these practices from previous approaches is that competitive management practices depend upon generating relationships and knowledge through interactions with others outside the firm. Strategic advantage comes not just from the firm's internal flow of knowledge but in how the firm is able to tap into and use this internal flow of knowledge in conjunction

BOX 3: **Create a work environment not just to accommodate, but to inspire**

Leading organisations understand the growing diversity of the future workforce; but they know that accommodating work schedules is simply not enough. Beyond part-time work and telecommuting, they are coming up with truly ground breaking ways to accommodate employees' diverse needs, while creating an inspirational work environment.

For companies' top performers, this is especially critical. Studies have consistently shown that top performers produce in value at least 100 to 150 per cent more than average performers in similar jobs. And today's high-potentials place great importance on having a balance between work and personal life. In a recent study on high-potentials and the factors that motivate them to excel at work, work/life balance ranked fourth in importance out of 20 total factors. According to one high-potential, 'work/life balance ranks up there with eating and breathing for me.'

Some companies are building work arrangements for a targeted pool of employees. They cater to a segment with the intensity of a targeted marketing campaign and build a miniculture and support network to sustain it. At Ernst & Young LLP, an accounting, tax, and legal services firm, employees create flexible schedules to accommodate personal and professional needs. Some work full-time part of the year and part-time the rest of the year. Employees using flexible scheduling are not hurt in terms of promotions and rewards, either. Ernst & Young has a philosophy that workers will be more productive and will produce higher quality work if they're not distracted by work/life balance concerns.

Sun Microsystems' 'iWork programme' offers employees across the globe a variety of choices for getting work done – in the office, at home or at drop-in centres. Employees armed with a 'SunRay' smart card, introduced more than a decade ago, can access the Internet and Sun's network from anywhere. This type of virtual flexibility has been widely embraced by Sun's employees. Nearly half of Sun's workforce of 15,000 work either from home, at drop-in centres or in Flex Zones within Sun office buildings. The programme enables them to be better able to accommodate their work/life needs and personal work styles. What's more, they have saved the company money on real estate and back-office support.

According to Daniel Pink, the most talented workers are in the driver's seat when it comes to job choices. Pink argues that 'today, talented people need organisations a lot less than organisations need talented people'. As a result, companies need to pay more attention to what truly drives and engages top talent and work hard to build an inspiring work environment and experience. Pink believes that many companies 'overlook how much people draw meaning and purpose and even pleasure, satisfaction, or challenge from their jobs'. Similarly, James Ware and Charles Grantham of the Work Design Collaborative write: 'For high-performing talent today, lifestyle has become just as important as work style; in many respects, the two are inseparable.'

Capital One pushes the notion of work environment one step further. Through the company's 'Future of Work' pilot project on the sixth floor of its McLean, Virginia, headquarters, employees get to experience the workplace of the future. Traditional enclosed offices and desks give way to movable workstations, islands of common space to encourage dialogue, and glass-enclosed meeting rooms. There are creative spaces with couches and toys to promote brainstorming and quiet spaces devoted to silent work. Associates have flexibility to work as residents in one location, as mobile workers moving from space to space, or as telecommuters. All are armed with Wifi-enabled laptops, voice-over-IP (Internet protocol) software phones, and portable printers. A leading member of the joint IT, HR and real estate team behind the initiative, Sallie Larsen, says 'Capital One is a culture that obsesses with taking it to the next step. The Future of Work is part of that'.

SOURCE: GANDOSSY, R. P., TUCKER, E. & VERMA, N. (HEWITT ASSOCIATES). 2006. Workforce wake-up call: your workforce is changing, are you? (*In* Gandossy, R. P. & Kao, T. *Staffing for the future: Next generation workforce management*. New Jersey: John Wiley & Sons:83–84. Used with permission.

with knowledge flows that occur outside the organisation (see Chapter 2 in this regard).[136-137] This can result in a workplace that is team based, where (core) employees are varied and transient in both organisational status and time relationships and management engages more in leveraging their resource than in managing them.[138] As noted, management needs to recognise that the ability of a firm to acquire, integrate, and release resources is critical for a constant flow of knowledge from diverse sources within and beyond the boundaries of the organisation. The challenge for managers is to ensure alignment of the goals of these employees and the goals of the firm; this alignment may result in organisations allowing key employees to go wherever they can be most productive and even helping them depart for a better job. The rationale behind this somewhat counter-intuitive view is that in the age of information-intensive industries, no organisation can compete without access to information from other organisations.[139] Content ex-employees join other information networks in their new employment, but still retain links with their former networks and can channel new information into those networks.[140] Increasingly the challenge for managing flexible patterns of work will be to strike a balance between maintaining the stock of intellectual capital and absorbing and exchanging new knowledge and employees through external networks.[141] This will continually affect the structure of organisations and, as a consequence, the way in which organisations manage the employment relationship. This draws attention to the impact of management's ability to derive competitive advantage from continually developing and exploiting both its knowledge stock and knowledge flows.

5.4.3 New perspectives – flexible workers need flexible managers

One of the most overlooked aspects of flexible patterns of work in this 'new' environment is the role and development of management. As Davenport and Prusak[142] have noted, the most dramatic improvements in knowledge-management capability will be human and managerial. The development of fluid organisations through informal and intuitive patterns of work needs a management base that has the skill to acquire, transform, and exploit knowledge. Management must have the leadership skills to harness new practices; shed old habits such as hierarchy, culture, and power; and empower continual change.[143-144]

These new capabilities can be developed only where management understands this and has the skills and knowledge to create such an environment. Addressing these issues requires the skill to make decisions about skill gaps and inform training and development requirements. It can also be linked to career management, which may facilitate and encourage staff to leave to gain more experience, whilst maintaining ties with the organisation or returning to the organisation in the future, with increased knowledge. As Kamoche and Mueller[145] have argued, this may make the organisation an attractive place to work – or in contemporary language, an employer of choice – that can attract high-quality knowledge workers because of its positive reputation, underpinned by sophisticated policies on employment.

Research by Macdonald[146] on headhunting practices for knowledge workers in the USA found that organisations that had developed a culture which encouraged employees to see their organisation as a supportive platform for advancing elsewhere, and for returning when opportunities become available, were likely to facilitate the growth of knowledge stocks within the firm. More recent Australian research has supported this, with Holland, Hecker, and Steen[147] finding that a medium-sized firm was able to attract employees by adopting such policies as employee mobility, training, development, and career management. As Scarbrough, Swan, and Preston[148] note:

It is significant, for example, that consultancies and other knowledge-intensive organisations do not strive for maximum levels of staff retention. Such firms might see a turnover level around 15–18 per cent as desirable, to be achieved if necessary by 'counselling out'. This allows a reasonable number of career opportunities and a continuous influx of fresh talent.

SOURCE: SCARBROUGH, H., SWAN, J. & PRESTON, J. 1999. *Knowledge management: A review of the literature.* London: Institute of Personnel and Development:18.

Thus it is management which acts as the catalyst in the through-flow of staff to enable the organisation continually to regenerate its knowledge base.[149]

Therefore, management skills and appreciation are central to understanding the unique and critical issues these new flexible patterns of work raise.[150] This being so, it is important that organisations invest resources in these employees; this investment is necessary to ensure that they continue to develop their knowledge, skill, and ability, so as to make certain that the organisation develops sustained competitive advantage through their human resources.

5.5 Advantages and disadvantages of flexible patterns of work

Much research and debate has surrounded the development of flexible patterns of work; however, less attention has been paid to the outcomes of these work patterns and practices. Emmott and Hutchinson[151–152] have attempted to address this omission by identifying the advantages and disadvantages (both real and potential) of flexible patterns of work.

5.5.1 The employer perspective on flexible patterns of work

The perceived advantages for employers in developing flexible patterns of work are that they:

- Enable employers to match organisational resources more closely with customer demand and product demand
- Reduce fixed costs (e.g. homeworkers do not require office space)
- Aid recruitment and retention
- Increase productivity – those working for a reduced period of time are likely to be less tired and stressed
- Reduce absence and turnover.

The most important factor for management in the adoption of flexible patterns of work is the ability to respond quickly to market demands with minimum disruption. This may take the form of moving employees from one job to another, or adjusting the level of human resources in response to fluctuation or changes in demand, as the market dictates. The use of homeworkers or telecommuters, and outsourcing or offshoring (see Chapter 1), where the place of work is incidental to the requirements of the job or where office space is at a premium, can provide substantial cost savings.

Flexible work patterns also allow the employer to cover changes in work requirements, as and when required, by integrating the various types of flexibility. Again, the ability to change the structure of the workforce or work patterns with minimal disruption is a key to efficient and effective utilisation of the available human resources. These work patterns can aid recruitment and retention by providing employees with employment opportunities which suit their requirements. These opportunities may have otherwise been unavailable because of other commitments (we shall discuss this later). In terms of productivity, the obvious problems of fatigue associated with working for long periods have been well documented in the literature on occupational health and safety.[153–154] Therefore, the attraction of reduced periods of work is an overall increase in productivity and shorter recovery time. In jobs that are repetitive or require high levels of mental alertness, the advantages are clear.[155]

For employers, the main disadvantages of flexible patterns of work include:
- Increased costs of training

- Higher direct costs (e.g. part-timers who receive pro-rata benefits)
- Administration that is more complex
- Communication difficulties
- The required management of the flexible workforce.

Development of these work patterns requires significant and long-term investment on the part of the organisation in ongoing training and development, in order to create and maintain the required skills, knowledge, and expertise.[156] These increased costs, combined with the more complex administration associated with managing these work patterns and the new (tenuous) psychological contract of gold-collar workers with the organisation, may diminish the perceived competitive advantage in developing flexibility to the extent that it is no longer a viable option. Multiple patterns of work and shifts may result in managers and employees not necessarily working at the same time for extended periods. This creates the potential for communication breakdowns.[157] Equally, the increased use of telecommuting and the use of virtual teams provide their own difficulties.

Finally, management of the flexible workforce requires a significant increase in planning and coordination and the support of senior management, if these patterns of work are to provide the organisation with a competitive advantage. Management also needs to develop a peripheral labour supply which can be 'plugged-in' with minimal disruption to the production process, or provide specialist skills. Management also needs to manage the variable nature of the employment relationship and the changing demands on internal and external labour, so as to retain and maintain these resources. For example, temporary employment could be used as an opportunity or prerequisite for a permanent position.[158] For the multi-skilled workforce there must be opportunities to use the skills developed to ensure they are maintained at a satisfactory level.

Where the task requires the bringing together of workers of differing backgrounds and terms and conditions, there is the potential for tension and commitment problems to develop. As Geary identified, using both permanent and temporary staff working closely together led to frequent problems and animosity between the groups. He elaborated[159]:

> In one instance, the tension between temporary and permanent employees was of such a degree that it compelled the supervisor to stop production for an afternoon so that she could take employees off the shop floor to resolve the differences.
>
> SOURCE: GEARY, J. 1992. Employment flexibility and human resource management. *Training, employment and society*, 6(2):251–270:259.

Geary[160] also noted that similar conflict elsewhere in the plant required the supervisors to spend increasing amounts of time in a close supervisory role, distracting them from their other roles and creating an atmosphere of mistrust. In addition, the ad hoc nature of the recruitment of temporary workers caused problems for supervisors, who complained of the quality and attitude of these employees, also citing an increasing sense of diminished control over the workforce. This case illustrates some of the potential difficulties in managing flexibility.

5.5.2 The employee perspective on flexible patterns of work

The main advantages for employees associated with flexible work patterns include:
- The ability to combine work with outside interests (e.g. career responsibilities or hobbies)
- Greater satisfaction with the job
- Improved motivation
- Less tiredness.

Flexibility can provide the opportunity to combine work with outside activities (which typically implies family commitments). This allows employees to maintain a presence in the workforce, which may not have otherwise been possible.[161] In addition, the increase in part-time work and flexible career paths, and the development of portfolio careers, allows employees to develop the right balance of work, career development, and outside commitments.

Greater satisfaction with the job and improved motivation are associated with employees who have the opportunity to develop their skill range (multi-skilling). The intrinsic opportunity to develop skills by undertaking a wider range of tasks and responsibilities fits in with the theories that underpin the motivational aspects of job design. It may also provide satisfaction for peripheral employees, as it provides them with the appropriate mix of work commitments and outside interests.

The major negative implications of flexible patterns of work for employees include:

• Unequal treatment in terms of pay and benefits
• Reduced opportunities in terms of career
• Limited opportunities for training
• The challenge to the 'psychological contract'
• Increased insecurity of jobs
• Increased stress.

To facilitate the development and the advantages of flexible patterns of work, the employment relationship is likely to be based upon a variation in terms and conditions, as the workforce becomes less uniform. The minimal obligation that the organisation has to the peripheral workforce may mean that their terms, conditions, and employment opportunities are significantly less favourable than those of the full-time, core workforce, despite the fact that they may do work demanding similar skills. These employees provide qualitative flexibility, therefore the very nature of this relationship places less obligation on the employer to invest in their training or development. They are therefore likely to be caught in a permanent pool of low-skilled workers with little opportunity to acquire new skills. For those employees on fixed-term contracts, casual or part-time work, the lack of entitlements, job insecurity, and increased stress go hand in hand with almost non-existent career prospects.

For multi-skilled employees, flexibility is generally interpreted as a skill formation and enhancement process, which provides the employee with relevant and up-to-date skills and therefore increased opportunity to progress within the organisation.[162] Critics of this approach to work organisation point to the de-skilling and work-intensification aspects of the downward enlargement of job profiles which fall within the umbrella term of multi-skilling.[163–167] Employees in this context provide efficiencies through cost-cutting rather than skill development. In an era of increasing shortages of skills, this approach may cause significant recruitment problems and retention problems.

The development of multi-skilling, which by its nature requires employees to increase their range of tasks, combined with the elimination of work restrictions, offers the employer the opportunity to do more with fewer employees, thereby increasing the potential for job insecurity. In addition, the constant change in work demands requires a continual reassessment and renegotiation of the employment relationship. This redefining of role or position of an employee with the organisation can undermine the relationship between the employee and employer. Combined with the increase in stress and potential for job insecurity, these patterns of work can threaten the security of the very employees for whom flexibility was intended as an enhancement.[168]

SUMMARY

This chapter discusses how the development of flexible work patterns requires a shift in approach in the management of human resources to ensure that organisations use and maintain these work patterns to their full potential. The variable nature of the employment relationship with regard to terms and conditions, and the changing demands in an era of skill shortages, requires HR managers to have the prerequisite skills and understanding to balance the changing requirements quickly and with minimal disruption. For example, where an organisation is seeking to develop internal flexibility it must ensure that it provides the training and development required to facilitate such changes. Where it brings a team together from the internal and external environment, management should ensure that terms and conditions are not so different that they create tension or motivation problems and commitment problems. However, these concerns also have to be considered and balanced within the context of attracting and retaining core employees who are highly skilled, in labour markets of skill shortages and strong competition (see *The War for Talent* – Chapter 6).

The development of these various forms of flexibility requires management to plan and be able to use these different work patterns on demand – this requires management to develop a strategic approach to labour requirements and to have the requisite skills to undertake this task. This may mean the development of a pool of subcontractors or part-time employees, who are available as and when required to maximise the utilisation of organisational resources. In addition, the development of such work practices requires the development of a participative and consensual style of management to support, rather than direct, an increasingly skilled workforce in a complex and dynamic environment.

From a senior-management perspective, Pettinger has identified several key themes to ensure the successful implementation, development, and maintenance of flexible patterns of work[169]:

- A long-term commitment to creating the necessary environment and conditions supported and resourced by top management
- A long-term view of the results desired; these do not happen overnight, and the benefits may not be apparent for months or, even, years
- A long-term commitment to creating the required skills, knowledge, attitudes, behaviour, and expertise, including training programmes.

The key model that has been developed to assist in the development of flexible patterns of work is the Institute for Employment Studies's core–periphery model or flexible-firm model. This model has attracted wide attention and criticism; however the core–periphery model has been acknowledged as a framework and a benchmark upon which organisations can draw to develop their own particular 'flexible firm', suited to localised products, markets, and workforces. To facilitate this approach to labour utilisation, there is a need for procedural changes in work practices, in particular the restrictions associated with lines of demarcation, a (re)combination of jobs, and the provision of mechanisms to support and encourage these changes, such as training and development.

Despite the controversy and criticism which surround the area of flexibility, the growing literature on the subject cannot be dismissed. In the same vein, Harvey notes[170] the following: 'The evidence for increased flexibility throughout the capitalist world is simply overwhelming. ... The argument that there is an acute danger of underestimating the significance of any trend towards flexibility ... stares most workers in the face.'

This chapter has explained that the emerging patterns of flexibility are wide and varied. It has noted that, despite this, research suggests that organisations are increasingly adopting the integrative development of multiple forms of flexible patterns of work. Organisations do this to enhance their effectiveness through more efficient utilisation of resources in response to an increasingly turbulent and competitive environment.

KEY CONCEPTS

• Cognitive flexibility	• Internal numerical flexibility
• Contractual flexibility	• Job sharing
• Distancing	• Location flexibility
• Financial flexibility	• Mobility flexibllity
• Flex zones	• Multi-skilling
• Flexibility	• Numerical flexibility
• Flexible firm	• Organisational flexibility
• Flexible patterns of work	• Procedural flexibility
• Flexible specialisation	• Regulatory flexibility
• Functional flexibility	• Virtual flexibility
• Gold-collar workers	• Work-time flexibility

CASE STUDY

Objective: To understand the important role flexible work practices can play within an organisation

Managing diversity for competitive advantage at Deloitte & Touche (now Deloitte.)

In 1992, Deloitte & Touche, LLP, was celebrating the tenth year in which approximately 50 per cent of its new hires were women. Because it takes nearly a decade to become a partner, the Big Six accounting firm based in Wilton, Connecticut, was now sitting back waiting for all the women in the pipeline to start making bids for partnership.

But something unexpected happened. Instead of seeing an increase in the number of women applying for partnership, Deloitte & Touche saw a decline. Talented women were leaving the firm and this represented a huge drain of capable people. In a knowledge-intensive business such as theirs, this problem went beyond social consciousness. The success of the firm was at stake. They could not afford to lose valued partners.

To address the problem, the company formed the Task Force on the Retention and Advancement of Women to pinpoint the reason women were leaving. The task force conducted a massive information gathering initiative, interviewing women at all levels of the company, even contacting women who had left the firm. The task force uncovered three main areas of complaint: (1) a work environment that limited opportunity for advancement, (2) exclusion from mentoring and networking, and (3) work and family issues.

The networking and mentoring concerns seemed to be the most troublesome. In a male-dominated business, men often network, sometimes to the exclusion of women. To tackle this problem, Deloitte & Touche retooled the work environment. It made changes such as a renewed commitment to flexible work arrangements, reduced workload and flexitime. The firm also developed plans for company-sponsored networking and formal career planning for women. In addition, the firm's 5 000 partners and managers attended two-day workshops called 'Men and women as colleagues' at a price to the company of approximately $3 million.

The results have been terrific. Retention of women at all levels has risen, and for the first time in the history of the firm, turnover rates for senior managers (just before making partner) have been lower for women than for men. In addition, in 1995 the company promoted its highest percentage of new partners who were women (21 per cent). Deloitte & Touche is basking in its new reputation as a women-friendly firm: It now has the most female employees in the Big Six (52 per cent of new hires). This gives them external recognition in the market place and not only helps them with recruiting but also gives them a laudable reputation with their customers. Apart from strictly diversity concerns, the business reasons for making these changes are coming home very quickly. For its efforts, Deloitte & Touche received *Personnel Journal*'s 1996 Optimas Award for Competitive Advantage.

Questions and activities

1. How did the problems at Deloitte & Touche occur in the first place?
2. Did the changes fix the underlying problems? Explain.
3. What other advice would you give Deloitte & Touche's managers?

SOURCE: BOHLANDER, G. 1996. Firm's diversity efforts even the playing field. *Personnel Journal*, January:56 (*In* Sherman, A., Bohlander, G. & Snell, S. 1998. *Managing human resources* 11th ed. Cincinnati, Ohio: South-Western Publishing (an ITP Company):35–36. Used with permission.

REVIEW QUESTIONS AND ACTIVITIES

1. A major goal implicit in the idea of flexible labour is to render HRM as a strategic activity. By this is meant a multifold process involving a number of issues. Discuss briefly.
2. Explain the major differences between numerical flexibility and functional flexibility.
3. Explain the major differences between financial flexibility and procedural flexibility.
4. What are the key advantages and disadvantages of flexible patterns of work from the employer's perspective?
5. What are the key advantages and disadvantages of flexible patterns of work from an employee's perspective?

6. Briefly discuss why is it important to develop and manage flexible patterns of work.
7. List 10 organisational and management practices organisations can use to determine whether they are ready for flex work.
8. Briefly outline the flexible-firm model, including a discussion of its merits and criticisms.
9. List the characteristics of the gold-collar worker and discuss how this new type of employee affects organisational flexibility.
10. Write a short essay on flexibility.

FURTHER READING

DYCHTWALD, K., ERICKSON, T. J. & MORISON, R. 2006. *Workforce crisis: how to beat the coming shortage of skills and talent.* Boston, Massachusetts: Harvard Business School Press.

GANDOSSY, R.P., TUCKER, E. & VERMA, N. 2006. *Workforce wake-up call: your workforce is changing, are you?* New Jersey: John Wiley & Sons.

REILLY, P. 2001. *Flexibility at work: Balancing the interests of employer and employee.* Hampshire: Gower Publishing.

WEB SITES

www.washington.edu/admin/hr/roles/mgr/flexwork/index.html – flexible work arrangements at the University of Washington

www.hr.upenn.edu/quality/worklife/flexoptions/training.asp – flexible work arrangements – University of Pennsylvania (Human Resources)

ENDNOTES

1. SENGENBERGER, W. 1992. Intensified competition, industrial restructuring and industrial relations. *International labour review*, 131(2):139–154.
2. LIEMT, G. V. 1992. Economic globalisation: labour options and business strategies in high labour cost countries. *International labour review*, 131(4–5):453–470.
3. KROLL, K. M. 2007. Let's get flexible. *HR magazine*, 52(4):97–100.
4. ATKINSON, J. 1984. Manpower strategies for flexible organisations. *Personnel management*, 28–31(August); MEISINGER, S. 2007. Flexible schedules make powerful perks. *HR magazine*, 52(4):12.
5. ATKINSON, J. 1987. Flexibility or fragmentation? The United Kingdom labour market in the eighties. *Labour & society*, 12(1):87–105.
6. HAKIM, C. 1987. Trends in flexible workforce. *Employment gazette*, 95(November):549–560.

7. HAKIM, C. 1990. Core and periphery in employers' workforce strategies: evidence from the 1987 ELUS survey. *Work, employment and society*, 4(2):157–188.
8. BLYTON, P. 1992. Flexible times?: recent trends in temporal flexibility. *Industrial relations journal*, 23(1):26–36; HARRIS, P. 2007. Flexible work policies mean business. *Training & development*, April:32–36.
9. BLYTON, P. & MORRIS, J. 1991. *A flexible future? Prospects for employment and organization.* Berlin: De Gruyter.
10. BLYTON, P. & MORRIS, J. 1992. HRM and the limits of flexibility. (*In* Blyton, P. & Turnbull, P. (eds). *Reassessing human resource management.* London: Sage:116–130.)
11. PROCTER, S. J., ROWLINSON, M., MCARDLE, L., HASSARD, J. & FORRESTER, P. 1994. Flexibility, politics and strategy: in defence of the model of the flexible firm. *Work, employment and society*, 8(2):221–242.

12. LEGGE, K. 1995. *Human resource management: Rhetorics and realities*. London: Macmillan.
13. URSELL, G. D. 1991. Human resource management and labour flexibility: some reflections based on cross–national and sectoral studies in Canada and the UK. (*In* Blyton, P. & Morris, J. 1991. *A flexible future? Prospects for employment and organization*. Berlin: De Gruyter:311–327:312.)
14. STOREY, J. 1991. Introduction: from personnel management to human resource management. (*In* Storey, J. (ed.), *New perspectives on human resource management*. London: Routledge:1–18.)
15. MCGRAW, P. 1997. HRM – history, models, process and directions. (*In* Kramar, R., McGraw, P. & Schuler, R. *Human resource management in Australia* 3rd ed. Melbourne: Longman:44–86.)
16. HAKIM, C. 1990. Core and periphery in employers' workforce strategies: evidence from the 1987 ELUS survey. *Work, employment and society*, 4(2):157–188.
17. BLYTON, P. & MORRIS, J. 1991. *A flexible future? Prospects for employment and organization*. Berlin: De Gruyter.
18. WOODS, S. 1989. *The transformation of work: Skill, flexibility and the labour process*. London: Unwin-Hyman; HISLOP, D. & AXTELL, C. 2007. The neglect of spatial mobility in contemporary studies of work: the case of telework. *New technology, work and employment*, 22(1):34–51.
19. ATKINSON, J. 1984. Manpower strategies for flexible organisations. *Personnel management*, 28–31(August).
20. ORGANISATION FOR ECONOMIC CO–OPERATION AND DEVELOPMENT (OECD). 1986. *Labour market flexibility*. Report by a high-level group of experts to the Secretary-General. Paris: OECD.
21. ORGANISATION FOR ECONOMIC CO–OPERATION AND DEVELOPMENT (OECD). 1990. *Labour market policies for the 1990s*. Paris, OECD.
22. GUEST, D. 1991. Human resource management: Its implications for industrial relations and trade unions. (*In* Storey, J. (ed.). *New perspectives on human resource management*. London: Routledge:41–55.); BAMBER, G. 1990. Flexible work organisation: inferences from Britain and Australia. *Asia Pacific journal of human resource management*, 28(3):28–44; BRODT, T. L. & VERBURG, R. M. 2007. Managing mobile work – insights from European practice. *New technology, work and employment*, 22(1):52–65.
23. PILBEAM, S. & CORBRIDGE, M. 2006. *People Resourcing – contemporary HRM in practice* 3rd ed. Harlow, England: Pearson Education Ltd.
24. ATKINSON, J. 1984. Manpower strategies for flexible organisations. *Personnel management*, 28–31(August):28.
25. TREU, T. 1992. Labour market flexibility in Europe. *International labour review*, 131(4):497–512. See also SELS, L. & HUYS, R. 1999. Towards a flexible future? The nature of organisational response in the clothing industry. *New technology, work and employment*, 14(2):113–128; TIENARI, J. & TAINIO, R. 1999. The myth of flexibility in organisational change. *Scandinavian journal of management*, 15:351–384; KOSSEK, E. E., BARBER, A. E. & WINTERS, D. 1999. Using flexible schedules in the managerial world: the power of peers. *Human resource management*, 38(1):33–46.
26. ATKINSON, J. 1984. Manpower strategies for flexible organisations. *Personnel management*, 28–31(August).
27. Ibid.
28. RIMMER, M. & ZAPPALA, J. 1988. Labour market flexibility and the second tier. *Australian bulletin of labour*, 14(4):564–591.
29. NATIONAL ECONOMIC DEVELOPMENT OFFICE (NEDO) 1986. *Changing work patterns*. Brighton: Institute of Manpower Studies/National Economic Development Office.
30. Ibid.
31. ORGANISATION FOR ECONOMIC CO-OPERATION AND DEVELOPMENT (OECD). 1986. *Labour market flexibility*. Report by a high-level group of experts to the Secretary-General. Paris: OECD.
32. RIMMER, M. & ZAPPALA, J. 1988. Labour market flexibility and the second tier. *Australian bulletin of labour*, 14(4):567.
33. BLYTON, P. 1992. Flexible times?: recent trends in temporal flexibility. *Industrial relations journal*, 23(1):26–36.
34. NELSON, L. & HOLLAND, P. 1999. The impact of 12 hour shifts: the views of managers and unions. *Asia Pacific journal of human resource management*, 37(3):27–34.
35. HERRIOT, P. 1998. The role of the HRM function in building a new proposition for staff. (*In* Sparrow, P. & Marchington, M. (eds). *Human resource management: The new agenda*. London: Financial Times/Pitman):106–114.)
36. ATKINSON, J. 1984. Manpower strategies for flexible organisations. *Personnel management*, 28–31(August):29.
37. BOYER, R. 1988. *The search for labour market flexibility: The European economies in transition*. Oxford: Clarendon Press.
38. WOODS, S. 1989. *The transformation of work: Skill, flexibility and the labour process*. London: Unwin-Hyman:1.
39. MATHEWS, J. 1989. *Tools of change: New technology and the democratisation of work*. Sydney: Pluto Press.
40. BAMBER, G. 1990. Flexible work organisation: inferences from Britain and Australia. *Asia Pacific journal of human resource management*, 28(3):28–44.
41. GRINT, K. 1991. *The sociology of work*. Cambridge: Policy Press.

42. RIMMER, M. & ZAPPALA, J. 1988. Labour market flexibility and the second tier. *Australian bulletin of labour*, 14(4):537.

43. ATKINSON, J. 1984. Manpower strategies for flexible organisations. *Personnel management*, 28–31(August).

44. HAKIM, C. 1987. Trends in flexible workforce. *Employment gazette*, 95(November):549–560.

45. MATHEWS, J. 1989. *Tools of change: New technology and the democratisation of work*. Sydney: Pluto Press.

46. PROCTER, S. J., ROWLINSON, M., MCARDLE, L., HASSARD, J. & FORRESTER, P. 1994. Flexibility, politics and strategy: in defence of the model of the flexible firm. *Work, employment and society*, 8(2):221–242.

47. BAMBER, G. 1990. Flexible work organisation: inferences from Britain and Australia. *Asia Pacific journal of human resource management*, 28(3):28–44.

48. Ibid.

49. SPARROW, P. & MARCHINGTON, M. 1998. Introduction: Is HRM in crisis? (*In* Sparrow, P. & Marchington, M. (eds). *Human resource management: The new agenda*. London: Financial Times/Pitman:3–20:19.)

50. MORRISON, D. 1994. Psychological contracts and change. *Human resource management*, 33(3):353–372.

51. GREENHAUS, J. H. & CALLANAN, G. A. 1994. *Career management* 2nd ed. Fort Worth: Dryden Press.

52. ROSSEAU, D. M. 1995. *Psychological contracts in organisations: Understanding written and unwritten agreements*. Thousand Oaks, C.A.: Sage.

53. ATKINSON, J. 1984. Manpower strategies for flexible organisations. *Personnel management*, 28–31(August).

54. SPARROW, P. & MARCHINGTON, M. 1998. Introduction: Is HRM in crisis? (*In* Sparrow, P. & Marchington, M. (eds). *Human resource management: The new agenda*. London: Financial Times/Pitman:3–20:19.)

55. GUEST, D. 1991. Human resource management: Its implications for industrial relations and trade unions. (*In* Storey, J. (ed.). *New perspectives on human resource management*. London: Routledge:41–55.)

56. HASSARD, J. & PARKER, D. 1993. *Postmodernism and organisations*. London: Sage. See for example 1998. *International journal of human resource management*, 9(3).

57. This section is based on the work done by Dychtwald, Erickson, & Morison and published in DYCHTWALD, K., ERICKSON, T. J. & MORISON, R. 2006. *Workforce crisis: How to beat the coming shortage of skills and talent*. Boston, Massachusetts: Harvard Business School Publishing:154–155.

58. NATIONAL ECONOMIC DEVELOPMENT OFFICE (NEDO) 1986. *Changing work patterns*. Brighton: Institute of Manpower Studies/National Economic Development Office.

59. HAKIM, C. 1987. Trends in flexible workforce. *Employment gazette*, 95(November):549–560.

60. BAMBER, G., BOREHAM, P. & HARLEY, B. 1992. *Economic and industrial relations outcomes of different forms of flexibility in Australian industry: An analysis of the AWIRS data*. Exploring industrial relations rurther analysis of AWIRS, 4 (Industrial Relations Research Series) (ed.). Canberra: AGPS Press:1–70.

61. THOMPSON, P. & MCHUGH, D. 1995. *Work organisation: A critical introduction* 2nd ed. London: Macmillan Business.

62. SPARROW, P. & MARCHINGTON, M. 1998. Introduction: Is HRM in crisis? (*In* Sparrow, P. & Marchington, M. (eds). *Human resource management: The new agenda*. London: Financial Times/Pitman:3–20:19.)

63. ATKINSON, J. 1984. Manpower strategies for flexible organisations. *Personnel management*, 28–31(August).

64. PROCTER, S. J., ROWLINSON, M., MCARDLE, L., HASSARD, J. & FORRESTER, P. 1994. Flexibility, politics and strategy: in defence of the model of the flexible firm. *Work, employment and society*, 8(2):221–242.

65. ATKINSON, J. 1984. Manpower strategies for flexible organisations. *Personnel management*, 28–31(August).

66. ATKINSON, J. & MEAGER, N. 1986. *New forms of work organisation*, Report 121. Brighton: Institute of Manpower Studies.

67. ATKINSON, J. & GREGORY, D. 1986. Is flexibility just a flash in the pan? *Personnel management*, September:26–29.

68. THOMPSON, P. & MCHUGH, D. 1995. *Work organisation: A critical introduction* 2nd ed. London: Macmillan Business:174–175.

69. ATKINSON, J. 1984. Manpower strategies for flexible organisations. *Personnel management*, 28–31(August).

70. NATIONAL ECONOMIC DEVELOPMENT OFFICE (NEDO) 1986. *Changing work patterns*. Brighton: Institute of Manpower Studies/National Economic Development Office.

71. WOODS, S. 1989. *The transformation of work: Skill, flexibility and the labour process*. London: Unwin-Hyman:1.

72. ATKINSON, J. 1984. Manpower strategies for flexible organisations. *Personnel management*, 28–31(August).

73. HAKIM, C. 1987. Trends in flexible workforce. *Employment gazette*, 95(November):549–560.

74. WOODS, S. 1989. *The transformation of work: Skill, flexibility and the labour process*. London: Unwin-Hyman:1.

75. ATKINSON, J. 1984. Manpower strategies for flexible organisations. *Personnel management*, 28–31(August):20.

76. MORRIS, J. & IMRIE, R. 1991. *Transforming buyer–supplier relations: Japanese style industrial practices in a Western context.* London: Macmillan.

77. ATKINSON, J. 1984. Manpower strategies for flexible organisations. *Personnel management*, 28–31(August).

78. ATKINSON, J. 1987. Flexibility or fragmentation? The United Kingdom labour market in the eighties. *Labour & society*, 12(1):87–105.

79. BLYTON, P. & MORRIS, J. 1991. *A flexible future? Prospects for employment and organization.* Berlin: De Gruyter.

80. BURGESS, J. 1997. The flexible firm and the growth of non-standard employment. *Labour & industry*, 7(3):85–102.

81. ATKINSON, J. 1984. Manpower strategies for flexible organisations. *Personnel management*, 28–31(August).

82. ATKINSON, J. 1985. The changing corporation. (*In* Clutterbuck, D. (ed.). *New patterns of work.* Aldershot: Gowers:13–34.)

83. POLLERT, A. 1988. Dismantling flexibility. *Capital and class*, (34):42–75.

84. POLLERT, A. 1991. The orthodoxy of flexibility. (*In* Pollert, A. (ed.). *Farewell to flexibility?* Oxford: Blackwell:3–31.)

85. MACINNES, J. 1988. The question of flexibility. *Personnel review*, 17(1):12–15.

86. HORSTMAN, B. 1988. Labour flexibility strategies and management style. *Journal of industrial relations*, 30(3):412–431.

87. HUNTER, L., MCGREGOR, A., MACINNES, J. & SPROULL, A. 1993. The flexible firm: strategy and segmentation. *British journal of industrial relations*, 31(3):383–407.

88. PROCTER, S. J., ROWLINSON, M., MCARDLE, L., HASSARD, J. & FORRESTER, P. 1994. Flexibility, politics and strategy: in defence of the model of the flexible firm. *Work, employment and society*, 8(2):221–242.

89. LEGGE, K. 1995. *Human resource management: Rhetorics and realities.* London: Macmillan.

90. BURGESS, J. 1997. The flexible firm and the growth of non-standard employment. *Labour & industry*, 7(3):85–102.

91. NATIONAL ECONOMIC DEVELOPMENT OFFICE (NEDO) 1986. *Changing work patterns.* Brighton: Institute of Manpower Studies/National Economic Development Office.

92. WOODS, S. 1989. *The transformation of work: Skill, flexibility and the labour process.* London: Unwin-Hyman:1.

93. PROCTER, S. J., ROWLINSON, M., MCARDLE, L., HASSARD, J. & FORRESTER, P. 1994. Flexibility, politics and strategy: in defence of the model of the flexible firm. *Work, employment and society*, 8(2):221–242.

94. MACINNES, J. 1988. The question of flexibility. *Personnel review*, 17(1):12–15.

95. POLLERT, A. 1988. Dismantling flexibility. *Capital and class*, (34):42–75.

96. POLLERT, A. 1991. The orthodoxy of flexibility. (*In* Pollert, A. (ed.). *Farewell to flexibility?* Oxford: Blackwell:3–31.)

97. BURROWS, R., GILBERT, N. & POLLERT, A. 1992. Introduction: Fordism, post Fordism and economic flexibility. (*In* Gilbert, N., Burrows, R. & Pollert, A. (ed.). *Fordism and flexibility.* London: Macmillan:1–12.)

98. HORSTMAN, B. 1988. Labour flexibility strategies and management style. *Journal of industrial relations*, 30(3):412–431.

99. HUNTER, L., MCGREGOR, A., MACINNES, J. & SPROULL, A. 1993. The flexible firm: strategy and segmentation. *British journal of industrial relations*, 31(3):383–407.

100. TRADE UNION COUNCIL (TUC). 1986. *Flexibility: A trade union response.* London: TUC.

101. BROOKES, B. 1990. Labour flexibility and employment law: the new order. *The economics and labour relations review*, 1(June):107–120.

102. TRADE UNION COUNCIL (TUC). 1986. *Flexibility: A trade union response.* London: TUC.

103. GRINT, K. 1991. *The sociology of work.* Cambridge: Policy Press.

104. HYMAN, R. 1991. The theory of production and the production of theory. (*In* Pollert, A. (ed.). *Farewell to flexibility?* Oxford: Blackwell:3–31.)

105. MACINNES, J. 1988. The question of flexibility. *Personnel review*, 17(1):12–15.

106. POLLERT, A. 1991. The orthodoxy of flexibility. (*In* Pollert, A. (ed.). *Farewell to flexibility?* Oxford: Blackwell:3–31.)

107. PENN, R. 1992. Flexibility in Britain during the 1980s: recent empirical evidence. (*In* Gilbert, N., Burrows, R. & Pollert, A. (eds) *Fordism and flexibility.* London: Macmillan:66–86.)

108. HUNTER, L., MCGREGOR, A., MACINNES, J. & SPROULL, A. 1993. The flexible firm: strategy and segmentation. *British journal of industrial relations*, 31(3):383–407.

109. LEGGE, K. 1995. *Human resource management: Rhetorics and realities.* London: Macmillan.

110. HAKIM, C. 1987. Trends in flexible workforce. *Employment gazette*, 95(November):549–560.

111. POLLERT, A. 1988. Dismantling flexibility. *Capital and class*, (34):42–75.

112. POLLERT, A. 1991. The orthodoxy of flexibility. (*In* Pollert, A. (ed.). *Farewell to flexibility?* Oxford: Blackwell:3–31.)

113. HORSTMAN, B. 1988. Labour flexibility strategies and management style. *Journal of industrial relations*, 30(3):412–431.

114. HUNTER, L., MCGREGOR, A., MACINNES, J. & SPROULL, A. 1993. The flexible firm: strategy and segmentation. *British journal of industrial relations*, 31(3):383–407.

115. WILKINSON, F. & WHITE, M. 1994. Product market pressures and employer responses. (*In* Rubery, J. & Wilkinson, F. (eds). *Employer strategies and the labour market.* Oxford: Oxford University Press:111–137.)

116. LEGGE, K. 1995. *Human resource management: Rhetorics and realities.* London: Macmillan.

117. NATIONAL ECONOMIC DEVELOPMENT OFFICE (NEDO). 1986. *Changing work patterns.* Brighton: Institute of Manpower Studies/National Economic Development Office.

118. WOODS, S. 1989. *The transformation of work: Skill, flexibility and the labour process.* London: Unwin-Hyman:1.

119. BAMBER, G. 1990. Flexible work organisation: inferences from Britain and Australia. *Asia Pacific journal of human resource management,* 28(3):28–44.

120. GARRAIIAN, P. & STEWART, P. 1992. *The Nissan enigma: Flexibility at work in a local economy.* London: Mansell.

121. PROCTER, S. J., ROWLINSON, M., MCARDLE, L., HASSARD, J. & FORRESTER, P. 1994. Flexibility, politics and strategy: in defence of the model of the flexible firm. *Work, employment and society,* 8(2):221–242.

122. BURGESS, J. 1997. The flexible firm and the growth of non-standard employment. *Labour & industry,* 7(3):85–102.

123. ACIRRT. 1999. *Australia at work: Just managing.* Sydney: Prentice Hall.

124. ROSSEAU, D. M. 1995. *Psychological contracts in organisations: Understanding written and unwritten agreements.* Thousand Oaks, C.A.: Sage.

125. NEWELL, S., ROBERTSON, M., SCARBROUGH, H. & SWAN, J. 2002. *Managing knowledge work.* Hampshire: Palgrave.

126. SCARBROUGH, H. & SWAN, J. 2003. Discourses of knowledge management and the learning organization. Their production and consumption. (*In* Easterby-Smith, M. & Lyles, M. (eds). *Handbook of organizational learning and knowledge management.* Oxford: Backwell.)

127. NONAKA, I., TOYAMA, R. & BYOSIERE, P. 2001. A theory of organizational knowledge creation: Understanding the dynamic process of creating knowledge. IPD South West London: Kingston Business School. [Paper.]

128. BARNES, D. 1999. *Perspectives on total rewards: Recruitment and retention.* New York: Towers Perrin.

129. STOREY, J. & QUINTAS, P. 2001. Knowledge management and HRM. (*In* Storey, J. (ed.). *Human resource management: A critical text.* London: Thomson Learning.)

130. HOLLAND, P., HECKER, R. & STEEN, J. 2002. Human resource strategies and organisational structures for managing gold-collar workers. *Journal of European industrial training,* 26:72–80.

131. ARNOLD, J. 1996. The psychological contract: A concept in need of closer scrutiny? *European journal of work and organizational psychology,* 5(4):511–520.

132. NEWELL, S., ROBERTSON, M., SCARBROUGH, H. & SWAN, J. 2002. *Managing knowledge work.* Hampshire: Palgrave.

133. STEEN, J. & INNES, P. 2000. *Fortress or sponge? Using organisational structure to manage the flow of information in Australian R&D intensive firms.* Tasmania: University of Tasmania. [School of Management Working Paper 20–01.]

134. GRANOVETTER, M. S. 1973. The strength of weak ties. *American journal of sociology,* 78(6):1360–1381.

135. TSOUKAS, H. 1996. The firm as a distributed knowledge system: a constructionist approach. *Strategic management journal,* 17:11–25.

136. SCARBROUGH, H. & SWAN, J. 2003. Discourses of knowledge management and the learning organization. Their production and consumption. (*In* Easterby-Smith, M. & Lyles, M. (eds). *Handbook of organizational learning and knowledge management.* Oxford: Backwell.)

137. HOLLAND, P., HECKER, R. & STEEN, J. 2002. Human resource strategies and organisational structures for managing gold-collar workers. *Journal of European industrial training,* 26:72–80.

138. STOREY, J. & QUINTAS, P. 2001. Knowledge management and HRM. (*In* Storey, J. (ed.). *Human resource management: A critical text.* London: Thomson Learning.)

139. MACDONALD, S. 1998. *Information for innovation.* Oxford: Oxford University Press.

140. MACDONALD, S. 1989. Headhunting in high technology. *Technovation,* 4:233–245.

141. MACDONALD, S. 1998. *Information for innovation.* Oxford: Oxford University Press.

142. DAVENPORT, T. H. & PRUSAK, L. 1998. *Working knowledge: How organizations manage what they know.* Boston: Harvard Business School Press.

143. HIBBARD, J. & CARILLO, K. M. 1998. Knowledge revolution: Getting employees to share what they know is no longer a technology challenge it's a corporate culture challenge. *Information week:*663.

144. SCARBROUGH, H. & SWAN, J. 2003. Discourses of knowledge management and the learning organization. Their production and consumption. (*In* Easterby-Smith, M. & Lyles, M. (eds). *Handbook of organizational learning and knowledge management.* Oxford: Backwell.)

145. KAMOCHE, K. & MUELLER, F. 1998. Human resource management and the appropriation-learning perspective. *Human relations,* 51:1033–1061.

146. MACDONALD, S. 1989. Headhunting in high technology. *Technovation,* 4:233–245.

147. HOLLAND, P., HECKER, R. & STEEN, J. 2002. Human resource strategies and organisational structures for managing gold-collar workers. *Journal of European industrial training,* 26:72–80.

148. SCARBROUGH, H., SWAN, J. & PRESTON, J. 1999. *Knowledge management: A review of the literature.* London: Institute of Personnel and Development:18.

149. STOREY, J. & QUINTAS, P. 2001. Knowledge management and HRM. (*In* Storey, J. (ed.). *Human resource management: A critical text.* London: Thomson Learning.)

150. SPARROW, P. & MARCHINGTON, M. 1998. Introduction: Is HRM in crisis? (*In* Sparrow, P. & Marchington, M. (eds). *Human resource management: The new agenda.* London: Financial Times/Pitman:3–20.)

151. EMMOTT, M. & HUTCHINSON, S. 1998. Employment flexibility: Threat or promise? (*In* Sparrow, P. & Marchington, M. (eds). *Human resource management: The new agenda.* London: Financial Times/Pitman.)

152. See also EVANS, J. S. 1991. Strategic flexibility for high technology manoeuvres: a conceptual framework. *Journal of management studies,* 28(1):69–89.

153. BENT, S. 1998. The psychological effects of extended working hours. (In Heiler, K. (ed.). *The 12 hour workday: Emerging issues.* Sydney: University of Sydney:27–33. [ACCIRT Working Paper 51.]

154. SPURGEON, A., HARRINGTON, J. M. & COOPER, C. L. 1997. Health and safety problems associated with long working hours: a review of the current position. *Occupational and environmental medicine,* 54(6):367–375.

155. BAKER, K., OLSEN, J. & MORISSEAU, D. 1994. Work practices, fatigue and nuclear power plant safety performance. *Human factors,* 36(2):244–257.

156. PETTINGER, R. 1998. *Managing the flexible workforce.* London: Cassell.

157. NELSON, L. & HOLLAND, P. 1999. The impact of 12 hour shifts: the views of managers and unions. *Asia Pacific journal of human resource management.*

158. ATKINSON, J. & RICK, J. 1996. *Temporary work and the labour market.* Report 311. Brighton: Institute of Employment Studies.

159. GEARY, J. 1992. Employment flexibility and human resource management. *Work, employment and society,* 6(2):251–270:259.

160. Ibid.

161. LEGGE, K. 1995. *Human resource management: Rhetorics and realities.* London: Macmillan.

162. ATKINSON, J. 1984. Manpower strategies for flexible organisations. *Personnel management,* 28–31(August).

163. POLLERT, A. 1988. Dismantling flexibility. *Capital and class,* (34):42–75.

164. POLLERT, A. 1991. The orthodoxy of flexibility. (In Pollert, A. (ed.). *Farewell to flexibility?* Oxford: Blackwell:3–31.)

165. TRADE UNION COUNCIL (TUC). 1986. *Flexibility: A trade union response.* London: TUC.

166. GARRAHAN, P. & STEWART, P. 1992. *The Nissan enigma: Flexibility at work in a local economy.* London: Mansell.

167. LEGGE, K. 1995. *Human resource management: Rhetorics and realities.* London: Macmillan.

168. HERRIOT, P. & ANDERSON, N. 1997. Selecting for change: how will personnel and selection psychology survive? (*In* Anderson, N. & Herriot, P. (eds). *International handbook of selection and assessment.* Chichester: John Wiley.)

169. PETTINGER, R. 1998. *Managing the flexible workforce.* London: Cassell:3–4.

170. HARVEY, D. 1989. *The conditions of post modernity.* Oxford: Blackwell:191.

6

Talent management – An HR challenge

Learning outcomes

After reading this chapter you should be able to:

▶ Define the concept 'talent'
▶ Discuss the changing dynamics of the workplace in the twenty-first century facilitating an increased emphasis on talent management
▶ List the five key areas to make talent a source of competitive advantage
▶ Discuss the reasons for the perceived increasing shortages of skills
▶ Discuss strategies for dealing with the 'war for talent'

Purpose

The purpose of this chapter is to introduce you to the concept of talent management.

Chapter overview

This chapter begins by exploring the changing dynamics of the workplace in the twenty-first century. It then looks at two issues, namely human capital theory and the resource-based view (RBV) of the company (we first discussed the RBV in Chapter 2). Thereafter it explores talent management and the reasons for the increasing worldwide shortages of skills. It finally takes a look at the building of a new paradigm to make talent a source of competitive advantage and discusses strategies for dealing with the 'war for talent'. The concluding case study illustrates how the theory contained in this chapter can be applied to a practical situation.

Introduction

In the first decade of the twenty-first century there is a growing recognition of the changing nature of the employment relationship.[1] The production base of advanced economies is evolving from having an industrial focus to having a focus on service and knowledge. This has contributed to a shift in the nature of work, and an increasing recognition of the individual employee as the primary source of competitiveness[2] (see Chapter 2). As a result of this focus on the employee, the HR function has the potential to assume an increasingly critical and dynamic role in generating a sustainable competitive advantage through people by focusing on the development of diverse policies, practices, and systems to attract, retain, and develop these key resources.[3]

The recognition of the role of HR has come at a time of major change in the nature of the labour market. Increasing shortages of skills in many advanced economies, combined with a generation of workers focused on employability rather than employment, have been the catalyst for a shift away from the traditional employer–employee relationship, and created a major change in the balance of power in this relationship.[4] In addition, declining birth rates in most countries over the last two decades have exacerbated, and will continue to exacerbate, the growing shortage in labour and skills – a shortage which is only now starting to become apparent.[5] Although, as both Cappelli[6] and Critchley[7] argue, this may be more to do with contemporary employment and retirement trends than demographic issues associated with growing shortages in labour and skills. Despite the differing perspective, it is clear that in this emerging world of work, if organisations are to remain competitive, the management of talented employees will be a key focus and fundamentally different to the latter half of the twentieth century.[8] Many recruitment advertisements ask for talented people, yet if organisations are lucky enough to recruit a talented individual, they often experience difficulty in engaging or retaining him or her.[9] This chapter explores the HRM trends and issues arising from the required new perspective associated with building and retaining human resources to build a sustained competitive advantage – also known as talent management.

6.1 Attraction and retention – a theoretical perspective

In recent years, the attraction and retention of employees have become increasingly significant aspects of contemporary HRM. A review of the literature reveals two theoretical perspectives which provide a framework for analysing the strategic approach linked to the long-term development of the organisation's human resources. The first is human capital theory, which links investment in the organisation's key asset, its employees, to increased productivity and sustained competitive advantage.[10] The strategic aspect is the long-term enhancement of the firm's resource base by linking employees' skill development with retention through training and development, career management, and progression.[11] This is also consistent with the second theoretical perspective, the RBV of the firm[12] (see Chapter 2). The focus of the RBV is on an organisation retaining and developing these human resources through investments such as human resource development (HRD) strategies. This retention and development will ensure that these assets become valuable, rare, and difficult to imitate, enhancing further the organisation's competitive advantage.[13] Many scholars have adopted these theoretical approaches in interpreting the essential elements in building a competitive organisational advantage.[14]

It is possible to link the strategic focus on the management and development of human resources to the deliberate promotion of HRD strategies as a catalyst for the attraction and retention of talented employees. This has led to an increased focus on HRM as a platform for building a competitive advantage. A critical element is the strategic development of diverse strategies for staff enhancement and development as important tools for both attraction and retention. Organisations taking the strategic course will seek a long-term and diverse approach to managing and investing in their human resources, to ensure that appropriate training and development are available to all employees.

The management of learning and knowledge within organisations in an ever more complex role for HRM in the creation of a competitive advantage – a theme which is increasingly reflected in the literature.[15] In a dynamic environment, this means that the organisations must commit resources to develop a diverse and adaptive approach, to ensure that each area within the organisation has access to appropriate levels of training and development to meet diverse organisational objectives.

6.2 Talent management and the demographic time-bomb

Talent management, which involves the cooperation and communication of managers at all levels, has become an imperative in the face of today's business challenges. In addition, talent-management processes must be more strategic, connected, and broad-based than ever before. Talent-management processes include workforce

planning, talent-gap analysis, recruitment, selection, education and development, retention, talent reviews, succession planning, and evaluation (see Figure 1.3 in Chapter 1 as well as Figure 6.1 below). To drive performance, deal with an increasingly rapid pace of change, and create sustainable success, a company must integrate and align these processes with its business strategies. By assessing available talent and placing the right people in the best roles, companies can survive and thrive in today's increasingly competitive environment.[16]

In attempting to quantify talent, Michaels, Handfield-Jones, and Axelrod[17] have argued in its broadest sense that, 'Talent is the sum of the person's abilities – his or her intrinsic gifts, skills, knowledge, experience, intelligence, judgement, attitude, character and drive. It also includes his or her ability to learn and grow.'

Talent management has become increasingly important in the more industrialised economies over the last two decades for a variety of reasons. Over the second half of the twentieth century, population trends across most industrialised

Figure 6.1 Talent-management system

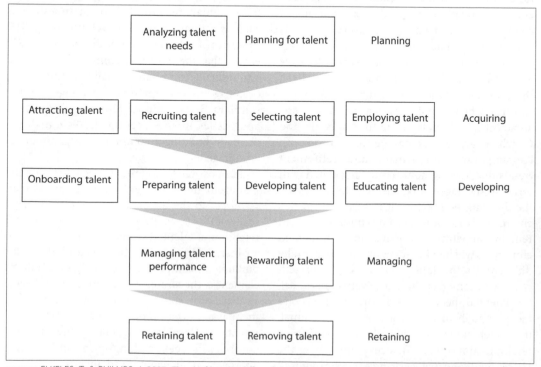

SOURCE: ELKELES, T. & PHILLIPS, J. 2007. *The chief learning officer: Driving value within a changing organisation through learning and development.* Oxford: Butterworth-Heinemann, an imprint of Elsevier:234. Used with permission.

countries revealed almost static populations and declining birth rates. In the period between 1990 and 2003 the population growth rates for most of these countries averaged 0,6 per cent per annum.[18] This has generated growing concern for the long-term supply of labour in the market as the first wave of baby boomers reaches retirement age. For the foreseeable future, under current strategies for employment, more people will be leaving the workforce than joining it.[19]

A global study by the Boston Consulting Group (BCG)[20] in 2003 estimated a shortfall in skilled labour worldwide of the order of 60 million by 2020. The USA will face a labour shortage of 17 million; Japan, 9 million; China, 10 million; Russia, 6 million; Germany, 3 million; France, 3 million; Spain, 3 million; and the UK, 2 million.

In 1998, research by McKinsey & Co. – entitled *The war for talent* and involving 77 companies and almost 6 000 managers and executives in the USA – highlighted the importance of the coming skill-shortage crisis. The report identified that the principal corporate resource over the next 20 years will be talent, which, due to identified demographic changes, will become increasingly difficult to find for which it will be costly to battle.[21] The research recommended a fundamental change in organisations' HR practices, including finding more imaginative ways to attract and retain this talent. The report also identified that 75 per cent of organisations in the survey either did not have enough talent or were chronically short of talent. This shortage was highlighted by another survey undertaken in 2006. In January 2006, staffing service provider Manpower Inc. conducted a *Talent Shortage Survey* of nearly 33 000 employers across 23 countries and territories. The survey asked employers which positions they had difficulty filling. The following results were found in order of importance[22]:

1. Sales representatives
2. Engineers
3. Technicians (primarily production and operations, engineering, and maintenance)
4. Production operators
5. Skilled manual trades (primarily carpenters, welders, and plumbers)
6. IT staff (primarily programmers and developers)
7. Administrative and personal assistants
8. Drivers
9. Accountants
10. Management and executives.

These scenarios, however, have been challenged. Both Cappelli[23] and Critchley[24], for example, have acknowledged the changing demographics but argue that the critical flaws in the scenarios suggested above are that they assume employment strategies and relationships will not adapt accordingly. As Cappelli argues[25]:

> Many of the studies that foresee labour shortages in the future assume retirement patterns will be unchanged, and that people will retire at the same age even as life expectancy and the ability to work longer go up ... Surely this is unrealistic for no other reason than financial resources for retirement may not allow it:
>
> SOURCE: CAPPELLI, P. 2005. Will there really be a labor shortage? (*In* Losey, M., Meisinger, S. & Ulrich, D. *The future of human resource management*. Virginia: Wiley & Sons:7–8.)

This is also supported by Critchley[26], who argues for a fundamental rethink in the nature of employment. He argues that:

- Firstly, the retirement concept in advanced economies and re-engagement of the post-50 age group or sector of the workforce needs to be re-examined.
- Secondly, polices need to be developed to attract and retain a multi-generational workforce.

What the McKinsey report and others, including Cappelli and Critchley, do agree upon is the need for more creative HR practices to attract and retain talented employees. In this context, the McKinsey report highlighted the changing psychological contract within the employment relationship, noting that employees will look for employability not employment, as we mentioned earlier, and will want to change jobs often. Critchley[27] also argues that psychological contracts and engagement profiles will be substantially different for older workers. These trends indicate that organisations that are prepared to focus on attracting and developing talent will be in a stronger position to retain key human resources as the so-called war for talent intensifies. It is also clear that the way organisations seek to retain these highly skilled resources will have to change. This places human resources at the centre of policy and systems development to achieve outcomes that promote the organisation as an employer of choice for increasingly discerning (potential) employees. The structural changes driving the 'war for talent' are widespread across many of the more industrialised market economies. This creates what Michaels, Handfield-Jones, and Axelrod[28] describe as a 'new' business reality, in which management skills and ability to embrace a new mindset are critical (see Tables 6.1 and 6.2).

6.3 Building a new paradigm

In their seminal work on talent management, Michaels, Handfield-Jones, and Axelrod[29] identified five key areas for organisations to act upon if they were going to be make talent a source of competitive advantage. These were:

- Embrace a talent mindset
- Craft a winning employee value proposition
- Rebuild your recruitment strategy
- Weave development into your organisation
- Differentiate and affirm your people.

The following section discusses these key areas more fully.

6.3.1 Embrace a talent mindset

The Mckinsey Group defines a talent mindset in holistic terms as follows[30]:

Table 6.1 The old and new realities of business

The old reality	The new reality
People need companies	Companies need people
Machines, capital, and geography are the competitive advantage	Talented people are the competitive advantage
Better talent makes some difference	Better talent makes a huge difference
Jobs are scarce	Talented people are scarce
Employees are loyal and jobs are secure	People are mobile and their commitment is short term
People accept the standard package they are offered	People demand much more

SOURCE: MICHAELS, E., HANDFIELD-JONES, H. & AXELROD, E. 2001. *The war for talent*. Boston, Mass.: Harvard Business School Press:6. Used with permission.

Table 6.2 The old and the new ways of doing things

The old way	The new way
HR is responsible for people management	All managers, starting with the CEO, are accountable for strengthening their talent pool
We provide good pay and benefits	We shape our company, our jobs, even our strategy to appeal to talented people
Recruiting is like purchasing	Recruiting is like marketing
We think development happens in training	We fuel development primarily through stretch jobs, coaching, and mentoring
We treat everyone the same and like to think that everyone is equally capable	We affirm all our people but invest differently in our A, B, and C players

SOURCE: MICHAELS, E., HANDFIELD-JONES, H. & AXELROD, E. 2001. *The war for talent*. Boston, Mass.: Harvard Business School Press:16. Used with permission.

> A talent mindset is a deep-seated belief that having better talent at all levels is how you out-perform your competition. It's the belief that better talent is a critical source of competitive advantage. It's the recognition that it is better talent that pulls all the other performance levers.
>
> SOURCE: MICHAELS, E., HANDFIELD-JONES, H. & AXELROD, E. 2001. *The war for talent*. Boston, Mass.: Harvard Business School Press:xi.

Whilst most organisations would like to see themselves in this context, many tend to adopt the old style of talent management, as indicated in Table 6.3.

A key element in the McKinsey report is that talent management is increasingly becoming an important role (if not the critical role) for the CEO – a role that cannot be delegated. In this context, the report's authors propose several key actions that leaders must take[31]:

- Get involved in people decisions
- Develop probing talent reviews

Table 6.3 The old talent mindset vs the new talent mindset

Old talent mindset	New talent mindset
A vague notion that 'people are our most important asset'	A deep conviction that better talent leads to better corporate performance
HR is responsible for people management	All managers are accountable for strengthening their talent pool
We do a two-day succession planning exercise once a year	Talent management is a central part of how we run the company
I work with people I inherit	I take bold actions to build the talent pool I need

SOURCE: MICHAELS, E., HANDFIELD-JONES, H. & AXELROD, E. 2001. *The war for talent*. Boston, Mass.: Harvard Business School Press:22. Used with permission.

BOX 1: Talent management: a CEO job

Talent management now features prominently on the CEOs's agenda, with many spending as much as half their time spotting, preparing and monitoring promising executives. In many cases, CEOs now also participate directly in development activities such as mentoring and teaching leadership skills.

A recent Whitepaper by the Economist Intelligence Unit, in cooperation with Development Dimensions International (DDI), found that CEOs believe strong talent management leads to improved financial performance, but they do not explicitly measure return on investment.

While talent management has traditionally been the domain of HR, the Whitepaper found that two factors largely account for increased CEO involvement in the past few years: the shift in focus towards intangible assets such as talent, and increased board scrutiny in relation to both ethics and performance.

'Now it is a strategic necessity for these executives not only to keep abreast of the latest developments in the company's talent programme but also to plot the strategy, own associated initiatives and regularly participate in events related to talent management', the Whitepaper found.

'As talent management has grown in importance in recent years, so has the role of HR departments. This is positive news for senior HR professionals who have long been seeking greater involvement in matters of strategic importance.'

The in depth survey involved 18 CEOs and two COOs from large companies across 10 countries, including the USA, the UK, France, Japan, China and Australia.

'Top executives now consider talent management one of the highest priorities,' said Nigel Holloway, research director for America at the Economist Intelligence Unit.

'The findings underscore that it is no longer a case of whether talent management is on the Board agenda, but ensuring the CEO receives adequate strategic support in tackling the issue,' he said.

SOURCE: *Adapted from DONALDSON, C. ECONOMIST INTELLIGENCE UNIT, SECTION – HUMAN RESOURCES. 2006. Issue 105, 30 May. Used with permission*

- Instil a talent-focused mindset within the organisation
- Invest real money in talent
- Be accountable for talent management.

As the issue of skill shortages intensifies, is this message starting to reach the top-management level of organisations? Research by the Economist Intelligence Unit on this issue appears to show this is increasingly the case (see Box 1 on the previous page).

6.3.2 Craft a winning employee value proposition (EVP)

An EVP is everything an employee experiences within an organisation, including intrinsic and extrinsic satisfaction, values, ethics, and culture. It is also about how well the organisation fulfils the employees' needs, expectations and aspirations[32] (see Figure 6.2).

Figure 6.2 The employee value proposition (EVP)

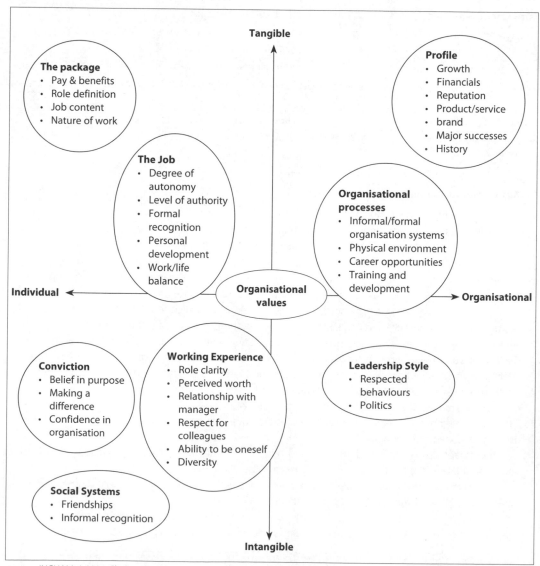

SOURCE: INGHAM, J. 2006. Closing the talent management gap. *Strategic HR review*, 5(3):2. Used with permission.

In their study, the McKinsey Group set out to determine what the employees in companies look for when making an employment decision. As Table 6.4 illustrates, the items with a strong causal relationship with satisfaction were exciting work, development, great company, and wealth and rewards.

It is evident from the results in Table 6.4 that intrinsic factors such as having interesting, challenging work that one is passionate about are rated highly by employees when they consider the place of employment. These factors are followed closely by good culture, commitment, support, and career advancement. It is interesting to note that pay and wealth creation were in the bottom quartile, suggesting that extrinsic factors are not the main drivers in attracting and retaining talent.

6.3.3 **Rebuild your recruitment strategy**

When managers restructure a recruitment strategy in the emerging market for labour, a critical issue is being able to understand the new workforce. This means that even in downturns in the market, it is imperative that managers maintain a creative recruitment-and-selection strategy as the skill shortage is a long-term proposition. Only in this way will organisations continue to absorb new talent. In this context, McKinsey differentiates the new from old approaches to recruitment, as Table 6.5 shows.

In terms of attraction, along with the primary areas of recruitment and selection, values and ethics act as important sources of attraction as employees become increasingly discerning about their employers. Macken[33], for example,

Table 6.4 What employees are looking for

Exciting work		Great company	
Interesting, challenging work	59%*	Company is well managed	48%
Work I feel passionate about	45%	Good relations with by boss	43%
Development		I like the culture and values	39%
Career advancement opportunities	37%	I trust senior management	39%
Long-term commitment to me	35%	**Wealth and rewards**	
Build skills to boost career	35%	Recognised, rewarded for my individual contribution	39%
Snr management commitment to me	30%	Substantial wealth creation opportunity	36%
High performance promoted	28%	High performers paid more	31%

* % of respondents who rate the item critical in their decision of which company to join or stay with it
SOURCE: MICHAELS, E., HANDFIELD-JONES, H. & AXELROD, E. 2001. *The war for talent*. Boston, Mass.: Harvard Business School Press:45. Used with permission.

Table 6.5 The old recruiting strategies vs the new recruiting strategies

Old recruiting strategies	New recruiting strategies
Grow your own talent	Pump talent in at all levels
Recruit for vacant positions	Hunt for talent all the time
Go to a few traditional sources	Tap many diverse pools of talent
Advertise to job hunters	Find ways to reach passive candidates
Specify a compensation range and stay within it	Break the compensation rules to get the candidates you want
Recruiting is about screening	Recruiting is about selling as well as screening
Hire as needed with no overall plan	Develop a recruiting strategy for each type of talent

SOURCE: MICHAELS, E., HANDFIELD-JONES, H. & AXELROD, E. 2001. *The war for talent*. Boston, Mass.: Harvard Business School Press:70. Used with permission.

notes the sophisticated use of blogs and Web sites by potential employees to find out about real organisational culture and values and points out that even organisations as large as Microsoft have expressed concern about internal bloggers and their effect on the future workforce and clients.

Sheahan[34] observes on this issue:

> Increased 'consciousness' and 'awareness' ... have a serious effect on the way organisations are perceived in the talent marketplace. If you have questionable business practices, do serious damage to the environment, and create negative social consequences through the operation of your business, you will be blackmarked by talented people. They will not only boycott the products of such companies, they won't want to work for them either.
>
> SOURCE: SHEAHAN, P. 2005. *Generation Y: Thriving and surviving with Generation Y at work.* Prahran: Hardie Grant Books:28.

Research undertaken by the recruitment agency Talent2 reinforces this point. A survey of 527 people on Web-related employment revealed that:

- Most job hunters (73 per cent) always use an Internet search engine to find information about the boss and the company
- Most job hunters (72 per cent) stated that the information obtained from searches has a bearing on the interview and a bearing on whether they decide to take the job
- A high proportion (86 per cent) of respondents indicated that this investigation allowed them to ask more job-related questions before accepting the position.[35]

In fact, some of these features have been noted in articles appearing in the business press. For example[36]:

> The advertisement shows a young man with long hair, hippie beads and casual pants at the edge of a beach. He looks ecstatic as he embraces the sea breeze under the heading 'Are you looking for a lifestyle change?' Coke's new campaign? A shot from Survivor? Or is Hugh Jackman enjoying a break back in Australia? Try a recruitment ad for a bank. Evidently being sales development manager for a northern Australian bank is as good as a sea change. Forget work stations, pin-striped suits and teller boxes. This bank wants you to think a day at the office feels like a day at the beach. Is this what it takes to attract good staff today?
>
> SOURCE: MACKEN, D. 2004. A sense of entitlement: the new worker wants it all. *Weekend financial review*, November 27–28. Melbourne: The Fairfax Group:17–18.

An understanding of how potential employees view or obtain information about the organisation can enhance the match between the person and the organisation, increasing organisation fit and retention. As Dale, as quoted in Keen[37], notes:

> The smart organisations are defining what type of person will fit with the organisation's culture. A lot of that is value-driven – not just what they are capable of doing, but what satisfies them. If someone is unmotivated, their skill set will walk out the door.
>
> SOURCE: KEEN, S. 2005. Interview with M. Dale – Hudson Consulting – National Practice Manager for Talent Management – Australia. *HR monthly*, February:18–24. Used with permission.

6.3.4 Weave development into your organisation

In this new era, employees are looking for work that provides opportunities and is challenging. However, this is often given lip service in many organisations, in particular those in the Anglo-

American region. As Michaels, Handfield-Jones, and Axelrod[38] note, 'Talent rarely arrives fully developed ... People posses vast amounts of potential that, when nurtured and challenged, can be brought to full bloom.' In other words, organisations must develop their talent at all levels and weave it into the culture (see Table 6.6). This requirement is closely linked to areas such as job design, job analysis, and team building, which contribute to the day-to-day experience on the job, determining what people actually do at work, and how effectively they do it. Boxall, Macky, and Rasmussen[39], in a review of the labour turnover and retention in New Zealand, identified that one of the main reasons why respondents left their employers was to pursue more interesting work elsewhere. In an environment characterised by skill shortages and an increasingly discerning workforce, it is imperative for employers to review how they construct jobs and connect jobs.

Another critical factor in the retention of skilled workers is the provision of training and development. Edgar and Geare's[40] study of aspects of HRM that are important to employees identified training and development to be of 'paramount' importance. Boxall, Macky, and Rasmussen[41] also identified training opportunities as a determining issue in the decision employees made to leave their employers. This identification reinforces the point that HRM and development assume an increasingly significant role in the retention of key employees. Resistance to investment in human resources may reflect the traditional approach of many organisations and industries, particularly those reliant on immigration and poaching to solve skill shortages. In addition, organisational resistance to heavy investment in career development may reflect the changing psychological contract between employers and employees. Employees are choosing to manage their own careers by moving between organisations. Employers may therefore be questioning the value of investing heavily in training and development opportunities for employees who may not stay.[42] Nevertheless, as Edgar and Geare[43] point out, training and development are still considered to be critical issues in employee retention and organisations would recognise them as important lures in the 'war for talent'.

6.3.5 **Differentiate and affirm your people**

We can link approaching the workforce as a diverse set of resources to what are called the 'hard' and 'soft' approaches to HRM. In terms of soft HRM, organisations:
- Invest heavily in star performers (the A team)
- Develop solid employees (the B team) to contribute their best to retain them
- Help poor performers (the C team) to improve their performance.

If the technique of soft HRM fails to change the performance of the C team, the organisation will use an exit strategy – hard HRM.

Note that this approach can be seen as producing a potential star-focused culture that undermines a team culture. Michaels, Handfield-

Table 6.6 The old approaches to development vs the new approaches to development

Old approaches to development	New approaches to development
Development just happens	Development is woven into the fabric of the organisation
Development means training	Development primarily means challenging experiences, coaching, feedback, and mentoring
The unit owns the talent	The company owns the talent; people move easily around the company
Only poor performers have development needs	Everyone has development needs and receives coaching
A few lucky people find mentors	Mentors are assigned to every high-potential person

SOURCE: MICHAELS, E., HANDFIELD-JONES, H. & AXELROD, E. 2001. *The war for talent*. Boston, Mass.: Harvard Business School Press:98. Used with permission.

Jones, and Axelrod, however, disagree, arguing that it simply involves recognition of an individual's achievement – as long as it is not overt it will not affect the performance of the organisation. Despite this, organisations should carefully consider the issue if they are considering embarking on such policies.

An important factor in differentiating and affirming employees is awareness of their diverse lifestyles and needs. Initially, the areas of work/life balance, family-friendly benefits, and diversity may be seen only as attraction strategies. Allowing employees the flexibility to meet personal needs also becomes an important retention factor by adding to an organisation's 'employer of choice' standing.[44]

Pocock[45] also makes the business case for a link between work/life balance and the attraction and retention of workers, and the ultimate competitive survival of a company. The increase in the number of women in the workforce, coupled with an ageing population base that requires part-time work or carers, elevates the need for organisations to support valued employees who have family responsibilities.

The focus on work/life balance has also been highlighted with regard to child-care problems and some parents' decision to return to work. Research by employers such as Toshiba and others has addressed this issue with their development of the Flexible Workplace Special Interest Group Research.[46]

Evidence of change in traditional professions such as law (noted for its long hours) highlights the sea change mentioned in the advertisement we discussed earlier in this chapter. Brown[47] mentions that Henry Davis York – a law firm based in Sydney Australia – reported that the development of flexible patterns of work, stemming from its internal survey on work/life balance in 2001, has been a key factor in improving retention. Indicators included an increase in return from maternity leave, low turnover, and employee feedback as identifiable criteria (see Chapter 5). Another key issue in building diversity is the opportunity to attract a wider range of talent. Writers such as Murray and Syed[48] and Orland[49] have highlighted the negative effect of not capitalising on workers

from a wide range of backgrounds. Companies employing diversely experienced employees are likely to be more creative and thus better able to meet the expectations of a diverse market. Given that organisations are operating in such a tight market for labour, such capacities would be highly advantageous. Thorne and Pellant[50] provide the following typical set of questions an organisation could use to rate its process for talent management:

1. Have we developed a definable organisation brand?
2. Do we actively demonstrate our values and brand in the way that we conduct our business?
3. Does this equally apply in the way we handle our people?
4. Are we committed to identifying and recognising talent at all levels in the organisation?
5. Do we have an infrastructure that allows individuals freedom to innovate, generate ideas and receive feedback?
6. Are we sure that our management structure is developing new talent and creating a coaching and learning culture?
7. Have we created an environment that attracts potential employees to want to come and work for us?
8. Do we welcome previous employees back?
9. Do we recognise the need for some employees to go?
10. Do we give honest, open and supportive feedback on performance?
11. Have we created internal forums that allow for healthy debate and discussion?
12. Do we undertake effective benchmarking with other organisations?
13. Do we know our retention rates?

14. Do we conduct exit interviews with all employees?
15. Do we encourage all our employees at all levels to identify other potentially talented people to join our organisation?
16. Do we actively share our experiences and demonstrate best practice to other organisations?
17. Do we have a diverse and multi-talented workforce?
18. Do we share our expectations of each other?
19. Do we actively champion talent?
20. Do we see talent management as one of the core pillars of our organisation development?

SOURCE: THORNE, K. & PELLANT, A. 2007. *The essential guide to managing talent: How top companies recruit, train and retain the best employees*. London: Kogan Page:137–138. Used with permission.

6.4 Talent management in practice

The following information[51] about SoftwareCo illustrates how an organisation can achieve sustained competitive advantage by embracing talent management.

SoftwareCo is a leading supplier of networking IT, providing support applications for the development of e-business. It is a worldwide organisation, with subsidiaries in each country. The company identified the issue of attracting and retaining IT staff as a major problem in the late 1990s. The key findings of a staff survey indicated that the employees required a challenging and stimulating environment in which to develop their skills. Many of these IT staff were aiming to develop careers as either (internal) project managers or (external) self-employed contractors. The key challenge for SoftwareCo was to provide a continuous range of project-management roles in house. It could not afford to lose employees who wanted to move into contracting. In response to this problem, SoftwareCo developed a partnering programme with its network of distributors and customers. This approach had the dual effect of providing partners with staff who were appropriately skilled to manage projects on site, whilst at the same time providing these staff with ongoing career-and-skill development. From an organisational perspective, it also allowed for growth in the core knowledge, skills, and ability of the organisation's IT employees. The programme also focused on attracting potential IT staff by providing them with in-house training and employment within both SoftwareCo and its partners. This helped the organisation become an employer of choice. For those wanting to become independent contractors, SoftwareCo embraced this by helping them set up their own businesses and then contracting them back to the organisation. This guaranteed work for the employees, whilst enabling SoftwareCo to have the same work done without the cost associated with full-time employees.

To facilitate the development of these work patterns and practices, the organisation restructured its organisational form. The organisational structure increasingly reflects the core–periphery model described in Chapter 5. The organisation developed the second periphery by subcontracting out its core employees to partner organisations.

The outcomes of the SoftwareCo approach were as follows. The success of the partnership agreement is reflected in the turnover of IT staff – around 5 per cent, down from 15 per cent (the industry average is 10 per cent). The achievements of this programme have resulted in its being included in the organisation's recruitment-and-selection process. In particular, SoftwareCo has identified a series of high-performance competencies that can deliver success at entry-level positions. These include customer service, problem solving, communication skills, team working, and project management. In terms of the developmental side of this approach, SoftwareCo has initiated training programmes in management to provide IT staff with the skills to advance their career paths into middle management and senior management. As one manager noted:

IT professionals need to have business, communication and leadership skills in order to fully understand their clients' mission statements and the role technology plays in meeting corporate goals and objectives. As an industry, we need to do a better job of teaching our people these skills because they are in fundamental building blocks for successful organisations. Those who ignore them are likely to fail.

SOURCE: BOXALL, P., MACKY, K. & RASMUSSEN, E. 2003. Labour turnover and retention in New Zealand: the causes and consequences of leaving and staying with employers. *Asia Pacific journal of human resources*, 41(2):195–214.

The company now has a waiting list of potential talent to employ.

SUMMARY

There is a clear indication that the negotiating position of employees in the workplace is increasing for the first time in a generation. This is beginning to have an impact on the employment relationship and subsequently, employment policies and practices as the 'war for talent' becomes increasingly intense. It is clear that the new workforce is discerning and skilled. Potential employees are exploring whether the organisation pays enough attention to them in terms of both opportunities and resources. Despite the rhetoric, it appears that organisations are still coming to terms with the management of talent as a source of competitive advantage. Over the next decade, it will be interesting to see whether there is any change in focus as labour markets tighten and workers become increasingly discerning.

KEY CONCEPTS

• Attraction	• Strategy
• Development	• Sustainable competitive advantage
• Employee value proposition (EVP)	• Talent
• Recruitment	• Talent management
• Resource-based view (RBV)	• Talent mindset
• Retention	

CASE STUDY

Objective: To understand the role and value of talent management within an organisation

Developing talent at Kyphon and Triage – different but similar

Introduction

Unlike the leaders of many Silicon Valley start-ups who dream of being acquired by a big player so they can cash out, Richard Mott, CEO of Kyphon Inc., believes his company can emerge as a giant in its own right. In fact, Mott and his board see almost limitless opportunities for growth for the Sunnyvale, Calif. company – but only if it can put workers with the right skills into the right jobs.

That may be easier said than done. Kyphon's skill needs are both specialized and broad. For example, the company has long relied on salespeople (called spine consultants) who are so well trained on its patented device for correcting painful spinal conditions that they can, in turn, teach surgeons what the product is – and how to use it in the operating room.

In addition to training employees on these specialized skills, Kyphon also needs to develop workers with a vast array of more commonly found skills – such as operations, accounting and HR. The company has rapidly outgrown its infrastructure and without such skills in place, further growth will be hampered. As a result, employee learning in a number of areas is vital for the organisation's continued growth and success.

Farther north, in San Francisco, Patricia Lee-Hoffman faces a similar challenge. Lee-Hoffman is a founding principal of Triage Consulting Group, a company that helps hospitals identify and recover outstanding medical insurance payments. New employees learn the company's custom process and techniques for identifying such funds, then travel extensively around the country to put the practice in use at client sites.

The challenge for Triage: Workers can't walk in the door knowing the company's specialized, but learnable, system. They must be taught – and quickly. The rigorous travel schedule (employees are on travel three weeks out of four) often leads to burnout and job churning, and annual attrition is 22 percent.

In this environment, time is the enemy, and getting workers up to speed quickly on the company's system is vital to business success. Triage tackles this through continuous training; new associates are taken out of the field about one week per month to receive ongoing instruction.

Similarities certainly exist between Triage and Kyphon. Both companies face an equally pressing need to train and develop employees, and both companies tackle that need effectively. (Kyphon fills 44 percent of its management positions through internal management promotions. In 2005, Triage filled all vacancies from within.)

Yet both organisations train and develop workers in ways that are different, and that are tailored to their specific business models and concerns.

Kyphon

Three years ago, when Rich Mott took the reins at Kyphon, the company – now six years old – had morphed from a fledgling start-up fueled on dreams and enthusiasm into a publicly traded company poised to become a global player. But management had not caught up, had not upgraded its administrative structure or clearly articulated its culture and values.

'We succeeded up to that point in spite of ourselves,' says Art Ferdinand, manager of R&D, who has been with Kyphon from the beginning. 'The company had no mission, vision or strategic plan.'

Among Mott's first priorities was implementing a strategy and articulating a vision that would attract and develop the leadership talent Kyphon required – and encourage those leaders to stay with the company for the long haul.

But when Mott looked to his chief HR officer for help, he ran into a problem: He didn't have one. 'We had a hard driving sales force, but no foundation, no executive structure – HR included – that could take us to the next step,' he recalls.

With world-class companies like Hewlett-Packard (HP) and General Electric as models, Mott established the position of vice-president of HR and hired former HP executive Steve Ham to fill the role. Ham had broad experience in HR and specialized expertise in training and development, and he had demonstrated a wide range of executive competencies as chief operating officer for the now-defunct women's American Basketball League.

Ham was a key element in Mott's strategy, one in which HR would play a central role. 'When you're in a business like ours, the HR dynamic is incredibly important,' Mott says. 'Education – training and teaching others – are key elements of our culture. It's a consistent theme. If our organisation doesn't continue to evolve and develop, it will fail.'

Anything Goes (Almost)

Under Mott and Ham, Kyphon's flexible, open-ended approach to employee development has become a highlight of the culture. The company values virtually any type of learning. From scientific training to lifestyle management, employees are encouraged to pursue knowledge in any format that suits them, in-house or outside, formal or informal. Support for learning extends to families of employees through a dependent education reimbursement program. This year, Kyphon will spend $4,075 per employee on training, up from $3,200 last year.

Erika Palmer, manager of R&D, who is a scientist by training, has been a beneficiary of this 'do whatever it takes' philosophy. She has been encouraged to take outside management courses as well as internal ones. 'There's responsibility on the employee to seek out opportunities, but support is also there from management in helping you find what you need,' she says.

'The culture encourages personal development,' agrees Maria Jenkerson, supervisor of operations. 'If I need courses in finance, budget management or anything else that would help prepare me, they'd let me do it. I do the same for my direct reports.'

In addition, training opportunities are proving to be a powerful recruitment and retention incentive. 'Given our growth path, individuals who want to advance can see promotions within a year,' says Ben Murdock, director of sales operations. Murdock began as a marketing intern in June 2000 right out of Bates College in Maine. He has moved up the ladder steadily, working in the field as a sales trainee, salesman and sales manager before assuming the director role.

'You get opportunities quickly, much faster than with other companies in our industry,' he says. 'Because we're growing so fast, our hiring profile is one where we're willing to take people with drive, passion and develop them.'

More than three-quarters of Kyphon's sales managers came up through the ranks, and, with a sales force that is expected to grow to 300 this year, more opportunities are certain.

Consolidating and Upgrading

When Ham arrived, HR was a bit player in talent development. Line managers developed their direct reports on an ad hoc basis, deciding when to send them to outside training programs or conferences. Sales, which hired almost half of the employees, was the exception: Its training was focused, tightly controlled and effective at producing spine consultants who could educate and sell to surgeons, Kyphon's primary customers.

Under Ham, HR assumed responsibility for all Kyphon training, sales included. He instituted a companywide talent review and succession planning exercise, asking the vice presidents to assess their staffs and identify gaps where training or education would be beneficial looking out on one- and three-year horizons.

'Now every area has identified its high-potential [employees],' he says. 'People were put in buckets – those who are ready for promotion now, those who need some time and those who do not appear to have the potential.'

Also, early on Ham created the position of

director of employee development. To fill that spot, he recruited Steve Gerhart, who had been running an employee development program for McKesson Corp., a Fortune 15 health care and information technology company.

Gerhart found the caliber of the sales training 'fabulous,' a veritable 'how to' case study. Easing any anxiety over a potential turf battle, he announced his intention to build on sales' successes by extending aspects of the training to the entire company.

What made the sales training so special? Personalized and continuous, it favoured an integrated approach – mentoring, classroom instruction and fieldwork. Spine consultants, all hired with medical device or pharmaceutical sales backgrounds, are given reading materials and are tested on those materials to ensure that they all have the same knowledge base. Once they pass the test, they receive two weeks of intensive classroom training in sales, product training and spinal conditions – such as injuries, diseases and the like. Then they travel in the field with a supervisor for a few weeks and finally are assigned to their territories.

Monthly, a manager travels their territory to mentor them, offering feedback. At various intervals, they return from the field for classroom training in management or advanced sales.

Gerhart was impressed by the spine consultants' passion. He wondered if there were ways to replicate for other employees what the spine consultants experienced daily in the field.

'Kyphon's mission is more tangible for us,' explains Brad Paddock, vice president of sales. 'We see the patients, often interact with them in the recovery room. We see them in debilitating pain, unable to move. One hour later, they're pain free. I've been in the recovery room where a patient has cried and said, "I can't believe it; you've given me my life back!" '

Integrated Training

True to his word, Gerhart, an able consensus builder, consolidated and innovated. He began by making the comprehensive sales, product and science orientation available to all staff. He found ways to bring patients on-site so

administrative staff can experience the same miracles that spine consultants see in the field. He has placed all in-house training under the umbrella of 'Kyphon University.'

Courses, which usually last one day or less, are open to everyone. 'People are more likely to attend if a program is in-house and [they] can complete it in an hour or so,' says Christina Catuanao, director of manufacturing.

Among the offerings in what promises to be an expanding curriculum: interviewing, situational leadership and emotional intelligence. In addition, Gerhart has continued to encourage managers to build personal education and development plans with their reports, supporting tutoring, coaching, travel to conferences, outside seminars and the like.

Catuanao, for example, encourages all of the 70 workers she supervises to include courses in their development plans. 'Some do; others choose not to. The important thing is that they know the opportunities are out there.'

Jenkerson, for one, seized the training opportunities given to her, with excellent results. Within her first year at the company, she took supervisor and project management courses offered by the American Management Association in San Francisco. She has also taken courses in interviewing and emotional intelligence through Kyphon University. 'Who would think that in less than two years, I'd be supervising operations?' she asks. 'I'm a great example of development.'

Triage Consulting Group

In contrast to Kyphon, which hopes to build loyalty and long-term commitments, Triage's employee life cycle is considerably shorter. Most employees view it as a good place to be for a while, but not for the long haul.

'Our business model is based on churning, hiring large numbers at the entry level and replacing them when they leave three or four years later,' explains Jeff Coolican, a manager.

The 200-person company has a relatively flat structure: six principals at the top, 23 managers reporting to them, 52 'senior associates' (fully trained consultants) below them, and more than 100 associates at the entry level.

Of all new associates, 70 percent make it to senior associate; those who leave tend to pull out a year or two after reaching that level.

Why do they leave? 'People go off to do cool things like graduate school or medical school,' says Dan Phippen, a manager.

For the Triage business model to work, the company has to get entry-level associates up to speed rapidly, then retain them long enough to justify the investment before they move on. An additional challenge is identifying and training select senior associates for manager slots and eventually preparing them to become principals.

Getting Worker Bees in the Field

Beginning associates come in with a blank slate. They need to master quantitative skills and gain working knowledge of health care issues.

'There isn't anything that Triage does that anyone has any idea about when they come out of college,' says senior associate Kristi Davis. 'I had no idea about co-pays; the medical jargon was a mystery.'

New associates also need training on how to cope with difficult interpersonal situations. When they go into the field, they find money that their clients overlooked – a situation that can breed resentment from the staff at client companies. Coping with that resentment can be a recurring issue, say associates.

To help new associates develop the skills they need, Triage conducts regular group training sessions. Each month or so, new hires are assigned to cohorts of 10 to 12 for orientation. During the next 21 months, they return together to complete 15 formal training modules. Initially the modules focus on the nuts and bolts of being a consultant. Later, there's more on project management skills. The format is interactive, featuring PowerPoint presentations, case studies and teamwork.

'We've got the same experience level but work at different sites,' Davis says. 'It makes us comfortable when we ask questions. There's real camaraderie.'

That was the design. 'We time the training to match their experience level, so they'll learn what they need to do to function on a project,' says Josh Kobal, a manager. 'We break it up because if we throw too much at them it won't stick.'

Peer Instruction

All modules are taught by Triage staff, most only a few years removed from the trainees. 'I like that the training is done by senior associates who have been here for at least two years,' says associate Emily McMahon. 'They know what they're talking about but aren't so removed from us. It's encouraging to know that in 20 months, I'll be where they are.'

Many consulting firms ship trainees off-site for three weeks of intensive classes; then they're done. Triage prefers the longer, combined module/field approach.

'We recognize that a lot of training will take place on-site and want to get them out there as soon as possible so they're not overwhelmed with information that they can't relate to,' Phippen says.

'When you go to training, you learn something you've never seen before; you remember parts, forget parts. In the field, you see something and it triggers the training in your mind. Sometimes you go into the training and you already had the experiences three weeks ago. The senior associate took you through it on-site; then the module reinforces it. You get a mix of both.'

Promotion Hook

Promotion is the carrot that keeps most associates in the fold. They know up front that if they stick it out for 21 months, they'll be promoted to 'senior associate' with a salary increase and a chance to run their own project.

'It's appealing because of the opportunity to move up,' says McMahon. 'It's not a dead end; promoting everyone gives you so much motivation.'

'When I look at what my peers are doing out of college, the fact that I'll be running my own project, supervising people, responsible for profits in 21 months seems pretty quick,' agrees associate Brian Friedlander. 'And I'll only be 24.'

Prescribed Training

Under Lee-Hoffman's lead, the company provides an estimated 100 hours of training annually for each employee. Unlike Kyphon, which values learning in general, even when it is not directly linked to the business, Triage needs to focus on training that is immediately job specific – particularly for entry-level workers. Not only must the company get these workers up to speed quickly before they leave, it also faces greater competition for market share than Kyphon and must stay more focused on generating immediate revenue.

Perhaps it's not surprising, then, that outside training does not receive unqualified support at Triage. Looking to pursue an outside degree? If you have time, which is unlikely, you'll have to do it on your own. Though Triage principals write effusive graduate school references, they discourage associates from attending. They believe school is an unnecessary diversion, that the real-life experience associates are getting on the job is preferable.

In-house training, however, is another matter. Partially to encourage staff to extend their tenure after achieving promotion, Triage offers seasoned senior associates – those who have managed at least three projects – the opportunity to enroll in an on-site 'Mini-MBA' program.

Offered by faculty from the University of California at Berkeley and designed specifically for Triage, it's divided into eight sections; each runs for two days. Topics include the U.S. health care system, negotiations and social responsibilities.

'The idea is to give them a more well-rounded health care background so they know what the client is dealing with,' Lee-Hoffman says. Attendees do not earn an MBA, but they do receive a certificate when they complete the program.

Building the Senior Team

Continuing education for senior associates and managers occurs at quarterly meetings, where outside experts brief staff on critical business and health care issues. In addition, Lee-Hoffman conducts 'next generation' leadership training for Triage's 23 managers, all former senior associates, preparing them to make the jump to principal. (So far no one has made it.) She leads skills workshops and brings in outside experts to assist, stressing the practical.

'We're having people deal with case studies that relate to our work,' she says. 'What do you do when a senior associate is in trouble? How do you make a toast? How do you make a speech at a retirement party?'

Overall, Lee-Hoffman believes Triage's programs are unparalleled in depth and quality. There's reason to believe she may be right. Clearly her passion for education is a major factor. 'I never wanted to stop being trained; that's why I do it,' she says. 'You need someone who loves to learn in charge. It wouldn't be fun for me unless I saw this talent develop.'

Questions and activities

1. What lessons did Steve Ham, Kyphon's vice president of HR, learn at Kyphon?
2. What characteristics would you say Kyphon and Triage share regarding the development of talent at their respective organisations?

SOURCE: GROSSMAN, R. J. 2006. Developing talent. *HR magazine*, 51(1):40–46, January. Used with permission.

REVIEW QUESTIONS AND ACTIVITIES

1. Discuss the changing dynamics of the workplace in the twenty-first century facilitating an increased emphasis on talent management.

2. How has the psychological contract between employees and employers been affected by the new era of HRM? Discuss.

3. Discuss the reasons for the perceived increasing shortages of skills.

4. Define the concept of 'talent'.

5. Discuss strategies for dealing with the potential 'war for talent' from a human capital perspective and resource-based perspective.

6. (a) List the key findings from the 1998 McKinsey report and its recommendations.
   (b) How has the scenario depicted in this report been criticised?

7. (a) Outline the critical characteristics of a talent mindset.
   (b) Outline how a talent mindset differs from the old view of management.

8. (a) Define an employee value proposition.
   (b) Outline the items McKinsey found to be strongly and causally related to employee satisfaction.

9. As Michaels, Handfield-Jones, and Axelrod have noted, in this new era of HRM, employees look for challenge and opportunities. Discuss how organisations can approach this through employee development.

10. (a) What are the key factors in making SoftwareCo an employer of choice?
    (b) Are these factors transferable to other organisations?

FURTHER READING

DYCHTWALD, K., ERICKSON, T.J. & MORISON, R. 2006. *Workforce crisis: How to beat the coming shortage of skills and talent.* Boston, Mass.: Harvard Business School Press.

THORNE, K. & PELLANT, A. 2007. *The essential guide to managing talent: How top companies recruit, train & retain the best employees.* London: Kogan Page.

STEDT, J. 2006. *Talent balancing: Staffing your company for long-term success.* Westport, Connecticut: Pralger Publishers, an imprint of Greenwood Publishing group.

STRINGER, H. & RUEFF, R. 2006. *Talent force: A new manifesto for the human side of business.* Upper Saddle River, N.J.: Prentice Hall.

WEB SITES

www.shrm.org/surveys – Society for Human Resource Management: 2006 Succession Planning Survey Report as well as the 2006 Talent Management Survey Report

www.humancapitalinstitute.org – Human Capital Institute

www.cornell.edu/iws – Institute for Workplace Studies

ENDNOTES

1. CRITCHLEY, R. 2004. *Doing nothing is not an option: Facing the imminent labor crisis.* Australia: Thomson-South Western; FULLERTON, H. & TOOSSI, M. 2001. Labor force projections 2010: steady growth and changing composition. *Monthly labor review,* 124(110):21–28, November; CAPPELLI, P. 2005. Will there really be a labor shortage? (*In* Losey, M., Meisinger, S. & Ulrich, D. *The future of human resource management,* Virginia: Wiley & Sons:5–14.)

2. BARNEY, J. 1991. Firm resources and sustained competitive advantage. *Journal of management,* 17:99–120; BOXALL, P. 1996. The strategic HRM

debate and the resource-based view of the firm. *Human resource management journal,* 6(3):59–75; BOXALL, P. & PURCELL, J. 2003. *Strategy and human resource management.* Basingstoke: Palgrave Macmillan.

3. CRITCHLEY, R. 2004. *Doing nothing is not an option: Facing the imminent labor crisis.* Australia: Thomson-South Western; HOLLAND, P., HECKER, R. & STEEN, J. 2002. Human resource strategies and organisational structures for managing gold-collar workers. *Journal of European industrial training,* 26:72–80.

4. LOSEY, M. 2005. Anticipating change: will there be a labour shortage? (*In* Losey, M., Meisinger, S. & Ulrich, D. *The future of human resource management*, Virginia: Wiley & Sons:23–37.); TSUI, A. S. & WU, J. B. 2005. The new employment relationship versus the mutual investment approach: implications for human resource management. (*In* Losey, M., Meisinger, S. & Ulrich, D. *The future of human resource management*, Virginia: Wiley & Sons:44–54); SALT, B. 2004. *The big shift* 2nd ed. South Yarra, Australia: Hardie Grant books; READY, D. A. & Conger, J. A. 2007. Make your company a talent factory. *Harvard business review*, 85(6):69–77.

5. OECD (2004). *Labour force statistics*. OECD, Paris. For non-OECD countries: Department of Economic and Social Affairs, United Nations.

6. CAPPELLI, P. 2003. Will there really be a labor shortage? *Organizational dynamics*, 3:15–24.

7. CRITCHLEY, R. 2004. *Doing nothing is not an option: Facing the imminent labor crisis*. Australia: Thomson-South Western.

8. Ibid.

9. THORNE, K. & PELLANT, A. 2007. *The essential guide to managing talent: How top companies recruit, train and retain the best employees*. London: Kogan Page:1; BERGER, L. A. & BERGER, D. R. 2004. *The talent management handbook*. New York: McGraw-Hill.

10. BARON, A. & ARMSTRONG, M. 2007. *Human capital management: Achieving added value through people*. London: Kogan Page; SMIT, A. 1998. *Training and development in Australia* 2nd ed. Sydney: Butterworth.

11. GARAVAN, T., MORELEY, M., GUNNIGLE, P. & COLLINS, E. 2001. Human capital accumulation: the role of human resource development. *Journal of European industrial training*, 25:48–68.

12. PENROSE, E. 1959. *The theory of growth of the firm*. Oxford: Blackwell; WANG, C. L. & AHMED, P. K. 2007. Dynamic capabilities: a review and research agenda. *International journal of management reviews*, 19(1):31–50, March.

13. BARNEY, J. 1991. Firm resources and sustained competitive advantage. *Journal of management*, 17:99–120; GARAVAN, T., MORELEY, M., GUNNIGLE, P. & COLLINS, E. 2001. Human capital accumulation: the role of human resource development. *Journal of European industrial training*, 25:48–68.; WALTON, J. 1991. *Strategic human resource development*. Great Britain: Pearson Education Limited.

14. BOXALL, P. & STEENVELD, J. 1999. Human resource strategy and competitive advantage: a longitudinal study of engineering consultancies. *Journal of management studies*, 36(4):443–463. DELERY, J. & SHAW, J. 2001. The strategic management of people in work organizations: review, synthesis and extension. *Research in personnel and human resource management*, 20:165–197; WRIGHT, P., DUNFORD, B. & SNELL, S. 2001. Human resources and the resource based view on the firm. *Journal of*

management, 27:701–721; GARAVAN, T., MORELEY, M., GUNNIGLE, P. & COLLINS, E. 2001. Human capital accumulation: the role of human resource development. *Journal of European industrial training*, 25:48–68; BOXALL, P. & PURCELL, J. 2003. *Strategy and human resource management*. Basingstoke: Palgrave Macmillan.

15. GARAVAN, T., MORELEY, M., GUNNIGLE, P. & COLLINS, E. 2001. Human capital accumulation: the role of human resource development. *Journal of European industrial training*, 25:48–68; HOLLAND, P. & DE CIERI, H. (Eds). 2006. *Human resource development: a contemporary perspective*. Australia: Pearson Education; HOMAN, G. & MACPHERSON, A. 2005. E-learning in the corporate university. *Journal of European industrial training*, 30(1):75–90; PRINCE, C. & STEWART, J. 2002. Corporate universities – an analytical framework. *Journal of management development*, 21(10):794–811; STEWART, J. & MCGOLDRICH, J. 1996. *Human resource development: perspectives, strategies and practice*. London: Financial Times Pitman Publishing.

16. This section was taken from MCCAULEY, C. & WAKEFIELD, M. 2006. Talent management in the 21st century: help your company find, develop and keep its strongest workers. *The journal for quality and participation*, 29(4):4, Winter; OAKES, K. 2006. The emergence of talent management. *Training & development*, 60(4):21–24; SILVERMAN, L. L. 2006. How do you keep the right people on the bus? Try stories. *Journal for quality and participation*, 29(4):11–15, Winter.

17. MICHAELS, E., HANDFIELD-JONES, H. & AXELROD, E. 2001. *The war for talent*. Boston, Mass.: Harvard Business School Press:xi; BOUDREAU, J. W. & RAMSTAD, P. M. 2005. Talentship, talent segmentation, and sustainability: a new HR decision science paradigm for a new strategy definition. *Human resource management*, 44(2):129–136, Summer; LOCKWOOD, N. R. 2006. Talent management: driver for organisational success. *HR magazine*, 51(6):2–11.

18. OECD. 2004. *Labour force statistics*. OECD: Paris. For non-OECD countries: Department of Economic and Social Affairs, United Nations.

19. CRITCHLEY, R. 2004. *Doing nothing is not an option: Facing the imminent labor crisis*. Australia: Thomson-South Western.

20. BOSTON CONSULTING GROUP. 2003. *India's new opportunity 2020 report*. Boston: Boston Consulting Group.

21. MICHAELS, E., HANDFIELD-JONES, H. & AXELROD, E. 2001. *The war for talent*. Boston, Mass.: Harvard Business School Press:xi.

22. JOERRES, J. & TURCQ, D. 2007. Talent value management. *Industrial management*, March/April:8–13.

23. CAPPELLI, P. 2003. Will there really be a labor shortage? *Organizational dynamics*, 3:15–24; CAPPELLI, P. 2005. Will there really be a labor

shortage? (*In* Losey, M., Meisinger, S. & Ulrich, D. *The future of human resource management*. Virginia: Wiley & Sons:5–14.)

24. CRITCHLEY, R. 2004. *Doing nothing is not an option: Facing the imminent labor crisis*. Australia: Thomson-South Western.

25. CAPPELLI, P. 2005. Will there really be a labor shortage? (*In* Losey, M., Meisinger, S. & Ulrich, D. *The future of human resource management*. Virginia: Wiley & Sons:7–8.)

26. CRITCHLEY, R. 2004. *Doing nothing is not an option: Facing the imminent labor crisis*. Australia: Thomson-South Western.

27. Ibid.

28. MICHAELS, E., HANDFIELD-JONES, H. & AXELROD, E. 2001. *The war for talent*. Boston, Mass.: Harvard Business School Press.

29. Ibid.

30. Ibid.

31. Ibid.

32. Ibid.

33. MACKEN, D. 2005. Twentysomethings will vote with their feet. *The weekend financial review*. November 19–20. Melbourne: The Fairfax Group:27; FRASE, M. J. 2007. Stocking your talent pool. *HR magazine*, 52(4):67–74, April.

34. SHEAHAN, P. 2005. *Generation Y: Thriving and surviving with Generation Y at work*. Prahran: Hardie Grant Books; GRIGORYEV, P. 2006. Hiring by competency models. *The journal for quality and participation*, 29(4):16–18, Winter; GOFFEE, R. & JONES, G. 2007. Leading clever people. *Harvard business review*, 85(3):72–79.

35. TALENT 2. 2005. *Employees snoop on bosses on Google*. September.

36. MACKEN, D. 2004. A sense of entitlement: the new worker wants it all. *Weekend financial review*, November 27–28. Melbourne: The Fairfax Group:17–18.

37. KEEN, S. 2005. Interview with M. Dale – Hudson Consulting – National Practice Manager for Talent Management – Australia. *HR monthly*, February:18–24.

38. MICHAELS, E., HANDFIELD-JONES, H. & AXELROD, E. 2001. *The war for talent*. Boston, Mass.: Harvard Business School Press:95–96.

39. BOXALL, P., MACKY, K. & RASMUSSEN, E. 2003. Labour turnover and retention in New Zealand: the causes and consequences of leaving and staying with employers. *Asia Pacific journal of human resources*, 41(2):195–214.

40. EDGAR, F. & GEARE, A. 2005. Employee voice of human resource management. *Asia Pacific journal of human resources*, 43(3):361–380; GROSSMAN, R. J. 2006. Developing talent. *HR magazine*, 51(1):40–46,

January; LANDES, L. 2006. Getting the best out of people in the workplace. *The journal for quality and participation*, 29(4):27–29, Winter.

41. BOXALL, P., MACKY, K. & RASMUSSEN, E. 2003. Labour turnover and retention in New Zealand: the causes and consequences of leaving and staying with employers. *Asia Pacific journal of human resources*, 41(2):195–214.

42. NOON, M. & BLYTON, P. 2002. *The realities of work* 2nd ed. Hampshire: Palgrave.

43. EDGAR, F. & GEARE, A. 2005. Employee voice of human resource management. *Asia Pacific journal of human resources*, 43(3):361–380.

44. LANDSBURY, R. & BAIRD, M. 2004. Broadening the horizons of HRM: lessons for Australia from the US experience. *Asia Pacific journal of human resources*, 42(2):147–155; LIDDICOAT, A. 2003. Stakeholder perceptions of family-friendly workplaces: an examination of six New Zealand organizations. *Asia Pacific journal of human resources*, 41(3):354–370.

45. POCOCK, B. 2005. Work–life 'balance' in Australia: limited progress, dim prospects. *Asia Pacific journal of human resources*, 43(2):198–209.

46. FLEXIBLE WORKPLACE SPECIAL INTEREST GROUP RESEARCH. 2005. *Flexible working: A guide to creating and managing a flexible workplace*. Toshiba, Australia.

47. BROWN, K. 2005. Putting the life back into work: the case of Henry Davis York. *Human resources*, July:22–23; MEISINGER, S. 2006. Talent management in a knowledge-based economy. *HR magazine*, 51(5):10.

48. MURRAY, P. & SYED, J. 2005. Succession management: trends and current practice. *Asia Pacific journal of human resources*, 43(2):210–224; CORSELLO, J. 2006. The future is now for talent management. *Workforce management*, 85(12):52–57.

49. ORLAND, R. 2000. Racial diversity, business strategy and firm performance: a resource-based view. *Academy of management journal*, 43(2):164–177.

50. THORNE, K. & PELLANT, A. 2007. *The essential guide to managing talent: How top companies recruit, train and retain the best employees*. London: Kogan Page:137–138.

51. BOXALL, P. , MACKY, K. & RASMUSSEN, E. 2003. Labour turnover and retention in New Zealand: the causes and consequences of leaving and staying with employers. *Asia Pacific journal of human resources*, 41(2):195–214.

7

Measuring human resource management within organisations

Learning outcomes

After reading this chapter you should be able to:

▶ Identify the key forces driving the use of scorecards within organisations
▶ List the three different scorecards available for measuring a company's performance
▶ Identify the components of the Balanced Scorecard, the HR Scorecard, and the Workforce Scorecard
▶ List the stakeholders needed to implement the scorecards successfully within organisations

Purpose

The purpose of this chapter is to introduce you to a number of instruments for measuring performance within organisations.

Chapter overview

This chapter starts by identifying three new performance-measurement instruments, known as Scorecards, in the business environment today, namely the Balanced Scorecard, the HR Scorecard, and the Workforce Scorecard. The chapter then considers each of these instruments in detail by looking at their composition and implementation, as well as at the stakeholders involved in each. The concluding case study illustrates how the theory contained in this chapter can be applied practically to companies.

Introduction

There is no doubt, as can be seen from Chapter 6, that knowledge workers have had a tremendous impact on the changing role of HR. Observers, both internal and external to organisations, have come to view a company's workforce as far more valuable than ever before. This situation has placed the HR function directly in the spotlight. Thus, HRM can no longer be an observer that can be removed or outsourced by the company, but must become a player on the field, in the game, with the ability to score.[1] The ability to score, according to Beatty, Huselid, and Schneier[2], necessitates a new understanding of the rules of the game, and a new perspective on what HR is to contribute, how its systems enable it to contribute, and how to measure its ultimate deliverables. In this chapter we shall explore how to measure the workforce, the HR function, and the company's leadership with respect to their impact on the workforce and, ultimately, the company's strategic success. Over the years, a number of measures have become available for this purpose. We shall examine three of the most popular measures, namely the Balanced Scorecard, the HR Scorecard, and the Workforce Scorecard.

7.1 The Balanced Scorecard

This approach, which is used by companies like Sears and American Express, was developed by Robert S. Kaplan and David P. Norton in the early 1990s.[3] In their Balanced Scorecard approach (see Figure 7.1), Kaplan and Norton allow managers to look at the business from four important perspectives, namely[4]:

1. A customer perspective
2. An internal perspective
3. An innovation and learning perspective
4. A financial perspective.

From the above it is clear that the Balanced Scorecard forces managers to focus on only a handful of measures that are most critical.

To activate the scorecard, managers translate the company goals relating to the four perspectives (these are normally generic issues which form part of any mission statement) into specific measures that reflect the factors that really matter. We shall briefly discuss this approach by referring to Figure 7.1[5]:

- *A customer perspective.* The question pertaining to the customer perspective is: how do customers see us? Managers can obtain the answer by measuring lead times (for example lead time measured from the time the company receives an order to the time it actually delivers the product or service to the customers), quality (the defect level), performance, service, and cost.[6] To do this, companies articulate goals for the components of time, quality, performance, service, and cost. They then translate these into specific measures (see Figure 7.2 on page 150). Goals for customer performance, for example, can include the following (in order to track the performance on any of these goals, the company can obtain the information either internally or externally from customers):
  > To get standard products to the market sooner
  > To improve customers' time to the market
  > To become the customers' supplier of choice through partnerships with them
  > To develop innovative products tailored to the customers' needs.
- *An internal perspective.* The question pertaining to the issue of an internal perspective is: what must we excel at? Thus, what must the company do internally to meet its customers' expectations? Managers can obtain the answer by determining the processes and competencies that are most critical for the company, and specifying measures for components such as cycle times, quality, employee skills, and productivity.[7] As was the case with the previous component, companies also here articulate goals for the following: cycle times, quality, employee skills, and productivity. They then translate these goals into specific measures for each

Figure 7.1 The Balanced Scorecard

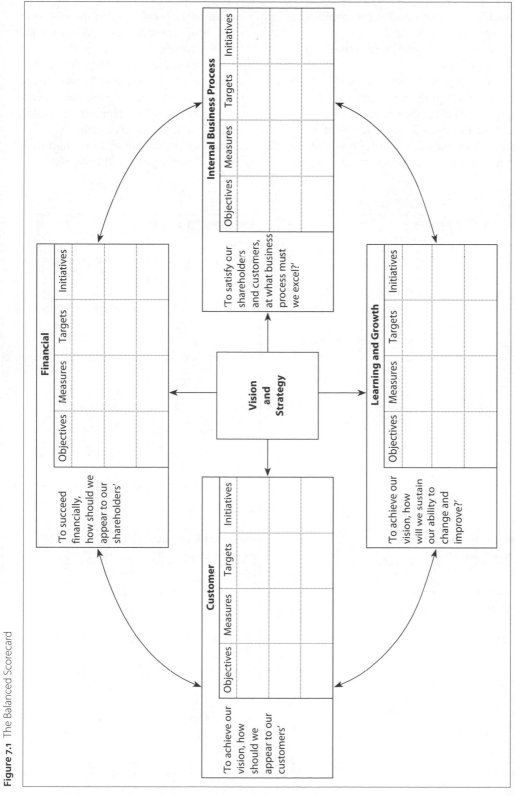

source: NIVEN, P. R. 2005. Driving focus and alignment with the balanced scorecard: why organisations need a balanced scorecard. *The journal for quality and participation*, 28(4):3, Winter. Used with permission.

(see Figure 7.2). Goals for this component can include, for example:

> To obtain a capability in submicron technology
> To obtain excellence in manufacturing
> To obtain productivity in design
> To introduce new products.

As much of the activity to achieve these goals takes place at the lower levels of the organisation, the company must bring the measures for these goals to the attention of the employees at these levels. By doing this, the company will ensure that the employees at these levels have clear targets for actions, decisions, and improvement activities that will enable the company to achieve its overall mission. The availability of information systems within an organisation can play an important role in monitoring progress in this regard.

Figure 7.2 ECI's Balanced Business Scorecard

Financial Perspective	
GOALS	MEASURES
Survive	Cash flow
Succeed	Quarterly sales growth and operating income by division
Prosper	Increased market share and ROE

Customer Perspective	
GOALS	MEASURES
New products	Percentage of sales from new products
	Percentage of sales from proprietary products
Responsive supply	On-time delivery (defined by customer)
Preferred suppliers	Share of key accounts' purchases
	Ranking by key accounts
Customer partnerships	Number of cooperative engineering efforts

Internal Business Perspective	
GOALS	MEASURES
Technology capability	Manufacturing geometry versus competition
Manufacturing excellence	Cycle time, unit cost, yield
Design productivity	Silicon efficiency, engineering efficiency
New product introduction	Actual introduction schedule versus plan

Innovation and Learning Perspective	
GOALS	MEASURES
Technology leadership	Time to develop next generation
Manufacturing learning	Process time to maturity
Product focus	Percentage of products that equal 80% of sales
Time to market	New product introduction versus competition

SOURCE: KAPLAN, R. S. & NORTON, D. P. 2005. The Balanced Scorecard: measures that drive performance. *Harvard business review*, 8(7):178. Used with permission.

- *An innovation and learning perspective.* The question pertaining to the innovation and learning perspective is: can we continue to improve and create value? Managers can obtain the answer by monitoring the company's ability to launch new products, create more value for customers, and improve operating efficiencies.[8] The previous two components of the Balanced Scorecard identified the parameters that the company should consider most important for competitive success. However, in this ever-changing world, continual improvements need to be made to existing products and processes, and companies have to have the ability to introduce entirely new products. One of a company's measures in this area could be, for example, the percentage of sales from new products (see Figure 7.2). If sales go down, the company can establish whether this fall is due to the design of the product. (Note that some organisations replace the innovation and learning perspective with a broader human-capital or people perspective.)
- *A financial perspective.* The question pertaining to the financial perspective is: how do we look to shareholders? Managers can obtain the answer by measuring cash flow, quarterly sales, growth, operating income by division, increased market share by segment, and return on equity.[9] To achieve this, companies articulate goals for these components. Typical financial goals have to do with profitability, growth, and shareholder value. They then translate these goals into specific measures (see Figure 7.2). Financial-performance measures indicate whether the company's strategy, implementation, and execution are contributing to bottom-line improvement.

Having looked at the different components of the Balanced Scorecard, we shall now briefly discuss some operational aspects of this process.

7.1.1 Compiling the Balanced Scorecard – who is responsible?

As the discussion of the individual components of the Balanced Scorecard earlier suggests, this process cannot be the responsibility of one person only. At least a Balanced Scorecard team should be responsible.[10] The question thus is: what will this team look like? Some of the important stakeholders in the team will undoubtedly be members of top management. This group is vital as it can influence change brought about by this process at the very top of the organisation. The literature also indicates that, besides this group, the higher the level of people an organisation can assemble from across the business units within it, the better. The advantages of this approach are obvious: with rank come experience, knowledge, credibility, and the ability to interact with the most senior executives at regular intervals.[11] Besides senior representatives from the business units within an organisation, senior members from support groups such as Human Resources, Finance, and Information Technology (IT) will also be necessary. According to Niven[12], conflict is at the heart of Balanced Scorecard development. Thus one trait all team members must possess is the ability to work comfortably in an atmosphere of conflict. Every team needs a leader. The Balanced Scorecard process is no exception; the leader can be called the Balanced Scorecard champion.[13] The responsibilities of this person will include scheduling meetings, tracking results, ensuring the distribution of materials, interacting with top management, and providing guidance on tough issues.[14] Thus, the compilation of the Balanced Scorecard team is a very important part of the execution of the Balanced Scorecard approach.

7.1.2 Implementing the Balanced Scorecard within an organisation

Once the process of compiling the Balanced Scorecard has been completed, the organisation needs to implement the Balanced Scorecard, i.e. cascade it down the organisation to all levels.[15]

(See Figure 7.3 in respect of the customer-perspective component of the scorecard.) However, this process is not simple; often, not only have employees never heard of the term 'Balanced Scorecard', but they also do not have a working knowledge of it. Thus, for successful implementation, organisations need to undertake some staff training.

One way of doing this is by making some articles on the topic available to the staff.[16] On completion of this, the employees can attend an information session. These sessions can address issues such as the origins of the scorecard, the four perspectives, and the implementation principles. Proper communication between everybody is absolutely essential. No scorecard can work unless managers link it to the budget of the company.[17] The linkage of the employees' pay to performance will also play an important role.[18] Once the organisation has implemented a Balanced Scorecard, it is important that the organisation holds the first review of results of the Balanced Scorecard within 60 days. Thereafter, the organisation should review and frequently discuss scorecard results throughout the organisation to achieve long-term success.

From the above discussion, it is clear that use of the Balanced Scorecard has a number of advantages, namely[19]:

- It brings together many of the competitive elements – e.g. becoming customer oriented, improving quality, and emphasising teamwork
- It guards against the underutilisation of assets by allowing management to see whether improvement in one area takes place at the expense of another area.

The literature shows that the Balanced Scorecard has grown in popularity in recent years. This is due to the fact that it meets the demands of a modern business world characterised by value creation stemming from intangible assets such as employee know-how, deep relationships with customers, and cultures capable of innovation and change.[20] However, even an excellent set of Balanced Scorecard measures cannot guarantee a winning strategy. According to Kaplan and Norton[21], the Balanced Scorecard can only translate a company's strategy into specific measurable objectives; a failure to convert improved operational performance, as measured

Figure 7.3 Cascading the Balanced Scorecard

Corporate Scorecard			
Perspective	Objective	Measure	Target
Customer	Provide safe, convenient transportation to our customers	Increase in number of passengers carried	10%

Fleet Services Scorecard			
Perspective	Objective	Measure	Target
Customer	Provide safe, convenient transportation to our customers	Percentage of taxi fleet available	90%

Maintenance Department Scorecard			
Perspective	Objective	Measure	Target
Customer	Provide safe, convenient transportation to our customers	Percentage of vehicle repairs completed within 24 hours	75%

SOURCE: NIVEN, P. R. 2005. *Balanced Scorecard diagnostics: Maintaining maximum performance.* Hoboken, N.J.: John Wiley & Sons:134. Used with permission.

in the scorecard, into improved financial performance should send management back to the drawing board to rethink the company's strategy or its implementation plans.

The foregoing makes it clear that the Balanced Scorecard places the strategy of the company – and not control efforts – at the centre of the process.[22] The measures are thus designed to pull employees towards the overall mission of the company.

The strength of the scorecard is that it provides a simple conceptual and diagnostic tool to ensure that companies utilise the right processes and people to drive customer and business performance – the goal of any company striving towards gaining a sustained competitive advantage.[23] To assist a company to determine whether the time is right to implement a Balanced Scorecard, Appendix 7.1 on page 166 includes an assessment tool.

7.2 The HR Scorecard

A recent development in the measurement area, which takes the Balanced Scorecard to the next level of sophistication, has been the arrival of the HR Scorecard. The HR Scorecard seeks to strengthen an aspect of the Balanced Scorecard approach which Norton and Kaplan acknowledge to be its weakest feature: the question of how best to integrate HR's role into the company's measurement of business performance.[24] The HR Scorecard is based on more than a decade of academic research on the relationship between HR and company performance. The HR Scorecard is grounded in the consulting work undertaken in a wide range of companies by Becker, Huselid, and Ulrich.[25] According to the authors, the HR Scorecard offers the following benefits[26]:

- It reinforces the distinction between HR doables and HR deliverables
- It enables control of costs and creation of value
- It measures leading indicators
- It assesses HR's contribution to strategy implementation and, ultimately, to the 'bottom line'

- It lets HR professionals effectively manage their strategic responsibilities
- It encourages flexibility and change.

7.2.1 Building an HR Scorecard

Organisations should not consider building an HR Scorecard as a one-time, or even an annual, event. To manage by measurement, human resource leaders must stay attuned to changes in the performance drivers that HR is supporting within the company. If these drivers change, or if the key HR deliverables that support them change, the scorecard must shift accordingly.[27] Table 7.1 on page 154 provides the seven steps needed to implement an HR Scorecard.

7.2.2 How does the HR Scorecard work?

The HR Scorecard helps to integrate HR into the organisational performance management and measurement system by identifying the points of intersection between HR and the organisation's strategy – in other words, strategic HR deliverables.[28] These are strategic HR outcomes that enable the execution of the organisation's strategy. The deliverables come in two categories:

- *HR performance drivers.* These are core people-related capabilities or assets such as employee productivity or employee satisfaction. It is important to note that there is actually no single correct set of performance drivers.[29] Each company identifies its own set, based on its unique characteristics and the requirements of its strategy-implementation process.
- *Enablers.* These reinforce performance drivers. For example, if a company identifies employee productivity as a core performance driver, then re-skilling might be an enabler.[30] However, it is important not to think here only in terms of HR-focused enablers in a company (those that influence the more central HR performance drivers), but to consider also how specific HR enablers reinforce performance drivers in the operations,

Table 7.1 Guidelines for implementing an HR Scorecard

Change Checklist Item	Guiding Questions for Change Sponsors	Suggested Guidelines for Implementation
1. Leading change	Who is in charge of the effort? Who sponsors? Who champions?	1. Need two sponsors (line manager, head of HR). 2. Require measurement champion: someone specializing in HR measurement. 3. Need advisory team to supervise work.
2. Creating a shared need	Why do the HR Scorecard? How does it fit with our business?	1. Create business case for HR and for HR measurement. 2. Share this case with line management and HR. 3. Allocate 3 to 5% of HR budget to measurement.
3. Shaping a vision	What is the desired outcome of the Scorecard?	1. Define desired outcomes of the HR Scorecard. 2. Prepare the key measures that will be tracked and monitored, and clarify how they will be tracked. 3. Define decisions that will be made using these measures. 4. Create a mechanism to collect the data behind the measures.
4. Mobilizing commitment	Who needs to support the project?	1. Identify key players whose support the project requires. 2. Figure out how to engage these key players so they will support it.
5. Building enabling systems	How do we build systems to sustain the change?	1. Put the right people on the project. 2. Ensure that we have the right incentives to do it. 3. Make sure that the HR measurement group reports to the right people. 4. Create a communication plan for HR measurement. 5. Invest in technology requirements to execute the HR Scorecard. 6. Make the financial investments required.
6. Monitoring and demonstrating progress	What will we use to track the implementation process?	Develop a project plan for HR measurement.
7. Making it last	How will we sustain the effort?	1. Start with simple measures. 2. Make the measures visible and applicable. 3. Post the measures. 4. Change the measures over time if required.

SOURCE: BECKER, B. E., HUSELID, M. A. & ULRICH, D. 2001. *The HR Scorecard: Linking people, strategy and performance*. Boston, Massachusetts: Harvard Business School Press:189. Used with permission.

customer, and financial segments of the organisation (see Figure 7.4).[31]

Figure 7.4 makes it clear that there are four major dimensions in the HR Scorecard, namely[32]:

- The key human resource deliverables that will leverage HR's role in a company's overall strategy (e.g. the extent to which employees' behaviour changes in ways that make a real difference to the business)
- The high-performance work system (e.g. the key HR policies and practices that must

be in place and implemented well to achieve the organisation's strategy)
- The extent to which that system is aligned with the company strategy (e.g. the extent to which the HR practices that a company deploys are internally consistent and not working at cross purposes and are really the right ones to drive organisational strategy)
- The efficiency with which the deliverables are generated (e.g. the extent to which managers are efficient in delivering HR services to the organisation).

Figure 7.4 Linking the HR Scorecard to the Business Scorecard

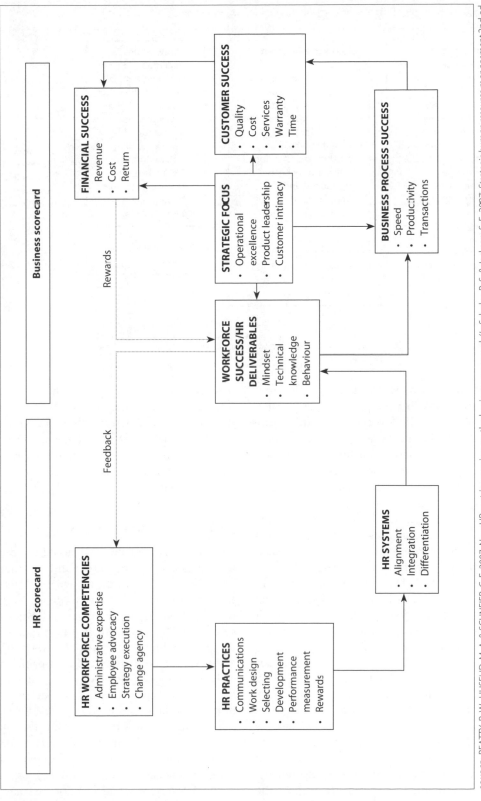

SOURCE: BEATTY, R. W., HUSELID, M. A. & SCHNEIER, C. E. 2007. New HR metrics: scoring on the business scorecard. (*In* Schuler, R. S. & Jackson, S. E. 2007. *Strategic human resource management* 2nd ed. Oxford: Blackwell Publishers:362.) Used with permission.

Figure 7.5 An example of an HR scorecard for a company's R&D function

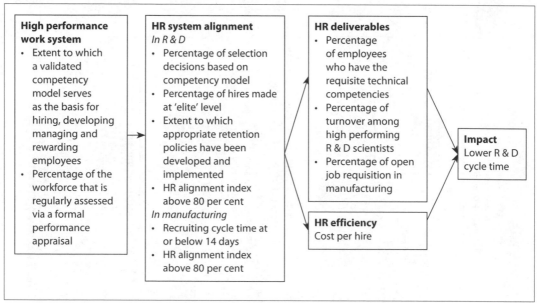

Figure 7.5 gives a basic idea of how an HR Scorecard might look in a company's R&D function (of course, an HR Scorecard for the entire company would include many more entries).

Finally, to be successful, the HR Scorecard requires investment in HR systems, the hiring of HR employees with the required competencies, the communication of the scorecard throughout the organisation, and the weaving of the HR results into reward and recognition systems (see figure 7.4). According to Beatty, Huselid, and Ulrich[33], the objective is to drive those types of workforce behaviour with substantial impact on business-process success that lead to customer success and, ultimately, result in financial success. Companies that are successful operationally and with their customers, according to the authors, should also experience financial success.[34] From the perspective of HR, it is a continuous feedback loop (see Figure 7.4). Financial success fuels the next new employee rewards. Customer success provides the feedback that enables the HR function to understand what needs to be done to build better (or different) HR workforce competencies, enhance HR practices, and determine the

necessary steps to improve the alignment, integration, and differentiation of HR systems.[35] All of this can be achieved only with a significant partnership with line management, which will enable line management also to be successful in delivering on its business model (e.g. the Balanced Scorecard).[36]

7.3 The Workforce Scorecard

Having implemented the Balanced Scorecard as well as the HR Scorecard within numerous organisations around the world, Huselid, Becker, and Beatty soon noticed, in their dealings with these organisations, that something was missing in this process.[37] It become obvious to them that it was not the activity that counts, but the impact of the activity on organisational outcomes that meant the most to companies. For example, the number of days of training provided was not important; what was important was the impact the training had on individuals and the organisation. The authors believed that companies needed a business strategy, a strategy for the HR function, and a workforce strategy.[38]

These strategies are operationalised in the Balanced Scorecard, the HR Scorecard, and the new proposed Workforce Scorecard respectively. Hence the Workforce Scorecard is a crucial lever in the strategy-execution process within companies. Figure 7.6 shows the integration of these scorecards.

7.3.1 The composition of the Workforce Scorecard

The Workforce Scorecard points out that workforce investments should help to execute strategy through the components of workforce mindset and culture, workforce competencies, and workforce behaviour.[39] These components become the link between strategy, HR investments, and the workforce, which leads to workforce success (see Figure 7.6).

We shall briefly look at the components of the Workforce Scorecard:

- *Workforce success.* This is the most important dimension of the Workforce Scorecard because it captures the 'bottom line' of the workforce performance.[40] These are the measures that reflect how well the workforce has contributed to the execution of the company's strategy. Typical measures here include the number and quality of customer complaints, the number of new distributors, and the response time for customer inquiries.[41]
- *Workforce mindset and culture.* The question in this area is two-fold: does the

Figure 7.6 Managing human capital to execute strategy

HR Scorecard ←	Workforce Scorecard ←		Balanced Scorecard
		Customer Success What specific customer desires and expectations must be satisfied?	Financial Success What specific financial commitments must be met?
	Leadership and Workforce Behaviours Are the leadership team and workforce consistently behaving in a way that will lead to achieving our strategic objectives?	Workforce Success Has the workforce accomplished the key strategic objectives for the business?	Operational Success What specific internal operational processes must be optimized?
HR SYSTEMS • Align • Integrate • Differentiate	Workforce Mindset and Culture Does the workforce understand our strategy and embrace it, and do we have the culture we need to support strategy execution?	Workforce Competencies Does the workforce, especially in the key or 'A' positions, have the skills it needs to execute our strategy?	
HR Workforce Competencies • Strategic partner • Change agent • Employee advocate • Administrative expert	HR Practices • Work design • Staffing • Development • Performance management • Rewards • Communication		

SOURCE: HUSELID, M. A., BECKER, B. E. & BEATTY, R. W. 2005. *The Workforce Scorecard: Managing human capital to execute strategy.* Boston, Massachusetts: Harvard Business School Press:4. Used with permission.

workforce understand the company strategy, and does the culture within the organisation support the execution of this strategy? Organisations create norms and expectations that the workforce needs to understand. This creates the culture of the organisation, which ultimately shapes employees' behaviour.[42] Managers can consequently measure and assess this culture in terms of its impact on the company's strategic success. Typical measures to use here include the extent to which the company strategy is clearly and widely understood, the extent to which the average employee can describe the company's HR strategy, and the extent to which employees take pride in working for the company.[43]

- *Workforce competencies.* The question in this area is: does the workforce have the skills it needs to execute the strategy? The competencies represent the knowledge, skills, and ability each employee possesses, and can also be measured and monitored.[44] Typical measures here include the effectiveness of information sharing among departments, the exposure of cross-functional job experiences, and the extent of organisation learning.[45]
- *Leadership and workforce behaviour.* The question in this area is: are the employees consistently behaving in a way that will lead to the achievement of the company's strategic objectives? To execute the strategy, leaders and employees must behave in ways consistent with the strategy.[46] These types of behaviour can be defined and measured to ensure that leaders and employees do what the strategy suggests needs to be done. Typical measures here are effectiveness in dealing with poor performers, percentage of employees making suggestions, and percentage retention of core-competency workforces.[47]

With these components in place, managers can answer the question of what measures to adopt and can now be held accountable not only for

their words and actions relative to people but also by the workforce's success, and for the mindset, capabilities, and types of behaviour they create.[48] Thus, companies can identify, target and develop, or move out managers who do not create workforce success (see Figure 7.6). It is important to mention here that while HR professionals and the HRM system lay the foundation for building the workforce into an strategic asset, the responsibility for workforce success increasingly falls on line managers who perform most of the workforce-management activities in any company.

7.3.2 Implementing the Workforce Scorecard

The successful implementation of the Workforce Scorecard is based, according to Huselid, Becker, and Beatty[49], on three challenges, namely:

- *The perspective challenge.* The question here is: do all our managers understand how workforce capabilities and behaviours drive strategy execution?
- *The metrics challenge.* The question here is: have we identified (and collected) the right measures of workforce success, leadership, workforce behaviour, workforce competencies, and workforce culture and mindset?
- *The execution challenge.* The question here is: do our managers have the access, capability, and motivation to use the data to communicate strategic intent and monitor progress towards strategy execution?

Bearing the above challenges in mind, we shall briefly look at the steps for practical implementation of the Workforce Scorecard within an organisation:

- *Step 1.* The first step in the process will be the development of a clear statement of the company's business strategies and the strategic capabilities needed to execute those strategies.
- *Step 2.* The next step will entail the identification of key jobs or 'A' positions as well as 'A' performance that will be required within these positions to execute

the company's strategy successfully.[50] This could be, for example, jobs in R&D, Manufacturing, Marketing etc. By using the components in the scorecard, measures for these components for the different areas can be developed. (Note that it is possible that the measures for the workforce mindset, workforce competencies, and workforce behaviour for the individual areas, e.g. R&D, can be largely the same, while measures for workforce success, for example, may differ considerably for these areas.)

- *Step 3.* The next step will involve the company's HRM system, which must elicit the needed competencies and types of behaviour from the workforce that ultimately drive the company's success. The tool that can be used here is the HR Scorecard. According to Huselid, Becker, and Beatty, the following are questions to ask here:

> Is our total investment in the workforce appropriate?
> Are our HR practices aligned with the business strategy, integrated with each other, and differentiated across employee groups, where appropriate?
> Have we designed and implemented strategically aligned, world-class HRM policies and practices throughout the business?
> Do our HR professionals have the skills they need to design and implement a world-class HRM system?

From the above process, it is clear that a team of people will have to be involved in this process if it is to be successful. The team must include the CEO and the executive team, line managers, the workforce, and HRM. Without them, the whole process is doomed.

SUMMARY

This chapter considered the new and innovative performance-measurement instruments – known as scorecards – found in the business world today. It discussed in detail the Balanced Scorecard, the HR Scorecard, and the Workforce Scorecard, focusing respectively on the business strategy, a strategy for the HR function, and a workforce strategy. The development of these scorecards promises great rewards, but their implementation is no easy task. It is clear that the potential for future growth and development of these scorecards is dramatic and that the work in this area continues, with the most exciting breakthroughs still to come.

KEY CONCEPTS

- Balanced Scorecard
- Balanced Scorecard champion
- Bottom line
- Competencies
- Custom perspective
- Deliverables
- Financial perspective
- High-performance work system
- HR Scorecard
- Human capital
- Information systems
- Innovation and learning perspective
- Internal perspective
- Knowledge workers
- Leadership and workforce behaviours
- Operating efficiencies
- Performance drivers
- Performance enablers
- Strategic success
- Workforce competencies
- Workforce mindset and culture
- Workforce Scorecard
- Workforce success

CASE STUDY

Objective: To indicate how HR can become more accountable within organisations

IBM's HR takes a risk

When Palmisano announced his signature Business Transformation initiative, he called for IBM to establish an 'on demand' global supply chain that provides customers with IBM products and services – software, hardware, business processing, consulting and more – wherever and whenever they need it. He then eliminated layers of management bureaucracy and moved the workforce closer to its global clients so that the company could compete on service delivery.

Today, under Palmisano, the IT giant generates more than $90 billion in revenues. With 330,000 employees, it is among the 15 largest publicly traded companies in the world.

Central to its resurgence is IBM's recognition that human capital is its most distinctive and manageable asset. Companies that rely on technological or manufacturing innovation alone cannot expect to dominate their markets indefinitely. Competitors can and do catch up. The quality and strategic deployment of talent is what separates winners from the also-rans.

That's why Palmisano chose to center IBM's business strategy on the belief that its people are, and will continue to be, IBM's key market differentiator. HR and talent management – not computers – are IBM's core business.

HR at centre stage

As a result of Palmisano's initiative, HR finds itself in the spotlight. No need to fight for a seat at the table. No struggle to convince line executives that HR should be their business partner. HR's job is to deliver the people, to establish a ready supply chain of talent that will outperform the competition from top to bottom, from the executive suite to the factory floor. Palmisano has made it clear that if the company begins to lose revenue or market share, HR's piece of the responsibility will come from not delivering the right people to the right jobs at the right time.

The game is not for the faint of heart. When IBM wins, HR gets to share the champagne; if the company loses, HR's head is on the block.

In this case, the head belongs to Randy MacDonald, senior vice president of HR. A seasoned HR executive, MacDonald has Palmisano's ear and the respect of his fellow executives in the C-suite. His fingerprints are all over the key strategic and operational decisions of the corporation. 'They know Randy can cut costs, fire people, call a spade a spade. He has a history in the way he has stood up to union drives and taken criticism for IBM's cuts in pensions and other benefits for retirees,' says Fred Foulkes, professor and director of the Human Resources Policy Institute at Boston University School of Management.

His success has earned him the confidence at the top level. 'The more success you have, the more license you're granted,' Foulkes explains.

MacDonald has taken that license and run with it. Foulkes says IBM's HR operation and MacDonald's business orientation are cutting-edge. 'Clearly a leader like Randy has enormous impact,' he says. 'He is among this generation's top HR leaders.'

Now, MacDonald is taking a big risk. He's gambling on a radical HR restructuring that must pan out for IBM to continue as a market leader. 'I don't mean to be arrogant about it, but this is leading-edge,' he claims. 'My team is doing things in the 21st century that nobody else has done. It's the wave of the future.'

HR's strategic gamble

Keeping the human capital supply flowing wherever it's needed is a daunting undertaking, one that MacDonald says is discussed in general HR circles but until now has not been done. The challenge led him to rethink the way HR delivers services. He says typical HR organisations operate out of silos – talent, learning, employee relations, benefits, diversity – a structure that's ineffective and inefficient. 'Blow it all up is my attitude. Don't think about silos; think about end-to-end process.'

True to his word, in December, MacDonald announced a worldwide, $100 million reorganisation of HR, the Workplace Management Initiative (WMI), which segmented the 330,000 employees into a layer cake of three customer sets. One layer consists of executive and technical resources, another holds managerial talent, and the third is rank-and-file employees.

Separate cross-functional HR teams serve each layer, by the end of this year, MacDonald says, 'We'll manage each person within each group as an asset and develop them accordingly. You'll have talent, learning and compensation people all managing people within their assigned levels.'

MacDonald says it's his responsibility to challenge the business plans of each unit in IBM. 'If I look at a three-year plan and it says we're going to enter new markets, I have to decide what skills we'll need three years from now to compete in these markets. I have to look at what existing skills I have that will become obsolete.'

Using metrics, MacDonald already knows his workforce breakdown. 'In three years, 22 percent of our workforce will have obsolete skills. Of the 22 percent, 85 percent have fundamental competencies that we can build on to get them ready for skills we'll need years from now.' The remaining 15 percent will either self-select out of IBM or be let go.

Roles and skill sets

No one at IBM is safe from being in that obsolete category. Everyone from top to bottom will be assessed and reassessed on their competency levels and placed where IBM needs them – whether it be in the United States, India or anywhere else IBM expands in the future. Those who are lacking necessary competencies will have the opportunity to be trained if they can and want to be.

Under WMI, every role that workers, managers and executives play – 490 in all – has been identified and defined. All IBM employees play at least one role, sometimes two, maybe even three. (For example, Ted Hoff, vice president for learning, is a learning leader and a

manager.) Internal analysts studied what people do in each role and determined the functional expertise or skill sets that the roles require in each job. There are 4,000 skill sets, all closely defined and measurable, and monitored by MacDonald and his HR team.

By the end of this year, each employee will have conducted a self-assessment and reviewed it with his or her manager to discuss the level of mastery the worker has achieved in each skill set. 'The manager will be sitting with a checklist of skills that you'll need for your job,' Hoff explains. 'This will provide precision about performance and also will offer a road map as to how we've developed each person. We're not measuring how well you perform on a written test. We're measuring how you've demonstrated mastery in each skill set through your performance.'

Ratings are made on a continuum from zero to three:
- Zero – You have not demonstrated a significant mastery of the skill set.
- One – You have demonstrated acquired knowledge, understand what's needed in the role and understand the bottom-line results that are being sought. But you have not yet applied it in a demonstrated way.
- Two – You have done something around the skill set that shows you have a level of mastery that has been applied.
- Three – You have achieved a mastery level demonstrated by the fact that you're not only proficient, but that you're developing others around it.

Assessments in hand, employees will be told where they stand. 'We'll tell you where we see your skill sets, which skills you have that will become obsolete and what jobs we anticipate will become available down the road,' MacDonald says. 'We'll direct you to training programs that will prepare you for the future.'

MacDonald says that the early warning system should be a morale booster. 'People will sit back and say, "I get this, you notified me. Now I've got time to do something about it." '

Yet some people won't. 'There's a segment that will choose to opt out; there's nothing I can do about it,' he says. 'There's a segment that can't get re-skilled; they don't have the intellectual capability or the drive to do it. But whatever happens, people will be able to decide for themselves. Three years from now, I can look people in the eye and say, "We told you, but you didn't do it." '

The purpose of the ratings is so that MacDonald can easily locate who at IBM has the skill set needed for an open position anywhere in the world and fill it quickly. It will mean employees will have less security about what their job will be and where it will be in the future. But, because the overall IBM business strategy is to meet customers' demands wherever they are, the IIR strategy has to follow.

Assembling the team

To fulfil this strategy throughout the global company, MacDonald had to assemble an HR team that is truly business-oriented. Karen Calo, vice president for global talent in Armonk, N.Y., supervises team talent directors who are assigned to work with the managing directors of IBM's line units such as Global Technology Services (GTS) and Global Business Services.

'The talent directors report to me but work directly with the business leader they're assigned to support,' she says. 'They do a lot of similar activities, helping to develop strategic and operations plans but in different contexts. If you're [a talent director] in Hardware, you may deal with issues relative to product life cycle; in a service business, you may be working on integrating solutions.'

The tie that binds all talent directors is knowledge of the individual business sectors. 'If you are an HR person who doesn't understand the business you're supporting, you can't be successful,' says Calo. 'You don't necessarily need an HR degree; you can always learn HR. Deep subject-matter expertise is important in some areas like compensation. But from a generalist standpoint, some of our most interesting hires come from outside HR.'

In recruiting for HR, Calo says she's 'intrigued by the business professional who really has been out there on the line who really understands the business, has good judgment and good common sense.'

Kari Barbar, vice president of learning, is an example. An experienced hardware engineer, Barbar, who is based in Research Triangle Park, N.C., recently transferred into HR to work directly with Mike Daniels, senior vice president of GTS in Somers, N.Y. 'Five years ago, I would not have considered leaving hardware development to move to HR,' she says. 'But now, I see that our ability to develop expertise is what distinguishes IBM from its competitors. In HR, I'm involved in driving the transition of the company.'

Barbar's job is to determine the professional and technical skills that her client, Daniels, requires to grow GTS. She must provide both the selection of talent and training of existing talent and demonstrate to Daniels' satisfaction that she has delivered value.

To help develop those skill sets across the board, last year, IBM spent more than $700 million training its workforce. Ninety-five percent of the funding came not from HR's budget, but from line managers' budgets. Putting the training line item on managers' budgets ensures that the training is connected to their business goals. At the end of the day, HR and MacDonald will have to produce evidence to the line managers who funded the training that it has helped to keep the pipeline flowing.

The pipeline also includes senior-level positions. Succession planning is a standing agenda item at Palmisano's monthly executive team meetings. Calo, Palmisano and his direct reports discuss the merits of candidates for any open senior-level position. 'We present a diverse slate of candidates who can fill the role, describe the competencies they have and those that are required for the position,' Calo says. 'After discussion and consensus within the Operating Team members, the position is filled.'

Going for broke

At this point, the rollout of WMI is just beginning and the jury is out on whether the new silo-less, integrated HR will make HR more effective. Even the usually confident MacDonald is uncertain. 'This is the first time in my life I'm afraid,' he says. 'The restructuring is so radical.' Still, he relishes his opportunity to run with the innovation. 'I'm here to lead, not follow,' he says.

And he urges other HR executives to follow his example and step up. 'I don't care if you're sitting on top at IBM or you're at a Fortune 1000 company. You are entrusted by the shareholders to protect the assets of the corporation that are human in nature. Don't worry about jargon like 'business partner'. You should be just like any other senior executive making a difference to your company.'

Questions and activities

1. It is not very clear from the information provided in the case study whether IBM is at present using any of the three scorecards – i.e. the Balanced Scorecard, the HR Scorecard, and the Workforce Scorecard – discussed in this chapter for performance-measurement purposes. Having evaluated the information in this case, would you say that IBM is ready to implement the three scorecards? Motivate your answer in detail.

2. If IBM does not use any of the scorecards, how would you advise the company to implement these scorecards? Write an essay on how you would suggest it goes about it.

SOURCE: GROSSMAN, R. J. 2007. IBM's HR takes risk. *HR magazine*, 52(4):56–59. Used with permission.

REVIEW QUESTIONS AND ACTIVITIES

1. Why has the role of HRM changed so dramatically over the past few years? Discuss briefly.
2. Briefly discuss the four perspectives of the Balanced Scorecard.
3. Write a short paragraph on who is responsible for compiling the Balanced Scorecard.
4. How would you go about implementing the Balanced Scorecard within your organisation?
5. What, in your view, is the strength of the Balanced Scorecard?

6. Briefly discuss the benefits of the HR Scorecard.
7. Write a short paragraph on how the HR Scorecard works by referring to the four dimensions of the scorecard.
8. What, in your view, are the attributes of a successful HR Scorecard? Briefly discuss.
9. Write a short paragraph on the rationale for the existence of a Workforce Scorecard within an organisation.
10. Briefly discuss the four components of the Workforce Scorecard.

FURTHER READING

NIVEN, P. R. 2006. *Balanced Scorecard: Step-by-step-maximising performance and maintaining results* 2nd ed. HoBoken, N.J.: John Wiley & Sons.

NIVEN, P. R. 2005. *Balanced Scorecard diagnostics: Maintaining maximum performance.* Hoboken, N.J.: John Wiley & Sons.

BECKER, B. E., HUSELID, M. A. & ULRICH, D. 2001. *The HR Scorecard: Linking people, strategy and performance.* Boston, Massachusetts: Harvard Business School Press:23.

HUSELID, M. A., BECKER, B. E. & BEATTY, R. W. 2005. *The Workforce Scorecard: Managing human capital to execute strategy.* Boston, Massachusetts: Harvard Business School Press.

OLVE, N-G., PETRI, E. J., ROY, J. & ROY, S. 2003. *Making scorecards actionable: Balancing strategy and control.* West Sussex: John Wiley & Sons.

WEB SITES

www.balancedscorecard.org/ – Balanced Scorecard Institute – devoted to the Balanced Scorecard approach

www.business-intelligence.co.uk/reports/hr_score/summary.asp – Business Intelligence Report – step-by-step guide on how to create an HR scorecard

www.oracle.com/applications/performance-management/ent/module/wrkfrc_scorecard.html – Peoplesoft – learn about the Workforce Scorecard

ENDNOTES

1. BEATTY, R. W., HUSELID, M. A. & SCHNEIER, C. E. 2007. New HR metrics: scoring on the business scorecard. (*In* Schuler, R. S. & Jackson, S. E. 2007. *Strategic human resource management* 2nd ed. Oxford: Blackwell Publishers:352.)
2. Ibid.
3. NIVEN, P. R. 2005. *Balanced Scorecard diagnostics: Maintaining maximum performance.* Hoboken, N.J.: John Wiley & Sons:16–17.
4. KAPLAN, R. S. & NORTON, D. P. 2005. The Balanced Scorecard: measures that drive performance. *Harvard business review,* 8(7):172–179.
5. This discussion is based on the work of R. S. Kaplan and D. P. Norton (2005) and based on the following

article: KAPLAN, R. S. & NORTON, D. P. 2005. The Balanced Scorecard: measures that drive performance. *Harvard business review,* 8(7):172–179.
6. KAPLAN, R. S. & NORTON, D. P. 2005. The Balanced Scorecard: measures that drive performance. *Harvard business review,* 8(7):175.
7. Ibid.:176. See also NIVEN, P. R. 2005. Driving focus and alignment with the Balanced Scorecard: why organisations need a Balanced Scorecard. *The journal for quality and participation,* 28(4):1–5.
8. KAPLAN, R. S. & NORTON, D. P. 2005. The Balanced Scorecard: measures that drive performance. *Harvard business review,* 8(7):177.
9. Ibid.:178.

10. NIVEN, P. R. 2005. Driving focus and alignment with the Balanced Scorecard: why organisations need a Balanced Scorecard. *The journal for quality and participation*, 28(4):42.
11. Ibid.:43. See also NIVEN, P. R. 2006. *Balanced Scorecard: Step-by-step-maximising performance and maintaining results.* HoBoken, N.J.: John Wiley & Sons.
12. NIVEN, P. R. 2005. Driving focus and alignment with the Balanced Scorecard: why organisations need a Balanced Scorecard. *The journal for quality and participation*, 28(4):44.
13. Ibid.:45.
14. Ibid.
15. Ibid.:135.
16. Ibid.:48–49.
17. Ibid.:139–141.
18. Ibid.:147–148.
19. KAPLAN, R. S. & NORTON, D. P. 1992. The Balanced Scorecard: measures that drive performance. *Harvard business review*, January/February:73.
20. NIVEN, P. R. 2005. Driving focus and alignment with the Balanced Scorecard: why organisations need a Balanced Scorecard. *The journal for quality and participation*, 28(4):xi.
21. KAPLAN, R. S. & NORTON, D. P. 2005. The Balanced Scorecard: measures that drive performance. *Harvard business review*, 8(7):179.
22. KAPLAN, R. S. & NORTON, D. P. 1992. The Balanced Scorecard: measures that drive performance. *Harvard business review*, January/February:79.
23. YEUNG, A. K. & BERMAN, B. 1997. Adding value through human resources: reorienting human resource measurement to drive business performance. *Human resource management*, 36(3):325.
24. BECKER, B. E., HUSELID, M. A. & ULRICH, D. 2001. *The HR Scorecard: linking people, strategy and performance.* Boston, Massachusetts: Harvard Business School Press:23.
25. Ibid.:xiii.
26. Ibid.:75–76.
27. Ibid.:77.
28. Ibid.:30.
29. Ibid.:31.
30. Ibid.:32.
31. Ibid.:33.
32. Ibid.:53. See also ELLIS, G. 2001. The HR Balanced Scorecard: linking strategy to people performance. *Management today*, 17(7):40–41.
33. BEATTY, R. W., HUSELID, M. A. & SCHNEIER, C. E. 2007. New HR metrics: scoring on the business scorecard. (*In* Schuler, R. S. & Jackson, S. E. 2007. *Strategic human resource management* 2nd ed. Oxford: Blackwell Publishers:362.)
34. Ibid.
35. Ibid.:364.
36. Ibid.
37. HUSELID, M. A., BECKER, B. E. & BEATTY, R. W. 2005. *The Workforce Scorecard: Managing human capital to execute strategy.* Boston, Massachusetts: Harvard Business School Press:xv.
38. Ibid.:3.
39. Ibid.:x.
40. Ibid.:6–8.
41. Ibid.:72.
42. Ibid.:9.
43. Ibid.:79–80.
44. Ibid.:9.
45. Ibid.:76–77.
46. Ibid.:8.
47. Ibid.:74.
48. Ibid.:xi.
49. Ibid. Based on the work of HUSELID, M. A., BECKER, B. E. & BEATTY, R. W. 2005. *The Workforce Scorecard: Managing human capital to execute strategy.* Boston, Massachusetts: Harvard Business School Press:14.
50. Ibid.:83–100.

Appendix 7.1

Assessing the need for a Balanced Scorecard

To complete the exercise, read each statement in Table A5 and determine how much you agree with what is stated. The more you agree, the higher the score you assign. For example, if you fully agree, assign a score of five points.

Table A5 Assessing the need for a Balanced Scorecard

1 2 3 4 5	1.	Our organisation has invested in Total Quality Management (TQM) and other improvement initiatives but we have not seen a corresponding increase in financial or customer results.
1 2 3 4 5	2.	If we did not produce our current Performance Reports for a month, nobody would notice.
1 2 3 4 5	3.	We create significant value from the intangible assets such as employee knowledge and innovation, customer relationships, and a strong culture.
1 2 3 4 5	4.	We have a strategy (or have had strategies in the past) but have a hard time successfully implementing it.
1 2 3 4 5	5.	We rarely review our performance measures and make suggestions for new and innovative indicators.
1 2 3 4 5	6.	Our senior management team spends the majority of its time together discussing variances from plan and other operational issues.
1 2 3 4 5	7.	Budgeting at our organisation is political and based largely on historical trends.
1 2 3 4 5	8.	Our employees do not have a solid understanding of our mission, vision, and strategy.
1 2 3 4 5	9.	Our employees do not know how their day-to-day actions contribute to the organisation's success.
1 2 3 4 5	10.	Nobody owns the performance measurement process at our organisation.
1 2 3 4 5	11.	We have numerous initiatives taking place at our organisation, and it's possible that not all are truly strategic in nature.
1 2 3 4 5	12.	There is little accountability in our organisation for the things we agree as a group to do.
1 2 3 4 5	13.	People tend to stay in their 'silos', and as a result we have little collaboration among departments.
1 2 3 4 5	14.	Our employees have difficulty accessing the critical information they need to serve customers.
1 2 3 4 5	15.	Priorities at our organisation are often dictated by current necessity or 'fire-fighting'.
1 2 3 4 5	16.	The environment in which we operate is changing, and in order to succeed, we too must change.
1 2 3 4 5	17.	We face increased pressure from stakeholders to demonstrate results.
1 2 3 4 5	18.	We do not have clearly defined performance targets for both financial and nonfinancial indicators.
1 2 3 4 5	19.	We cannot clearly articulate our strategy in a one-page document or 'map'.
1 2 3 4 5	20.	We sometimes make decisions that are beneficial in the short term but may harm long-term value-creation.

Scoring key:

20–30: If your score fell in this range you most likely have a strong performance measurement discipline in place. The programme has been cascaded throughout your organisation to ensure that all employees are contributing to your success, and it is linked to key management processes.

31–60: You may have a performance measurement system in place but are not experiencing the benefits you anticipated or need to succeed. Using the Balanced Scorecard as a Strategic Management System would be of benefit to you.

61–100: Scores in this range suggest difficulty in successfully implementing your strategy and meeting the needs of your customers and other stakeholders. A Balanced Scorecard system is strongly recommended to help you focus on the implementation of strategy and align your organisation with overall goals.

Source: NIVEN, P. R. 2005. (26–27) Balanced Scorecard diagnostics: Maintaining maximum performance. Hoboken, N.J.: John Wiley & Sons. Used with permission.

8

Ethical issues and challenges in human resource management

Learning outcomes

After reading this chapter you should be able to:

▶ Define the concepts 'ethics' and 'business ethics'
▶ Identify and discuss the ethical dimensions of a strategic HRM paradigm
▶ Explain the ethical decision-making frameworks of utilitarianism, Kantian deontology, justice, and rights and be able to apply them to the HR function and activities
▶ Identify and discuss issues that arise in the employment relationship from the perspective of utilitarianism, Kantian deontology, justice, and rights
▶ Discuss the role of HR professionals in the management of corporate ethics programmes

Purpose

The purpose of this chapter is to explore the ethical issues and challenges that arise in the practice of HRM.

Chapter overview

The chapter begins with an explanation of the term 'ethics' and its relevance to enterprises in the South African business and social environment. It goes on to introduce ethical dimensions of a strategic HRM paradigm. These dimensions include the loyalties that HR professionals have to the enterprises that employ them and that may directly conflict with the interests of organisational members or be contrary to the values of their professional code of conduct. To help HR professionals resolve the problem of multiple loyalties, as well as to identify and resolve myriad ethics issues that arise in the employment relationship, the chapter will explain and discuss four major ethical decision-making frameworks. Thereafter, it will explore the literature on the role of HR professionals in the management of corporate ethics programmes and corporate ethics cultures. The concluding case study illustrates how the theory contained in this chapter can be applied to a practical situation.

Introduction

Several chapters in this book have discussed how the HR function has evolved from an ancillary administrative service to a strategic partnership, and have considered the attendant changes in the role of the HR professional. One area which has not received attention is ethics. This chapter will address the ethical dimensions of the HR function and HR activities, and the ethical challenges associated with a strategic HR paradigm. It will also introduce ethical decision-making frameworks and discuss the role of HR in developing and implementing corporate ethics programmes. Chapter 9 will address such programmes in more detail and, in particular, the concepts of corporate citizenship and corporate governance. Before we address these issues, we shall clarify the meaning of the term 'ethics' and its relevance to the management of enterprises, both domestically and globally.

8.1 Ethics and the South African business environment

Most definitions characterise ethics as referring to standards of conduct or codes of conduct for specialised groups.[1] Thus, we refer to the ethics of accountants or the code of ethics for the HR profession. The term 'ethics' is also used to denote the field of moral philosophy. Moral philosophy or philosophical theories of ethics are concerned with principles of conduct that govern behaviour. These theories or principles provide the ultimate ground of justification for ethical beliefs about right and wrong behaviour. Singer, a renowned moral philosopher, explains[2]:

Ethics deals with values, with good and bad, with right and wrong. We cannot avoid involvement in ethics for what we do and we don't do is always a possible subject of ethical evaluation. Anyone who thinks about what he or she ought to do is, consciously or unconsciously, involved in ethics.

SOURCE: SINGER, P. (Ed.). 1993. *A companion to ethics.* Oxford: Basil Blackwell:v.

Business ethics (or management ethics) focuses on moral standards as they apply to organisations and the behaviour of organisational members. Most decisions in business, particularly those relating to HR, have an ethical component. Business ethics thus requires an integrated approach to decision making. An integrated approach recognises that managers must take the moral point of view as well as make economically sound decisions and act within applicable law.

The moral point of view requires people to act impartially and in accordance with reason, rather than on the sole basis of self-interest or tradition. If ethics is about relationships between people, then business ethics is about relationships between stakeholders and the recognition that their divergent interests must be accommodated.

Decisions must also be understood as involving different levels of analysis, including the individual, the organisational, the professional, the business system, and societal levels.[4-5] Employment equity is a case in point.

Business ethics has two important anchors in South African-based public and private enterprises. The first is the Constitution's founding values of human dignity, the achievement of equality, and the advancement of human rights and freedom.[6] In the post-apartheid twenty-first century, these values are highly salient to the practice of HRM. For example, the recognition that all people are of equal importance has implications for the deployment of human resources by HR professionals and other managers. The second anchor is the *King (II) report on corporate governance*[7], which has been instrumental in moving ethics onto the agenda of corporate boards in South African-based enterprises.

However, the *Business ethics South Africa 2002 survey*[8] reported that many enterprises face high levels of risk, through paying lip-service to ethics management. Similarly, the *King Report* recognised that many enterprises need to put in place training programmes to develop ethical competency and to develop organisational processes that embed ethics into organisational cultures and operations.

The HRM activities of recruitment, selection, training and development, compensation, and performance management are not only a means to gaining competitive advantage; they are also important vehicles for promulgating an ethical culture. This chapter will now focus on the ethical dimensions of the strategic HR paradigm and HR activities, as well as developing competencies for ethical decision-making. (Many institutes, professional bodies, and Web sites are dedicated to ethics in the workplace. If you would like to do further research on the topics this chapter raises, the Web sites listed in Table 8.1 are a useful starting point. The resources they provide will help you to undertake further research on the topics covered in this chapter and to undertake ethics initiatives in your enterprises. Many of these Web sites provide hundreds of annotated links to other Web sites, as well as links to research articles and large amounts of other useful content.)

Table 8.1 Web site resources for ethics and HRM

Web site	Details
www.amanet.org	The American Management Association
www.kpmg.co.za and www.tisa.org.za	Ethics Survey – 2001 Ethics in Practice by KPMG and Transparency International, South Africa to measure the extent to which South Africa's public services, private corporations and civil society organisations succeeded in establishing ethics management practices
www.ethics.org.au	The St James Ethics Centre, Australia provides consultancy services to enterprises, the Corporate Social Responsibility Index, and papers on various business ethics topics
www.shrm.org	Society of Human Resource Management, USA
www.siopsa.org.za	Society of Industrial and Organisational Psychology of South Africa
www.ahri.com.au	Australian HR Institute
www.sabpp.co.za	South African Board for Personnel Practice (professional HR institute)
www.hrcosa.co.za	Human Resource Council of South Africa
www.apso.co.za	Association of Personnel Service Organisations of SA
www.ethicsa.org	The Ethics Institute of South Africa
www.acts.co.za	Acts Online
www.ibe.org.uk	Institute of Business Ethics in the UK
www.corpwatch.org	Corporate Watch activists
www.bsr.org	Business for Social Responsibility
www.web-miner.com/busethics.htm	The definitive Web site resource for business ethics research by Sharon Stoeger
www.humanresourcesmagazine.com.au	*Human resources* magazine, an Australian bi-weekly publication for the HR profession
www.cauxroundtable.org/	Caux Round Table Principles of enterprises engaged in global business
www.utilitarianism.com/	Provides information, book chapters, and articles on utilitarianism
http://faculty.frostburg.edu/phil/forum/Kant.htm	Provides information about Kant's theory of ethics
www.sweatshops.org and www.sweatshopwatch.org	Provides information on sweatshops around the world
www.eben.org	Links to ethics organisations, university programmes, and research institutes
www.ethics.org	Ethics Research Center (ERC) in Washington, D.C.; access to National Business Ethics Survey, Ethics Toolkit and other valuable resources

8.2 Ethical dimensions of a strategic HRM paradigm

Chapter 1 introduced the early paradigms of HRM and the evolution of the strategic HRM paradigm, while Chapter 4 explored the basic principles and various models of strategic HRM. Although some have questioned the extent to which the HR profession has practiced strategic HRM[9], there is some evidence that the transition from administrative functions to the strategic planning role is in progress. For example, the *2006 Strategic HR Management Survey*, conducted by the USA-based Society for Human Resource Management (SHRM)[10], reported that more than 50 per cent of HR professionals indicated that strategic planning is part of their function.

In this section our attention turns to the ethical dimensions of the changing paradigms of HRM. This involves two related, but distinct, problems. The first is the problem of dual loyalties and the second is the role of the HR professional in an integrity-based approach to strategic business partnership. These problems arise because the transformation of the HR function has left unresolved tensions between the aims of the traditional welfare, administrative, and service roles and the aims of a new strategic role. In particular, the current emphasis on strategic HRM heightens the potential conflict of loyalties for HR professionals who have to balance their dual membership in the HR profession grounded in the values of 'fair and efficient' management of people and in the corporate environment focused on values which have more to do with economic rationalism.[11] The HR function has developed out of a concern for the individual, the enterprise, and society in response to relevant management and social problems of the day. HR practices have been driven by multiple values, including efficiency, competitiveness, care, respect for individuals, rights, and justice. As long as HR professionals are concerned with both the management of systems and the management of people, it is difficult to see how they will be able give up any one of these values. Operationalising the proper balance between conflicting values remains

complex and goes to the heart of strategically managing human resources with integrity. For example, do the means employed by HR professionals condone corporate ends and can those ends be justified? Moreover, to be regarded as a profession, HR practitioners must have a degree of independence commensurate with their exercising critical analyses of corporate policies and practices in the service of the public good.

8.2.1 The problem of dual loyalties

HR executives who are expert in both financial and people skills are in a strong position to balance judgments of economic rationality with social responsibility. However, both anecdotal and research evidence suggest that some HR practitioners find this position burdensome. They see conflict between the understanding of themselves as 'friends of the workers' and their new role as management's instruments of competitive advantage.[12] Three examples from the research literature serve to illustrate this point:

- Firstly, studies have consistently found that respondents cite pressure to meet unrealistic or overly aggressive business objectives and deadlines as the most likely factor to cause organisational members to compromise their companies' ethical standards. For example, this response was reported by 70 per cent of respondents to the 2006 AMA/HRI survey[13], 48 per cent of respondents to the 2003 SHRM/ERC survey[14], and 50 per cent of respondents in a 2007 Australian study.[15]
- Secondly, Schwoerer, May, and Benson's study of 785 members of the Society for Human Resource Management in the USA found that 'many organisations report difficulty establishing a balanced and coherent strategy between employee and employer rights'.[16]
- Thirdly, Hendry suggests that in the UK it has been difficult for HR managers to act as a 'neutral go-between' and that the HR manager 'became more unequivocally the representative of management, counter-

balancing the power of trade unions and individual rights enshrined in legislation'.[17]

Hendry's suggestion is congruent with many UK researchers who have been critical of the unitarist and managerialist views of HR, maintaining instead that workers and managers have different interests. The unitarist assumption that the interests of employees are the same as those of their employers gives rise to the view that the proper employee–employer relationship is one of partnership.[18-20] This contrasts with the pluralist perspective that recognises the possibility of diverse interest groups and sources of loyalty or, even worse, inevitable conflict between employers and employees. A paradigm shift from pluralism to unitarism is problematic. On the one hand, treating human resources as valued assets, integrating HR policies into the business strategy, and striving for employee commitment through the management of culture, rather than seeking compliance with rules and regulations, can be viewed as beneficial to both employees and employers. On the other hand, these practices may allow labour to be used as business needs dictate and can therefore be thought of as serving primarily the interests of employers.[21] Moreover, when corporate ethics and corporate culture are seen solely as systems for controlling behaviour, they function at the lowest level of moral development. Not surprisingly, then, the nature and role of socialisation in the workplace raises myriad ethical issues for HR professionals charged with developing corporate cultures and embedding ethics into them. These issues arise because the process of socialisation or induction into an organisation's culture tends to move beyond fostering knowledge of cultural norms and values to promoting the internalisation of corporate values by individual members. As Hoffman[22] has noted, it is moral autonomy that enables corporate cultures to be critiqued.

Developing strategies and policies that protect employees' interests, yet balance operational and human resource needs, is a difficult mandate because it requires HR professionals to quantify the contribution of human resources to organisational performance in ways that do not compromise respect for, and the dignity of, individual organisational members. It is not surprising, therefore, that HR professionals may experience some ambivalence about the pursuit of competitive advantage, particularly when one considers that HR activities such as staffing, compensation, and training have a direct impact upon organisational members in a way that other business functions – e.g. sales, marketing, finance, and production – do not.[23]

8.2.2 HR professional codes of conduct

When faced with conflicts of dual loyalties many professionals turn to their profession's code of ethics for guidance. Professional codes of conduct serve as 'moral anchors', embody a profession's values, help it to establish an ethical climate, and provide a framework for evaluating alternative courses of action.[24] Professional codes of conduct can also reassure stakeholders (the public, employees, managers, and shareholders) that a profession's activities are underpinned by moral principles, and provide stakeholders with a benchmark by which to evaluate the ethical performance of a profession.

Traditionally, professional codes of ethics for professions such as accountancy, architecture, engineering, journalism, medicine, pastoral counselling, public administration, social work, and education have recognised that loyalty is owed to affected stakeholders in the following order of priority:

1. The public (including employees and consumers)
2. The profession
3. The client and employer
4. The individual professional.[25-26]

However, this has not always been the case with HR professional bodies. Prior to 2006, the code of ethics for SHRM, which has a membership in excess of 120 000, took a balanced approach to the multiple responsibilities its members have to internal and external stakeholders, but gave primacy to the fair and equal treatment of employees and the public interest.[27] This was in contrast to the pre-2006 *Charter of Professional Standards* from the Australian Human

Resources Institute (AHRI), which addressed the problem of primary responsibility by stating that the first responsibility of HR professionals was to their employer.[28] The South African Board for Personnel Practice (SABPP) is a professional body for managers, practitioners, consultants, academics, and students in the field of HRM and has a membership of over 7000. The pre-2006 *Code of Professional Conduct* from the SABPP somewhat ambiguously stated that, 'registered members of the human resources profession are obliged to uphold certain standards in their practice, both in the interests of the public and their calling'.[29]

Recently, all three of these professional HR bodies, in consultation with their respective members, revised their codes of ethical and professional standards. Both SHRM and AHRI bypassed the issue of dual loyalties and instead now refer to standards and values such as advancing the profession, honesty, integrity, confidentiality, justice, competence, lawfulness, and organisational capability. However, at its board meeting in August 2006, the SABPP approved in principle a new *Code of conduct* which appears to recognise directly the problem of conflicting or dual loyalties and gives a clear statement on them to its members (see Box 1 on the next page). In part, the SABPP code states[30]:

> Our first responsibility is to meaningfully transform the lives of those men and women that are employed by the organisations we serve. We have a further responsibility to contribute to the success and sustainability of the organisations that employ us or that we render a service to. It is our responsibility to comply with the expectations of our profession and fellow practitioners. We accept responsibility for the outcomes of our actions and interventions. In this we contribute to the greater goodness of society.
>
> SOURCE: SOUTH AFRICAN BOARD FOR PERSONNEL PRACTICE (SABPP). 2007. *Code of conduct*. [Online.]. Available: www.sabpp.co.za. 1 July 2007.

The code also emphasises the obligation of HR professionals to uphold respect for the dignity of all persons and empowers them to be vigilant and aggressive in this pursuit. For example, the code states[31]:

> We are unwaveringly committed to tolerance, respect for human dignity and upholding the human rights as prescribed by the constitution of the country. We treat all our stakeholders with respect … We stand in service of … those organisations that remunerate us for our professional contribution … We have an obligation to prevent breaches of principles of respect and to assertively object to such violations when they occur.
>
> SOURCE: SOUTH AFRICAN BOARD FOR PERSONNEL PRACTICE (SABPP). 2007. *Code of conduct*. [Online.]. Available: www.sabpp.co.za. 1 July 2007.

The SABPP's revised *Code of conduct* appears to hold in tension the plurality of values it has inherited from multiple traditions. These include not only HRM paradigms, but also South Africa's Constitution. In doing so the code is an important vehicle for providing direction and counsel to the HR profession in South Africa as it moves forward to meet local and global contemporary challenges, including the demands of a strategic HRM paradigm.

8.2.3 An integrity-oriented approach to strategic business partnership

The second ethical dimension of a strategic approach to HRM concerns the roles undertaken by HR professionals in regard to corporate ethics. A study conducted in the USA by SHRM and the Commerce Clearing House (CCH)[32] suggests that:

- The dominant role performed by HR professionals in workplace ethical issues is that of monitoring for policy and legal compliance

BOX 1: The South African Board for Personnel Practice (SABPP) *Code of Conduct*

Preamble

We value what we can offer as a profession and recognise the stewardship role of the profession and its members. This role is embodied in the norms and principles we stand for. The purpose of this code is to entrench the obligation we have as professional HR practitioners to uphold the profession's norms and principles and to conduct our activities in a professional and ethical manner. To ensure the trust of all our stakeholders, we strive to build the reputation of the profession and its members through the values of responsibility, integrity, respect and competence.

Our ethical identity

As members of the profession of Human Resource Management in South Africa, we actively pursue the ideals of professionalism and are therefore ethically obliged to
- Bring meaning and quality of worklife to the people we serve in our professional capacities
- Ensure the sustainability of the organisations that we serve
- Make a difference to the communities we touch.

Our ethical values

Responsibility

Our first responsibility is to meaningfully transform the lives of those men and women that are employed by the organisations we serve. We have a further responsibility to contribute to the success and sustainability of the organisations that employ us or that we render a service to. It is our responsibility to comply with the expectations of our profession and fellow practitioners. We accept responsibility for the outcomes of our actions and interventions. In this we contribute to the greater goodness of society.

Integrity

As HR practitioners we are committed to exemplary ethical conduct that is characterised by honesty, objectivity, fairness of judgement, consistency of action and loyalty to our profession and the organisations and communities we engage with. We aim to grow the profession in a controlled and responsible manner. In that we strive to attract to the profession members with sound moral character and integrity.

Respect

We are unwaveringly committed to tolerance, respect for human dignity and upholding the human rights as prescribed by the constitution of the country. We treat all our stakeholders with respect and protect them from harm. We stand in service of our profession and its membership, those organisations that remunerate us for our professional contributions, and the communities we affect. We have an obligation to prevent breaches of principles of respect and to assertively object to such violations when they occur. We respect the confidentiality of information that is entrusted to us.

Competence

Professional registration of HR practitioners is a privilege afforded to individuals that have met the criteria for registration. We are committed to ensure professional credibility by actively evaluating and protecting the quality of professional education and training of those aspiring to enter the profession. We aspire to uphold the highest standards of continued professional development and improvement of competence of members of the profession. We enact this aspiration through role modelling and mentorship. It is our professional duty to integrate and apply sound human resource management principles, policies and practices in all aspects of people management and to assess the value that we add. We strive to formulate generally accepted HR practices that adhere to criteria of scientific and feasibility proportions. It is our quest to build the field of human resource management by promoting and supporting rigorous research.

SOURCE: SOUTH AFRICAN BOARD FOR PERSONNEL PRACTICE (SABPP). 2007. *Code of conduct*. [Online.]. Available: www.sabpp. co.za. 1 July 2007. Used with permission.

- The least dominant roles are those of employee advocate, educator, and questioning the ethical dimensions of managerial decisions.

The results of the survey are shown in Table 8.2. Whilst the role of monitoring for legal compliance is important, it is a narrow role and remains focused on a reactive administrative approach to both ethics and HR.

Although the 2006 SHRM survey cited above reported an increase in HR's involvement at the strategic level, it also reported that more than 80 per cent of survey respondents felt their department's focus on administrative duties, rather than on strategy, limited their ability to contribute at the strategic level. In the HR literature it is argued that an emphasis on the administrative–service role frustrates a transformation of the HR function.[33–34] The business-ethics literature generally recognises that the law specifies an ethical minimum and that ethics involves more than minimal legal compliance.[35]

One reason for the emphasis on legal compliance may be that the HR profession has left the business of ethics to external bodies – either the law or unions. As a result, many HR policies and practices relating to workplace rights, bribery, global human rights, and the environment are designed to avoid lawsuits, union conflict, and consumer boycotts. The common misconception that ethics is primarily concerned with avoiding wrongdoing can obfuscate an important dimension of ethics; ethics is also guidelines for the constructive

Table 8.2 Ethics roles played by HR professionals – perceived frequency and effectiveness

HR role and function	Very frequent %	Very effective %
Monitoring: HR monitors organisational conduct for compliance with laws and policies.	78	66
Modelling: HR attempts to increase ethical conduct by serving as an ethical role model.	78	58
Advisory: HR advises organisational members on ethics standards and polices.	67	58
Organisational: HR defends the organisation's actions when confronted by outside agencies.	58	69
Investigative: HR investigates unethical/ethical situations and complaints.	51	63
Advocacy: HR acts on behalf of employees; HR protects employees from reprisals from management.	50	58
Educative: HR trains or disseminates information on ethics policy.	42	35
Questioning: HR acts to question the ethical dimensions of management's decisions.	41	42

SOURCE: Adapted from SOCIETY FOR HUMAN RESOURCE MANAGEMENT. 1991:4 (*In* Carey, L. E. 1999. Ethical dimensions of a strategic approach to HRM: an Australian perspective. *Asia Pacific journal of human resources*, 37(3):57.) Used with permission.

role that decision-makers can play in an organisation.[36]

A second reason for an emphasis on legal compliance may be that the HR profession has not adequately addressed ethics in the training and professional development of HR practitioners. Without an understanding of ethical principles, the emerging role of ethics for the HR practitioner is likely to become locked into the administrative–supportive HR paradigm, rather than a strategic one.[37-38] This point is similar to Beer's[39] observation that the most formidable obstacle to the transformation of the HR function is the lack of high-level analytical and interpersonal skills in many HR professionals. Certainly it is easier to monitor behaviour for compliance with legal and organisational guidelines than to engage in complex philosophical debates germane to ethical issues. The issues of junior wage rates and employment-equity compliance illustrate this point. Monitors need only administer the policy according to a manual; they avoid the complexities of comparative worth, distributive justice, and hourly wage rates based on skill-level, regardless of personal characteristics such as age, gender, and race. Similarly, monitors may be more interested in a prescribed monetary figure to determine when legitimate entertainment becomes bribery than in understanding the principles which censure bribery while condoning limited gift-giving. Monitoring and legal compliance have more to do with standardising behaviour than with ethical decision-making. Ethical decision-making requires three qualities which can be developed or enhanced through education:

1. The ability to perceive ethical issues in a situation
2. The ability to engage principled reasoning and problem-solving strategies
3. A personal resolve to act ethically.

Josephson[40] refers to these qualities as ethical consciousness, ethical competency, and ethical commitment. In Section 8.3 we shall discuss ethical principles or frameworks for decision making.

A strategic HRM paradigm calls for HR professionals to move beyond the roles of 'policy police and regulatory watchdog'[41] to business partner. Whilst the concept of 'business partner' is an attractive one, it must be remembered that it may be associated with a unitarist perspective and the expectation that HR professionals should demonstrate their contribution to the bottom line could easily overshadow any commitment to balance competing interests. This is particularly problematic when codes of practice for HR professionals reflect a unitarist view. Likewise, recent empirical studies which have expressed interest in investigating the effectiveness of values-oriented ethics programmes over compliance-oriented ethics programmes tend to speak of shared values throughout the organisation, without due regard for the pluralist–unitarist debate.[42-43] One way around this problem may be to adopt De George's[44] notion of integrity. The term is a useful one because it avoids some of the negative connotations that many attach to the terms 'ethics' and 'morality', while at the same time it suggests that acting ethically 'extends beyond satisfying the bare moral minimum'.[45] Paine also speaks about integrity as a governing ethic[46]:

> [F]rom the perspective of integrity, the task of ethics management is to define and give life to an organisation's guiding values, to create an environment that supports ethically sound behaviour, and to instill a sense of shared accountability among employees.
>
> SOURCE: PAINE, L. S. 1994. Managing for organizational integrity. *Harvard business review*, March–April:111.

Extending the notion of 'business partner' to include integrity means that HR executives should integrate ethics into strategic decision-making. As integrity-based business partners, senior HR executives would need to develop the presently underutilised roles of questioner and educator in ethical matters. The execution of these roles requires the high-level analytical skills referred to earlier, in particular Josephson's[47] ethical consciousness, competency, and commitment. Integrity-based business partners would question, for example, the exploitation of workers in any strategic plan which suggested the payment of below-subsistence wages, even in situations where it was legal to do so. Ethical values can influence which business opportunities organisations accept, as well as the design of operating systems, including those related to risk-taking, hiring, compensation, performance management, and safety. For example, in 2003 South Africa's 'Big Four' banks (ABSA, First National, Nedcor, and Standard Bank) developed the *Financial Sector Charter*, which is a voluntary initiative designed to address the issue of Black Economic Empowerment (BEE) in the financial-services industry and to reverse previous inequalities arising from apartheid. In particular, the charter aims to increase access to finance and banking services, including home-loan finance for poorer South Africans previously denied access, and to promote diversity within management ranks.[48] Too often, enterprises fail to make ethics a 'before-profit concern' and consequently fail to recognise the role ethics plays in achieving entrepreneurial success and avoiding costly errors.[49]

An HR approach to business partnership that is based on integrity would combine concern for the competitive use of human capital with managerial responsibility for the ethical dimensions of an enterprise's strategic operations. Without an integrity-oriented approach to business partnership, there is the danger that HR professionals may continue in the administrative–service role under the guise of being strategic players.

8.3 Ethical decision-making frameworks[50]

The integration of ethics into strategic HRM decision-making requires HR executives to be fully capable of identifying the social and ethical issues attached to alternative business strategies and to be fully capable of resolving them in HR practices.[51] Earlier we noted the three qualities

Josephson[52] identified as essential to ethical decision-making: ethical consciousness, competency, and commitment. In this section we shall turn our attention to ethical competency, which is the ability to engage in ethical reasoning to explore and resolve ethics issues and dilemmas. To engage in ethical reasoning, HR practitioners can draw on two widely accepted normative theories of ethics, namely:

- *Teleology*. This theory is concerned with understanding the consequences of actions for the common good.
- *Deontology*. This theory is concerned with understanding duties, justice, and rights.

The essential elements of each theory are summarised in Table 8.3.

8.3.1 The consequences of actions: Teleological theory

Teleological theory stresses the consequences which result from an action or practice. For this reason it is also known as consequentialism. The most widely accepted form of consequentialist reasoning is utilitarianism (see Table 8.3.) The classical statements of utilitarianism are found in the writings of Bentham and Mill in the nineteenth century. However, the utilitarian tradition remains influential today, especially in the areas of economics and business, public policy, and government regulation.

For the utilitarian, the right thing to do is that which maximises the greatest good for the greatest number of people. The greatest good is determined by weighing all the good consequences against all the bad consequences for all those the action directly and indirectly affects for the foreseeable future. The means by which the greatest utility is achieved is only of importance insofar as it affects the outcome. For this reason, it is often said that under utilitarianism, the end justifies the means. For example, if psychometric testing results in the greatest good, utilitarianism will accept that the means to that end may involve breaching individual privacy rights.

Act utilitarianism and rule utilitarianism are refinements of the utilitarian theory, nevertheless

Table 8.3 Summary of ethical frameworks for moral reasoning and decision making

Ethical framework and principle	Strengths	Weaknesses
Utilitarianism (consequentialism) The greatest good for the greatest number (net utility) (Teleological theory)	1. Looks at *all* the consequences on *all* those affected by the action. 2. Is universalistic not egoistic. 3. Values efficiency. Consistent with profit maximisation and is easy for managers to understand.	1. Difficult to predict and quantify all the consequences. 2. Can result in unfair distributions of the common good. 3. The end (net utility) can justify the means. 4. Individual rights can be overlooked for net outcomes.
Kantian duty (nonconsequentialism) Universal respect for autonomous beings (Deontological theory)	1. Protects the individual from being used as a means to an end. 2. Consistent with the golden rule, 'do unto others as you would have them do unto you'. 3. Firm standards that do not depend on results.	1. Can be difficult in practice to make the means/end distinction. 2. The tests of universalisability and respect for autonomous beings may not be sufficient. 3. Only rational beings have moral worth (not animals, etc.).
Justice Due process and due outcome Rawls's egalitarianism: fair distribution of benefits and burdens Nozick's entitlement theory: Uphold property rights and liberty	1. Attempts to allocate resources and costs fairly and objectively. 2. Protects those who lack representation and provides basic welfare. 3. Is consistent with a democratic approach and Kant. 4. Upholds rights of liberty and property.	1. Can encourage a sense of entitlement that reduces risk, innovation and productivity. 2. Can result in reducing rights of some in order to accommodate rules of justice. 3. Emphasises freedom over other values. 4. Unjust treatment of disadvantaged.
Moral rights Individual entitlements which impose obligations on others.	1. Protects the individual from harm. 2. Imposes obligations on others either not to interfere or to promote other's welfare. 3. Consistent with universal human rights.	1. Can be misinterpreted resulting in selfish behaviour. 2. Can promote personal liberties that impede productivity and efficiency. 3. Difficult to balance conflicting rights.

SOURCE: CAREY, L. E. 2007. *Profits and principles: The operationalisation of corporate ethics in Australian enterprises*. Canberra, Australia. University of Canberra. (Ph.D. thesis.) Used with permission.

each decides right and wrong on the basis of the consequences of an action. The difference is over whether a utility analysis should be applied to every action whenever it occurs (act utilitarianism) or to classes of actions (rule utilitarianism). Faced with the choice of breaking a contract, every time the question of breaking a contract arose the act utilitarian would have to weigh up all the good and bad consequences for all those the action effects. The rule utilitarian, looking to past consequences of breaking contracts, might develop the rule that 'generally breaking contracts leads to more harm than good, therefore, in this case, breaking a contract is wrong'. Proponents of utilitarianism have also differed over what should count as good. For example, Bentham focused on pleasure and Mill on happiness. However, contemporary utilitarians argue for a pluralistic interpretation of the good, including satisfaction of individual preferences.

Take care not to confuse the concept of the greatest good for the greatest number as the equivalent of the greatest good for the enterprise.

For this reason, it is important to differentiate utilitarianism from egoism. Although egoism is a form of consequentialism, it does not meet the criteria of logical coherence, impartiality, consistency with basic moral intuitions, explanatory adequacy, and concern for the facts – all of which are necessary for a good moral theory.[53] Under egoism, the right action is that which maximises self-interest. To defend one's course of action by appealing to self-interest is hardly likely to be seen as publicly defensible. Yet individuals and enterprises frequently appeal to egoistic reasoning, either overtly or covertly. For example, an enterprise which justifies a breach of safety by appealing only to its need to cut costs would be employing reasoning typical of egoism. Utilitarianism requires HR practitioners to implement policies and practices which produce the greatest benefit for society and not those which produce only the greatest benefit to the enterprise. This does not, however, preclude management from taking actions which yield the largest profit.[54] For example, to meet the challenge of declining profits and market share, an enterprise might consider downsizing and an extensive retrenchment programme. Some good would result from the lower labour costs, which might also mean that more people could purchase lower-priced goods or the enterprise could become more attractive to investors. Thus while some people stand to lose, others stand to gain. The utilitarian (especially an act utilitarian) would condone labour cutbacks so long as net utility was maximised (the end justifies the means). It must be stressed however, that net utility must be the aggregate of consequences for all stakeholders involved in the labour cutbacks.

Utilitarianism is a useful decision-making tool for HR practitioners since it requires consideration of collective, as well as individual, interests, and the formulation of alternatives based on the greatest good for all parties affected by the decision, and it quantifies the costs and benefits of alternatives for the affected groups.[55] With its emphasis on the collective good, utilitarianism is compatible with traditional African values of communitarianism, consensus, and co-existence.[56] The ubuntu principle of reciprocity and interdependence reflects the communitarian nature of South Africa. Mbiti translates the term as 'I am, because we are; and since we are, therefore I am'.[57] However, the main weaknesses of utilitarianism are that the principles of justice and rights are secondary and therefore, in theory, could be ignored, and individual interests may be sacrificed for the greater good. Critics of utilitarianism would never justify abrogation of human rights and unequal access to education, employment, housing, and health care for a minority, even if doing so maximised overall utility. Because individuals live in a community and the community is made up of individuals, utilitarianism is best understood as complementary to deontology rather than as a rival theory.

8.3.2 The importance of duty to others: Deontological theory

Deontological theories of ethics stress the importance of an individual's duty toward others, rather than consequences. Deontological reasoning is therefore known as non-consequentialist (see Table 8.3). It emphasises the concept of duties and challenges management to treat every stakeholder with respect and integrity rather than viewing them instrumentally for the collective good. The concepts of 'human rights' and 'justice' are based on deontology.

The most widely recognised statement of deontology is found in the writings of the eighteenth-century German philosopher Kant. Kant was both an absolutist and a rationalist and believed that human reason could 'work out a consistent set of moral principles that cannot be overridden'.[58] Reason is central to Kantian ethics and has three key characteristics:

1. *Consistency*. This requires that moral actions must not be self-contradictory. Bribery, for example, is self-contradictory.
2. *Universality*. This requires that one treats others the way one wants to be treated and

does not make an exception in matters relating to oneself. This is akin to the 'golden rule'. For example, one ought to respect the integrity of the tendering process and not attempt to gain an unfair advantage for oneself by offering a bribe.
3. *It is a priori.* Reason is a priori (not derived from experience).[59] Bribery is wrong regardless of whether or not one wins contracts.

Kant reasoned that a moral principle or law must follow a particular form. It must:
1. Be possible for it to be made consistently universal
2. Respect rational human beings as ends in themselves
3. Respect the autonomy of rational beings.

These three criteria make up Kant's categorical imperative or absolute principle from which second order principles or rules can be derived. For Kant, actions and principles which fail to meet any one of these criteria cannot be regarded as moral. Note, however, that Kant does not claim that one must never use people for a purpose; he states only that one never merely uses them as a means to an end. Kant is not opposed to the hiring of labour, for example, so long as employees autonomously agree to work and are paid a fair wage. The logic underlying Kant's categorical imperative is an important reminder to HR decision-makers that the humanity of individuals 'must be considered above the stakes, power or consequences of our actions'.[60] In post-apartheid years, an age where technology and economic rationalism can dehumanise individuals in the guise of efficiency, this is an important reminder.

Ross[61] later expanded Kant's single-rule theory to address the problem of conflicting duties. Ross's 'prima facie duties' require managers to choose between conflicting duties on the basis of which is the more fundamental or obligatory. For example, an HR manager may have a duty to respect an individual employee's right to smoke, as well as to ensure that other employees have a safe working environment; however, the latter is the more obligatory duty.

8.3.3 Fairness: The idea of justice

The notion of justice is often expressed in terms of fairness and equality, while issues involving questions of justice are divided into four categories: distributive, procedural, retributive, and compensatory. Understanding these different aspects of justice is important to HR practitioners responsible for enacting policies in relation to the conventional HR activities, as well as specific issues such as workplace surveillance, drug testing, affirmative action, workplace bullying or harassment, discipline, and change management. Enterprises perceived to be just are likely to be able to attract and retain the best employees, reduce stress and conflict in the workplace, and create organisational cultures that promote efficient and satisfying workplaces.

- *Distributive justice.* Distributive justice is of particular importance to HRM since it is concerned with the fair distribution of society's benefits and burdens through the major societal institutions, which include business and government enterprises. The following are all issues related to distributive justice: disparities between executive salaries and those of their subordinates; inequalities based on gender or race; profit-sharing schemes; pay for performance bonuses; redundancy packages; and the use of cheap labour. The effects of perceived inequity on attitudes and behaviour in the workplace have been the subject of a substantial body of research in the literature on management.[62–65]

  Philosophers have identified a number of relevant properties for a just distribution of society's benefits and burdens. These properties include equality, individual need, individual rights, individual effort, societal contribution, and merit. Libertarian and egalitarian theories of distributive justice have been proposed in the face of these divergent appeals to justice. Libertarians identify justice with liberty and so emphasise free choice and freedom from interference. They denounce utilitarians' concern for aggregate social well-being and instead believe people should receive economic rewards directly in proportion to their free contributions to the production of those rewards.[66] Friedman[67] and his narrow view of corporate social responsibility are in the libertarian tradition.

Nozick's defence of the libertarian understanding of justice is the most widely recognised.[68] Nozick's defence involves two important concepts: entitlement and liberty. Nozick's view of entitlement builds upon Locke's notion of negative property rights. It claims that a just distribution of property is one where people have acquired their property justly. This requires four conditions:

> What is held in common (water, grain, fish, fruit, grass, etc.) becomes private property when one has mixed one's labour with it
> One cannot claim that which is held as private property by another
> One cannot claim more than one needs (no waste)
> One must leave enough for others, i.e. one's possession of private property cannot leave others worse off.

The liberty principle allows for only minimal intervention by governments in the free market and does not support a taxation system that redistributes wealth to the poor.

Unlike libertarians, egalitarians support a broad socio-economic view of corporate social responsibility and emphasise the concept of fairness. Egalitarians base their view of justice on the proposition that all human beings are equal in some fundamental aspect, and in virtue of this equality, each person has an equal claim to society's benefits and burdens. One of the most influential proponents of egalitarianism is Rawls.[69] Following the Kantian tradition, Rawls argued that under the conditions of rationality, desire to promote one's own interests and impartiality (people would not know their gender, race, personal talents, characteristics, and luck), all would agree on two fundamental principles of justice. The principles are:

> Each person is to have equal right to the most extensive basic liberty compatible with similar liberty for others.
> Social and economic inequalities are to be arranged so that they are both (a) reasonably expected to be to everyone's advantage (especially the least advantaged) and (b) attached to positions and offices open to all.[70]

Furthermore, Rawls argued that the first principle (equal liberty) should take priority over the second and that part b of the second principle should take priority over part a. Thus, egalitarians would not support the very large discrepancies that sometimes exist between the salaries of CEOs and their workers on the shop floor, unless those workers had an equal opportunity to reach positions such as a CEO, and unless the inequalities meant that the least well-off workers were better off than they would be under any other system.

Rawls's theory of justice has important implications in the South African context. For example, people's basic liberties such as the right to vote, hold property, due process, and education, as well as freedom of speech, movement and other civil liberties, must be as extensive as equity allows and cannot be sacrificed for utilitarian ends. More specifically, Rawls's theory provides important principles for the development of the traditional HR activities of recruitment, selection, employee development, and performance management.

• *Procedural justice.* Rather than focusing on outcomes (Rawls's distributive justice), procedural justice is concerned with the processes used to make decisions and implement workplace controls, e.g. in relation to selection, compensation, promotion, dismissal, and dispute resolution. Research suggests there are two aspects which employees see as particularly important to procedural justice. The first concerns clearly identified rules and standards which are applied consistently across time and other persons, for example written performance-appraisal standards and grounds for dismissal. The second calls for a flexible approach, including employee participation in decision-making procedures, and processes that allow mistakes or poor decisions to be appealed.[71-76]

- *Retributive justice*. Retributive justice is concerned with the imposition of penalties and punishment upon individuals and enterprises who cause harm to others. An important criterion for applying this principle of justice is that the punishment must fit the crime. For example, a bank teller who is found to have taken home a few office supplies for personal use ought to receive a lesser sanction than one found to have misappropriated bank funds.

- *Compensatory justice*. Compensatory justice involves compensating people for any harm or loss they have suffered. The most controversial forms of compensation are the preferential treatment or affirmative-action programmes that attempt to remedy past injustices by giving groups that suffered past discrimination preference in hiring, training, and promotion policies. The controversy arises largely because the principle of compensatory justice generates demands which conflict with the demands made by the principle of equity. Some have argued that when the argument for compensatory justice is combined with the principle of equity in the long term and the principle of the greatest good for the greatest number, then there is sufficient justification for overriding the principle of equity for some in the short term.[77]

The controversy over affirmative action is compounded when affirmative-action programmes are of the strong type, e.g. quota based, rather than the weaker form, which upholds the merit principle first and then applies affirmative action. In Australia, the weaker form of affirmative action is practised. In countries where the stronger version is practised, e.g. the USA, India, and South Africa, there has been some criticism that organisations may not appoint the best candidate, thereby limiting efficiency. Such criticism is a reminder that it is best to think of HR activities as an integrated suite. For example, employee-development programmes need to support affirmative-action programmes. In South Africa, many government and company policies are now based on the need to redress the wrongs of the past and correct systemically based imbalances that developed during the apartheid years. For example, the Employment Equity Act (No. 55 of 1998) states that the purpose of the act is not only to achieve equal opportunity by eliminating discrimination, but also to implement 'affirmative action measures to redress the disadvantages in employment experienced by designated groups in order to ensure their equitable representation in all occupational categories and levels of the workforce'.[78] An understanding of rights theory will help to explain further why people are entitled to compensation when their rights have been violated.

8.3.4 Individual entitlements: Rights

Kant's emphasis on respect for autonomous rational human beings as ends in themselves provides a strong basis for a theory of rights. To claim a right is to claim that one is ethically entitled to something and this places a duty on other people to act (or refrain from acting) in a way which brings about the fulfilment of one's right. Rights can be classified as either negative or positive. Negative rights are liberty rights (e.g. the right to privacy); positive rights are claim or welfare rights (e.g. the right to employment at a living wage). Most specific rights are derived from the three major Lockean rights of life, liberty and property.

One criticism of a rights approach is that it opens the way for people to claim a right to 'anything and everything'.[79] However, properly understood rights can be limited both by the concept of equality and the concept of a hierarchy of rights.[80] An example of the former is that an employee is not entitled to individual supervision, only to his or her fair share of supervision. An example of the latter is that the right to life is more fundamental than the right to property and, hence, the rights of employees to a safe workplace can override an employer's right to liberty or an individual employee's right to smoke as he or she pleases.

Understanding, implementing, and protecting employee rights is essential to good HRM practice. In developed countries, many employee rights are enshrined in law and some rights are institutionalised in international agreements such as those with the International Labour Organisation (ILO). Groups that monitor human rights are likely to report human-rights violations by multinational enterprises operating in less-developed countries, and, through the medium of the World Wide Web, these violations are reported widely – often to the detriment of the offending multinational. Table 8.4 presents the major types of employee rights in the workplace and the relevant HR activities. Although many of these rights must be balanced against the rights of employers, some rights of employees – such as the right to a living wage and a safe workplace – are non-negotiable.

8.3.5 Convergence across normative ethical theories

While significant differences exist between utilitarianism and deontology, these differences are often exaggerated, particularly when one considers that different theories often lead to similar views about the right action to take. Moreover, the strength of one theory often acts as a balance to the weakness of another and therefore, rather than affiliate with 'one best theory', managers stand to learn from them all.[81]

In summary, our discussion of ethical theory generates four key questions that HR managers can usefully employ to evaluate prospective responses to ethical challenges and dilemmas they may face:

1. Who is affected and how? Which action will result in the greatest good for the greatest number of people affected by it? (utilitarianism)
2. Is the action one that universally respects autonomous rational beings as ends in themselves? (Kantian deontology)
3. Is the action one that treats all stakeholders fairly? (justice)
4. Is the action one that upholds fundamental human rights? (rights)

To illustrate the way in which ethical theory can help to resolve workplace dilemmas, let us consider the case of an HR manager of a large retail department store, who has been asked to respond to significant amounts of employee theft, using high-tech multi-directional zoom cameras that can be hidden in ceilings and are so small they can film through a pinhole. Firstly, this scenario raises issues of privacy, dignity, working conditions, discrimination, due process, control over employees, property rights, and the common good. Secondly, the monitoring of employees by video surveillance or other means requires a delicate balance between the right of the employer to protect property, staff, and business interests, and the right of the employee to be free from invasions of privacy, in particular, to determine what, to whom, and how much information about themselves shall be available to others. It is also necessary to weigh considerations of harm caused to customers, who may have to bear some of the cost of theft in the form of higher prices, against the potential harm to employees.

A utilitarian analysis would have to weigh positive consequences that might come from surveillance against potential negative consequences, such as increasing stress, undermining morale, and creating distrust and suspicion between employees and management. A utilitarian focus might view the occasional adverse impact on an employee as regrettable, but acceptable, providing the surveillance resulted in net utility.

Table 8.4 Employee rights and related HR activities

Employee rights	HR activities
Right to work Right not to be dismissed without just cause Right to equal employment opportunity Right to employability Right to due process Rights regarding plant closings	Fair treatment in recruitment and selection Employee development programs Fair performance management programs Affirmative action programs Sexual and racial harassment prevention Due processes in cases of dismissal or termination Grievance policies and hearings
Right to a fair wage	Management of compensation (developing pay and job structures, performance related pay, profit sharing, group incentives) based on concepts of equity and distributive justice
Right to healthy and safe working conditions Right to be informed of risks and harms	Occupational health and safety programs to prevent harm and respect human life Safety audits Safety training Working conditions Management of sick leave Discipline for breaches
Right to privacy	Data protection procedures Due process in video surveillance practices Due process in drug testing and genetic screening practices Work–life balance Email access notification (based on concepts of respect, fairness, autonomy)
Right to free speech Right to organise and strike	Whistleblowing policies (including anonymity and confidentiality and no retribution) Negotiation with unions and union members
Right to due process	Communication of policies Employee participation and representation Transparency in decision-making processes Grievance procedures
Right to meaningful work	Employee participation Employment empowerment New forms of work Job enrichment Employee development programs Social programs

SOURCE: CAREY, L. E. 2007. *Profits and principles: The operationalisation of corporate ethics in Australian enterprises.* Canberra, Australia. University of Canberra. (Ph.D. thesis.) Used with permission.

From a justice perspective, the HR manager, in consultation with management, could first consider factors in the workplace that might contribute to employee theft. Rather than use electronic surveillance, it may be possible to use conventional HR practices to reduce substantially the incidence of employee theft. For example, a substantial body of research suggests that employee theft is often a reaction to perceived inequity of rewards and to feelings of injustice in the workplace.[82–83] Ordinary and reasonable methods of supervision are preferable to extraordinary methods such as video surveillance, and especially covert surveillance.

If the HR manager uses video surveillance, then it would be useful for him or her to organise a 'round table' discussion with other senior managers, representatives of employees and unions, and experts in surveillance and security, to draw up policies, procedures, and practices that protect the legitimate interests of all parties. A deontological perspective of justice and respect for the rights of autonomous beings, might focus on matters such as:

- The extent of employee consultation regarding the conduct, purposes, and uses of surveillance
- The manner in which managers collect information and the relevance of its uses
- The security of video recordings and the length of their retention
- Employee access to recordings
- The rights of employees to explain recorded behaviour
- Ensuring video surveillance is limited to its original purposes
- The release of video recordings to third parties.[84]

A focus on these matters would help to ensure that surveillance, if used, is limited to the issue at hand – in this case employee theft – and that employees have the opportunity to give or withhold their informed consent.

The matter is more problematic if the surveillance is covert. One view is that if the surveillance is a response to a suspected illegal activity, then managers may justify it, provided areas such as staff rooms, bathrooms, and changing rooms are surveillance-free. Velasquez[85] suggests that extraordinary methods of investigation, such as covert surveillance, are permissible only when the following conditions have been met:

- The problem can be solved in no other manner
- The problem is serious and there is good reason to believe that the extraordinary method will put an end to the problem

- The method will be stopped after the wrongdoer has been identified or when it is clear that the method will not work
- All non-relevant data collected in the course of the surveillance is disregarded and destroyed
- The error rate of the device is taken into account and information collected from devices with known error rates are verified by reliable, independent means.

In reviewing this analysis, we emphasise that ethical theories do not provide formulae for correct decision-making. Rather, they provide a means of analysis for arriving at a reasoned judgement concerning the propriety of alternative courses of action. Managers could apply the same analysis to myriad issues in ethics, e.g. judging the ethicality of drug testing in the workplace, performance measurement and evaluation systems, training and development policies, diversity programmes, bonus schemes, retrenchment programmes, and disciplinary measures.

Judging with integrity requires careful reasoning by taking into account consequences, duties, justice, and rights and weighing them in cases of conflict. Only when managers act in accordance with this balanced and reasoned judgement do they act with integrity.[86]

As we noted earlier, research shows that when employees perceive workplace practices to have integrity, there is a positive impact on employee morale, motivation, loyalty, commitment, recruitment, and turnover, all of which positively impact the bottom line of enterprises.[87-88] However, managers should take care not to shift the rationale for ethical HR policies and procedures from one grounded in principles of justice and rights to one grounded solely in economic rationalism.

8.4 **Ethical issues and challenges in the workplace**

Traditionally, the primary responsibility of the employer to the employee was to pay a fair wage and, in return, employees were expected to give their employers a fair day's work. However, this model is too simple to address the many ethical issues and challenges that arise out of the interplay between employers and employees in contemporary workplaces. Many see the failure to recognise ethics issues when they arise (ethical consciousness) as one of the main reasons why good people do bad things. For example, the SHRM survey of HR professionals (which we referred to earlier) reported that the most serious ethical problems for HR professionals, and the ones with which they dealt with the least success, came from decisions made by managers who used factors other than job performance as the basis for decisions in hiring, training, pay, promotion, and discipline.[89] Whereas the previous section concentrated on ethical reasoning for ethical competency in decision-making, the following section will review the ethics issues and challenges that arise with respect to the HR activities of selection, compensation, and promotion of employees.

8.4.1 Selection

Effective and fair selection practices for the strategic deployment of highly motivated and competent employees are an important vehicle for enterprises to gain competitive advantage. In making selection decisions, HR practitioners must ensure that they treat all job applicants fairly. A significant body of research in the HRM and ethics literature covers issues of fairness, equal opportunity, affirmative action, and discrimination – relating to gender, race, ethnicity, marital status, religion, disability, and age – in the selection process.[90] These issues are particularly problematic for selection, although they also arise in the areas of compensation, career development, and discipline. Selection practices typically include screening, the employment interview, and psychometric testing, all of which can be viewed as strategic tools supporting business strategy.

- *Screening.* Screening begins with the following:
  - › *A job description.* This provides details about a job's duties, responsibilities,

working conditions, and physical requirements.
- › *A job specification.* This describes the qualifications, skills, educational experience, and physical attributes needed to successfully undertake the job.

To protect individuals against discrimination, employment legislation in most developed countries, including South Africa[91], does not allow gender, race, ethnicity, marital status, religion, or age to appear in job specifications or recruitment advertising (unless it is specifically related to the requirements of the job) on the basis that these items potentially exclude job candidates on grounds not related to the job. For example, the aim of the Employment Equity Act (No. 55 of 1998) in South Africa is to achieve equality in employment and, therefore, economic equality. HR professionals must also be careful not to screen out disabled applicants who are capable of carrying out the job. A successful screening process is one that ensures there is a pool of suitable candidates who have all been treated fairly with regard to their right to equal opportunity for employment. The screening out of unsuitable or less-suitable candidates must be done on the basis of job-relevant criteria for it to be considered fair.

- *The employment interview.* Despite possible shortcomings, the employment interview remains the most widely used tool for selection and is often the first point of formal contact between a potential employee and an enterprise.[92] Interviews can vary in structure from unstructured to semi-structured to structured, although since the early 1980s the structured interview has been the dominant form because it is more reliable and valid.[93] Structured interviews standardise questions and processes across interviews with different candidates. Therefore, they are considered to be fair, since each candidate has the same opportunity and the process minimises interviewer bias.

The issue of fairness in job interviews has been widely discussed in the literature, although the emphasis has been on discrimination arising from non-relevant criteria for jobs. A number of authors have suggested ways in which the employment interview can avoid charges of discrimination. These include:

> Conduct the interview along professional lines
> A panel of interviewers who represent key organisational perspectives, including those of minority groups, should conduct interviews
> All interviewers should be trained in areas of perceptual bias, discrimination, relevance of criteria, intrusive questioning, abuse of power, and cultural differences
> Interviews should be consistent to allow comparison between candidates
> Interviews should not be used to assess abilities which can be more accurately assessed by other means.

A critical component of ethical interviewing for employment is the standardisation and objectification of the interview. Although these will not guarantee the elimination of discrimination and harmful practices, they are essential steps for HR practitioners who seek to interview ethically. Such practices may also benefit the enterprise through the acquisition of 'the right people in the right place at the right time' and the avoidance of high costs associated with litigation, absenteeism, turnover, and poor morale.

• *Psychometric testing*. This is another screening-and-selection tool enterprises, especially larger ones, often use. The most common types measure ability (cognitive, mechanical or psychomotor) and personality, but may also include drug testing, health screening, and, more recently, genetic testing. Although genetic testing is still in its early stages of development and adoption, employers can now test an employee for about 50 genetic traits that indicate a potential to develop certain diseases such as breast cancer, colon cancer, and cystic fibrosis or be affected by certain occupational hazards, such as toxins.[95] The ethical implications of genetic testing are huge, mostly because there is a danger that 'the risk of disease will be treated as a disease'.[96] However, in principle, genetic testing and drug testing raise the same questions as ability and personality tests:

> Are the tests valid and reliable?
> Is the test job-relevant?
> Are the tests culturally based?
> Has the tester gained informed consent?
> Are the interests of the enterprise and the general public sufficient to justify an encroachment upon individual privacy?[97]

Ethical issues abound in the use of employment testing. In addition to the issues of fairness and discrimination discussed above, an individual's right to privacy is problematic. Included in the notion of privacy are psychological privacy (relating to one's inner life), physical privacy (relating to one's space and time), and autonomy to determine when, how, and what information is communicated about oneself to others.[98] When conducting psychometric testing, HR professionals must safeguard the interests of enterprises and candidates by upholding the rights of those they test to:

> Informed consent
> Not be harmed or unfairly disadvantaged by the process of assessment (or testing)
> Full information about the purpose and results of the assessment
> Suitable preparation for the process of assessment
> Not be subjected to assessment processes which have systematic bias, high rates of error, or unwarranted

discrimination, or which are not relevant to the job
> Confidentiality
> Secure storage of test data and results
> Destruction of results when no longer needed
> Counselling, especially in the case of drug, health, and genetic testing.[99]

The literature on organisational behaviour reports that very few studies have found significant correlations between personality-test scores and job performance. Not only is the concept of personality difficult to define and measure, but personality tests are also vulnerable to social desirability bias.

In the USA, these findings, as well as equal-employment legislation and judicial rulings against the use of personality tests, have greatly limited the use of personality tests as job predictors.[100] Commenting on the rights of job candidates in regard to employment testing, Anderson[101] notes that in Sweden

> employee representatives are present when psychologists' reports are considered, candidates are informed of their results before these results are made available to the hiring organisation
> candidates can have their results destroyed should they wish to withdraw their application.

In South Africa, two streams of legislation control the use of psychological tests by employers.[102] The first stream involves acts that deal with individual rights. These acts include the Constitution of the Republic of South Africa (1996), the Labour Relations Act (No. 66 of 1995 (as amended)), and the Employment Equity Act (EEA) (No. 55 of 1998) (as amended). The second stream of legislation addresses the scope, responsibilities, and duties of professional psychologists. Under an early draft of the EEA, all psychological testing of employees was banned. However, the final legislation states[103]:

[P]sychological testing and other similar assessments of an employee are prohibited unless the test or assessment being used –
(a) has been scientifically shown to be valid and reliable,
(b) can be applied fairly to all employees,
(c) is not biased against any employee or group.

SOURCE: SOUTH AFRICA. 1998. *Employment Equity Act*, No. 55 of 1998. Section 8. Pretoria: Government Printer.

The issue of discrimination figures prominently in the selection process. Considerations of justice and rights play an important role in ensuring that managers treat all candidates fairly and assure them of equal opportunity for employment. In addition to the issue of discrimination, if jobs are to be truly fair, the selection process must also recognise that it provides an opportunity for a potential employee to select the organisation. Thus, employees have the right to know the conditions of their employment. These include compensation, career development, and possible termination. Only when the conditions of employment have been made clear is the selection process, and subsequent employment agreement, truly fair.

8.4.2 Compensation

The right to fair compensation, often referred to as the right to a living wage, is derived from the right to life, the right to employment, and the right to respect.[104] For some, a just wage is simply whatever the market determines. Traditionally, however, a just wage has involved a mix of variables, including merit or contribution to the enterprise, need, effort, the nature of particular jobs (for example, some are more dangerous, socially undesirable, or lacking in security), bargaining power of unions, laws governing minimum wages, the capability and profitability of the enterprise, and, more recently, concern with equality, and conditions of the labour market.

In recent years, HR practices in the area of compensation have undergone a number of developments. These developments include the use of performance pay and other contingent systems of reward; the flattening of pay scales with fewer, but broader, pay grades; and flexible cafeteria-style benefit systems.[105] The HR literature generally recognises that the new approach to compensation, often referred to as 'new pay', is more suitable to today's changing organisational environments and structures than are the older methods of pay related to job-evaluated pay structures, time, and seniority. These older methods suited hierarchical organisations operating in predictable environments. In particular, it is advocated that new pay is 'strategic pay', i.e. it both flows from and implements an enterprise's business strategy.[106] Therefore, writers on new pay recommend :

- Significantly increasing the proportion of pay contingent on performance
- Making base salaries only moderately competitive in order to increase the potency of variable pay
- Broadening the range of incentive schemes to include linking pay to group and organisational performance as well as individual performance
- Identifying new performance measures of business success
- Introducing flexibility to compensation plans so that rewards extend beyond monetary ones to include prizes and recognition.[107-108]

While there is much to commend in the new-pay model, Heery[109] argues that, from an ethical perspective, these developments in compensation practice are potentially flawed. He says they represent a 'movement towards greater risk in remuneration' (because from an employee perspective, salaries and benefits are less secure and predictable) and a 'movement away from employee representation' (in the setting of

policies and practices relating to compensation systems). The increase in employee risk and a decrease in independent employee representation associated with the new pay are cause for ethical concern and are the focus of our discussion on compensation.

Firstly, the most basic moral principle in ethics is 'do no intentional harm'. Yet the new-pay model is a threat to both the economic and the psychological well-being of employees. This is because it increases the risk of financial instability, and an inability to predict one's income relative to one's financial commitments is likely to cause emotional anxiety. Secondly, the twin themes of procedural and distributive justice have a long history in both ethics and HR theory and practice in areas such as job evaluation, reward systems, and collective bargaining. As we noted earlier, procedural justice is concerned with fair processes and distributive justice is concerned with fair outcomes; both dimensions are essential for a compensation strategy to be considered ethical. From a procedural-justice viewpoint, a significant problem with the new-pay model is that it links rewards to performance measures valued by management and, yet, often these measures are not entirely under the control of an individual. For example, the measures may be tied to group performance or customer satisfaction. The new-pay model is also open to perceived and real subjective judgements about performance on the part of management and provides 'little scope for independent representation of employee interests'.[110] From the viewpoint of distributive justice, there are problems not only with increased economic risks, but also with the transfer of risk from employers to employees.

The unitarist–pluralist debate is a complex one beyond the scope of this chapter. We can, however, state that whilst employer and employee interests are never likely to be completely identical, it may be that aspects of the new-pay model offer mutual benefits to both employers and employees. Indeed, some writers argue that employees have a right to share in the financial success of their enterprises.[111] HR managers involved in formulating and implementing compensation programmes should consider the new-pay model not only as a strategic tool for furthering business strategy, but also as a tool which, used in conjunction with principles of ethical management of pay, can help to secure a balance between the interests of employers and those of employees. The pivotal point of such a balance is the notion of acceptable risk. Employees have an interest in stable and predictable incomes, as well as in the opportunity to benefit from profit sharing through contingency-based compensation programmes. Heery[112] suggests that principles of acceptable risk include:

- The use of variable pay to supplement, not to replace, wages and salaries
- Commitment to the provision of employee benefits that provide economic security
- The use of rigorous measures of performance, which are under the control of employees, when implementing variable pay schemes
- Transparent systems for pay, which are widely communicated, regulated, and monitored throughout an enterprise
- The implementation of appeal processes
- The involvement of employee representatives in the formulation, implementation, and evaluation of variable pay schemes.

Distributive justice also raises issues of fairness in regard to the growing gap between executive pay and average rates of pay. For example, Australian data show that for the period 1992–2002, executive remuneration rose from 22 times average weekly earnings to 74 times average weekly earnings.[113] In many organisations throughout Europe, the USA and Australia, recent developments in corporate governance and accountability have led to higher standards of transparency regarding the ways in which the remuneration of senior executives is structured and related to performance. However, what those performance measures should be remains a contentious issue.

Procedural and distributive justice and the absence of economic and psychological harm are critical components of fair and equitable compensation strategies, and compensation strategies that are perceived to be fair and equitable are central to employee motivation and self-esteem. When developing new compensation strategies to drive the business strategy, HR managers can discharge their responsibilities to both management and employees by balancing employer interest in contingent pay with employee interest in stable and predictable income. Principles of ethical management of pay help to identify acceptable levels of risk and the task of minimising harm while maximising benefits for all stakeholders.

8.4.3 Promotion and performance management

As with selection and compensation, the key ethical issue in managing the promotion of employees is fairness. The difficulty is in determining the criteria that should serve as the basis for fair promotion procedures. While there is debate over how much weight to give to the criteria of seniority and job qualifications, it is widely recognised that promotion should normally be on the basis of job-related criteria, especially performance, and that procedures should not discriminate against employees on the basis of inappropriate criteria such as gender, race, and religion. Employees may not have a right to promotion, but they do have a right to fair evaluations and consideration for promotion. They also have a right to be informed of the reasons for lack of promotion in those situations where they might reasonably expect it.[114] Commenting on the debate over promotion based on loyalty to senior employees or on the basis of qualifications, Shaw notes: 'A policy that provides promotions strictly on the basis of qualifications seems heartless, whereas one that promotes seniority alone seems mindless.'[115] Promotion is one more example where HR practitioners are challenged to 'merge dual responsibilities in a way that is beneficial to the firm and fair to all concerned'.[116]

Related to promotion is the issue of performance management. Typically, systems of performance management involve the setting of performance objectives, the measurement of performance against these objectives, the identification of developmental support, and a review process to develop performance and subsequent objectives. Managers may use performance management as a decision-making tool for the distribution of performance-related pay and promotion. A common criticism of performance-management systems is that they raise issues of privacy, dignity, discrimination, and power and control over employees, particularly performance-management systems that use surveillance technology to gather data about workplace performance. To ensure that performance-management programmes are ethically sound, managers must ensure that these systems reflect the principles of respect for the individual, procedural fairness, and transparency of decision making. Legal obligations concerning issues of fairness and employee rights can be met by HR practices such as:

• The development of valid, reliable, and transparent performance-appraisal systems that include specified performance criteria, such as position descriptions and performance goals
• Formal and documented review processes
• Written advice to employees in the case of inadequate performance, including information about processes in place to assist with performance improvement and procedures and consequences for non-compliance.

Our discussion of the ethical issues and challenges in employee selection, compensation, and promotion, demonstrates the critical role that HRM plays in the effective and fair management of human capital. An understanding of the ethical dimensions of a strategic approach to HRM suggests that HRM cannot be strategic unless it is ethical.

The values of fairness and respect for persons are integral to effective job screening, interviews, and testing; salary and benefits determination; performance appraisals; and promotion policies that are accurate, honest, and relevant. It is through the fair implementation of these HR activities that enterprises are able to attract and retain a superior workforce for sustained competitive advantage.

8.5 The role of HR professionals in the operationalisation of corporate ethics programmes[117]

Over the past decade, corporate governance and the operationalisation of corporate ethics programmes have been in the spotlight of governments, corporate boards, and research by academics. The literature on responsibility for corporate ethics programmes reveals two broad themes:

• The first is that responsibility for corporate ethics programmes has been assigned to existing functional areas of management – primarily HR departments in Australia, Canada, South Africa, and the USA, and legal departments or corporate services in the UK.
• The second is that to be effective, corporate ethics programmes must have the support of top-level management.

The following section will provide an overview of research on the role of HR professionals in the operationalisation of corporate ethics programmes.

Despite the enormous growth in corporate ethics programmes, the ethics process does not yet seem to have evolved into a separate function, although in many large enterprises, ethics or compliance officers and executives with ethics responsibilities have been introduced. The ethics and HR literature contains research (not empirically based) that suggests that the HR function ought to take on the role of ethical stewardship, with some writers suggesting that HRM has a special role to play in the formulation, communication, monitoring, and enforcement of an enterprise's ethics programme.[118] The USA-based literature on business ethics generally presents the view that the HR function, along with finance and law, is the appropriate locus of responsibility for an enterprise's ethics programme.[119-121] Donaldson[122] places HR at the top of this triangle, arguing that 'seventy percent of the responsibility for values and ethics should fall to HR'. This is not surprising when one considers that ethical issues are people issues and HR activities are instrumental to the development and maintenance of corporate ethical cultures. For example, performance management and reward systems can hold employees accountable for ethics performance, as well as for their financial performance. Whether the role of the HR manager is that of strategist or conscience of the organisation is a contentious issue and influenced by the culture and structure of an organisation, as well as by the status and credibility of the HR function and its specialists.[123]

Empirical studies have investigated whether ethics initiatives and strategies for ethics management should be HR driven. The 1997 SHRM/ERC[124] survey found that 70 per cent of HR professionals are involved in formulating ethics policies for their enterprises and 69 per cent are a primary resource for their enterprises' ethics initiatives. Focus groups of HR managers in the USA support the view that it is appropriate for HRM to take responsibility for workplace ethics.[125] However, the SHRM respondents did not regard ethics as the sole responsibility of HRM. When asked to indicate the degree to which they thought other units or positions should be responsible for ethical leadership, 96 per cent of HR professionals said the CEO, 93 per cent functional vice-presidents, 90 per cent immediate supervisors, 77 per cent the board of directors, and 65 per cent legal counsel. When asked which functional areas should have responsibility for the administration of corporate codes of conduct, 37 per cent of CEOs answered HR, 19 per cent law, and 9 per cent senior management. In assigning responsibility for revising corporate codes of conduct, 40 per cent cited HR, 31 per cent law and 10 per cent the company director or president.

Canadian[126-127], Australian[128], and South African[129] surveys provide some support for these findings. The *2001 South African Ethics Survey* conducted by KPMG and Transparency South Africa found that 59 per cent of the 166 respondents reported the appointment of a senior-level manager whose role specifically included responsibility for ethics initiatives. In

78 per cent of these cases the responsibility was part of another position, and in most cases it was the additional responsibility of the HR manager. A 2007 study of the operationalisation of ethics in Australian enterprises found that the HR function currently has the primary responsibility for the formulation, communication (dissemination and training), and monitoring and enforcement phases of corporate ethics programmes, although other departments and different levels of management do share responsibility for corporate ethics programmes. The study also found that respondents indicated that:

- All functions and personnel should have more responsibility than they currently have for corporate ethics programmes
- The CEO should have primary responsibility for the formulation and communication phases
- Business-unit managers should have primary responsibility for the monitoring and enforcement phases.

Robertson and Schlegelmilch[130] report that enterprises in the UK are more likely to communicate ethics policies through senior executives than through HR departments. Their results show that the CEO and Managing Director have 'primary responsibility' for communicating ethics policies and codes in 69 per cent of the UK enterprises and 42 per cent of the USA enterprises. This compares to the HR function which had 'primary responsibility' for communicating ethics policies in 15,7 per cent of the UK enterprises and 33,2 per cent of the USA enterprises. These findings are supported by Weaver, Trevino, and Cochran[131] in the USA and the IBE surveys in the UK.[132] Weaver, Trevino, and Cochran's study of Fortune 1000 enterprises found that CEOs in USA companies typically had very minimal responsibility for communicating with respondents about ethics-related issues and that responsibility for ethics education rested with ethics officers, HR staff, and legal counsel. The IBE surveys for 1998, 2001, and 2004 found that in 44–46 per cent of the UK companies, the Company Secretary or legal department was responsible for administering a company's code of ethics. This is in contrast to the reported 16 per cent in 2004, 20 per cent in 2001, and 12 per cent in 1998 for responsibility resting with HR departments.

Overall, these empirical findings recognise that HRM is well positioned to make an important contribution to creating, implementing, and sustaining ethical organisational behaviour within a strategic HR paradigm. HR professionals have specialised expertise in the areas of organisational culture, communication, recruitment, training, performance management, leadership, motivation, group dynamics, organisational structure, and change management –

all of which are key factors for integrating ethics into all aspects of organisational life and for developing positive corporate ethics cultures. For example, studies have found that the most common sources of pressure to compromise ethics standards in organisations are related to conflicts of interest (a superior's directive, meeting overly aggressive business objectives, and helping the organisation to survive).[133-134] HRM plays a critical role in ensuring that employees have, and are aware of, recourse to such pressure. At the same time, the findings suggest that responsibility for ethical leadership should cut across all functions and managerial levels, including line and senior managers.

SUMMARY

This chapter explains that in an era of increasing competitive pressures, the pursuit of strategic and fair HR practices inevitably raises myriad ethical dilemmas and conflicts of duties, which are often complex. Ethical dilemmas rarely resolve themselves and unexamined personal value systems lack the necessary rigour. It is therefore imperative that HR practitioners take steps to develop their competencies in identifying ethical issues and engaging in sound moral reasoning so that they can represent the interests of all organisational stakeholders, including employees, management, the community, and society.

This chapter has presented the view that HR practitioners who are sensitive to ethical issues and who are well versed in the elements of ethical theory will be able to respond creatively to the ethical challenges that confront them, as well as make a significant contribution to an enterprise's ethical infrastructure, thereby limiting the occurrence of costly (human and financial) ethical breaches. In this way ethics has the potential to be an integral component to a strategic approach to the fair and effective management of an enterprise's human resources.

KEY CONCEPTS

• Apartheid	• Integrity
• Autonomy	• Just cause
• Categorical imperative	• Justice
• Compensatory, distributive, procedural, and retributive justice	• Kantian deontology
• Consequentialism	• Libertarian
• Deontology	• Non-consequentialism
• Discrimination	• Normative ethical theory
• Dual loyalties	• Pluralist
• Due process	• Prima facie duties
• Egalitarian	• Professional codes of conduct
• Egoism	• Psychometric testing
• Employment at will	• Teleology
• Ethics	• Unitarist
• Human rights	• Utilitarian

CASE STUDY

Objective: To understand the importance of ethical issues in the execution of HRM practices

Voluntary Resignations at Orbolay

Joe Mercer is one of several HR managers working for Orbolay, a large multinational corporation in the resources industry. Despite a resources boom, the company's financial performance has been poor over the past five years. For example, the company's annual earnings estimate has fallen to below US$7 a share, from last year's US$11,45 a share, on earnings of US$6,5 billion. New estimates for the second quarter earnings are now below US$2,60 a share, compared with last year's US$4,45, or US$1,85 billion. This continues a trend begun almost five years earlier.

To remain competitive, the company has had to cut costs and that has meant a drastic reduction in its global workforce. The company now employees approximately 315 000 workers compared to a high of 350 000 five years ago. The reduction was achieved through a voluntary programme that gave incentives to employees who sought work at other companies. This was done to honour a 'no firings' pledge the company had upheld ever since its founding decades before. The voluntary programmes included incentives for early retirement and expenses incurred if an employee took a job with another non-competitive company. Despite the uptake of voluntary departures, the programme has not been without problems. In particular, senior management now recognises that too many of the company's good workers have taken advantage of the incentives, while many weaker employees have remained. An internal study done by the company's industrial psychology department has concluded that productivity was down 20 percent among remaining workers, mainly because many of the best employees have left the company.

Nevertheless, Joe was surprised to hear the director of HRM announce at today's group meeting that the accounting department had recommended cutting the workforce by another 14 000 to reduce further profit loss. This has created a problem for HR: how to cut the workforce while honouring the 'no firing' pledge and still hang on to the best workers.

Joe was even more surprised to learn that the director of HRM had already put in place a number of policies. First, she asked her HR managers to 'encourage' certain targeted employees to leave the company. Second, she announced that many of the weaker employees were to be laid off indefinitely, thereby technically adhering to the no-firing policy. However, a certain number of targeted employees cannot be laid off because of the terms of their contracts. It is these employees whom Joe and his HR colleagues are being told to 'encourage' to leave. The director explained that the policies would become effective in four weeks' time and that they should remain confidential until that time – the delay was to avoid any negative publicity prior to the next board meeting (which is to be held in the following fortnight).

The director then provided the five HR managers with a memo that outlined these policies and also listed four expendable employees from each of their departments. The list ended with this statement: 'You are to convince said employees that seeking employment elsewhere would be to their best interest.' The director of HRM went on to explain to the HR group managers that it was up to them to convince the employees to leave and that if they felt that some of the people on the list were there by mistake, they could prepare a memo outlining their objections and suggesting alternate names to be placed on the list. She also noted that those employees who left would be given two weeks' severance pay for every year they had worked at the company, in addition to the mandatory severance pay. However, this offer would be good only for those who left voluntarily within one month of the policy's announcement. After that, there would be no additional severance pay for employees who left voluntarily or who were fired. Further, she announced that it was the HR managers' job to inform marginal employees who wanted to stay that their pay might be cut or that they might be fired eventually. The HRM director finished her verbal report with a clear statement that a dim view would be taken of HR managers who could not 'encourage' the targeted employees to move on.

Back in his office, Joe felt deeply troubled by the whole situation. On the one hand, he was aware that the best hope for the company's continued economic survival was to cut back its workforce. On the other hand, doing so seemed to violate the spirit of the no-firing policy. As he stared at the list of names that appeared on the memo, Joe became even more troubled. At least two of the four employees named on the list from his own department were employees he considered to be well above average. Joe thought to himself, 'If someone had to be on the list, I could think of at least two other people whose work is marginal. How did the Director decide who was to be listed.' He also wondered how on earth he was to go about 'encouraging' people to leave jobs they had held, in all four cases, for at least five years.

Joe then looked over the names of the employees from other departments and his heart sank even further. Only the previous week he had played cricket with Pete Briely. Pete was an engineer at Orbolay and had been there about seven years. Joe didn't see much of Pete at work, but when their local cricket clubs played against each other, they shared a beer afterwards. The previous Saturday, Pete had told Joe how he

and his wife were expecting their third child and as a consequence had put their house on the market and had organised finance to purchase a larger one that they had been admiring. Although the mortgage payments would be steep, especially without a second income until Pete's wife returned to work, they were looking forward to these new beginnings. They expected to sign the purchase contract over the next week or two.

Joe decided to call the other HR managers. They all agreed that it seemed clear that the company was not simply encouraging voluntary participation. Rather, it was pressuring certain employees into quitting, thus making the no-firing policy a mere sham. However, if they failed to carry out the company's orders, they knew that they would be looked upon as marginal. They told Joe that they didn't know how they should proceed.

Questions and activities

1. Identify and discuss the implications of Joe's dual roles as employer representative and employee activist.
2. Analyse the ethical issues and dilemmas faced by the HR managers at Orbolay from utilitarian, Kantian, rights, and justice perspectives.
3. Discuss how ethical theories can help inform good practice of HRM activities.
4. Given your analysis and discussion, how would you proceed if you were Joe?

REVIEW QUESTIONS AND ACTIVITIES

1. Identify the important concepts involved in a definition of business ethics. How are these concepts relevant in the context of South Africa?
2. What is the problem of dual loyalties and why does it arise? Provide an example of dual loyalties that an HR professional might encounter.
3. Evaluate the appropriateness of the professional code of conduct of the South African Board for Personnel Practice (SABPP). How effective is the code in providing guidance to HR professionals who face the problem of dual loyalties? Why?
4. Outline the main features of an integrity-based approach to a strategic HR paradigm.
5. Explain and evaluate the utilitarian and deontological approaches (Kant, justice and rights) to ethics and discuss their relevance to HRM. Illustrate your discussion with reference to examples in South African workplaces and society.
6. Discuss the ethical issues that may arise within the traditional HR activities of employee selection, compensation, and promotion.
7. Discuss the issues that managers should address in formulating a company's policy on employee privacy.
8. The moral issues surrounding affirmative action are controversial. Discuss the pros and cons of affirmative-action programmes. In your view, are affirmative-action programmes morally justified or is employment-equity legislation sufficient to address the problem of discrimination? Why?
9. Identify and discuss the key justice and rights issues in contemporary South Africa. How would Mill, Kant, Rawls, and Nozick address them? How do South African enterprises deal with them?
10. In your view, what is the proper role of HR professionals in the operationalisation of corporate ethics programmes? Why?

FURTHER READING

PINNINGTON, A., MACKLIN, R. & CAMPBELL, T. 2007. *Human resource management ethics and employment.* Oxford: Oxford University Press.

TREVINO, L. K. & NELSON, K. A., 2007. *Managing business ethics: Straight talk about how to do it right* 4th ed. Hoboken, N.J.: John Wiley & Sons Inc.

WINSTANLEY, D. & WOODALL, J. (Eds.). 2000. *Ethical issues in contemporary human resource management.* Basingstoke: MacMillan.

VELASQUEZ, M. G. 2006. *Business ethics concepts and cases* 6th ed. Upper Saddle River, N.J.: Pearson.

WEB SITES

www.web-miner.com/busethics.htm – articles and publications on business ethics

www.sabpp.co.za – South African Board for Personnel Practice

www.tisa.org.za – Transparency International South Africa (anti-corruption site, includes hotline)

ENDNOTES

1. BOATRIGHT, J. 2007. *Ethics and the conduct of business* 5th ed. Upper Saddle River, N.J.: Pearson.
2. SINGER, P. (Ed.). 1993. *A companion to ethics.* Oxford: Basil Blackwell:v.
3. ROSSOUW, G. J. 1997. Business ethics in South Africa. *Journal of business ethics*, 16:1539–1547.
4. BOATRIGHT, J. 2007. *Ethics and the conduct of business* 5th ed. Upper Saddle River, N.J.: Pearson.
5. WOOTEN, K. C. 2001. Ethical dimensions in human resource management: An application of a multi-dimensional framework, a unifying taxonomy and applicable codes. *Human resource management review*, 11(1&2):159–175.

6. SOUTH AFRICA. 1996. *Constitution of the Republic of South Africa* [Online]. Available: www.info.gov.za/documents/constitution/index.htm. 20 September 2007. [Laws.]

7. INSTITUTE OF DIRECTORS. 2002. *Second King Report on corporate governance for South Africa.* Johannesburg: Institute of Directors.

8. STRASHEIM, P. 2004. *HR, ethics, compliance risks & fair labour practices: ethical dilemmas, an ethical safety algorithm and recommendations for a way forward.* [Online.] Available: www.workinfo.com/free/Downloads/169.htm. 18 August 2007. See also TREVINO, L. K. & BROWN, M. E. 2004. Managing to be ethical: debunking five business ethics myths. *Academy of management executive*, 18(2):69–81; VEIGA, J. F., GOLDEN, T. D. & DECHANT, K. 2004. Why managers bend company rules. *Academy of management executive*, 18(2):84–89; CARROLL, A. B. 2004. Managing ethically with global stakeholders: a present and future challenge. *Academy of management executive*, 18(2):114–120.

9. FISHER, C. & DOWLING, P. J. 1999. Support for an HR Approach in Australia: the Perspective of Senior HR Managers, *Asia Pacific journal of human resources*, 37(1):1–19. See also LEPAK, D. P. & COLAKOGLU, S. 2006. Ethics and strategic human resource management. (*In* Deckop, J. R. (Ed.). 2006. *Human resource management ethics.* Greenwich, Connecticut: Information Age Publishers:27–45.)

10. SOCIETY FOR HUMAN RESOURCE MANAGEMENT (SHRM). 2006. *2006 Strategic HR management survey.* [Online.] Available: www.shrm.org/surveys. 6 October 2007.

11. CAREY, L. 1999. Ethical dimensions of a strategic approach to HRM. *Asia Pacific journal of human resources*, 37(3):53–68. See also WEAVER, G. R. 2004. Ethics and employees: Making the connection. *Academy of management executive*, 18(2):121–125.

12. CAREY, L. 1999. Ethical dimensions of a strategic approach to HRM. *Asia Pacific journal of human resources*, 37(3):53–68.

13. AMERICAN MANAGEMENT ASSOCIATION. 2006. *The Ethical Enterprise.* [Online.]. Available: www.amanet.org. 16 September 2007.

14. SOCIETY FOR HUMAN RESOURCE MANAGEMENT/ETHICS RESOURCE CENTER (SHRM/ERC). 2003. *Business ethics survey.* [Online.]. Available: www.shrm.org. 21 August 2007.

15. CAREY, L. E. 2007. *Profits and principles: The operationalisation of corporate ethics in Australian enterprises.* Canberra, Australia. University of Canberra. (Ph.D. thesis.)

16. SCHWOERER, C. E. , MAY, D. R. & BENSON, R. 1995. Organisational characteristics and HRM policies on rights: exploring the patterns of connections. *Journal of business ethics*, 14(7):531–549.

17. HENDRY, C. 1994. Personnel and human resource management in Britain. *Zeitschrift für personalforschung*, 8(3):209–238.

18. BEER, M. 1997. The transformation of the human resource function: resolving the tension between a traditional administrative and a new strategic role. *Human resource management*, 36(1):49–56.

19. LEGGE, K. 1995. *Human resource management: Rhetoric and realities.* Houndmills: Macmillan.

20. DYER, L. & KOCHAN, T. A. 1995. Is there a new HRM? Contemporary evidence and future directions. (*In* Downie, B. and Coates, M. (eds). *Managing human resources in the 1990s and beyond.* Ontario: IRC Press:132–63.

21. STOREY, J. 1995. *Human resource management: A critical text.* London: Routledge.

22. HOFFMAN, M. 1986. What is necessary for corporate moral excellence? *Journal of business ethics*, 5:233–242.

23. CAREY, L. 1999. Ethical dimensions of a strategic approach to HRM. *Asia Pacific journal of human resources*, 37(3):53–68.

24. WARD, S. P., WARD, D. R. & WILSON, T. E. 1996. The code of professional conduct: Instructional impact on accounting students' ethical judgement. *Journal of education for business*, 71:147–155. See also PINNINGTON, A., MACKLIN, R. & CAMPBELL, T. 2007. Introduction: ethical human resource management (*In* Pinnington, A., Macklin, R. & Campbell, T. (eds). *Human resource management: Ethics and employment.* Oxford: Oxford University Press:1–20.)

25. BROOKS, L. J. 1995. *Professional ethics for accountants.* St. Paul: West Publishing.

26. WINDT, P., APPLEBY, P., BATTIN, M. , FRANCIS, L. & LANDESMAN, B. 1989. *Ethical issues in the professions.* Englewood Cliffs: Prentice Hall.

27. SOCIETY FOR HUMAN RESOURCE MANAGEMENT (SHRM). 1995–96. *Membership services directory.* Alexandria, VA: SHRM.

28. AUSTRALIAN HUMAN RESOURCES INSTITUTE (AHRI). 2007. [Online.]. Available: www.ahri.com.au. 13 October 2007.

29. SOUTH AFRICAN BOARD FOR PERSONNEL PRACTICE (SABPP). 2007. [Online.]. Available: www.sabpp.co.za. 1 July 2007.

30. Ibid.

31. Ibid.

32. SOCIETY FOR HUMAN RESOURCE MANAGEMENT (SHRM). 1991. *Human resource management.* Alexandria: SHRM:1–2.

33. BEER, M. 1997. The transformation of the human resource function: resolving the tension between a traditional administrative and a new strategic role. *Human resource management*, 36(1):49–56.

34. ULRICH, D. 1998. A new mandate for human resources. *Harvard business review*, 76(1):124–134.

35. STONE, C. D. 1975. Why the law can't do it. (*In* Beauchamp, T. & Bowie, N. 1993. *Ethical theory and business* 4th ed. New Jersey: Prentice Hall:162–166.)

36. JOSEPHSON, M. 1988. Ethics and business decision making. (*In* W. M. Hoffman, W. M., Frederick, R. E. & Schwartz, M. S. 2001. *Business ethics readings and cases in corporate morality* 4th ed. New York: McGraw-Hill:87–94.)

37. CAREY, L. 1999. Ethical dimensions of a strategic approach to HRM. *Asia Pacific journal of human resources,* 37(3):53–68.

38. More recently a growing number of universities across Africa are beginning to incorporate ethical issues into their business school courses, particularly in their MBA programmes.

39. BEER, M. 1997. The transformation of the human resource function: resolving the tension between a traditional administrative and a new strategic role. *Human resource management,* 36(1):49–56.

40. JOSEPHSON, M. 1988. Ethics and business decision making. (*In* W. M. Hoffman, W. M., Frederick, R. E. & Schwartz, M. S. 2001. *Business ethics readings and cases in corporate morality* 4th ed. New York: McGraw-Hill:87–94.)

41. ULRICH, D. 1998. A new mandate for human resources. *Harvard business review,* 76(1):124–134.

42. PAINE, L. S. 1994. Managing for organizational integrity. *Harvard business review,* March–April:106–117.

43. WEAVER, G. R., TREVINO, L. K. & COCHRAN, P. L. 1999. Corporate ethics programs as control systems: influences of executive commitment and environmental factors. *Academy of management journal,* 42(1):41–57.

44. DE GEORGE, R. T. 1993. *Competing with integrity in international business.* New York: Oxford University Press.

45. Ibid.:6.

46. PAINE, L. S. 1994. Managing for organizational integrity. *Harvard business review,* March–April:111.

47. JOSEPHSON, M. 1988. Ethics and business decision making. (*In* W. M. Hoffman, W. M., Frederick, R. E. & Schwartz, M. S. 2001. *Business ethics readings and cases in corporate morality* 4th ed. New York: McGraw-Hill:87–94.)

48. COETZEE, J. 2005. *Banking the unbanked in South Africa: the practical implications on branch banking.* [Online.]. Available: www.essa.org.za/ download/2005Conference/Coetzee.pdf. 16 July 2007.

49. KEY, S. & POPKIN, S. J. 1998. Integrating ethics into the strategic management process: doing well by doing good. *Management decision,* 36(5):1–9.

50. The discussion on ethical decision-making frameworks is based on CAREY, L. E. 2007. *Profits and principles: The operationalisation of corporate ethics in Australian enterprises.* Canberra, Australia. University of Canberra. (Ph.D. thesis.):26–70.

51. NOE, R. A. , HOLLENBECK, J. R. , GERHART, B. & WRIGHT, P. W. 1997. *Human resource management: Gaining a competitive advantage.* Burr Ridge, Illinois: Irwin.

52. JOSEPHSON, M. 1988. Ethics and business decision making. (*In* W. M. Hoffman, W. M., Frederick, R. E. & Schwartz, M. S. 2001. *Business ethics readings and cases in corporate morality* 4th ed. New York: McGraw-Hill:87–94.)

53. BEAUCHAMP, T. L. & CHILDRESS, J. F. 1994. *Principles of biomedical ethics* 4th ed. New York: Oxford University Press.

54. KEHOE, W. J. 1993. Ethics in business: theory and application. *Journal of professional services marketing,* 9(1):13–25.

55. WEISS, J. W. 1998. *Business ethics: A stakeholder and issues management approach* 2nd ed. Fort Worth: Dryden

56. WEST, A. 2006. Theorising South Africa's corporate governance. *Journal of business ethics,* 68:433–448.

57. MBITI, J. 1989:110 (*In* WEST, A. 2006. Theorising South Africa's corporate governance. *Journal of business ethics,* 68:439.)

58. POJMAN, L. P. 1995. *Ethical theory, classical and contemporary readings* 2nd ed. Belmont, C.A.: Wadsworth:253.

59. DE GEORGE, R.T. 1999. *Competing with integrity in international business.* New York: Oxford University Press.

60. WEISS, J. W. 1998. *Business ethics: A stakeholder and issues management approach* 2nd ed. Fort Worth: Dryden:76.

61. ROSS, W. D. 1930. *The right and the good.* Oxford: Clarendon Press.

62. DITTRICH, J. E. & CARRELL, M. R. 1979. Equity perceptions, employee job satisfaction, and department absence and turnover rates. *Behaviour and human performance,* 24:29–40.

63. HATFIELD, E. & SPRECHER, I. 1982. Equity theory and behaviour in organisations. (*In* Bacharach, S. & Lawler, E. (eds). *Research in the sociology of organisations.* Greenwich: JAI Press:95–124.)

64. DORNSTEIN, M. 1991. *Conceptions of fair pay: Theoretical perspectives and empirical research.* New York: Praeger.

65. COWHERD, D. M. & LEVINE, D. I. 1992. Product quality and pay-equity between lower-level employees and top management: An investigation. *Administrative quarterly,* 37:302–325.

66. NOZICK, R. 1974. The entitlement theory. (*In* Beauchamp, T. & Bowie, N. 2001. *Ethical theory and business* 6th ed. Upper Saddle River, N.J.: Prentice Hall:657–661.)

67. FRIEDMAN, M. 1970. The social responsibility of business is to increase its profits. (*In* Beauchamp, T. & Bowie, N. 2001. *Ethical theory and business* 6th ed. Upper Saddle River, N.J.: Prentice Hall:51–55.)

68. NOZICK, R. 1974. The entitlement theory. (*In* Beauchamp, T. & Bowie, N. 2001. *Ethical theory and business* 6th ed. Upper Saddle River, N.J.: Prentice Hall:657–661.)

69. RAWLS, J. 1971. *A theory of justice*. Cambridge, M.A.: Harvard University Press.

70. Ibid.:60.

71. GREENBERG, J. 1986. Determinants of perceived fairness of performance evaluations. *Journal of applied psychology*, 71:340–342.

72. GREENBERG, J. 1987. A taxonomy of all justice theories. *Academy of management review*, 12:9–22.

73. OSIGWEH, C. A. B. 1991. Toward an employee responsibilities and rights paradigm. *Human relations*, 43(12:):1277–1309.

74. FOLGER, R. & KONOVKSY, M. A. 1989. Effects of procedural and distributive justice on reactions to pay raise decisions. *Academy of management journal*, 32:115–130.

75. COOPER, C. L. , DYCK, B. & FROHLICH, N. 1992. Improving the effectiveness of gainsharing: The role of fairness and participation. *Administrative science quarterly*, 37:471–491.

76. KIDWELL, R. E. & BENNET, N. 1994. Employee reactions to electronic control systems: The role of procedural fairness. *Group & management*, 19(2):203–218.

77. BEAUCHAMP, T. & BOWIE, N. (Eds.) 2004. *Ethical theory and business* 7th ed. Englewood Cliffs, N.J.: Prentice Hall.

78. SOUTH AFRICA. 1998. *Employment Equity Act, No. 55 of 1998*. Pretoria: Government Printer. [Laws.]; SOUTH AFRICA. 1996. *Constitution of the Republic of South Africa*. Pretoria: Government Printer. [Laws.] (The Act defines 'designated groups' as meaning black people, women and people with disabilities.)

79. VON GLINOW, M. A. 1996. On minority rights and majority accommodations. *Academy of management review*, 21(2):346–350.

80. VAN HOOFT, S., GILLAM, L. & BYRNES, M. 1995. *Facts and values*. Sydney: Maclennan & Petty.

81. BEAUCHAMP, T. L. & CHILDRESS, J. F. 1994. *Principles of biomedical ethics* 4th ed. New York: Oxford University Press.

82. GREENBERG, J. 1990. Employee theft as a reaction to underpayment inequity: the hidden cost of pay cuts. *Journal of applied psychology*, 75:561–568.

83. HOLLINGER, R. D. & CLARK, J. P. 1983. *Theft by employees*. Lexington, M.A.: Lexington Books.

84. PRIVACY COMMITTEE OF NEW SOUTH WALES. 1995. *Invisible eyes: Report on video surveillance in the workplace*. Sydney: Privacy Committee of New South Wales.

85. VELASQUEZ, M. G. 2002. *Business ethics* 5th ed. Upper Saddle River, N.J.: Prentice Hall.

86. CLARK, G. L. & JONSON, E. P. 1995. *Management ethics theory, cases and practice*. Pymble, N.S.W.: Harper Educational.

87. KRAMER, R. 2004. Corporate social responsibility … a challenge for HR? *Human resources*. [Online.]. www.humanresourcesmagazine.com.au/articles/22/0c01d22.asp. 24 February, 28 September

2007. The author refers to research involving three surveys across Europe and the USA and a survey involving 25 countries.

88. WILSON, A. 1997. Business and its social responsibility. (*In* Davis, P. (ed.) *Current issues in business ethics*. London: Routledge.)

89. SOCIETY FOR HUMAN RESOURCE MANAGEMENT (SHRM). 1991. *Human resource management*. Alexandria: SHRM.

90. For an introduction to the literature on employee' rights and duties within a firm, see DE GEORGE, R.T. 1999. *Competing with integrity in international business*. New York: Oxford University Press; BEAUCHAMP, T. & BOWIE, N. 2001. *Ethical theory and business* 6th ed. Upper Saddle River, N.J.: Prentice Hall; SHAW, W. H. & BARRY, V. 2001. *Moral issues in business* 8th ed. Belmont, C.A.: Wadsworth.

91. For example, Chapter 2 of the *Constitution of the Republic of South Africa* (1996) contains a Bill of Rights which in part states: 'The state may not unfairly discriminate directly or indirectly against anyone on one or more grounds, including race, gender, sex, pregnancy, marital status, ethnic or social origin, colour, sexual orientation, age, disability, religion, conscience, belief, culture, language and birth.'

92. IVANCEVICH, J. M. 1995. *Human resource management* 6th ed. Chicago: Irwin.

93. ELDER, R. W. & FERRIS, G. R. (Eds.) 1989. *The employment interview: Theory research and practice*. London: Sage.

94. See, for example, PEARN, S. & SEEAR, L. 1988. cited in Winstanley, D. & Woodall, J. (Eds.) 2000. *Ethical Issues in contemporary human resource management*. Basingstoke: Macmillan.

95. VELASQUEZ, M. G. 2002. *Business ethics* 5th ed. Upper Saddle River, N.J.: Prentice Hall.

96. BEAUCHAMP, T. & BOWIE, N. 2001. *Ethical theory and business* 6th ed. Upper Saddle River, N.J.: Prentice Hall:261. See also KUPFER, J. 1993. The ethics of genetic screening in the workplace. (*In* Beauchamp, T. & Bowie, N. 2001. *Ethical theory and business* 6th ed. Upper Saddle River, N.J.: Prentice Hall:303–310.)

97. SHAW, W. H. 1999. *Business ethics*. Belmont, C.A.: Wadsworth.

98. WEISS, J. W. 1998. *Business ethics: A stakeholder and issues management approach* 2nd ed. Fort Worth: Dryden

99. BAKER, B. & COOPER, J. (*In* Winstanley, D. & Woodall, J. (Eds.) 2000. *Ethical Issues in contemporary human resource management*. Basingstoke: MacMillan.)

100. MITCHELL, T., DOWLING, P., KABANOFF, B. & LARSON, J. R. 1988. *People in organisations: An introduction to organisational behaviour in Australia*. Sydney: McGraw-Hill.

101. ANDERSON, G. 1991. Selection. (*In* Towers, B. (ed.). *The handbook of human resource management.* Oxford: Blackwell.)

102. MAUER, K. 2000. Psychological test use in South Africa. [Online.]. www.pai.org.za/. 16 August 2007.

103. SOUTH AFRICA. 1998. *Employment Equity Act, No. 55 of 1998.* Section 8. Pretoria: Government Printer. [Laws.]

104. DE GEORGE, R.T. 1999. *Competing with integrity in international business.* New York: Oxford University Press.

105. HEERY, E. 1996. Risk, representation and the new pay. *Personnel review,* 25(6):54–65.

106. LAWLER III, E. E. 1995. The new pay: a strategic approach. *Compensation and benefits review,* July/August:14–22.

107. HEERY, E. 1996. Risk, representation and the new pay. *Personnel review,* 25(6):54–65.

108. KINNIE, N., HUTCHINSON, S. & PURCELL, J. 2000. Fun and surveillance: the paradox of high commitment management in call centres. *International journal of human resources,* 11(5):967–985.

109. HEERY, E. 1996. Risk, representation and the new pay. *Personnel review,* 25(6):54–65.

110. Ibid.:178.

111. KELLY, J. & KELLY, C. 1991. 'Them and us': social psychology and the new industrial relations. *British journal of industrial relations,* 29(1):25–48.

112. HEERY, E. 1996. Risk, representation and the new pay. *Personnel review,* 25(6):54–65.

113. DE CIERI, H., KRAMER, R., NOE, R., HOLLENBECK, J., GERHART, B. & WRIGHT, P. 2005. *Human resource management in Australia* 2nd ed. North Ryde, Australia: McGraw Hill.

114. DE GEORGE, R.T. 1999. *Competing with integrity in international business.* New York: Oxford University Press.

115. SHAW, W. H. 1999. *Business ethics.* Belmont, C.A.: Wadsworth:216.

116. Ibid.

117. Section 8.5 is based on CAREY, L. E. 2007. *Profits and principles: The operationalisation of corporate ethics in Australian enterprises.* Canberra, Australia. University of Canberra. (Ph.D. thesis.):168–171.

118. WINSTANLEY, D., WOODALL J. &. HEERY, E. 1996. Business ethics and human resource management themes and issues, *Personnel review,* 25(6):5–12.

119. EDWARDS, G. & BENNETT, K. 1987. Ethics and HR: standards in practice, *Personnel administrator,* 32(12):62–66.

120. DRISCOLL, D. & HOFFMAN, W. M. 1998. HR plays a central role in ethics programs, *Workforce,* 77(4):121–123.

121. WILEY, C. 1998. Reexamining perceived ethics issues and ethics roles among employment managers, *Journal of business ethics,* 17(2):147–161.

122. DONALDSON, T. (cited in Digh, P. 1997. Shades of Gray in the Global Marketplace. *HR magazine,* 42(4):90–98). See also OFFSTEIN, E. H. & DUFRESNE, R. L. 2007. Building strong ethics and promoting positive character development: the influence of HRM at the US Military Academy at West Point. *Human resource management,* 46(1):95–114.

123. FOOTE, D. & ROBINSON, I. 1999. The role of human resources manager: strategist or conscience of the organisation? *Business ethics: a European review,* 8(2):88–98.

124. SOCIETY FOR HUMAN RESOURCE MANAGEMENT/ETHICS RESOURCE CENTER. 1997. *Business ethics survey report.* Alexandria: SHRM/Ethics Resource Center.

125. WILEY, C. 1998. Reexamining perceived ethics issues and ethics roles among employment managers, *Journal of business ethics,* 17(2):147–161.

126. BROOKS, L. J. 1995. *Professional ethics for accountants.* St. Paul: West Publishing.

127. LINDSAY, R. M., LINDSAY, L. M. & IRVINE, B. V. 1996. Instilling ethical behaviour in organizations: a survey of Canadian companies. *Journal of business ethics,* 15(4):393–410.

128. CAREY, L. E. 2007. *Profits and principles: The operationalisation of corporate ethics in Australian enterprises.* Canberra, Australia. University of Canberra. (Ph.D. thesis.)

129. KPMG & TRANSPARENCY SOUTH AFRICA. 2002. *Ethics Survey – 2001 ethics in practice.* South Africa: KPMG Inc. South Africa.

130. ROBERTSON, D. & SCHLEGELMILCH, B. 1993. Corporate institutionalization of ethics in the United States and Great Britain. *Journal of business ethics,* 12:301–312.

131. WEAVER, G. R., TREVINO, L. K. & COCHRAN, P. L. 1999. Corporate ethics practices in the mid-1990s: an empirical study of the Fortune 1000. *Journal of business ethics,* 18(3):283–294.

132. WEBLEY, S. & LE JEUNE, M. 2005. *Corporate use of codes of ethics 2004 survey.* London: Institute of Business Ethics.

133. CAREY, L. E. 2007. *Profits and principles: The operationalisation of corporate ethics in Australian enterprises.* Canberra, Australia. University of Canberra. (Ph.D. thesis.)

134. VICKERS, M. R. 2005. Business ethics and the HR role: past, present and future HR. *Human resource planning,* 28(1):26–32.

9

Corporate social responsibility, ethics, and governance: Implications for corporate citizenship and HRM[1]

Learning outcomes

After reading this chapter you should be able to:

▶ Distinguish between the concepts 'corporate social responsibility', 'corporate ethics programmes' and 'corporate governance'
▶ Explain and discuss the shareholder and stakeholder models of corporate social responsibility and how the two models reflect different theories of the corporation
▶ Identify the key components of an effective corporate ethics programme and explain how they impact upon the implementation of corporate social responsibility
▶ Discuss recent global initiatives in corporate governance
▶ Discuss the implications of good corporate citizenship for the HR function

Purpose

The purpose of this chapter is to explore the nature of corporate social responsibility, citizenship, and governance.

Chapter overview

This chapter begins with an overview of the arguments in the literature for diverse viewpoints on corporate social responsibility (CSR). These views range from a narrow classical economic view to varying degrees within the socio-economic view that include both negative and affirmative duties of corporations to stakeholders. These viewpoints can be characterised as the shareholder and stakeholder models of CSR, respectively. The chapter indicates that the concepts of CSR, corporate ethics programmes, and corporate governance are related, but different. The term 'corporate citizenship' is sometimes used interchangeably with the term 'CSR' and is sometimes used to encapsulate all three concepts.

The chapter then explores research findings on corporate ethics programmes and considers the most effective elements of ethics programmes for corporations. It then discusses recent initiatives in corporate governance, including those pertaining to South Africa in the wake of the second *King Report*. Finally, this chapter recognises how the concept of corporate citizenship brings together the themes of CSR, ethics, and governance and examines the implications for the HR function. The concluding case study illustrates how the theory contained in this chapter can be applied to a practical situation.

Introduction

The proper role of business in society and how that role should be regulated have been the subject of much debate in the literature on business ethics. One of the major developments in management thought in the latter part of the twentieth century was the recognition that enterprises have social responsibilities beyond those of profit maximisation and legal obligations. This development has required management to take into account the diverse needs of individuals and groups that have an interest in the operations of their enterprises, rather than focus solely on the interests of shareholders. To operationalise accountability to multiple stakeholders, enterprises in Australia, Canada, China, Europe, South Africa, the UK, the USA, and elsewhere, have embarked on corporate ethics programmes that include the introduction of written standards of ethical business conduct, compliance programmes, and board-level ethics committees.

Research on corporate ethics programmes has resulted in a substantial body of literature about the content of these programmes. Academics do not always agree, however, on how far corporate responsibilities to multiple stakeholders should extend, and corporations do not always succeed in fulfilling the obligations they acknowledge. When corporations fail to self-regulate, government regulation often follows. For example, in the face of major failures in corporate ethics at the beginning of the new millennium – e.g. at Enron – the US government enacted the Sarbanes–Oxley Act of 2002. In the wake of other corporate failures globally, corporate governance programmes have evolved, both in structure and status. However, in both theory and practice, organisations and academics have given insufficient consideration to the philosophical foundations and assumptions that underpin corporate governance initiatives.[2] A theory of corporate social responsibility is a prerequisite to a well-articulated stance on corporate governance and is also the foundation of corporate ethics programmes.

In recent years some have used the concept of corporate citizenship as an extension of the earlier work on corporate social responsibility and the role of business in society. Some writers suggest that corporate citizenship encompasses corporate social responsibility, corporate ethics programmes, and corporate governance.[3] Other writers suggest business practitioners favour the term 'corporate citizenship', while 'corporate social responsibility' and 'stakeholder theory' have wider acceptance in the academic literature.[4] A review of company documents shows that, indeed, many companies publicly refer to themselves as good corporate citizens. For example, ABN Amro's corporate Web site states that 'we are a responsible institution and a good corporate citizen'; BHPBilliton's 2007 *Annual Report* declares that its strategy includes being valued as a good corporate citizen; and Boeing's Web site identifies good corporate citizenship as a key value at Boeing. ExxonMobil, Ford, Nike, Nokia, Toyota, and Unilever are further examples of companies that consider themselves to be good corporate citizens.[4] Cultural differences might also account for a preference for one term or another. For example, in South Africa, academe seems to favour 'corporate citizenship', whereas in the USA and Australia, writers use the term 'corporate social responsibility'. Whatever term is used, the landscape is vast. Therefore, although the different aspects of corporate citizenship overlap, it is useful to distinguish the key domains both theory and practice attribute to them.

- *Corporate Social Responsibility (CSR).* Definitions of CSR abound. Typically, they refer to Carroll's 1999 definition, which identified the economic, legal, ethical, and philanthropic (discretionary) responsibilities that enterprises have towards their stakeholders.[5] For example, the World Council for Sustainable Development states that CSR involves not only a commitment to behave ethically and to contribute to economic development, but also a commitment to improve the quality of life of the workforce and their families, the local community, and society at large.[6] This definition plays a role in the Corporate Responsibility Index, an instrument initially developed in the UK, but now used globally, to provide detailed information to enterprises which volunteer to be indexed for the purpose of improving their actual performance in corporate responsibility.[7] Similarly, the Commission of the European Communities on the responsibilities of corporations defined CSR as 'a concept whereby companies integrate social and environmental concerns in their business operations and in their interaction with their stakeholders on a voluntary basis'.[8] Often, debates about CSR are seen in terms of the proper balance between obligations to shareholders and obligations to stakeholders. Currently, many large enterprises have an office for corporate environmental and social responsibility and almost all multinational enterprises practise triple-bottom-line reporting (financial, social, and environmental) in their annual reports. Figure 9.1 illustrates a range of the diverse stakeholders with

whom companies might engage. It is not exhaustive, but rather illustrates the broad range of interactions.

- *Corporate ethics programmes.* The programmes that enterprises institute to manage ethics, legal compliance, and social responsibilities are widely referred to as corporate ethics programmes. They provide an integrative function by defining boundaries of acceptable behaviour, stimulating and supporting organisational ethical behaviour, and providing early-warning mechanisms to identify and address potential problems. Written standards of ethical business conduct are the cornerstone[9–10] and essential foundation of corporate ethics programmes. Purcell and Weber[11] were early exponents of corporate ethics programmes and in the late 1970s wrote about the importance of institutionalising ethics into business. They define the institutionalisation of ethics as follows:

Figure 9.1 Diverse stakeholders with whom companies might engage

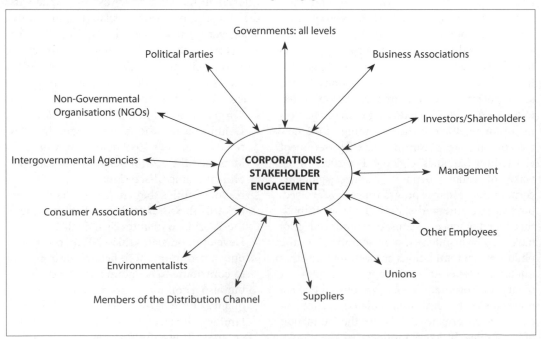

SOURCE: EUROPEAN FOUNDATION FOR MANAGEMENT DEVELOPMENT. 2005. *Globally responsible leadership: A call for engagement.* European Foundation for Management Development: 29. Used with permission.

[I]ntegrating ethics, formally and explicitly into daily business life … into company policy formulation at the board and top management levels and through a formal code … [and] into all daily decision making and work practices, down the line at all levels of employment.

SOURCE: PURCELL, H. & WEBER, J. 1979. (Cited in Sims, R. R. 1991. The institutionalization of organizational ethics. *Journal of business ethics*, 10:493.)

- *Corporate governance*. Corporate governance refers to the policies, practices, and mechanisms that shareholders, executive managers, and boards of directors use to manage themselves and fulfil their responsibilities to stakeholders, including investors. Since the early 1990s, corporate governance has grown in importance and acceptance. Like CSR, people now expect enterprises to include a section on corporate governance in their annual reports. For example, Unilever's corporate Web site includes a 60-page document on corporate governance.[12] Transparency, compensation, accountability, independence, and board diversity are key dimensions of policies and practices regarding corporate governance. However, like CSR, corporate governance is also concerned with topics such as employment practices, environmental policies, and community involvement.

- *Corporate citizenship*. Most definitions of corporate citizenship utilise Carroll's work on CSR.[13] For example, Maignan and Ferrell define corporate citizenship as 'the extent to which businesses meet the economic, legal, ethical and discretionary responsibilities imposed on them by their stakeholders'.[14] Harned, President of the Ethics Resource Centre based in Washington, DC, argues that organisational ethics (internal corporate ethics programmes) and CSR (ethical activities conducted outside the

corporation for the benefit of society) are independent of each other, but corporate citizenship requires both.[15] In a special edition of the *Journal of corporate citizenship* on Africa, the editors identify typical issues on the agenda of corporate citizenship.[16] They include eradicating poverty, improving governance, tackling corruption, enforcing labour standards, protecting human rights, preventing resource depletion, controlling industrial pollution, ensuring environmental conservation, upholding business ethics, and creating supply-chain integrity. The editors then state that a major difference between corporate citizenship in developed countries and less-developed countries, such as those in Africa, is that in developing countries the issues are 'in-your-face' and 'a daily reality, an unavoidable part of doing business'.[17] However, knowing at what stage of development a company is, and what challenges it faces in advancing citizenship, can be of great value. A proposed model to assist in this regard is contained in Appendix 9.1 to this chapter.

Having defined each of these terms, we shall now explore them in more detail. We shall begin with CSR. An important focus of the CSR debate is on distinguishing legitimate from illegitimate moral demands on corporate conduct by evaluating whether or not those demands are consistent with moral principles and values that underlie all moral institutions, including business.

9.1 Corporate social responsibility

The concept of CSR has evolved over time. However, while there is evidence of concern by business for social responsibility over centuries, the concept of CSR as a core construct primarily developed in the literature over the last 50 years. In this body of literature, a number of different viewpoints offer intense debate about what properly constitutes the social responsibilities of corporations and whether those responsibilities should be codified in voluntary written standards or codified in law.[18]

Following Carroll's widely cited model of CSR, referred to above, which identified economic, legal, ethical, and philanthropic (discretionary) responsibilities, and authors who have taken a similar approach, one can group the viewpoints on CSR into three broad types[19-20], as follows (Table 9.1 summarises them):

- *A view that corporations ought to maximise profits in view of their sole responsibility to shareholders and that market forces and the law are the determinants of ethical conduct.* This view is generally referred to as the narrow classical economic view of CSR. We shall explain it in more detail below.
- *A socio-economic view.* This view argues that corporations are responsible for the consequences of their actions in a sphere beyond that of profit making. This sphere includes the responsibility to do what is right and fair. For example, Davis refers to

'businessmen's [sic] decisions and actions taken for reasons at least partially beyond the firm's direct economic or technical interest'.[21] Camenisch[22] goes further. While recognising that the essential elements of business are profit and the provision of goods and services, Camenisch argues that it is the responsibility of business to ensure that the products and services it provides do not negatively impact on human flourishing, nor irresponsibly use limited and non-renewable resources.

- *A broad or maximal view.* This view refers to the obligations of corporations to act in ways that enhance total socio-economic welfare and even solve social problems.

Carroll argues that the three viewpoints are non-sequential stages and that 'each is to be fulfilled at all times'.[23] Sethi[24] and Wood[25], however, recognise that social expectations about the responsibilities of corporations to society may vary across time and cultures. We

Table 9.1 Three viewpoints on corporate social responsibility

Corporate social responsibility viewpoints	Approaches	Key references
Narrow classical economic (Shareholder model)	• Maximisation of shareholder value, uphold the law and ethical custom, enlightened long-term value maximisation	Friedman, 1970
Socio-economic (Stakeholder model)	• Profitability and legal compliance • Moral minimum of do no harm (negative duties) • Moral minimum of prevent harm (affirmative duties) • Uphold issues of justice and rights • Respect for all stakeholders as ends in themselves • Social contract	Simon, Powers & Gunnemann, 1972; Arrow, 1973; Stone, 1975; Evan & Freeman, 1988; Bowie & Duska, 1990; Goodpaster, 1991, 1996; West, 2006
Broad, maximal (Stakeholder model)	• Profitability and legal compliance • Moral minimum with affirmative duties • Uphold justice and rights of all stakeholders • Active role in social issues and contributing to the betterment of society through improving social conditions	Davis, 1973; Carroll, 1999, 2000; Mulligan, 1993; Wood, 1991; 2002; Porter & Kramer, 2002; Prahalad & Hammond, 2002

SOURCE: CAREY, L. E. 2007. *Profits and principles: The operationalisation of corporate ethics in Australian enterprises.* Canberra, Australia. University of Canberra: 98. (Ph.D. thesis.) Used with permission.

shall discuss the three viewpoints in detail below.

The values which underlie these different viewpoints on CSR derive from normative ethical theory (see Chapter 8) and are therefore prescriptive beliefs for right and wrong. The ethical values include:
- Social utility through profit maximisation
- Nonmaleficence
- Care for others
- Prevention of harm (accountability)
- Respect for individual rights, including life, property, and freedom rights
- Justice
- Responsible citizenship
- Beneficence.

9.1.1 The narrow classical economic view of CSR

The narrow classical economic view of CSR is most often associated with free market enthusiasts and is still influential today, especially among economists. The most well-known proponent of this view is the Nobel-winning economist Friedman.[26] The essence of Friedman's philosophy is that the sole responsibility of business is to maximise profits within the law and the 'rules of the game' (coercion and fraud are disallowed) and that governments ought not to interfere in the workings of the free market beyond providing a minimal state of order and securing public welfare. There are two premises underlying this philosophy. The first is a link between capitalism and freedom. The second is that corporations are not moral agents, but legal entities only and that whilst they can be held legally responsible for actions, they cannot be held morally responsible. Not surprisingly, the literature on business ethics is replete with critiques of the free market or narrow classical economic view generally, and Friedman's arguments specifically. Shaw[27] states that in the period 1970 to 1988, there were at least 1 000 attempts in the literature to discredit Friedman's position.

In support of his classical economic view, Friedman offered two arguments, which we shall discuss in detail. They are:

- The 'free society' argument
- The so-called 'agent–principal argument' and the associated 'taxation argument'.

Friedman's first argument in support of his classical economic view is the 'free society' argument. This argument states that any obligations placed on business to spend resources on concerns other than the pursuit of profit (within the law) are at odds with the principles of a free society. In his 1970 essay he asserted that 'the doctrine of "social responsibility" … does not differ in philosophy from the most explicitly collectivist doctrine'.[28] Furthermore, Friedman claimed that businesspeople who defend the idea of CSR undermine the basis of a free society and are 'unwitting puppets' of socialism and that 'capitalism is a necessary condition for political freedom'.[29] The free society that Friedman is defending here is a free-market economic system, characterised by open and free competition for resources, numerous buyers and sellers who have perfect information and who are all rational utility maximisers, and the absence of external costs and market regulation.

Critics of the market approach argue that these characteristics are absent from the market and therefore the laws of supply and demand cannot reign supreme and ought not to define CSR. For example, Arrow[30], also an economist, rejects Friedman's conclusion on the basis that a mandate to maximise profits ignores the reality of imperfect competition and results in an unequal distribution of income, a decline in altruism, and social inefficiencies due to the problems of an imbalance of knowledge between buyers and sellers and of uncosted externalities such as pollution. Other critics have argued that the classic defence of the free-market system is undermined because manufacturers create the demand for the products they make, thereby encouraging excessive and unsustainable levels of consumption.[31]

In recognition of market failures, critics recommend the use of government regulation, taxation, legal liability, and voluntary initiatives, including codes of ethics, to institutionalise the social responsibilities of corporations. Other writers[32] point to the limits of relying on legal standards alone for determining CSR. These limits include the degree of influence that corporations are able to exercise in both shaping regulatory law and influencing legal outcomes and the reactive, rather than proactive, nature of the law. Moreover, while the law prescribes what cannot be done, it does not prescribe what ought to be done.

Attempts have been made to defend the free-market or classical economic view of business responsibilities by reference to utilitarianism and two rights-based arguments, as follows:

- *A utilitarian defence of the free-market system.* As we identified in Chapter 8, utilitarianism is the ethical theory that utility ought to be maximised in the long run. The utilitarian defence of the classical economic view of the responsibilities of business is that the free-market approach is the best means to achieve the goal of maximising net happiness or the well-being of society as a whole. The justification is Smith's well-known 'invisible hand' and its role in harmonising self-interested behaviour to secure an end (public interest) that is not part of anyone's intention.[33] However, there is evidence to suggest that commonly held views of Smith's understanding of ethics and economics misrepresent his work. For example, Werhane and others have argued that for Smith, self-interest is not the highest virtue and economic gain is not the highest goal; instead, justice is the crowning virtue.[34] These authors point out that while Smith showed how individuals pursuing their economic interests in the free marketplace would propel society towards wealth and greatness, he concluded in *The wealth of nations* that economic actors must exercise prudence, benevolence, and restraint; respect the rights of others; and operate according to principles of justice. Moreover, they suggest that an earlier and less well-known work by Smith, *The theory of moral sentiments*, provides the context for

Smith's later work and that to read the latter without the former misrepresents Smith's understanding of individualism and society. In *The theory of moral sentiments*, Smith sought to develop an ethical theory based on a theory of human nature. For Smith, the defining ethic or virtue is not self-interest, but 'sympathy' or compassion. Smith understood sympathy as 'the capacity for entering imaginatively into the feelings of others and allowing the sympathy to guide our own actions'.[35] Objectivity (Smith refers to the 'impartial spectator') and, indeed, conscience are established by one's ability to evaluate one's own actions as others would evaluate them. Friedman's emphasis on maximising one's own interests – in this context, those of shareholders – without regard for how this might harm others falls short of the utilitarian principle and Kant's test of universalisability and respect for autonomous human beings (we explored this issue in Chapter 8).

- *A rights-based defence of the free-market system.* The two rights-based arguments used as a defence for the narrow classical economic view of CSR are liberty and property rights.

  > *The argument from liberty.* This argument is that individuals have the right not to be interfered with in their affairs, including with respect to their economic affairs, and that any interference by governments or others would infringe on their rights to property. This is essentially Nozick's argument for his libertarian approach to justice (see Chapter 8).

  > *The argument from property rights.* This argument is related to the argument from liberty. Proponents of this view argue that the owners of a corporation hold private property rights to use as they see fit (within the law and without committing fraud or deception). According to this argument, if the owners wish to pursue the goal of profit maximisation, then any action

or legislation that impedes this goal is an illegitimate restriction on the property rights of the owners of the corporation. Thus, proponents conclude that while managers have a duty to maximise profits for the shareholders of the corporation, governments and others have a duty not to interfere with the corporate pursuit of profit. For Friedman, the property rights of individual shareholders are inviolable. However, as we identified in Chapter 8, the principle of equality limits rights and when different rights of different people are in conflict, those rights most closely associated with the right to life have priority over those founded on rights to liberty and property.

Friedman's second argument in support of the classical economic view of CSR is the so-called 'agent–principal argument and the associated 'taxation argument': 'The manager is the agent of the individuals who own the corporation … and his [sic] primary responsibility is to them.'[36] Here he claims that corporate executives are the employees of shareholders and as such have a primary fiduciary responsibility to protect their interests, which, Friedman claims, is to maximise profits. At the same time, for Friedman, management's only responsibility is the protection of shareholders' interests: 'There is one and only one social responsibility of business … to increase its profits so long as it stays within the rules of the game.'[37] The claim is that corporate executives who spend the corporation's resources on social concerns do not maximise profits for the corporation (shareholders). Friedman arrives at this claim by arguing that in cases where an executive spends the corporation's resources on social concerns that do not maximise profits for the corporation, the executive 'is in effect imposing taxes, on the one hand [by reducing returns to owners], and deciding how the tax proceeds shall be spent, on the other [by lowering wages or adding costs to customers]'.[38] For Friedman this is akin to stealing from shareholders, unless contributions to charity are done as a public-

relations exercise for the purpose of increasing profits. Moreover, for Friedman, imposing taxes and spending the revenue on social concerns is a governmental function, not a corporate function, and when corporate officers become involved in community activities and public policy, they are acting outside their area of competence. These matters, claims Friedman, are best handled through the political process and left to elected and trained civil servants.

The literature reports that most people do not find Friedman's taxation argument against CSR very compelling. This is partly because managers do not have a responsibility to earn the greatest amount of profit without regard for the means by which the profit is made, and partly because shareholders may be interested in the social dimensions of their portfolio investments, as well as in their financial returns. The success of ethical investment portfolios are testament to this. Moreover, there is a growing body of research evidence that suggests a positive correlation between CSR and corporate financial performance.[39] Also, rather than viewing socially responsible behaviour as theft, one can view it as a kind of payment for the unpaid social costs of doing business.

In regard to the agent–principal argument, there are problems with Friedman's synonymous use of 'primary' and 'only', his emphasis on 'maximisation' of profits, and his failure to acknowledge that 'primary' implies that there might be other interests to consider. Such interests often require management to forgo the goal of maximum profit, in favour of a good profit, as well as just wages, safe working conditions, and good environmental practices. Criticisms of Friedman's agent–principal and taxation arguments and his free-society argument have led not only to a broader view of CSR, but also to the view that ethics should be institutionalised from within corporations. Whilst the literature is in agreement that corporations should be socially responsible, there is still much debate about what those responsibilities are. At a minimum, the broader socio-economic view acknowledges the interests and rights of multiple stakeholders who need to be protected from harm.

9.1.2 The socio-economic view of CSR

The second viewpoint in the CSR debate argues that stakeholder interests and expectations should be more explicitly incorporated in the organisation's purposes even when doing so results in reduced profitability.[40] The literature refers to it as the neo-classical view or socio-economic view of CSR. Some formulations of the socio-economic view include only the moral minimum, described as the responsibility to make a profit without causing harm. However, Simon, Powers, and Gunnemann[41], in requiring the moral minimum from corporations, make the important distinction between negative injunctions and affirmative duties and argue that the standard of a 'moral minimum' requires both.

This understanding of the moral minimum for corporations requires not only that they do no harm – such as 'do not pollute' (duties of nonmaleficence) – but also that corporations prevent harm from occurring. BHPBilliton's environmental policy provides a good example of affirmative duties. It states that its policy is to ensure it has management systems to identify, control, and monitor environmental risks arising from its operations and to conduct research and establish programmes to conserve resources, minimise waste, improve processes, and protect the environment.[42]

However, the obligation to prevent harm is not open ended. Simon, Powers, and Gunnemann present the view that it is limited by the criteria of need, proximity, capability, and last resort. Profitability is included as a function of capability. These criteria serve to bring direction and coherence to corporate social policy.

Other formulations of the socio-economic view of CSR recognise issues of rights and justice and how these may require corporations to forgo some profit in the interests of all who have a stake in a business's operations. The recognition of stakeholder rights is central to the concept of stakeholder theory, which has become popular with many writers on business ethics.[43] For example, Johnson identified a 'multiplicity of interests' when he stated[44]:

> [A] socially responsible firm is one whose managerial staff balances a multiplicity of interests. Instead of striving only for larger profits for its stockholders, a responsible enterprise also takes into account employees, suppliers, dealers, local communities, and the nation.
>
> SOURCE: JOHNSON, H. L. 1971. *Business in contemporary society: Framework and issues.* Washington, D.C.: Wadsworth:50.

Stakeholder theory has been justified by appeals to Kant, rights, justice, and utilitarianism. There is also wide support in the literature for the view that strategically managed firms can and ought to take into account broad stakeholder-based interests.[45] It is argued that by attending to such interests, corporations build intangible assets such as goodwill, reputation, trust, loyalty, and opportunities for innovation.

Taking account of the various themes within the socio-economic view of CSR, Bowie and Duska offer a revision of the classical economic view, stating[46]:

> [B]usiness has a primary responsibility to make a profit, but in doing so cannot resort to coercion or fraud, and must respect the rights of all those who have a stake in the business, treating them justly and fairly, compensating for past injuries, doing no harm, and, where required, preventing harm.
>
> SOURCE: BOWIE, N. E. & DUSKA, R. F. 1990. *Business ethics* 2nd ed. Englewood Cliffs, N.J.: Prentice Hall:41.

Missing from Bowie and Duska's reformulation is the obligation for corporations to contribute to solving social problems. To consider legitimate constraints on profit making, Bowie and Duska employ Frankena's four principles of prima facie duties of beneficence.[47] Frankena presented these duties in ascending order, with the implication that the more difficult the duty, the more likely it is to be understood as an ideal rather than a strict moral obligation. Frankena's duties in ascending order are:

1. Avoiding harm
2. Preventing harm
3. Removing harm
4. Promoting good.

Bowie and Duska's reformulated view is supported by advocates of the socio-economic view who argue that while companies are responsible for any wrongdoing they cause, they are not obliged to take responsibility for solving social problems, such as community health and education, although they may undertake such activities if they wish to do so. The main arguments put forth by these neo-classicists are that:

- Corporations do not have the resources to solve social problems
- In a competitive market, competitive pressure will prevent well-intentioned companies from involvement in solving social problems
- It is unrealistic to expect corporations to address systemic problems such as inflation, pollution, and unemployment.

However, even on Friedmanite grounds, one can defend philanthropic and social activities by corporations since, paradoxically, acting ethically and responsibly may end up being more profitable.[48] This is the view of enlightened self-interest through corporate investment in community involvement with a view to long-term profit maximisation. For example, drawing on the philosophy of its founders, Texas Instruments defines itself as a good corporate citizen that gives back to the communities in which it operates, making them better places in which to live and work and 'in turn making them better places to do business'.[49] This supports the recent work of Porter and others[50] in using Porter's earlier work on competitive advantage to argue that corporate activities aimed at improving society may result in creating contexts of competitive advantage. Nevertheless, there is an important difference between Friedman's view and the socio-economic view: 'The Friedmanite treats

stakeholders well in order to make a profit, while the stakeholder theorist treats stakeholders well because it is the right thing to do.'[51]

9.1.3 The broad maximal view of CSR

The third view of CSR obliges corporations to take on maximal duties (duties of beneficence) of CSR. According to this view, a corporation's responsibilities include shaping society and solving social problems caused wholly or in part by the corporation. The Millennium Poll on Corporate Social Responsibility[52] interviewed over 25 000 people in 23 countries on 6 continents about their expectations of corporations. Two of the most significant findings of the global survey are that the majority of citizens, in all but three of the countries surveyed, thought companies should go beyond the Friedmanite view of profit making and obeying the law, and the majority thought that corporations, in addition to making a profit and obeying laws, should make a positive contribution to society.

The maximal account of social responsibility is based on the argument that corporations are powerful institutional members of society, which places an obligation on them to use their social power for good ends. For example the largest 100 companies in the world have annual revenues that exceed the gross domestic product of 50 per cent of the world's nation states, 359 corporations account for 40 per cent of world trade, and 10 corporations control almost every aspect of the worldwide food chain.[53]

A key assumption in this proposition is that society entrusts business with significant resources to accomplish its goals and expects business to manage these resources prudently. The question then arises as to whether competent trusteeship can be assured through compliance with voluntary codes of behaviour, rather than enforced through legal constraints. The maximal view is also based on an understanding that corporate citizenship, like individual citizenship, involves civic duties and responsibilities, duties of gratitude for the benefits corporations receive from society, and the responsibility to contribute positively to society.

Wood suggests that while corporations are not responsible for solving all social problems, they are responsible for the consequences related to their primary and secondary areas of involvement with society.[54] This is similar to Simon, Powers, and Gunnemann's criterion of proximity in relation to preventing harm. For example, according to Wood's principle and Simon, Powers, and Gunnemann's criteria, while car manufacturers may not have a responsibility to become involved in literacy programmes, they do have a responsibility for helping to solve the problems of vehicle safety and the environment and, therefore, it is appropriate for them to become involved in programmes related to driver education, recycling, and pollution reduction. However, Wood also recognises that the inter-relationship of business and society may justify social responsibilities beyond a corporation's primary and secondary involvements. Thus, if the car manufacturer in the example above is dependent on migrant workers, then a literacy programme would be a relevant responsibility.

Unilever's campaigns on hand-washing, established in partnership with UNICEF and the London School of Hygiene and Tropical Medicine, provide a good example of obligations to solve social problems when they are within a corporation's primary area of business activity. The campaigns were established to help combat childhood deaths from diarrhoea. The hand-washing campaigns initially ran in India, but Unilever has extended them to Bangladesh and East Africa. The United Nations estimates that more than 5 000 children die every day from diarrhoeal diseases. The so-called 'health awakening' campaigns involve a two-prong approach whereby Unilever funds hygiene-education programmes and makes its Lifebuoy soap affordable to local communities. To date, the programmes have helped around 80 million people in 28 000 Indian villages become more aware of basic hygiene, stressing the importance of hand-washing with soap. Working in partnership with local and national stakeholders, the five-year campaign aims to educate a total of 200 million people – 20 per cent of the population. In 2006 Unilever reported that its sales of Lifebuoy soap increased by almost seven per cent, with particularly strong growth in the eight Indian states where Unilever launched the programme.[55]

Unilever is also involved in community activities outside its primary area of business. For example, in South Africa, Unilever factories have begun diverting food waste to make compost that people then use in community vegetable gardens. Local people can grow vegetables in the community garden and sell the produce. This provides a source of income for people and helps to feed local communities. It also helps to reduce waste sent to landfill and reduces the cost of waste disposal for Unilever.[56]

9.1.4 Current developments in CSR

In view of the evolution of CSR to date, one can identify a number of trends likely to shape CSR in the decade ahead, namely:

- First, there is a growing recognition that CSR and business ethics are intertwined; thus, corporate ethics programmes are likely to focus on preventing harm as well as initiatives to do good, and to focus not only internally on primary stakeholders, but also externally on external stakeholders, including the community
- Second, business ethics and CSR initiatives will be strategically focused
- Third, there is likely to be an increase in both mandatory and voluntary reporting and, perhaps, government regulation
- Fourth, there is likely to be greater public expectation about corporate leadership in solving social problems
- Fifth, there is an increased focus on the effectiveness of corporate ethics initiatives and best-practice corporate ethics programmes; it is in this sense that CSR programmes combine principles, processes, and outcomes.

In the following two sections we shall discuss the processes within corporate ethics and governance programmes that corporations have adopted to help ensure high levels of CSR and ethical business conduct.

9.2 **Corporate ethics programmes**

The programmes that enterprises have instituted to manage ethics, legal compliance, and social responsibilities in order to be good corporate citizens are widely referred to as corporate ethics programmes, corporate values programmes, compliance programmes, and social responsibility programmes.[57] As the introduction identified, corporate ethics programmes – an umbrella term used in the literature – provide an integrative function by defining boundaries of acceptable behaviour, stimulating and supporting organisational ethical behaviour, and providing early-warning mechanisms to identify and address potential problems. They are sometimes referred to as both formal and soft organisational control systems.[58]

Written standards of ethical business conduct are regarded as the cornerstone and 'essential foundation' of corporate ethics programmes. An important function of written standards is that they make a company's values explicit. By doing so, they provide ethical justifications to guide the resolution of dilemmas at both the individual level and the organisational level.

Although written standards are central to a corporate ethics programme, the evidence shows that merely having written standards, such as a code of conduct, is insufficient.[59] Written standards of ethical business conduct must be aligned with an enterprise's organisational structures, culture and leadership. Some argue that unethical managerial behaviour disclosed in large high-profile companies is not due to anomalies, but rather, is institutionalised through corporate planning systems, especially those resulting in pressures on individual managers.[60]

Consequently, writers often emphasise the need to institutionalise ethical principles and values through an organisation's culture. They perceive ethical cultures to be vehicles for enabling and producing shared understandings among organisational members about proper behaviour.

9.2.1 **Operationalising corporate ethics programmes**

Over the past three decades there has been a dramatic increase in the number of enterprises that have embarked on corporate ethics programmes. These programmes have been the subject of numerous studies by the business ethics research community in the USA, the UK, Canada, Australia, Europe, and Asia.[61] The more recent research has focused on the operationalisation of corporate ethics programmes and their effectiveness. The operationalisation of corporate ethics programmes refers to the mechanisms and processes enterprises use to integrate ethics into organisational structures, organisational cultures, and decision-making practices of employees. An analysis of the current body of literature suggests there are three primary components of a corporate ethics program: the formulation, communication, and monitoring and enforcement of written standards. The body of literature also enables the identification of particular factors associated with each component.

- *Formulation phase*. The formulation component of a corporate ethics programme can include the following:
  - ▸ Consideration of the types of written standards of ethical business conduct that a corporation will develop
  - ▸ How frequently the standards are revised
  - ▸ Whether they are developed in consultation with organisational members or external consultants, or both
  - ▸ The values reflected in the written standards
  - ▸ The issues they address
  - ▸ The organisational positions or units responsible for the formulation of the written standards.

The following points summarise the key findings in the literature in relation to the formulation phase:
  - ▸ Written standards of ethical business conduct include codes of ethics, codes of conduct, codes of practice, value statements, corporate credos, and policy

documents on specified issues.

➤ Currently, almost all large enterprises worldwide have at least one of these written standards and many have several.

➤ Typically, written standards include definitions of ethical and unethical conduct; professional standards and directives; identification of stakeholders and their rights; commitments to fairness, equity, employee safety, the environment, and social responsibility; stipulations on the proper use of company resources, conflicts of interest, privacy, confidentiality, improper payments, gifts, and whistle-blowing; sanctions and other methods for the enforcement of standards; and advice on interpreting and implementing the standards.

➤ When designing and developing written standards, managers should consider the specific ethics issues that a company and its employees are likely to face. The written standards will then be relevant to the company's operating environment.

➤ Written documents are enhanced by the provision of examples about ethics issues and dilemmas that employees are likely to face in their daily work relationships and how those dilemmas can be resolved.

➤ It is best to develop written standards in a consultative and participatory manner with employee involvement in all stages of the process.

➤ Once formulated, written standards should not be stagnant. There should be ongoing and regular revision of ethics documents.

➤ Corporate ethics programmes can have different orientations, including values and compliance. Compliance programmes typically emphasise legal statutes and contracts, provide training in rule compliance, and set sanctions for non-compliance. Values-based corporate ethics programmes focus on core ideals

and types of behaviour that reflect ideals, such as 'respect for all persons'. While a values orientation has a larger unique impact on desired outcomes, the orientations are complementary.

➤ Values written standards typically include fairness, respect, integrity, honesty, trustworthiness, social responsibility, quality, equality, the keeping of promises, autonomy, care for the environment, and good citizenship.

➤ The involvement of senior-level management in the formulation phase is critical for the acceptance of written standards throughout an organisation. However, different organisational units share responsibility for the formulation phase, and most often it is delegated to the HR function.

• *Communication phase.* The communication phase of corporate ethics programmes is concerned with:

➤ The distribution of written standards to stakeholders (internal and external)

➤ Training programmes to educate employees about the nature, provisions, and requirements of the standards

➤ Who receives ethics training and how frequently

➤ Mechanisms for obtaining advice about implementing written standards at the individual and organisational levels

➤ The organisational positions or units responsible for the dissemination of ethics programmes.

The literature suggests that the majority of enterprises taking specific steps to instil ethics into organisational decision making are focusing on the first component, the formulation of written standards, and in particular on codes of ethics. The implementation of the communication component of corporate ethics programmes is generally reported to be incomplete.[62] Particularly problematic is the issue of training.

Surveys consistently show that while almost all large corporations have written standards of ethical business, training in those standards is provided by 30 per cent to 65 per cent of those corporations. Surveys also reveal that the most common form of ethics training in corporations is that conducted as part of employee induction or orientation programmes. The depth and breadth of such ethics training is questionable. When organisations do provide ethics training, the majority of employees report that they frequently use such training to guide their decisions and conduct at work and that the training prepares them to handle ethically sensitive situations. Studies have also found that while there is a good match between the ethics issues written standards of ethical business conduct address and those ethics training addresses, many companies do not adequately address ethics issues that employees perceive to be of concern to them. For example, in one study respondents indicated that out of a list of 25 ethics issues, sexual harassment and equality in employment were ranked the two most frequently addressed ethics issues in their company's written standards and ethics training.[63] However, the same issues ranked ninth and fifth, respectively, as a current issue, and thirteenth and sixth, respectively, as a future issue. Conversely, the use of information systems and environmental issues ranked second and fourth, respectively, as a current issue and first and second, respectively, as a future issue, but were ranked between seventh and ninth as the issues written standards and training programmes most frequently addressed. One explanation for the discrepancy may be that HRM had primary responsibility for the formulation of written standards and ethics training and its focus was on HR-related ethics issues, particularly ones that involved legal compliance. The ranking of occupational health and safety as the third-most-frequent issue addressed in written standards and training programmes supports this explanation.

Lack of opportunity to discuss ethics issues in the workplace can lead to 'moral stress'. Consequently, organisations increasingly provide mechanisms whereby employees can obtain advice and information regarding workplace ethics.[64] In addition to providing written standards, organisations increasingly provide advice by means of dedicated telephone advice lines, ethics officers, ethics committees, consultants, email, intranet services, and company Web sites. Electronic communication has helped to overcome the problem of distributing written standards to employees of overseas subsidiaries and of providing them in multiple languages. BHPBilliton, for example, provides some of its documents in nine different languages. Electronic communication via the World Wide Web also facilitates the communication of corporate ethics policies and practices to external stakeholders and the regular updating of those policies and practices.

- *Monitoring and enforcement phase.* The monitoring and enforcement component of corporate ethics programmes is concerned with:
  › The methods used to monitor compliance with written standards
  › The effectiveness of these methods
  › Actions an enterprise might take in the case of ethics misconduct
  › Whether or not ethics compliance is a formal part of an organisation's reward and performance management programmes
  › The organisational positions or units responsible for compliance monitoring and enforcement.

International studies dating from 1993 to 2005 show that enterprises appear to be somewhat inactive in monitoring and enforcing ethical behaviour and that the compliance measures in place appear to be somewhat superficial. For example, they may require only a periodic sign-off, be focused on punishment for wrongdoing rather than linked to performance management, or not have ethics infrastructure such as ethics committees and ethics officers.[65] A lack of emphasis on the communication and monitoring and enforcement aspects of corporate ethics programmes raises important questions about the extent to which ethics is embedded into an organisation's culture, routines and processes, and, therefore, the motivation that enterprises are providing their employees to behave ethically.

In recent years, the provision of mechanisms for reporting unethical practices or raising questions about ethical dilemmas in the workplace has gained increased attention. In both the USA and the UK, all corporations listed on the relevant stock exchanges must provide a code of business conduct that includes a means for employees to raise ethical issues in a confidential manner. In the UK, the number of companies reporting a mechanism for employees to ask questions concerning their company's code increased from 66 per cent in 1995 to 88 per cent in 2004.[66] Similarly, in 2004, 88 per cent of companies reported that employees could raise these issues in confidence, although only 46 per cent provided a helpline. Moreover, high-profile corporate financial scandals have spawned a wave of corporate governance initiatives in the USA, Australia, South Africa, European countries (e.g. Ireland, the UK, and others), and elsewhere. These corporate governance initiatives include evolving laws and self-regulated best practices. Under new corporate governance structures, senior management and boards of directors are beginning to address proactively the oversight issues their companies face. We shall discuss corporate governance issues in Section 9.3.

9.2.2 Effectiveness of corporate ethics programmes

A fundamental issue in the operationalisation of corporate ethics programmes is their effectiveness and how to measure it. However, while codes of ethics are both widely used and researched, little is known about their effectiveness. There is agreement that ethics is hard to measure and that any evaluation of a corporate ethics programme must go beyond cost accounting or savings from fewer lawsuits. Assuming that effectiveness of codes and corporate ethics programmes relates to ethical behaviour, measures of effectiveness and ethical behaviour must first determine what behaviour is ethical in the normative sense. A number of studies have attempted to verify the influence of codes of ethics and ethics programmes on behaviour. Schwartz[67] reported on 22 such studies and concluded the findings were mixed. Ten of the studies found codes were effective in influencing behaviour and another 10 studies found they were not. The remaining two studies found the relationship to be weak. However, most of the studies suffered from flawed methodologies.

While the earlier literature generally suggests one cannot meaningfully measure effectiveness of corporate ethics programmes, recent literature argues that one can measure effectiveness and that it involves both processes and outcomes.[68] With regard to processes, in the USA the federal sentencing guidelines, first implemented in 1991 and revised in 2004, have been influential in setting benchmarks for identifying processes required for an effective corporate ethics programme. The guidelines are designed to achieve just punishment, offer sufficient deterrence, and encourage the development of internal mechanisms to prevent and identify unethical and illegal behaviour. To assist corporations to develop such internal mechanisms, the guidelines identify seven minimal processes that a company's operating structure must incorporate. These processes are:

1. The establishment of standards and procedures tailored to the needs, size, and operating environment of an enterprise
2. Communication of compliance standards and procedures to all employees, regardless of level, and training appropriate to each employee's role and responsibility
3. Periodic auditing, monitoring, and evaluation of all aspects of the programme and the implementation of internal consultative and reporting mechanisms

4. Promotion and consistent enforcement through positive incentives and appropriate discipline
5. Appropriate and timely responses in cases of a violation
6. Oversight by senior management
7. Careful screening of personnel to whom authority is delegated.

A number of surveys have shown that the major impact of the guidelines has been the creation or enhancement of corporate ethics programmes by numerous companies, both in the USA and worldwide.[69] The greatest impact of the guidelines is thought to be on ethics training, ethics officers, ethics offices, and ethics hotlines. However, perhaps even more significantly, the guidelines have important implications for corporate culture and corporate self-governance and responsibility.

Weaver and Trevino[70] state that enterprises often implement the processes stipulated by the *US Federal Sentencing Guidelines for Organisations* without first identifying desired outcomes from their investment in corporate ethics programmes, beyond reduced penalties should they be found guilty of misconduct, and without a systematic evaluation of ethics programmes. While recognising that ethics programmes might influence other outcomes, they posit that the outcomes they have identified are the most salient in the context of most corporate ethics programmes.

The seven outcomes are:

1. Low levels of observed unethical behaviour
2. High levels of employee awareness of ethical issues that arise in the workplace
3. High levels of willingness to seek ethics advice within the company
4. High levels of willingness and sense of comfort about delivering bad news to superiors
5. High levels of reporting ethics violations to management
6. High levels of effective ethical decision making that is based on a company's ethics programme

7. High levels of employee commitment to the organisation because of its values.[71]

In order to investigate the relationship between the dynamics of a formal ethics programme process and outcomes, Trevino, Weaver, and Toffler[72] surveyed over 10 000 randomly selected employees in 6 large USA companies. The companies were drawn from a variety of industries and the employees represented a variety of organisational levels. The research found that the most significant organisational processes associated with the seven outcomes were a values orientation, a combined values and compliance orientation, formal mechanisms that allowed employees to raise concerns, follow-through on those concerns by the organisation, performance appraisals that included ethics, and ethical-culture factors. Ethical-culture factors were the most significant influential factors and included leadership (leaders that genuinely cared about ethics), fair treatment of employees, the perception that ethics and values could be spoken about openly and integrated into decision making, reward systems that supported ethical conduct, and an organisational focus on all stakeholders rather than on self-interest.

The body of research literature on corporate ethics programmes suggests they do influence employee behaviour and that organisations should develop corporate ethics programmes by implementing a range of processes related to the formulation, communication, monitoring, and enforcement of written standards of ethical business conduct. Ethics programmes act as control systems by identifying legal and ethical requirements, providing enabling mechanisms and monitoring for compliance. Together, these establish a corporate ethics culture. The case of Enron serves as a reminder that an enterprise with a commendable code of ethics can count for naught unless mainstream organisational structures support the code and unless the enterprise embeds the code's ethos into the culture and spirit of its management and employees. In implementing a corporate ethics programme, companies should establish measurable programme objectives in order to evaluate programme effectiveness and they should also, when required, amend the processes and review the objectives.

9.3 Corporate governance

Corporate governance is not a new concept, but large-scale corporate scandals and collapses around the globe, and the development of international market economies, have been catalysts for renewed interest in corporate governance. Consequently, during 2002–2004, 28 countries throughout the world implemented new corporate governance codes on best practice.[73] These have focused corporate boards on governance and compliance issues, which include attention to organisational culture, and refocused CSR issues from the limited shareholder model to the broader stakeholder model. Most new initiatives on corporate governance, particularly in the Anglo-American world, reflect a strategic or instrumental stakeholder analysis which considers stakeholders' interests in terms of corporate economic outcomes for the purpose of improving corporate profitability. However, some aspects, such as those pertaining to the environment, take a 'multi-fiduciary approach' which considers stakeholders' interests equally with shareholders' interests, thereby potentially compromising the profitability of a corporation.[74] The broader stakeholder approach is more common in the European and Japanese approach to corporate governance, which strongly upholds the concepts of obligation, family, and consensus.[75]

9.3.1 Corporate governance and its importance

Corporate governance refers to the processes which direct and control enterprises and hold them to account. It is concerned with the performance of enterprises for the benefit of shareholders, stakeholders, and economic growth. Corporate governance focuses on the conduct of boards of directors, managers, and shareholders. It encompasses authority,

accountability, stewardship, leadership, direction, and control exercised in the enterprise.

Definitions of corporate governance abound, but the common themes are shareholder rights, stakeholder rights, disclosure and transparency, executive management, and board accountability. The corporate governance framework includes business ethics and CSR. The Organisation for Economic Co-operation and Development (OECD) has defined corporate governance as[76]:

> ... a set of relationships between a company's management, its board, its shareholders and other stakeholders. Corporate governance provides the structure through which the objectives of the company are set, and the means of attaining those objectives and monitoring performance are determined. Good corporate governance should provide proper incentives for the board and management to pursue objectives that are in the interest of the company and its shareholders and should facilitate effective monitoring.

SOURCE: OECD, 2004. *OECD Principles of corporate governance.* Paris: OECD:11.

As we have already indicated, fraud and abuse have led to a greater awareness of the need for good corporate governance. Bosch[77] states that good governance is important for two reasons. The first is that 'investor protection has increased with the enormous surge in share ownership' and the second is that the creation of wealth can be increased by 'improving the performance of honestly managed and financially sound companies'.[78]

Research in Australia has shown that investors are prepared to pay a premium for companies that are well governed and that, overall, companies with good corporate governance achieved better share prices.[79] There is broad agreement in the literature that corporate governance can have a fundamental impact on the prosperity of not only companies, but also nation states. Arthur Levitt, the former

Chairperson of the US Securities and Exchange Commission, expressed this view, stating[80]:

> [I]f a country does not have a reputation for strong corporate governance practices, capital will flow elsewhere. If investors are not confident with the level of disclosure, capital will flow elsewhere. If a country opts for lax accounting and reporting standards, capital will flow elsewhere. All enterprises in that country will suffer the consequences.
>
> SOURCE: INSTITUTE OF DIRECTORS IN SOUTHERN AFRICA. 2002. *King Committee on Corporate Governance.* Parktown, South Africa: Institute of Directors in Southern Africa:9.

Good governance is also important because it enables predictability, transparency, participation, and accountability.[81] Predictability refers to the consistent interpretation and enforcement of rules, procedures, and regulations. Transparency enhances predictability and quality decision making by ensuring that all relevant information is available and disclosed to all relevant stakeholders. Transparency serves participation by providing stakeholders with the necessary information to participate in decision-making processes and practices. Finally, accountability requires enterprises to account for their actions. The account should explain the appropriateness, legality, and morality of corporate actions. To support accountability practices, corporations should identify who is accountable, to whom they are accountable, and for what they are accountable. The essence of good corporate governance is accountability. Figure 9.2 indicates the five pillars of corporate governance as well as issues which need to be addressed in each. By attending to these elements an organisation can develop an integrated and robust corporate governance process.

9.3.2 Theories of corporate governance

Historically, the same persons owned and managed businesses. In many countries – e.g. many in Asia, Australia, and Europe – family-owned firms, or small firms where managers are high-percentage owners, remain the dominant form. However, the development of the modern corporation has led to a separation of ownership and management control, thereby creating an agency relationship. In such an agency relationship, there exists a potential conflict of interest between shareholders and managers. Corporate governance involves aligning the interests of top-level management with those of the shareholders (and other stakeholders) through mechanisms that address the appointment of directors, executive compensation, and a corporation's structure and strategic direction.[82]

The agency, steward, and stakeholder theories of governance reflect different assumptions about the nature of the relationship between owners and managers. Consequently, each of these theories emphasises different aspects of corporate governance. When one theorises about different approaches to corporate governance, it is important to consider first the assumptions underlying them. The three theories are outlined below (even though we have already addressed them in the earlier section on CSR).

- *Agency theory.* Agency theory suggests that because professional managers have superior knowledge and expertise, they may act opportunistically and gain advantage of the firms' owners (shareholders). In other words, managers (agents) may maximise their personal interests (typically short-term increases in market value), rather than maximise the interests of shareholders (principals) (market value over the long term). It has been suggested that the 'excesses' of the profligate 1980s represented the inherent problems with agency relationships and led to the push for more public accountability on the part of managers.[83]
- *Stewardship theory.* Stewardship theory recognises managers as trustworthy stewards of the resources entrusted to them. Unlike agency theory, it does not hold that there is a conflict of interest

Figure 9.2 The five pillars of corporate governance

Corporate Governance				
Culture	**Leadership**	**Alignment**	**Structure**	**Systems**
Aspects of culture that can work against good governance	Aspects of leadership that can work against good governance	Aspects of alignment that can work against good governance	Aspects of structure that can affect good governance	Aspects of systems that can affect good governance
• Unethical behaviour • Excessive internal rivalry • Intolerance of failure • Propensity for risk-taking • Secretiveness • Persecution of people who speak up (whistle-blowers)	• Recklessness • Ruthlessness • Being a bullying leader • Egotism • Self-promotion • Insensitivity to the company culture • Single-mindedness • Irrational behaviour • The leader's integrity	• Inability to align key functions and their responsibilities in the face of rapidly changing environments • Conflicts between functions • Gaps in responsibility	• Appointing large numbers of insiders on boards • Having a wrong structure of board oversight committees which is conducive to fraud	• Lack of strong financial controls • Deficient internal control systems • Weak IT systems
Questions to probe whether the company culture supports good governance	Questions to assess the governance abilities of leaders	Questions to judge whether the organisational alignment of capabilities is conducive to stronger good governance	Questions to judge whether the structure is conducive to good governance	Questions to review the existing systems and their contribution to control, reporting, and risk management
• Are the company beliefs and values openly articulated in mission statements, and do these include ethical concerns? • Does the culture temper drive for entrepreneurship and success with a tolerance for occasional failure? • Do employees feel free to bring problems to executives without fear of adverse consequences? • Is the organisation unduly concerned with meeting short-term earnings targets, and are fear and extreme pressure associated with missing numerical goals?	• Is the leadership considered charismatic and possessing extraordinary powers? • Does the leadership show an absence of reflection and unrealistically assess opportunities and constraints in the business environment? • Are leaders committed to developing the highest standards of corporate governance, managerial judgement and independence of mind in their followers?	• Do the company's recent actions and performance show evidence of unfocused and misaligned priorities? • Do the board, senior executives and top management teams collectively have an understanding of the best practices in corporate governance and internal reporting and how these may be aligned? • Have the responsibilities of senior executives and governance committees been properly aligned to ensure compliance with regulations?	• Are the roles of chairman and CEO combined? If so, how are any conflicts of interest managed? • Is there an appropriate degree of diversity, and are outsiders on the board? • Does the organisational structure provide an effective system of checks and balances for governance and strategic decision-making?	• Does the company have an effective and standardised system of internal controls and financial reporting? • Does the company regularly assess changes in the business and regulations environments that have an effect on internal control systems? • Is the organisation attempting to improve strategic risk management?

Culture	Leadership	Alignment	Structure	Systems
• Do incentive plans in any way encourage or condone unacceptable unethical and illegal behaviours?	• Does the leadership show sensitivity to the needs of all important organisational stakeholders (internal and external)? • Does the board ensure leaders are measured and motivated not only by stock valuations, but also by longer-term strategic and ethical considerations?	• Is there regular communication between internal auditors, external auditors, and senior executives? • Do strategic planning processes encourage an appropriate balance of conservatism with entrepreneurship and risk avoidance with opportunity seeking?	• Are there strong roles for internal auditors with an appropriate structure of reporting to senior executives and board committees? • Is the responsibility for assessment of internal controls structured throughout the organisation?	• What systems are currently in place to identify, assess, and mitigate risks across the organisation? • Is the organisation attempting to implement a framework and systems for IT governance that will be acceptable?
How to address critical cultural weaknesses	How to address critical leadership weaknesses	How to improve alignment	How to improve structure	
• Implementing new and stronger controls • Restructuring incentive systems • Educating employees • Creating communication programmes • Providing individual and team coaching	• Using values-based leadership • Setting an example • Establishing clear expectations of ethical conduct • Providing feedback, coaching, and support regarding ethical behaviour • Recognising and rewarding behaviours that support organisational values • Being aware of individual differences among subordinates • Establishing leadership training and mentoring	• Ensuring strategy-making processes, aligning performance objectives with risk propensity and regulatory demands on the firm • Aligning organisational changes and structural redesign with regulatory compliance and desired ethical standards of behaviour • Designing new information and knowledge-management systems to support enterprise management • Creating new senior management integrating roles • Training and developing management to raise awareness about compliance issues throughout the organisation	• Understanding the changing nature of risk organisations face as they grow and evolve • Understanding how major structural transformations lead to changes in strategic risk exposure • Designing improved strategic risk management practices into structural change programmes	

SOURCE: Adapted from DREW, S. A., KELLY, P. C AND KENDRICK, T. 2006. Class: five elements of corporate governance to manage strategic risk. *Business horizons*, 49: 127–138 and DREW, S. A. 2005. Risk management: the five pillars of corporate governance. *Journal of general management*, 34(2):29, Winter. Used with permission.

between managers and owners. Rather, as stewards, managers will work to achieve the objectives of shareholders (profits and share prices) and in so doing satisfy their personal needs. Consequently, stewardship theorists focus on governance structures that facilitate and empower, rather than on those that simply monitor and control.

- *Stakeholder theory*. According to stakeholder theory, corporations serve a broader social purpose than their responsibilities to shareholders. Under stakeholder theory, boards of directors are accountable for the interests of all stakeholders. These include not only employees, suppliers, and customers, but also the disadvantaged and the natural environment. This accountability requires a board's performance to be measured by metrics other than shareholders' wealth and profit. The 'Balanced Scorecard'[84] approach to management performance is a good example of performance evaluation aligned to the needs of multiple stakeholders.

9.3.3 Governance standards and principles

The renewal in corporate governance mostly originated in the USA and the UK, but quickly influenced developments in other European countries, in Australia, and in South Africa. The most significant corporate governance from various organisations in these countries include:

- King I (1994) and King II (2002) – *King report on corporate governance and King report on corporate governance for South Africa* (reports of the King Committee on Corporate Governance)
- OECD principles (1999, 2004) (*Organisation for Economic Co-operation and Development principles of corporate governance*)
- SOX (2002) (*Sarbanes–Oxley Act*, USA)
- CCUK (2003) (*Combined code on corporate governance*, UK)
- ASXGCP (2003, 2007) (*Australian Stock Exchange corporate governance principles and recommendations*)

- AS, 8000-2003 (one of the five parts of 'Standards Australia') (*Australian corporate governance standards*).

Most of these governance principles have focused on large listed companies, but the organisations responsible for them argue that the principles are also relevant to smaller companies, public enterprises, and not-for-profit enterprises. The following section outlines the key elements of corporate-governance principles covered by the OECD, and those operating in the UK, the USA, Australia, and South Africa.

- *OECD principles of corporate governance (1999, 2004)*. The OECD principles published in 1999 were the first international code of corporate governance approved by governments. Although the principles were widely adopted, numerous corporate failures around the turn of the century had undermined public trust in companies and financial markets. As a result, in 2002, representatives of the 30 OECD member countries, as well as representatives from other interested non-member countries, came together for the purpose of revising the OECD principles. The revised principles, reworked from five to six, were released in 2004. The principles cover the following areas:
  - ▸ Ensuring the basis for an effective corporate-governance framework
  - ▸ The rights of shareholders and key ownership functions
  - ▸ The equitable treatment of shareholders
  - ▸ The role of stakeholders in corporate governance
  - ▸ Disclosure and transparency
  - ▸ The responsibilities of the board.[85]

The main areas of revision included the strengthening of investors' rights by granting shareholders a more active role in the nomination and removal of board members, the independence and accountability of external auditors, whistle-blower protection, the expansion of the duties of board members and clarification of the fiduciary nature of a board's primary responsibilities. The focus of the principles appears to be on governance problems arising from the separation of ownership (institutional and individual shareholders) and control (corporate management and boards). As we indicated earlier, the OECD principles have served as a reference point for countries when developing their own governance principles.

- *Corporate governance in the UK.* In the UK during the period 1992 to 2003, a number of committees were established by various financial and government bodies to report and make recommendations on corporate governance. The major reports include the following[86]:
  - > *The Cadbury report (1992).* This report, by a committee chaired by Sir Adrian Cadbury, is internationally recognised as having been seminal in the development of corporate governance in the UK and elsewhere. Many of its recommendations have been incorporated into the *Combined code of corporate governance* (1998, 2003) as well as the OECD principles and the corporate-governance codes of countries such as Australia and South Africa.
  - > *The Greenbury report (1995).*
  - > *The Hampel report (1998).*
  - > *The Higgs report (2003).*
  - > *The Combined code of corporate governance* (CCUK) (1998, 2003). Since the CCUK of 2003 also incorporates the major recommendations of the

Greenbury, Hampel, and Higgs reports, we shall limit the remainder of our discussion on corporate governance in the UK to the CCUK of 2003. The CCUK (1998) consolidated the principles and recommendations of the Cadbury, Greenbury, and Hampel reports. It was revised in 2003 following the Higgs report. The CCUK is divided into two sections. The first contains 14 main and supporting principles and provisions for companies, while the second contains 3 main and supporting principles and provisions for shareholders. Some of the main principles and reforms of the 2003 CCUK are shown in Table 9.2.

- *Corporate governance in the USA.* Like the UK, the USA has produced a number of standards related to corporate governance. The most well known and influential of these is the Sarbanes–Oxley Act (SOX) of 2002. SOX was enacted in response to the perceived crisis in corporate governance following the failure of internal controls to stop fraud in high-profile companies such as those of Enron and WorldCom. Particularly problematic was the finding that the organisation Arthur Anderson had Enron and WorldCom as clients in its consulting services and external client services. The amount of consulting services that Arthur Anderson conducted did not allow its auditing service to act independently from its consulting business.

Table 9.2 Main principles and reforms of the *Combined code of corporate governance* (2003)

- At least half of the board of directors should comprise non-executive directors
- The CEO should not be the chairperson of the board and should be independent
- The board, its committees, and directors should be subject to annual performance reviews
- Levels of remuneration should be sufficient to attract, retain, and motivate directors of high quality, but should not be excessive
- A significant proportion of executive directors' remuneration should be linked to corporate and individual performance
- At least one member of the audit committee is to have recent and relevant financial experience
- Formal and transparent procedures are to be adopted for the appointment of new directors to the board and for fixing the remuneration packages of directors
- All directors should receive induction on joining the board and should regularly update and refresh their skills and knowledge.

An important requirement of SOX is auditor independence. The act restricts firms engaging in accounting from both auditing and consulting services. It also prohibits insider trading and company loans to executive officers and directors. SOX requires independence of corporations' board committees, management assessment of internal controls, and personal certification of financial reports by CEOs and CFOs (Chief Financial Officers) with associated criminal liability.

SOX applies to all public companies listed on the US Stock Exchange. However, some states within the USA have adopted, or are considering adopting, similar provisions to those found within SOX, to apply to private companies. SOX has been subject to criticism, mostly because of the costs of compliance. For example, the American Institute of Certified Public Accountants has estimated that SOX has resulted in a 32 per cent increase in the costs of internal auditing.[87]

However, SOX has been successful in changing corporate-governance practices. For example, studies show that board evaluations are becoming more commonplace (a PricewaterhouseCoopers study reported an increase from 33 per cent in 2002 to 73 per cent in 2004[88]), boards are more independent (the Business Roundtable survey showed that 82 per cent of companies say their boards are at least 80 per cent independent[89]), and external directors are more active in attending board meetings (the Business Roundtable survey reported that in 2004, 68 per cent of companies said their independent directors met at every board meeting, compared to 55 per cent in 2003[90]).

- *Corporate governance in Australia.* The *Australian corporate governance standards*, commonly referred to as 'Standards Australia', consist of five standards. These are:
   › AS 8000-2003 Good governance principles

  › AS 8001-2003 Fraud and corruption control
  › AS 8002-2003 Organisation codes of conduct
  › AS 8002-2003 Corporate social responsibility
  › AS 8004-2004 Whistle-blower protection for entities.

Standards Australia are intended to establish and maintain ethical cultures through self-regulation and benchmarks against which stakeholders (including shareholders) can assess an enterprise's performance.

The AS 8000-2003 standard on good corporate governance is similar to the UK CCUK of 2003 in that it includes guidance on developing a governance policy, the roles and responsibilities of a board, executive and board remuneration, disclosure and transparency obligations, shareholders' ownership and voting rights, and shareholder responsibilities. AS 8000-2003 states that the major objective of good governance should be to improve organisational performance, identify and manage risks, strengthen shareholder and community confidence in an entity, improve the transparency and accountability of an organisation, and assist in the prevention and detection of fraudulent behaviour. Thus the good-governance principles offer a generic framework that applies to private, public, and not-for-profit enterprises of all sizes in order to enhance organisational performance and reputation.

A number of laws and institutions in Australia complement the guidelines on corporate governance within Standards Australia. These include the *Trade Practices Act* (1974), the *Prices Surveillance Act* (1983), the Australian Competition and Consumer Commission (ACCC), the Australian Securities and Investments Commission (ASIC) and the Australian Stock Exchange (ASX). The ASX formed a Corporate Governance Council and in 2003 issued its *Principles for good corporate governance and best practice recommendations*. The principles were revised in 2007.[91] These principles are similar to those codified in Standards Australia, but also require that all listed companies provide a statement in their annual report about their corporate governance practices. These include practices such as:

> Board procedures for nominating directors
> Fair, responsible, and transparent executive remuneration
> Director independence and tenure
> Board performance reviews
> Management of business risk through establishment of internal control systems
> Establishment of audit committees composed of non-executive directors
> The use of external auditors
> Committee structures
> Establishment of a code of conduct that recognises obligations to non-shareholder stakeholders
> Provision of effective communication to shareholders.

• *Corporate governance in South Africa.* South Africa's principal corporate governance reports are the *King report on corporate governance* (King I), issued in 1994, and the *King report on corporate governance for South Africa* (King II), issued in 2002. King II was initiated partly in response to the global changes in corporate governance discussed above and partly to take into account changes in the South African legal, political, and economic environments that followed the post-apartheid period. Both reports came from committees chaired by Mervyn King, who claimed: 'South Africa has taken the lead in defining corporate governance in broadly inclusive terms.'[92] As we identified earlier, an inclusive approach to corporate governance is one whereby companies consider the interests of myriad stakeholders. King II justifies an inclusive approach to corporate governance by appeal to improved economic efficiency for

companies, current socio-economic conditions in South Africa, and traditional African values.

King II opens with a quotation from Sir Adrian Cadbury which starts with a definition of corporate governance as being 'concerned with holding the balance between economic and social goals and between individual and communal goals', and continues, '… the aim is to align as nearly as possible the interests of individuals, corporations and society'.[93] King II then goes on to state that the King I advocated 'good governance in the interests of a wide range of stakeholders' with regard to 'good financial, social, ethical and environmental practice'.[94] A later section of King II states that the King Committee's unanimous view is that an inclusive approach to corporate governance is fundamental to doing business in South Africa 'where many of the country's citizens disturbingly remain on the fringes of society's economic benefits'.[95] The inclusive approach is then placed within the context of South Africa's culture and dominant values. For example, King II refers to the African experience of collectiveness over individualism, consensus rather than dissension, co-existence rather than prejudice, and an inherent belief in fairness for all human beings.

However, while King II purports to advocate an inclusive approach to corporate governance, several of its guidelines reflect an Anglo-American approach which tends toward the shareholder model or, at best, an instrumental stakeholder approach to governance. West suggests that the shareholder or instrumental stakeholder view of corporate governance rests on the primacy of individuals' rights to private property and is therefore inappropriate to societies, such as South Africa, that place greater value on communal rights and requirements of duties.[96] Moreover, West argues that the elevation of shareholder interests above urgent needs of social justice (stakeholder interests) conflicts with African values of consensus and communitarianism. An example of the instrumental stakeholder approach can be seen in King II's discussion of accountability and responsibility. The report states[97]:

> [T]he stakeholder concept of being accountable to all legitimate stakeholders must be rejected for the simple reason that to ask boards to be accountable to everyone would result in their being accountable to no one. The modern approach is for a board to identify the company's stakeholders, including its shareholders, and to agree policies as to how the relationship with those stakeholders should be advanced and managed in the interests of the company.
>
> SOURCE: INSTITUTE OF DIRECTORS IN SOUTHERN AFRICA. 2002. *King Committee on corporate governance.* Parktown, South Africa: Institute of Directors in Southern Africa:paragraph 5.1.

In this passage and throughout King II, it appears that the principle of accountability is primarily applicable to shareholders, but not to other stakeholders. Rossouw[98] has also commented on the 'continuities and discontinuities' between King II's philosophical premises and King II's recommendations. He notes, for example, that the entire section dealing with boards and directors makes no mention of stakeholders, and that the section on integrated sustainability reporting does not include stakeholders in internal and external social reporting requirements. Also, the only matter specified for directors in their annual reports is financial reporting. It appears then that while King II does incorporate aspects of stakeholder theory into the Anglo-American model of corporate governance, it does not fully embrace the inclusive approach it advocates.

In keeping with global initiatives in corporate governance, King II refers to seven characteristics of good corporate governance. These are:

> Discipline
> Transparency
> Independence
> Accountability
> Responsibility
> Fairness
> Social responsibility.

These characteristics are then developed into principles and guidelines to promote high standards of corporate governance in South Africa. The topics covered by King II are very similar to those addressed in the UKCC and the OECD principles. They include boards of directors (a balance of executive and non-executive members 'of whom sufficient should be independent of management so that shareowner interests can be protected'[99] and transparent appointment processes), directors' remuneration, internal control and risk management, and the adoption of accounting and auditing standards. In addition, King II contains a section on integrated sustainability reporting, a topic increasingly on the agenda of corporate boards worldwide. The reporting requirement is for companies to report annually on their social, transformation, ethical, safety, health, and environmental policies and practices.

Although the guidelines of King II are voluntary, the Johannesburg Securities Exchange (JSE) has made them a listing requirement. Research undertaken in 2004 shows that of the JSE top 200 companies, 60 per cent claimed to have fully adopted the requirements of King II and 90 per cent claimed they would fully comply in the future.[100] Whilst King I and King II have been catalysts for significant improvements in the governance of South African corporations, challenges remain. In response to these challenges Vaughn and Ryan[101] offer five recommendations they believe would further enhance the governance reforms to date. The recommendations are as follows:

- Regulating private funding of political parties
- Strengthening regulations that monitor takeovers
- Improving accountability (independence) of boards of directors
- Motivating institutional investors to monitor corporate governance actively
- Educating current and future business leaders about the importance of transparency, accountability, fairness, responsibility, and independence.

9.4 Corporate citizenship: Implications for the HR function

We have referred to corporate citizenship as an umbrella term that embraces CSR, corporate ethics programmes, and corporate governance. It is therefore a comprehensive and complex concept. Corporate citizenship policies, practices, and mechanisms aim to influence the attitudes, behaviour, and performance of an organisation's internal and external stakeholders. Corporate citizenship initiatives also aim to make corporations more effective and more satisfying places to work in, and contribute to what is sometimes known as 'human flourishing'. Therefore, corporate citizenship shares much in common with HRM and has enormous implications for the HR function.

Assessing the effectiveness of an enterprise's corporate citizenship, particularly in terms of valid and reliable measurements, has been problematic. The Center for Corporate Citizenship at Boston College in the USA is involved in launching a new assessment tool (The Corporate Citizenship Assessment Tool™) that is intended to help enterprises manage corporate-citizenship practices in order to better integrate corporate-citizenship efforts into company culture and strategic planning. The assessment tool is based on a series of questions relating to three dimensions of corporate citizenship. These are:

- Community – non-commercial activities that address social and environmental challenges from the very local to the global

- Products and services – commercial activities that find market solutions to social and environmental challenges
- Operations – responsible business practices that integrate a commitment to corporate citizenship across all business units and corporate functions.

These three dimensions suggest that corporate-citizenship programmes are an interdisciplinary endeavour. The HR function is well placed to provide leadership, not only in assessing corporate performance, but also in advancing new corporate-citizenship initiatives that move corporations beyond economic transactional relationships, philanthropy, and compliance to integrated social partnerships and self regulation. The following sections will discuss the relationship between HRM and corporate citizenship in more detail.

9.4.1 Corporate social responsibility and HRM

A stakeholder understanding of CSR involves listening and responding to stakeholders' interests and concerns. It puts people at the centre and builds relationships of mutual trust and mutual benefit. It requires corporations to operate in ways that not only avoid harming people, but which have a positive impact on people's health and safety, quality of life, and personal growth.[102] In the case of employees, this involves HRM practices associated with equal employment opportunity, diversity, job security, compensation, occupational health and safety, industrial relations, performance and remuneration, and work–life balance. In global operations, it involves managing human rights, particularly those relating to child labour, wage exploitation, basic health and safety, empowerment, and quality of life.

In our earlier discussion of current trends in CSR (see Section 9.1.4), we noted that business ethics and CSR initiatives will increasingly be strategically focused. A good illustration of a strategically focused CSR initiative is the HIV/Aids programme at Eskom. Eskom Holdings Limited is a South African electricity public utility, established in 1923 as the Electricity

Supply Commission. The utility is the largest producer of electricity in Africa, is among the top seven utilities in the world in terms of generation capacity, and is among the top nine in terms of sales. As an organisation conducting its business exclusively in South Africa and other countries in Africa, Eskom is actively involved in the management of HIV/Aids and its effects on its employees, as a strategic priority.[103] It is estimated that 26,6 million people in sub-Saharan Africa live with HIV, of which 4,7 million live in South Africa; 1 500 new infections occur every day; and more than half of these are in the 20- to 30-year age group. The impact of these infections and deaths on society is devastating. HIV/Aids also affects the sustainability of business, through, for example, a reduction in available workers, loss of experienced workers and their skills, strained labour relations, and declining morale in employees. Eskom has estimated that each new infection will cost the company four to six times the annual salary per individual infected and that during the period 2006–2010, existing HIV infections will cost seven per cent of the payroll per annum. To minimise the impact of HIV/Aids on employees and the business, Eskom has developed a set of HIV/Aids programmes for its employees, contractors, suppliers, and customers. The programmes include learning materials, educational programmes, medical training of appropriate personnel, and community projects. The company says that while the programmes are financially onerous, the costs are insignificant when compared to the impact of HIV/Aids.

Some criticise the stakeholder theory for its lack of guidance on how to manage and balance competing interests of different stakeholders. However, the stakeholder theory does provide guidance about myriad CSR issues and expectations of stakeholders. One can glean many of these issues from a review of corporate codes of conduct presented above. By way of summary, we present Coghill, Black, and Holmes's five key stakeholder groups and a number of attendant issues, many of which are HR related:

- Employees: recruitment and selection, compensation and benefits, training, occupational health and safety, work–life balance, diversity, sexuality in the workplace, minority hiring practices, responsible redundancy, use of temporary and casual workers, and workplace culture. By attending to these issues, corporations stand to benefit from reduced turnover and improvements in morale in the workplace, productivity, and employee identification with the firm, which in turn are likely to reduce the risk of fraud and unethical behaviour.
- Suppliers: ethical sourcing, prompt payment, use of migrant and child workers, doing business with oppressive regimes, and human rights of outsourced workers.
- Customers: product manufacturing (human rights of workers, product safety, safety standards), labelling and packaging, marketing and advertising practices, and pricing.
- Communities: traditional philanthropy, community investment and development, partnerships between employees and communities, environmental issues, and donations to political parties.
- Investors: identifying sources of social and environmental risk.

SOURCE: COGHILL, D., BLACK, L. & HOLMES, D. 2005. *Submission to the Parliamentary Joint Committee on Corporations and Financial Services,'Inquiry into Corporate Social Responsibility'.* Canberra, A.C.T.: Parliamentary Joint Committee on Corporations and Financial Services, Parliament of Australia.

9.4.2 Corporate ethics programmes and HRM

In Chapter 8, we looked at the role of HR professionals in operationalising corporate ethics programmes. In doing so, we noted that in Australia, Canada, South Africa, and the USA, HR departments play a central role in developing and maintaining corporate ethics programmes. In the following section, our focus will be on the contribution that HRM can make to the formulation, communication, and monitoring and enforcement of written standards of ethical business conduct.

When many companies develop and revise written standards of ethical business conduct, they do so in consultation with employees. Typically this involves HRM in organising focus groups or workshops where employees at all levels come together to identify and discuss key corporate values, behavioural indicators of values, and the ethics issues which employees most frequently face. The engagement of organisational members in the formulation of written standards is essential for the standards' relevance and acceptance and, therefore, effectiveness. As we noted earlier, when HRM is involved in developing written standards (and training programmes), it is important that ethics issues not be limited to specific HRM issues – e.g. equity, sexual harassment, and occupational health and safety – but also include those of primary concern to employees in their daily work practices – e.g. the environment, use of information systems, and conflicts of interest.

We identified earlier that while most large enterprises have at least one written standard, many do not pay sufficient attention to providing training about these standards. There is wide agreement in the research literature that HRM currently has most responsibility for training programmes in organisational ethics and is also a primary source of advice and information for employees regarding workplace ethics. However, it is not clear if HR managers and HR staff are adequately trained in more complex ethics matters. Also, when training is provided, most often it is conducted as part of a general orientation programme. It is unlikely that such training would equip employees with all the skills and competencies necessary to respond to ethical situations they may face during their tenure with the organisation. However, it is reasonable to assume that ethics training as part of an orientation programme would:

- Convey to new employees an organisation's commitment to its values and ethical business conduct as stated in its written standards
- Raise new employees' awareness of ethical issues that may arise in the conduct of their daily work
- Provide information about organisational resources available to employees when faced with conflicts or observed breaches of the standards
- Inform employees of linkages between ethical business practice and sanctions, rewards, and performance management.

HRM could make a significant contribution to corporate ethics programmes by, firstly, undertaking ethics training, and secondly, implementing more in-depth training programmes, particularly for employees who are involved in complex ethical decision-making. In some organisations HRM is involved in developing ethics-education material that also comprises organisational-specific case studies. This material is then widely distributed via intranet services, handbooks, and company Web sites. For example, Telstra is an Australian telecommunications and information-services company with over 52 000 employees. It has harnessed the advantages of e-learning technology to provide desktop training on a range of ethics issues to all employees. This training is designed to be interactive and to address typical ethics issues that arise in the workplace. The Telstra HR and legal departments wrote most of the ethics dilemmas the programme includes. They based the dilemmas on past experiences of organisational members. These online programmes have the advantage that employees can access them at times to suit their schedules and needs and regardless of their geographic location. In the UK, a survey conducted in 2004 found the use of corporate Web sites to publicise corporate codes of ethics had increased from 5 per cent in 1998 to 26 per cent in 2001, and to 63 per cent in 2004.[104]

HR professionals can also make a strong contribution to corporate ethics programmes by initiating creative and meaningful ways to link ethics and organisational values to performance management and reward programmes. Reward systems are said to be the single most important influence on employee behaviour. However, most surveys in this area reveal that approximately 50 per cent of companies currently link ethics to performance management and only very few link ethics to reward programmes. Surveys also reveal that while organisations frequently punish misconduct, they rarely reward good conduct. Most managers find it difficult to conceive of meaningful ways in which to reward good conduct. However, rewarding ethical behaviour is possible if managers take a longer-term view. For example, some Australian multinational enterprises are currently using a performance-management system whereby they dismiss employees who meet their financial targets but fail to address corporate values in the process, while the enterprises counsel and retain, albeit sometimes on probation, those who fail in their financial targets but who operate in line with corporate values. HRM needs to investigate ways to use the tools of reward and performance-management programmes innovatively to shape, maintain, and develop ethical cultures that support ethical types of behaviour. A lack of ethics infrastructure fails to nurture an organisation's ethics culture and employees' motivation to live the standards.

9.4.3 Corporate governance and HRM

The corporate-governance codes described in this chapter indicate that one can identify superior governance in terms of transparency, accountability, responsibility, and independent oversight in matters relating to corporate financial, ethical, social, and environmental performance. The uniformity of corporate-governance codes across different countries suggests there is the emergence of international 'soft law' governing the expected conduct of enterprises. Much of the reform in corporate governance has focused on the role and duties of directors. A board's main functions include defining a company's purpose, formulating its strategy and policies, appointing the chief executive officer, monitoring and assessing the performance of the executive team, and assessing the board's performance. The traditional HRM activities of recruitment and selection, training and development, and performance management and remuneration have a critical role to play in the development and maintenance of good corporate-governance practices, not only in terms of boards of directors, but also in terms of improving shareholder value through the development of intellectual capital and upholding a company's responsibilities to stakeholders, in particular its employees.

There is agreement amongst different corporate-governance codes that a 'balanced board' is desirable and, therefore, diversity is sought in board membership in terms of skills, experience, backgrounds, and personalities. There is also agreement that the appointment of the chairperson of the board is crucial as it is the chairperson who is a key determinant of creating a culture of integrity and ensuring board effectiveness. The Royal Commission which investigated the collapse of the Australian insurance company HIH found the chief executive, Ray Williams, appointed friends and associates to the board. This practice contributed to a culture of compliance whereby the board simply followed the recommendations of senior management, without due assessment of risk.[105] Despite important similarities between corporate ethics and corporate culture, they are not synonymous. The distinguishing feature of ethical discourse is not the standardisation of behaviour, but the joint promotion of community (belonging) and autonomy. Corporate culture can only be ethical if it seeks to make autonomy a fundamental feature.

The issue of board-member independence versus board-member knowledge and expertise is contentious. Lorsch[106] has argued that some conflict of interest is a price worth paying for more knowledge and expertise. His point is that when the majority of board members have no conflicts of interest and a focus on the interests of the company and its shareholders, they are likely to be members who know little about the company or its industry and who, because of their other commitments, have little time to devote to board and company affairs. Insofar as both qualities are important to board integrity, HRM has an important role to play in providing objective recruitment and selection processes for independent and diverse board members, providing orientation training and ongoing development opportunities for the board, and assessing the board's performance for both independent oversight and effectiveness.

Board remuneration is another area of importance for HRM. In addition to a base salary, remuneration packages for directors typically include bonuses, share options, and retirement benefits. Corporate-governance codes provide guidelines for policies and practices relating to executive remuneration, while some aspects of director remuneration are subject to government regulation. For example, the *Australian Corporations Act* (No. 50 of 2001) requires that shareholders approve a director's remuneration and that the details be disclosed in a company's financial statements. Remuneration committees may also assist in the determination and review of remuneration packages. The Australian Stock Exchange (ASX) guidelines recommend that remuneration committees be composed of a majority of independent directors and have a formal charter that sets forth the committee's role and responsibilities.

Press articles have widely reported and discussed levels of remuneration for directors. Many directors perceive that their responsibilities and risks have increased under new guidelines and regulations about governance, but that they are not adequately compensated for these increases in responsibility. At the same time, changes in corporate-governance requirements have resulted in an increase in demand for independent directors. Consequently, HRM has an important role in leading and advising remuneration committees about competitive, fair, and equitable remuneration for directors.

The monitoring and measurement of board performance is related to remuneration. Performance appraisals require that performance indicators be identified. Such indicators should include financial and non-financial metrics. For example, in addition to a company's share price, performance measures could include such things as compliance with regulations and standards, transparency, leadership, shaping long-term strategy, and balancing the interests of different stakeholders.

SUMMARY

This chapter first presented three different viewpoints on corporate social responsibility (the narrow economic view or shareholder view, the socio-economic view, and the maximal view). It then discussed three key phases of corporate ethics programmes (formulation of written standards, communication of standards, and monitoring and enforcing of standards) and how one might evaluate programme effectiveness. The chapter then focused on international developments in corporate governance, including developments in the UK, the USA, the Organisation for Economic Co-operation and Development, Australia, and South Africa. Finally, the chapter discussed the implications of corporate social responsibility, corporate ethics programmes, and corporate governance for the HR function.

KEY CONCEPTS

- Affirmative duties
- Corporate citizenship
- Corporate ethics programmes
- Corporate governance
- Corporate social responsibility
- Corporate Social Responsibility Index
- Maximal view of CSR
- Moral minimum
- Narrow classical economic view of CSR
- Shareholder model
- Socio-economic view of CSR
- Stakeholder model
- Stakeholder theory
- Triple-bottom-line reporting

CASE STUDY

Objective: To understand the importance of a proactive programme for stakeholder engagement in the building of strong relationships between parties with a view of good corporate governance

Constructive relationships bring tangible benefits at Anglo Platinum

Driving sustainability

The Anglo Platinum Group is the world's leading primary producer of platinum group metals. Its operations comprise six mines, two smelters, a base metals refinery and a precious metals refinery, located in the Limpopo and North West provinces of South Africa. The Group's mining operations are divided into three centres: Mokopane (Potgietersrus), Lebowa and Rustenburg, the latter being the location of the base and precious metal refining activities as well.

The company's overarching sustainability objective is to operate these mining interests within the framework of striving to be a responsible corporate citizen. With a clear commitment to sustainable development, Anglo Platinum endeavours to create maximum social and economic value, and to minimise adverse impacts on the natural environment. But as CEO Ralph Haverstein explains, sustainable development is a co-operative effort. 'It is not a matter of ticking the boxes on a nine-point scorecard and being reluctant compliers with a charter. Instead it is something we undertake willingly in partnership with government, communities, our employees, our suppliers, our customers and our business partners.'

Adding value through relationships

One of the key avenues for pursuing the principles and practices of sustainable development is to develop constructive relationships with a broad stakeholder base. This includes investors, employees, trade unions, customers, business partners, contractors, suppliers, NGOs, government bodies, educational institutions, and local communities.

Anglo Platinum understands that achieving growth for shareholders is best undertaken through considered regard for the interests of all stakeholders. Local communities that host the mining interests of Anglo Platinum are a specific example.

Formalising engagement

Whilst Anglo Platinum's Rustenburg operations have been involved in community dialogue for many years, its approach to stakeholder engagement was only formalised in late 2000. Prior to this, much of the engagement with stakeholders was reactive, driven by events and issues that impacted surrounding communities. This reactive approach often resulted in heated debates and unsatisfactory outcomes.

Recognising that regular dialogue with local communities plays an important role in enhancing local relationships and minimising disruption to operations, Anglo Platinum has over the last four years developed a structured and proactive stakeholder engagement programme.

Mapping the terrain

The first step in structuring the programme was an extensive stakeholder mapping process. Stakeholders were defined as all individuals and groups who may be positively or negatively affected by the company's operations. Local communities were defined as those communities within a 50km radius of the mine's operations.

The mapping process then identified potential impacts for stakeholder groups as well as the level of capacity of these stakeholders to participate in an engagement process. In some instances, capacity-building was undertaken with stakeholder groups to ensure that they could effectively participate in the process.

Communication is key

The stakeholder engagement approach is broadly communicated to all employees and business partners through the company's Code of Ethics and Business Principles. Anglo Platinum and the stakeholders further identified the most appropriate method and frequency of engagement per specific group. To this end, a range of communication strategies were developed to communicate with each group, to maximise the quality of interactions. Radio, meetings, forums, posters, open days, workshops, local newspapers and traditional leadership structures are all used to communicate with stakeholder groups in the appropriate language and manner.

Group communication with all stakeholders is undertaken through a twice-yearly open day at which the company is available for questioning across a range of issues. In addition, monthly meetings are held with the community development forum to discuss pertinent issues, including educational needs, access to health care, environmental issues, HIV/Aids and BEE procurement.

> Anglo Platinum's sustainable development targets are inextricably interwoven with its business strategy. Similarly, its sustainable development programmes are shaped by its business strategy.

Positive spin-offs

In partnership with the local municipality, Anglo Platinum has also contributed to the local integrated development planning process and provided input into local economic development (LED) initiatives. Working at this level the company is able to play an important facilitator role as a key stakeholder in sustainability planning for the region. Through the stakeholder engagement programme, Anglo Platinum has also established mutually beneficial relationships with locally empowered businesses. These relationships have served both to stimulate local business and assisted the mine in meeting its preferential procurement targets.

Essential tools

Anglo Platinum has developed an innovative solution to manage the diverse range of stakeholder interactions at its Rustenburg operation. All stakeholder names, contact information as well as details of issues raised and responses are recorded on a management system application called IsoMetrix. This system allows for effective tracking and monitoring of all stakeholder interactions, and has proved to be an indispensable management tool in dealing effectively with stakeholder queries and ensuring issues are indeed resolved.

Stakeholder engagement has also been included as a key performance area (KPA) in Operations Managers' contracts. Integrating this area of responsibility into the highest level of operational management has ensured that all issues are monitored and dealt with appropriately.

A virtuous cycle

While it is not possible to quantify the exact impact of the stakeholder engagement programme, its major benefits are clear: An inclusive and proactive approach to stakeholder engagement preserves Anglo Platinum's licence to operate, maintaining its competitive edge as the investor, business partner and employer of choice in the region.

Moreover, the company has found that its stakeholder engagement activities have enhanced employee morale. Employees believe that the integrity of operations has improved and are proud to be associated with a company that listens and responds to its stakeholders. As a result, Anglo Platinum is better able to recruit and retain good quality staff.

Looking ahead

Although mine closure is not expected for at least another 70 years, discussion about economic diversification and biophysical rehabilitation is already underway. This is testament to the fact that relationships between stakeholders have strengthened and matured. With a strong awareness of a mutually dependant relationship, the mining company can walk boldly into the future.

Reducing sulphur emissions

By working closely with community stakeholders, Anglo Platinum has developed a comprehensive SO_2 emissions-reduction programme at the Waterval Smelter, including development of a new ACP converter plant at a cost of over one billion rand.

During construction and commissioning of the new plant, a mutually beneficial solution was agreed with the community – namely an interim operating arrangement for the old plant. This included establishing a community organisation that was paid to assist in emission monitoring on a 24 hour basis.

When atmospheric dispersion conditions caused the emission plume to descend to ground level, they would use the dedicated hotline to alert the plant. This provided control mechanisms in addition to electronic monitoring to ensure that the number of converters in stack would be reduced, thereby limiting emissions until atmospheric conditions improved.

Questions and activities

1. Read through the case study and compile a list of all the possible stakeholders you think would be involved with Anglo Platinum at its various mining operations.
2. Explain in one sentence the significance of each of these stakeholders to the company.
3. Indicate what you think the most appropriate methods would be for engaging with those stakeholders.

SOURCE: FREEMANTLE, A. P. 2005. (Editor). This case study originally appeared in: *The good corporate citizenship: Pursuing sustainable business in South Africa*, June 2005. 2nd ed. Cape Town: Trialogue:106–107. Reproduced with kind permission from Trialogue (Pty) Ltd (www.trialogue.co.za).

REVIEW QUESTIONS AND ACTIVITIES

1. Explain Friedman's main arguments for his view that the purpose of a corporation is to maximise profits for shareholders. What criticisms can be made of Friedman's arguments?
2. What is the 'moral minimum' and what is the relevance of 'affirmative duties'?
3. Explain the socio-economic view of corporate social responsibility and how it differs from the maximal view of corporate social responsibility.
4. What arguments can be given in support of the maximal view? Do you agree with them? Why?
5. What is your view about corporate social responsibility and the role of corporations in society?
6. Draw up a list of possible stakeholders with whom companies could interact.
7. Discuss the five pillars of corporate governance and the issues which need to be addressed within each of these pillars.
8. What is corporate governance and why is it generally important? Specifically, why is corporate governance important to South Africa?
9. The King II report on corporate governance aspires to an 'inclusive' approach to corporate governance whereby enterprises are asked to consider the interests of myriad stakeholders. In your view, does the King II report end up being more shareholder focused than stakeholder focused? Why and what are the implications?
10. Identify and discuss ways in which the HR function can contribute to corporate citizenship through implementing programmes in corporate social responsibility, corporate ethics, and corporate governance.

FURTHER READING

CARROLL, A. B. 2000. A commentary and an overview of key questions on corporate social performance measurement. *Business and society*, 39(4):466–479.

COLLINS-CHOBANIAN, S. 2005. *Ethical challenges to business as usual.* Upper Saddle River, N.J.: Pearson–Prentice Hall.

INSTITUTE OF DIRECTORS IN SOUTHERN AFRICA. 2002. *King committee on corporate governance.* Parktown, South Africa: Institute of Directors in Southern Africa.

JACKSON, I. A. & NELSON, J. 2004. *Profits with principles.* New York: Currency Doubleday.

DU PLESSIS, J., MCCONVILL, J. & BAGARIC, M. 2005. *Principles of contemporary corporate governance.* Melbourne, Australia: Cambridge University Press.

PRAHALAD, C. K. & PORTER, M. E., 2003. *Harvard business review on corporate responsibility.* Boston MA: Harvard Business School Press.

THE CONFERENCE BOARD. 2007. *Corporate governance handbook 2007: Legal standards and board practices.* Cambridge M.A.: InfoEdge.

TREVINO, L. K. & NELSON, K. A, 2007. *Managing business ethics* 4th Ed. Hoboken, N.J.: John Wiley & Sons.

WEST, A. 2006. Theorising South Africa's corporate governance. *Journal of business ethics*, 68:433–448.

WOOD, D. J. 2002. *Business citizenship: From individuals to corporations.* USA: Ruffin Series in Business Ethics, Society for Business Ethics:59–94.

WEB SITES

www.bccc.net/ – The Centre for Corporate Citizenship at Boston College

www.unisa.ac.za/ccc – Corporate Citizenship Centre at the University of South Africa

www.oecd.org/dataoecd/32/18/31557724.pdf – *OECD principles of corporate governance* (2004)

www.ecgi.org/codes/all_codes.htm – Corporate governance codes in various countries (including Australia, South Africa, the UK, the USA and many others)

http://ca.geocities.com/busa2100/miltonfriedman.htm and http://www.acir.yale.edu/pdf/EthicalInvestor.pdf (print only pages 15–26) – Readings in corporate social responsibility

ENDNOTES

1. This chapter is based on CAREY, L. E. 2007. *Profits and principles: The operationalisation of corporate ethics in Australian enterprises*. Canberra, Australia. University of Canberra. (Ph.D. thesis.)

2. WEST, A. 2006. Theorising South Africa's corporate governance. *Journal of business ethics*, 68:433–448.

3. MATTEN, D. & CRANE, A. 2003. *Corporate citizenship: Towards an extended theoretical conceptualization*. Research Paper Series No. 5. Nottingham, UK: International Centre for Corporate Social Responsibility, Nottingham University.

4. ALTMAN, B. W. & VIDAVER-COHEN, D. 2000 corporate citizenship in the new millennium: foundation for an architecture of excellence. *Business and society review*, 105(1):145–169; ABN Amro. [Online] Available: www.abnamro.com. 16 January 2008; BHPBilliton. 2007. *Annual Report*. [Online] Available: www.bhpbilliton.com/bb/home.jsp. 16 January 2008; Boeing. [Online] Available: http:/www.boeing.com. 16 January 2008.

5. CARROLL, A. B. 1991. The pyramid of corporate social responsibility: Toward the moral management of organisational stakeholders. *Business horizons*, 34:39–48; CARROLL, A. B. 1999. Corporate social responsibility. *Business and society*, 38(3):268–296.

6. JAMALI, D. & MIRSHEK, R. 2006. corporate social responsibility (CSR): Theory and practice in a developing context. *Journal of business ethics*, 72:243–262.

7. See, for example, The St James Ethics Center's Web site, which provides data on Australian corporations that have been indexed (www.ethics.org.au).

8. COMMISSION OF THE EUROPEAN COMMUNITIES (CEC). 2002. *Corporate social responsibility: A business contribution to sustainable development*. CEC: Brussels: 3.

9. SIMS, R. R. 1991. The institutionalization of organizational ethics. *Journal of business ethics*, 10:493–506.

10. WEBER, J. 2006. Implementing an organizational ethics program in an academic environment: the challenges and opportunities for the Duquesne University schools of business. *Journal of business ethics*, 65:23–42

11. PURCELL, H. & WEBER, J. 1979. (Cited in Sims, R. R. 1991. The institutionalization of organizational ethics. *Journal of business ethics*, 10:493–506.)

12. HURST, N. E. 2004. *Corporate ethics, governance and social responsibility: Comparing European business practices to those in the United States*. Santa Clara: Markkula Center for Applied Ethics, Santa Clara University. See also BENZ, M. & FREY, B. S. 2007. Corporate governance: what can we learn from public governance? *The academy of management review*, 32(1):92–104; Unilever. [Online] Available: www.unilever.com/ourcompany/investorcentre/corp governance. 16 January 2008.

13. CARROLL, A. B. 1999. Corporate social responsibility. *Business and society*, 38(3):268–296.

14. MAIGNAN, I. & FERRELL, O. C. 2000. Measuring corporate citizenship in two countries: the case of the United States and France. *Journal of business ethics*, 28:283–297. See also GARDBERG, N. A. & FOMBRUN, C. J. 2006. Corporate citizenship: creating intangible assets across institutional environments. *The academy of management review*, 31(2):329–346.

15. HARNED, P. J. 2005. A word from the president: corporate social responsibility and organizational ethics. *Ethics today online*, 3(9). Ethics Resource Center. [Online.] http://rtbrain.com/ethics/today/et v1n31102.html. 16 January 2008.

16. JOURNAL OF CORPORATE CITIZENSHIP (EDITORS). 2005. Corporate citizenship in Africa, introduction. *Journal of corporate citizenship*, 18:18–20.

17. Ibid.:19. See also MIRVIS, P. & GOOGINS, B. 2006. Stages of corporate citizenship, *California management review*, 48(2):104–126, Winter.

18. See, for example, BARNARD, C. I. 1938. *The functions of the executive*. Cambridge, M.A.: Harvard University Press; BOWAN, H. R. 1953. *Social responsibilities of the businessman*. New York: Harper & Row; DAVIS, K. 1973. The case for and against business assumption of social responsibilities. *Academy of management journal*, 1:312–322; FRIEDMAN, M. 1970. The social responsibility of business is to increase its profits. (*In* Beauchamp T. L. & Bowie, N. E. 1997. *Ethical theory and business* 5th ed. Upper Saddle River, N.J.: Prentice Hall:56–61); SIMON, J. G., POWERS, C. W. & GUNNEMAN, J. P. 1972. The responsibilities of corporations and their owners. (*In* Beauchamp T. L. & Bowie, N. E. 1997. *Ethical theory and business* 5th ed. Upper Saddle River, N.J.: Prentice Hall:61–76); EVAN, W. M. & FREEMAN, R. E. 1988. A stakeholder theory of the modern corporation: Kantian capitalism. (*In* Beauchamp T. L. & Bowie, N. E. 1997. *Ethical theory and business* 5th ed. Upper Saddle River, N.J.: Prentice Hall:75–84); MULLIGAN, T. 1993. The moral mission of mission. (*In* Beauchamp T. L. & Bowie, N. E. 1993. *Ethical theory and business* 4th ed. Englewood Cliffs, N.J.: Prentice Hall:65–75); CARROLL, A. B. 1999. Corporate Social Responsibility. *Business and society*, 38(3):268–296; CARROLL, A. B. 2000. Ethical challenges for business in the new millennium: corporate social responsibility and models of management morality. *Business ethics quarterly*, 10(1):33–42; WOOD, D. 2002. *Business citizenship: from individuals to organizations*. USA: Ruffin Series in Business Ethics, Society for Business Ethics:59–94.

19. CARROLL, A. B. 1999. Corporate Social Responsibility. *Business and society*, 38(3):268–296.

20. See, for example, MAIGNAN, I. & FERRELL, O. C. 2000. Measuring corporate citizenship in two countries: the case of the United States and France. *Journal of business ethics*, 28:283–297.

21. DAVIS, K. 1960. Can business afford to ignore social responsibilities? *California management review*, 2:70.

22. CAMENISCH, P. F. 1981. Business ethics: on getting to the heart of the matter. *Business and professional ethics journal*, 1:59–69.

23. CARROLL, A. B. 1999. Corporate Social Responsibility. *Business and society*, 38(3):280.

24. SETHI, S. P. 1975. Dimensions of corporate social performance: an analytical framework. *California management review*, 17(3):58–65.

25. WOOD, D. J. 1991. Corporate social performance revisited. *Academy of management review*, 16(4):691–718.

26. FRIEDMAN, M. 1970. The social responsibility of business is to increase its profits. (*In* Beauchamp T. L. & Bowie, N. E. 1997. *Ethical theory and business* 5th ed. Upper Saddle River, N.J.: Prentice Hall.)

27. SHAW, W. H. 1988. A reply to Thomas Mulligan's critique of Milton Friedman's Essay 'The social responsibility of business is to increase its profits'. *Journal of business ethics*, 7:537–543.

28. FRIEDMAN, M. 1970. The social responsibility of business is to increase its profits. (*In* Beauchamp T. L. & Bowie, N. E. 1997. *Ethical theory and business* 5th ed. Upper Saddle River, N.J.: Prentice Hall:32)

29. FRIEDMAN, M. 1962. *Capitalism and Freedom*. Chicago: University of Chicago Press:10.

30. ARROW, K. J. 1973. Social responsibility and economic efficiency. *Public policy*, 21, Summer.

31. See, for example, PACKARD, V. 1958. *The hidden persuaders*. New York: Pocket Books; GALBRIETH, K. 1985. Persuasion and power. (*In* Desjardins, J. R. and McCall, J. J. (Eds). *Contemporary issues in business ethics*. Belmont, C.A.:Wadsworth Publishing Company:142–147.)

32. See, for example, STONE, C. 1975. *Where the law ends: The social control of corporate behavior*. N.Y.: Harper and Row.

33. SMITH, A. 1776. Inquiry into the nature and causes of the wealth of nations. (Cited in Wilson, J. Q. 1989. Adam Smith on business ethics. *California management review*, 32(1):59–72.)

34. WERHANE, P. 2000. Business ethics and the origins of contemporary capitalism: Economics and ethics in the work of Adam Smith and Herbert Spencer. *Journal of business ethics*, 24(3):185–198.

35. WILSON, J. Q. 1989. Adam Smith on business ethics. *California management review*, 32(1):70.)

36. FRIEDMAN, M. 1970. The social responsibility of business is to increase its profits. (*In* Beauchamp T. L. & Bowie, N. E. 1997. *Ethical theory and business* 5th ed. Upper Saddle River, N.J.: Prentice Hall:57.)

37. Ibid.:55.

38. Ibid.:57.

39. See, for example, GRIFFIN, J. J. & MAHON, J. F. 1997. Corporate social performance: research directions for the 21st century. *Business and society*, 39(4):479–493; WADDOCK, S. A. & GRAVES, S. B. 1997. The corporate social performance–financial performance link. *Strategic management journal*, 18(4):303–320; ROMAN, R., HAYIBOR, S. & AGLE, B. R. 1999. The relationship between social performance and financial performance. *Business and society*, 38(1):109–125; ORLITZKY, M., SCHMIDT, F. L. & RYNES, S. 2004. Corporate social and financial performance: a meta analysis. *Organization studies*, 24(3):403–411; VERSCHOOR, C. C. 2005. Is there financial value in corporate values? *Strategic finance*, 87(1):17–18.

40. JOHNSON, G. & SCHOLES, K. 1997. *Exploring corporate strategy* 4th ed. Hemel Hempstead: Prentice Hall.

41. SIMON, J. G., POWERS, C. W. & GUNNEMAN, J. P. 1972. The responsibilities of corporations and their owners. (*In* Beauchamp T. L. & Bowie, N. E. 1997. *Ethical theory and business* 5th ed. Upper Saddle River, N.J.: Prentice Hall:61–76.)

42. BHP BILLITON. 2005. *Health, safety, environment and community management standards*. Melbourne, Australia: BHPBilliton:2.

43. EVAN, W. M. & FREEMAN, R. E. 1988. A stakeholder theory of the modern corporation: Kantian capitalism. (*In* Beauchamp T. L. & Bowie, N. E. 1997. *Ethical theory and business* 5th ed. Upper Saddle River, N.J.: Prentice Hall:75–84.)

44. JOHNSON, H. L. 1971. *Business in contemporary society: Framework and issues*. Washington, D.C.: Wadsworth:50.

45. COGHILL, D., BLACK, L. & HOLMES, D. 2005. *Submission to the Parliamentary Joint Committee on Corporations and Financial Services, 'Inquiry into Corporate Social Responsibility'*. Canberra, A.C.T.: Parliamentary Joint Committee on Corporations and Financial Services, Parliament of Australia.

46. BOWIE, N. E. & DUSKA, R. F. 1990. *Business ethics* 2nd ed. Englewood Cliffs,N.J.: Prentice Hall:41.

47. FRANKENA, W. 1973. (Cited in BOWIE, N. E. & DUSKA, R. F. 1990. *Business ethics* 2nd ed. Englewood Cliffs,N.J.: Prentice Hall:41.)

48. BOWIE, N. E. 1991. New directions in corporate social responsibility. *Business horizons*, 34:56–65.

49. TEXAS INSTRUMENTS. Corporate social responsibility. [Online.]. Available: http://www. ti.com/corp/docs/company/citizen/index.shtml. 16 January 2008.

50. PORTER, M. E. & VAN DER LINDE, C. 1995. Green and competitive: Ending the stalemate. *Harvard business review*, 73(5):120–133; PORTER, M. E. & KRAMER, M. R. 2002. The competitive advantage of corporate philanthropy. *Harvard business review*, 80(12):56–69; PRAHALAD, C. K. & HAMMOND, A. 2002. Serving the world's poor, profitably. *Harvard business review*, 80(9):48–57.

51. BOWIE, N. E. 1991. New directions in corporate social responsibility. *Business horizons*, 34:59.

52. ENVIRONICS INTERNATIONAL LTD. 1999. *The millennium poll on corporate social responsibility.* [Online.]. Available: http://www.mori.com/polls/1999/millpoll.shtml. 16 January 2008.

53. MCINTOSH, M., LEIPZIGER, D., JONES, K. & COLMAN, G. 1998. *Corporate citizenship.* London: Financial Times Pitman Publishing.

54. WOOD, D. 1991. Corporate social performance revisited. *Academy of management review*, 16(4):691–718.

55. UNILEVER. Lifebuoy promotes handwashing with soap to improve health. [Online.]. Available: www.unilever.com. 16 January 2008.

56. Merck's commitment to eliminate river blindness in Africa and Latin America is a further example of a corporate social responsibility practice within a corporation's primary area of business. See, for example, MERCK. Commitment to society. [Online.]. Available: www.merck.com/about/feature_story/05192004_mectizan.html. 16 January 2008 or MERCK. Merck expands its commitment to eliminate river blindness. [Online.]. Available: www.merck.com/about/cr/policies_performance/social/mectizan_donation.html. 21 Septermber 2007.

57. WEAVER, G. R. & TREVINO, L. K. 1999. Compliance and values oriented ethics programs: influences on employees' attitudes and behaviour. *Business ethics quarterly*, 9(2):315–335.

58. WEAVER, G. R., TREVINO, L. K. & COCHRAN, P. L. 1999. Corporate ethics programs as control systems: Influences of executive commitment and environmental factors. *Academy of management journal*, 42(1):41–57.

59. TREVINO, L. K., WEAVER, G. R. & TOFFLER, B. L. 1999. Managing Ethics and Legal Compliance: What Works and What Hurts. *California management review*, 41(2):131–151.

60. TREVINO, L. K. & YOUNGBLOOD, S. A. 1990. Bad apples in bad barrels: a causal analysis of ethical decision-making behavior. *Journal of applied psychology*, 75:378–385; ASHKANASY, N. M., WINDSOR, C. A. & TREVINO, L. K. 2006. Bad apples in bad barrels revisited: Cognitive moral development, just world beliefs, rewards, and ethical decision-making. *Business ethics quarterly*, 16(4):449–473.

61. See, for example, ETHICS RESOURCE CENTER. 1994, 2000, 2003, and 2005. *National business ethics survey.* Washington, D.C.: Ethics Resource Center; ROBERTSON, D. & SCHLEGELMILCH, B. B. 1993. Corporate institutionalization of ethics in the United States and Great Britain. *Journal of business ethics*, 12(4):301–309; WEAVER, G. R. 1995. Does ethics code design matter? Effects of ethics code rationales and sanctions on recipients' justice perceptions and content recall. *Journal of business ethics*, 14:367–385; LINDSAY, R. M., LINDSAY, L. M. & IRVINE, B. V. 1996. Instilling ethical behavior in organizations: A survey of Canadian companies. *Journal of business ethics*, 15(4):393–410; WEBLEY, S. & LE JEUNE, M. 2005. *Corporate use of codes of ethics 2004 survey.* London: Institute of Business Ethics; SCHWARTZ, M. S. 2004. Effective corporate codes of ethics: perceptions of code users. *Journal of business ethics*, 55:323–343; O'DWYER, B. & MADDEN, G. 2006. Ethical codes of conduct in Irish companies: a survey of code content and enforcement procedures. *Journal of business ethics*, 63:217–236; SINGH, J. B. 2006. A comparison of the contents of the codes of ethics of Canada's largest corporations in 1992 and 2003. *Journal of business ethics*, 64:17–29; TREVINO, L. K., WEAVER, G. R. & TOFFLER, B. L. 1999. Managing ethics and legal compliance: what works and what hurts. *California management review*, 41(2):131–151; SOCIETY FOR HUMAN RESOURCE MANAGEMENT/ETHICS RESOURCE CENTER (SHRM). 2000. *Business ethics survey report.* Alexandria, V.A.: Society for Human Resource Management and Ethics Resource Center.

62. WEBLEY, S. & LE JEUNE, M. 2005. *Corporate use of codes of ethics 2004 survey.* London: Institute of Business Ethics; ETHICS RESOURCE CENTER. 2005. *National business ethics survey.* Washington, D.C.: Ethics Resource Center.

63. CAREY, L. E. 2007. *Profits and principles: The operationalisation of corporate ethics in Australian enterprises.* Canberra, Australia. University of Canberra. (Ph.D. thesis.)

64. WEBLEY, S. & LE JEUNE, M. 2005. *Corporate use of codes of ethics 2004 survey.* London: Institute of Business Ethics; ETHICS RESOURCE CENTER. 2005. *National business ethics survey.* Washington, D.C.: Ethics Resource Center.

65. ROBERTSON, D. & SCHLEGELMILCH, B. B. 1993. Corporate institutionalization of ethics in the United States and Great Britain. *Journal of business ethics*, 12(4):301–309; LINDSAY, R. M., LINDSAY, L. M. & IRVINE, B. V. 1996. Instilling ethical behavior in organizations: A survey of Canadian companies. *Journal of business ethics*, 15(4):393–410; WEBLEY, S. & LE JEUNE, M. 2005. *Corporate use of codes of ethics 2004 survey.* London: Institute of Business Ethics.

66. WEBLEY, S. & LE JEUNE, M. 2005. *Corporate use of codes of ethics 2004 survey.* London: Institute of Business Ethics.

67. SCHWARTZ, M. S. 2004. Effective corporate codes of ethics: perceptions of code users. *Journal of business ethics*, 55:323–343.

68. TREVINO, L. K., WEAVER, G. R. & TOFFLER, B. L. 1999. Managing ethics and legal compliance: what works and what hurts. *California management review*, 41(2):131–151; SCHWARTZ, M. S. 2004. Effective corporate codes of ethics: perceptions of code users. *Journal of business ethics*, 55:323–343; ETHICS RESOURCE CENTER. 2005. *National*

business ethics survey. Washington, D.C.: Ethics Resource Center.

69. IZRAELI, D. & SCHWARTZ, M. S. 1998. What can we learn from the U.S. Federal sentencing guidelines for organizational ethics? *Journal of business ethics,* 17(9–10):1045–1055.

70. WEAVER, G. R. & TREVINO, L. K. 1999. Compliance and values oriented ethics programs: influences on employees' attitudes and behaviour. *Business ethics quarterly,* 9(2):315–335.

71. TREVINO, L. K., WEAVER, G. R. & TOFFLER, B. L. 1999. Managing ethics and legal compliance: what works and what hurts. *California management review,* 41(2):131–151.

72. Ibid.

73. WEBLEY, S. & LE JEUNE, M. 2005. *Corporate use of codes of ethics 2004 survey.* London: Institute of Business Ethics.

74. GOODPASTER, K. E. (*In* West, A. 2006. Theorising South Africa's corporate governance. *Journal of business ethics,* 68:433–448.)

75. WEST, A. 2006. Theorising South Africa's corporate governance. *Journal of business ethics,* 68:433–448.

76. ORGANISATION FOR ECONOMIC CO-OPERATION AND DEVELOPMENT. 2004. *OECD Principles of corporate governance.* Paris: OECD:11. See also DREW, S. A. W. 2005. Risk management: the five pillars of corporate governance. *Journal of general management,* 31(2):19–36, Winter; DALTON, D. R. & DALTON, C. M. 2006. Going dark. *Journal of business strategy,* 27(1):5–6; DREW, S. A. W. KELLEY, P. C. & KENDRICK, T. 2006. Five elements of corporate governance to manage strategic risk. *Business horizons,* 49:127–138.

77. BOSCH, H. 2002. The changing face of corporate governance. *UNSW law journal,* 25(2):270–293.

78. Ibid.:271.

79. See, for example, ibid. and HORWATH PTY LTD. 2004. *Horwath 2004 corporate governance report.* Newcastle: University of Newcastle, Australia.

80. INSTITUTE OF DIRECTORS IN SOUTHERN AFRICA. 2002. *King committee on corporate governance.* Parktown, South Africa: Institute of Directors in Southern Africa:9. See also HUTTON-WILSON, D. 2001. Corporate governance: critical challenges for South Africa. *Management today,* 17(7):8–13, August.

81. SHALIER, G. 2004. *Introduction to corporate governance in Australia.* Frenchs Forest: Australia: Pearson.

82. HITT, M. A., IRELAND, R. D. & HOSKISSON, R. E. 2007. *Strategic management* 7th ed. Ohio: Thomson, South-Western, U.S.

83. KIEL, G. C. & NICHOLSON, G. J. 2003. *Boards that work: A new guide for directors.* Australia: McGraw Hill. See also PHAROAH, A. 2003. Corporate reputation: the board room challenge. *Corporate governance,* 3(4):46–51.

84. KAPLAN, R. S. & NORTON, D. P. 1996. *The balanced scorecard.* Boston: Harvard Business School Press.

85. ORGANISATION FOR ECONOMIC CO-OPERATION AND DEVELOPMENT. 2004. *OECD Principles of corporate governance.* Paris: OECD.

86. These reports and codes are available at the following Web site: http://www.ecgi. org/codes/all_codes.htm.

87. MARDEN, R. & EDWARDS, R. 2005. The Sarbanes–Oxley 'axe'. *The CPA journal,* April:6–10.

88. HEMPHILL, T. A. 2005. The Sarbanes–Oxley Act of 2002. *Journal of corporate citizenship,* 20:23–26.

89. Ibid.

90. Ibid.

91. For details see the following Web site: www.asx.com. au/corporategovernance.

92. BARRIER, M. 2003. (Cited in West, A. 2006. Theorising South Africa's corporate governance. *Journal of business ethics,* 68:433.)

93. INSTITUTE OF DIRECTORS IN SOUTHERN AFRICA. 2002. *King committee on Corporate governance.* Parktown, South Africa: Institute of Directors in Southern Africa.

94. Ibid.:paragraph 4.

95. Ibid.:paragraphs 36–37.

96. WEST, A. 2006. Theorising South Africa's corporate governance. *Journal of business ethics,* 68:433–448.

97. INSTITUTE OF DIRECTORS IN SOUTHERN AFRICA. 2002. *King Committee on corporate governance.* Parktown, South Africa: Institute of Directors in Southern Africa:paragraph 5.1.

98. ROSSOUW, G. J. , 2005. The philosophical premises of the second King report on corporate governance. *Koers,* 70(4):727–744.

99. INSTITUTE OF DIRECTORS IN SOUTHERN AFRICA. 2002. *King Committee on corporate governance.* Parktown, South Africa: Institute of Directors in Southern Africa: paragraph 2.2.1.

100. VISSER, W. 2005. Corporate citizenship in South Africa. *Journal of corporate citizenship,* 18:29–38.

101. VAUGHN, M. & RYAN, L. V. 2006. Corporate governance in South Africa: a bellwether for the continent? *Corporate governance,* 14(5):504–512.

102. JACKSON, I. & NELSON, J. 2004. *Profits with principles.* New York: Currency Doubleday.

103. RAMBHAROS, M. 2005. Managing HIV/Aids at Eskom. *Journal of corporate citizenship,* 18:25–27.

104. WEBLEY, S. & LE JEUNE, M. 2005. *Corporate use of codes of ethics 2004 survey.* London: Institute of Business Ethics.

105. ROYAL COMMISSION. 2003. The failure of HIH Insurance. [Online.]. Available: www.hihroyalcom. gov.au/finalreport/. 24 July 2006.

106. BERNHUT, S. 2004. Leader's edge: An interview with Professor Jay Lorsch, Harvard Business School. *Ivey business journal,* September–Ocober:1–5.

Appendix 9.1

Proposed model of stages of corporate citizenship

In their article 'Stages of Corporate Citizenship', Mirvis and Googins propose a model to help companies determine at what stage of development their corporate citizenship activities are. The proposed model appears in Table A6, and we shall discuss it with the article as point of departure.

In the proposed model, the developmental path of citizenship in companies is tracked along five stages namely:

- Elementary (stage 1)
- Engaged (stage 2)
- Innovative (stage 3)
- Integrated (stage 4)
- Transforming (stage 5).

Besides focusing on these stages, the model also focuses on seven dimensions of citizenship, which appear on the left side of the model. These dimensions, as indicated in the model, vary at each stage of development. Before we look at the individual stages of the model, note that various forces play a role in how citizenship develops in a specific company. Aspects that play a role include various forces in society, industry dynamics, cross-sector influences, and a company's culture.

We shall now briefly look at the stages of the model:

- *Stage 1 – Elementary.* At this stage the citizenship activity is episodic and its programmes undeveloped. This can be attributed to the scant awareness of what corporate citizenship is all about, as well as the lack of interest from top management in the issue. The mindset of these companies often focuses on simple

Table A6 Mirvis and Googins's model of stages of corporate citizenship

Dimensions of citizenship	Stage 1 Elementary	Stage 2 Engaged	Stage 3 Innovative	Stage 4 Integrated	Stage 5 Transforming
Citizenship concept	Jobs, profits and taxes	Philanthropy, Environmental protection	Stakeholder management	Sustainability or Triple bottom line	Change the game
Strategic intent	Legal compliance	License to operate	Business case	Value proposition	Market creation or Social change
Leadership	Lip service, Out of touch	Supporter, In the Loop	Steward, On Top of it	Champion, In Front of it	Visionary, Ahead of the pack
Structure	Marginal: Staff driven	Functional ownership	Cross-functional coordination	Organisational alignment	Mainstream; Business driven
Issues management	Defensive	Reactive, Policies	Responsive, Programs	Pro-active, Systems	Defining
Stakeholder relationships	Unilateral	Interactive	Mutual Influence	Partnership	Multi-organisation Alliances
Transparency	Flank protection	Public relations	Public reporting	Assurance	Full disclosure

SOURCE: MIRVIS, P. & GOOGINS, B. 2006. Stages of corporate citizenship. *California management review*, 48(2):108, Winter. Used with permission.

compliance with the laws and industry standards.

- *Stage 2 – Engagement.* At this stage, the company normally wakes up and starts adopting a new outlook on its role in society. Top managers begin to take an interest and monitor what is going on by studying community, environmental, and social issues and requiring staff units to perform to higher standards.
- *Stage 3 – Innovation.* In stage 3, citizenship-related programmes are planned, funded, and launched. These typically start in functional units. Managers also begin to monitor social and environmental performance, and issue public reports on the results.

- *Stage 4 – Integrated.* In stage 4, boards of directors are increasingly setting standards and monitoring corporate performance. In operational terms, this involves setting targets, establishing key performance indicators, and monitoring performance through balanced scorecards.
- *Stage 5 – Transformative.* In the last stage, companies seldom operate alone in the social and environmental realm. They now partner extensively with other businesses, community groups, and non-governmental organisations (NGOs) to address problems, reach new markets, and develop local economies.

10

Human resource management and the electronic era

Learning outcomes

After reading this chapter you should be able to:

▶ Define the concept 'e-business'
▶ Describe the design of an e-business strategy
▶ Define the concept 'electronic HRM', also known as 'E-HR'
▶ Distinguish between the different levels of HR intranets
▶ Identify the advantages and disadvantages of E-HR
▶ Discuss the effects of technology on several key HRM functions

Purpose

The purpose of this chapter is to indicate the impact of e-technology on companies and the HRM function.

Chapter overview

This chapter starts by focusing on the role that e-technology plays within an organisation. It considers how to implement this technology within a company. Thereafter it looks at the impact it has on the HRM function. The discussion focuses on some important HRM functions such as recruitment, selection, training, performance management, and compensation. The concluding case study illustrates how the theory contained in this chapter can be applied practically to companies.

Introduction

Experts have predicted that very early in the twenty-first century, the portion of the economy driven by the electronic medium will be greater than that driven by industrial companies.[1] In this 'new economy', it is inevitable that the way companies do business, are managed, and are organised will change dramatically. The impact of Web-technologies such as the Internet, intranets, and extranets on, for example, universal connectivity, is already apparent.[2] These new developments will also affect the competitive advantage of companies. In view of this new and important initiative, we shall in this chapter look first at the impact of the electronic era (e-era) on business in general. Thereafter, we shall discuss the developments taking place within the area of HRM, the so-called E-HR.

10.1 The impact of the electronic era on business

The introduction makes it clear that electronic business (e-business) will form the basis on which organisations will conduct business in the future. Organisations that understand the impending demands of the Internet economy stand the greatest chance for success with their e-transformation. Of course they must do more than just be aware of these changes; they must develop new 'best practices' to address them.[3]

10.1.1 What does e-business mean?

According to Brache and Webb[4], e-business is about doing business digitally – everything from buying and selling on the Web, to extranets that link a company to suppliers, to intranets that enable an organisation to manage its knowledge better, to enterprise-resource-planning systems that streamline an enterprise's supply chain, to electronic customer support, to automated order tracking.

A similar viewpoint is shared by Karakanian[5] when she states:

... e-business is the overall business strategy that redefines the old business models and uses digital media and network technology to optimise customer value delivery. It relies on Internet-based computing which is the platform that supports the open flow of information between systems. It capitalises on an existing technology backbone consisting of front-end and back-end enterprise business systems; it makes effective use of component technology and interacts with customers via business portals established over the Internet. Technology is used in this case both as the actual cause and also driver of business strategy. It is used not only to develop the product or the service but also to provide better choices to customers along with enhanced delivery options.

SOURCE: KARAKANIAN, M. 2000. Are human resources departments ready for E-HR? *Information systems management*, 17(4):36.

Thus, an e-business initiative, to be done well, requires dramatic changes in strategy, organisational processes, relationships, and systems. It also requires significant changes to the way in which employees work.[6]

10.1.2 Where does a company start on the e-business path?

To find the answer to this question, we shall look at the important work of Feeny[7], published in his article 'Making business sense of the e-opportunity'. Feeny suggests that companies interested in e-business should first construct a coherent map identifying the areas where Web-based technology could be introduced. The author suggests three core areas or domains – which one can almost see as generic – that business should look at. These include e-operations, e-marketing, and e-services. He suggests that e-operations and e-marketing should receive the most urgent attention as they

Figure 10.1 Three e-business opportunity domains and their components

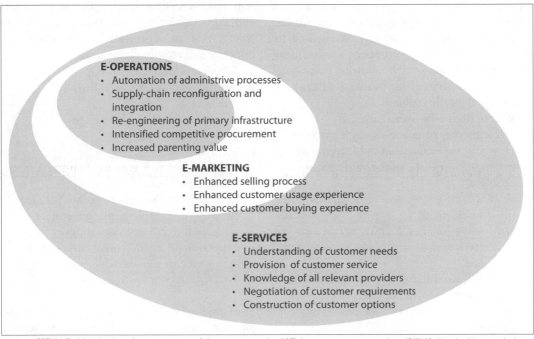

E-OPERATIONS
- Automation of administrive processes
- Supply-chain reconfiguration and integration
- Re-engineering of primary infrastructure
- Intensified competitive procurement
- Increased parenting value

E-MARKETING
- Enhanced selling process
- Enhanced customer usage experience
- Enhanced customer buying experience

E-SERVICES
- Understanding of customer needs
- Provision of customer service
- Knowledge of all relevant providers
- Negotiation of customer requirements
- Construction of customer options

SOURCE: FEENY, D. 2001. Making business sense of the e-opportunity. *MIT sloan management review*, 42(2):41. Used with permission.

provide the most certain rewards. He further suggests that it is important to distinguish clearly between these three domains as they each require their own distinctive framework for identifying ideas that can bring a competitive advantage to a given context.[8] Figure 10.1 shows the three domains and some of their components.

We shall now briefly look at each of the three domains individually[9]:

- *E-operations*. This covers Web-based initiatives that improve the creation of existing products. Of importance is the way a business manages itself and its supply chain. An example is the improvement of a company's purchasing by posting requirements on a Web site and having suppliers bid electronically.
- *E-marketing*. This covers Web-based initiatives that improve the marketing of existing products. Aspects of importance are the way the organisation delivers products and the scope of support services. An example is the online bookshop

Amazon notifying customers of new book-buying options based on a profile of previous purchases.

- *E-services*. This covers Web-based initiatives that provide customer-affiliated services. Aspects of importance are, for example, the new ways to address an identified set of customer needs. An example is shopping robots which search the Internet to find the best deals available. A number of new dotcom businesses are currently active in this area.

Having identified these domains within a company, we shall consider the question of what should happen next.

10.1.3 **Formulating an e-business strategy**

After formulating a corporate strategy, a company's top executives should develop an e-business strategy.[10] Just as strategies for marketing, manufacturing, and HR follow the company strategy, so also should an e-business strategy be formulated; it is important that the company strategy contains a framework for the company's e-business strategy. According to Brache and Webb[11], a company's e-business strategy should answer the following questions:

- What objectives of our business strategy can be digitally enabled?
- Where does e-business (not just e-commerce) fit in our strategic priorities?
- How will we ensure that the Internet does not make our niche in the value chain obsolete?
- How will we protect our customer base in the digital world?
- How will e-business help us attract new customers in the markets our strategy has targeted?
- How will we interface electronically with our customers? Our suppliers? Ourselves?
- What role will our Web site play? How will people find it?
- How will we ensure that we have the systems and technological capabilities to implement this vision?
- How will we ensure that we have the processes to implement it?
- How will we ensure that we have the human capabilities to implement this vision?
- What are the priorities among our digital initiatives?
- What is our plan for making this all happen?

When a company has completed all these activities, the next phase entails actually implementing the e-business strategy within the company.

10.1.4 Implementing the e-business strategy

Due to the nature of Web-based technology, change within the 'new economy' will be almost immediate whereas, in most cases, change in the old business paradigm was incremental.[12] As organisations will have to change the way in which they approach their customers, and how they market, order, track, and deliver their products or services, they will have to build rapidly the business and technical architectures required, as well as develop the new cultures and skills needed.[13] This means, according to Neef[14], that an organisation-wide e-business initiative will require expertise in:

- E-business strategies
- Leading operational-level business practices
- Process and technical redesign
- Data management
- Security
- Specialist services such as Web-marketing and design
- Knowledge-management techniques for choosing and implementing business information and decision-support tools
- Supply-chain management, supplier management, and strategic sourcing
- System-to-system integration.

Thus, finding and keeping the right skills is just one obstacle for managers hoping to implement an e-business strategy successfully. The literature[15] identifies a number of other issues that need attention during this process. We shall briefly consider these.

- *Gain the support of top management.* As with any change that takes place within an organisation, the support of top management, as well as that of other key players in the organisation, is vital. This will help to minimise delays in decision making when implementing the necessary changes, and working across existing functional, geographical, and company boundaries.
- *Establish a cross-functional project team.* Driving the implementation of the e-strategy successfully will also require the establishment of a cross-functional project team. It has been proved that creating a dedicated team of people produces the quickest results. Such a team will consolidate new ideas as well as coordinate and manage the efforts between the different parts of the organisation. It will also be important to have both a technical and a non-technical component within the project team, given the technical matters – e.g. management information system

(MIS) – and non-technical aspects – i.e. business processes and change-management initiatives. The success of such a project team depends on its leader. This person needs to understand how the business works and has to believe in the project passionately. Besides the project leader, team members must also be selected. Here it is vital to select team members who are optimistic and enthusiastic about the project. According to Butler[16], the ideal e-business team member possesses leadership qualities, creativity, and strong interpersonal skills, and is also able to influence co-workers and supervisors. It will also be a good idea to appoint at least two individuals (e.g. consultants) from outside the organisation.

- *Draw up a communication plan.* A proper communication plan is necessary to indicate to the employees why the company is initiating the project, how the project will be done, what the likely outcome will be, and how those affected will be treated. Not only top-down communication is necessary, but also bottom-up communication. The organisation should invite employees – as well as customers, suppliers, and other affected groups – to be involved throughout the project.

- *Obtain own budget.* One cannot underestimate the importance of having a budget. This will ensure that a smooth transition takes place. Having a budget under someone else's existing budget, so that questions are regularly asked regarding whether the expenditure is necessary, will not work. The project team must have its own budget approved by top management.

- *Create a transition plan.* The following will enable the organisation to implement the e-business strategy successfully: acknowledging the way employees' work will change and creating a transition plan covering new activities and jobs, changes to reporting structures, and, when necessary, changes to incentive and reward systems and the retraining of staff.

- *Evaluate the process.* An organisation needs to monitor its implemented e-strategy to determine the extent to which it achieves its objectives. Despite efforts at objectivity, the process of formulating a strategy is largely subjective. Thus, the first substantial test of a strategy comes only after implementation. The project team must watch for early signs of marketplace response to their actions. They must also provide monitoring and control methods to ensure that the organisation follows the e-business strategy as planned.

As Figure 10.2 indicates, e-business success within an organisation is dependent on a number of issues, namely:

- The presence of a business strategy

Figure 10.2 The four elements of e-business success

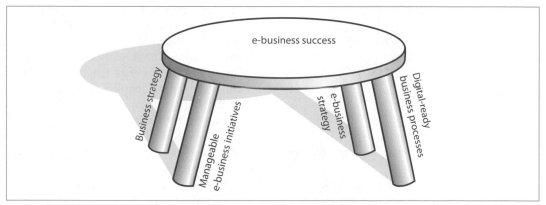

SOURCE: BRACHE, A. & WEBB, J. 2000. The eight deadly assumptions of e-business. *Journal of business strategy*, 21(3):17, May/June. Used with permission.

- An e-business strategy
- Manageable e-business initiatives
- Digital-ready business processes.

Just as the idea of e-business has captured the attention and imagination of the business world, the world of HR is also rapidly progressing toward an electronic-delivery concept, sometimes referred to as E-HR. In the following section we shall look at this new development.

10.2 The impact of the electronic era on HRM

There is no doubt that Web technology is changing every aspect of the way in which a company conducts its business. It is also transforming the way in which companies manage their employees[17], and thus is changing the way in which HR professionals do their job. As a result, HRM has become the latest partner in the Web development known simply as E-HR.[18] What does E-HR entail?

10.2.1 Describing E-HR

According to Karakanian[19], E-HR is:

> ... the overall HR strategy that lifts HR, shifts it from the HR department and isolated HR activities, and redistributes it to the organisation and its trusted business partners old and new. E-HR ties and integrates HR activities to other corporate processes such as finance, supply chain and customer service. Its promise is that HR is the owner of the strategy and when required it is the service broker as opposed to the provider.
>
> SOURCE: KARAKANIAN, M. 2000. Are human resources departments ready for E-HR? *Information systems management*, 17(4):36.

What this definition is trying to identify is that E-HR[20]:

- Demands HRM to do its homework
- Requires executive participation

- Needs an excellent appreciation of technology and the use of technology
- Requires a well-developed and integrated human-resource information system (HRIS)
- Needs to use wisely the network of technologies and various communication channels such as the Web, wireless, and, perhaps, kiosks.

The HRIS will thus form the backbone of the HRM system. This system will interface with the organisation's intranet and will connect to HR service suppliers and business partners via an extranet as well as have links to the Internet via HR portals (single points of access).

This whole process will allow cost-effective universal access to HR data by all authorised parties, including employees, managers, executives, HR service providers, relevant communities, corporate customers, and the public at large. It will also reduce the distance between the HR department and its internal customers.[21] For example, an e-procurement system might use HR data to establish rules about authorisations and approvals, while an e-operations system might access HR data to tweak staffing levels or help the company plan an expansion more effectively. It might also play a central role in designing a more efficient production or sales method.[22]

10.2.2 Advantages of E-HR

From the literature it is clear that taking HRM online can achieve vast improvements in efficiencies (see Box 1 on the next page). This process strategy, according to Collett[23], is becoming known as 'B2E' – the automation of the entire business-to-employee relationship via the Internet in ways that enhance employee productivity and workforce return on investment. For example, one of the largest organisations in the USA, Oracle Corporation, has made significant cost savings in the transformation of its HRM. Many routine day-to-day administrative tasks have been taken online, freeing the HR department to focus on more important issues.[24]

BOX 1: Ways in which HRM can benefit from electronic systems

- Portals can create a single interface for accessing key data.
- Online recruiting can eliminate paperwork and speed up the hiring process.
- Employee self-service can automate record keeping.
- A Web-accessible knowledge base can reduce questions to the HR department or a call centre.
- Electronic benefits enrolment lets employees sort through options faster, while reducing paperwork and questions for HRM.
- Electronic payroll can cut costs and make data more easily accessible.
- Trading exchanges and e-market places can reduce the costs of products and services.
- E-procurement can eliminate catalogues and manual processes that are expensive and slow.
- Electronic travel and expense reporting can crumple the paper glut and speed up reimbursements to both employees and the company.
- Online retirement planning can help employees map out their future, while reducing questions and paperwork for HRM.
- Online learning can slash travel costs and make training available anytime, anywhere.
- Competency management can help an organisation identify strengths and weaknesses.

SOURCE: GREENGARD, S. 2000. Net gains to HR technology. *Workforce*, 79(4):46. Used with permission.

10.2.3 Disadvantages of E-HR

Despite the positive aspects of E-HR the previous section mentions, there is also a negative side to this process. This involves the security of the HR data. HR-related information is perhaps more critical than any other because it involves private and highly sensitive individual data. According to Karakanian[25], the disclosure and cross-border movement of HR data is a critical issue to be managed very carefully, based on country- and organisation-specific, as well as individual, authorisations. Thus data and multiplatform security aspects are perhaps the most serious factors an organisation needs to consider during the formulation of its E-HR strategy.

10.2.4 HR intranet sites

With reference to the earlier domains of Web application (see Section 10.1.2), we note that E-HR will play a crucial role in the e-operations domain of the company. However, for the HR Web site to achieve its full potential it is important to understand the levels of Web site development and how effectiveness increases as the site evolves to the higher level of sophistication. For this purpose we shall focus on the work of Chamine[26], published in his article 'Making your intranet an effective HR tool'. We shall discuss the four types of HR intranet sites Chamine identifies, namely:

1. *Brochureware.* Normally at the launch of a Web site, a company posts most of its written materials on the site and consequently uses the site as an electronic bulletin board. Under these circumstances employees are bombarded with a great deal of information. For a busy employee who is looking for a simple piece of information, this can be very time consuming and frustrating. Under these conditions, this format does not take advantage of the integrated, interactive, and personalised capabilities of Web technology.

2. *Transactional.* When the enormous potential of the intranet is appreciated, by allowing employees to conduct transactions online, the site moves up in capability. Typical online transactions include changing personal information, registering for courses, submitting expense reports, reviewing vacation information and leave, reviewing and updating benefit selections, and applying for other jobs in the company. New types of technology have enabled the creation of truly

engaging, easy-to-use applications for self-service.

3. *Integrated*. Here multiple sites are linked together to create a seamless experience for the user. The challenge at this stage is how to integrate the various services in a way that makes sense to the employee.

4. *Personalised*. The ultimate goal is to create a truly individualised experience for each user by providing unique content based on the person's profile: Is the person a manager, supervisor or hourly worker? In what region does he or she work? To which benefits package is he or she entitled? What are the person's unique skills, motivations, and objectives for career advancement?

Box 2 below gives some tips for an effective intranet site.

As employees explore and use an integrated personalised HR intranet site, their productivity and retention are likely to increase due to the immediate delivery of services or information to them. According to Chamine[27], the Web site in effect becomes the face of HRM and has the ability to make a significant and personal impact on individuals, thereby helping them to make a more meaningful contribution to the organisation.

In the next section, we shall look at some E-HR applications in practice.

10.2.5 **E-HR in practice**

This section is based on a number of authors' work, which was published in *The brave new world of EHR*, edited by Gueutal and Stone. In this section we shall look at the effects of technology on several key HR functions, e.g. recruitment, selection, training, performance management, and compensation.

BOX 2: Tips for an effective intranet site

- *Make it user-friendly.* Look at the site through the eyes of employees, not through the eyes of an HR professional. Employees often complain that HR information is presented in language and structure that only makes sense to HRM. Employees want to be able to quickly find learning opportunities that meet their individual needs.

- *Make it unique.* Don't just transfer text from paper – use the capabilities of intranet technology to make the site compelling, interactive and personalised.

- *Make it useful.* Integrate and link HR services wherever possible. Graphics, navigation and links should make sense and be appealing to employees so that they are pulled into other areas of the site that might otherwise be ignored or overlooked.

- *Do not reinvent the wheel.* Use already-developed online tools and invest in creating new custom tools only when necessary. The Information Technology Association of America recently reported that dozens of new intranet applications are coming to the market each month. Many services can be outsourced to specialised providers, minimising internal HRIS requirements.

- *Update it.* Consistently change and update the HR home page with new information and fresh graphics to encourage employees to keep visiting it. One company features a 'banner ad' for HR services that changes each time the employee visits the site. Another greets the employees by name and uses detailed database information to alert them to an upcoming deadline for benefit changes or an internal seminar that they might find interesting.

- *Get feedback.* Solicit lots of feedback from your users. As with any product, it is critical to know what your customers think.

- *Be creative.* Remember, in order to make your employees enthusiastic and consistent intranet users, your site must have the snap, crackle and pop Internet users have come to expect.

SOURCE: SANDLER, S. (Ed). 1998. *HR focus*, December:12, 212/244-0360. http://www.ioma.com. CHAMINE, S. 1998. Making your intranet an effective HR tool. *HR focus*, December:12. Article9992. Reprinted by permission © *HR focus*

- *E-recruitment and e-selection.* No organisation can function without people, and the attraction and retention of highly talented employees remains a challenge. To aid in this process, companies are increasingly making use of E-HR systems such as Web-based job sites, portals, and kiosks to attract applicants.[28] According to Stone, Lukaszewski, and Isenhour, the most common practices used for online recruitment involve:
  1. Adding recruitment pages to existing company Web sites
  2. Using specialised recruitment Web sites, e.g. job portals and online job boards
  3. Developing interactive tools for processing applications such as online applications and automatic email responses
  4. Using online screening techniques such as keyword systems, online interviews, and personality assessment.[29]

Job postings are also done on the internal network (intranet) of the company. Companies derive a number of benefits from using e-recruiting, namely:

- ➤ It increases the effectiveness of the recruitment process by reaching larger numbers of qualified people
- ➤ It reduces recruitment costs
- ➤ It decreases and streamlines cycle times of the administrative process
- ➤ It enables the company to evaluate the success of its recruitment strategy.[30]

It is thus clear that e-recruiting has numerous benefits for an organisation. However, despite these benefits, there are a number of dysfunctional or unintended consequences of e-recruiting, e.g.:

- ➤ The computerised system may make the recruitment process more impersonal and inflexible
- ➤ Some groups may not have access to computerised systems or even have the skills to use them
- ➤ Some applicants may see the online system as more likely to invade their personal privacy and this may reduce their willingness to apply.[31]

To overcome these obstacles, an organisation can do the following:

- ➤ Restrict unauthorised access to data gathered online
- ➤ Restrict disclosure of data to only that required for decision-making purposes
- ➤ Develop systems that are culturally sensitive
- ➤ Align the system with the strategic goals of the company
- ➤ Provide sufficient evidence on the system about the company
- ➤ Design the site so that it is easy to use.[32]

Once an employee is recruited, he or she must next move through the selection process. The implementation of any selection process is complex, and the integration of technology to use in this process even more complex, especially when testing is one of the critical steps in the process. According to Kehoe, Dickter, Russell, and Sacco[33], organisations can follow a number of steps when implementing the e-selection process, namely:

- ➤ *Step 1.* Draw-up a flow chart of the current assessment process.
- ➤ *Step 2.* Draft the desired flow process that will result from the e-selection process – from this step process improvements, efficiencies, and cost savings should be evident (e.g. the new process will involve fewer staff).
- ➤ *Step 3.* Consider how the various new stakeholders and clients (recruiters, administrators etc.) will use the system.
- ➤ *Step 4.* Choose a new technology-enabled scoring system – with e-selection the scoring should be rapid or instantaneous, test results should be readily combinable with other test results, and score reports that are readily interpretable and printable should be available. Important also here is the equivalence of the previous paper-and-pencil system with the new one. Rules regarding the interpretation of the score results must also be determined (e.g. 'definitely hire', 'possibly hire', and 'definitely reject').

> *Step 5.* An issue organisations also need to address is how to prepare the candidate for the test (e.g. provide a few practice items). This will help with test anxiety.

> *Step 6.* Train the employees who will be responsible for administering the process.

Figure 10.3 indicates a typical process for e-recruitment/e-selection.

• *E-training.* As we indicated earlier, knowledge workers play an important part in the competitiveness of companies. Unfortunately, a reality of today's rapid explosion of knowledge is that the knowledge workers' possess becomes obsolete.[34] How can this process be stopped?

The answer lies in training. Training makes learning and relearning essential if employees are to keep abreast with the latest developments in their fields. However, there is also a growing demand from companies for just-in-time training, as well as for cost-effective ways of delivering it.[35] In this area, the appearance of the World Wide Web has provided trainers with greater flexibility in the way they design and implement training (e.g. anywhere and any time) and thus makes e-training a reality.[36] E-learning is a concept that has appeared within this domain over the past few years and is gaining greater momentum. According to Swart, Mann, Brown, and Price[37], this concept can be defined as follows:

> Learning that is delivered, enabled or mediated by electronic technology, for the explicit purpose of training in organi-sations. It does not include stand alone technology based training such as the use of CD Rom.

Figure 10.3 A typical e-recruitment/e-selection process

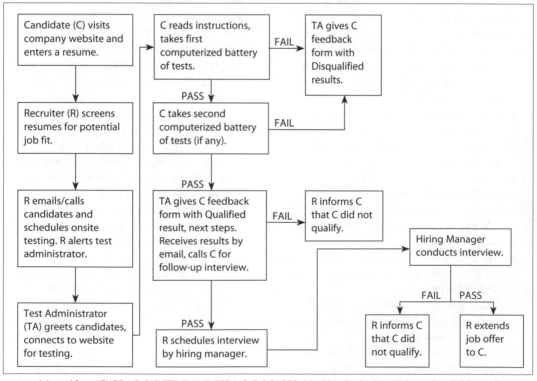

SOURCE: Adapted from KEHOE, J. F., DICKTER, D. N., RUSSELL, D. P. & SACCO, J. M. 2005. E-selection. (*In* Gueutal, H. G. & Stone, D. L. (Eds). *The brave new world of E-HR*. San Francisco: Jossey Bass, an imprint from John Wiley & Sons:88.) Used with permission.

What types of e-learning exist? According to Silberman[38], e-learning has different forms, which can be separated into four distinct categories, namely:

> *Independent e-learning.* This is asynchronous – all learning does not have to take place at the same time, i.e. participants can take the course when and where they choose. Examples are Web- and computer-based training.
> *Group-based e-learning.* This is synchronous – participants communicate at the same time. Examples are video training, Webcasts, and Webinars.
> *Virtual classroom.* This is asynchronous and synchronous. Examples are discussion boards, chatrooms, and electronic breakout groups.
> *Blended learning.* This is asynchronous and synchronous. An example is e-learning combined with instructor-led training in a classroom.

How does one access e-learning programmes? The literature identifies two main ways to access e-learning programmes: through a company intranet or through learning portals on the Internet.[39] Learning portals are like online libraries; they offer courses on a wide variety of topics, from time management to customer-service training to courses on spreadsheets.

We shall now take a closer look at the e-learning concept. According to Driscoll[40], the justification for investing in e-learning programmes has both strategic and tactical dimensions. From a strategic perspective, the following are important:

> The existence of a global workforce
> Shorter product-development cycles
> Managing flatter organisations
> Adjusting to the needs of employees
> Retaining valuable workers
> Increasing productivity and profitability.

From a tactical perspective the following are important:

> Reducing travel and related costs
> Enabling learning any time and any place
> Providing just-in-time learning
> Leveraging the existing infrastructure
> Enabling delivery independent of a platform
> Providing tools for tracking and record keeping
> Making updates easy.

Table 10.1 indicates some benefits and some disadvantages of e-learning.

Given these benefits and disadvantages of e-learning, what would the characteristics of a successful e-learning programme be? According to Wilcock[41], the following need to be present:

> *A technically robust delivery platform.* A reliable company intranet or online Web-based system must be available, offering fast download times.
> *An intuitive user interface.* Navigation through the system should be simple and obvious.
> *Online coaching support.* Fast feedback from e-learning systems must be available. Online coach facilitation through discussion groups and regular personal contact must be part of the system.
> *A high level of interactivity.* Online tests and quizzes should be available to provide instantaneous feedback to learners.

Thus, e-learning involves not only providing trainees with content, but also giving learners the ability to control what they learn, the speed at which they progress through the programme, and, even, when they learn. This type of learning also allows learners to collaborate or interact with other trainees and experts, and it provides links to other learning resources such as reference material, company Web sites, and other training programmes.[42] It may also include various aspects of training administration, such as course enrolment, the testing and evaluation of trainees, and the monitoring

Table 10.1 Benefits and disadvantages of E-learning

Benefits	Disadvantages
High degree of interaction between the learner and materials	Requires specific equipment to run the programmes
Understanding can be assessed before the learner moves on	Access to a computer is needed for each learner
Feedback can be tailored to the learner's decisions	Development time can be high
Topics can be accessed in an order which suits the learner	Specialist expertise may be required to design and write the programme
Potential for adapting the learning style to the user's needs	Hardware may be expensive
Relatively easy to update text and graphics	Not good at conveying attitudes or behaviour
Ready means of testing	Some learners find it difficult to read text from a screen
Standardized form of training	Can be inappropriate as a single medium for longer applications
Attractive to many learners	Learner may be unable to comprehend learning material
Learner can use material at his/her own pace	Learning process cannot be followed or modified by tutor following production
Computer aided learning programmes are flexible regarding usage time	Learning programmes may be unreliable
The possibility of using different kinds of material	High-level infrastructure and equipment needed Time spent on studies is reduced, meaning less time spent away from the workplace

When to use:
Good for simulations
Procedural training – adds interest and interaction, particularly the ability to check your responses to activities and tasks
Decision-making 'games' – 'action mazes'
Keyboard training
Tutorials for software packages
Management of learning

SOURCE: SWART, J., MANN, C., BROWN, S. & PRICE, A. 2005. *Human resource development: Strategy and tactics.* Oxford: Elsevier Butterworth-Heinemann:302. Copyright Elsevier, used with permission.

of the trainees' learning processes. Text, video, graphics, and sound can be used to present course content. Note that e-learning does not simply mean putting existing training courses and materials on a Web site. According to Mathis and Jackson[43], the following steps need to be followed:

➤ *Step 1.* Convert the training content into electronic form.
➤ *Step 2.* Modularise the content to enable the trainees to complete segments of it.
➤ *Step 3.* Measure the learning, track usage and evaluate training to see whether it meets the objectives set.

Undoubtedly, E-learning will have a major impact on HRM and training within companies.

• *E-HR-based performance management.* There is no doubt that employers want employees who perform their jobs well. An effective performance-management system increases the likelihood of such performance. However, to date, the performance-management process has largely been a paper exercise, which has become fairly cumbersome in many organisations. With the arrival of the World Wide Web, intranets, and extranets, performance management can now take place through the direct involvement of technology. It is important that, when using technology in this area, managers make sure that employees are satisfied with the system, i.e. that they feel that they are being treated fairly. If ratees are dissatisfied, or perceive a system as unfair, they will have diminished motivation to use the evaluation information emanating from the system to improve their performance.[44] The question then is: how can technology contribute to performance management?

According to Cardy and Miller[45], the following two ways are possible:

> *Measurement of an employee's performance via computer monitoring.* This can occur as an unobtrusive and rote mechanical process which relies on minimal input from individuals beyond their task performance. Examples of areas where this can take place are at a call centre or in a data-capturing environment. In this environment the very act of performing a job simultaneously becomes the measure of how well a job holder accomplishes it. For example, keystrokes, time on the task, and number of calls made are recorded and at once become both job content and appraisal content. This is generally known as computerised performance monitoring (CPM). An important aspect here is that this system must be able to balance quantitative performance data with systems factors. For example, an employee who delivers high-quality customer service over the telephone could generate positive responses from the public that could foster return business even though objective call duration alone might not capture this fact. Thus, a process that also incorporates acknowledgement of system factors such as call complexity would put work performance in perspective.[46] As this is the kind of performance a company seeks to encourage, finding an appropriate

objective balance benefits not only the performer in terms of fairness, but also the organisation from an outcome point of view. According to Cardy and Miller[47], one way to overcome these constraints is to incorporate CPM into a type of management-by-objectives (MBO) approach. For example, a supervisor can have a meeting with an employee to review the CPM data, discuss tactics for raising performance (if required), and jointly solve problems regarding current procedures. This will make CPM a more positive experience. An advantage of this system is that it permits a greater span of control because it facilitates the accurate collection of performance data without requiring managers to spend significant time observing each individual worker's actual performance on the job.[48]

> *The use of technology as a tool to facilitate the process of writing reviews or generating performance feedback.* Examples here include multi-rater appraisals that supervisors or team members generate online and off-the-shelf appraisal packages that actually construct an evaluation for a manager.[49] This particular approach occurs more often where jobs require personal judgment and high discretion and are open-ended tasks for which real-time performance monitoring is not an option. Also, here the employees' perception regarding the fairness of the system is important. There are several ways of achieving technological enhancement of performance-management systems in this option. According to Cardy and Miller[50], one method is to incorporate appraisal as part of a software system for overall enterprise resource planning (ERP). The advantage of this approach is that it comprises a wide variety of company data – e.g. financial, operations etc. – that managers can view in ways that would otherwise not have been

possible.[51] By exploring the company data, and by analysing competencies for individuals, groups of workers or departments, HR practitioners can identify high performers and spot gaps in skill and competency. It is also possible to analyse pay levels relative to performance. Besides the ERP software system, company intranets or the Internet may also be utilised.[52] In this case, a performance-evaluation process may begin with email messages to relative stakeholders coordinating the programme. Following this, the participants can nominate potential evaluators who can provide feedback about them. The system can, for example, automatically limit the number of people an evaluator may rate. The evaluator will then receive a password, which will enable him or her to enter a 'secure Web site' to complete the evaluation.[53] Once the evaluation is complete, the system will collect the feedback, which will be assembled into reports and sent electronically to the ratees. The advantage of this process is that the employees can be evaluated more frequently.

Another positive feature of this type of process is that many of the software packages also include a training component for the rater. This does not only save the company money but ensures that the reports generated by the rater are of high standard.[54] In addition, the ratees can also automatically access online developmental suggestions and become aware of training opportunities within the company. The system will also enable the ratees to track their own progress over a series of evaluations. Many of the software packages also allow users to click buttons on a screen for each rating and simultaneously create sentences and paragraphs of text. If, for example, the ratings within an individual factor are high or low or varied at both ends of the scale, the program can

prompt the evaluator to review the rating and add his or her own comments.[55] Some packages also contain enormous databases of prewritten text, allowing raters to upgrade automatically to a more positive evaluation or downgrade to a more negative one.[56] The systems can also send evaluators the reports of other raters to see how closely they agree with the other ratings.

All these options have the potential to make the performance-evaluation process less daunting for frontline managers, engineers, scientists or others who often strongly resist the time and effort spent on this activity. Thus, the numerous benefits of online performance appraisal are clear, but companies can reap them only if they consider the issues of trust, fairness, system factors, computer literacy, and training of both the raters and the ratees.

- *E-compensation*. For many employees, a lifelong commitment to one employer is no longer an option.[57] This view holds serious implications for companies. Without talented staff, companies cannot realise organisational competitiveness. Thus, the role of compensation has become an important tool for attracting, retaining, and motivating the talent needed for survival over the long term. The management of this process has, in view of technological developments within the HRM field, also undergone major changes and today the literature refers to e-compensation.

According to Dulebohn and Marler[58], E-compensation tools can enhance the practice of designing and administering compensation programmes in three ways:
  ➤ The tools can increase access to critical information on compensation, without the need to involve specialised IT staff – users can simply access key information on an as-needed basis
  ➤ The tools enable around-the-clock availability of meaningful compensation information to senior managers, HR

managers, and employees

> The tools can streamline cumbersome bureaucratic tasks, through the introduction of workflow functionality and real-time information processing.

The tools thus enable an organisation to gather, store, manipulate, analyse, utilise, and distribute compensation data and information.[59] Thus, what distinguishes e-compensation from previous compensation software is that e-compensation is Web based, rather than client–server based or stand-alone PC-based. It also allows managers and employees to perform data entry and data processing remotely, e.g. through self-service portals. Many software companies supply electronically advanced job-analysis and job-evaluation techniques for companies to use in the establishment of their compensation structures.[60] These components form the building blocks of a proper compensation programme. A job-analysis system known as the Common Metric Questionnaire (CMQ), designed by Personnel Systems and Technology Corporation, enables, for example, companies to describe accurately both managerial as well as nonmanagerial occupations.[61] Some software systems can also specify the number and type of compensable factors, the number of levels within each factor, and the points associated with the factors (the process known as job evaluation). Because the system is Web enabled, HR specialists can electronically distribute information to target employees or managers via the company intranet.[62] The intranet technology therefore enables organisations to decentralise the responsibility for job evaluation and job analysis to the desktop of a manager. These software packages, in many instances, also include information on salary surveys which can be used as benchmarks for different jobs within a company.[63] One company, PeopleSoft, for example, offers a comprehensive Web-enabled compensation-planning programme that can coordinate and integrate information from both internal pay structures and external market data to design pay structures effectively and efficiently.[64] Thus through e-compensation tools organisations can adapt to shifting demands for information in this area of HRM.

SUMMARY

With the advent of Web technology there has been a significant shift in the way companies are managed, organised and, most importantly, valued. This chapter provided guidelines to assist businesses grappling with understanding and implementing the new technology – the electronic or e-business phenomenon. The chapter also focused on the way in which technology impacts on the management of people within organisations – the so-called E-HR.

In reality, E-HR touches every corner of a business and therefore requires new tools – such as portals, intranets, and extranets – to consolidate, manage, and deliver information efficiently to its stakeholders. Ultimately, HRM must be aware of the dynamics of e-business in the marketplace if it is to be successful.

KEY CONCEPTS

- Asynchronous
- Brochureware
- B2E (business to employee)
- Cross-functional team
- Computerised performance monitoring (CPM)
- Common Metric Questionnaire (CMQ)
- E-business
- E-business strategy
- E-compensation
- E-HR
- E-marketing
- E-operations
- E-services
- E-recruitment
- E-selection
- E-learning
- E-performance management
- E-training
- Enterprise resource planning (ERP)

- Electronic medium
- Extranet
- Human resource information system (HRIS)
- HR portals
- Integrated
- Internet
- Intranet
- Kiosks
- Management information system (MIS)
- Management by objectives (MBO)
- New economy
- Personalised
- Portals (single points of entry)
- Security
- Synchronous
- Transactional
- Transition plan
- Web

CASE STUDY

Objective: To understand the role of training in an advanced technological environment

Training at Sunrise Inc.

Sunrise Inc. is a large brokerage company operating out of Sandton, Gauteng. The company was founded in 1908 by Patrick Johnson Sr, great-grandfather of the current CEO. Sunrise Inc. offer a complete line of insurance services for both individuals and business firms. As is true with other insurance companies, Sunrise Inc emphasises sales. In fact, more than half of all employees are involved in sales to some degree.

Because the sales activity is so important, the company spends a considerable amount of time, effort and money on sales training. Its training director, Tom Wilson, is constantly on the lookout for new training techniques that can improve sales and profits. He recently attended a workshop on new training techniques and heard about a new approach named 'E-training' which seems to have some promise. On returning to the company, he immediately scheduled a meeting with his boss, Cathy Adams, Executive Director for human resources at Sunrise Inc., to discuss the possibility of implementing E-training within the company.

Cathy: Come in Tom. What's this I hear about a new training technique?

Tom: Well, as you know, Cathy, I always try to keep up to date on the latest in training techniques so that we can remain competitive. I attended this workshop last week and the issue of E-learning, a new approach in training, was presented to the audience present by a consultancy company, Train for the Future. Apparently this technique saves companies time as well as money. For instance, we do not have to send our sales people away to be trained; it can all happen right here! I have already worked out a preliminary budget for such a system here at Sunrise Inc. and it looks very feasible. I thought that I'd run it by you.

Cathy: How much will it cost to implement?

Tom: For the first phase it will be about R3 million.

Cathy: I don't know. Tom. That sounds a little steep to me. Besides, Oscar [the CEO], has been bugging me again about the results of our last training effort. He wants to know whether all the money we are spending on sales training is really paying off. As you know, sales and profits are down this quarter and Oscar is looking for places to cut corners. I am afraid that if we cannot demonstrate a pay-off somehow for our training courses, he is going to pull the rug out from under us.

Tom: But we evaluate all our training programmes! The last one got rave reviews from all the participants.

Cathy: That's true. Tom, but Oscar wants more proof than just the reactions of the salespeople. He wants something more tangible. Now, before we buy into any new training technique, I want you to draw up a report on what our present training is costing us.

Questions and activities

1. What is meant by the statement that training is extremely 'faddish'?
2. How can Sunrise Inc. avoid becoming a victim of the faddishness of the training business?
3. Draw up a brief report that Tom can present to Cathy on why e-learning should be implemented at Sunrise Inc. Discuss issues such as the benefits and disadvantages of such a system. Also give a brief overview of what the e-learning system entails.

REVIEW QUESTIONS AND ACTIVITIES

1. Briefly describe what e-business means.
2. Feeny suggests that companies interested in e-business should first construct a coherent map identifying the areas where Web-based technology could be introduced. Discuss briefly.
3. According to Brache and Webb, a company's e-business strategy should answer a number of questions. Briefly discuss some of these issues.
4. Write a short essay on the implementation of an e-business strategy.
5. Do you think the establishment of a cross-functional project team is very important when implementing an e-business strategy? Explain briefly why you think so.
6. Write a short essay on E-HR.
7. Discuss the benefits and disadvantages of implementing e-learning within a company.
8. Four types of HR intranet sites are identified by Chamine. Discuss each site briefly.
9. Write a short essay on E-HR based performance management.
10. Briefly explain a typical e-recruitment process and e-selection process.

FURTHER READING

GUEUTAL, H. G. & STONE, D. L. (Eds). *The brave new world of E-HR*. San Francisco: Jossey Bass, an imprint from John Wiley & Sons

SWART, J., MANN, C., BROWN, S. & PRICE, A. 2005. *Human resource development: Strategy and tactics*. Oxford: Elsevier Butterworth-Heinemann.

PLOYHART, R. E., SCHNEIDER, B. & SCHMITT, N. 2006. *Staffing organisations: Contemporary practice and theory*. New Jersey: Lawrence Erlbaum Associates Inc. Publishers.

WEB SITES

www.pstc.com – Personnel Systems and Technology Corporation (PSCT): examples of Web-based job-analysis tools

www.cmqonline.com – Web-based questionnaire to describe both managerial and nonmanagerial occupations

www.knowledgepoint.com – Job-analysis product accessed over the Web; provided by the Knowledgepoint company

www.hr-software.net/cgi/jobevaluation – online point-method job-evaluation instrument

www.jpsmanagement.com – JPS Management Consulting: questionnaires to collect information from job incumbents

ENDNOTES

1. SHARMA, P. 2000. E-transformation basics: key to the new economy. *Strategy & leadership*, 28(4):27–31.
2. FEENY, D. 2001. Making business sense of the e-opportunity. *MIT sloan management review*, 42(2):40–50.
3. SHARMA, P. 2000. E-transformation basics: key to the new economy. *Strategy & leadership*, 28(4):30.
4. BRACHE, A. & WEBB, J. 2000. The eight deadly assumptions of e-business. *Journal of business strategy*, 21(3):13, May/June. See also PIERPOINT, H. W. 2000. Preventing e-business pain. *Strategy & leadership*, 28(2):39–41.
5. KARAKANIAN, M. 2000. Are human resources departments ready for E-HR? *Information systems management*, 17(4):36.
6. NEEF, D. 2000. Hiring an e-team. *Journal of business strategy*, 21(6):17.
7. FEENY, D. 2001. Making business sense of the e-opportunity. *MIT sloan management review*, 42(2):40.
8. Ibid.: 41.
9. Ibid.
10. BRACHE, A. & WEBB, J. 2000. The eight deadly assumptions of e-business. *Journal of business strategy*, 21(3):15, May/June.
11. Ibid.

12. BUTLER, A. S. 2000. Developing your company's new e-business. *Journal of business strategy*, 21(6):38. See also MARINI, D. P. 2000. Needed: an electronic business model for HR functions. *Employee benefit news*, 14(1):22–25.

13. NEEF, D. 2000. Hiring an e-team. *Journal of business strategy*, 2(6):18.

14. Ibid.

15. The discussion here will be based mainly on the following two articles: BUTLER, A. S. 2000. Developing your company's new e-business. *Journal of business strategy*, 21(6):38–42 and NEEF, D. 2000. Hiring an E-team. *Journal of business strategy*, 21(6):17–21.

16. BUTLER, A. S. 2000. Developing your company's new e-business. *Journal of business strategy*, 21(6):40.

17. COLLETT, C. 2001. Business-to-employee: Automating the HR function. *CMA management* (October):21. See also ROBERTS, B. 2001. E-learning: new twist on CBT. *HR magazine*, 46(4):99–106.

18. MONGELLI, L. 2000. Companies turn to the Web for their HR needs. *Incentive*, 174(5):10. See also GOODGE, P. 2001. Pure and simple. *People management* (8 March):6; PICKARD, J. 2000. HR shows scant interest in e-business, survey says. *People management*, 6(11):13–18; PICKARD, J. 2000. Electronic future for HR. *People management*, 6(14):11: PICKARD, J. 2000. Electronic future for HR. *People management*, 6(12):24–30.

19. KARAKANIAN, M. 2000. Are human resources departments ready for E-HR? *Information systems management*, 17(4):36.

20. Ibid.

21. Ibid.:37.

22. GREENGARD, S. 2000. Net gains to HR technology. *Workforce*, 79(4):46. See also KAY, A. S. 2000. Recruits embrace the internet. *Information week*, 778:72–75; CULLEN, B. 2001. E-recruiting is driving HR systems integration. *Strategic finance*, 83(1):22–25; HANSEN, K. A. 2001. Cybercruiting changes HR. *HR focus*, October:13–14; THORNBURG, L. 1998. Computer-assisted interviewing shortens hiring cycle. *HR magazine*, 43(2):73–79; ANDREWS, J. D. & FREEMAN, S. 2001. E-lessons learned. *CA magazine*, September:22–26; PETERS, K. 2001. Five keys to effective e-recruiting. *Ivey business journal*, 65(3):8–11, January/February; WALDRON, P. V. 1999. Managing HR on the Web. *Chain store age*, 75(12):160; MASSYN, V. 2002. E-HR: a human achievement. *People dynamics*, 18(10):38–39, October; HORWITZ, S. 2000. Considering human resources in the new e-economy. *People dynamics*, 18(9):38–39, September; SCHREYER, R. & MCCARTER, J. 2001. 10 steps to effective internet recruiting, *HR focus*:6.

23. COLLETT, C. 2001. Business-to-employee: Automating the HR function. *CMA management* (Canada), October:21. See also WELLS, S. J. 2001. Communicating benefits information online. *HR magazine*, 46(2):69–76; MORAN, J. V. 2000. Top ten e-learning myths. *Training & development*, 54(9):32–33; GALAGAN, P. A. 2000. Getting started with e-learning. *Training & development*, 54(5):62–64. GALAGAN, P. A. 2000. The e-learning revolution. *Training & development*, 54(12):50–56; STIFFLER, M. A. 2001. Incentive compensation and the Web. *Compensation & benefits review*, January/February:15–19; POLLARD, E. & HILLAGE, J. 2001. Exploring e-learning. *Report 376 – a study supported by the IES Research Club*. [Online.]. Available: http://www.employment–studies.co.uk/summary/376sum.html. 17 August 2007:1–4; TYLER, K. 2001. E-learning: not just for e-normal companies anymore. *HR magazine*, 46(5):82–88, May; CHRISTIE, M. 2000. Forging new employee relationship via E-HR. *HR focus*, 77(12):13–14.

24. COLLETT, C. 2001. Business-to-employee: Automating the HR function. *CMA management* (Canada), October:22.

25. KARAKANIAN, M. 2000. Are human resource departments ready for E-HR? *Information systems management*, 17(4):37–38. See also ULRICH, D. 2000. From e-business to E-HR. *Human resource planning*, 23(2):1–20; CURRIE, M. B. & BLACK, D. 2001. E-merging issues. *Ivey business journal*, January/February:18–22.

26. CHAMINE, S. 1998. Making your intranet an effective HR tool. *HR focus*, December:11–12. See also WILSON, J. 1999. Internet training: the time is now. *HR focus*, March:6; BROOKS, M. K. 1998. HR intranets an ROI strategy. *HR focus*, August:13–14; GREENGARD, S. 2001. IOHR technology trends for 2001. *Workforce*, 80(1):20; JOSSI, F. 2001. Taking on the E-HR plunge. *HR magazine*, 46(9):97–103; MEADE, J. 2001. Dot-com fall out. *HR magazine*, 46(9):86–93.

27. CHAMINE, S. 1998. Making your intranet an effective HR tool. *HR focus*, December:12.

28. STONE, D. L., STONE-ROMERO, E. F. & LUKASZEWSKI, K. 2003. The functional and dysfunctional consequences of human resource information technology for organisations and their employees. (*In* Stone, D. L. (Ed.). *Advances in human performance and cognitive engineering research*. Greenwich, CT: JAI Press:37–68.)

29. STONE, D. L., LUKASZEWSKI, K. M. & ISENHOUR, L. C. 2005. E-recruiting: online strategies for attracting talent. (*In* Gueutal, H. G. & Stone, D. L. (Eds). *The brave new world of E-HR*. San Francisco: Jossey Bass, an imprint from John Wiley & Sons:22–53.)

30. COBER, R. T., BROWN, D. J., LEVY, P. E., KEEPING, L. M. & COBER, A. L. 2003. Organisational websites: website content and style as determinants of organisational attraction. *International journal of selection and assessment*, 11:158–169.

31. HARRIS, M. M., VAN HOYE, G. & LIEVENS, F. 2003. Privacy and attitudes toward internet-based selection systems: a cross-cultural comparison.

International journal of selection and assessment,
11:230–236.

32. STONE, D. L., LUKASZEWSKI, K. M. & ISENHOUR, L. C. 2005. E-recruiting: online strategies for attracting talent. (*In* Gueutal, H. G. & Stone, D. L. (Eds). *The brave new world of E-HR.* San Francisco: Jossey Bass, an imprint from John Wiley & Sons:48–49.)

33. KEHOE, J. F., DICKTER, D. N., RUSSELL, D. P. & SACCO, J. M. 2005. E-selection. (*In* Gueutal, H. G. & Stone, D. L. (Eds). *The brave new world of E-HR.* San Francisco: Jossey Bass, an imprint from John Wiley & Sons.)

34. SALAS, E., DE ROUIN, R. E. & L. LITTRELL, L. N. 2005. Research-based guidelines for designing distance learning: what we know so far. (*In* Gueutal, H. G. & Stone, D. L. (Eds). *The brave new world of E-HR.* San Francisco: Jossey Bass, an imprint from John Wiley & Sons:104–137.)

35. CASIO, W. F. 2006. *Managing human resources: Productivity, quality of work life, profits* 7th ed. New York: McGraw-Hill:286–288.

36. BRAY, T. 2006. The training design manual. London: Kogan-Page:237–238.

37. SWART, J., MANN, C., BROWN, S. & PRICE, A. 2005. *Human resource development: Strategy and tactics.* Oxford: Elsevier Butterworth-Heinemann:297.

38. SILBERMAN, M. 2006. *Active training: A handbook of techniques, designs, case examples and tips* 3rd ed. San Francisco: Pfeiffer, an imprint of John Wiley:191.

39. CASIO, W. F. 2006. *Managing human resources: Productivity, quality of work life, profits* 7th ed. New York: McGraw-Hill:285.

40. DRISCOLL, M. 2002. *Web-based training: Designing e-learning experiences.* San Francisco: Jossey Bass/Pfeiffer:6.

41. WILCOCK, L. 2002. E-learning – promises and pitfalls. *Open learning today.* British Association for Open Learning. [Online.] Available: www.baol.org.uk. 11 July 2007:52.

42. NOE, R. A. & SIMMERING, M. J. 2002. Training and development in virtual organisations. (*In* Heneman,

R. L. & Greenberger, D. B. (Eds). *Human resource management in virtual organisations.* Greenwich, Connecticut: Information Age Publishing:189.)

43. MATHIS, R. L. & JACKSON, J. H. 2003. *Human resource management* 10th ed. Mason, Ohio: South Western a division of Thomson Learning.

44. CARDY, R. L. & MILLER, J. S. 2005. EHR and performance management: a consideration of positive potential and the dark side. (*In* Gueutal, H. G. & Stone, D. L. (Eds). *The brave new world of E-HR.* San Francisco: Jossey Bass, an imprint from John Wiley & Sons:138–165.)

45. Ibid.

46. Ibid.

47. Ibid.:145.

48. Ibid.:142.

49. Ibid.:151.

50. Ibid.:147.

51. Ibid.:148.

52. Ibid.:148.

53. Ibid.:148.

54. Ibid.:149.

55. ADAMS, J. T. III. 1995. Four performance packages add ease and speed to evaluations. *HR magazine,* 40:151–155.

56. Ibid.:154.

57. DULEBOHN, J. H. & MARLER, J. H. 2005. E-compensation: the potential to transform practice? (*In* Gueutal, H. G. & Stone, D. L. (Eds). *The brave new world of E-HR.* San Francisco: Jossey Bass, an imprint from John Wiley & Sons:166–189.)

58. Ibid.:167.

59. Ibid.:167.

60. Ibid.:171.

61. Ibid.:172.

62. Ibid.:173.

63. Ibid.:176.

64. Ibid.:184.

11

Change management and building the learning organisation

Learning outcomes

After reading this chapter you should be able to:

▶ Identify the forces that trigger change in organisations
▶ Describe the barriers to organisational change and how to overcome them
▶ Specify three important steps to follow to implement change successfully within organisations
▶ Discuss the role of the learning organisation and its benefits to all stakeholders
▶ Describe the five subsystems within a learning organisation
▶ Identify the role of the chief learning officer (CLO) within an organisation

Purpose

The purpose of this chapter is to introduce you to the concept of change management and to discuss how to establish a learning organisation to enhance change on a continuing basis.

Chapter overview

This chapter starts by looking at the causes (triggers) of organisational change. It then considers the barriers to change and makes some recommendations on how to overcome these barriers. It proposes the use of a model known as 'The Strategic Organisational Change (SOC) framework', with a view to implementing change within organisations successfully. Thereafter it considers the establishment of a learning organisation. It addresses the characteristics and benefits of this type of organisation and also considers a model managers can use to establish such an organisation; it discusses the role of the CLO in this regard. The concluding case study illustrates how the theory contained in this chapter can be applied practically to companies.

Introduction

It is clear from looking at the numerous new developments within the HRM field thus far discussed in this text that the twenty-first century belongs to human resources and organisational capabilities. According to Sims[1], the quality of people and their engagement will increasingly be key factors in organisational vitality, survival, and growth. If HRM is to play a meaningful role within organisations and to continue to make a significant contribution to the bottom line, it will need to make numerous changes to its traditional role. But how does change impact on the human resources of an organisation and affect the HRM contribution? The scenario in the box below provides an example to illustrate this point[2].

A major financial institution has identified improved customer service as a key strategic thrust required for survival in an increasingly competitive market. The company is undertaking various change initiatives aimed at building a customer centric organisation such as implementing leading edge call-centre technology, introducing Internet banking and re-engineering business processes to increase efficiency and focus on the customer.

SOURCE: BOTHA, J-A. & GROBLER, P. 2006. *Only study guide for strategic and international human resource management (AAHR01–F) for the advanced programme in human resource management.* Pretoria: Centre for Business Management, University of South Africa:141.

From this scenario, it is clear that these changes have a direct impact on how HRM will have to operate in future. Thus, HRM will also need to undergo changes to support these new company initiatives. The actions on the HRM side may, for example, range from mere improvements in existing processes without significant reference to the strategic focus of the organisation (e.g. redesigning the performance-appraisal cycle and process) to multifaceted large-scale initiatives aimed at supporting changes in the business strategy (e.g. culture change or restructuring in support of the company's strategy). How can HRM then address these new initiatives required from it? Effecting these changes successfully requires HRM to adopt some change-management principles. However, although change in today's world is inevitable, the rate of success reported in the literature seems to be low, as the following examples illustrate[3]:

- One-half to two-thirds of major corporate change initiatives are deemed failures[4]
- Less than 40 per cent of change efforts produce positive change[5]
- Eighty per cent of mergers are considered unsuccessful after five years[6]
- One-third of major change efforts either do not work or actually make the situation worse[7]
- Only five per cent of companies undertaking significant organisational change avoided substantial disruptions and finished on time.[8]

To address these issues, this chapter will focus on change management principles, the creation of the learning organisation, and the role of the chief learning officer (CLO).

11.1 Change management

As the introduction indicated, change is inevitable if a company is to remain competitive in the turbulent business environment of today. This change also impacts on the HRM approach within a company. The question thus is: what triggers change within an organisation?

11.1.1 The triggers to organisational change

The literature identifies a range of triggers to organisational change. According to Dawson[9], these triggers can come from within and outside the organisation. The author identifies the following internal and external triggers resulting in organisational change:

- *Internal triggers to change.* These include the following:
  - › *Technology.* The term 'technology' can

be used broadly here to refer to the use of new machinery and tools and the associated way in which managers design work within organisations to produce goods and services.

> *The changing nature of customers.* The needs of consumers change constantly, necessitating new products and services.

> *People.* New HRM initiatives such as team-based working arrangements necessitate the retraining and multi-skilling of employees.

> *Administrative structures.* Managers need to undertake the restructuring of administrative processes and the redefining of authority relationships to accommodate new work practices.

• *External triggers to change.* These include the following:

> *Political.* Government laws and regulations – e.g. employment laws, pricing regulations etc. – can impact on an organisation.

> *Economic.* No business functions in isolation, and economic growth, interest rates, and the level of unemployment can impact on the way business is conducted. The internationalisation of business can also have a major impact on how business is conducted.

> *Social.* Organisations consist of people, and changes in their lifestyle can impact on how they are managed. Other issues of importance here are population growth, age distribution of the population, and leisure interests.

> *Technological.* The rate of technological developments can also impact on organisations – e.g. the computerisation of business processes etc.

It is clear that change is not a one-off process but is instead a continuous process taking an organisation from its present state to a future state. The scale of change, as well as its scope, differs from organisation to organisation. Identifying the triggers of change and implementing processes to address them should suffice. Why then is change often so unsuccessful? In the next section we shall discuss the issue of why change is often unsuccessful.

11.1.2 Barriers to organisational change

In answering the question posed above, the literature indicates that individuals and organisations are not inherently resistant to change.[10] They put up barriers only when they perceive the change to be threatening. They therefore react to the threat and not to the change. Whether they perceive change as threatening or not will depend on the way managers introduce it. According to Gilley and Gilley[11], common barriers to change have their roots in three main areas, namely:

• The organisational system (structure, policies, procedures etc.)
• Leadership and management (philosophies, capabilities, and actions)
• The human dimension.

Table 11.1 indicates common barriers these three main areas exhibit.

The 'human dimension' column in Table 11.1 lists 'inherent human resistance to change' as a barrier. Eccles (as quoted in Dawson[12]) identifies the following 13 possible causes of resistance from employees:

• Failure to understand the problem
• Dislike of a solution because an alternative is preferred
• A feeling that the proposed solution will not work
• Unacceptable personal costs of the change
• Insufficient rewards
• Fear of being unable to cope with the new situation
• Threatened destruction of existing social arrangements by the change
• Erosion of sources of influence and control
• Repellent new values and practices
• Low level of willingness to change
• Suspicious view of management's motives for change
• Higher value placed on other interests than on the new proposals
• Reduced power and reduced career opportunities.

Table 11.1 Common barriers to change

System Barriers	Leadership/Management Barriers	Human Dimension Barriers
Differing organisation values.	Inability or unwillingness to handle resistance when it occurs.	Inherent human resistance to change.
Dysfunctional culture.	Lack of skill or ability necessary to effectively implement change.	Lack of skill or ability necessary to effectively implement change.
Organisational immune system.		
Supervisors/managers attempt to change employees when, in fact, the system may need changing.	Poor or short-term leadership.	
	The change is ill-conceived (e.g., seen as a quick fix or as a solution to a symptom – not to the actual problem).	Faulty assumptions regarding change.
Ineffective policies or procedures.		
Employees are not involved in the decision-making.	Lack of management support or commitment to change.	
The change initiative team isn't communicating appropriately.	Lack of trust between management and employees.	
	No one is in charge or accountable.	
Insufficient resources (human, technical, financial, etc.) to support the change.	Differing organisational values.	
	Lack of agreed-upon organisational vision, mission, or strategy.	
Internal conflict over resources.	Dysfunctional culture.	
	Faulty assumptions regarding change.	
	Few leaders or managers understand the complexities of the change process, implementation techniques, or human reactions to change.	
	The change is poorly implemented (e.g., lacks structure, planning, resources, etc.).	
	Organisations fail to identify and mitigate potential barriers (including people) to the change.	
	Supervisors/managers attempt to change employees when, in fact, the system may need changing.	
	Managers and executives are often powerful resistors while employees are often blamed.	
	Employees are not involved in the decision-making.	
	The change initiative team isn't communicating appropriately.	
	Lack of consequences for inadequate performance.	
	Lack of rewards for change.	
	The change is conceived, implemented, and managed from a purely technical stance and without understanding of the human influence on its success or failure.	
	Insufficient resources (human, technical, financial, etc.) to support the change.	
	Internal conflict over resources.	

SOURCE: GILLEY, A. & GILLEY, J. W. 2007. Organisational development and change. (*In* Sims, R. R. (Ed.). *Human resource management: Contemporary issues, challenges and opportunities.* Charlotte, North Carolina: Information Age Publishing:509–510.) Used with permission.

Symptoms of resistance to change include the following:

- Withdrawal
- Aggression
- Arguing
- Negativity
- Blaming
- Gossip
- Slowdown of work
- Sabotage of the change effort
- Increased absenteeism.[13]

Having identified the barriers to change, an organisation's next step is to implement interventions to overcome them. In the next section we shall discuss this step.

11.1.3 **Overcoming barriers to change**[14]

As Table 11.1 indicates, there are barriers to change in at least three main areas within an organisation. Thus, managers need to devise interventions or strategies to address these issues if an organisation is to survive and thrive over the long term. Table 11.2 shows strategies Gilley and Gilley identify for leaders, managers, and HRM professionals to overcome these obstacles to change.

There is no doubt, as the discussion of these strategies suggests, that the HR professional plays a vital role in this regard. Table 11.2 also makes it clear that change managers need certain skills if they are to function effectively and efficiently. These can include social

Table 11.2 Overcoming barriers to change

Enhance your skills.	Increase your understanding of and skills in change implementation and techniques, including the human factor.
Determine what should be changed.	Strategy, structure, culture, systems, or people? Ensure that the focus on the change is needed and appropriate.
Create a context for change.	Sell the change. Help others understand why change is needed, who it will benefit, and consequences of failure to change.
Know your people.	What is his/her predisposition to change? How will he/she react and why? Which fears are rational? What coping skills does he/she possess? How will he/she personally benefit from the change?
Model the change.	Honestly support, champion, and live the change.
Remove obstacles in the system.	Identify and eliminate obstacles embedded within organisational policies, procedures, people, and structure.
Understand and plan for resistance.	Understand that change is difficult. Identify and address the root cause of reasons for an individual's resistance. Engage him/her in that area. Channel passions constructively.
Involve people at all levels in all stages of change.	From design to implementation to evaluation, involvement and participation lead to commitment. Employee involvement only in the implementation stage contributes to failure of the initiative.
Communicate, communicate, communicate.	Provide those impacted by the change with routine, sufficient information at all stages. Encourage questions and act on feedback.
Provide support.	Provide resources, allow mistakes, protect/defend your people when necessary.
Reward change efforts.	Recognize and reward individuals, groups, and departments for their efforts (even if initially unsuccessful).
Create a culture of organisational development and change.	Engage in the above actions routinely; live continuous, incremental, beneficial change.

SOURCE: GILLEY, A. & GILLEY, J. W. 2007. Organisational development and change. (*In* Sims, R. R. (Ed.). *Human resource management: Contemporary issues, challenges and opportunities*. Charlotte, North Carolina: Information Age Publishing:512.) Used with permission.

relationship skills, communication skills, persuasive skills, presentation skills, problem-solving skills, and planning skills.[15] According to Higgs and Rowland[16], managers should also possess the following eight change-management competencies in order to be successful:

- Change initiation
- Change impact
- Change facilitation
- Change leadership
- Change learning
- Change execution
- Change presence
- Change technology.

Thus far, we have addressed the following issues pertaining to organisational change: the triggers that initiate change, barriers to organisational change, and interventions and strategies for overcoming the barriers to change. The following question now arises: how can change actually be successfully implemented within an organisation? This will be the focus of the next section.

11.1.4 A strategic organisational change (SOC) framework

Leading change within organisations is extremely difficult. However, change is inevitable for ongoing organisational success. Clearly, an organisation needs some form of framework to drive this process successfully. Having looked at numerous frameworks or models presented in the literature, we have decided to examine more closely the framework or model developed by Auster, Wylie, and Valente and discussed in their book *Strategic organisational change: Building change capabilities in your organisation.*[17] This framework or model covers all the aspects of change, from building commitment, to leveraging what is already working well, to navigating the politics and emotions of change, to working through the implementation details and inspiring ongoing learning (the focus of the next section).

The framework in Figure 11.1 distils nine different dimensions of change to address the three essential questions of any change, namely:

- Where are we now?
- What do we need to change?
- How will we implement those changes and build in dynamism?

We shall now briefly discuss these three questions.

- *Where are we now?*[18] Working from left to right in Figure 11.1, this is the first question posed. Organisations can answer this question by doing two things: firstly, continuously assess the external environment, and secondly, understand the present state of the organisation, e.g. identify what is working well and what not. (For a discussion of issues in the external environment, see section 11.1.1 above.) This process will help the company establish whether it is still in line with what is going on outside the organisation. As far as the internal organisation is concerned, managers need to establish what is working well so that they do not tamper with this during the change process. They need to analyse operational dimensions such as strategy, leadership, structure, HR practices, physical layout, technology, and culture (see Figure 11.1).
- *What changes do we need to make?*[19] This is the second question. From the previous discussion, it is clear that one of the changes will involve solving the present problems in the organisation. However, besides doing this, managers also need to position the organisation for future success. As Figure 11.1 indicates, each of the various dimensions from strategy to leadership to structure can reveal an array of possible changes which it might make sense to pursue. Once managers have generated a range of possible alternatives, they can evaluate each one to find the optimal path for change.
- *How are we going to implement these changes and build in dynamism?*[20] This question addresses the issue of implementation. Here managers need to

Figure 11.1 The strategic organisational change (SOC) framework

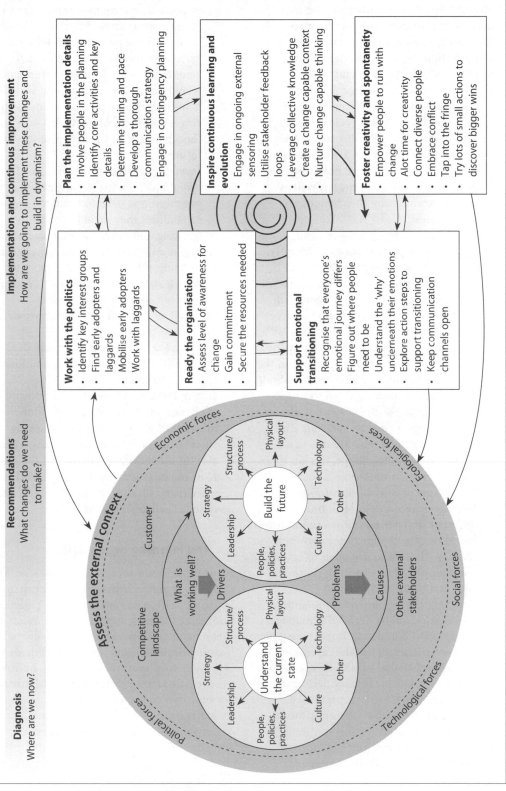

SOURCE: AUSTER, E. R., WYLIE, K. K. & VALENTE, M. S. 2005. *Strategic organizational change: Building change capabilities in your organisation*. Houndmills: Palgrave Macmillan:176. Used with permission.

attempt everything from ensuring the necessary resources and commitment to navigating the political dynamics of the organisation. Some of the steps in this process include the following:

> *Getting ready for change.* Readying the organisation for change involves securing the necessary resources needed for the process or finding ways to work with limited resources. It also means involving all parties and obtaining the commitment of all parties as well as understanding why the changes are being made.

> *Working with the politics of change.* Different people see things differently. For this reason, people will try and push their agendas they see fit. This will inevitably result in the emergence of politics. To ensure successful change, managers need to work effectively with the political dynamics in the company. Identifying influential people within the organisation who are also excited about the change, and using them to propel the change forward, is essential. Besides this, managers need to make an effort to convince those who are not so sure of the value of the change, to gain their commitment as well.

> *Supporting emotional transitioning.* Managers need to establish how different individuals in the organisation feel about the change. They can then leverage those who are open to change and help the others to work on their personal barriers to change.

> *Planning the implementation details.* The change can be derailed if managers do not plan it in detail. Important issues here for managers to take care of are the pacing and timing of the change, who will be responsible for key deliverables, how the changes will impact on customers, and what communication channels are used.

> *Fostering creativity and spontaneity.* Although the details of change is

important, managers do not have to plan for everything. Effective change leaders let the people work with the various elements of change, which can sometimes result in unexpected positive results. This type of approach will also help to develop a passion amongst the employees for change, which will be to the advantage of the organisation in the future.

> *Inspiring continuous learning and evolution.* To achieve continued success, organisations have to build the ongoing capabilities they need for continuous learning and evolution. Successful organisations continuously engage in ongoing external scanning, develop strong stakeholder-feedback loops, and leverage collective knowledge.

We shall address this issue in more detail in the next section.

From the above discussion it is clear that the SOC framework offers a unique approach to change. It enables the stakeholders both to see the complexity of change and to work through all the different facets necessary for achieving success, not only for current change, but also for the inevitable changes of the future. How organisations use the framework will depend on the specific situations and change challenges they face.

11.2 **The learning organisation**

As the previous section indicates, change-capable organisations inspire continuous learning. These organisations are generally known as learning organisations. What does this mean and how can organisations become learning organisations? We shall address these issues in this section. However, before we proceed, it is important first to distinguish between two concepts in the literature, namely 'organisation learning' and 'the learning organisation'. According to Mabey, Salaman, and Storey[20]:

- The term 'the learning organisation' is used to characterise an enterprise in which learning is open-ended, takes place at all levels, and is self-questioning
- 'Organisation learning' is a descriptive device to explain and quantify learning activities and events taking place within an organisation.

Thus, one critical distinction between an organisation that learns and the learning organisation seems to be that in the latter, individual leaning activities feed and integrate with broader and deeper learning processes in the organisation, while this is not the case with organisation learning. What, then, are the characteristics of a learning organisation and does a learning organisation have any benefits for its stakeholders?

11.2.1 Characteristics and benefits of a learning organisation

According to Marquardt[21], the learning organisation possesses the ability to adapt, renew and revitalise itself continuously in response to the changing environment – a vital component for organisational change, which we discussed earlier. Marquardt identifies the following characteristics of such an organisation:

- Learning is accomplished by the organisation as a whole
- Employees within the organisation recognise the importance of current and future success of ongoing learning
- Learning is a continuous, strategically used process that is integrated and runs parallel to work
- There is a focus on creativity and generative learning in the organisation
- Systems thinking is fundamental in a learning organisation
- The organisational climate encourages, rewards, and accelerates individual and group learning
- Employees network in an innovative manner that resembles a community both inside and outside the organisation
- Everyone is driven by a desire for quality and continuous improvement
- Employees have uninterrupted access to information and data.[22]

Having all these characteristics present in an integrated whole provides benefits for an organisations stakeholders. Table 11.3 shows some of the benefits of a learning organisation.

11.2.2 Building a learning organisation

Clearly, becoming a learning organisation is absolutely a prerequisite if an organisation is to

Table 11.3 Benefits of a learning organisation

• Anticipate and adapt more readily to environmental influences
• Accelerate the development of new products, processes and services
• Become more proficient at learning from competitors and collaborators
• Expedite the transfer of knowledge from one part of the organisation to another
• Learn more effectively from its mistakes
• Make greater use of employees at all levels of the organisation
• Shorten the time required to implement strategic changes
• Stimulate continuous improvement in all areas of the organisation
• Attract the best workers
• Increase worker commitment and creativity

SOURCE: MARQUARDT, M. J. 2002. *Building the learning organisation: Mastering the five elements for corporate learning.* Palo Alto, C.A.: Davies-Black Publishing:32. Used with permission.

remain competitive. But moving from a non-learning organisation to a learning organisation is no simple task. It requires, amongst other things, cooperation between numerous stakeholders. It also needs a person to oversee the process. This person is normally known as a chief learning officer (CLO) (see Section 11.3). But how can companies then move from a non-learning mode to become a learning organisation? To answer this question, we shall look at the 'Systems learning organisation model' developed by Marquardt and discussed in his book *Building the learning organisation: Mastering the five elements for corporate learning*.[23] Thousands of companies around the world have successfully adopted this model, which is practical and workable. The model consists of five related subsystems (see Figure 11.2). These are learning, organisation, people, knowledge, and technology.[24] (Note that all five of the subsystems are necessary to sustain a viable ongoing learning organisation.) As Figure 11.2 shows, the subsystems within the model consist of a number of elements/components. We shall briefly discuss each of these by referring to Figure 11.2.

- *The learning subsystem*[25]. At the core of the learning organisation is learning. Learning can occur at three levels, namely:
  - › *Individual level.* This refers to changes

Figure 11.2 The learning organisation model

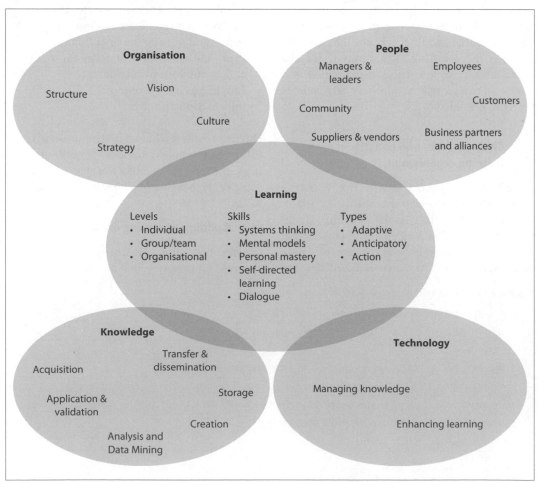

SOURCE: Adapted from MARQUARDT, M. J. 2002. *Building the learning organisation: Mastering the five elements for corporate learning*. Palo Alto, C.A.: Davies-Black Publishing:24–31. Used with permission.

in skills, insights, knowledge, attitudes, and values acquired through self-study.

> *Group or team level.* Group or team learning involves an increase in knowledge, skills, and competencies accomplished by and within groups.

> *Organisational level.* Organisational learning is the enhanced intellectual and productive capability gained through commitment.

A learning organisation develops the capacity to encourage and maximise learning on all three levels. Besides these levels of learning, there are three types of learning, namely:

> *Adaptive learning.* This happens when people reflect on past experiences and then modify future actions.

> *Anticipatory learning.* This involves acquiring knowledge from envisioning various futures and determining ways to achieve that future.

> *Action learning.* This involves reflecting on reality on a present, real-time basis, and applying the knowledge in developing individuals, groups, and the organisation.

Note that these types of learning are not exclusive of one another, but that an individual, group or organisation may employ more than one type at the same time.[26] As Figure 11.2 shows, besides the levels and types of learning, five key skills are also needed for initiating and maximising learning within a company if it is to attain ultimate business success. These five key skills are:

> *Systems thinking.* This is a conceptual framework to make full patterns clearer and determine how to change them.

> *Mental models.* These are deeply ingrained assumptions that influence people's views and actions in the world.

> *Personal mastery.* This indicates a high level of proficiency in a subject or skill area.

> *Self-directed learning.* Everybody is aware of, and enthusiastically accepts

responsibility for, being a learner.

> *Dialogue.* This denotes a high level of listening and communication between people.[27]

Other important issues here, but not shown in the model, are:

> The speed of learning (how quickly the organisation is able to complete each learning cycle)

> The depth of learning (the degree of learning the organisation achieves at the end of the cycle)

> The breadth of learning (how extensively the organisation is able to transfer the new insights and knowledge).[28]

Thus, for the learning component to make a contribution to the company, the following needs to be done:

> Develop modular, reuseable learning content

> Increase the ability to learn how to learn

> Develop the discipline of organisational dialogue

> Design career-development plans for employability

> Establish self-development programmes

> Build team learning skills

> Encourage and practise systems thinking

> Utilise scanning and scenario planning

> Expand multicultural and global mindsets and learning

> Change the mental model of learning.[29]

• *The organisation subsystem.* This is the setting within which the learning process occurs. To change to the new focus, a company's structure and strategies must change dramatically.

Four components can be distinguished here, namely[30]:

> *Vision.* The vision encompasses a company's hopes, goals, and direction for the future.

> *Culture.* The culture refers to an organisation's values, beliefs, practices, rituals, and customs.

> *Strategy.* The strategy relates to action,

plans, methodologies, tactics, and steps employed to achieve a company's vision and goals.[31]

> *Structure.* The structure includes a company's departments, levels, and configurations.

Thus, for the organisational component of making a contribution to the process of becoming a learning organisation, the following needs to take place:

> Use future-search conferences to develop a vision
> Gain support from top management
> Create a corporate climate of continuous learning
> Re-engineer policies and structures around learning
> Reward individual and team learning
> Incorporate learning in all policies and procedures
> Establish centres of excellence
> Measure financial and nonfinancial areas as a learning activity
> Create time and space for learning
> Make learning intentional at all times everywhere.[32]

• *The people subsystem.* People are pivotal to learning organisations because only people have the capacity to learn. People are the agents who take information and transform it into valuable knowledge for personal and organisational use.[33] The people subsystem in the learning organisation consists of the following components:

> Managers and leaders that carry out coaching, mentoring, and modelling roles and, therefore, are responsible for enhancing learning opportunities for the people around them
> Employees who are empowered and expected to learn, plan for their future competencies, and take action and risks to solve problems.[34]

The learning organisation also recognises that customers can be a fertile source of information and ideas and thus should be closely linked with the organisation learning systems.[35] Other important external groups include: business partners and alliances that can share their competencies and knowledge, suppliers and vendors, and community groups such as social, educational, and economic agencies that can share in providing and receiving learning.[36]

Strategies for empowering and enabling people within the learning organisation include:

> Encouraging leaders to model and demonstrate learning
> Inviting leaders to champion learning processes and projects
> Empowering employees to learn and produce
> Instituting personnel policies that reward learners
> Creating self-managed work teams
> Balancing learning and development needs
> Encouraging and enhancing customer participation
> Maximising learning from business partners and alliances
> Building long-term learning partnerships with suppliers and vendors
> Providing educational opportunities for the community.[37]

• *The knowledge subsystem.* Companies need knowledge in order to increase their ability to improve products and services.[38] The knowledge subsystem in the learning organisation consists of the following components:

> Acquisition (the collection of existing data and information from inside and outside the organisation)
> Creation (generating new knowledge through a number of different processes)
> Storage (the coding and preservation of the organisation's valued knowledge for easy access by employees at any time)
> Analysis and data mining (analysing data as well as reconstructing, validating, and inventorying it)
> Transfer and dissemination (the movement of information by mechanical, electronic, and interpersonal means)

> Application and validation (the use and assessment of knowledge by members of the organisation).[39]

Thus, for knowledge to play an important role in the learning organisation, the following steps need to be taken:

> Share responsibility for collecting and transferring knowledge
> Systematically capture relevant external knowledge
> Organise internal learning events
> Be creative about thinking and learning
> Encourage and reward innovation
> Train staff in knowledge storage and retrieval
> Maximise knowledge transfer across boundaries
> Develop a knowledge base around organisational values and learning needs
> Create mechanisms for collecting and storing learning
> Transfer classroom learning to on-the-job utilisation.[40]

- *The technology subsystem.* The technology subsystem is made up of supporting integrated technological networks and information tools that enable access to, and exchange information and learning.[41] This subsystem includes technical processes, systems and structures for collaboration, coaching, coordination, and other knowledge skills. It encompasses electronic tools and advanced methods of learning.[42] Two major components here are:
  > *Technology for managing knowledge.* This refers to computer-based technology that gathers, transfers, and codes information.
  > *Technology for enhancing learning.* This involves the utilisation of video, audio, and computer-based multimedia training for the purpose of delivering and developing knowledge and skills.[43]

For technology to play an important role in the learning organisation, the following steps need to be taken:

> Encourage and enable staff to connect to the information highway
> Develop multimedia, technology-based learning centres
> Develop and use a variety of distance-learning technologies
> Use technology to capture internal and external knowledge and ideas
> Acquire and develop competencies in groupware and in self-learning technology
> Install electronic performance-support systems
> Plan and develop a just-in-time learning system
> Build internal courseware technology and capability
> Use intranets for training
> Increase capabilities of management and HR staff.[44]

From the above discussion, it is clear that if it is to become a learning organisation, an organisation needs an understanding of, and commitment to, mobilising all five subsystems of the model. Taking the specific steps to build a learning organisation requires well-orchestrated planning on the part of many people in the organisation.

However, maintaining this new higher level of learning power is perhaps as challenging as initiating the process. Appointing a CLO to oversee this process might well be a good idea. In the next section we shall look more closely at the CLO.[45]

11.3 The chief learning officer (CLO)

In many circles, the rise of the position of CLO, also known as the chief knowledge officer (CKO), as a senior corporate position is seen as a recent phenomenon. General Electric and Coca-Cola, two of the world's major companies, were the first to hire such individuals.[46] These individuals are normally part of the HR departmental structure and report directly to the head of HRM and the CEO of the company[47] (see Box 1 on the next page, entitled 'Help wanted: Chief Knowledge Officer', for an example of an advertisement for a CKO).

The sample advertisement in the box on the next page makes it clear that the CLO (or CKO)

BOX 1: WANTED: Chief Knowledge Officer

Rapidly growing corporation with aggressive expansion goals seeks CKO to manage organisation's intellectual assets to gain competitive advantage. Will report to CEO.

RESPONSIBILITIES: Design and implement a knowledge-learning culture and a knowledge-learning infrastructure. Tie together the information in the corporation's databases, historical records, file cabinets, and intranet, as well as employees' informal knowledge that has yet to be identified or recorded in a systematic way. Draw from external information sources, such as the Internet and public databases. Align and integrate diverse groups and functions in order to leverage knowledge management strategically across the entire corporation. Use technology to support knowledge capture, sharing and retention.

QUALIFICATIONS: Successful candidate must be an evangelist for the value of knowledge sharing among employees. Must have a strong sense of vision and business strategy, and be able to partner with senior managers. Ability to conduct complex strategic needs assessments and use personal influence to IT networks.

SOURCE: BONNER, D. 2000. Enter the chief knowledge officer. *Training & development*, 54(2):39. Used with permission.

plays a vital role in building and sustaining the high-level learning organisation, as we discussed it in the previous section. In the next section we shall discuss the characteristics of such a person.

11.3.1 Characteristics of a chief learning officer

Recent studies have identified a number of characteristics most prevalent for CLOs. For example, knowledge officers[48]:

- Must have circulated through the company and must have developed a holistic perspective
- Must be able to energise the organisation and function as cheerleaders to build momentum behind the knowledge initiatives
- Must be able to withstand a multitude of pressures
- Must feel rewarded by other people's accomplishments
- Must have a good relationship with the head of HRM.

Although the CLO appears to be a rare type of person, the identification, appointment, and training of the CLO is of utmost importance to the company. What is the role of the CLO? We shall discuss this next.

11.3.2 The role of the chief learning officer

The CLO can influence the organisation in several ways (see Table 11.4 on what CLOs do in some of the major companies in the world). One way is rapidly to generate new knowledge, ideas, and solutions to problems throughout the organisation by means of the information technology we mentioned earlier (refer to section 11.2).

In today's highly competitive global environment, the organisation needs knowledge workers more than knowledge workers need the organisation, and the role of the CLO in this process is thus indispensable. The good news is that the number of CLOs continues to grow worldwide.[49]

Table 11.4 What the CKO/CLO does

Roles, responsibilities, and activities	Andersen: Knowledge manager	BP Norway: Knowledge manager	CIA: CKO	Clarica: Other	Entovation: CKO	Enquiva: CLO	Foreign Bank: CKO	IBM (UK): CKO/CLO	Lancaster: Other (CLO)	Luxury Retail: CKO	Mem. Hermann: CLO	Millbrook: CLO	Plante & Moran: Other	SAIC: CLO	Sedgwick: CLO	7 Schools: Other (CLO)	Stock Trade: CKO/CLO	Zerox: CLO
Align/integrate diverse functions or groups	X	X	X	X	X	X	X	X	X	X	X	X	X	X	X	X		X
Best practices/benchmarking (utilized or developed)	X	X	X	X	X	X		X	X	X	X	X	X	X	X	X		X
Business objectives & performance (developed or supported)	X	X	X	X		X		X		X	X	X	X	X	X		X	X
Career planning/staff or professional development	X				X						X	X		X	X			X
Change manager role	X	X	X	X	X	X		X			X	X	X	X	X			X
Communications/build networks/use personal influence	X	X	X	X	X	X		X	X		X	X	X	X				
Continuous and/or consistent learning systems highlighted	X	X	X	X	X	X		X	X		X	X	X	X	X			X
Corporate or in-house universities/learning lab	X				X						X			X	X			
Create/lead expert teams	X	X	X			X		X	X					X	X			X
Culture development for learning and/or knowledge	X	X	X	X	X	X		X			X	X	X		X	X		X
Customer service orientated	X	X	X	X	X	X	X	X	X	X	X	X	X	X	X	X	X	X
Employee orientation programme											X		X		X			
Employee retention/recruitment programmes							X		X				X					
Executive education and/or action learning					X	X			X	X		X						
Financial knowledge management																	X	
Identify critical areas for improvement/needs analyses	X	X	X	X	X	X	X	X	X	X	X	X	X	X	X	X	X	X
Knowledge-content activities (capture, share & retain)	X	X	X	X	X	X	X	X	X	X	X	X	X	X	X	X	X	X
Knowledge-structure (tools, manage infrastructure)	X	X	X	X	X			X		X	X			X			X	X
Leverage corporate-wide learning and/or knowledge	X	X	X	X	X	X	X	X	X	X	X	X	X	X	X	X	X	X
Organisation effectiveness consulting/OD activities	X	X	X			X					X	X	X					
Partnerships with senior management/others	X	X	X	X	X	X			X		X	X	X	X	X	X	X	X
Project management activities		X			X						X	X						X
Sales/marketing/business development	X			X		X					X	X					X	X
Strategic planning & implementation	X	X	X	X	X	X	X		X		X	X	X	X	X			X
Technology for learning/knowledge (developed or supported)	X	X	X		X	X		X			X	X	X	X	X			X
Training & education/ workshops/retreats/meeting leader		X	X	X	X		X	X	X	X	X	X	X	X	X			
Visionary/champion for organisational learning and/or KM	X	X	X	X	X	X	X	X	X	X	X	X	X	X	X			

SOURCE: BONNER, D. 2000. Enter the chief knowledge officer. *Training & development*, 54(2):37. Used with permission.

SUMMARY

This chapter addressed the issues of change management and building the learning organisation. The organisational fight for survival encompasses many fronts and to address these challenges successfully, organisations need to make changes. A planned, ongoing process of change provides a framework through which individuals and their organisations engage in well-planned change initiatives proactively, continuously, slowly, and incrementally. An inherent component of this process is learning.

To obtain and sustain competitive advantage in this new environment, companies will have to learn better and faster from both successes and failures. They will need to transform themselves continuously into learning organisations, to become places in which groups and individuals at all levels continuously engage in new learning processes.

KEY CONCEPTS

• Barriers to change	• Planning skills
• Change management	• Presentation skills
• Chief knowledge officer (CKO)	• Problem-solving skills
• Chief learning officer (CLO)	• Social-relationship skills
• Communication skills	• Strategic organisational change (SOC) framework
• Learning organisation	• Systems learning organisational model
• Organisation learning	• Triggers for change
• Persuasive skills	

CASE STUDY

Objective: To understand the HR role in the reengineering process within and organisation

The role of HR in re-engineering and change at Siemens Rolm

Siemens Rolm Communications, based in Goodwood, Cape Town, is an operating company for Siemens, the electrical- and electronics-systems supplier. Rolm, which employs 5 800 people, was previously owned by IBM, but in 2000, when the company was losing money, IBM sold Rolm. As the new owners, executives at Siemens were determined to turn the company around, but they realised that to do so would require a lot of changes. Because Siemens is a knowledge-based company, it had to restructure itself as a learning organisation to stay competitive in the new business environment.

To start the change process, Bonnie Hatchcock, Chief Director of HRM, put together a team of managers to design a new appraisal process. The new system raised the bar on performance and encouraged employee self-development. The company CEO, Karl Geng, was committed to tracking appraisals of key players. The company also worked on a cultural transformation that emphasised speed, guts, and dramatic moves. More than 60 managers – in small groups across South Africa – attended a two-day 'world class management institute' development conference that reinforced the message. Finally, the company re-engineered its pay and rewards policies. HRM carved out a portion of the merit budget pool to award to employees who had advanced their skills in the previous period. In addition, the new flexible rewards programme was instituted to allow managers to award up to R10 000 to employees who 'go the extra five miles'.

As the company is evolving into a learning organisation, HRM itself is becoming a new creature, one that brings Siemens Rolm's bid for excellence to fruition. Hatchcock asks HRM people to work on three skills: business mastery, change and process mastery, and personal credibility. To accomplish this, HR has torn down the 'silos' between staffing, training, compensation, and the like and reorganised into five business-driven teams. The Strategy and Design team studies Siemens Rolm's business plans and sets HRM strategies that complement those plans. The Consulting Services group helps influence the company's culture and decides how best to deploy people to meet HRM goals. The HR Programme Integration area ensures that HR managers clone their expertise across the company, so it can maintain its own best practices system. The Education division assists with employee development and the HR Service Centre handles employees' day-to-day administrative HRM questions.

According to Bonnie Hatchcock, 'We can't just think of ourselves as support. We have to be right out there.' These efforts, taken together, have helped turn the company around, and, in 2006, the company won the IPM's Award for Managing Change.

Questions and activities

1. How can HRM practices help Siemens Rolm become a learning organisation?
2. What other methods might help the HRM organisation develop the competencies it needs?
3. What problems, if any, do you see in the Siemens Rolm change strategy?

SOURCE: Adapted from SHERMAN, A., BOHLANDER, G. & SNELL, S. 1998. *Managing human resources* 11th ed. Cincinnati, Ohio: International Thomson Publishing – South Western College Publishing:34 35. Used with permission.

REVIEW QUESTIONS AND ACTIVITIES

1. Provide examples of internal and external triggers to organisational change. 2. Common barriers to change can be rooted in three main areas. Briefly discuss. 3. List a number of possible causes for employees resisting change in companies. 4. What are typical symptoms of resistance to change, from an employee's perspective? 5. Write an essay on how to overcome barriers to change within organisations. 6. Auster, Wylie, and Valente have designed a strategic organisational change (SOC) framework to assist companies in the successful implementation of change.	Write a short essay on this framework by referring to the three questions posed in the framework. 7. Distinguish between the concepts 'organisation learning' and the 'learning organisation'. 8. List nine characteristics of a learning organisation. 9. Briefly discuss the 'Systems Learning Organisation Model' developed by Marquardt, by referring to the five subsystems of the model. 10. Write a short essay on the CLO found in many organisations today.

FURTHER READING

AUSTER, E. R., WYLIE, K. K. & VALENTE, M. S. 2005. *Strategic organizational change: Building change capabilities in your organisation.* Houndmills: Palgrave MacMillan.

MARQUARDT, M. J. 2002. *Building the learning organisation: Mastering the five elements for corporate learning* 2nd ed. Palo Alto: Davies-Black Publishing.

ELKELES, T. & PHILLIPS, J. 2007. *The chief learning officer: Driving value within a changing organisation through learning and development.* Burlington, M.A.: Butterworth-Heinemann an imprint of Elsevier.

WEB SITES

www.solonline.org/ – Society for Organisational Learning: provides info on various issues pertaining to learning

www.tipp.co.za/training_change_management.htm – Company providing change-management training

ENDNOTES

1. SIMS, R. R. (Ed). 2007. *Human resource management: Contemporary issues, challenges and opportunities.* Charlotte, North Carolina: Information Age Publishing:IX.
2. BOTHA, J-A. & GROBLER, P. 2006. *Only study guide for strategic and international human resource management (AAHR01–F) for the advanced programme in human resource management.* Pretoria: Centre for Business Management, University of South Africa:141.
3. GILLEY, A. & GILLEY, J. W. 2007. Organisational development and change. (*In* Sims, R. R. (Ed.). *Human resource management: Contemporary issues, challenges and opportunities.* Charlotte, North Carolina: Information Age Publishing:495.)
4. BEER, M. & NOHRIA, N. 2000. *Breaking the code of change.* Boston, Massachusetts: Harvard Business School Press.
5. PORRAS, J. I. & ROBERTSON, P. J. 1983. Organisation development: theory, practice and research. (*In* Dunnette, M. D. & Hough, L. M.

(Eds). *The handbook of industrial and organisational psychology*, (3). Palo Alto, C.A.: Consulting Psychologist Press:719–822.)
6. GILLEY, A. & GILLEY, J. W. 2007. Organisational development and change. (*In* Sims, R. R. (Ed.). *Human resource management: Contemporary issues, challenges and opportunities.* Charlotte, North Carolina: Information Age Publishing:495.)
7. BEER, M., EISENSTAT, R. A. & SPECTOR, B. 1990. Why change programmes don't produce change. *Harvard business review*, 68(6):158–166.
8. JOHNSON-CRAMER, M. E., PARISE, S. & CROSS, R. L. 2007. Managing change through networks and values. *California management review*, 49(3):85–109.
9. DAWSON, P. 2004. *Understanding organisational change: The contemporary experience of people at work.* London: Sage Publications; JOHNSON-CRAMER, M. E., PARISE, S. & CROSS, R. L. 2007. Managing change through networks and values. *California management review*, 49(3):85–109; NOLAN, S. 2007. The tricky business of change

management. *Strategic HR review*, 6(3 ():2, March/
April; YARBERRY, W. A. 2007. Effective change
management: ensuring alignment of IT and business
functions. *Information systems security*, 16:80–89;
SCALZO, N. J. 2006. Memory loss? Corporate
knowledge and radical change. *Journal of business
strategy*, 27(4):60–67.

10. CARNALL, C. A. 2003. *The change management
toolkit*. London: Thomson Learning:2.

11. GILLEY, A. & GILLEY, J. W. 2007. Organisational
development and change. (*In* Sims, R. R. (Ed.).
*Human resource management: Contemporary issues,
challenges and opportunities*. Charlotte, North
Carolina: Information Age Publishing:509.)

12. DAWSON, P. 2004. *Understanding organisational
change: The contemporary experience of people at
work*. London: Sage Publications:19.

13. GILLEY, A. & GILLEY, J. W. 2007. Organisational
development and change. (*In* Sims, R. R. (Ed.).
*Human resource management: Contemporary issues,
challenges and opportunities*. Charlotte, North
Carolina: Information Age Publishing:504.)

14. This section is based on GILLEY, A. & GILLEY, J.
W. 2007. Organisational development and change.
(*In* Sims, R. R. (Ed.). *Human resource management:
Contemporary issues, challenges and opportunities*.
Charlotte, North Carolina: Information Age
Publishing:511–513.) See also SIRKIN, H. L.,
KEENAN, P. & JACKSON, A. 2005. The hard side
of change management. *Harvard business review*,
October:109–118; HUGHES, M. 2007. The tools
and techniques of change management. *Journal of
change management*, 7(1):37–49; GRAVELLS, J.
2006. The myth of change management: a reflection
on personal change and its lessons for leadership
development. *Human resource development
international*, 9(2):283–289; WINDSOR, P.
2007. Successful change management. *The AIIM
guide to ECM purchasing*:82–84: GREENER, T.
& HUGHES, M. 2006. Managing change before
change management. *Strategic change*, 15:205–212;
BOGAARD, L. 2006. How to align employees'
behaviour during change management programs.
Business communicator:10–11; WOODWARD, N. H.
2007. To make changes, manage them. *HR magazine*,
52(5):63–67.

15. CARNALL, C. A. 2003. *The change management
toolkit*. London: Thomson Learning:107–113.

16. HIGGS, M. & ROWLAND, D. 2000. Building
change leadership capability: the quest for change
competence. *Journal of change management*,
1(2):116–134.

17. AUSTER, E. R., WYLIE, K. K. & VALENTE, M. S.
2005. *Strategic organizational change: Building change
capabilities in your organisation*. Houndmills: Palgrave
MacMillan:176. Used with permission.

18. Ibid.:9.

19. Ibid.:11.

20. Ibid.:11–13. See also KOTTER, J. P. 2007. Leading
change: why transformation efforts fail. *Harvard
business review*, January:96–103; LEYBOURNE,
S. A. 2006. Managing change by abandoning
planning and embracing improvisation. *Journal
of general management*, 31(3):11–29; MABEY, C.,
SALAMAN, G. & STOREY, J. 1999. *Human resource
management: A strategic introduction* 2nd ed. Oxford:
Blackwell Publishers:312.

21. MARQUARDT, M. J. 2002. *Building the learning
organisation: Mastering the five elements for corporate
learning*. Palo Alto, C.A.: Davies-Black Publishing:31.

22. Ibid.:31–32.

23. Ibid.

24. Ibid.:24.

25. Ibid.:24–25.

26. Ibid.:43.

27. Ibid.:26.

28. Ibid.:54–55.

29. Ibid.:65–72.

30. Ibid.:26.

31. Ibid.:27–28.

32. Ibid.:104–109.

33. Ibid.:111.

34. Ibid.:112–120.

35. Ibid.:123.

36. Ibid.:124–126.

37. Ibid.:132–137.

38. Ibid.:139.

39. Ibid.:30.

40. Ibid.:170–175.

41. Ibid.:177.

42. Ibid.

43. Ibid.:31.

44. Ibid.:204–208.

45. Ibid.:209.

46. MARTINEZ, M. N. 1998. The collective power.
HR magazine, February:88. See also ELKELES, T.
& PHILLIPS, J. 2007. *The chief learning officer*.
Oxford: Butterworth Heinemann – an imprint from
Elsevier:ix.

47. Ibid.:90. See also SARVARY, M. 1999. Knowledge
management and competition in the consulting
industry. *California management review*,
41(2):95–107, Winter.

48. DAINTRY, D. 1998. Knowledge champions. *UMI
article*, 12(4), November. Clearing-house number
1639500:1. See also ARGOTE, L. & INGRAM, P.
2000. Knowledge transfer: a basis for competitive
advantage in firms. *Organisational behaviour and
human decision processes*, 82(1):150–169, May.

49. ELKELES, T. & PHILLIPS, J. 2007. *The chief learning
officer*. Oxford: Butterworth Heinemann – an imprint
from Elsevier:ix. See also KETTER, P. 2006. CLO
path. *Training & development*, August:33–34.

12

Human resource management – An international dimension

Learning outcomes

After reading this chapter you should be able to:

▶ Understand the different issues posed by operating HRM internationally
▶ Discuss some of the underlying academic debates in international human resource management (IHRM)
▶ Debate the duality raised by the simultaneous need for standardisation and localisation of HRM
▶ Identify some of the new features of IHRM that are changing the way organisations operate
▶ Understand the way in which organisations manage international transfers of employees

Purpose

The purpose of this chapter is to introduce you to some new thinking in the field of international human resource management.

Chapter overview

This chapter sets out by exploring some key debates in the field of IHRM. It starts by addressing some of the key academic issues in the field, namely the universal and contextual paradigms, the issue of convergence versus divergence, and the aspect of cultural and institutional influences. It then explores the nature of IHRM and some of the key developments occurring in the field. Finally, it takes a sharp look at international assignments. The concluding case study illustrates how the theory contained in this chapter can be applied to a practical situation.

Introduction

The world is becoming increasingly global. Of course, there are organisations like the Roman Catholic church that can claim to have been global for hundreds of years, but it is the extent and the speed of change that is significant now. It is not just jeans and hamburgers that are found all over the world. Changes in technology – and, particularly, perhaps, in capital markets – have led to an increasing influence of some countries over others. The growing influence of internationalisation on organisations, both large and small, is beyond dispute. In these circumstances, increased knowledge about the specifics of management across borders – including knowledge of how organisations operating internationally handle HRM issues – has become a prominent issue for social scientists in the same way as it has become a key issue for all kinds of managers.[1]

Is HRM part of, or separate from, these trends? There is a real sense in which one might expect HRM to be the most local of management practices – this, after all, is where institutional factors such as the differences in labour markets and educational standards, differences in employment legislation and differences in trade union presence and power can be most obviously seen. HRM is also, because it is the part of management most tightly tied to people, the area of management in which people experience cultural differences most profoundly. However, the spread of internationally operating organisations brings with it a spread of employment practices, with these organisations unwilling to keep 'reinventing the wheel' to cope with local sensibilities and determined to spread what are seen as successful practices throughout their operations. As in other areas of HRM, there are tensions and balances – and few clear-cut answers.

12.1 Three key debates

HRM is universal, since every organisation has to utilise and, hence, in some way, manage human resources. Chapter 1 outlined the origin of the subject and the approaches that

organisations have developed. These approaches, or variations of them, are used in, perhaps, most universities and business schools around the world.

However, approaches to HRM, and the practice of HRM, vary across the world. We can use the analogy of a telescope: we can take either a very close look at things, which reveals important details, but blurs, or loses completely, a wider perspective, or we can adjust the focus screw and take a wider view, but if we do this we lose some of the detail.[2] Neither view is wrong: each is useful for particular purposes. In this chapter, we take a wider perspective, looking at how organisations that operate in many countries cope with the cultural and institutional differences they find.

To do this, we shall begin by exploring some of the key debates in IHRM. These are the conceptual paradigms that underlie how the topic is understood, the issue of convergence and divergence, and the issue of the explanatory factors for the differences found. These conceptual distinctions provide a platform on which to explore not only how organisations are handling IHRM but also the factors creating change in IHRM.

12.1.1 The universalist and contextual paradigms in HRM

People do things differently in different countries. The differences include differences in the way in which people conceptualise HRM, the research traditions through which they explore it, and the way in which organisations conduct it. In conceptual and research terms, two different (ideal type) paradigms have been classified as the universalist paradigm and the contextual paradigm.[3] The notion of paradigm is used here in Kuhn's (1970) sense as an accepted model or theory, and with the corollary that different researchers may be using competing models or theories.[4] It is to some degree the difference between these paradigms, lack of awareness of them, and the tendency for commentators to drift from one paradigm to another, which has led to the debates about the very nature of HRM as a field of study, as noted in Chapter 1.

- *The universalist paradigm.* This paradigm is dominant in most textbooks, universities, and business schools, especially in the USA, a country that has significant power in influencing the world's thinking. It is a 'scientific' approach. HRM is seen as a science and, as in other sciences, the aim is to discover universally applicable laws.[5] This paradigm assumes that the purpose of the study of this area of the social sciences, HRM, and, in particular, SHRM, is to improve the way that organisations strategically manage human resources.[6] Thus, the widely cited definition by Wright and McMahan states that SHRM is 'the pattern of planned human resource deployments and activities intended to enable a firm to achieve its goals'[7] (see Chapter 4). Methodologically, research based on the universalist paradigm is deductive, i.e. it involves generating carefully designed questions capable of leading to proof or disproof, the elements of which one can measure in such a way that one can subject the question itself to the mechanism of testing and prediction. Built into this paradigm is the assumption that research is not 'rigorous' unless it is drawn from existing literature and theory, focused around a tightly designed question which can be proved or disproved to be 'correct', and contains a structure of testing that can lead on to prediction. The research base centres mostly on a small number of private-sector 'leading edge' exemplars of 'good practice' – often large multinationals, generally from the manufacturing and, specifically, the high-tech sector.
- *The contextual paradigm.* This paradigm, by contrast, is idiographic, and looks not for universal laws but for an overall understanding of what is contextually unique and why. In HRM, it focuses on understanding what is different between and within HRM in various contexts and what the antecedents of those differences

are. Hence, the research mechanisms used are inductive. Here, theory is drawn from an accumulation of data collected or gathered in a less directed (or constrained) manner than would be the case under the universalist paradigm. Research traditions are different: focusing less upon testing and prediction than upon the collection and interpretation of evidence. There is an assumption that if things are important, they should be studied, even if testable prediction is not possible or the resultant data are complex and unclear. The policies and practices of the 'leading edge' companies (something of a value-laden term in itself) which are the focus of much HRM research and literature in the USA are of less interest to researchers in the contextual tradition than is the identification of the way labour markets work and what the more typical organisations are doing. As a contributor to explanation, this paradigm emphasises external factors as well as the actions of management within an organisation. Thus, it explores the importance of such factors as culture, ownership structures, labour markets, the role of the state, and trade-union organisation as aspects of the subject rather than as external influences upon it. That authors of many of the seminal management and, even, HRM texts write as if the analysis applies at all levels: what Rose called 'false universalism'.[8] These texts are produced in one country and tend to base their work on a small number of by now well-known cases. This can become a problem when people elsewhere unthinkingly adopt the analysis or prescriptions in those texts. The cultural hegemony of US teaching and publishing, particularly in the US journals, means that readers and students in other countries often utilise these texts. US-based literature searches, now all done on computer of course, tend to show little writing outside the universalist tradition. For analysts and practitioners elsewhere – with interests in different sectors, countries and so on –

many of these descriptions and prescriptions fail to match their reality. It is not that either paradigm is necessarily correct or more instructive than others, but that the level and focus needs to be specified to make the analysis meaningful.

12.1.2 Convergence and divergence in HRM

A second key issue concerns the question of whether the differences between societies in the way that organisations manage people are being reduced as globalisation increases. The early management theorists thought that a form of 'social Darwinism' would mean that successful management practices would 'crowd out' less successful ones and so management practices would inevitably converge towards the most efficient, and therefore they argued for the US model.[9] A widespread emphasis on the benchmarking practices of organisations, and attempts at the diffusion of 'best-practices', have been noted.[10] They have contributed to shaping similar forms of organisations across countries as well as similar curricula in business education.

One theoretical possibility, therefore, is that as policies of market deregulation and loosening state control are spreading from the USA to the rest of the world, firms everywhere move towards North American HRM.[11] Another possibility is that different regional models of HRM may be created, so that powerful economic groupings – such as the European Union (EU), which is developing employment laws that have to be adopted in all its 27 countries – may develop their own models of HRM.[12]

There are other theoretical possibilities: one is that organisations are so locked into their respective national institutional settings that no common model is likely to emerge for the foreseeable future. Since HR systems reflect national institutional contexts and cultures, and these do not respond readily to the imperatives of technology or the market, each country will continue to be distinctive.[13] The literature often refers to divergence theories, but what is usually meant is 'non-convergence': no one seems to be arguing that countries are becoming even more

dissimilar. Managers in each country operate within a national institutional context and a shared set of cultural assumptions. Neither institutions nor cultures change quickly, and they rarely change in ways that are the same as those of other countries. Hence managers within one country behave in a way that is noticeably different from managers in other countries. Even superficially universal principles (e.g. 'profit' and 'efficiency'), may be interpreted differently in different countries.[14] A final set of theoretical possibilities is that there is convergence in some aspects of HRM but not in others.

Recent research has drawn a distinction between directional convergence (where the same trends are visible in different nations, but they may not be getting more alike) and final convergence (where the countries are actually becoming more similar).[15] In HRM, there are clearly common trends, at least in the more industrialised countries, towards a greater professionalism in the HRM function and in the growth of practices such as more sophisticated recruitment and the use of contingent pay practices. However, there is no sign of countries becoming more alike in the way that they manage their human resources.

12.1.3 Cultural and institutional explanations of differences in HRM

One question this raises is: why are there differences, which seem to persist over time, between countries?[16] In broad terms, there are two competing sets of explanations: the cultural and the institutional. In other words, are the differences between countries 'sustained because people find it repulsive, unethical or unappealing to do otherwise ... [or] ... because a wider formal system of laws, agreements, standards and codes exist?'[17]

Exploring different cultures is not easy, because 'culture is one of those terms that defy a single all-purpose definition and there are almost as many meanings of culture as people using the term'.[18] Organisations represent 'cultural communities', but so do much wider groupings.[19] Often, these will reflect national boundaries, but this is by no means always the case. Thus, countries such as Belgium, Spain, and Switzerland contain communities speaking different languages, with different religions and different legislation, and seeming, at least to the citizens there, sharply different in their approach to life. In Africa and in the Middle East, cultural groups were divided by colonial map-makers; the individuals in those groups may have more cultural similarities with groups in countries across the national border than they do with other citizens of their own country. In many countries, however, especially the longer-established ones and those within coherent geographical boundaries (e.g. islands), culture equates to country – and that is certainly the assumption the research into workplace values makes.[20]

The 'culturalist' school includes many different approaches, but they have in common the notion that it is not possible to depart radically from established rules and norms. They see culture as shared by individuals as a means of conferring meaning on, and adding sense to, social interactions. The national culture provides a persistent boundary, horizon or 'segment' to the life of individuals, which enables them to make sense of their world. When companies try to operate against a national culture, their local subsidiary in that country may find 'ways around' or adaptations of the company policy so as to fit in with the expectations and values of people in that country.

Many different researchers have found geographically based – usually national – differences in deep-seated values about what is good or bad, honest or dishonest, fair or unfair, etc.[21] These perceptions affect the way people – especially, perhaps, managers – in a country view the world. There is, of course, an interrelation between cultural-level and individual-level values; each individual is different but the aggregation of their approaches makes what is acceptable and desirable in one country different from what is acceptable or desirable in another.[22] HRM is concerned with interactions between people at different hierarchical levels within an organisation, so these cultural differences will inevitably be reflected in differences in the way organisations manage people.

In contrast to the cultural approach, the institutional perspective assumes that the institutions of a society are what keeps the society distinctive.[23] Social arrangements in a nation are always distinct; many of the institutions are likely to shape the social construction of an organisation. Thus, the wealth of a society, the general and vocational education system, employment legislation, and the amount of informal working in an economy will all impact on the way that organisations can conduct HRM. Since these vary from country to country, so HRM in countries will vary. As with the culture effects, there seems to be a kind of societal recipe against which it is possible to go, or ignore, but only at a cost. Most people, or most organisations, generally do not do so.

The recognition of institutional differences is not new, but there is increasing research in this area.[24] This research notes that, for example, there are variations between countries' typical patterns of ownership.[25] Public ownership is not widespread in the USA, but in many northern European or African countries it continues to be the main provider of work in the formal sector. And private-sector ownership may not mean the same thing. In many of the southern European countries and in South America, for example, large corporations, even, are owned by single families. In many African and Asian countries, large proportions of the population are outside the formal employment scheme, whereas this is rare in the richer countries of the 'North'. Each of these factors – and many other institutional differences in terms of labour and educational markets, legislation, trade unionism etc. – will have important implications for IHRM experts.

Perhaps neither an exclusively 'culturalist' nor an exclusively 'institutional' approach can be satisfactory. Many of the 'cultural' writers see institutions as being key artefacts of culture, reflecting deep underlying variations in the values that they see between societies; many 'institutional' writers include culture as one of the institutional elements explaining differences. Institutions cannot survive without legitimacy, but the way they operate also affects the views of a society's people about what is legitimate. In the end, the two explanations simply explore the same factors from different points of view.[26]

Within the organisational literature, HRM is one of the areas where organisations are most likely to maintain a 'national flavour' and is the point at which business and national cultures have the sharpest interface.[27] This therefore presents a dilemma for companies internationally operating. On the one hand, they want to get the advantages of integration – ensuring that HRM policies and practices are as far as possible similar in all countries – as this brings benefits of scale, brings benefits of learning across the organisation (no 'reinventing the wheel'), and ensures fairness and equity. On the other hand, they have to be sensitive to national differences. Organisations have to adapt some policies and practices to local contexts. For example, the cultures and laws surrounding equal opportunities in the USA, the European Union, and South Africa are very different, even if the intentions may be similar. Companies operating in all these countries may well have active diversity and non-discrimination policies, but these policies will have to be differently applied in each place if the company is not to find itself a target for activists, or even taken to court, with all the resultant bad publicity. The company may have more scope in dealing with cultural differences: it does not have to hire 'typical' people from the country and can seek employees who are closer to its own attitudes, it can undertake socialisation and training, and it can dismiss people who do not share its philosophy. Even here, however, multinational corporations' (MNCs) room for manoeuvre may be limited: cultures are deep-seated and might be hard to tease out.

12.2 IHRM: What is special about 'international'?

In the dynamic and international world of the twenty-first century, organisations, from both the public and the private sectors, need to operate across national borders. How are they to handle this national diversity in the way they manage their people? The complexities of

international business are no longer restricted to MNCs but are also of concern for small to medium-sized enterprises (SMEs), international joint ventures (IJVs), and not-for-profit organisations.[28-29] Indeed, a comprehensive understanding of global operations would also incorporate learning from international family business units, overseas networks of entrepreneurs, and, even, illegal gangs, all of which have learned how to operate globally.[30]

The theories of IHRM – the way in which organisations manage their staff across country boundaries – have not developed in line with the growth of globalisation. There is still much room for better understanding of successful HRM practices in an international context.[31] Whilst there is an increasing amount of research on IHRM, and whilst organisations recognise that this is of practical importance to HR managers, some have criticised the work as focusing too narrowly on functional activities and as lacking appropriate theoretical structures.[32] The essence of the critique, in summary, is that the current literature in international HRM defines the field too narrowly and is influenced by a discussion of concepts and issues with little backing in systematic research. Critics argue that a new field of IHRM studies should be built around a broader set of questions. They argue that an assessment is needed of what the term 'IHRM' means, how to conceptualise it, and what areas and activities it includes, and that researchers need to model its drivers and enablers.

IHRM originally consisted of three major clusters of inquiry:

- The international transfer of staff, specifically focused on expatriation
- The conduct of people management in companies operating internationally, most typically in multinational organisations
- Comparisons of HRM policies and practices across different countries.[33]

All three streams of discussion have grown in size, differentiation and depth.

The majority of studies in the area have traditionally focused on expatriation: cross-border assignments of employees, lasting for a significant period of time.[34] Indeed, for many organisations and many commentators, IHRM and expatriate management are virtually synonymous. This is understandable; expatriates are among the most expensive human resources in any internationally operating organisation and they are almost invariably in crucial positions for the organisation. They have, and their management involves, issues and problems that go beyond those of most other employees. And yet the understanding of expatriates and the management of expatriates is less complete than that of other employees, and expatriates are often far from the best-managed employees. We shall return to this issue.

However, IHRM covers a far broader spectrum than the management of expatriates. It involves the worldwide management of people. Several researchers have proposed detailed models of how IHRM fits into the overall globalisation strategy of organisations. Adler and Ghadar[35] suggest that organisations need to follow very different IHRM policies and practices, according to the relevant stage of international corporate evolution, which they identify as domestic, international, multi-national, and global. Linking this with the attitudes and values of top management at headquarters (classified by Heenan and Perlmutter[36] as ethnocentric, polycentric, regio-centric, and geocentric – see Table 12.1), they outline how organisations could adapt their HRM approaches and practices to fit the external environment in which the firm operates, and its strategic intent. Some have criticised these categories on the grounds that:

- They imply a development from earlier to later categories, which may not be the case
- They imply, without evidence, that the earlier stages are less appropriate or effective
- They give equal weight to the various categories, when in practice the vast majority of organisations are clearly ethnocentric.[37]

Schuler, Dowling, and De Cieri[38] offer an integrative framework for the study and understanding of strategic international human resource management (SIHRM) that goes beyond theories of SHRM based in the domestic context and incorporates features unique to the international context.[39] They define SIHRM as[40]:

> ... human resource management issues, functions and policies and practices that result from the strategic activities of mul-tinational enterprises and that impact on the international concerns and goals of those enterprises.
>
> SOURCE: SCHULER, R., DOWLING, P. J. & DE CIERI, H. 1993. An integrative framework of strategic international human resource management. *International journal of human resource management*, 4(4):720.

Table 12.1 Four approaches to international human resource management

Aspect of the enterprise	Orientation			
	Ethnocentric	**Polycentric**	**Regiocentric**	**Geocentric**
Standard setting, evaluation, and control	By home country headquarters	By local subsidiary management	Coordination across countries in the region	Global as well as local standards and control
Communication and coordination	From HQ to local subsidiary	Little among subsidiaries, little between subsidiary and HQ	Little between subsidiary and HQ, medium to high among subsidiaries in region	Totally connected network of subsidiaries and subsidiaries with headquarters
Staffing	Home country managers	Host country managers	Managers may come from nations within region	Best people where they can be best used

SOURCE: HEENAN, D. A. & PERLMUTTER, H. V. *Multinational organizational development*. Addison-Wesley Publishing Company:18–19. © 1979 by Addison-Wesley Publishing Company. Used with permission.

The breadth of issues involved is illustrated by a framework linking SIHRM orientations and activities to the strategic components of multinational enterprises (MNEs).[41] The framework comprises inter-unit linkages and internal operations (see Figure 12.1). The authors argue that the key determinant of effectiveness for MNEs is the extent to which their various operating units across the world are differentiated and, at the same time, integrated, controlled, and coordinated.[42] As we have indicated, the link between, on the one hand, strategy–structure configuration in MNEs and the demands for global integration and, on the other, the need for local responsiveness, is a recurring theme in the literature. Most organisations require an element of both, but where global integration and coordination are important, subsidiaries need to be globally integrated with other parts of the organisation and strategically coordinated by the parent.[43] HRM practices that are, as far as possible, common across the organisation will be appropriate. In contrast, where local responsiveness is important, subsidiaries will have far greater autonomy and there is less need for integration. Hence, in such cases, the organisation will gain little from trying to coordinate HRM at the global level.

Evidence of different solutions adopted by MNEs to the problem of tension between differentiation and integration – otherwise termed the 'global vs local' – dilemma, results from the influence of a wide variety of exogenous and endogenous (external and internal) factors. Exogenous factors include:

- Industry characteristics, such as type of business and technology available
- The nature of competitors, and the extent of change

Figure 12.1 Factors in strategic international human resource management

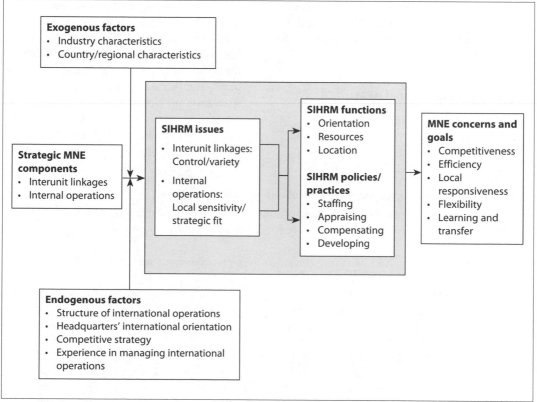

SOURCE: Reprinted from SCHULER, R. S. 2000. The internationalization of human resource management. *Journal of international management*, 6(3):252. With permission from Elsevier Science.

- Country and regional characteristics, such as political, economic, and socio-cultural conditions, and legal requirements.

Endogenous factors include:
- The structure of international operations
- The international orientation of the organisation's headquarters
- The competitive strategy being used
- The MNE's experience in managing international operations.

A practical issue to which the literature pays little attention concerns what it is possible for headquarters to know about its local operations (see Box 1 below). Whatever controls there are can always be circumvented: in practice, subsidiaries have some flexibility in how they respond.[44]

Recent research focuses on the drivers and enablers of HRM in MNEs.[45] Using the term 'global HRM' (GHRM) rather than the more familiar terms 'IHRM' or 'SIHRM' to emphasise the wider nature of the topic, these researchers summarise their findings in a model of IHRM (see Figure 12.2).

12.2.1 The drivers of global HRM

The drivers of GHRM are as follows:
- *Efficiency.* This involves, for example, the outsourcing of business processes and a high degree of centralisation. The organisations involved here focus on shared service centres, centres of excellence, and E-HR as the key delivery mechanisms for global HRM. The extensive ramifications of global HRM restructuring will have a significant effect on the roles and career paths of HR professionals. This has clear implications in terms of the level of expertise sought at selection and the amount of training the organisation gives.
- *Global provision.* This comprises two key elements – building a global presence and e-enabling management. Organisations are striving to build a global presence. For example, Rolls-Royce identified the fact that the market for aircraft engines was increasing globally, with much of the business in North America. It was important for Rolls-Royce to have a presence there. That meant moving a considerable portion of its operations there. This move, in turn, implied an extended role for the HRM function, which had to arrange the transfer of specialists, the redundancy of others (in the UK home base), and the recruitment of new specialists (in North America). For e-enabling management see Chapter 10. From the international HRM viewpoint, one of the outcomes of e-enabling HRM is

---

BOX 1: What can an organisation know about its local operations?

An organisation's operation thousands of kilometres away in another continent states: 'Sorry, but such a policy would be against the law here.' How is a manager outlining a new policy to judge the statement?
- Should headquarters check whether this is in fact the case – with consequences for local people's perception of how much the organisation trusts them?
- Should headquarters take the statement at face value – with the consequence that the policy is not applied in that country and idiosyncratic local practices continue?
- Should headquarters insist that the subsidiary implements the policy – with the possibility that the subsidiary may get taken to court?

It is, perhaps, this kind of 'on-the-ground' dilemma that brings the academic debate home to practitioners. As one international HR director has said, 'It's a bit like a pendulum: what seems to be just a small adjustment at the top can turn out to be a major change out at the edge of the organisation.' His suggestion was that headquarters just had to put people they trusted in charge of the local HRM operation – and trust them to follow the purposes, even if not the actual processes, of HRM policy.

Figure 12.2 Model of global HRM

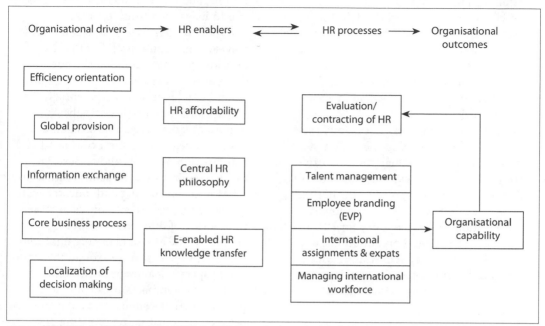

SOURCE: BREWSTER, C., SPARROW, P. & HARRIS, H. 2005: Towards a new model of globalizing HRM. *International journal of human resource management,* 16(6):950. Used with permission.

that local HRM specialists, line managers, and, even, employees around the globe can access the same material. The electronic capability tends to swing the HRM pendulum in the direction of centralisation and integration.

- *Information exchange and organisational learning.* These also comprise two key elements – knowledge transfer and management, and the forging of strategic partnerships. So far, the possibilities of GHRM as the process which adds to and helps exploit the knowledge stock, and particularly the powerful intrinsic knowledge stock, have not been fully developed. This is largely, perhaps, because information-technology specialists have driven much of the knowledge-management debate. Capturing and sharing explicit knowledge puts pressure on company intranets and on the technology, but the HRM function also has to grapple with the intrinsic knowledge – held in people's heads – that is often the

key to competitive advantage. Forging strategic partnerships is a second important factor related to the issue of information exchange and organisational learning. The not-for-profit charity Action Aid, for example, has as a central part of its strategy the aim of decentralising its activities to local operations and local staff. This has involved working closely with other aid groups to ensure the delivery of the necessary support.

- *Core business process convergence.* This involves the HRM response to the creation of core business processes and the movement away from country-based operations towards business-line driven organisations. Convergence around core business processes is not automatically associated with centralisation. Moreover, the HR function does more than just respond to this phenomenon and is often a key part of the re-orientation of the strategy. For example, as Shell changed its business focus from oil extraction to retailing, and identified centres of excellence around the world, HRM had to arrange the staffing, the procedures and the policies to put that change in place and embed it within the organisation. In another example, BOC set up a Pacific-based operation and HRM had to ensure that it worked.

- *Localisation*. In practice, not many firms seem to be incorporating the option of decentralisation into their strategic-driver recipe. However, though not common, this does exist. It is widespread in the not-for-profit and charity sectors, for example. The ramifications of such a policy for HRM are extensive. The central organisation can be reduced to a few key staff dealing with the top and the internationally rotating employees. Otherwise, HRM has to decentralise too.

12.2.2 The enablers of global HRM

The enablers of GHRM are as follows:

- *HRM affordability*. This is about the need to deliver global business strategies in the most cost-effective manner possible. For nearly all organisations, the costs of labour are the largest single element of operating costs. Thus, as cross-national organisations have to be increasingly aware of their competitive position and ensure that they reduce their costs to a minimum consistent with organisational efficiency, they examine both the people employed and the activities they undertake, to identify their added value. MNEs are devoting much attention to ensuring that people are where they can be most cost-effective and that central overheads are as low as possible. In many cases, this has led to a redeployment of activities from higher-cost countries to lower-cost ones, especially those where there is a well-educated population, or at least a high enough number of educated people for the needs of the MNE.
Arguably, the growth spurts in Eastern

Europe, and most dramatically in China and India, started from this base.

- *Central HRM philosophy*. This consists of two elements: centralisation of HRM decision-making and industry-wide convergence of HRM practice. The transfer and mutual learning from potentially very varied global practice is critically important. Some organisations aim to develop a degree of central command and coordination over this knowledge. For many organisations, the centralisation of HRM decision-making and industry-wide convergence clashes with the requirement to be aware of differences between countries. The aim of many organisations is to adopt the best from around the world whilst operating a decentralised and distributive approach to global best practice. Perhaps almost inevitably, the line between standardisation (creating best practice from around the world) and centralisation (assuming that best practice is either found at headquarters or needs to be controlled from there) is blurred. It is not uncommon for the people managing HRM at the centre of the MNE to argue that they are doing the first, whilst people in the subsidiaries see only the second.

- *E-enabled HR and knowledge transfer*. This is increasingly a critical component in terms of IHRM positioning. The HRM department's role as knowledge-management champion has three key elements: capitalising on the e-enablement of HRM, the pursuit of knowledge transfer and management, and the building of a global HRM presence. Organisations are spending billions of dollars on e-enabled HRM around the world, but no multinational organisation will claim that it is really making the most of E-HR. Just as individuals often have facilities on their mobile phones that they almost never use, so MNEs often buy hugely expensive E-HR systems and then fail to exploit them to the full. Nevertheless, the ability for any HRM specialist anywhere in the world to access data, for example, on employees who are expert in certain subjects, to contact them in real time, and to enable the organisation to draw on that expertise, has improved efficiency considerably. Such examples could be multiplied many times over.

12.3 International transfers

One of the traditional areas of IHRM – and one that still has a key impact on the field in terms both of academic research and of the implications for organisations and individuals – concerns the issue of moving people around the world. All international organisations struggle with the problems created by the need to fill and manage important assignments that may not be in the home country. Organisations usually choose expatriates, also known as parent-country nationals (PCNs), to fill these key positions, for example country manager or financial controller, or technical-specialist roles. These positions are important to the success of the organisation. The people involved are invariably expensive to service, perhaps costing three or four times as much as a similar posting at home and often far more than a local appointment would cost. At the same time, assignments in the overseas subsidiaries are rarely other than a very small proportion of the overall organisational staffing. Because the numbers are low, it is difficult for all but the largest international organisations to develop expertise and policies in dealing with other employees. The increasing pressure to cut costs has exacerbated the problem. Many large organisations have done so by reducing the number of expatriates, only to find later that this has caused very significant problems of communication, coordination, and control. Smaller and younger organisations face a different situation, but one that can lead to the same problem: how to decide which assignments to localise and which to fill with expatriates.

Organisations often handle key international assignments as unique events. It is true, of course, that each case is different – but not so different that the organisation cannot learn from the accumulation of cases, nor so different that organisations cannot develop generic guides based upon past experience. Very often the 'one-off' approach arises because, except in the very largest organisations, there is no coherent framework on which to base decisions. Each situation becomes a problem and the line manager has to use his or her personal knowledge of individuals to try to fill the gap. This is partly why the research into expatriate selection often fails to identify any systematic approach. The reality is that managers often take such decisions (or at least initiate them) in the corridor or at a social gathering as the result of one manager 'knowing' someone who could fill their one vacancy.[46]

An organisation might undertake international assignments for a variety of reasons:
* To enhance the control of the centre
* To underline the importance of the country to the local government
* To provide skills not existing in that geographical location
* To provide opportunities for management development
* To internationalise the managerial cadre.

Furthermore, there is evidence that there are variations between firms in the use of expatriates, based on size, organisational age, and nationality.[47] A developing strand of the literature discusses expatriation in terms of knowledge transfer: the ability of the organisation to move information and understanding from one country to another.[48] This is seen as a key task and one that organisations can undertake through a variety of mechanisms, but is not without its problems.[49–50]

12.3.1 International transfers: Cheaper and/or better

In this section we shall discuss two approaches to international transfers:
* *Doing it more cheaply.* In this regard, we shall consider alternatives to expatriation.
* *Doing it better.* In this regard, we shall discuss the expatriate cycle.

We shall start by examining the issue of 'doing it more cheaply' and consider alternatives to expatriation. Expatriation is always expensive. Expatriates tend to be paid more than other staff, even at the same level; they get substantially more benefits; their transfer may involve a partner and a family and it will certainly involve a disproportionate amount of specialist HRM support and senior management time. Many established MNEs are looking carefully at their budgets and trying to reduce the costs involved.

One approach is to negotiate more toughly. Many organisations use 'salary clubs' (groups of international organisations sharing pay and cost-of-living information), which, in effect, allow them to set the terms and conditions of staff – for particular locations and levels of staff. This is increasingly being challenged: whilst MNEs see the benefits of ensuring that their staff are able to 'hold their own' with other equivalent level expatriates, they are also seeing the benefits of negotiating hard about terms and conditions: 'If you are the right person, and really want this job, you will take it on these terms: if not we will look elsewhere.' At the same time, expatriates themselves are getting more 'streetwise' about their employability. They know that good expatriates are in short supply and intend to negotiate a good deal. The result is that the standard deal of a set package for a set job in a set location is being replaced by the kind of negotiation that goes on elsewhere.

Increasingly, international organisations are employing expatriates on local terms and conditions. This is of particular relevance in the EU and is happening amongst both university graduates (e.g. biochemists recruited from Italy to work in Eastern England on the same terms as they would have been had they come from Scotland) and managerial employees. In Europe there is comparatively little unemployment, a rough equivalence of living standards and facilities, and an absence of legal formalities and constraints for transfers within the countries of the EU, where, for example, citizens of other European countries do not require work permits. Hence, organisations have good reasons for trying to localise terms and conditions of staff

transferring between European countries. A particular group of employees of MNEs, which has been little studied, is made up of the many who end up working for one of their national organisations after having made their own way to the host country. This group of self-initiated foreign employees (SEs) is probably much bigger than had previously been understood and is only now beginning to be researched.[51]

There has been increasing interest in the use of third-country nationals (TCNs): individuals who are not from either headquarters or from the host country.[52] They have a number of advantages:

• Their use reduces criticism of the organisation as ethnocentric
• They emphasise the organisation's commitment to developing and using talent wherever it may be
• They are usually considerably cheaper
• They often have a cultural awareness that can be beneficial.

Thus, a UK MNE may gain advantages from using Malaysian Muslims in Arab countries, or Portuguese employees in Brazil, for example. In both cases, the TCNs will have a cultural advantage over home country (British) expatriates. However, assumptions here can be dangerous: there are innumerable stories of Overseas Chinese being sent in to the People's Republic of China, for example, and, because they have fewer excuses, receiving a much rougher ride than Westerners would have done.

Of course, many international workers are not expatriates. These are the short-term assignees, international commuters, frequent flyers, and international project teams. Their number is considerable and, at least amongst larger organisations, is growing faster than the number of expatriates, though there is growth in all forms.[53] In many ways, these employees share the same stresses as expatriates, particularly in terms of their social lives and family pressures, and yet they never move their homes or get many of the benefits of expatriation.

Organisations recruit some people specifically for short-term assignments and some are sent from within the existing home-country labour force. The advent of easier and cheaper travel and improvements in communications technology have led to a surge in such arrangements in recent years. The duration of such assignments varies, depending on purpose, company, and sector. In most cases, assignments will last less than a year – normally anything from a few weeks to six months. The main reasons for short-term assignments are skills transfer and management development, so managerial control is not as important as it is for long-term international assignments.[54] Thus, compared to the traditional expatriate assignments, the main advantages of project assignments are – especially in Europe, where there is no need for work or residence permits – flexibility, simplicity, and cost-effectiveness. Goals for short assignments are easier to set and evaluate than those for longer assignments.[55] That said, remuneration and administration, as well as costs associated with short-term assignments, can create severe problems.[56]

The international commuter phenomenon is becoming more widespread: managers live at home in, say, Austria during the weekend and travel to Hungary every Monday, returning home every Thursday night or Friday morning. In parts of Africa, many aid organisations house their employees' families in safer countries, while the employees 'commute' to the more dangerous country where they work on a regular basis. The effects on their home lives and the implications this has for local staff perceptions of the degree of commitment to the country they work in are significant and negative.

Many more people, throughout the world, travel frequently: visiting company operations or customers in other countries for a few hours or days on a regular basis. The costs to the organisation and the benefits that such travel brings are debatable. In many cases these trips are unmonitored from any central source, agreement to such trips being the prerogative of the line manager. The effect is that the organisation has no overall idea of how much it spends on such frequent flyers – and no idea of the benefits. Some organisations have teams of

people flying around the world on regular assessment projects, enabling them to balance central knowledge with local control.[57] They believe that 'hands-on' and 'face-to-face' are still the best ways to do business.

Some have argued that the development of information and communication technology (ICT) will render both international transfers and international travel redundant. Why go to a country when it is easier, safer, and cheaper to video-conference with the people there? With the growth of ICT in individual economies, the argument has some strength – undoubtedly the future will see more video-conferencing and more use of email etc. However, familiar arguments apply: in many cases, face-to-face meetings are more effective. Just as ICT technology has made a comparatively limited difference to working practices within individual countries, so the fact that business travel has grown significantly just as international ICT has developed may be less a function of ignorance or the desire for foreign travel than of a recognition that the social side of management is critical to success. An understanding of negotiating skills, for example, will tell that it is more difficult to say 'No' face to face than it is by fax or email. In these circumstances, international travel by sellers makes a lot of sense. It is well-known that teamwork is better fostered by meetings than by even the best video-conferencing. Amongst many companies which make considerable use of 'virtual project teams', there is a firm belief that the members of the team should meet in person at the beginning of the project in order to ensure that the 'distance' phases of the work are fully effective.[58]

The cheapest option, of course, is usually the employment of local people. There is a strong case to be made that the reason that the employment of local people is so rare in management circles is less to do with internationalising the management cadre than with the remnants of colonialism or racial assumptions of superiority.[59] The argument that international assignments are part of developing international awareness and understanding in the management team would be stronger if there were better evidence that organisations utilise and exploit the knowledge they can gain from these arrangements: in fact, it seems that international assignments are usually seen as little more than an interlude away from headquarters. It is assumed that it is at headquarters that the real action takes place. International experience is discounted.[60] In practice, most organisations fail to release the capabilities and expertise of their local employees.

Having examined the issue of 'doing it more cheaply', we shall now turn to the issue of 'doing it better' and discuss the expatriate cycle. Whilst the forms of international assignment are all growing, so is the use of traditional expatriation. Research into expatriation has, in general, followed the traditional expatriate 'cycle', with, interestingly, early attention given to the earlier stages of the assignment and a successively developing focus on the later and more complex issues of adjustment, monitoring of performance, and repatriation. 'Doing it better' at each stage of the cycle will lead to greater cost-effectiveness overall.

- *Selection*. Research into the selection of expatriates has generally focused on the more 'visible' aspects of these issues, such as the criteria used in selection decisions.[61] Researchers have found that, in practice, technical expertise and domestic track record are by far the two dominant selection criteria. Factors such as language skills and international adaptability come further down the list in all studies, though some evidence shows that these have more importance for European organisations than for those in the USA.[62] Recent research into recruitment systems indicates that these criteria are constructs of international HR departments: in practice, decisions on expatriation are taken by line managers (who often simply ignore the criteria).[63]
- *Training and development programmes*. Such programmes for expatriates are, surprisingly, more apparent by their absence than their presence. They are more common in European MNEs than in US ones, and in Europe they include some

interesting and cost-effective alternatives to formal training programmes, e.g. pre-appointment visits and briefings by returned expatriates.[64-65]
- *Adjustment*. There have been a number of studies into the issues of expatriate adjustment.[66] Increasingly, those who study adaptation have been moving away from the most widely used 'three-factor' approach that tries to distinguish between the overlapping area of work, interaction, and general adjustment.[67] While it is essential for a functioning household to be well adjusted to the economic environment regarding consumption of goods and services, for example, there has been discussion as to how far adjustment should go in the workplace and where the expatriate's allegiance should lie.[68]
- *Pay and rewards*. These are critical components in ensuring maximum return from human resources throughout the whole international organisation but, as 'technical' issues related to tax and pension regimes, they have tended to be the domain of consultants rather than researchers, though some researchers have made important contributions. Recent writing in Europe has been concerned with central pay policies and their link to business goals, whilst allowing for sensitivity to business, cultural, and other influences at subsidiary-unit level. Differences in international rewards are seen as a consequence not just of cultural differences, but also of differences in institutional influences, national business systems, and the role and competence of managers in the sphere of HRM.[69-70]
- *Performance measurement and management*. The whole question of performance measurement and management in multinational companies involves a complex range of issues. Research to date suggests that rigorous performance-appraisal systems for expatriates are far from universal.[71] This is perhaps surprising, given the high costs of

expatriate underperformance and the growing tendency to see expatriates as key human assets. European firms, in particular, seem to be paying more attention to this aspect of expatriation.[72] In part, this reflects the growing use of international assignments for development purposes in European multinationals and the greater integration of expatriation into the overall career-development process in European firms. In part, however, it also represents the difficulty of establishing performance criteria for posts aimed at fulfilling multiple objectives.

• *Repatriation.* The repatriation of expatriates has been identified as a major problem for multinational companies, but is still comparatively underresearched.[73] For many MNEs, this problem has become more acute in recent years because expansion of foreign operations took place at the same time as the rationalisation of HQ operations; there are few unfilled positions suitable for expatriates in the majority of companies. From the repatriate perspective, other problems associated with re-integrating into the home country are loss of status, loss of autonomy, loss of career direction, and a feeling that international experience is undervalued by the company. There is growing recognition that where managers see companies dealing unsympathetically with the problems expatriates face on re-entry, managers will be more reluctant to accept the offer of international assignments.[74] It has been reported that 10–25 per cent of expatriates leave their company within 12 months of repatriation, a figure which is notably higher than for equivalent non-expatriates.[75-76] Yet whilst it is widely accepted that the costs of expatriate turnover are considerable, very few firms have effective repatriation programmes. One study of a cohort of Finnish expatriates found that most had received great value from their international assignment, but that within a year many

had left their firm and many others wanted to leave.[77] Recent research in Europe situates repatriation in the context of career development and loss of corporate knowledge.[78] The focus now is on seeing the expatriation phase as part of an individual's career, rather than seeing repatriation as the end of the process.

12.4 **Strategy and attention to detail**

The complexities of IHRM are a reflection of the lack of simple answers to the questions involved in managing HRM generally, and the extra level of difficulty added by internationalism. There are unlikely to be exact or final answers to the questions IHRM raises. However, senior executives in multi-national enterprises can do much to ensure that their organisations learn from the available research understanding. (And, incidentally, researchers can learn much by paying closer attention to experience and expertise within MNEs.)

Many international organisations struggle with the issues of which elements of their HR policies and practices they can centralise and which they can decentralise. The literature shows an ongoing debate about the extent to which MNEs bring new HRM practices into a country, in comparison to the extent to which they adapt their own practices to those of the local environment. In practice, of course, there is always an interplay between the two, and both factors apply to some degree.

Research into IHRM has tended to focus on expatriation and, even more narrowly, on the pay and conditions of expatriates. HR managers in MNEs have to start examining their use of human resources internationally according to the same criteria they would apply to national HRM. When MNEs ask themselves the following basic questions, they will be able to improve the way in which they manage their human resources internationally:

• What kind of people do we need working for us in these locations?
• How do we ensure that we get the best people in the most cost-effective manner?

- How do we ensure that we monitor their performance and unlock their potentialities as fully as possible?

- In this particular context, would that involve the international transfer of people?
- If so, what is the best mechanism for making that effective?

SUMMARY

This chapter examines the additional complexities created for HR managers when organisations conduct business internationally. It addresses the critical issues of what can be managed from the centre and what has to be held locally. The international transfer of employees remains a key and complicated topic, but MNCs are taking a much more globalised view of their management of people, trying to ensure that they get the best from them and provide them with the best opportunities to contribute to the organisation.

KEY CONCEPTS

• Contextual paradigm	• International HRM (IHRM)
• Convergence	• International joint ventures (IJVS)
• Cultural approach	• Multinational companies (MNCs)
• Divergence	• Multinational enterprises (MNEs)
• E-enabling HRM	• Polycentric
• Endogenous factors	• Regiocentric
• Ethnocentric	• Repatriation
• Exogenous factors	• Salary clubs
• Expatriation	• Self-initiated foreign employees (SEs)
• Geocentric	• Strategic HRM (SHRM)
• Global HRM (GHRM)	• Strategic international HRM (SIHRM)
• Globalisation	• Third-country nationals (TCNs)
• Information and communication technology (ICT)	• Universalist paradigm
• Institutional perspective	

CASE STUDY

Objective: To understand the role of HRM in an international business environment

Global HR at McDonald's

One of the best-known companies worldwide is McDonald's Corporation. The fast-food chain, with its symbol of the golden arches, has spread from the United States into 91 countries. With more than 18000 restaurants worldwide, McDonald's serves 33 million people each day. International sales represent an important part of McDonald's business, and more than 50% of the company's operating income comes from sales outside the United States. To generate these sales McDonald's employs more than 2 million people.

Operating in so many different countries means that McDonald's has had to adapt its products, services, and HR practices to legal, political, economic, and cultural factors in each one of those countries. A few examples illustrate how adaptations have been made. In some countries, such as India, beef is not acceptable as a food to a major part of the population, so McDonald's uses lamb or mutton. To appeal to Japanese customers, McDonald's developed teriyaki burgers. Separate dining rooms for men and women are constructed in McDonald's restaurants in some Middle Eastern countries. HR practices must adapt to different cultures. Before beginning operations in a different country, HR professionals at McDonald's research the country and determine how HR activities must be adjusted. One method of obtaining information is to contact HR professionals from other US firms operating in the country and ask them questions about laws, political factors, and cultural issues. In addition, the firm conducts an analysis using a detailed outline to ensure that all relevant information has been gathered. Data gathered might include what employment restrictions exist on ages of employees and hours of work, what benefits must be offered to full-time and part-time employees (if part-time work is allowed), and

other operational requirements. For instance, in some of the former communist countries in Eastern Europe, employers provide locker rooms and showers for their employees. These facilities are necessary because shower facilities, and even consistent water supplies, are unavailable in many homes, particularly in more rural areas around major cities. Also, public transportation must be checked to ensure employees have adequate means to travel to work. Once a decision has been made to begin operations in a new country, the employment process must begin. Often, McDonald's is seen as a desirable employer, particularly when its first restaurant is being opened in a country. For instance, in Russia, 27000 people initially applied to work at the first McDonald's in Moscow. Because customer service is so important to McDonald's, recruiting and selection activities focus on obtaining employees with customer service skills. For worker positions such as counter representative and cashier, the focus is to identify individuals who will be friendly, customer service-oriented employees. A 'trial' process whereby some applicants work for a few days on a conditional basis may be used to ensure that these individuals will represent McDonald's appropriately and will work well with other employees.

For store managers, the company uses a selection profile emphasising leadership skills, high work expectations, and management abilities appropriate to a fast-paced restaurant environment. Once applicant screening and interviews have been completed, individuals are asked to work for up to a week in a restaurant. During that time, both the applicants and the company representatives evaluate one another to see if the job 'fit' is appropriate. After the first group of store managers and assistant managers are selected, future managers and assistant managers are chosen using internal promotions based on job performance.

Once the restaurants are staffed, training becomes crucial to acquaint new employees with their jobs and the McDonald's philosophy of customer service and quality. McDonald's has taken its Hamburger University curriculum from the United States and translated it into 22 different languages to use in training centres throughout the world. Once trainers and managers complete the training, they then conduct training for all employees selected to work at McDonald's locations in the foreign countries.

Questions and activities

1. Identify cultural factors that might be important in a training programme for food handlers at McDonald's in Saudi Arabia.

2. Rather than focusing on the differences, what similarities do you expect to exist among McDonald's customers and employees in both the United States and abroad?

SOURCE: MATHIS, R. L. & JACKSON, J. H. 2003. *Human resource management* 10th ed. Mason, Ohio: South Western, a division of Thomson Learning:603–604. Used with permission.

REVIEW QUESTIONS AND ACTIVITIES

1. Briefly define the concept of strategic international human resource management (SIHRM).
2. Write a short essay on expatriates.
3. Briefly discuss the 'universal' and 'contextual' paradigms in HRM.
4. Briefly discuss the four approaches to IHRM by referring to the following aspects of the organisation: staffing; communication and coordination; and standard setting, evaluation, and control.
5. Write a short essay on the 'institutional' perspective in IHRM.
6. Write a short essay on the 'drivers' of GHRM.
7. Give a detailed discussion of the alternatives to expatriation.
8. Write a short paragraph on the repatriation of expatriates.
9. Briefly discuss the issue of culture in IHRM.
10. Write a short paragraph on the 'enablers' of GHRM.

FURTHER READING

TOH, S. M. & DENISI, S. 2005. A local perspective to expatriate success. *Academy of management executive*, 19(1):132–146.

BREIDEN, O., MIRZA, H. R. & MOHR, A. T. 2005. Coping with the job abroad. *International studies of management & organisation*, 34(3):5–26.

ANDOL-SEK, D. M. & STEBE, J. 2005. Devolution or (de) centralisation of HRM function in European organisations. *The international journal of human resource management*, 16(3):311–329.

MEZIAS, J. M. & SCANDURA, T. A. 2005. A needs-driven approach to expatriate adjustment and career development: a multiple mentoring perspective. *Journal of international business studies*, 36:519–538.

GONG, Y., SHENKAR, O., LUO, Y. & NYAW, M. K. 2005. Human resources and international joint venture performance: a system perspective. *Journal of international business studies*, 36:505–518.

WEB SITES

www.shrmglobal.org – Society of Human Resource Management Global Forum

www.Berlitz.com – Berlitz International (language and cultural adjustment training and information provided by this well-known firm)

www.etiquetteintl.com – Etiquette International (this professional firm works with organisations to make their employees more effective and professional when working with other cultures)

ENDNOTES

1. SPARROW, P. R., BREWSTER, C. & HARRIS, H. 2004. *Globalising HR*. London: Routledge.
2. BREWSTER, C. 2007. Comparative human resource management. (In Storey, J. (ed.) *Human resource management: A critical text* 3rd ed. London: Thomson.)
3. BREWSTER, C. 1999. Strategic human resource management: The value of different paradigms. *Management international review*, Special Issue 1999, 3(39):45–64.
4. KUHN, T. 1970. *The structure of scientific revolutions.* Chicago: University of Chicago Press.
5. SMITH, C. & MEISKINS, P. 1995. System, society and dominance effects in cross national organisational analysis. *Work, employment and society*, 9(2):241–67.
6. ULRICH, D. & SMALLWOOD, N. 2005. HR's new ROI: return on intangibles. *Human resource management*, 44(2):137–142; WRIGHT, P. M. & MCMAHAN, G. C. 1992. Theoretical perspectives for strategic human resource management. *Journal of management*, 18(2):295–320.
7. WRIGHT, P. M. & MCMAHAN, G. C. 1992. Theoretical perspectives for strategic human resource management. *Journal of management*, 18(2):298.

8. ROSE, M. J. 1991. Comparing forms of comparative analysis. *Political studies*, 39:446–462.

9. DRUCKER, P. 1950. *The new society: The anatomy of the industrial order*. New York: Harper; HARBISON, F. & MYERS, C. A. 1959. *Management in the industrial world: An international analysis*. New York: McGraw Hill.

10. MARCHINGTON, M. & GRUGULIS, I. 2000. Best practice human resource management: perfect opportunity or dangerous illusion?, *International journal of human resource management*, 11(6):1104–1124; WRIGHT, P. M. & BREWSTER, C. 2003. Editorial. Learning from diversity: HRTM is not Lycra. *International journal of human resource management*, 14(8):1299–1307.

11. SMITH, C. & MEISKINS, P. 1995. System, society and dominance effects in cross national organisational analysis. *Work, employment and society*, 9(2):241–67.

12. BREWSTER, C. 2004. European perspectives on human resource management. *Human resource management review*, 14(4):365–382; SPARROW, P. & HILTROP, J.-M. 1994. *European human resource management in transition*. Hemel Hempstead: Prentice Hall.

13. DIMAGGIO, P. J. & POWELL, W. W. 1983. The iron cage revisited: Institutional isomorphism and collective rationality in organisational fields. *American sociological review*, 48:147–160.

14. HOFSTEDE, G., VAN DEUSEN, C. A., MUELLER, C. B. & CHARLES, T. A. 2002. What goals do business leaders pursue? A study in fifteen countries. *Journal of international business studies*, 33(4):785–803.

15. MAYRHOFER, W., MÜLLER-CAMEN, M., LEDOLTER, J., STRUNK, G., & ERTEN, C. 2002. The diffusion of management concepts in Europe – conceptual considerations and longitudinal analysis. *Journal of cross-cultural competence & management*, 3:315–349; MAYRHOFER, W. & BREWSTER, C. 2005. European human resource management: researching developments over time. *Management revue*, 16(1):36–63.

16. BOXALL, P. 1995: Building the theory of comparative HRM. *Human resource management journal*, 5(5):5–17.

17. SORGE, A. 2004. *Cross-national differences in human resources and organization* (*In* Harzing, A.-W. & Van Ruysseveldt, J. (Eds). *International human resource management*. London: Sage.)

18. AJIFERUKE, M. & BODDEWYN, J. 1970. Culture and other explanatory variables in comparative management studies. *Academy of management journal*, 35:154.

19. FUKUYAMA, F. 1995. *Trust: Social virtues and the creation of prosperity*. New York: Free Press; SAKO, M. 1998. Does Trust Improve Business Performance? (*In* Lane, C. & Bachmann, R. (Eds). *Trust within and between organizations*. Oxford: Oxford University Press.)

20. See, for example, HOFSTEDE, G. 2001. *Culture's consequences: comparing values, behaviours, institutions, and organizations across nations* 2nd ed. Thousand Oaks: Sage; HOUSE, R. J., HANGES, P. J., JAVIDAN, M., DORFMAN, P. W. AND GUPTA, V. 2004. *Culture, leadership and organizations: the GLOBE study of 62 societies*. New York: Sage; SCHWARZ, S. H. 1992. Universals in the content and structure of values: Theoretical advances and empirical tests in 20 countries. (*In* Zanna, M. P. (Ed.). *Advances in experimental social psychology*, 25, New York: Academic Press); SCHWARZ, S. H. 1994. Beyond individualism/collectivism: new cultural dimensions of values. (*In* Kim, U., Triandis, H. C., Kagitcibasi, C., Choi, S. C., Yoon, G. (Eds). *Individualism and collectivism*. London: Sage); SPONY, G. 2003. The development of a work-value model assessing the cumulative impact of individual and cultural differences on managers' work-value systems: empirical evidence form French and British managers. *International journal of human resource management*, 14(4):658–679.

21. See, for example, HOFSTEDE, G. 2001. *Culture's consequences: comparing values, behaviours, institutions, and organizations across nations* 2nd ed. Thousand Oaks: Sage; HOUSE, R. J., HANGES, P. J., JAVIDAN, M., DORFMAN, P. W. & GUPTA, V. 2004. *Culture, leadership and organizations: the GLOBE study of 62 societies*. New York: Sage.

22. SCHWARZ, S. H. 1994. Beyond individualism/collectivism: new cultural dimensions of values. (*In* Kim, U., Triandis, H. C., Kagitcibasi, C., Choi, S. C., Yoon, G. (Eds). *Individualism and collectivism*. London: Sage); SPONY, G. 2003. The development of a work-value model assessing the cumulative impact of individual and cultural differences on managers' work-value systems: empirical evidence form French and British managers. *International journal of human resource management*, 14(4):658–679.

23. AMABLE, B. 2003. *The diversity of modern capitalism*. Oxford: Oxford University Press; BREWSTER, C., WOOD, G., BROOKES, M. AND VAN OMMEREN, J. 2006. What determines the size of the HR function?: a cross-national analysis. *Human resource management*, 45(1):3–21; BROOKES, M., BREWSTER, C. & WOOD, G. 2005. Social relations, firms and societies: a study of institutional embeddedness. *International sociology*, 20(4):403–426; FERNER, A. & QUINTANILLA, J. 1998. Multinationals, national business systems and HRM: the enduring influence of national identity or a process of 'Anglo Saxonization'. *International journal of human resource management*, 9(4):710–31; GOODERHAM, P., NORDHAUG, O. & RINGDAL, K. 1999. Institutional and rational determinants of organizational practice: human resource management in European firms. *Administrative science quarterly*, 44(3):507–531; HALL, P. & SOSKICE, D. 2001. *Varieties of capitalism*. Oxford University Press:

Oxford; TREGASKIS, O. & BREWSTER, C. 2006. Converging or diverging? A comparative analysis of trends in contingent employment practice in Europe over a decade. *Journal of international business studies*, 37(1):111–126; WHITLEY, R. 1999. *divergent capitalisms: The social structuring and change of business systems.* Oxford: Oxford University Press.

24. ROZENZWEIG, P. M. AND SINGH, J. V. 1991. Organizational environments and the multinational enterprise. *Academy of management review*, 16(2):340–361.

25. BREWSTER, C. 2004. European perspectives on human resource management. *Human resource management review*, 14(4):365–382.

26. Ibid.; SORGE, A. 2004. *Cross-national differences in human resources and organization (In* Harzing, A.-W. & Van Ruysseveldt, J. (Eds). *International human resource management.* London: Sage.)

27. ROSENZWEIG, P. M. & NOHRIA, N. 1994. Influences on human resource management practices in multinational corporations. *Journal of international business studies*, 25(2): 229–252.

28. FAULKNER, D., PITKETHLY, R. & CHILD, J. 2002. International mergers and acquisitions in the UK 1985–94: a comparison of national HRM practices. *International journal of human resource management*, 13(1):106–122, February; CYR, D. 1995. *The human resource challenge of international joint ventures.* Westport: CT Quorum Books; CYR, D. & SCHNEIDER, S. 1996. Implications for learning: human resource management in East–West joint ventures. *Organization studies*, 17(2):201–226; LU, Y. & BJORKMAN, I. 1997. HRM practices in China – Western joint ventures: MNC standardization versus localization. *International journal of human resource management*, 8(5): 614–628; SCHULER, R. S. 2001. Human resource issues and activities in international joint ventures. *International journal of human resource management*, 12(1): 1–52, February.

29. BREWSTER, C. & LEE, S. 2006. HRM in not-for-profit international organisations: different, but also alike. (*In* Larsen H. H. & Mayrhofer, W. (Eds). *European human resource management.* London: Routledge:131–148.)

30. PARKER, B. 1998. *Globalization and business practice: Managing across boundaries.* London: Sage.

31. See, for example, DOWLING, P. J., SCHULER, R. S. & WELCH, D. 1994. *International dimensions of human resource management.* Belmont, C.A.: Wadsworth; SCHERM, E. 1995. *Internationales personalmanagement.* Munich, Vienna; BOXALL, P. 1995: Building the theory of comparative HRM. *Human resource management journal*, 5(5):5–17; HARZING, A.-M. & VAN RUYSSELVELDT, J. (Eds). 2004. *International human resource management: An integrated approach.* Sage: London; SPARROW, P. R., BREWSTER, C. & HARRIS, H. 2004. *Globalising HR.* London: Routledge; STAHL, G. & BJORKMAN,

I. (Eds). 2006. *Handbook of research in international HRM.* London: Edward Elgar.

32. KOCHAN, T., BATT, R. & DYER, R. 1992. International human resource studies: a framework for future research (*In* Lewin, D., Mitchell, O. S. & Sherer, P. D. (Eds). *Research frontiers in industrial relations and human resources.* Madison: Industrial Relations Research Association.)

33. DOWLING, P. J. 1999. Completing the puzzle: issues in the development of the field of international human resource management. *Management international review*, 39:27–43.

34. See, for example, BLACK, J. S., GREGERSEN, H. B & MENDENHALL, M. E. 1992. *Global assignments.* San Francisco: Jossey-Bass; SCHELL, M. E., & SOLOMON, C. M. 1997. *Capitalizing on the global workforce: A strategic guide to expatriate management.* New York: McGraw-Hill; HARTL, K. 2003. *Expatriate women managers, gender, culture and career.* Muenchen and Mering: Rainer Hampp Verlag; DOWLING, P. J., SCHULER, R. S. & WELCH, D. 1994. *International dimensions of human resource management.* Belmont, C.A.: Wadsworth.

35. ADLER, N. & GHADAR, F. 1990. International strategy from the perspective of people and culture: The North American context. (*In* Rugman, A. (Ed.) *Research in global strategic management*, 1. Greenwood, Connecticut: JAI Press.)

36. HEENAN, D. & PERLMUTTER, H. 1979. *Multinational organisation development.* Reading M.A.: Addison-Wesley.

37. MAYRHOFER, W. & BREWSTER, C. 1996. In praise of ethnocentricity: Expatriate policies in European multinationals. *International executive*, 38(6):749–778, November/December.

38. SCHULER, R., DOWLING, P. J. & DE CIERI, H. 1993. An integrative framework of strategic international human resource management. *International journal of human resource management*, 4(4):717–764.

39. SUNDARAM, A. K. & BLACK, J. S. 1992. The environment and internal organization of multinational enterprises. *Academy of management review*, 17(4):729–757; ADLER, N. J. & BARTHOLOMEW, S. 1992. Managing globally competent people. *Academy of management executive*, 6(1):52–64.

40. SCHULER, R., DOWLING, P. J. & DE CIERI, H. 1993. An integrative framework of strategic international human resource management. *International journal of human resource management*, 4(4):720.

41. We have preferred the term 'multinational enterprise (MNE)' to the perhaps more familiar term 'multinational corporation (MNC)' because we want to include intergovernmental, public sector, and not-for-profit organisations in our analysis.

42. PUNNETT, B. J. & RICKS, D. A. 1992. *International business.* Boston, Mass: PWS-Kent; GHOSHAL, S.

1987. Global strategy: an organizing framework. *Strategic management journal*, 8:425–440; GALBRAITH, J. R. 1987. Organization design. (*In* Lorsch, J. (Ed.). *Handbook of organization behavior.* Englewood Cliffs, N.J.: Prentice Hall:343–357.)

43. EVANS, P., PUCIK, V. AND BARSOUX, J.-L. 2002. *The global challenge. frameworks for international HRM.* Chicago: McGraw–Hill/Irwin.

44. OLIVER, C. 1991. Strategic responses to institutional processes. *Academy of management review*, 16:145–79.

45. SPARROW, P. R., BREWSTER, C. & HARRIS, H. 2004. *Globalising HR*. London: Routledge; BREWSTER, C., SPARROW, P. & HARRIS, H. 2005: Towards a new model of globalizing HRM. *International journal of human resource management*, 16(6):949–970.

46. HARRIS, H. & BREWSTER, C. 1997. The coffee machine system: how international selection really works. *International journal of human resource management*, 10(3):488–500.

47. TUNG, R. 1982, Selection and training procedures of US, European and Japanese multinationals. *Human resource management*, 23:129–143; WAXIN, M. F. 2004. Expatriates' interaction adjustment: the direct and moderator effects of culture of origin. *International journal of human intercultural relations*, 28:61–79.

48. BONACHE, J. & BREWSTER, C. 2001. Knowledge transfer and the management of expatriation. *Thunderbird international business review*, 43(1):145–168.

49. MÄKELÄ, K. & BREWSTER C. 2008 (forthcoming). *Interpersonal relationships as conduits of interunit interaction within multinationals: how well do different types of relationships work?*

50. RIUSSALA, K. & SMALE, A. 2007. Predicting stickiness factors in the international transfer of knowledge through expatriates. *International studies on management and organization*, 20(2):234–246.

51. SUUTARI, V. & BREWSTER, C. 2000. Making their own way: international experience through self-initiated foreign assignments. *Journal of world business*, 35(4):417–436; SUUTARI, V. & BREWSTER, C. 2003. Repatriation: evidence from a longitudinal study of careers and empirical expectations among Finnish repatriates. *International journal of human resource management*, 14(7):1132–1151.

52. PUNNETT, B. J., & RICKS, D. A. 1992. *International business.* Boston: Kent Publishing Co.

53. BREWSTER, C., HARRIS, H. AND PETROVIC, J. 2001. Globally mobile employees: managing the mix. *Journal of professional HRM*, 25:11–15.

54. PELTONEN, T. 2001. New forms of international work: An international survey study, Results of the Finnish Survey. Oulu, Finland: University of Oulu.

55. TAHVANAINEN, M., WORM, V. & WELCH, D. 2005. HR implications of short-term international assignments. 8th IHRM conference:14–17 June. Cairns. [Competitive paper.]

56. PELTONEN, T. 2001. New forms of international work: An international survey study, Results of the Finnish Survey. Oulu, Finland: University of Oulu.

57. BONACHE, J. & CERVINO, J. 1997. Global integration without expatriates. *Human resource management journal*, 7(3):89–100.

58. ZIMMERMANN, A. & SPARROW, P. 2007. Mutual adjustment processes in international teams. *International studies in management and organizations*, 20(2):256–278.

59. HAILEY, J. & HARRY, W. 2007. Localisation: a strategic response to globalisation. (*In* Brewster, C., Sparrow, P. & Dickmann, M. (Eds). *International HRM: A European perspective.* London: Routledge.)

60. BONACHE, J. & BREWSTER, C. 2001. Knowledge transfer and the management of expatriation. *Thunderbird international business review*, 43(1):145–168.

61. See reviews in DOWLING, P. J., SCHULER, R. S. & WELCH, D. 1994. *International dimensions of human resource management.* Belmont, C.A.: Wadsworth; MENDENHALL, M. & ODDOU, G. 1985. The dimensions of expatriate acculturation: a review. *Academy of management review*, 10(1): 39–47.

62. TUNG, R. 1982, Selection and training procedures of US, European and Japanese multinationals. *Human resource management*, 23:129–143; SUUTARI, V. & BREWSTER, C. 1998. The adaptation of expatriates in Europe: evidence from Finnish companies, *Personnel review*, 27(2):89–103.

63. HARRIS, H. & BREWSTER, C. 1997. The coffee machine system: how international selection really works. *International journal of human resource management*, 10(3):488–500.

64. TUNG, R. 1982, Selection and training procedures of US, European and Japanese multinationals. *Human resource management*, 23:129–143; TORBIORN, I. 1982. *Living abroad*. New York: Wiley; EHNERT I. & BREWSTER, C. 2008. An integrative framework for pre-departure preparation. (*In* Brewster, C., Sparrow, P. & Dickmann, M. (Eds). *International HRM: Contemporary issues in Europe* 2nd ed. London: Routledge.)

65. BREWSTER, C. & PICKARD, J. 1994. Evaluating expatriate training. *International studies of management and organisation*, 24(3):18–35; SUUTARI, V. & BREWSTER, C. 1998. The adaptation of expatriates in Europe: evidence from Finnish companies, *Personnel review*, 27(2):89–103.

66. See, for example, BLACK, J. 1991. Returning expatriates feel foreign in their native land. *Personnel*, 68(8):32–40; BIRD, A. & DUNBAR, R. 1991. *The adaptation and adjustment process of managers on international assignments.* Stern Working Paper. New York: New York University; MENDENHALL, M. & ODDOU, G. 1985. The dimensions of expatriate acculturation: a review. *Academy of management review*, 10(1): 39–47.

67. BLACK, J. S. & KAERINASAI, O. 1994. Factors related to Japanese repatriation adjustment. *Human relations*, 47(12):1489–1508; BLACK, J. S. & STEPHENS, G. K. 1989. The influence of the spouse on American expatriate adjustment and intent to stay in Pacific rim overseas assignments. *Journal of management*, 15(4):529–544.

68. BREWSTER, C. 1995. The paradox of expatriate adjustment. (*In* Selmer, J. (Ed). *Expatriate management: New ideas for international business*. Westport, C.T.: Quorum Books.)

69. BRADLEY, P. C., HENDRY, C., & PERKINS, S. 1999. Global or multi-local?: the significance of international values in reward strategy. (*In* Brewster, C. & Harris, H. (Eds). *International HRM: Contemporary issues in Europe*. London: Routledge).

70. SPARROW, P. 1998. International reward systems: to converge or not to converge? (*In* Brewster, C. & Harris, H. (Eds). *International HRM: Contemporary issues in Europe*. London: Routledge.)

71. SCHULER, R. S., FULKERSON, J. R. & DOWLING, P. J. 1991. Strategic performance measurement and management in multinational corporations. *Human resource management*, 30:365–392.

72. LINDHOLM, N., TAHVANAINEN, M. & BJORKMAN, I. 1999. Performance appraisal of host country employees: Western MNEs in China. (*In* Brewster, C. & Harris, H. (Eds). *International HRM: Contemporary issues in Europe*. London: Routledge.)

73. PELTONEN, T. 1999. Repatriation and career systems: Finnish public and private sector repatriates in their career lines. (*In* Brewster, C. & Harris, H. (Eds). *International HRM: Contemporary issues in Europe*. London: Routledge.); SUUTARI, V. & BREWSTER, C. 2003. Repatriation: evidence

from a longitudinal study of careers and empirical expectations among Finish repatriates. *International journal of human resource management*, 14(7):1132–1151.

74. SCULLION, H. 1993. Creating international managers: recruitment and development issues. (*In* Kirkbride, P. (Ed.). *Human resource management in Europe*. London: Routledge.)

75. ADLER, N. J. 1991. *International dimensions of organizational behavior* 2nd ed. Belmont, California: Wadsworth Publishing Company; BLACK, J. S. 1992. Coming home: The relationship of expatriate expectations with repatriate adjustment and job performance. Human relations, 45:95–99; BLACK, J. S., GREGERSEN, H. B. & MENDENHALL, M. E. 1992. Toward a theoretical framework of repatriation adjustment. *Journal of international business studies*, 23(4):737–60; SUUTARI, V. & BREWSTER, C. 2003. Repatriation: evidence from a longitudinal study of careers and empirical expectations among Finnish repatriates. *International journal of human resource management*, 14(7):1132–1151.

76. BLACK, J. S. & GREGERSEN, H. B. 1999. The right way to manage expats. *Harvard business review*, 77(2):52–63.

77. SUUTARI, V. & BREWSTER, C. 2003. Repatriation: evidence from a longitudinal study of careers and empirical expectations among Finish repatriates. *International journal of human resource management*, 14(7):1132–1151.

78. PELTONEN, T. & NEOVVIUS, M. 1998. Repatriation and career systems: Finnish public and private sector repatriates in their career lines. (*In* Brewster, C. & Harris, H. (Eds). *International HRM: Contemporary issues in Europe*. London: Routledge.)

13

The role of human resource management in the new millennium

Learning outcomes

After reading this chapter you should be able to:

▶ Describe the workplace of the new millennium
▶ Explain the redesign of the role of HRM
▶ Identify the competencies required of the HR professional of the future
▶ Describe the structure of the HR department of the future

Purpose

The purpose of this chapter is to introduce you to the role of human resource management in the new millennium.

Chapter overview

This chapter focuses on the new role of HRM within organisations. It begins with a discussion of the important changes taking place within the workplace. It next discusses the necessity to reposition the HR function and looks at tactics which can be used to assist with this process. Thereafter it discusses the competencies HR professionals need to manage this new environment of work and also looks at the new HRM structure which will accommodate these changes. The concluding case study illustrates how the theory contained in this chapter can be applied to a practical situation.

Introduction

The discussion in this book thus far has made it clear that organisations are facing numerous challenges. These challenges require new and innovative responses; this requirement has a direct effect on the world of work within organisations (see Figure 13.1), and also impacts not only on employees' working lives, but also on their future survival. In this book, we have discussed issues and activities through which to address these challenges, but the question now is: how will the future work environment look, and, specifically, what impact will it have on HR professionals and HR departments? In this chapter we shall address the workplace of the new millennium, the redesign of the role of HRM, the competencies required of the HR professional of the future, and the structure of the HR department of the future.

13.1 The workplace of the new millennium

In this section we shall look at the following important work:

- That of Barner, published in his article 'The new millennium workplace: seven changes that will challenge managers and workers'
- That of Barnatt, published in his article 'Office space, cyberspace and the virtual organisation'[1]
- That of Gandossy, Tucker, and Verma, published in their book *Workforce wake-up call: Your workforce is changing, are you?*[2]

Barner's research identifies seven changes, expected over the next few years, that will reshape the work environment. These include[3]:

- The virtual organisation
- A just-in-time workplace

Figure 13.1 Business challenges and their impact on people and HR departments

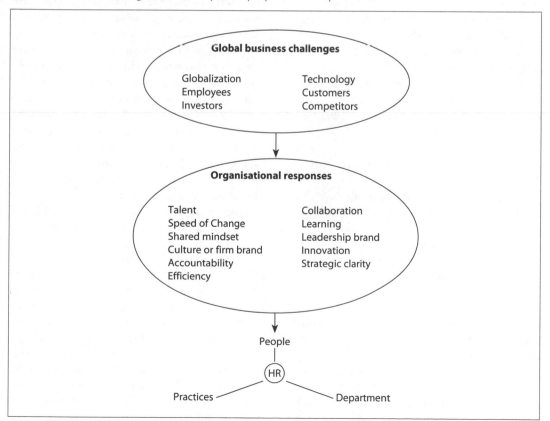

SOURCE: ULRICH, D., BROCKBANK, W. & JOHNSON, D. 2007. *Human resource competency study*. Society for Human Resource Management Annual Conference. Las Vegas: USA, 26 June. [Lecture notes from a paper.] Used with permission.

- The ascendancy of knowledge workers
- Computerised coaching and electronic monitoring
- The growth of worker diversity
- An ageing workforce
- The birth of a dynamic workforce.

We have already mentioned many of these issues in Chapters 1 to 12, but to understand their HR implications better, a closer investigation is necessary.

13.1.1 The virtual organisation

As we indicated earlier in this book, organisations are already using electronic technology to link their members at different work sites, and their members are communicating with each other via these systems. This type of operation is known as a virtual organisation. Virtual organisations exhibit a number of characteristics[4]:

- They are reliant on the medium of cyberspace (the medium in which electronic communications flow and computer software operates)
- They are enabled via new computing and communications developments
- They initially exist only across conventional organisational structures.

The growth in this area can be attributed to developments such as[5]:

- The rapid evolution of electronic technology in the area of video, audio, and text information
- The worldwide spread of computer networks, as a result of globalisation
- The growth of home offices (telecommuting).

For management as well as HR professionals, these developments hold a number of important challenges for the future.

From a management perspective, issues such as effective communication and planning will need attention as the face-to-face approaches which have worked well over the years disappear. In addition, to capitalise on the flexibility and speed through these networks, managers and team members will have to form clear agreements from the outset regarding issues such as performance expectations, team priorities, communication links, and resource allocation.[6] Other problems that may arise include possible misunderstandings and interpretations as a result of email correspondence. Email allows messages and computer files to be sent electronically from computer to computer over a network. The advantage of email is that it cuts down on paper use and increases the speed of messages.[7] According to Barnatt, the computer giant Microsoft sees its email system as the carrier of its culture. The company is expanding so rapidly that it is reliant on email as the glue to hold its employees together.[8-10]

The redistribution of power within the organisation can also be problematic. For example, with electronic networks, individuals can skip levels in the chain of command and give senior managers direct feedback on problems or successes, which is not the case in many conventional organisations.[11]

As a result of the computer networks, faster decision making and easier access to company information are also possible. However, the speed of decision making may place great pressure on individuals who do not possess the necessary skills to function within such environments. At the same time, those who thrive in such an environment will find themselves in a strong competitive position in the networked marketplace.[12]

From an HRM point of view, the virtual organisation also holds a number of challenges. For example, the ways in which organisations have approached recruitment and career development in the past will change rapidly. More companies and employees are using the Internet to match jobs and candidates.[13] If the information on individuals is up to date and correct, no skill within a company can go unnoticed. The Internet also helps management to put together people with specific skills via cross-functional teams to solve problems. This was impossible with the outdated information systems and rigid organisational structures of the past. Flexibility is thus the new goal.

Easy access to relevant information will mean that individuals will also be able to plan their own career moves within the company, thus utilising the available talent to the benefit of both the company and the individual.[14]

With multiple teams, the rigid, traditional job description will also have to disappear. Job descriptions are not flexible enough for the constantly changing world of new strategies, customer requirements, and membership of multiple teams. To fill this gap, companies will follow the competency-based approaches more enthusiastically. Competencies can and should be organised into menus that individuals and teams can use to describe their work and conduct people practices.[15]

With workers working at distant sites, problems can also arise regarding the appraisal system the organisation uses and the manner in which it compensates these individuals. HR managers will have to devise innovative methods to address these unique situations.

13.1.2 The just-in-time workforce

The growth in temporary workers and just-in-time workers, and the outsourcing of a large number of organisational functions, has resulted in companies using more temporary workers.

HR professionals utilising these types of worker will have to find new ways to motivate them, as serious problems in performance and morale will occur. Research in the USA indicates that conflict between permanent staff and temporary staff can easily occur where, for example, organisations pay permanent staff for production outputs while giving a flat hourly rate to temporary employees, as we mentioned in an earlier chapter.[16] Due to their employment contract, temporary workers cannot be motivated by the traditional methods of promotion, merit increases or, even, profit-sharing programmes. To overcome these problems, management and HR professionals will have to spend more time and money on providing training, giving such workers greater access to company information and a bigger role in decision-making. Thus, in the workplace of the future, HR professionals will have to look at issues such as the orientation and training of just-in-time workers.[17]

13.1.3 The ascendancy of knowledge workers

As the world moves rapidly away from manufacturing into the services sector, HR managers will have to rethink their traditional approaches to directing, coaching, and motivating employees. Thus, the emerging knowledge worker in this new environment will be a unique individual whom the organisation must nurture to enable it to gain the competitive edge it desires.[18]

As companies continue to become flatter, they will retrench individuals who do not add value. Gone are the days when companies paid individuals only for performing managerial tasks. Managers and employees will have to make a strong commitment to lifelong learning and skill advancement to achieve job security in the new work environment. As these new knowledge workers become more mobile, HR managers will continually have to educate and train new employees in company culture and values.[19]

13.1.4 Computerised coaching and electronic monitoring

The growth in electronic systems over the coming years will allow employees to become fully independent. Easier control by managers over work employees perform may result in employees feeling manipulated and exploited, placing the relationship between the manager and employee under great pressure.[20] Employees will also be able to learn more rapidly, e.g. by placing solutions to problems in a central database which can be accessed globally. Employees will also become less dependent on managers for coaching, training, and performance feedback, resulting in the redesign of managers' jobs. The operation of the electronic networks 24 hours a day will make it difficult for employees to draw a line between work and home, which may result in domestic problems. Employees' right to privacy may also be invaded as a result of the permanent presence of the network system in the home environment.[21]

13.1.5 The growth of worker diversity

The mobility of workers between countries has increased enormously over the years. Individuals with specific skills (e.g. computer specialists and chartered accountants) are sought throughout the world.[22] Increasingly, companies are setting up manufacturing and assembly plants worldwide and smaller companies are expanding into international markets.

For the first time, managerial staff will come into contact with multicultural groups and will need to adapt to different work expectations and communication styles. Companies will highly value workers who are able to operate successfully in these diverse environments.[23] HR professionals will find it necessary to provide sensitivity training to help managers understand the needs and perspectives of different members in these work groups.

13.1.6 The ageing workforce

In the past, companies were, to a large extent, reluctant to employ older workers, as they saw them as less productive, less flexible, and more expensive.[24] Older workers were also denied challenging jobs. However, with the lack of skills in numerous areas, companies are again employing older workers because of their experience and maturity. These workers are also more flexible about taking part-time and odd-hour shifts than younger workers are. However, the implications are that younger managers may find themselves threatened when managing older staff. In this situation, HR managers must arrange for these managers to undergo training in managing teams and communication skills, to enable them to extract the best efforts from older teams.[25]

13.1.7 The birth of the dynamic workforce

The processes and methods of performing work are no longer fixed but fluid. This situation requires workers to adapt continuously. Thus, over the next few years, managerial performance will be based less on the ability to direct and coordinate work functions and more on improving key work processes through innovative thinking on a continuous basis.[26] This new dynamic environment will require workers to jump quickly into new ventures and manage temporary projects.

13.2 The redesign of the HRM role

From the previous discussion, it is obvious that if HRM is to address these changes successfully, the traditional role it has played until now will not work in the future. Therefore, the redesign of the HRM role is necessary. Galbraith[27], as quoted by Kesler[28], argues that the function must be repositioned much in the same way as a company would reposition itself to become more competitive.

One method organisations have used to achieve this has been the re-engineering of HR processes. However, although re-engineering will reduce waste and result in more satisfied internal clients, it will not change the fundamental role that HR professionals play in the business or the value HR professionals add to shareholders.[29]

Research suggests that, to be successful, HR professionals must first work with top management to contract for a new or realigned role, before pursuing the re-engineering route. Thus, this must take place after the contract process. Kesler identifies three tactics that organisations can follow to achieve success[30]:

• Contracting with line management for a new role for HR
• Identifying and developing new HR competencies
• Redesigning HR work, systems, and the organisation.

All these components cannot achieve change alone; organisations need to do them in conjunction with one another. As Kesler remarks[31]:

> Contracting for new roles without competencies to deliver is pointless; redesigning or eliminating work without a consensus from the client organisation leads to confusion and dissatisfied clients.
>
> SOURCE: KESLER, G. C. 1995. A model and process for redesigning the HRM role, competencies, and work in a major multinational corporation. *Human resource management*, 32(2):230, Summer.

What do these individual elements entail? Let us take a brief look.

13.2.1 Contracting new roles

It is important that organisations, when contracting new roles to be performed, involve the internal clients who will be served. Thus, organisations need to approach several stakeholders. These can include employees, middle management, functional top executives, HR and top line management. The process must also be a two-way dialogue in which the client managers influence, and are influenced by, their HRM providers. The business needs to develop a process whereby it identifies HR priorities through intense involvement of both HR and line management.[32]

Establishing the priority HR practice areas and outputs line managers desire is not enough. HRM and line managers must also agree on how the HRM role will actually change in the new environment, beyond the re-engineering effort of the HRM processes. The question that must be asked is: what value will HRM truly add?[33] For example, in the case of training and development, will the HRM role be to enable employees to be better businesspeople or will it merely deliver a number of individual training programmes?[34] Thus, establishing this fundamental orientation of HRM work is critical if it is truly going to redesign itself for the new challenges.

Kesler has proposed a 'performance capabilities' (PC) model[35] that will help in this regard (see Table 13.1). As Table 13.1 shows, the model consists of a continuum of six value-adding roles, each of which is a distinct competency. The roles – from left to right in the model – are[36]:

Table 13.1 The performance capabilities model: defining the fundamental role of HRM

Greater leveraged roles			Less leveraged roles		
1 **Catalytic influence**	**2** **Diagnostic assessment**	**3** **Innovating processes, structure**	**4** **Assurance of standards**	**5** **Administration and services**	**6** **Problem-solving**
'Partnering role'			**'Transactional role'**		
• Enable others • Knowledge-based • Performance-based quality • Distributed resources • Enhance business performance • Knowledge transfer to line • Highly integrated with business process • Non-linear work – focus design on outcomes and competencies • Early life cycle			• Service others (or remove administrative barriers) • System-based • Conformance-based quality • Consolidated resources • Economy of scale/cost (commodity) • Few specialists/admin transferred to line • Parallel, stand-alone • Linear work – process map and redesign (for consolidation, elimination, automation) • Late in the life cycle		

SOURCE: KESLER, G. C. 1995. A model and process for redesigning the HRM role, competencies, and work in a major multinational corporation. *Human resource management*, 34(2):237, Summer. Reprinted by permission of Wiley-Liss Inc., a subsidiary of John Wiley & Sons, Inc.

- Catalytic influence
- Diagnostic and fact-based analysis
- Innovating business structures and processes
- Assurance standards
- Administration and services
- Problem-solving.

Roles one to three generally exert more leverage, as the model indicates. Here a partnership between HRM and line people creates benefits to the line organisation that are greater than the immediate efforts of the HR staff member.[37] Roles four to six, however, have less leverage because they are more transactional in nature and are less likely to add value to the money invested. Most HR departments view their current activities and resources as falling in the 'controlling, administering, and problem-solving' roles. However, the value of the various roles can be determined only in the context of a given company and its needs.[38] However, for the business strategy to be successful, the partnership-orientated performance capabilities (roles 1 to 3) must support the business strategy more directly than the service-transactions portion of the continuum (roles 4 to 6) does. The most effective use of resources is served when the continuum is utilised effectively.[39]

Activating the left side of the model first will normally reduce the resources consumed on the right side of the continuum later, according to Kesler.[40] For example, labour-relations planning and joint facilitation of the labour-management process will usually result in less problem-solving regarding labour relations. Thus, to be effective, the HR role which normally starts on the right side of the model (roles four to six) must move to the left (roles one to three), where conditions are best accomplished. Thus both halves of the model must be delivered to the appropriate extent and in a highly competent manner to be successful.[41]

To implement the discussion between line and HR managers, Kesler provides a further extension of the model shown in Table 13.1. He does this by placing HRM practice areas and the performance capabilities on an HR processes grid in which a dialogue can take place in order to[42]:

- Contract for priority, value-added roles, while influencing the expectations of internal clients
- Identify a set of required competencies that reflect those priorities
- Redesign the work and processes.

Table 13.2 shows Kesler's HR grid, which was completed by the US company Whirlpool's North American Appliance Group (NAAG). This grid will provide a tool for repositioning the HRM function by answering the following questions[43]:

- What is the HRM work that needs to be performed?
- Who are the best people to perform it?
- Where does the HRM organisation clearly add the most value?
- What are the specific outputs required, and in what time frames?
- What is the relationship between line and HRM staff in these major practice areas?
- How are we allocating resources among the cells of the grid?
- What can we stop doing?

Getting answers to these questions for the future state will form the basic contract with the line organisation. The process by which to obtain these answers can consist of scanning for competitive success factors to implement the business strategy, benchmark visits to other companies, interviews with focus groups within the company (e.g. managers across diverse units and group functions), and surveys among the staff (using questionnaires on the HR process grid).[44] For example, the survey can ask respondents to identify which cells in the grid should be further emphasised and which should be de-emphasised over the next number of years, given specific business strategies. Responses to other questions could determine what activities could be eliminated, consolidated or automated, either at the business-unit or other levels. After gathering the data, feedback meetings must be held and final decisions made. It is interesting to note that, in the Whirlpool case, middle management emphasised the maintenance or service-orientated portions of

Table 13.2 HR grid at Whirlpool's North American Appliance Group (NAAG)

	Catalytic influence	Diagnostic and analysis	Innovative process, structure and plans	Assurance of service	Admin and service	Problem-solving
Organisation design						
Talent pool management						
Training and education						
Employee involvement						
Rewards and recognition						
Well-being and morale						
Communication						

Key:

Increase	No change	Decrease
	Future emphasis	

SOURCE: KESLER, G. C. 1995. A model and process for redesigning the HRM role, competencies, and work in a major multinational corporation. *Human resource management*, 34(2):244, Summer. Reprinted by permission of Wiley-Liss Inc., a subsidiary of John Wiley & Sons, Inc

the grid. The team involved in this process must try to use the information from other more successful companies to increase the support for the partnering (the left side of the model) elements of the grid. After the discussions, a two-to-five-year plan can be drawn up, HR processes re-engineered, and staff competencies developed.[45]

13.2.2 Competencies

Besides new roles, additional competencies to support the new role – for example leadership, strategic planning, and business know-how – must also be developed, as we indicated earlier. In many HRM organisations these competencies will be unknown to the HRM staff.[46] The discussion in section 13.3 provides more details in this area.

13.2.3 Redesign of the HRM process and structure

The final step is the redesign of the HRM function. Here re-engineering plays a vital role, as it does in the other functional areas within the organisation. In most organisations the re-engineering action redirects the staff responsibilities away from functional work to client-centred consulting, while the HRM structure is realigned to focus on administrative service centres and internal HRM consulting organisations.[47] See section 13.4 for more details.

13.3 The competencies the future HR professional will require

As we indicated earlier, one of the tactics by which to reposition the HRM function includes the development of competencies for the HR employees. Competency refers to an individual's demonstrated knowledge, skills, and abilities.[48] The literature indicates that researchers have done little work to identify, conceptually or empirically, competencies HR professionals require.[49] Many companies follow the approach whereby either the insights of senior managers or other internal customers define competencies for HR professionals.

Ulrich, Brockbank, Yeung, and Lake propose that HR professionals demonstrate competence when they add value to their business. They can do this by delivering to their business ideas, programmes, and initiatives that can assist it to compete. Thus, the value of HR professionals resides in their ability to create a competitive advantage. If HR professionals develop the competencies to design and deliver practices which build organisational capability, they create and sustain unique sources of competitive advantage.[50]

Ulrich, Brockbank, and Johnson, from the Ross School of Business at the University of Michigan, developed a six-domain framework for conceptualising HR competencies (see Figure 13.2). They based the model on results obtained in a major Human Resource Competency Study (HRCS), which they undertook in conjunction with the RBL group. The framework consists of the following elements: talent manager and organisational designer, culture and change steward, strategy architect, operational executor, business ally, and credible activist.[51]

We shall now take a brief look at these elements. (Please note that the following work is based on the notes of a lecture given at the Society for Human Resource Management Annual Conference held in Las Vegas in June 2007 in the USA.[52])

13.3.1 Talent manager and organisational designer

In this domain, the HR professional must be active in the management of talent and the design of the organisation. Talent management focuses on how individuals enter and move up,

across or out of the organisation, while organisation design focuses on the structure, governance, and processes that shape how an organisation works. Good talent without a supporting organisation will not be sustained, and a good organisation will not operate without good talent. HR professionals who are successful in this area will have the following capabilities:

- Able to develop talent for today and tomorrow
- Able to design reward systems
- Able to shape the organisation
- Able to foster communication within the organisation.[53]

13.3.2 Culture and change steward

In this domain, the HR professional must recognise, articulate, and shape a company's culture. Culture involves the values, beliefs, and artefacts of an organisation. As a steward of culture, the HR professional must respect the past culture and also help shape a new culture. HR professionals who are successful in this area will have the following capabilities:

- Able to facilitate change
- Able to craft a culture
- Able to enact a culture
- Able to personalise a culture.[54]

13.3.3 Strategy architect

In this domain, the HR professional knows how to influence and implement the business strategy. To achieve this goal, the HR professional facilitates strategic-alignment change by turning what needs to be done into what is actually done. HR professionals who are successful in this area will have the following capabilities:

- Able to engage customers
- Able to sustain strategic agility.[55]

13.3.4 Operational executor

In this domain the HR professional administers the day-to-day work of managing people within an organisation. This goal is achieved by drafting, adapting, and implementing policies. To achieve credibility, the HR professional needs to do this

Figure 13.2 Six domains to become a successful HR professional

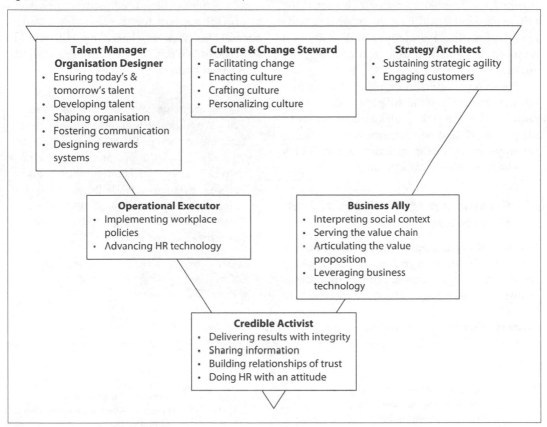

SOURCE: ULRICH, D., BROCKBANK, W. & JOHNSON, D. 2007. *Human resource competency study.* Society for Human Resource Management Annual Conference. Las Vegas: USA, 26 June. [Lecture notes from a paper.] Used with permission.

task flawlessly and base it on the consistent application of policies. HR professionals who are successful in this area will have the following capabilities:
- Able to implement workplace policies
- Able to advance HR technology.[56]

13.3.5 Business ally

In this domain, the HR professional contributes to the success of the business by knowing the social context or setting in which the business operates. HR professionals who are successful in this area will have the following capabilities:
- Able to interpret the social context
- Able to serve the value chain
- Able to articulate the value proposition
- Able to leverage the business technology.[57]

13.3.6 Credible activist

In this domain, the HR professional is both credible (respected, admired, listened to) and active (offers a point of view, takes a position, challenges assumptions). HR professionals who are successful in this area will have the following capabilities:
- Able to deliver results with integrity
- Able to share information
- Able to build relationships of trust
- Able to do HR with an attitude.[58]

The domains within which the HR professional must operate have been identified. The question now is: what competencies must the HR professional possess to be successful within these domains? The essential competencies underlying these domains are summarised in

Figure 13.3. The figure makes it clear that the HR professional will have to possess a wide range of skills, knowledge, and traits not required previously. Thus a great challenge lies ahead!

The different roles to be played by the new HR department and the different competencies required by the HR professional have been identified. All that now remains is to determine the appearance of the structure within which the HR professional will operate.

13.4 **The structure of the HR department of the future**

For the HR department to function successfully and survive the tremendous changes taking place within organisations, it needs to undergo major restructuring. Thus, reorganisation

should better position the function to enable it to provide support for the changing business needs. This view is shared by Hilborn (an associate of William M. Mercer in Philadelphia, USA), who remarks[59]:

> HR departments have been evolving away from a traditional functional design to a team based model. The traditional design typically includes a vice president of HR, then a manager of compensation and benefits, a manager of HRIS and payroll, a manager of employment and so on. However, the emerging model is more like a three-legged stool.

SOURCE: Quoted in JOINSON, C. 1999. Changing shapes. *HR magazine*, 44(3):41–48.

Figure 13.3 Competencies for the HR professional of the future

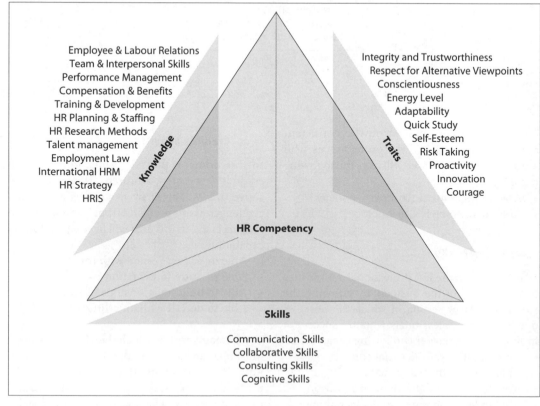

Employee & Labour Relations
Team & Interpersonal Skills
Performance Management
Compensation & Benefits
Training & Development
HR Planning & Staffing
HR Research Methods
Talent management
Employment Law
International HRM
HR Strategy
HRIS

Knowledge

Integrity and Trustworthiness
Respect for Alternative Viewpoints
Conscientiousness
Energy Level
Adaptability
Quick Study
Self-Esteem
Risk Taking
Proactivity
Innovation
Courage

Traits

HR Competency

Skills

Communication Skills
Collaborative Skills
Consulting Skills
Cognitive Skills

SOURCE: Adapted from MCEVOY, G. M., HAYTON, J. C., WARNICK, A. P., MUMFORD, T. W., HANKS, S. H. & BLAHNA, M. J. 2005. A competency-based model for developing human resource professionals. *Journal of management education*, 29(3):393, June. Used with permission from the Copyright Clearance Centre.

Figure 13.4 Emerging HR organisational model

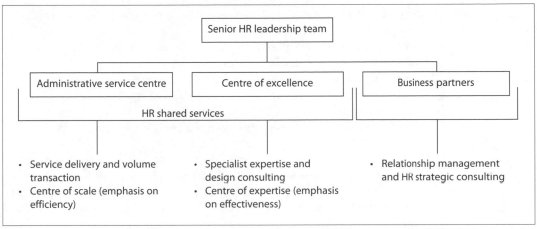

SOURCE: JOINSON, C. 1999. Changing shapes. *HR magazine*, 44(3), March. Republished with permission of *HR magazine*. Permission conveyed through the Copyright Clearance Center, Inc.

Hilborn's emerging HR organisational model appears in Figure 13.4. The model clearly shows the three legs mentioned in the previous paragraph, namely[60]:

- *An administrative service centre.* This is responsible for processing the payroll, benefits, and other administrative aspects, and also focuses on the efficiency in transaction functions.
- *A centre of excellence.* This concentrates on design rather than transactions and will have line managers as its customers. The emphasis here is on effectiveness.
- *Business partners.* The third leg comprises the HR business partners. These employees do not get involved in transactions but, instead, act as consultants and planners, linking the business with appropriate programmes.[62–64]

Another new development, besides this one in the structure of the HR department within organisations, is that an increasing number of large and multinational organisations are moving to shared services models in delivering the HR function.[65] The rationale for this is that it is commonly believed that the adaptation of an HR shared services model can transform the role of HRM by enabling the HR function to be more strategic at the corporate level and more cost-effective at the operational level. In terms of orientation, the literature identifies two broad types of HR shared services[66]:

- According to Cooke[67], the first is the set of shared services set up by large organisations, such as consultancies, to provide HR services both to their own organisation and to external client organisations as an outsourcing business.
- The second refers to those set up by large and often multinational or multisite organisations that aim to restructure their HR service provision through recentralisation and the creation of an internal market system – i.e. having a small HR team at the corporate level with HR service centres in the company with a self-help, online HR information system.

Numerous examples exist where the first type of shared services is working well, however, a number of problems have arisen regarding the second, more recent, option of shared services. For example, in many instances researchers found that a mismatch existed between the employees' expectations of HR services and the services they actually received.[68] This resulted in a negative perception of the utility of the HR shared services centre. This finding suggests that it is important to think through the implications of change for the role of the HR function, the impact on employee work processes, and the

Table 13.3 Key questions to consider when adopting HR shared services centres

I Strategic issues	1. What rationale exists for setting up the shared services centre, in addition to cost savings through synergy? What are the alternatives?
	2. Is the HR shared services model really more cost effective when hidden costs are calculated? What are potential indirect costs and how can they be measured?
	3. Are you going to look at the shared services centres of other firms before you set up your own? For example, will you engage in market research or benchmark exercise?
	4. If yes, how will you do it? What criteria will you use?
	5. What are the perceived benefits and disadvantages of the new service provision for the stakeholders?
	6. How will the shared services centre affect the role of HR strategy in the corporate strategy?
	7. How will the relationship between the HR professionals and line managers be reshaped?
	8. How should the HR function reconcile or manage its two roles: providing HR support services to the employees and line management and providing strategic input to the corporate strategy?
II Managing the change process	9. How will different groups of people be affected by the change (e.g., line managers, HR managers, HR officers, and individuals) who receive the services?
	10. How will the change process be managed?
	11. How will resistance to change be expressed and managed?
	12. What training is needed for different groups of employees?
III Operational issues (the business of the shared services centre)	13. What services will the shared services centre provide and how will the work be organized?
	14. How will the shared services centre interact with line managers and the corporate HR professionals to deliver a holistic package of HR services that will provide both operational services and strategic influence at the corporate level?
	15. What will be the internal contractual arrangements (e.g., service-level agreements, key performance indicators) between the centre and divisions of the firm?
IV HR policy and practice for the HR staff in the shared services centre	16. Will the setting up of the shared services centre lead to recentralization of the HR function and specialization of HR officers' skill portfolios?
	17. Will the HR staff lose any jobs as a result of the change?
	18. Will it be necessary to recruit new HR staff for the centre due to staff turnover (e.g., if staff refuse to be relocated) or new skill requirements (e.g., IT and customer management skills rather than HR specialists skills)?
	19. How will the following HR policies and practices be different from what they were before the change?
	(a) recruitment
	(b) training and development
	(c) skill/competence requirement
	(d) work organisation and responsibility
	(e) their role in the client department/establishment
	(f) terms and conditions
	(g) career pattern.
	20. In particular, what career pattern will exist for HR personnel, and what are the advantages and difficulties for their career progression within the organisation and within the broader labour market (as compared to the three typologies of an HR career pattern: vertical, zigzag, and parachuting)?
	21. How will the centre manage its work organisation to avoid the 'sweatshop and tight surveillance' image and nature of call-centre work that have been widely criticized?

SOURCE: COOKE, F. L. 2006. Modeling an HR shared services centre: experience of an MNC in the United Kingdom. *Human resource management*, 45(2):225. Used with permission.

way in which employees will experience the HR services.[69] Table 13.3 shows a number of key questions that Cooke has provided, and which a company needs to ask when it decides to move to an HR shared services approach. The information provided in Table 13.3 makes it clear that moving from a traditional HR delivery model to an HR shared services model involves major organisational change and careful management.[70]

Companies need to think through many strategic and operational issues. Given the high cost, financially as well as emotionally, in moving to a shared services model (second option), companies need to take a holistic approach and carry out sophisticated financial calculations to weigh up the cost of insourcing versus outsourcing.[71]

SUMMARY

This chapter looked at the important changes that will take place within the workplace over the next few years. It has also indicated the role the HR function will play. To be successful, the HR function will have to be repositioned. The chapter listed various tactics which can assist with this process.

The chapter also highlighted issues pertaining to the competencies HR professionals need to manage the new HR function, as well as the new HR structure which will accommodate these changes.

KEY CONCEPTS

• Administrative service centre	• Electronic monitoring
• Ageing workforce	• Just-in-time workforce
• Ascendancy of knowledge workers	• Operational executor
• Business ally	• Partnering
• Business partner	• Redesign
• Centre of excellence	• Restructuring
• Change processes	• Shared services model
• Change steward	• Strategy architect
• Competencies	• Talent manager
• Computerised coaching	• Value-added roles
• Credible activist	• Virtual organisation
• Culture	• Worker diversity
• Dynamic workforce	

CASE STUDY

Objective: To understand the role of the HR department in a changing environment

A change in HR

GE Fanuc is a manufacturer of products for factory automation and control. Headquartered in Johannesburg with 1 500 employees, the HR department primarily performed administrative support activities. But when Dawid Ellis took over as Senior Executive Director of Human Resources, he and his staff began by restructuring and decentralising the IIR entity so that each functional area of the company has an HR manager assigned to it. The HR managers were expected to be key contributors to their areas by becoming knowledgeable about the business issues faced by their business functional units. Today, HR managers participate in developing business strategies and ensure that human resource dimensions are considered. For instance, the HR manager for manufacturing has HR responsibilities for 600 employees.

In that role, she contributes to workflow, production, scheduling, and other manufacturing decisions. It also means that she is more accessible to and has more credibility with manufacturing workers, most of whom are hourly workers. Making the transition in HR management required going from seven to three levels of management, greatly expanding the use of cross-functional work teams and significantly increasing training.

To ease employee and managerial anxieties about the changes, GE Fanuc promised that no employees would lose their jobs. Managers and supervisors affected by the elimination of levels were offered promotions, transfer to other jobs in GE Fanuc, or early retirement buyouts.

Additionally, employees were promised profit sharing, which has resulted in up to three weeks additional pay in profit sharing bonuses in some years. The test of the change is in the results. GE Fanuc's revenue is up almost 18%. More than 40 work teams meet regularly to discuss work goals, track their performance against established measures, and discuss problems and issues. Employee turnover is also extremely low in most areas.

Questions and activities

1. What possible problems do you see with this approach for HRM in other organisations?
2. Compare this approach to HRM with the involvement of HR in operations in a job you have had.

SOURCE: MATHIS, R. L. & JACKSON, J. H. 2004. *Human resource management* 10th ed. (international student edition). Mason, Ohio: South Western, a division of Thomson Learning:47–48. Used with permission.

REVIEW QUESTIONS AND ACTIVITIES

1. Discuss the important challenges facing management and HR professionals regarding the development of virtual organisations.
2. Briefly explain Kesler's performance-capabilities model.
3. Ulrich, Brockbank, and Johnson recently identified six domains which can serve as a framework for identifying competencies for HR professionals. Briefly discuss.
4. Write a short paragraph on the concept of the 'HR shared services model'.
5. Explain Hilborn's emerging HR organisational model.
6. Provide a list of the seven changes, identified by Barner, that will take place over the next number of years and will reshape the work environment.
7. HR professionals will have to find new ways to motivate the just-in-time workforce. Discuss briefly.
8. Write a short paragraph on the challenges facing HR professionals regarding computerised coaching and electronic monitoring in the new workplace.
9. List Kesler's three tactics that can be followed in the redesign of the HRM role.
10. Write a short paragraph on the ageing workforce.

FURTHER READING

GANDOSSY, R. P., TUCKER, E. & VERMA, N. 2006. *Workforce wake-up call: your workforce is changing, are you?* Hoboken, N.J.: John Wiley & Sons.

DOMSCH, M. E. & HRISTOZOVA, E. 2006. *Human resource management in consulting firms.* Hamburg: Springer.

WARNER, M. & WITZEL, M. 2004. *Managing in virtual organisations.* London, Thomson Learning.

WEB SITES

www.shrm.org – Society for Human Resource Management (for latest research results pertaining to the changing environment of HRM)

www.gilgordon.com – site for issues such as telecommuting, telework, and alternative officing

www.prosgateway.com/www/index2.html – links to HR related Web pages

ENDNOTES

1. BARNER, R. 1996. The new millennium workplace: seven changes that will challenge managers and workers. *Futurist*, 30(2):14–18, March/April. [Online.] Available: http://gateway.ovid.com/server5/ovidweb. 10 October 2007. See also GIBSON, R. (ed). 2000. *Rethinking the future.* London: Nicholas Brealey Publishing; ULRICH, D. 1998. A new mandate for human resources. *Harvard business review* (Jan/Feb):124–134; BARNATT, C. 1995. Office space, cyberspace and virtual organisation. *Journal of general management*, 20(4):78–91, Summer.

2. GANDOSSY, R. P., TUCKER, E. & VERMA, N. 2006. *Workforce wake-up call: Your workforce is changing, are you?* Hoboken, N.J.: John Wiley & Sons.

3. BARNER, R. 1996. The new millennium workplace: seven changes that will challenge managers and workers. *Futurist*, 30(2):14–18, March/April. [Online.] Available: http://gateway.ovid.com/server5/ovidweb. 10 October 2007.

4. BARNATT, C. 1995. Office space, cyberspace and virtual organisation. *Journal of general management*,

20(4): 83, Summer; GANDOSSY, R. P., TUCKER, E. & VERMA, N. 2006. *Workforce wake-up call: Your workforce is changing, are you?* Hoboken, N.J.: John Wiley & Sons:xiv–xv.

5. BARNER, R. 1996. The new millennium workplace: seven changes that will challenge managers and workers. *Futurist*, 30(2):14–18, March/April. [Online.] Available: http://gateway.ovid.com/server5/ovidweb. 10 October 2007.

6. Ibid.

7. BARNATT, C. 1995. Office space, cyberspace and virtual organisation. *Journal of general management*, 20(4): 83, Summer.

8. Ibid.

9. PRUIIT, S. & BARRET, T. 1993. Corporate virtual workspace. (*In* Benedikt, M. (Ed). *Cyberspace: First steps.* Cambridge, M.A.: MIT Press.)

10. LLOYD, B. 1990. Office productivity – time for a revolution. *Long range planning*, 23(1):66–79.

11. BARNER, R. 1996. The new millennium workplace: seven changes that will challenge managers and

workers. *Futurist*, 30(2):14–18, March/April. [Online.] Available: http://gateway.ovid.com/server5/ovidweb. 10 October 2007.

12. Ibid.
13. Ibid.:3.
14. Ibid.
15. MCLAGAN, P. A. 1997. Competencies: the next generation. *Training & development*, 51(5):2. [Online.] Available: http://gateway.ovid. com/server3/ovidweb. 14 September 2008.
16. BARNER, R. 1996. The new millennium workplace: seven changes that will challenge managers and workers. *Futurist*, 30(2):14–18, March/April. [Online.] Available: http://gateway.ovid.com/server5/ovidweb. 10 October 2007.
17. Ibid.; GANDOSSY, R. P., TUCKER, E. & VERMA, N. 2006. *Workforce wake-up call: Your workforce is changing, are you?* Hoboken, N.J.: John Wiley & Sons:xiii–xiv.
18. BARNER, R. 1996. The new millennium workplace: seven changes that will challenge managers and workers. *Futurist*, 30(2):14–18, March/April. [Online.] Available: http://gateway.ovid.com/server5/ovidweb. 10 October 2007; GANDOSSY, R. P., TUCKER, E. & VERMA, N. 2006. *Workforce wake-up call: Your workforce is changing, are you?* Hoboken, N.J.: John Wiley & Sons:xviii–xxiii.
19. BARNER, R. 1996. The new millennium workplace: seven changes that will challenge managers and workers. *Futurist*, 30(2):14–18, March/April. [Online.] Available: http://gateway.ovid.com/server5/ovidweb. 10 October 2007.
20. Ibid.:5.
21. Ibid.
22. Ibid.; GANDOSSY, R. P., TUCKER, E. & VERMA, N. 2006. *Workforce wake-up call: Your workforce is changing, are you?* Hoboken, N.J.: John Wiley & Sons:xv–xvii.
23. BARNER, R. 1996. The new millennium workplace: seven changes that will challenge managers and workers. *Futurist*, 30(2):14–18, March/April. [Online.] Available: http://gateway.ovid.com/server5/ovidweb. 10 October 2007.
24. Ibid.:5; GANDOSSY, R. P., TUCKER, E. & VERMA, N. 2006. *Workforce wake-up call: Your workforce is changing, are you?* Hoboken, N.J.: John Wiley & Sons:xii–xiii.
25. BARNER, R. 1996. The new millennium workplace: seven changes that will challenge managers and workers. *Futurist*, 30(2):14–18, March/April. [Online.] Available: http://gateway.ovid.com/server5/ovidweb. 10 October 2007.
26. Ibid.; GANDOSSY, R. P., TUCKER, E. & VERMA, N. 2006. *Workforce wake-up call: Your workforce is changing, are you?* Hoboken, N.J.: John Wiley & Sons:87–94.
27. GALBRAITH, J. 1992. Positioning human resources as a value-adding function: the case of Rockwell

International. *Human resource management*, 31(4):287–300.

28. KESLER, G. C. 1995. A model and process for redesigning the HRM role, competencies, and work in a major multinational corporation. *Human resource management*, 32(2):229–252, Summer.
29. Ibid.:230.
30. Ibid.
31. Ibid.
32. Ibid.:231.
33. Ibid.:236.
34. Ibid.
35. Ibid.
36. Ibid.
37. Ibid.
38. Ibid.
39. Ibid.
40. Ibid.
41. Ibid.
42. Ibid.:238.
43. Ibid.
44. Ibid.:239–246.
45. Ibid.
46. Ibid.:231–232. See also BAILL, B. 1999. The changing requirements of the HR professional – implications for the development of HR professionals. *Human resource management*, 38(2):171–176; BARBER, A. E. 1999. Implications for the design of human resource management – education, training and certification. *Human resource management*, 38(2):177–182; HUNTER, R. H. 1999. The new HR and the new HR consultant: Developing human resource consultants at Andersen Consulting. *Human resource management*, 38(2,):147–155; GONZALES, B., Ellis, Y. M., Riffel, P. J. & Yager, D. 1999. Training at IBM's human resource service center: Linking people, technology and HR processes. *Human resource management*, 38(2):135–142; HEINEMAN, R. L. 1999. Emphasizing analytical skills in HR graduate education: the Ohio State University MLHR program. *Human resource management*, 38(2):131–134; BROCKBANK, W., ULRICH, D. & BEATTY, R. W. 1999. HR professional development: creating the future creators at the University of Michigan Business School. *Human resource management*, 38(2):111–118; DYER, W. G. 1999. Training human resource champions for the twenty-first century. *Human resource management*, 38(2):119–124.
47. KESLER, G. C. 1995. A model and process for redesigning the HRM role, competencies, and work in a major multinational corporation. *Human resource management*, 32(2):232, Summer.
48. ULRICH, D., BROCKBANK, W., YEUNG, A. K. & LAKE, D. G. 1995. Human resource competencies: an empirical assessment. *Human resource management*, 34(4):473–495.
49. Ibid.:474. See also ATHEY, T. R. & ORTH, M. S. 1999. Emerging competency methods for the future. *Human resource management*, 38(3):215–226;

HOFRICHTER, D. A. & MCGOVERN, T. 2001. People, competencies and performance: clarifying Means and Ends. *Compensation & benefits review*, July/August:34–38; ULRICH, D. & EICHINGER, R. W. 1998. Delivering HR with an attitude, professional, that is. *HR magazine*, June:154–160; MCEVOY, G. M., HAYTON, J. C., WARNICK, A. P., MUMFORD, T. V., HANKS, S. H. & BLAHNA, M. J. 2005. A competency-based model for developing human resource professionals. *Journal of management education*, 29(3):383–402, June.

50. ULRICH, D., BROCKBANK, W., YEUNG, A. K. & LAKE, D. G. 1995. Human resource competencies: an empirical assessment. *Human resource management*, 34(4):473–495. See also ULRICH, D. & BROCKBANK, W. 2005. *The HR value proposition*. Boston, Massachusetts: Harvard Business School Press.

51. GROSSMAN, R. J. 2007. New competencies for HR. *HR magazine*, 52(6,):58–62.

52. ULRICH, D., BROCKBANK, W. & JOHNSON, D. 2007. *Human resource competency study*. Society for Human Resource Management Annual Conference. Las Vegas: USA, 26 June. [Lecture notes from a paper.]

53. Ibid.

54. Ibid.

55. Ibid.

56. Ibid.

57. Ibid.

58. Ibid.

59. Quoted in JOINSON, C. 1999. Changing shapes. *HR magazine*, 44(3):41–48.

60. Ibid.:44.

61. Ibid.

62. Ibid. See also MARQUES, J. F. 2006. The new human resource department: a cross functional unit. *Human resource development quarterly*, 17(1):117–123, Spring.

63. BOBROW, W. 1998. Is your HR department in shape to support your business strategies? *Bobbin*, 39(8,):64–68.

64. PETERS, J. 1997. A future vision of human resources. (*In* Ulrich, D., Losey, M. R. & Lake, G. (Eds). *Tomorrow's HR management*. New York: John Wiley:250–258.) See also Hiltrop, J.-M. 2006. A diagnostic framework for building HR capability in organisations. *Strategic change*, 15(7/8):341–351, November–December.

65. COOKE, F. L. 2006. Modeling an HR shared services centre: experience of an MNC in the United Kingdom. *Human resource management*, 45(2):211.

66. Ibid.:212.

67. Ibid.

68. Ibid.:224.

69. Ibid.

70. Ibid.

71. Ibid.

Glossary

Asynchronous Learning
Interactions between instructors and learners on an intermittent basis with a time delay in between; an example is self-paced courses on the Internet.

Balanced Scorecard
A carefully selected set of quantifiable measures derived from a company's strategy, which can be used as the basis for awarding incentive pay.

Change management
An ongoing process enabling a company to anticipate and respond to changes taking place in its external and internal environments and to enable employees to cope with the changes.

Cognitive flexibility
The mental frame of reference required to perform effectively in the job and the level of cognitive skill required.

Communication
The process of exchanging information between a sender and a receiver.

Compensatory justice
Compensating people for any harm or loss they have suffered.

Competencies
Basic characteristics of individuals, which are necessary for successful performance, taking into consideration the nature of the tasks and the organisational context.

Competitive advantage
A condition that enables a company to claim certain customers from its competitors as a result of the fact that it can operate in a more efficient or higher quality manner.

Contingency approach
Allows for multiple ways of doing things to fit different circumstances.

Corporate Social Responsibility (CSR)
Involves not only a commitment to behave ethically and to contribute to economic development, but also a commitment to improve the quality of life of the workforce members and their families, the local community, and society at large.

Corporate ethics programmes
Integrating ethics formally and explicitly into daily business life, into company-policy formulation at the board and top-management levels, and, through a formal code, into all daily decision-making and work practices, down the line at all levels of employment.

Corporate governance
A set of relationships between a company's management, its board, its shareholders, and other stakeholders. Corporate governance provides the structure through which the objectives of the company are set, and the means of attaining those objectives and monitoring performance.

Corporate citizenship
The extent to which businesses meet the economic, legal, ethical, and discretionary responsibilities imposed on them by their stakeholders.

Culture
A set of actions, values, understandings, and ways of thinking, transmitted socially and shared by the majority of members of a company and taught to new employees as correct.

E-business
Doing business electronically by using the Internet.

E-HR
The processing and sending of HR information by making use of computer networking and the Internet.

E-leadership
A social influencing process mediated by advanced information systems to produce a change in attitudes, feelings, thinking, behaviour, and performance with individuals, groups, and organisations.

E-learning
Conducting training online by making use of the Internet or a company intranet or extranet.

E-marketing
Web-based initiatives that improve the marketing of existing products.

Employee value proposition (EVP)
Everything an employee experiences within an organisation, including intrinsic and extrinsic satisfaction, values, ethics, and culture. It is also about how well the organisation fulfils employees' needs, expectations and aspirations.

E-operations
Web-based initiatives that improve the creation of existing products.

E-recruitment
Online recruitment agents and sites established by companies for advertising their own vacancies.

E-services
Web-based initiatives that provide customer-affiliated services.

Ethics
A set of standards of conduct and moral judgments that help to determine right and wrong behaviour.

Extranet
A collaborative Internet-linked network that allows employees access to information provided by external entities such as suppliers and customers.

Functional flexibility
Abolishing skill barriers and utilising workers on a variety of jobs in response to market demand.

High-performance work system
A customer-driven system in which technology, organisational structure, people, and processes all work together with the common focus on customer satisfaction.

HR Scorecard
Linking human resource initiatives to business strategies, resulting in significant increases in shareholder value.

HR strategy
Human resource policies and practices designed to facilitate the implementatation of strategic business plans.

Human capital
The knowledge, skills, and abilities of employees, which have economic value to a company.

Human resource information system (HRIS)
A computer system used to acquire, store, manipulate, analyse, retrieve, and distribute information related to an organisation's people, jobs, and costs for purposes of control and decision-making.

Intranet
An internal company Web site that operates over the Internet (behind a firewall) and links employees to company-wide information sources.

Leadership
The process of influencing people within an organisational context to direct their efforts toward particular goals.

Learning organisation
An organisation that empowers its people to learn effectively and collectively inside and outside the organisation to achieve the results they desire.

Legalistic period
The 1960s and 1970s saw an unprecedented amount of legislation in the social and employment area, which had a major impact on the workplace and the roles and responsibilities assumed by the personnel officer.

Management by objectives (MBO)
A process that relies on goal setting to establish objectives for the organisation as a whole, and thereafter for each department, manager, and individual, thus providing a measure for each individual's contribution to the success of the company.

Mechanistic period
The 1940s and 1950s, when manufacturing was the driving force in industry; this period saw the birth of the personnel and industrial relations profession.

Numerical flexibility
Matching employee numbers to fluctuating production levels or service requirements as a result of economic activity.

Organisational learning
Learning of employees within an organisation through corporate-wide commitment to and opportunity for continuous improvement.

Organistic period
The 1980s, during which issues such as globalisation, mergers, acquisitions, re-engineering, and downsizing were taking place. These activities brought about radical changes in the workplace and created an environment in which the HRM function faced numerous challenges.

Paradigm
A common framework from which to view reality, based on fundamental assumptions, which establishes boundaries and principles within a particular field.

Psychological contract
A set of unwritten expectations and understandings of what an employee expects to contribute in an employment relationship and what the employer will provide the employee in exchange for those contributions.

Reneging
The term for what happens when either party to a psychological contract knowingly breaks a promise to the other.

Repatriation
The transfer of an employee back home from an international assignment.

Resource-based view
View that sees a company as a bundle of resources that enables it to conceive and implement strategies that will lead to above-average returns.

Retributive justice
The imposition of penalties and punishment upon individuals and enterprises who cause harm to others.

Self-control
The ability to keep disruptive emotions and impulses under control.

Self-directed work team (SDWT)
A team of individuals assigned a cluster of tasks, duties, and responsibilities to be accomplished.

Strategic human resource management
Linking HRM policies, practices, and processes with the strategic goals and objectives of the company in order to improve business performance.

Strategic international human resource management (SIHRM)
HRM issues, functions, and policies and practices that result from the strategic activities of multinational enterprises and that impact on the international concerns and goals of those enterprises.

Strategic period
The 1990s, during which strategic thinking and planning emerged as the most prominent activity to deal with the continual change faced by organisations.

Strategy
The means by which an organisation seeks to meet its objectives; a strategy focuses on significant long-term goals rather than day-to-day operating matters.

Synchronous learning
Transmission and interaction of information and knowledge in real time.

Talent
The sum of the person's abilities – his or her intrinsic gifts, skills, knowledge, experience, intelligence, judgement, attitude, character, and drive; it also includes his or her ability to learn and grow.

Talent management
The sourcing (finding talent), screening (sorting of qualified and unqualified applicants), selection (assessment and testing, interviewing, reference and background checking etc. of applicants), on-boarding (offer, acceptance, badging and security, payroll, facilities etc.), retention (measures to keep the talent that contributes to the success of the organisation), development (training, growth, assignments etc.), deployment (optimal assignment of staff to projects, lateral opportunities, promotions etc.), and renewal of the workforce with analysis and planning as the adhesive, overarching ingredient.

Talent mindset
A deep-seated belief that having better talent at all levels is how to outperform the competition; the belief that better talent is a critical source of competitive advantage; the recognition that it is better talent that pulls all the other performance levers.

Teleological theory
Stresses the consequences which result from an action or practice.

Third-country nationals
Citizens of one country, working in another country and employed by an organisation headquartered in a third country.

Triple bottom line
While a company's bottom-line traditionally refers to its financial profit or loss, triple bottom-line refers to the need to consider also social and environmental impacts; this triple bottom-line measures the financial, social, and environmental impact of business.

Virtual teams
Groups of geographically and organisationally dispersed co-workers assembled using a combination of telecommunications and information technologies to accomplish an organisational task.

Visionary leadership
The ability to take charge and inspire with a compelling vision.

Workforce Scorecard
Indicates in a clear manner how to turn strategy into strategy execution by focusing on elements of workforce success that can then be tracked and monitored.

Subject index

Author index